W9-CRT-041

Iraqi Security Forces

Iraqi Security Forces

A Strategy for Success

ANTHONY H. CORDESMAN

with the assistance of
Patrick Baetjer

Published in cooperation with the
Center for Strategic and International Studies,
Washington, D.C.

PRAEGER SECURITY INTERNATIONAL
Westport, Connecticut • London

Library of Congress Cataloging-in-Publication Data

Cordesman, Anthony H.
    Iraqi security forces : a strategy for success / Anthony H. Cordesman ;
with the assistance of Patrick Baetjer.
      p. cm.
    Includes bibliographical references (p.).
    ISBN 0-275-98908-9 (alk. paper)
    1. Iraq War, 2003.   2. Postwar reconstruction—Iraq.   3. Iraq—Armed Forces.
I. Baetjer, Patrick. II. Title.
    DS79.769.C67 2005
    956.7044'31—dc22   2005017188

British Library Cataloguing in Publication Data is available.

Library of Congress Catalog Card Number: 2005017188
ISBN: 0-275-98908-9

First published in 2006

Praeger Security International, 88 Post Road West, Westport, CT 06881
An imprint of Greenwood Publishing Group, Inc.
www.praeger.com

Printed in the United States of America

The paper used in this book complies with the
Permanent Paper Standard issued by the National
Information Standards Organization (Z39.48–1984).

Contents

Tables/Figures

TABLES

FIGURES

Acknowledgments

THE DATA in this book are based on a number of interviews and communications inside and outside of Iraq with U.S., other coalition, Iraqi, Turkish, and Arab officials and officers that cannot be sourced or attributed. It would have been impossible to write this analysis, however, without extensive support from those actively involved in the effort to create a modern and free Iraq.

Where possible, official sources and on-the-scene press reports are referenced to support the analysis and conclusions involved. There have been many criticisms of press reporting from those who have not been in Iraq. In practice, this work could not have been written without the courage and objectivity of the reporters who actively covered the story in the field, often at considerable risk to themselves.

Several research assistants played a key role in researching other aspects of this book, in draft portions of the analysis, and in developing the tables and graphs. This is a collaborative effort in many ways, and Bobby Roshan and Stephen Lanier deserve special recognition for their efforts.

Note on Sources and Methods

Two TECHNICAL points: First, the database used to allow the author to tie given parts of the analysis to given interviews and press reports sometimes required the original spellings used in the source to be used in the text. In any case, there is no standard or correct transliteration of Arabic, Kurdish, or historical place names into English.

Second, most of the numbers available on various aspects of Iraq are highly uncertain. In general, the figures quoted by a given source were left as reported, and no effort was made to reconcile them. The reader should be aware that numbers presented in this work are approximate at best and there are many uncertainties and contradictions in the data.

Introduction

W HATEVER ONE may think of the reasons for going to war in Iraq, the fact is that Iraq, the United States and its allies, and the world must deal with the consequences. History is now far more important for what it can teach about solutions to Iraq's problems than for individuals' efforts to second-guess or assign blame. No one can alter the past, and the Iraqi people deserve a future, not a failed state or civil war.

This analysis focuses on one aspect of that future, and one that is still very much a work in progress: constructing Iraqi military, security, and police forces that can provide an essential element of nation-building and stability. It does, however, build upon a broader analysis of what went wrong and right in U.S. planning for the invasion of Iraq, the execution of the invasion, and its aftermath. This is essential to understand the nature of the opportunities that now exist for creating effective forces and security in Iraq and the limits upon them.

More generally, the lessons of Iraq may apply to many future cases. This may well be a century of asymmetric wars, where stability operations and nation-building will be at least as critical to the grand strategic outcome as conventional fighting. There are no real experts in these fields, and it is important to learn from past successes and mistakes.

Saddam Hussein's "Powder Keg"

Many of the problems Iraq now faces were inevitable. The fall of Saddam Hussein would have exposed deep fracture lines in an impoverished Iraq, almost regardless of how it occurred. One key legacy of the British "divide and rule" tactics that formed the state was minority Arab Sunni rule over a state that had an Arab Shi'ite majority of some 60 percent of the population, with Kurdish, Turcoman, and other minorities that made up another 20 percent. Iraq's violent politics had further compounded these problems by bringing a leader to power who never tolerated political dissent and began the bloody purging and suppression of all organized political resistance when he took full power in 1979. Iraq came to be ruled by a small, largely rural Sunni Arab elite that used the Ba'ath Party and the state to maintain its power.

Its economy remained relatively undeveloped, agriculture was never modernized or made productive, and inefficient state industries undercut development, as did a rigid state-controlled financial sector and a mix of barriers to trade and outside investment. Worse, the economy effectively became a command kleptocracy, where Saddam Hussein used the nation's wealth to secure power and support his ambitions and his ruling elite exploited its position for its own personal benefit.

The nation was impoverished and driven into massive debt in the early 1980s by Saddam Hussein's invasion of Iran and his efforts to seize its oil-rich territory in the southwest of Iran. Eight years of war crippled the development of Iraq's infrastructure, education, and efforts to properly develop its oil wealth.

The politics of the Iran-Iraq War, which lasted from 1980–1988, were essentially the politics of ruthless repression. Political dissent of any kind became even more dangerous. Kurdish efforts to exploit the war and achieve some degree of autonomy or independence were met with murder, the use of poison gas, and "ethnic cleansing." Hundreds of thousands of Arab Shi'ites were driven out of the country, and many formed an armed opposition with Iranian support. While most of the remaining Arab Shi'ites remained loyal, their secular and religious leaders were kept under constant surveillance and sometimes imprisoned and killed. The marshy areas along the Iranian border were a key center of the fighting between Iran and Iraq but still became a sanctuary for deserters and Shi'ite opposition elements.

In 1990, Saddam Hussein's efforts to solve his economic problems by invading Kuwait led to a devastating military defeat, a massive new burden of reparations for the war, and then to more than a decade of UN and international sanctions that further crippled every aspect of the nation's development.

Iraq's defeat in the Gulf War in 1991 did more than further impoverish the country. Uprisings in the Shi'ite areas in the south were suppressed with all of the regime's customary violence and then followed by a mix of repression and low-level civil war that lasted until Saddam was driven from power. While this conflict received only limited attention from the outside world, it often involved significant local clashes between Iraqi government forces and those of Shi'ite opposition movements based in, and backed by, Iran. The post–Iraq War discovery of mass graves of Shi'ite fighters and civilians is a grim testimony to how serious this "quiet" fighting could be. This struggle further divided Shi'ite and Sunni but also left a lasting legacy of anger against the United States and Britain for not supporting the uprisings against Saddam and protecting the Shi'ites.

A similar set of uprisings in the Kurdish north created a flood of refugees into Turkey following the defeat of the Kurds and forced the United States to use airpower to protect the Kurds and create an international aid effort to support them. This gave the Kurds a level of protection the Arab Shi'ites lacked but left them in a kind of limbo where they had de facto autonomy but lived with nearly one-third of Iraq's military forces deployed on the edge of their "security zone."

Divisions between the two main Kurdish factions, headed by Masoud Barzani and Jalal Talibani, led to low-level fighting and even to one faction supporting an attack by Saddam on the other. The end result, however, was to further increase the Kurdish desire for independence while keeping many dispossessed Kurds out of their original homes in areas like Kirkuk and Mosul.[1]

From 1991 until the Coalition invasion in 2003, Saddam Hussein created still further political problems by encouraging tribal divisions and favoring those tribes and clans that supported his rule and regime. He exploited religion by increasingly embracing Islam publicly and privately favoring Sunni factions and religious leaders that supported him, while penalizing Shi'ite religious leaders and centers he saw as a threat. At the same time, funds were poured into Sunni areas in the western part of the country, government and security jobs were given to Sunnis, and scarce resources went into military industries that heavily favored Sunni employment. The result was to distort the economy and urban structure of Iraq in ways that favored Sunni towns and cities in areas like Tikrit, Samarra, Fallujah, Ramadi, and other largely loyalist Sunni towns.

Saddam Hussein made every effort to use the UN sanctions that followed the Gulf War as a political weapon. The regime manipulated rationing, control of imports, state funds, and the UN Oil-for-Food program for its own benefit, further undercutting economic development. The funding of education, medical services, and infrastructure was used as a political weapon in an effort to break out of UN sanctions by exploiting the suffering of the Iraqi people. It also was used selectively to favor key power centers like Baghdad and major potential centers of urban unrest, while leaving other areas with limited or no essential services like water, power, and sewers.

Rather than seek to restore and develop the nation's oil and gas wealth, existing fields were overproduced, funds were redirected for the use of the regime, and exports were manipulated to obtain kickbacks and get political support from nations like Syria. These efforts were cloaked by a propaganda campaign blaming the United States, United Nations, outside powers, and UN sanctions for all of the mistakes of the regime.

By comparison, Tito's regime in the former Yugoslavia was both progressive and benign. At the time, the U.S.-led Coalition that invaded Iraq was divided by far greater pressures and had far less capability for political leadership. It was a time bomb waiting to explode, fueled both by its original heritage of ethnic and sectarian division and over twenty years of direct misrule by Saddam Hussein.

America's Strategic Mistakes

The United States made major strategic mistakes in preparing to deal with this situation. It did demonstrate that it could fight the war it planned to fight: a conventional, regional war with remarkable efficiency, at low cost, and very quickly. The problem was that the United States chose a strategy wherein postconflict goals were unrealistic and impossible to achieve, and it planned only for the war it wanted to fight and not for the "peace" that was certain to follow. Its most obvious mistake was its basic rationale for going to war: a threat based on intelligence estimates of Iraqi efforts to create weapons of mass destruction that the United States later found did not exist. At a grand strategic level, however, the Bush administration and the senior leadership of the U.S. military made the far more serious mistake of wishing away virtually all of the real-world problems in stability operations and nation-building and making massive policy and military errors that created much of the climate of insurgency in Iraq.

The full chronology of what happened is still far from clear, and it's far easier to accuse specific U.S. leaders than it is to understand what really happened or assign responsibility with any credibility. It is clear, however, that many of the key decisions involved were made in ways that bypassed the inter-agency process within the U.S. government, ignored the warnings of U.S. area and intelligence experts, disregarded prior military war and stability planning by the U.S. Central Command (USCENTCOM), and ignored the warnings of policymakers and experts in other key Coalition states like the United Kingdom.

At the same time, it is clear that too much credence was given to ideologues and true believers in the ease with which such a war could be fought and in effective nation-building. These included leading neoconservatives in the office of the secretary of defense, the office of the vice president, and some officials in the National Security Council, as well as in several highly politicized "think tanks." The same was true of various Iraqi exile groups that grossly exaggerated the level of Iraqi popular support for a "liberating" invasion and the ease with which Saddam Hussein's regime could be replaced, underestimating both the scale of Iraqi's ethnic and sectarian divisions and economic problems. These problems were compounded by leadership within the office of the secretary of defense that put intense pressure on the U.S. military to plan for the lowest possible level of U.S. military deployment and then for delays in that deployment because of the political need to avoid appearing precipitous to the United Nations. At the same time, the leadership of the U.S. military actively resisted planning for, and involvement in, large-scale and enduring stability and nation-building activity and failed to plan and deploy for the risk of a significant insurgency.

The fact that the United States failed to plan for meaningful stability operations and nation-building was the most serious strategic mistake that led to the insurgency and crime that are the focus of this analysis, but these mistakes were compounded by others, including the following:

- A failure to accurately assess the nature of Iraqi nationalism, the true level of cultural differences, and the scale of Iraqi problems. This failure of strategic assessment included the failure to see the scale of Iraq's ethnic and sectarian differences, its economic weaknesses and problems, the difficulty of modernizing an infrastructure sized more to 16 to 17 million than the current population of 25 to 26 million, unrealistic estimates of "oil wealth," the probable hard-core support for the former regime in Sunni areas, secular versus theocratic tensions, the impact of tribalism, the impact of demographics in a society so young and with so many employment problems, and a host of other real-world problems that became U.S. and Coalition problems the moment Coalition forces crossed the border.
- The failure to plan and execute effective broader information operations before, during, and after the invasion to win the "hearts and minds of Iraqis" and to persuade them that the Coalition came as liberators that would leave rather than occupiers who would stay and exploit Iraq and that the Coalition would provide aid and support to a truly independent government and state. A secondary failure was to anticipate and defuse the flood of conspiracy theories certain to follow Coalition military action.
- The failure to create and provide anything approaching the kind and number of civilian elements in the U.S. government necessary for nation-building and stability operations. These problems were particularly serious in the State Department and other civilian agencies, and much of the civilian capability the United States did have was not recruited or willing to take risks in the field.
- The failure to plan and execute efforts to maintain the process of governance at the local, provincial, and central level, to anticipate the risk that the structure of government would collapse and the risk of looting, or to create a plan for restructuring the military, police, and security forces—all of which needed to be proclaimed and publicized before, during, and immediately after the initial invasion to win the support of Iraqi officials and officers who were not linked to active support of Saddam Hussein and past abuses—and to preserve the core of governance that could lead to the rapid creation of both a legitimate government and security.
- Broad failures by what a leading officer involved in planning operations in Iraq described as "quiescent U.S. military and intelligence community leaders who observed the distortion/cherry picking of data that lead to erroneous conclusions and poor planning" but failed to press their case or force the issue.
- Overreliance on exile groups with limited credibility and influence in Iraq.
- The failure to anticipate and prepare for Iraqi expectations after the collapse of Saddam's regime and for the fact that many Iraqis would

oppose the invasion and see any sustained U.S. and Coalition presence as a hostile occupation.

- Miscalculating UN, NATO, and Coalition support and transit through Turkey.
- The failure to provide the personnel and skills necessary to secure Iraqi rear areas and urban areas as the Coalition advanced and to prevent the massive looting of government offices and facilities, military bases, and arms depots during and after the fighting—a process that effectively destroyed the existing structure of governance and security without making any initial effort to replace it. It was not until May 2003, roughly two months after the fall of Baghdad, that a 4,000-man U.S. military police effort was authorized for deployment to Baghdad, and it then took time to arrive. No serious effort to rebuild Iraqi police forces took place until June 2004, in spite of mass desertions right after the fighting and the turmoil caused by disbanding the Ba'ath Party and military and security forces.[2]
- The creation of only a small cadre of civilians and military in the Office of Reconstruction and Humanitarian Assistance (ORHA), many initially recruited only for three-month tours. ORHA planned to operate in an Iraq where all ministries and functions of government remained intact. It was charged with a largely perfunctory nation-building task, given negligible human and financial resources, and was neither allowed meaningful liaison with regional powers nor integrated with the military command. Effective civil-military coordination never took place between ORHA and the U.S. command during or after the war, and its mission was given so little initial priority that it did not even come to Baghdad until April 21, 2003—twelve days after U.S. forces—on the grounds that it did not have suitable security.
- The failure not only to anticipate the threat of insurgency and outside extremist infiltration, in spite of significant intelligence warning, but also to deploy elements of U.S. forces capable of dealing with counterinsurgency, civil-military operations, and nation-building as U.S. forces advanced and in the immediate aftermath of the collapse of the regime. Regional commands were created based on administrative convenience rather than need, and most of the initial tasks of stability operations and nation-building were left up to improvisation by individual local commanders who had minimal or no expert civilian support.
- Replacing ORHA after the fall of Saddam Hussein with the Coalition Provisional Authority (CPA) and suddenly improvising a vast nation-building and stability effort, recruiting for and funding such an operation with little time for planning, and then attempting to carry out the resulting mission along heavily ideological lines that attempt to impose American methods and values on Iraq.
- Placing the CPA and U.S. commands in separate areas, creating large, secure zones that isolated the U.S. effort from Iraqis, and carrying out only limited coordination with other Coalition allies.

- Staffing the CPA largely with people recruited for short tours and often chosen on the basis of political and ideological vetting rather than experience and competence.
- A lack of language and area skills and training on the part of most U.S. military forces and of intelligence capabilities designed to provide the human intelligence (HUMINT), technical collection, analytic capabilities, and "fusion" centers necessary for stability, counterterrorist, and counterinsurgency operations.
- A failure to assess honestly the nature and size of the Iraqi insurgency as it grew and became steadily more dangerous.
- Planning for premature U.S. military withdrawals from Iraq before the situation was clear or secure with major reductions initially planned to begin some three months after the fall of Saddam's regime, rather than planning, training, and equipping for a sustained period of stability operations.
- A failure to react to the wartime collapse of Iraqi military, security, and police forces and focus immediately on creating effective Iraqi forces—a failure that placed a major and avoidable burden on U.S. and other Coalition forces and compounded the Iraqi feeling that Iraq had been occupied by hostile forces.
- Planning for several years of occupation once the CPA was created and for a situation where a U.S.-led Coalition could improve its own values and judgments about the Iraqi people, politics, economy, and social structure over a period of some three years rather than expedite the transfer of sovereignty back to Iraq as quickly as possible. The record is mixed, but the CPA only seems to have decided in October 2003 to expedite the transfer of sovereignty after the insurgency had already become serious, and its choice of June 2004 for doing so was largely arbitrary. Even then, it failed to make its plans sufficiently convincing for many of the Iraqi people.

It is true that foresight is far more difficult than "twenty-twenty hindsight." Many, if not most, of the factors that could lead to these problems were, however, brought to the attention of the president, National Security Council, State Department, Department of Defense, and intelligence community in the summer and fall of 2002. No one accurately prophesized all of the future, but many inside and outside government warned what it might be. The problem was not that the interagency system did not work in providing many key elements of an accurate assessment, it was that the most senior political and military decision makers ignored what they felt was negative advice out of a combination of sincere belief, ideological conviction, and political and bureaucratic convenience.

The cost to the United States, its allies, and Iraq has been high. Over time, these failures have helped push the United States to the limit of the ground forces it can easily deploy. They helped cause the death of well over 1,500

Americans and other Coalition forces after Saddam had fallen and the wounding of well over ten thousand. They also helped to kill and wound tens of thousands of Iraqis. Furthermore, they laid the groundwork for many of the problems in creating effective Iraqi forces, and that responsibility cannot be allocated to the U.S. military and civilians in the field.

The Importance of Creating Effective Iraqi Military, Security, and Police Forces

It is still unclear what the outcome of the U.S.-led Coalition's invasion of Iraq will be and whether a stable, unified, and pluralistic Iraq can emerge out of the overthrow of Saddam Hussein's dictatorship. Iraq's political process, unity, and inclusiveness remain uncertain. A major insurgency and pervasive, violent crime continue to threaten Iraqi nation-building. Without substantial progress at both the political and force development levels, serious civil conflict is still a major possibility. Moreover, outside Islamic extremists present a major threat, and states as diverse as Iran, Turkey, and Syria either support elements of the insurgency or are potential threats to Iraq's stability.

More than two years after the fall of Saddam Hussein in April 2003, Iraq suffers from deep and growing violent divisions between its Shi'ite Arabs, Sunni Arabs, Kurds, Turcomans, and other minorities. The divisions among its Shi'ite majority remain serious, as well as the divisions over how secular and how Islamic Iraq's government and society should be. Tribal and other local divisions further threaten the country.

Governance is weak at the central and local levels. The transfer of power back to a sovereign Iraqi government and elections have helped give the government enhanced legitimacy, but elections do not substitute for the ability to govern, an effective rule of law, or the ability to protect the population and ensure human rights.

The collapse and looting of the government during and immediately after the war destroyed much of the structure of governance that existed under Saddam Hussein, and the U.S.-led Coalition was slow to make effective efforts to replace it. Iraq's elections have had value, but the newly elected officials lack experience, unity, and a common agenda for action. Iraq is a demonstration that elections held in nations without real political parties, experienced leaders, a stable economy, and a middle class present massive problems in creating an operating government—compounded in this case by parties based more on sectarian and ethnic faction than any practical program for governing.

Economic instability adds to Iraq's problems with security and governance. Massive outside aid, high oil prices, and a legacy of revenue from the regime of Saddam Hussein have still left Iraq a relatively poor state, and much of its economy and industry have collapsed—creating levels of direct and disguised unemployment ranging from 30 percent to 60 percent, depending on the age group and governorate involved.

The Five Key Elements of Victory

The end result is a situation where there are five key elements to any kind of "victory" in Iraq, both for the Iraqi people and for the United States and its Coalition allies:

- Establishing a pluralistic Iraqi government capable both of governing and providing security to the people of Iraq and finding a new balance of political power acceptable to the Arab Shi'ites, Arab Sunnis, Kurds, Turcomans, and other minorities. This means effective governance at the local, regional, and national levels.
- Creating effective Iraqi military, security, and police forces—eventually replacing all Coalition forces—capable of bringing security to the entire country and capable of conducting effective operations while winning the support of the vast majority of the Iraqi people.
- Providing effective aid, debt and reparations relief, and Iraqi economic reform efforts that—coupled with effective security—move the nation onto the path to stable economic development where wealth and economic growth are distributed in ways that meet the needs of all of Iraq's people.
- Developing a new national consensus that legitimizes Iraq's post–Saddam Hussein government and social structure and that can find a "golden mean" between the different goals and expectations of its different ethnic and religious elements.
- Finding a new balance of relationships with Iraq's neighbors that will ensure that they do not threaten Iraq or interfere in its affairs, while making it clear that Iraq no longer poses a threat to any neighboring state.

"Tipping Years" to Build Effective Forces

Building effective Iraqi military, security, police, and security forces is only one of these five elements, but it is an element that is critical to the creation of a legitimate government in Iraq and to establishing the stability and security vital to Iraq's political and economic development. In many ways it is the precursor to legitimacy, political stability and success, and economic recovery and development.

U.S. and Coalition efforts to build such forces are still very much a work in progress, and it may be years before the full history of these efforts becomes public and their short-term and ultimate successes become apparent. Many of the details of U.S. and other Coalition efforts remain classified, and the views of Iraqis are very difficult to determine. Enough is known, however, to raise major questions about the initial U.S. approach to the task and describe some aspects of this effort as a tragic failure. There is still a serious risk of failure at the political, economic, and security levels, and even serious civil war or the emergence of a failed state.

At the same time, many of the initial mistakes the United States and Coalition made after the fall of Saddam Hussein have been corrected. Important changes have taken place, and these changes have become far more promising since June 2004. They may well prove to be the key to giving Iraqis the security they need for nation-building.

No one can yet talk about "tipping points" or claim victory at this point in time. In fact, the period between 2005 and the end of 2007 are likely to be "tipping years" that test Iraq's political development and cohesion as well as how successful Iraq's new forces are and the adequacy of U.S. and other Coalition plans to strengthen them. It may also take a decade to give Iraq all of the military and police capabilities it needs—provided that the political and economic conditions are created to make this possible.

Military history also warns that force development is a history of successes and reversals, not some smooth evolution to success. That said, there is real hope and the possibility that the successful development of Iraqi forces may provide major lessons for future efforts at coalition-building, nation-building stability operations, counterinsurgency, and counterterrorism.

1 The Importance of the Initial Failures in Grand Strategy and Strategic Assessment

The Background to the Effort to Create Effective Iraqi Military, Security, and Police Forces

EXPERTS DISAGREE on many aspects of the Iraq War, including the ways in which America's strategic mistakes led to the initial failures in creating effective Iraqi military, security, and police forces. Failures occurred in spite of the fact that the United States had spent well over $5.8 billion by May 2005 to develop these forces, and the president had to request another $5.7 billion to accelerate their development.[1] There is broad agreement, however, among virtually all analysts who have examined the way in which the United States went to war in Iraq and dealt with its Coalition allies and Iraqi exile groups that the United States did not properly prepare for stability and nation-building operations and failed to anticipate the threat of terrorism and insurgency.

This should not have happened. It is clear to anyone who participated in the process that the interagency studies conducted before the war led to many warnings from serving officials, former military officials, military intelligence officers, and area experts that nation-building and instability could present major risks. This included intelligence warnings that Saddam Hussein's regime was preparing for insurgency and resistance if Coalition forces defeated Iraq's regular military forces and forced the regime to give up overt power and get out of Baghdad.

While it may be years before the full record is declassified, the Bush administration had ample strategic and tactical warning of what might occur, much of it coming from interagency efforts led by the State Department. It seems to have chosen to disregard such warnings because some senior policy officials believed their vision of Iraq was far more correct than the warnings they were given. There are also strong indications that the administration ignored the portions of previous U.S. Central Command (USCENTCOM) war plans that called for stability operations and much larger force levels than the administration chose to deploy and that the policy cluster in the Department of Defense chose to ignore much of the advice it was given by the State Department and the intelligence community when the Department of Defense was given operational authority for stability operations in late 2002 and early 2003.

The Department of Defense not only ignored the risk of terrorism and insurgency, it did little to realistically plan to create stability. It had no clear plans to secure government offices and maintain the process of governance. It was not organized and manned to provide local security, prevent looting, or seize exposed arms depots. The original office charged with reconstruction—the Office of Reconstruction and Humanitarian Assistance (ORHA)—was never given significant manpower and financial resources, and its head, General Jay Garner, was initially given a three-month appointment. The United States planned to inherit stability, not achieve it, and to begin major force reductions within a few months following Saddam's fall. The preservation or creation of effective Iraqi military, security, and police forces was never a serious part of the prewar, wartime, or immediate postwar U.S. planning effort.

It is also clear that the United States and the Coalition were slow to react as terrorism and insurgency became serious problems and that they underestimated the scale of Iraqi resentment and hostility that occurred as a result of the invasion and the problems that followed.

The "Turkish Question"

There still is no detailed public record of what the United States planned for as it went to war or how much its plans differed from any previous USCENTCOM plans for effective occupation and stability operations. Secretary of Defense Donald Rumsfeld did say in March 2005, however, that he felt much of the problem of insurgency and terrorism came from the fact that Turkey did not allow U.S. forces and the Fourth Infantry Division to advance through Iraq from the north and occupy Sunni towns and cities as it moved south toward Baghdad.[2]

There may be some validity to these claims, although much of the U.S. miscalculation about how easy it would be to obtain Turkish consent seems to have come from precisely the same policymakers who underestimated the stability and nation-building problems in Iraq. The additional U.S. manpower in the equivalent of a four-brigade force would almost certainly have had a major impact in suppressing Ba'ath and rear-area activity in the North and areas like the "Sunni Triangle."

A Turkish analyst presents the Turkish position as follows:

> While using the Turkish soil for the operations in Northern Iraq was one of the centerpieces of invasion strategy, there was minimal consideration for the complexity of Turkey's decision. One of the chief reasons for the Turkish refusal was the loss incurred during the Gulf War. Promises by U.S. officials to fully compensate Turkish economic losses during early 1990s in return for their cooperation in the Gulf War were not fulfilled. [The] Turks' request for the compensation of $30 billion loss from the Gulf War remained mostly unanswered.

U.S. diplomats were not cognizant of the disappointment much of the Turkish establishment and public felt when the George H. W. Bush and Bill Clinton administrations failed to compensate or reward Turkey for its substantial sacrifices during the 1991 Operation Desert Storm and subsequent Operation Northern Watch operations, which signaled to the larger Turkish audience that Washington did not care for its friends. Faced with an unresponsive Washington that expected them to cooperate fully for the second time, most Turkish members of parliament felt like Turkish collaboration was taken for granted. While some decision makers in Turkey advocated for allowing the U.S. troops to enter the country and for the Turkish troops to participate in the Coalition, there was widespread concern in the country for incurring new economic losses that would not be compensated, akin to Gulf War losses.

Another factor for the Turkish Parliament's decision was the American diplomacy. Turkey's participation in the 2003 Iraq War was highly desirable to the United States from both a military and diplomatic perspective. Yet the State Department failed to engage in high-level diplomacy with its Turkish counterpart. Aside from a brief 2001 visit, Secretary of State Colin Powell did not travel to Turkey until a month after the National Assembly's vote. Powell's failure to visit Turkey in late 2002 and early 2003—while he visited Angola, Cape Verde, and Colombia—was indicative of the failure in American public diplomacy.

Both the State Department and the U.S. Embassy in Ankara mishandled American approach to Turkey in other ways. In February 2003 Powell dispatched Ambassador Marisa Lino to lead negotiations. Lino's competency in negotiations is highly criticized. While she had experience in Syria and Iraq and was ambassador to Albania, she had little experience in Turkey. As the head of the U.S. delegation negotiating military memoranda of Turkish-American cooperation in Iraq, Lino created an antagonistic and dishonest image. Simultaneously, though, Ankara's choice of Ambassador Deniz Bolukbasi, well known for his nationalistic sentiments, as head of the Turkish team was also unfortunate. While Ankara and Washington eventually reached an agreement, the lack of personal chemistry and cooperation between [the] two ambassadors soured the atmosphere.

The bulk of responsibility for the erosion of bilateral relations in the wake of the war is attributable to the U.S. Embassy in Ankara. During prewar negotiations Ambassador W. Robert Pearson leaked comments about Turkey to the American and Turkish press. He ignored the private warnings of Turkish diplomats that the presence of American diplomats in the Turkish Grand National Assembly on the day of the vote would create a nationalist backlash against the American deployment. He also shocked policymakers when, shortly before his departure, he mentioned at a diplomatic reception that he had spent the day before the vote playing golf with a famous Turkish businessman.

Neither Pearson nor his staff made an effort to defend the case for American policy to the Turkish press. While anti-American journalists were often invited to embassy functions with little mention of their provocation, many prominent pro-American reporters and officials were excluded from these functions. Perhaps unintentional, such moves nevertheless demoralized Turkish proponents of American policy.

At the same time, no detailed plans seem to have existed to give such U.S. forces a major role in stability operations and nation-building. This mission was only tasked as a minor role for the U.S. Army and Marine Corps forces advancing northward out of Kuwait, and the United States seems to only have anticipated irregular Iraqi resistance from forces like Saddam's Fedayeen as it closed on Baghdad—not as a serious problem in the South. Moreover, a number of senior U.S. military and intelligence officials have stated off the record that the United States expected far more Iraqi units to defect or stand aside and did not consider the sudden collapse of Iraqi military, security, and police forces to be a risk.

Warning Indicators before and after the Fall

No one provided precise warnings as to the kind of insurgency that would develop in the country before, during, or immediately after the fall of Baghdad and Saddam's regime. Many inside and outside of government did warn, however, that the United States and Coalition would at best be greeted as liberators for a matter of months and that the United States would immediately begin to face hostility from an extremely nationalistic country while having to deal with deep religious and ethnic divisions. Many warned of the possibility of having to deal with some form of insurgency, and Defense Intelligence Agency (DIA) and other elements of the intelligence community warned that Saddam Hussein's regime might be preparing for such insurgency and dispersing arms and munitions.

As has been touched upon earlier, U.S. intelligence detected indicators that Saddam Hussein was seriously planning for a possible armed resistance if he lost control of Iraqi cities before the war and that some Iraqi security forces were planning for armed resistance if the regime fell. It was also aware that arms were being distributed to groups like the Popular Army before the Coalition invasion began. During and immediately after the fighting, the United States became aware that some 900 munitions sites and 10,000 arms caches—in excess of 650,000 tons of munitions—were scattered around the country. It was clear from the start that many had been "looted" and that the Coalition did not have the manpower to rapidly secure the rest. While the Coalition eventually claimed to have destroyed and secured most of the munitions, as of October 2004 it could not account for some 250,000 tons of munitions.

In short, there was ample intelligence and other warning indicators that showed how important it would be to create effective Iraqi military, security, and police forces. There were also clear warnings of how lethal an insurgency or terrorism could be and how easy it would be to obtain weapons and explosives. Moreover, public opinion polls conducted following the fall of Saddam Hussein provided ample warnings of the kind of hostility that an "occupation mentality" on the part of the Coalition might create, and it was clear what might happen in a highly militarized society once the regime fell.

The United States chose to continue to ignore or undervalue these indicators for most of the rest of 2003. This was partly the result of the ideological belief of many officials and advisers in the office of the secretary of defense, office of the vice president, and National Security Council that Iraqis would see the Coalition as a liberator, and that the people wanted "transformation" into a Western-style democracy and economy. It was partly the result of the fact that (1) the U.S. military saw warfare in terms of quick, decisive uses of overwhelming force against the conventional forces of a state, (2) resisted nation-building and peacemaking operations, and (3) was unprepared for lasting counterinsurgency missions.

It was also partly the result of the fact that the Bush administration listened to exile groups that promised Iraqis would see the Coalition as liberators, that Iraqis saw themselves as Iraqis and not in terms of sect or ethnicity, and that governance and economic development would not encounter major security problems. The administration chose to ignore warnings about the political legacy of over thirty years of Ba'ath Party and Saddam Hussein dictatorship and the fact Britain had forged Iraq out of elements of the Ottoman Empire on the basis of divide-and-rule tactics and that the regimes that followed had never established a power structure based on any fair equity for Iraq's Shi'ite majority or its Kurdish, Turcoman, and other minorities.

The Importance of Iraqi Public Opinion and Hostility and Distrust of Coalition Forces

The Bush administration badly misread Iraqi attitudes and perceptions before, during, and after the war, the problems the United States and Coalition would face as occupation forces, and Iraqi desire to see the security mission performed by Iraqis. Some elements of Iraq did greet the advancing Coalition forces as liberators but scarcely with the fervor and broad popular base that the U.S. officials shaping the invasion expected. Almost no Iraqis, however, wanted the Coalition to stay as occupiers or to be "transformed" from the outside.

The nature of the Coalition efforts that followed also ensured that much of its activity would be seen as imposing U.S. goals and values. This was particularly true because the United States initially did not provide any clear vision of how and when it would transfer sovereignty back to the Iraqi people, did not provide any clear schedule for doing so, did not make it clear whether or not it would seek permanent bases in Iraq, and did not provide a clear and consistent schedule for local elections or national elections. While the record is still unclear, the United States seems to have planned until the fall of 2003 for some three years of occupation and shifted its plans to transfer true sovereignty back to Iraqi in June 2004 only after it was already facing a rising insurgency.

The inevitable Iraqi backlash against the U.S.-led occupation was compounded by the fact that two critical groups had good reason to oppose the Coalition efforts. One was the Sunni Arab elements that suddenly lost the privileges and power they had had since the founding of Iraq, especially under

Saddam Hussein and the Ba'ath Party. The second were those Arab Shi'ites who wanted to create their own version of Iraq, especially those who wanted a more Islamic state in which they would play a dominant role.

At the same time, most Iraqi Arabs made it clear they had a strong nationalist resentment of any lasting Coalition military presence. From the start of the occupation Iraqi public opinion made it clear that training effective Iraqi military, police, and security forces should not be treated as a luxury or a sideshow. Regardless of how many Iraqis did or did not welcome the fall of Saddam Hussein, one public opinion poll after another showed that Coalition forces quickly came to be seen by many Iraqis as occupiers—and as occupiers unable to bring security.

Many Iraqi expectations of what the Coalition should and could do for them were unrealistic, and many of their criticisms of the Coalition and Coalition forces were unfair. The reality was that Iraqis were all too aware that the United States had failed to secure the country, key government offices, and key cultural centers. In their eyes the United States failed to show that it would reconstitute an effective Iraqi government and security structure, and police services and personal security remained at risk.

Coalition Operations = "Occupier" Operations = Anger and Friction

It is not surprising that the presence of Coalition forces created a natural friction with the population, particularly in Sunni Arab areas. Most U.S. and allied forces had little experience with Iraqi culture and history or with Islam. They were superb conventional-war fighters, but they had limited training and equipment for counterinsurgency and counterterrorism missions.

U.S. counterinsurgency, counterterrorism, and civil-military operations initially had limited effectiveness, frequently involved the detainment of innocent Iraqis and "collateral damage," and alienated otherwise friendly Iraqis. The United States saw the insurgents as a limited force with limited popular support that could be defeated without creating strong and highly effective Iraqi armed forces, and it badly underestimated the personal security problem.

The United States and the Coalition did not see the need to rush the creation of effective Iraqi military, police, and security forces—in spite of the developing scale of the military problem and polls showing that two-thirds of Sunnis and one-third of Shi'ites opposed war, while 33 percent of Sunnis and 11 percent of Shi'ites supported attacks on the Coalition.

Early Warning of the Need for Effective Iraqi Forces and True Interoperability: The Polls before the Transfer of Power

Polls consistently showed from June 2003 onward that the number one concern of Iraqis was personal security for themselves and their families and that crime was an even larger concern than terrorism or insurgency. Concerns over jobs, medical care, and education came next, and politics lagged significantly behind. It should have been clear from the start that creating effective

Iraqi police for local security and to fight crime was as critical as creating Iraqi security forces to take over counterinsurgency missions and removing or minimizing the signs of the Coalition as "occupiers."

The patterns in the earlier polls may be summarized as follows:

- First poll conducted in Iraq in August 2003 by Zogby International revealed that just over 50 percent of Iraqis felt that the United States would "hurt" Iraq over the next five years and that a slightly greater number thought "democracy is a Western way of doing things and it will not work here." *Some 31.6 percent felt that Coalition forces should leave within six months; 34 percent said within one year; and 25 percent said within two years.* In addition, just fewer than 60 percent felt that Iraq should determine its political future alone and without the help of the Coalition.[3]

- Some of these findings were substantiated by a poll conducted in May 2004 by the BBC, ABC News, the German network ARD, and NHK in Japan. Among these, while more than half said that life was better a year ago under Saddam, "only 25 percent expressed confidence in the US/UK occupation forces and 28 percent in both Iraq's political parties and the CPA."[4]

- *USA Today*/CNN/Gallup polls published in April 2004 revealed further developments in Iraqi perceptions of U.S. policy, presence, and operations. *Among these was that "53 percent say they would feel less secure without the Coalition in Iraq, but 57 percent say the foreign troops should leave anyway," while 71 percent of the respondents identified Coalition troops as "occupiers."*[5]

- In the April 29, 2004, *USA Today* poll cited earlier, many Iraqis considered American troops to be arrogant and insensitive:
  - 58 percent said [Coalition force] soldiers conduct themselves badly or very badly
  - 60 percent said the troops show disrespect for Iraqi people in searches of their homes, and 42 percent said U.S. forces have shown disrespect toward mosques
  - 46 percent said the soldiers show a lack of respect for Iraqi women
  - 11 percent of Iraqis say Coalition forces are trying hard to restore basic services such as electricity and clean drinking water

- US/Oxford polls show 78 percent of Iraqis had no confidence in Coalition forces in October 2003 and 81 percent in June 2004—and these figures included the Kurds.

Iraqi Views Harden: The Polls in 2004

The patterns in later polls are equally clear. The comparison of more recent poll data in table 1.1 was developed by Rick Barton and Sheba Crocker of CSIS and again clearly reflects trends in Iraqi attitudes that reinforce the warning that only Iraqi police and security forces can provide the political dimension of victory, no matter how well U.S. and other Coalition forces do at the military and tactical levels.

Such polls are not an argument that stability operations and nation-building were or are impossible in Iraq or any other nation. A poll by the Independent Republican Institute (IRI) during February and March 2005—conducted long into the occupation and after both the transfer of sovereignty back to Iraqis in June 2004 and Iraq's first real election on January 30, 2005—showed that some 61.5 percent of Iraqis felt the nation was now moving in the right direction versus 13.8 percent who "don't know" and 23.2 percent who think the nation is moving in the "wrong direction." (The poll had a wide sampling of different ages, sexes, and sectarian and ethnic groups and a 25 percent Sunni response but covered fifteen of Iraq's eighteen provinces or governorates and did not include the areas with the heaviest insurgent activity.)[6]

More generally, Iraqis showed considerable realism about the time progress would take. Only 56 percent thought things would be better in six months, and 29.6 percent thought things would be worse. Some 70 percent thought things would be better in a year, and 16 percent thought things would be worse. A total of 79 percent thought things would be better in five years, and only 4 percent thought things would be worse.

The poll also showed that Iraqis felt the three most important things in their lives were patriotism (74 percent), family (68 percent), and security (63 percent). The next ranked area was "individual freedom," at a little over 30 percent. All other values (physical health, education, position in society, wealth, and love) ranked from 18 percent to 4 percent. Interestingly, the call for the highest priority for more government action was improved electricity (57 percent), followed by unemployment (42 percent). Security was a major area, but crime had the highest priority (24 percent) in that category, followed by national security (22 percent) and terrorists (21 percent).

It was striking, however, that this poll never asked Iraqis about their attitude toward the occupation forces and occupation or whether wanting the Multinational Force–Iraq (MNF–I) out was a major reason for their support of the elections. There were Shi'ite anti–U.S. presence demonstrations after the elections, and a number of leading candidates made the earliest feasible departure of U.S. forces a major part of their campaigns during the elections.[7]

Moreover, the results of similar IRI polls reflected a 50 to 51 percent feeling that Iraq was moving in the wrong direction until the transfer of sovereignty in June 2004, and this declined to 32 percent in the winter of 2004 as the Iraqi political process took hold in spite of a rise in insurgency and criminal activity.[8] Some 26 percent of those showing a positive result in February and March 2005 gave sovereignty and the elections as the main reason for moving in the right direction, and some 22 percent cited their opposition to the old regime. Only 9.8 percent believed security was improving. In contrast, some 13 percent of

TABLE 1.1
Iraqi Public Opinion Polls: Iraqi Faith in Iraqi Forces versus Hostility to Coalition Forces (numbers in percentages)

IIACSS: How much confidence do you have in the [new] Iraqi police to improve the situation in Iraq?

	Jan. 2004	Apr./May 2004	May 2004
Great deal	44.80	47.90	47.30
Fair amount	35.00	29.60	28.70
Not very much	6.70	8.60	5.70
None at all	11.00	11.20	15.80

Source: IIACSS, Department of State, CPA, "National Poll of Iraq."

Iraqi Perception
Oxford: How much confidence do you have in the [new] Iraqi police?

	Oct./Nov. 2003	Feb. 2004	Mar./Apr. 2004	June 2004
Great deal	19.70	27.60	33.00	35
Quite a lot	30.60	43.30	39.20	39
Not very much	33.40	20.60	17.60	20
None at all	16.30	8.50	10.20	7

Source: Oxford Research International, "National Survey of Iraq."

Attitudes toward Iraqi Army Forces
IIACSS: How much confidence do you have in the [new] Iraqi Army to improve the situation in Iraq?

	Jan. 2004	Apr./May 2004	May 2004
Great deal	34.70	36.50	32.90
Fair amount	28.40	25.00	28.50
Not very much	9.70	9.90	8.60
None at all	17.20	17.80	20.10

Source: IIACSS, Department of State, CPA, "National Poll of Iraq."

Oxford: How much confidence do you have in the [new] Iraqi Army?

	Oct./Nov. 2003	Feb. 2004	Mar./Apr. 2004	June 2004
Great deal	16.00	19.70	24.40	24
Quite a lot	30.10	42.20	46.70	50
Not very much	34.30	27.50	17.10	20
None at all	19.50	10.70	11.80	6

Source: Oxford Research International, "National Survey of Iraq."

Attitudes toward U.S. and Coalition Forces
Oxford: How much confidence do you have in the [U.S. and UK] occupation forces?

	Oct./Nov. 2003	Feb. 2004	Mar./Apr. 2004	June 2004
Great deal	7.60	8.70	7.00	6
Quite a lot	13.60	19.00	18.40	14
Not very much	22.20	25.60	22.30	30
None at all	56.60	46.80	52.30	51

Source: Oxford Research International, "National Survey of Iraq."

IIACSS: How much confidence do you have in [Coalition] forces to improve the situation in Iraq?

	Jan. 2004	Apr./May 2004	May 2004
Great deal	11.60	2.60	1.50
Fair amount	16.70	4.40	8.20
Not very much	13.70	4.70	6.10
None at all	53.30	83.50	80.60

Source: IIACSS, Department of State, CPA, "National Poll of Iraq."

those who felt Iraq was moving in the wrong direction cited the presence of occupation forces as the main reason, and 60.2 percent cited security.

Limited sampling in other surveys indicates that if the survey had covered the areas with strong support for insurgency, the presence of occupation troops would have dominated negative opinion in those areas. The Sunni areas that could be surveyed never showed more than 33 percent support for "moving in the right direction" between May 2004 and March 2005. Such support also dropped to 15 percent in September 2004 and then to 12 percent in January 2005, although it rose sharply to 33 percent when it became clear that elections would be held and a truly independent Iraqi government would be created.

At the same time, attitudes were more positive in the more secure Shi'ite and Kurdish areas, and much depended on exactly who was being polled. For example, MNSTC–I [Multinational Security Transition Command–Iraq] reports a poll was conducted of Iraqi women in early 2005 that indicated that 46 percent worried about crime and insurgency, 12 percent feared the Coalition, and, according to MNSTC–I statements, 40 percent feared nothing at all. The sample size, however, is unclear as are the exact questions that were asked of the women.[9]

"Disbanding" Iraqi Forces

In practice, the United States initially did little to create the kind of Iraqi forces that Iraqis wanted and the Coalition needed. The CPA announced that it was dissolving the former regime's military and security forces on May 23, 2003, and planned to create a new set of national self-defense capabilities for Iraq.[10] This decision, however, did little more than recognize a fait accompli.

U.S. forces had shattered much of the Republican Guard force and regular army in the South. Coalition airpower used some 18,000 guided air-to-surface munitions and thousands of unguided weapons, most against military targets. Imagery of Iraqi military facilities shows that many were essentially destroyed during the fighting, and others were looted, relooted, and looted again—often to the point of being totally unusable.

Most of the regular forces dependent on conscripts had collapsed because of mass desertions; the heavier units in the regular army were largely ineffective and suffered from both desertions and massive looting. The Republican Guard and Special Republican Guard units had been defeated in the field and were too politicized to preserve. Additionally, many of the Iraqi police vanished during the collapse of virtually every aspect of governance. Few facilities survived intact, most equipment was looted, and what remained was generally unsuited to the needs of forces that could serve a post–Saddam Hussein Iraq.

Only those who flew over Iraqi military and police installations and bases after the war or who actually walked through some of their remains can appreciate just how badly looted they were. With a few exceptions, like some of the facilities at Taji, the armed forces not only were gone, they had nothing to come back to. The police that did return often had empty buildings with no arms, furniture, communications, or vehicles. Moreover, many facilities simply did not suit a democratic and volunteer force. Barracks and other facilities paid minimal attention to the needs of enlisted men and other ranks.

Saddam Hussein fell from power on April 9, 2003, and the Iraqi military, security, and police forces had largely disintegrated by the middle of April 2003. The decision to formally disband the Ba'ath Party was taken on May 16, 2003—more than a month after the fall of Saddam Hussein and the virtual disintegration of Iraqi forces. Ambassador Paul Bremer did not issue Order No. 2, the Dissolution of Entities, which "abolished" the Iraqi Army along with the security forces and several other ministries, until March 23, 2003.

Ambassador Bremer, the former head of the Coalition Provisional Authority (CPA), described this situation in early 2005 as follows:

> Recently some Monday morning quarterbacks have questioned the Coalition's decision to "disband" Saddam's army and bar senior Ba'athists from government jobs after we liberated Iraq. These were the right decisions. They served an important strategic purpose and recognized realities on the ground.... Conservative estimates are that Saddam's security and intelligence forces killed at least 300,000 of their fellow countrymen.... During my time in Iraq, Iraqi citizens from all over the country, from every sect, religion, and ethnic group, repeatedly praised the de-Ba'athification and disbanding of Saddam's security forces as the Coalition's most praiseworthy decisions.... There was a practical side to our decision, too. By the time Baghdad and Tikrit fell, the Iraqi army had already disbanded itself. There was not a single organized Iraqi military unit intact after mid-April 2003.... In many military bases at Liberation not a single brick was left standing on another. No base was usable without major repairs.[11]

Disbanding the Corrupt and Incapable

Force quality is also a key issue. Many Sunni Iraqis talk about the competence of Iraqi forces and how well they would have performed if they had been preserved and recalled. Anyone who watched Iraqi forces operate during the Iran-Iraq War, however, became aware of the deep ethnic and sectarian divisions in Iraqi forces and that the regime often punished competence and professionalism rather than rewarded it.

The uprisings following the Gulf War triggered a continuing series of purges in the Iraqi military that lasted until Saddam's fall, while a vast number of promotions inflated the ranks of senior officers and filled slots with loyalists and incompetents. The security services grew in size and ruthlessness, the regular police were kept largely a passive tool of the regime, and promotion of all the military, security, and police forces increasingly became a matter of loyalty. Regular military forces became tied down in garrison duty along the Iranian border and opposite the Kurdish security zone in the North and declined sharply in capability. Units like the Republican Guard and security forces were used to attack the Kurds and in an enduring low-level civil struggle with the Shi'ite resistance in the South.

The "culture" of the Iraqi military was a key problem. Junior officers were trained *not* to show initiative and others failed to actively support their men or "lead forward." Aggressive and active mid-rank officers were seen as a threat by their superiors. Noncommissioned officers had little status or training and were not the key partners of their offices. Conscripts were given minimal training and support and sometimes were subjected to harsh conditions. The active army of 1980–1988 had become a politicized, barracks-oriented force by 2003. Illiteracy, poor physical condition, and appointment by nepotism and favoritism were common in both the military and police. Tests and exams were minimal. Men who supposedly had training were often passed or promoted because of influence or to avoid "shaming" a failure. Poor officers stayed on indefinitely.

As one senior U.S. expert put it, "The police ranked eleventh out of Iraq's eleven security services and had minimal pay, training, and equipment. They feared any form of interference with government activity and were largely passive and station-bound. Investigations and prosecution had to be paid for by complainants coming to the station, and follow-on investigations and prosecutions could become corrupt bidding contests between opposing sides, followed by feuds and revenge. Corruption, favoritism, and nepotism were endemic. The lack of a retirement system also meant many older police stayed on indefinitely and 'phantoms' stayed on police lists after their death to pay their widows."

The end result was that far too many of the military, security, and police personnel that served under Saddam lacked the training, leadership, and motivation to act as the kind of military, security, and police forces Iraq needed in the post-Saddam era. Deputy Secretary of State Richard Armitage, speaking on this issue, commented that "the units that existed previous to the invasion are not ones that were trained in the type of skills that we necessarily prize, to include a respect for the lives of civilians and civilian property."[12]

There were still some outstanding Iraqi leaders and force elements in each service, but the vast majority were poorly trained, lacked effective leadership and organization, and were designed more to protect the regime—at the cost of corruption, self-interest, and inertia—and not the nation. The services were vastly overstaffed with senior officers who were used to getting privileges but not to leading and taking initiative.

The "De-Ba'athification and De-Saddamization" of Iraqi Forces

Nevertheless, the decision in May 2003 to abolish the Ba'ath Party and then to remove former regime officials; disband military, security, and police personnel; and remove other supporters—including many teachers—as parts of a postwar "de-Ba'athification" program had serious effects. Many Iraqis felt (and still feel) that Ambassador Bremer and the CPA chose to carry out "de-Ba'athification" in sweeping and all-inclusive ways that included large numbers of middle-ranking level three and level four Ba'ath members and excluded many Iraqi's who had had no choice other than to go along with Saddam's regime or join the Ba'ath Party. It sent the message that they were being excluded from a role in the new Iraq, and since so many ordinary jobs—like that of teacher—were included in "de-Ba'athification," this reinforced Iraqi fears and concerns.

The decision also helped further alienate Arab Sunnis. Ambassador Bremer, the head of the Coalition Provisional Authority, seems to have made this decision after limited consultation with Washington. Certainly it was clear to Iraqis at the time that the United States and CPA were reacting to pressure from Shi'ite exile groups like the one led by Ahmed Chalabi, and many saw this as a sign that Sunnis would no longer have a major role in governing Iraq. Certainly the end result was to further alienate an already hostile Sunni leadership and largely exclude—rather than co-opt—senior Iraqis in both the military and security services.

One senior leader of the effort to create effective Iraqi forces puts it this way:

> The disenfranchisement of the Sunnis through the process of de-Ba'athification and the dissolution of the Police Force and the Army was a mistake. The Sunnis, in particular, were left with nothing and without hope, having been the ruling elite. Opinion on the Army is very much divided, but my own view is that we should have put what we could in cantonments—no matter how smashed up they were—fed them, provided tentage, generators whatever—purged the upper ranks and run a subtle info-ops campaign that did not show then as comprehensively outmaneuvered and defeated but one that had eventually surrendered. All very easy with hindsight of course but relevant in relation to what we might do in future conflicts.

These problems were compounded by the near collapse of the Iraqi economy, the looting of most military and police facilities, mass desertions of the military and police during and immediately after the war, and the loss of the government and military jobs upon which many Sunnis depended. The CPA was then slow to offer former military and security officers retirement or pay and slow to make good on the offer. There was little understanding that the impact would be far worse in the Sunni areas where such jobs, government investment, and military industries virtually dominated the local economy.

In the process the CPA and Iraqi Interim Government (IIG) disbanded all of the special security and intelligence services and excluded many competent former Ba'ath and career military and police officers and personnel from eligibility for the new military and security services. This included many innocent Iraqis who had simply gone along with the former regime to survive or because of the very national threats that developed during the Iran-Iraq War. While the overall manning of Iraqi leadership cadres consisted of timeservers, uniformed bureaucrats, and men seeking their own advantage, there were still many in these cadres who had served with honor in previous wars. It also seems that

Arab Sunnis were much more likely than Arab Shi'ites to be purged or blocked from jobs because of connections to the Ba'ath Party, and the process likely entailed at least some corruption on the part of the Iraqi officials involved.

The end result was a legacy that created serious and interrelated problems when it came to creating postwar military, security, and police forces, including the following:

- Most of Iraq's preinvasion police came back after the invasion, but far too many were timeserving instruments of regime security with little training and competence and were largely passive. Its security forces were much better trained and equipped but had been largely active instruments of regime repression. They did not go along to get along; they were key parts of the problem, but they were both the only forces trained for counterinsurgency and counterterrorism, and they were largely Sunni elements trained to be insurgents once excluded from power. The end result was that untrained police had to support the military, while trained ex-intelligence and security personnel were pushed into becoming insurgents.

- The armed forces had many elements that were effective and were not regime loyalists and that could later be recruited into the police and security forces. They had effectively disintegrated during the war, so they were a pool of talent to draw upon—rather than a disbanded force—but they were keys to creating effective forces, avoiding a Sunni-Shi'ite split, and avoiding driving another group of skilled manpower into the insurgency.

- De-Ba'athification blocked the U.S. teams developing the military, security, and police forces from recruiting many of the most experienced leaders and military personnel for much of the first year of the occupation. Some of the best and most qualified personnel could not be recruited. This, in turn, ensured there were few stable unit elements with proven leaders and personnel, and no amount of training and equipment can substitute for experienced leadership and the level of unit integrity that creates mutual loyalty among those assigned. Essentially, the United States and the Iraqi government ended up emphasizing sheer throughput in terms of numbers of personnel going through a grossly inadequate training system without bothering to give them any place to go.

- The near collapse of much of Iraq's economy following the invasion, coupled with the disbanding of the armed forces and much of the government, put tremendous pressure on young men to join the armed forces, security forces, and police regardless of their personal goals and ambitions. It then placed them in a society undergoing political, economic, and social turmoil—as well as a society experiencing a growing insurgency. Inevitably, large numbers of men joined for all the wrong reasons, often had no incentive to take risks, did not take training and discipline any more seriously than they were forced to, focused on family and local problems, and had little reason to be loyal. Some became informers or supporters of the insurgency.

It is interesting to note, however, that current Iraqi military and police officials and officers seem to be less critical of the "disbanding" of the military and security forces by the CPA than other Iraqis. They have lived with the real-world shortcomings in Saddam's forces and acknowledge that the war, desertions, and looting left few units and facilities intact and that most were not worth preserving. Many do, however, blame de-Ba'athification for failing to retain key personnel or anticipate what would happen to those with no political and career options.

Many of the Iraqis involved in creating Iraq's new forces also acknowledged that Shi'ite exile elements in the Interim Government had considerable responsibility for the pressure they put on the CPA to take a hard-line stand on de-Ba'athification—and did not simply blame U.S. officials. Such Iraqis also felt that the Interim Government made a major error in not reaching out to Ba'ath and Sunni elements who had had to go along with Saddam's regime and in allocating positions in fixed shares to Shi'ite Arabs, Kurds, and Sunni Arabs, rather than trying to create a national government.

The Initial Ideological Approach to Creating Iraqi Military, Security, and Police Forces

The United States did more than fail to plan for an effective effort to secure the country or to develop effective Iraqi forces before or during the invasion. It failed to deal with the risk—and then with the reality—of a growing insurgency effort for nearly a year after the fall of Saddam Hussein. This is in many ways due to the fact that a relatively small group of "neoconservatives," rather than the interagency process, dominated planning for the stability and nation-building phases following the fall of Saddam Hussein and that the Department of Defense was put in charge of the operation.

Part of the reason for this failure is that the problem of dealing with the Iraqi Army and security forces was handled largely by ideologues that had an unrealistic grand strategy for transforming Iraq and the Middle East. Their strategic assessments of Iraq were wrong in far more important ways than their assessment of the potential threat posed by Iraq's weapons of mass destruction. They were fundamentally wrong about how the Iraqi people would view the U.S. invasion. They were wrong about the problems in establishing effective governance, and they underestimated the difficulties in creating a new government that was legitimate in Iraqi eyes. They greatly exaggerated the relevance and influence of Iraqi exiles and greatly underestimated the scale of Iraq's economic, ethnic, and demographic problems.

They did not foresee the impact of the war on America's overall structure of alliances and on world opinion. They fundamentally misread the linkages between the invasion of Iraq, the Arab-Israeli conflict, and the fighting in Afghanistan. They did not foresee its impact on the Middle East and the Islamic world, the resulting decline in support for the war on terrorism, or the risk that Islamists inside and outside Iraq could become part of an insurgent threat. They failed to see that Iraqi Shi'ites might welcome the Coalition as liberators but not as occupiers and that they were almost certain to divide into factions and could present another insurgent risk. They saw military action by the Department of Defense as a workable substitute for effective coordination and action by all the agencies of government. Above all, they failed to see the importance of serious stability operations and nation-building; they did not plan effectively for the risk of insurgency; and they assumed that they were so right that America's allies and the world would soon be forced to follow their lead.

The end result was that they had no practical grand strategy beyond Saddam's fall, and their strategic assessments were slow to improve thereafter. Many neoconservatives wasted a year after the Coalition's apparent military victory, living in a state of ideological denial. The United States effectively occupied Iraq as proconsuls, rather than rushing to create a legitimate government and effective Iraqi military and security forces. U.S. aid efforts faltered in a mix of bureaucratic fumbling and uncoordinated, ideologically driven plans to make the Iraqi economy "American." They failed to rush aid in where it might have bought acceptance and stability—a fault only corrected much later when the U.S. military implemented effective emergency aid as part of its Commander's Emergency Relief Program (CERP), and the State Department and Department of Defense restructured aid plans to provide quick reaction funds and reprogram money to meet urgent needs.

No analysis of the successes and failures in creating effective Iraqi forces can ignore the impact of these failures. What realism there is in the present U.S. approach to the "war after the war" in Iraq was thrust upon the neoconservatives managing the Iraq War after the fall of Saddam Hussein. Ironically, to the extent that the United States may be evolving a workable approach to a grand strategy that evolution has been shaped largely by the people that neoconservatives chose to ignore in going to war in the first place. The adaptation to the political and military realities in Iraq has come from military, State Department, and intelligence professionals.

Problems in the Culture of the U.S. Military

The U.S. military, however, must share part of the blame. The U.S. military talked "asymmetric war," but it planned and organized for conventional war. It entered the Iraq War focused on conventional combat, high-technology warfare, and short wars in which the use of decisive force was assumed to produce decisive results.

At almost every level it lacked training in grand strategy in any practical terms. It failed to learn from the lessons of being unprepared for conflict termination in the Gulf War of 1991 and the practical problems of nation-building in Bosnia and Kosovo. Its leadership largely saw stability operations, nation-building, creating security, and dealing with local military and security forces as secondary missions that diverted and locked down scarce military resources.

The U.S. military never planned for an effective occupation of the country and never planned for extensive civil-military operations or to create the kind of area expertise, military police, and human intelligence (HUMINT) resources it might need. It focused on the military dimension of battle and forgot the fundamental principle that all victory is ultimately political in character. In doing so, it seems to have ignored or put aside at least some of the prior contingency planning by USCENTCOM, the command with real expertise in the area.

While some senior U.S. officers in Washington did warn that massive occupation forces would be needed, this seems to have been more to argue for large war-fighting forces or as a counter to the enthusiasm of ideologues than the result of detailed analysis and planning. In general, the military, as well as the civilians, did not plan for successful conflict termination or stability operations, and it focused on early withdrawal rather than the range of missions that might occur. U.S. officers indicate that the operational plan called for rapid withdrawals from Iraq after Saddam's fall—with some plans calling for a rapid reduction to 30,000 troops—rather than for an effective stability and security effort. It is also all too clear that the U.S. military did not plan either to provide U.S. forces training and equipment for counterinsurgency missions or to provide the kind of training cadres and facilities necessary to help Iraqi forces.

The U.S. military—like most of the world's militaries—focuses on its own priorities and force developments. Its exceptional level of professionalism and technology, however, often has the negative effect of making it reluctant to cooperate fully with allies and to develop true interoperability. When it does, it tends to do so only with proven, highly professional partners like Britain and Australia.

Some U.S. field commanders did see the need to establish "interoperability" with the Iraqis, particularly in gaining local political support, HUMINT, translation skills, and so forth. A few saw early on that the counterinsurgency, security, and police missions required a different kind of interoperability that would make the development of Iraqi forces critical to nation-building, security, and counterinsurgency missions. The U.S. military culture was not prepared for such interoperability at the start of the occupation, however, and it took roughly a year of developing insurgency to make senior U.S. military commanders in Washington and the Gulf region understand the essential importance of allies. In the process they repeated many of the mistakes made in Vietnam and Lebanon—forgetting, if they ever knew, the lessons of those operations.

At a different level the top leadership of the U.S. military failed to establish effective links to the civil occupation authority in the Office of Reconstruction and Humanitarian Assistance (ORHA) before, during, and immediately after the fighting that toppled Saddam Hussein. It then tolerated, if not encouraged, the poor relations between Bremer, the CPA, General Ricardo Sanchez, and the field commanders for the year that followed. The lack of interagency cooperation in Washington had its mirror image in the field, made worse by two leaders who proved unable to develop an effective working relationship on a personal or staff level.

It is fair to argue that the fundamental failure of the interagency process to coordinate the efforts of the Department of Defense with those of the State Department and other civilian agencies lies with the president, his national security advisor, the secretary of defense, and the secretary of state. There is no question, however, that the military did not see the need for "jointness" at the civil-military level in the field and that this inevitably complicated virtually every aspect of the effort to create effective Iraqi forces, to link the effort to create them to the effort to create effective Iraqi governance, and to implement key aspects of the U.S. aid program.

Failures at the U.S. Advisory and Civilian Assistance Level: The Problem of the Security Forces and Police

Other kinds of failures took place at a different level on the civilian side of the aid process—failures that contributed to training the wrong kinds of forces and providing support for the insurrection. The Bush administration made the task of the CPA and aid officials extraordinarily difficult by failing to create any meaningful plans for nation-building before or during the war, by failing to create effective civilian structures to assist in nation-building and recruiting suitable personnel in advance, and by failing to develop and budget for anything approaching a meaningful aid program.[13]

Stability operations require strong and effective police forces even in climates where there is no political instability or threat from terrorists and insurgents. In practice almost all of Iraq's elite police and law enforcement functions were part of the security services the regime used to protect itself and repress the Iraqi people, and these functions were totally decoupled from the regular police. The regular police were corrupt, passive, badly undertrained and poorly educate, and often physically incapable or overage. As a report by the inspector generals of the State Department and Department of Defense notes:

> Three levels of police existed under the previous regime: Non-Commissioned Officers (NCOs), Assistant Officers, and Officers. At the most basic level, NCOs possessed little formal education, normally only completing primary school. When hired, they were trained within their provincial area in an unstructured program that could last up to three months. Standards and length of training varied widely from province to province. Upon graduation, NCOs were responsible for most of the daily contact with Iraqi citizens. NCOs were the first responders to calls for service and were responsible for dealing with disputes and for the maintenance of public order.

At the mid-grades, Assistant Officers completed secondary school education, usually from the Police High School, and then underwent on-the-job training. They were normally assigned to various administrative functions within the Iraqi Police Force. They would only respond to serious crimes and only in a supervisory capacity. Their duties usually consisted of administrative work for the Officer corps. Officers were also secondary school graduates, but were further educated at the Police Professional College in Baghdad, undergoing a three-year course of instruction. Upon graduation, the Officers received the equivalent of a Bachelor's degree in police science; however, the curriculum was steeped in military doctrine and training. After graduation, the academy Officers were posted around the country and normally served in the assigned region for the rest of their careers. Traditional training in leadership, management, and command and staff functions was not institutionalized.

... even more than the military, the Iraqi police during the Saddam Hussein era were perceived to be corrupt and brutal implementers of oppression. Accordingly, an early decision of the CPA was to cashier police officers closely tied to the former regime. Other members of the IPS [Iraqi Police Service] abandoned their duties or were casualties of the conflict. Only about 30,000, mostly low-ranking police remained on duty as a residual force—a number clearly insufficient to enforce law and order even had stability been established.[14]

The Iraqi police initially were seen as a minor aspect of the security mission— and largely in terms of training a police force with a respect for the rule of law and human rights. The Iraqi police largely deserted in April 2003 during the fighting. Many voluntarily returned to duty during May 2003, but the CPA made no real effort to vet them or review their performance. The CPA's director of police was tasked with providing rush training to get as many police on the streets as quickly as possible with no real vetting.[15]

It took the Coalition well over a year to realize that the police and security forces were critical to stability and to any form of effective Iraqi governance and reconstruction. The Coalition sometimes found itself reacting to an Iraqi lead in creating elite counterinsurgency security forces and training the regular police for a combat mission that went well beyond ordinary police work. Even then, priority was given to the military, although the police and security forces involved substantially more manpower, and no defeat of the terrorists or insurgents could be secured without their lasting presence.

A study by the inspector generals of the State Department and Department of Defense indicates the following problems:

The deficit of policemen was only one of the myriad problems that confronted Coalition planners after the June 2004 transition from the CPA to the Iraqi Interim Government (IIG). More vexing is the growth of terrorism and insurgency that continue to challenge both Coalition military forces and the nascent Iraqi military and police forces. Faced with this situation, Coalition officials perceived a primary objective should be the fastest possible creation of a sizeable police force.

... As a result of the conflict in 2003 and the ensuing state of chaos and looting, much of the IPS [Iraqi Police Service] infrastructure was destroyed or badly damaged. Many of the IPs [Iraqi police] who served during the Saddam Hussein era abandoned their positions, were casualties of war, or were cashiered.

... Consistent with the CPA goal of erasing troublesome aspects of the Hussein regime, command and control of the remnants of the police force were decentralized. This further diluted cohesion and effectiveness of the residual force.... The CPA decision to cleanse the political system of Hussein sympathizers—notably, the "de-Ba'athification" effort—effectively decapitated the IPS of its standing leadership. Even though some former police officers have been reincorporated into the force, it was necessary to start almost from scratch to build a new police force. The result was a "bottom-up" approach with primary emphasis on minimal basic training.

... On May 2, 2003, the Office for Reconstruction and Humanitarian Assistance (ORHA—the predecessor of the CPA) called for police in Baghdad to return to work. Coalition force commanders made similar announcements for secured areas outside the capital. In June 2003, the CPA and MOI [Ministry of Interior] issued a directive that all police officers had to return to work no later than July 3. Those failing to do so were subject to immediate termination. According to International Criminal Investigation Training Assistance Program (ICITAP) officials, about 38,000 had returned to the IPS as of July.

... To bolster the force, an additional 30,000 police were recruited by Coalition Joint Task Force 7 (CJTF–7) and the Major Subordinate Commanders (MSCs). The driving objective was to get "boots on the ground." In doing so, the CPA enunciated minimal requirements for entry into the IPS.... Subsequently, to meet MNSTC–I training quotas, two patterns of recruiting evolved. Iraqis did most of the recruiting in the Baghdad area. Coalition forces (working through the major subordinate commands or MSCs) were in charge of recruiting in the rest of the country. Iraqi recruiters appear to have enforced minimum requirements as enunciated by CPA, while the MSCs sent to JIPTC [Jordan International Police Training Center] some recruits who did not meet those minimum standards.

... the Coalition Provisional Authority (CPA) took the first steps to assist the Ministry of Interior (MOI) in developing an Iraqi Police Service (IPS) that would be a respected force based on public trust and confidence. Creating this force from the brutal and corrupt remnants of the Saddam regime police would probably have required dissolution of the entire force and slow rebuilding into a force that echoed the new democratic ideals of Iraq. The security situation, however, dictated rapid infusion of police into the cities and governorates, a requirement that mandated an accelerated training program. To optimize required quantity and equally important quality, CPA designed a program based on the International Criminal Investigation Training Assistance Program (ICITAP) "Kosovo" model that would give police recruits eight weeks of training. They planned to complement the eight-week basic program with a structured on-the-job training program guided by an experienced mentor.

In order to meet the capacity required, two academies were established: the Baghdad Public Safety Academy (more recently renamed the Baghdad Police

College) and an academy in Jordan, outside Amman, the Jordan International Police Training Center (JIPTC). Several regional academies were subsequently added. The basic training instructional program consisted of two distinct, but integrated, components: academy training and field training. New police recruits would spend two months at one of the academies, training in modern policing methods. New cadets would receive 320 standardized hours of intensive education in modern policing techniques. The basic course would include academic and practical training in firearms (pistols), defensive tactics, and emergency vehicle operation. The academic instruction also included policing in a democracy, constitutional framework, human rights, use of force, police ethics and code of conduct, gender issues, community policing, traffic accident management, etc.

For recruits who completed the academy courses, the concept prescribed subsequent participation in a structured field training program, focusing on the practical application of the coursework and seeking further development of proactive, service-oriented policing skills. During this probationary period, newly graduated cadets were to be paired one-on-one with a senior Iraqi Police Service (IPS) Field Training Officer (FTO), who would function as a mentor. International Police Advisors (later renamed International Police Liaison Officers (IPLOs) would oversee the program. The concept consisted of four phases conducted over a six-month period involving daily, weekly, and monthly evaluations by senior IPS FTOs.

The CPA plan relied upon building a foundation in the classroom, but also counted on the structured and mentored training that was to occur in the months following graduation. In March 2004, the Civilian Police Assistance Training Team (CPATT) was established, and an initial Field Training Coordinator Program was implemented locally in Baghdad. Unfortunately, the deteriorating security environment, coupled with a dearth of experienced IPS and insufficient numbers of International Police Liaison Officers (IPLOs), precluded full implementation of the mentoring program.

At the outset of the CPA effort to build IPS capacity, the assumption—even to some extent, the reality—was that training could be molded within a rapidly stabilizing political and security environment. The unexpected virulence and scope of subsequent terrorism and insurgency induced changes in the program, but such modifications ... lagged [behind] the "street reality" in Iraq.

A CPA decision to decentralize command and control of the IPS has had unintended consequences. Decentralization was consistent with the intent to disperse political power. Commendable in concept, the emerging result within the IPS is a pattern of fiefdoms, subject to political machinations. An example of this political maneuvering is the situation of competing chiefs of police in Najaf where one responds to the provincial governor, the other to the MOI.

Pay problems have been an equally troubling result of decentralization. Under the CPA designed system, much of the central government's funding is allocated to the provincial governors. Thereafter, the monies are sub-allocated to respective elements, such as the police. Accordingly, each provincial chief of police controls his share of sub-allotted funds. Allegations of mismanagement and corruption in the disbursement of pay for IPs, equipment purchases, etc., are credible.[16]

In practice a great many men were rushed into service with minimum vetting, inadequate training and equipment, a failure to reorganize the regular police to make them functional, and no controls on corruption and "phantom" personnel. Coordination between the Department of State and Department of Defense training efforts and the newly forming Iraqi Ministry of Interior and Ministry of Defense was poor at best. The flow of Coalition aid was grossly inadequate, and Iraq did not have a budget to make the new force work. The police were not properly trained, equipped, or facilitated for counterinsurgency and counterterrorism missions, and little serious effort was made to add the elite forces needed for these missions because of the fear that they would end up being the same kind of repressive tools of the regime that they were under Saddam Hussein. It was not until April 2004 that the Coalition fully recognized that the field training that was originally planned could not deal with the insurgency and terrorism, and even then the Coalition was "reluctant to increase the length of basic training because of the urgent need to build IPS capacity and get policemen on the streets."[17] State Department, USAID, and Department of Justice aid efforts were organized around the idea that regular police forces should be created as soon as possible to replace reliance on outside forces and the armed forces. The U.S. Congress also pressed hard to keep the U.S. military role in training paramilitary forces to a minimum, largely as a legacy of problems in Latin America and elsewhere during the cold war. This reflected a legitimate concern with the human-rights abuses that can occur when military or paramilitary forces become involved in police functions.

According to the General Accountability Office (GAO), it was not until May 2004 that a national security presidential security directive was issued that gave CENTCOM the responsibility of directing all U.S. government efforts to organize, train, and equip the Iraqi security force, which led to the Multinational Security Transition Command–Iraq, operating under MNF–I, being given a clear lead on all Coalition efforts.[18]

In several critical instances the United States did not listen to its own advisers in the field, even as the problems of crime, terrorism, and insurgency continued to grow. According to research by Robert M. Perito, the Department of Justice sent a team from its International Criminal Investigative Training Assistance Program (ICITAP) to Iraq in May 2003. It also focused on creating a conventional police force, not addressing the problems of terrorism, insurgency, and mass organized crime. It did recognize that the Iraqi police could not function effectively and called for the deployment of some 6,600 international police advisers with 360 police trainers in a police academy and in total a 2,500-man international police force organized into ten units to support Coalition military forces in reaching stability and training Iraqis.[19]

A Bush administration review of these recommendations, however, felt such requirements were exaggerated, and they were largely put aside. Similarly, the White House deferred a State Department recommendation for a 1,000-person team until fall—by which time the insurgency had become a serious problem. Action then had low priority. U.S. police advisers were obtained on a contract basis from DynCorp for a 500-person force, although they were precluded from actual police action and did not begin to arrive until the spring of 2004. There were only 283 deployed in June 2004, and the rise in attacks discouraged both U.S. recruiting and any allied presence.

Ultimately, a small six-person Department of Justice team was asked to remain under the direction of Bernard Kerik, the former police commissioner of New York City, working for the Iraqi Ministry of Interior in isolation from the efforts in the Ministry of Defense. The U.S. team not only had responsibility for creating a virtually new Iraq Police Service (IPS) but also Iraq's fire and emergency response forces and border police—a total of roughly 100,000 men. Equipment deliveries were also slow and inadequate—only about half of the short-term requirement for weapons, vehicles, and communications equipment had actually been delivered by June 2004.[20]

Some other aspects of the police training effort were more effective, although it should be stressed that such efforts initially trained police only for operations in a permissive environment, where even serious organized crime was not seen as a threat. (Some estimates put the level of criminal violence so high that it killed some 10,000 Iraqis between April 2003 and April 2004.)[21] The training efforts did not include effective vetting, providing proper equipment, getting rid of large numbers of incompetent officers, or adapting from failures, and many illiterate, physically weak, overage, and corrupt personnel continued to be retained. The United States and its allies also lacked the language skills, area skills, and manpower to perform such training functions and could not discriminate easily between civilians, criminals, and insurgents. This sometimes led to the killing, wounding, and detainment of innocent Iraqis when U.S. and other Coalition forces did perform such functions.[22]

A further major problem developed over time because the small Iraqi border force had never been effective, and border security had always been the function of the military, security, and intelligence forces. Most of Iraq's some 240 border "forts" were looted and abandoned during the Coalition advance, and most of the 614-man force deserted along with customs and other border officials. There was no planning to deal with this situation, and only one man from the Department of Justice police advisory team could initially be assigned. The Department of Homeland Security was forced to rush in a team to provide a few days of training for immigration and customs procedures to a thirty-person U.S. military team. Many of the U.S. military involved in immigration training had only about three hours of formal instruction and no language or area skills. As the insurgency developed, priority was given to military and police training, and efforts to create an effective, new Department of Border Enforcement (DBE) under the Ministry of Interior did not begin until the late spring of 2004.

The U.S. police advisers did succeed in developing a training course for the Iraqi police called the Transition Integration Program (TIP). This was a three-week course for rehired police who came back into service in large numbers in May and June 2003. It was administered by U.S. military police and gave some 30,000 to 40,000 limited training by December 2004, although a large part of the training was more in human rights and the rule of law than modern police work. It is also not clear how many of those credited with attending the course actually attended.

In December 2003 a Department of Justice–approved program began to function at the Jordan International Police Training Center, based to some extent on a much longer sixteen-week course developed for the Kosovo Police Service School. The eight-week course pushed some 2,500 recruits through every month and did so with minimal vetting and examination of qualifications, sometimes graduating personnel that neither met course standards nor attended the entire course.

They then received no follow-up training, and efforts to create a field training program using DynCorp police advisers were not put into practice because of the rising security threat. The end result was that 120,000 men were recruited back into the police force, at least 30,000 of whom were either unqualified or simply took pay (if they actually existed), and the government then had to offer retirement and other incentives to get rid of many of the police who had been so rapidly recruited. One result was a $60 million buyout program to cut the size of the police force by 25 percent—a program that came to involve an additional element of favoritism and corruption.[23]

This inadequate approach to nation-building would have been unworkable at any time and was little more than a disaster when there were already major threats to the police from militias, insurgents, organized terrorists, and large criminal elements. The transition to stability requires well-armed and well-protected security forces in large numbers that can coordinate directly with the military and handle serious threats. Trying to create regular police forces and constant reliance on the military—a lesson that became brutally clear in the Balkans and in Afghanistan long before the United States became involved in Iraq—are recipes for disaster.

Creating additional light-guard forces like the Facilities Protection Service (FPS) was treated as a low-level task that was as important in terms of employing Iraqis as creating effective units. The police and the bulk of the security forces were given grossly inadequate training, equipment, facilities, transport, and protection, and were hampered by a lack of the kind of structured leadership and emphasis on "unit integrity" necessary to equip police units to protect themselves and fight.

The end result was to waste nearly a year until police and security force training were better integrated with the military training effort and until the U.S.

military advisory team was given responsibility for planning the kind of security and police force Iraq needed—the kind of forces which the Iraqi Ministry of the Interior and U.S. civilian advisers were incapable of planning and creating. It then left General David Petraeus and the Iraqi government with a legacy of vast numbers of men with few real qualifications, the wrong kind of training, and ones that had been recruited without proper vetting and often without proper regard to even elementary qualifications like physical condition and literacy.

Problems in Governance and Iraq's Economy and Society

Another set of problems that contributed to the difficulties in creating effective Iraqi military, security, and police forces involved governance and economic and societal factors. Effective security efforts require effective governance at every level. They require coordination at the central government level to ensure they are properly financed, given clear direction, and that coordination takes place between the ministry leading the armed forces (Ministry of Defense) and the police and paramilitary security forces (Ministry of Interior). Effective planning and direction must take place at the regional and local levels, and more importantly, there must be local government to support, give direction to, provide effective services, and win the support of the local people.

Police and security forces can never be effective by themselves. They must serve a local government and the local population to win popular support, or they find themselves isolated and locked into a fortress and defensive mentality. They also are inherently vulnerable. They have to move, they have families, and they have relatives. In most cases, they are local. Leaving such forces vulnerable and unsupported has several major effects: it leads to constant desertions and turbulence within local forces, resulting in alliances with threat elements for self-preservation, corruption to try to buy security and status, and to cases in which the security and police forces use excessive violence without really knowing who the enemy is.

In practice there is still no effective governance in much of Iraq, and serious efforts to address these problems only began to be solved after the Iraqi Interim Government (IIG) took power in June 2004. Coordination problems still exist within ministries and between the defense, interior, and finance ministries. The central government cannot give effective direction and leadership, implement policy or react effectively to local requests, and above all move money and resources on anything like a timely basis.

Many regional and local governments are weak or ineffective. In many cases the local government serves its own interest, and in high threat areas the local government often simply does not function or will not confront the insurgents or other threats. Insurgent sympathizers have penetrated the government at many levels, corruption is common, and senior officials are often unwilling or reluctant to replace incompetent or corrupt subordinates until they fail so conspicuously that they create major security problems.

All of these problems were made worse, however, during the first year of Coalition occupation. The "green zone" mentality of the CPA and its focus on Baghdad meant that there was little effective leadership and help at the regional and local level. Some State Department officials and other civilians did outstanding personal work, but the U.S. civilian teams in the field were far too small to help compensate for the lack of effective local government or to provide the U.S. military with the kind of support it needed in any part of the nation-building and aid process. In terms of local governance and local police and security operations, the collapse of the Saddam Hussein regime left a vacuum that U.S. civilians were not available to fill and that the U.S. military was not trained to deal with. Therefore, criticizing Iraqi forces—particularly the police and security forces—for failing to perform under these conditions is both unfair and misses virtually every relevant lesson for nation-building.

The Iraqi View: Failure to Foresee Insurgency, Not Postwar Disbandment, Is the Key Problem

There is no way to comprehensively survey Iraqi defense officials and officers, but discussions with a number of officials and officers in 2004 do provide further insight into the problems that occurred during the initial stages of the U.S. and Coalition effort to create effective Iraqi military, security, and police forces. These Iraqis are less critical of the "disbandment" and "de-Ba'athification" of the military and security forces by the CPA than outside Iraqis. They acknowledge that the war, desertions, and looting left few units and facilities intact and that most were not worth preserving.

Some did blame de-Ba'athification for failing to retain key personnel or to anticipate what would happen to those with no political and career options. Many of the Iraqis involved did feel, however, that Shi'ite exile elements in the Interim Government had considerable responsibility for the pressure they put on the CPA to take a hard-line stand on de-Ba'athification—and did not simply blame U.S. officials. Such Iraqis also felt that the Interim Government made a major error in not reaching out to Ba'ath and Sunni elements who had had to go along with Saddam's regime and in allocating positions in fixed shares to Shi'ite Arabs, Kurds, and Sunni Arabs, rather than trying to create a national government.

In general, the Iraqi officials and officers involved in creating Iraqi forces saw the most serious problem behind the lack of effectiveness of Iraqi forces until late 2004 as the result of a failure on the part of the CPA and the U.S. military to anticipate the threat of a major insurgency and the failure to train and equip regular military, security, and police forces for this mission.

They stressed that the initial goals in creating new Iraqi military and security forces were to avoid the abuses of the past and to avoid creating a threat to democracy. As a result, the pace and scale of the military effort was slow to the point of reaching only token levels. The military was being shaped as a light border defense force that would only emerge with anything approaching serious capabilities long after the Iraqis finished drafting a constitution and had successfully created a new democratic government.

Similarly, the development of police and security forces was placed under the Ministry of the Interior, and little coordination took place with the military effort under the Ministry of Defense. Security forces were given minimal paramilitary and intelligence elements, and most were initially assigned to low-grade facility protection forces like the Iraqi Civil Defense Corps (ICDC)—the predecessor to the National Guard. The ICDC was recruited locally with little attention to manpower quality and had minimal equipment and facilities provided.

Iraqi military and security forces were developed and deployed by each of the five major division areas under the Multinational Security Transition Command—Iraq (MNSTC–I), to meet the priorities and security needs of the MNSTC–I rather than a new, sovereign Iraqi government. This led to a lack of any cohesive follow-up to the initial training efforts and an inevitable dependence on MNF–I forces for equipment and all forms of serious combat, service, and logistical support.

Iraqi police forces were created and recruited with minimal coordination and seen as little more than "beat cops" that required token training and equipment. In general, they were not shaped to deal with looting and Iraq's rapidly growing crime problems, much less the problem of security. They were created on a "helter-skelter" basis—with little equipment and training and minimal facilities. Much of this effort occurred at local levels with little attention to manpower quality, and the Ministry of the Interior often had no serious picture of the strength of given local police forces, much less any picture of their quality and leadership. Many police were chosen by local leaders more as a matter of patronage than as part of an effort to create effective forces, and corruption and favoritism were rampant. Vetting was little more than a "by guess and by God" effort, and little attention was paid to past training, education, and physical condition—problems that were equally serious in the ICDC/National Guard.

At a technical level the Iraqis involved in these efforts feel that the United States was far too slow to provide anything like adequate numbers of experienced personnel, to see that the police and security effort had to be coordinated with the military effort, and to understand that the mission was counterterrorism and counterinsurgency and not building conventional military and police forces. They note that most initial cadres had no knowledge of how to deal with Iraqis or a different culture, that the high levels of rotation meant that personnel did not have the necessary on-the-job training and personal contacts, and that the United States and MNSTC–I constantly changed focus and were different in each of the five major operational areas under MNSTC–I control.

The Legacy

The end result of these complex forces is that the U.S.-led Coalition initially tried to restrict the development of Iraqi armed forces to a token force geared to defend Iraq's borders against external aggression. It did not try to create police forces with the capability to deal with serious insurgency and security challenges. As time went on, it ignored or did not give proper priority to the warnings from U.S. military advisory teams about the problems of organizing and training Iraqi forces and in giving them the necessary equipment and facilities.

The United States failed to treat the Iraqis as partners in the counterinsurgency effort for nearly a year after the fall of Saddam Hussein and did not attempt to seriously train and equip Iraqi forces for proactive security and counterinsurgency missions until April 2004—nearly a year after the fall of Saddam Hussein and two-thirds of a year after a major insurgency problem began to emerge.[24] Moreover, the United States did not react to the immediate threat that crime and looting presented throughout Iraq almost immediately after the war and which made personal security the number one concern of the Iraqi people. It acted as if it had years to rebuild Iraq using its own plans, rather than months to shape the climate in which Iraqis could do it.

2 The Growth and Character of the Insurgent Threat

BOTH U.S. POLICYMAKERS and the U.S. military initially lived in a state of near denial over the rise of terrorism and insurgency. The United States assumed for much of the first year after the fall of Saddam Hussein that it was dealing with a limited number of insurgents that Coalition forces would defeat well before the election. It did not see the threat level that would emerge if it did not provide jobs or pensions for Iraqi career officers or co-opt them into the nation-building effort. It was slow to see that some form of transition payments was necessary for the young Iraqi soldiers who faced massive, nationwide unemployment. The United States still failed to acknowledge the true scale of the insurgent threat and the extent to which popular resentment of Coalition forces would rise if it did not act immediately to rebuild a convincing mix of Iraqi military and security forces.

The United States failed to establish the proper political conditions to reduce Iraqi popular resentment of the Coalition forces and create a political climate that would ease the task of replacing them with effective Iraqi forces. It failed to make clear to the Iraqi people that the United States and Britain had no economic ambitions in Iraq and would not establish permanent bases or keep Iraqi forces weak to ensure their control. In fact, Lieutenant General Jay Garner, the first American administrator in Iraq, suggested in early 2004 that U.S. forces might remain in Iraq for "the next few decades," adding that securing basing rights for the United States should be a top priority.[1]

Failing to Admit the Scope of the Problem through Mid-2004

As a result, the United States failed to come to grips with the Iraqi insurgency during the first year of U.S. occupation in virtually every important dimension. It was slow to react to the growth of the insurgency in Iraq, to admit it was largely domestic in character, and to admit it had significant popular support.

The U.S. military and intelligence effort in the field did begin to understand that the terrorist and insurgent threat was serious and growing by the fall of 2003.

For all of 2003 and most of the first half of 2004, however, senior U.S. officials and officers did not act on this plan or respond effectively to the growing insurgency. They kept referring to the attackers as terrorists, kept issuing estimates that they could not number more than 5,000, and claimed they were a mixture of outside elements and die-hard former regime loyalists (FRLs) who had little popular support. The United States largely ignored the previous warnings provided by Iraqi opinion polls and claimed that its political, economic, and security efforts were either successful or would soon become so. In short, the United States failed to honestly assess the facts on the ground in a manner reminiscent of Vietnam.

As late as July 2004, some senior members of the Bush administration still seemed to live in a fantasyland in terms of their public announcements, perception of the growing Iraqi hostility to the use of Coalition forces, and the size of the threat. Its spokespeople were still talking about a core insurgent force of only 5,000 when many Coalition experts on the ground in Iraq saw a core of at least 12,000 to 16,000. They also ignored signs of Sunni versus Shi'ite tension and growing ethnic tension in the north.

Such U.S. estimates of the core structure of the Iraqi insurgency ignored the true nature of the insurgency. The United States was dealing with a mixture of Iraqi nationalism, Sunni resentment and anger, and popular opposition to any form of Western occupation. The problem was broad support, not a small group of "bitter enders." From the start there were many part-time insurgents and criminals who worked with insurgents. In some areas volunteers could be quickly recruited and trained, both for street fighting and terrorist and sabotage missions. As in most insurgencies, "sympathizers" within the Iraqi government and Iraqi forces, as well as the Iraqis working for the Coalition, media, and nongovernmental organizations (NGOs), often provided excellent human intelligence without violently taking part in the insurgency. Saboteurs can readily operate within the government and every aspect of the Iraqi economy.

From the start Iraqi and foreign journalists provided an inadvertent (and sometimes deliberate) propaganda arm, and media coverage of insurgent activity and attacks provided a de facto command and communications net to insurgents. This informal "net" provides warning, tells insurgents what attacks do and do not work, and allows them to coordinate their attacks to reinforce those of other insurgent cells and groups. As in all insurgencies, a race developed, this one between the insurgents and the Coalition and Iraqi Interim Government forces to see whose strength could grow faster and who could best learn from their enemies.

Evolving Threat Tactics and Pressure on Government Forces

During the summer and fall of 2003, Iraqi insurgents emerged as effective forces with significant popular support in Arab Sunni areas and developed a steadily more sophisticated mix of tactics. In the process, as Chapter 11 and the Chronology describe in detail, a native and foreign Islamist extremist threat also developed, which deliberately tried to divide Iraq's Sunni Arabs from its Arab Shi'ites, Kurds, and other Iraqi minorities. By the fall of the 2004 this had some elements of a low-level civil war, and by June 2005 it threatened to escalate into a far more serious civil conflict.

There are no reliable unclassified counts of insurgent attacks and incidents or of the casualties on both sides—an issue also discussed in depth in Chapter 11. The United States only publicly reported on its own casualties, and the Iraqi government stopped making its own estimates public. Estimates of insurgent casualties are also tenuous at best.

The NGO Coordinating Committee on Iraq, however, did make useful rough estimates of the patterns of attack between September 2003 and October 2004. These patterns seem broadly correct and both illustrate key patterns in the fighting and the need for competent and combat-capable Iraqi government military, security, and police forces:

- From September 2003 through October 2004 there was a rough balance between the three primary methods of attack—namely, improvised explosive device (IED), direct fire, and indirect fire—with a consistent but much smaller number of vehicle-borne improvised explosive devices (VBIED). Numbers of attacks varied significantly by month. There was a slow decline from well over 400 attacks each by improvised explosive device (IED), direct-fire weapons, and indirect-fire weapons to around 300. There was also, however, a slow increase in attacks using VBIEDs.
- Attack distribution also varies with a steadily rising number of attacks in the area of Mosul in the North. Baghdad, however, has been the scene of roughly twice as many attacks and incidents as the other governorates with 300 to 400 a month on average. Al Anbar, Salah-al-din, and Ninewa have had roughly one-third to one-half as many. Babil and Diyala average around one hundred per month; lower levels of attack have taken place in Tamin and Basra.
- Since the Shi'ite fighting with Sadr has ceased, the peak of insurgent activity in the South has declined. There have been relatively low levels of attack in the Karbala, Thi-Qar, Wassit, Missan, Muthanna, Najaf, and Qaddisyaa governorates.
- Irbil, Dahok, and Sulaymaniyah are northern governorates administrated by the two Kurdish regional governments (KRGs) and have long been relatively peaceful.
- Attacks fit a broad pattern during the day, although 60 percent of the attacks reported are unspecified. Of those that do have a specific time reported, 10 percent are in the morning, 11 percent in the afternoon, and 19 percent at night.

A rough estimate of targets and casualties from September 2003 to October 2004 is shown in table 2.1 and helps illustrate the continuing diversity of the

TABLE 2.1
**Illustrative Patterns in Targeting and Casualties (September
2003 to October 2004)**

Target	Number of Attacks/Incidents	Killed	Wounded
Coalition forces	3,227	451	1,002
Coalition air convoy	49	55	32
CPA/U.S. officials/Green Zone	206	32	60
Diplomatic mission	11	7	9
Local authority	31	56	81
Contractor	113	210	203
Civilian	180	1,981	3,467
Criminal and suspect	49	31	972
ICDC	58	191	310
Kurd Army	31	25	8
Police	209	480	1,012
UN	67	2	3
IO	1	2	0
NGO	5	5	11
Journalist	8	27	38
Interpreter	7	17	6
Public property	182	5	15
Unspecified	43	1	1

attacks and that far more than American casualties were involved from the start
of the conflict.

Political, Psychological, and Information Warfare Lessons

The goals and methods of the strategy and tactics the insurgents used evolved
steadily after the summer and fall of 2003. Almost from the beginning Iraqi
insurgents, terrorists, and extremists exploited the fact that the media tends to
focus on dramatic incidents with high casualties, gives them high publicity, and
spends little time analyzing the patterns in insurgency. The fact that there were
different groups of insurgents and terrorists also led the patterns of insurgent
activity to evolve in ways that included a steadily wider range of tactics that each
group of actors exploited whenever it found them to be convenient and which all
groups of attackers could refine with time.

Insurgents came to exploit the following methods and tactics relating to
political, psychological, and information warfare:

- *Attack the structures of governance and security by ideological, political, and
  violent means.* Use ideological and political means to attack the legitimacy
  of the government and the nation-building process. Intimidate and subvert
  the military and security forces. Intimidate and attack government officials
  and institutions at the national, regional, and local levels. Strike at infrastructure, utilities, and services in ways that appear to show that the government
  cannot provide essential economic services or personal security.

- *Create alliances of convenience and informal networks with other groups to attack the United States, various elements of the Iraqi interim government, the elected government, and efforts at nation-building.* The informal common fronts operate on the principal that the "enemy of my enemy" is my temporary friend. At the same time movements "franchise" to create individual cells and independent units, creating diverse mixes of enemies that are difficult to attack.
- *Attack Iraqi elites and ethnic and sectarian fault lines; use them to prevent nation-building and governance by provoking civil war.* As the United States and the Coalition phased down their role and a sovereign Iraqi government increased its influence and power, insurgents increasingly shifted the focus of their attacks to Iraqi government targets, as well as Iraqi military, police, and security forces. At the same time, they stepped up attacks designed to prevent Sunnis from participating in the new government and to cause growing tension and conflict between Sunni and Shi'ite and Arab and Kurd.

There are no clear lines of division between insurgents, but the Iraqi Sunni insurgents focused heavily on attacking the emerging Iraqi process of governance, while Islamist extremist movements used suicide-bombing attacks and other bombings to cause large casualties among the Shi'ite and Kurdish populations—sometimes linking them to religious festivals or holidays and sometimes to attacks on Iraqi forces or their recruiting efforts. They also focused their attacks to strike at leading Shi'ite and Kurdish political officials, commanders, and clergy. Targeting groups like Shi'ites and Kurds, using car bombings for mass killings, and hitting shrines and festivals all force the dispersal of security forces, make the areas involved seem insecure, undermine efforts at governance, and offer the possibility of using civil war as a way to defeat the Coalition and the Iraqi Interim Government's efforts at nation-building.

For example, a step up in Sunni attacks on Shi'ite targets after the January 30, 2005, election, led some Shi'ites to talk about "Sunni ethnic cleansing." This effect was compounded by bloody suicide bombings, many of which had some form of government target but killed large numbers of Shi'ite civilians.[2] These attacks included instances in which fifty-eight corpses were dumped in the Tigris River and nineteen largely Shi'ite national guardsmen were found dead in a soccer stadium in Haditha. They also included a bombing in Hilla on March 1, 2005, that killed 136—mostly Shi'ite police and army recruits.[3]

Similar attacks were carried out against the Kurds. While the Kurds maintained notably better security over their areas in the North than existed in the rest of the country, two suicide bombers still penetrated into a political gathering in Irbil on February 1, 2004, killing at least 105. On March 10, 2005, a suicide bomber killed fifty-three Kurds in Kirkuk. On May 3, 2005, another suicide bomber—this time openly identified with

the Sunni extremist group Ansar al-Sunna—blew himself up outside a
recruiting station in Irbil, killing sixty and wounding at least 150 others.[4]
At the same time, other attacks systematically targeted Kurdish leaders
and Kurdish elements in Iraqi forces.

By May 2005 this began to provoke Shi'ite reprisals in spite of efforts
by Shi'ite leaders to avoid this, contributing further to the problems in
establishing a legitimate government and national forces. Sunni bodies, as
well as Shi'ite ones, began to be discovered in unmarked graves, and
killings struck at both Sunni and Shi'ite clergy.[5]

• *Link asymmetric warfare to crime and looting; exploit poverty and economic
  desperation.* Use criminals to support attacks on infrastructure and nation-
  building activity, raise funds, and undermine security. Exploit unemployment to strengthen dedicated insurgent and terrorist cells. Blur the lines
  between threat forces, criminal elements, and part-time forces.

• *Attack petroleum and oil facilities, electric power, water, and other critical
  infrastructure.* Attacks on power and water facilities both offset the impact
  of U.S. aid and cause Iraqi anger against the government. Al Qa'ida and
  Ba'athist groups found oil facilities and pipelines to be particularly attractive targets because they deny the government revenue, affect both power
  and Iraqi ability to obtain fuel, get extensive media and foreign business
  attention, and prevent investment in one of Iraq's most attractive assets.[6]

The impact of this activity is regularly reflected in the histograms in
the Department of Defense's *Iraq Weekly Status Report.* For example, the
April 27, 2005, edition shows that electric power generation remained far
below the U.S. goal and usually below the prewar level from January 1,
2004, to April 21, 2005. Crude oil production averaged around 2.1 MMBD
from February through April 2005—compared with the goal of 2.5
MMBD and a prewar peak of 2.5 MMBD in March 2003. Exports averaged
only about 1.3 to 1.4 MMBD from January to April 2005, largely because of
pipeline and facility sabotage—although record oil prices raised Iraqi export
revenues from $5.1 billion in 2003 to $17 billion in 2004 and $6.2 billion
in the first four months of 2005.

The continuing threat to electric facilities forced many Iraqis to rely on
home or neighborhood generators even in the areas with power because
of rolling power cuts in most areas and major shortages in others. It was
also a reason that the United States was only able to spend $1 billion of
$4.4 billion in programmed aid money on the electricity sector by the end
of April 2005 and $261 million out of $1.7 billion on the petroleum
sector.[7]

Sabotage and theft helped cripple many of the country's 229 operating
water plants by the spring of 2005, and some 90 percent of the municipalities in the country lacked working sewage processing plants, contaminating
the main sources of water as they drained into the Tigris and Euphrates
Rivers. The Iraqi Municipalities and Public Works Ministry calculated in

April 2005 that it provided water to some 17 million Iraqis (70 percent of the population), and supplies were so bad that some 30 percent of the 17 million did not have access to drinkable water. Many projects had to be canceled, and $1 billion of the $3.65 billion allocated in U.S. aid had to be diverted to security needs. There were a total of fifteen water project starts in 2004, but none were planned for 2005.[8]

- *Strike at U.S. and other aid projects to undermine Iraqi acceptance of the MNSTC–I and the perceived legitimacy of the Iraqi government.* It is unclear just how systematic such attacks have been, but a report by the special inspector general for Iraq reconstruction indicates that at least 276 civilians working on U.S. aid projects had been killed by March 31, 2005, and at least 2,582 had been wounded. The number of contractors killed also rose by 19 percent (to 44) in the first quarter of 2005. The cost impact is also high. The report indicates that the security costs of USAID funded aid projects were only 4.2 percent of the total cost from March 2003 to February 2004 but rose to 22 percent during the final nine months of 2004.[9] Other reports indicated that contractors had filed 2,919 death and injury claims for U.S. and foreign workers between the beginning of the war on March 19, 2003, and May 10, 2003, with 303 killed.[10]

- *Exploit Arab satellite television as well as traditional media—Islamist movements and other insurgents learned how to capture maximum exposure in regional media, use the Internet, and above all, exploit the new Arab satellite news channels.* Insurgents and terrorists also pay close attention to media reactions, and tailor their attacks to high-profile targets that make such attacks "weapons of mass media."

- *Maintain a strategy of constant attrition, but strike hard according to a calendar of turning points and/or at targets with high political, social, and economic impact.* Insurgents and Islamists learned the importance of a constant low-level body count and the creation of a steady climate of violence. This forces the United States into a constant, large-scale security effort; makes it difficult for Iraqi forces to take hold; puts constant pressure on U.S. and Iraqi forces to disperse; and ensures constant media coverage.

At the same time insurgents and Islamists showed a steadily more sophisticated capability to exploit holidays, elections, and other political events and sensitive targets both inside the countries that are the scene of their primary operations and in the United States and the West. Attacks on Kurdish and Shi'ite religious festivals are cases in point.

So was an attack on Abu Ghraib prison, the site of many media reports on the abuse of Iraqi prisoners on April 2, 2005. The prison still held some 3,446 detainees, and the insurgent attack, conducted by forty to sixty insurgents, lasted nearly forty minutes and was large and well organized enough to wound twenty U.S. troops.[11]

- *Focus on large U.S. installations.* As the insurgents became better organized, they moved from hit-and-run firings at U.S. installations to much larger and better organized raids that could capture major media attention even when these largely failed. The major Zarqawi organization raid on Abu Ghraib prison in early April 2005 was an example of such a raid.[12] As the Chronology at the back of this book shows, suicide bombing and infiltration attacks on the "Green Zone," the Coalition's safe area in Baghdad, and at other major U.S. military facilities in areas like Mosul were also incorporated. The use of Iraqi uniforms, security, and army vehicles, false IDs, and intelligence gained from infiltrators also became more sophisticated.

- *Push "hot buttons."* Try to find forms of attack that provoke disproportionate fear and "terror" to force the U.S.-Iraqi forces into costly, drastic, and sometimes provocative responses. Terrorists and insurgents have found that attacks planned for maximum political and psychological effects often have the additional benefit of provoking overreaction. Hamas and the Palestinian Islamic Jihad exploited such tactics throughout the peace process.

  An example of such attacks that put constant pressure on Americans, demonstrated insurgent "strength," and got high-profile media attention was the long series of attacks on the secure areas in the "Green Zone" in Baghdad and along the road from that zone to the Baghdad airport.

  Attacking the airport road was an almost perfect way of keeping up constant psychological and political pressure. It passed through a hostile Sunni area and was almost impossible to secure from IEDs, VBIEDs, rocket and mortar attacks, and sniping without pinning down large numbers of troops. This helps explain why there were well over one hundred attacks on targets moving along the road from January 30 through May 4, 2005.[13]

- *Game regional, Western, and other outside media.* Use interview access, tapes, journalist hostage takings and killings, politically led and motivated crowds, drivers and assistants to journalists, and timed and targeted attacks to attempt to manipulate Western and outside media. Manipulate U.S. official briefings with planted questions.

- *Use Americans and other foreigners as proxies.* There is nothing new about using Americans and other foreigners as proxies for local regimes or attacking them to win support for ideological positions and causes. There has, however, been steadily growing sophistication in the timing and nature of such attacks and in exploiting softer targets such as American businessmen in the country of operations, in striking at U.S. and allied targets in other countries, or in striking at targets in the United States. It is also clear that such attacks receive maximum political and media attention in the United States.

- *Attack the United Nations, NGOs, embassies, aid personnel, and foreign contractor business operations.* Attacking such targets greatly reduces the ability to carry out nation-building and stability operations to win hearts and minds. Attacking the "innocent" and curtailing their operations or driving organizations out of the country have become important focuses of insurgents and Islamist extremist attacks.

- *Kidnap, kill, and/or intimidate women and cadres of foreign workers.* Killing and kidnapping women, particularly those working in NGOs and aid projects, gets great media attention and leads some organizations to leave the country. Kidnapping or killing groups of foreign workers puts political pressure on their governments, gets high local and regional media attention, and sometimes leads governments to stop their workers from going to Iraq.

  Counts of kidnappings in Iraq and analyses of responsibility are necessarily uncertain and sharply undercount the number of kidnappings of Iraqis—many of which are never reported. An analysis of kidnappings from April 1, 2004, to January 31, 2005, showed, however, that there were 264 foreign civilian kidnappings. Some forty-seven were killed, fifty-six remained missing, 150 were released, five escaped, and a total of six were rescued. Given the fact that there were some 100,000 expatriates in Iraq at the time, this meant a roughly 1 in 380 chance of being kidnapped, and roughly 20 percent of the foreigners kidnapped were beheaded or otherwise killed.[14]

- *Kidnap, kill, and/or intimidate professionals, Iraqi media, and members of the intelligentsia.* Steady killing and intimidation of individual professionals, media figures, and intelligentsia in threatened areas offers a series of soft targets that cannot be defended but where a cumulative pattern of killing and intimidation makes governance difficult, creates major problems for security and police forces, weakens the economy, and exacerbates the general feeling of insecurity to the point where people lose faith in the Iraqi government, Coalition, and political process. According to the head of the Iraqi journalists' syndicate, Shihab al-Tamimi, kidnappings and assassinations targeting Iraqi journalists surged in the weeks leading up to the January 30 election.[15]

  The U.S. State Department report on human rights for 2004 states that the Ministry of Human Rights claimed that at least eighty professors and fifty physicians were assassinated during 2004. Reporters Without Borders noted that thirty-one journalists and media assistants were killed during the year. Universities also suffered from a wave of kidnappings. Researchers, professors, administrators, and students were all victims, including some who disappeared without a trace.[16]

- *Use "horror" attacks, atrocities, and alienation.* Whether or not the tactics were initially deliberate, insurgents in Iraq found that atrocities like beheadings and desecrating corpses are effective political and psychological weapons for those Islamist extremists whose goal is to divide the West from the Islamic world and create an unbridgeable "clash of civilizations."

  Experts have long pointed out that one of the key differences between Islamist extremist terrorism and previous forms of terrorism is that they are not seeking to negotiate with those they terrorize but rather to create conditions that can drive the West away, undermine secular and moderate regimes in the Arab and Islamic worlds, and create the conditions under which they can create "Islamic" states, according to their own ideas of "Puritanism."

This is why it serves the purposes of Islamist extremists, as well as some of the more focused opponents of the United States and the West, to create mass casualties and carry out major strikes or carry out executions and beheadings, even if the result is to provoke hostility and anger. The goal of Osama Bin Laden and those like him is not to persuade the United States or the West, it is rather to so alienate them from the Islamic and Arab world that the forces of secularism in the region will be sharply undermined and Western secular influence can be controlled or eliminated. The goal of most Iraqi insurgents is narrower, to drive the United States and its allies out of Iraq, but involves many of the same methods.

Seen in this context, the more horrifying the attack or incident the better, even if it involves Iraqi military, security, and police forces. Simple casualties do not receive the same media attention. They are a reality of war. Killing (or sometimes releasing) innocent hostages does grab the attention of the world media. Large bombs in crowds do the same, as does picking targets whose innocence or media impact grabs headlines. Desecrating corpses, beheading people, and similar acts of violence get even more media attention—at least for a while.

Such actions also breed anger and alienation in the United States and the West and provoke excessive political and media reactions, more stringent security measures, violent responses, and all of the other actions that help instigate a "clash of civilizations." The United States and the West are often provoked into playing into the hands of such attackers.

At the same time, any attack or incident that garners massive media coverage and political reactions appears to be a "victory" to those who support Islamist extremism or those who are truly angry at the United States—even though the actual body count is often low, and victory does not mean creating stronger forces or winning political control. Each such incident can be used to damage the U.S. and Western view of the Arab and Islamic worlds.

- *"Body dumps" and "mystery killings" became a variation on this theme.* The bodies of Iraqi forces and other Iraqis would be dumped in areas like rivers, soccer stadiums, and other public places where they were found without any clear picture of who had killed them and why and even sometimes who the bodies were. In mid-March 2005, for example, some eighty bodies, many of whom were police officers and soldiers, were found in four dumps in Iraq. Somewhat ironically, a small dump of seven bodies of Zarqawi loyalists, seemingly killed by other Sunnis, were found the same week.[17]

- *Deprive the central, regional, and local governments of efforts to expand legitimacy. Attack nation-building and stability targets.* There is nothing new about attacking key economic targets, infrastructure, and aspects of governance critical to the functioning of the state in an effort to disrupt its economy, undermine law enforcement and security, and encourage instability. Iraqi insurgent and Islamist attacks on aid workers and projects and their role in encouraging looting, sabotage, and theft did, however, demonstrate a growing sophistication in targeting stability efforts and tangible progress in aid and governance. These tactics also interact synergistically with the above tactics.
- *Confuse the identity of the attacker; exploit conspiracy theories.* Insurgents and Islamists learned that a mix of silence, multiple claims to be the attacker, new names for attacking organizations, and uncertain levels of affiliation made it harder for the United States to respond. They also produced more media coverage and speculation. As of yet, the number of false-flag operations has been limited. However, in Iraq and elsewhere attacks have often been accompanied by what seem to be deliberate efforts to advance conspiracy theories to confuse the identity of the attacker or to find ways to blame defenders of the United States for being attacked. In addition, conspiracy theories charging the United States with deliberately or carelessly failing to provide an adequate defense have been particularly effective.
- *Seek to create sanctuaries like Fallujah, and take shelter in mosques, shrines, and high-value targets and targets with high cultural impact.* Again, exploiting facilities of religious, cultural, and political sensitivity is not a new tactic. However, as operations against Sadr and in Fallujah have shown, the tactics raise the media profile, create a defensive deterrent, and can be exploited to make the United States seem anti-Islamic—or to be attacking a culture and not a movement.
- *Exploit, exaggerate, and falsify U.S. attacks that cause civilian casualties, collateral damage, friendly fire against local allies, and incidents where the United States can be blamed for being anti-Arab and anti-Islam.* Terrorists and insurgents have found they can use the media, rumor, and conspiracy theories to exploit the fact that the United States often fights a military battle without proper regard for the fact it is also fighting a political, ideological, and psychological war. Real incidents of U.S. misconduct, such as the harsh treatment of detainees and prisoners, and the excessive security measures are cases in point. So, too, are careless political and media rhetoric by U.S. officials and military officers. Bin Laden, the Iraqi insurgents, and other opponents all benefit from every Western action that unnecessarily angers or frustrates the Arab and Islamic worlds. They are not fighting to influence Western or world opinion; they are fighting a political and psychological war to dominate Iraq and the Arab and Islamic worlds.

- *Kidnap, kill, and attack official envoys and diplomats from Muslim countries seeking to engage the Jafari government.* This limits the ability of the elected government to establish international legitimacy and credibility. Governments whose personnel suffer an attack may not have the will to continue to pursue relations in the face of domestic discontent over any casualties and over the Iraq War in general. Such attacks can make the Iraqi government look powerless.
- *Kill members of the constitutional committee.* The goal of this is to discourage participation or, in the case of the Sunni delegation, deprive the committee of the necessary numbers of Sunni participants to move forward. Proceeding without the requisite numbers of Shi'ites, Sunnis, and Kurds would thus bring the committee's legitimacy into question.

Lessons about Methods of Attack and Combat

There is no clear division between the mix of insurgent and terrorist tactics focused on the political and psychological nature of war and those that focus on directly attacking targets like Multinational Force–Iraq (MNF–I) and Iraqi government forces, Iraqi and Coalition officials, and the Iraqi economy and nation-building process. The insurgents again made major adaptations in their tactics and methods of attack, including the following, which still further increased the problems of creating effective Iraqi forces:

- *Mix crude and sophisticated IEDs.* Hezbollah should be given credit for having first perfected the use of explosives in well-structured ambushes, although there is nothing new about such tactics—the Afghans used them extensively against the Soviets. Iraq has, however, provided a unique opportunity for insurgents and Islamist extremists to make extensive use of improvised explosive devices (IEDs) and vehicle-borne improvised explosive devices (VBIEDs) by exploiting its massive stocks of arms. The insurgents were able to draw on large stocks of explosives as well as large bombs and artillery shells. Nearly 400 tons of HMX and RDX plastic explosives disappeared from the Qaqaa weapons facility alone after the fall of Saddam Hussein's regime.

    The Iraqi attackers also learned to combine their extensive use of low-grade IEDs, more carefully targeted and sophisticated IEDs, very large car bombs, and other devices to create a mix of threats and methods that is much more difficult to counter than reliance on more consistent types of bombs and target sets.[18]

    The insurgents based many of their initial efforts on relatively simple weapons designs, some of which seem to have been adapted from the Arabic translations of U.S. field manuals on booby traps and similar improvised devices. The insurgents soon learned, however, to use more sophisticated detonators and triggering systems to counter U.S. electronic countermeasures and increase their distance away from the bomb. According to one report, only 10 percent of the IEDs used in Iraq as of May 2005 were modeled on the pressure-detonation devices shown in U.S. Army Field Manual 5-31 and in a direct Iraqi translation published in 1987.[19] Insurgents had also learned how to make crude shaped charges to attack U.S. armored and other vehicles.

The insurgents also pay close attention to U.S. intelligence collection methods and counter-IED operations and change their behavior accordingly. They also use improved methods of concealment, like digging holes in a road and then "paving over" the hole. Other methods have included stealing police, military, and government vehicles and uniforms and IDs to penetrate secure areas and linking bombings to ambushes with rifles and rocket-propelled grenades (RPGs)—or additional IEDs—to attack the response force.

In September 2004 General Richard Cody, the U.S. army vice chief of staff, stated that some 500 to 600 IEDs were then going off each month, and roughly half either harmed U.S. personnel or damaged U.S. vehicles.[20] While Coalition forces claimed to find some 30 to 40 percent of IEDs and render them safe, by May 2005 they also reported that the number of IED incidents had steadily climbed to some thirty per day.

Lieutenant General James T. Conway, director of operations in the U.S. joint staff, stated in May 2005 that a total of 70 percent of all Coalition casualties to date since the fall of Saddam Hussein had been caused by IEDs, an effort that had been so successful that the United States announced that even "uparmored" Humvees were unsafe in high-threat areas and were being replaced with heavily armored five-ton "gun trucks."[21] An analysis by the Iraq Coalition Casualty Count showed that IEDs had killed 336 Americans by various suicide or car bombs, as of April 29, 2005.[22]

IEDs accounted for 189 of 720 U.S. combat deaths in 2004—about 26 percent. Deaths caused by IEDs rose by more than 41 percent during the first five months of 2005, compared with a similar period in 2004, and accounted for 51 percent of the 255 combat deaths as of June 9, 2005. There were eighty-five deaths attributed to IEDs in the first five months of 2004 and 120 in 2005. This was a primary reason that the number of "uparmored" Humvees in U.S. forces rose from around 200 in the summer of 2004 to 9,000 in June 2005.[23]

Similar data are not available on Iraqi casualties, a larger percentage of whom seem to have been hit by suicide bombers and in ambushes, but the Chronology to this analysis (at the back of this book) shows there have been many effective attacks. For example, three Iraqi soldiers were killed and forty-four were wounded in a single VBIED bomb attack on their bus on April 6, 2005.[24] Iraqi military, security, and police are particularly vulnerable because they have little or no armor and often must move into insecure facilities or go on leave in unprotected vehicles simply to perform routine tasks like bringing money to their families in a cash-in-hand economy.

- *Use mixed attacks, and seek to ambush military and emergency forces in follow-on attacks.* Iraqi insurgents steadily improved their ability to carry out complex attacks where an IED might be set off, and then either more IEDs or other methods of attack would be used against rescuers and follow-on forces. Alternatively, an ambush might be used to lead U.S. and Iraqi forces into an area with IEDs.

  By the spring of 2005 insurgents increasingly used such mixed attacks to strike at U.S. facilities. For example, they used a mix of gunmen, suicide car bombs, and a large fire truck filled with explosives to attack a U.S. marine base at Camp Gannon at Husaybah near the Syrian border on April 11, 2005.[25] On May 9, 2005, they used a hospital at Haditha as an ambush point and then attacked the responding U.S. forces with suicide bombs. This mix of unpredictable attacks, many slowly built up in ways difficult for U.S. intelligence methods to detect, has greatly complicated the operations of U.S. and Iraqi forces, although it has scarcely defeated them.

- *Adapt technology to match updates in Coalition defense capabilities.* The summer of 2005 brought an increase in "shaped-charge" explosives, evidence that the insurgency was benefiting from technical support from Iran. The design is the same as those used by the Iranian-supplied Lebanese militia Hezbollah, and the weapons are far more effective at piercing armor than previous designs. The number of American troops killed by IEDs spiked during the summer, with thirty-five deaths in May, thirty-six in June, and thirty-nine in July.[26] Another adaptation that has increased the lethality of insurgent IED attacks was the increased size of the weapons, a response to the up-armoring of U.S. vehicles. Initially, IEDs in Iraq were small charges composed of single 60-mm and 81-mm mortars. Insurgents have since increased the size to 122-mm and 152-mm and are using buried 500- and 1,000-lb airplane bombs to effect an explosive upward force that can render current up-armoring useless.[27] The thirty-nine deaths by bombing in July 2005 was the largest to-date monthly toll since the war began.

- *Adapt targets to place maximum pressure on Iraqi social and political apparatuses.* Insurgents have adapted their tactics as well, focusing greater attention on Iraqi military forces and police. In January 2005, 109 Iraqi police and military were killed through insurgent activity. By May, this number had spiked to 259, and by July, to 304.[28] As the Iraqi constitutional process unfolded—which the Sunnis were largely absent from due to their widespread boycott of the Parliamentary election—sectarian violence became increasingly apparent. Sunni attacks on Iraqi security and political figures increased as radicals sought to derail the political process. On August 19, 2005, three Sunni election workers were kidnapped in Mosul, driven to Al Noor, and executed before a throng of people gathered before the Al Noor Mosque. Of the election workers murdered, one was identified as Faris Yunis Abdullah, a senior official in the mostly Sunni Iraqi Islamic

Party. The three men were posting placards encouraging Iraqis to vote in the October 15 election when they were abducted.[29]

- *Carry out sequential ambushes.* The insurgents increasingly carry out complex mixes of sequential ambushes to draw in and attack Iraqi and U.S. responders to the initial or follow-on attacks.
- *Develop complex mixes and ambushes using small arms and light weapons.* At least through the spring of 2005 insurgents did not make effective use of looted, guided antitank weapons and had only been able to down one aircraft with "manportable" surface to air missiles (MANPADS).[30] They did, however, steadily improve their tactics from single-fire ambushes to multiple firings of RPGs against the same target, mixes of firing positions, and sequential fire points, ambushes, and defenses—mixing small arms, RPGs, and light automatic weapons.
- *Use "swarming" techniques and attacks on vehicles.* The quality of urban and road ambushes improved strikingly in Iraq, as did the ability to set up rapid attacks and exploit the vulnerability of soft-skinned vehicles. Insurgents also learned to "swarm" Coalition forces by rushing in from different points or firing simultaneously from multiple locations. In some cases, a single vehicle could take eight RPG rounds in a short encounter. Particularly in built-up areas, these tactics could destroy or disable even heavy armor like the Abrams tank and posed a major threat to lighter armored vehicles, as well as exposed infantry.
- *Implement tactics such as suicide bombs, car bombs, and mass bombings.* The use of such tactics has increased steadily since 1999, in part due to the high success rate relative to alternative methods of attack. Exploding vehicles account for approximately 60 percent of Iraqi police and recruit fatalities.[31] It is not always clear that suicide-bombing techniques are tactically necessary. In many cases, timed devices might produce the same damage. Events in Iraq have shown, however, that suicide bombers still have a major psychological impact and gain exceptional media attention. They also serve as symbols of dedication and commitment, can be portrayed as a form of Islamic martyrdom, and attract more political support and attention among those sympathetic to the cause involved.

  The cost of suicide bombers has also been low. It seems that most are not Iraqis and are recruited from outside Iraq by various Islamist organizations. The limited evidence available indicates that many are chosen because they can be persuaded to seek Islamic martyrdom, and they do so collectively and without trying to call great public attention to themselves. They act as "force multipliers" for relatively small Islamic extremist groups because a single volunteer can use a strap-on bomb or a single vehicle filled with explosives, penetrate a crowded area or high-profile target area, and then set off an explosion producing high casualties. Even when such attacks fail to reach their target the explosion often gets intense public and media attention.

- *Develop teams of stay behinds and diehards and suicide squads.* During and after Fallujah, insurgents increasingly had teams stay behind who seem to have been prepared to die or to seek martyrdom. Many were Iraqis. Their willingness to defend a building or small area with suicidal determination and no regard for retreat often inflicted higher casualties on MNF–I and Iraqi forces.

- *Make better use of light weapons like automatic weapons, RPGs, and mortars; attack from remote locations or use timed devices.* While much will depend on the level of insurgent and Islamist extremist access to arms, Iraq and Afghanistan have seen a steady improvement in the use of systems like mortars, antitank weapons, rockets, and timed explosives. They have also seen improvements in light weapons and the increasing use of armor-piercing ammunition as cheap ways of attacking body armor, vehicles, and penetrating walls.

- *Make effective use of snipers.* Iraqi insurgents initially had very poor marksmanship and tended to fire off their weapons in sustained and poorly armed bursts. With time, however, they not only developed effective snipers but trained spotters, learned how to position and mix their snipers with other elements of Iraqi forces, and developed signals and other communications systems like them in tactical operations. Overall, fire discipline and marksmanship remained poor through the late spring of 2005, but sniper elements became steadily more effective, and the overall quality of insurgent fire discipline and marksmanship was generally no worse than that of Iraqi soldiers, security personnel, and police. Snipers acquired new types of rifles, antiarmor ammunition, and body armor from outside Iraq, indicating they might have both support and training from Islamist extremists. Islamist Web sites also began to include interactive sniper "training" data as a recruiting tool and crude training aid.[32]

- *Attack lines of communication (LOCs), rear areas, and support activity.* Iraqi insurgents soon found that dispersed attacks on logistics and support forces often offer a higher chance of success than attacks on combat forces and defended sites and make the Coalition fight wars based on "deep support" rather than "deep strikes" beyond the forward edge of battle areas (FEBA).

  In some cases insurgents also chose routes like the road from the Green Zone and central Baghdad to the airport that the Coalition and government forces could not avoid, where constant attacks both harassed operations and became a political statement and symbol of Iraq's lack of security. These "ambush alleys" allowed the insurgents to force a major Iraqi or MNF–I defensive effort at relatively little cost.

- *Strike at highly visible targets with critical economic and infrastructure visibility.* Water and power facilities have a broad political, media, economic, and social impact. Striking at critical export-earning facilities like Iraq's northern export pipeline from the Kirkuk oil fields to the IT-1A storage tanks near Baiji, where oil accumulates before it is pumped further north to Ceyhan, has sharply affected the government's revenues, forced it to create special protection forces, and gained world attention.

- *Kill Iraqi elites and "soft targets."* The insurgents soon found it was far easier to kill Iraqi officials and security personnel and their family members than Americans. They also found it was easier to kill mid-level officials than better-protected senior officials. In some areas simply killing educated elites and/or their family members—doctors, professionals, and so forth— could paralyze much of the nation-building process, create a broad climate of insecurity, and force U.S. and Iraqi forces to disperse resources in defensive missions or simply have to stand aside and tolerate continued attacks.

- *Target elections, the political process, and governance.* Elections and the local presence of government are soft, dispersed targets with operations critical to political legitimacy. Hitting these targets helps derail the political process, gets media visibility, offers vulnerable "low hanging fruit," and intimidates the government and population in much wider areas than those subjected to direct attack.

- *Strike at major aid and government projects after completion; break up project efforts when they acquire visibility or have high levels of employment.* Insurgents and terrorists often simply struck at the most vulnerable projects, but they seem to have learned that timing their attacks, looting, sabotage, and intimidation to strike when projects are completed means the Coalition and government aid efforts have maximum cost with minimum effect. They struck at projects when the security forces protecting workers and aid teams were no longer there. This often led the local population to blame the Coalition or government for not keeping promises or providing the proper protection. Alternatively, breaking up project efforts when they began to have maximum local visibility and employment impact had many of the same effects.

- *Hit the softest element of Iraqi military, security, and police forces.* The insurgents found they could strike at men on leave, their families, recruits, those seeking to enlist, green troops, trainees, and low-quality units with limited fear of effective retaliation. High-profile mass killings got major media attention. Moreover, not only were isolated forward elements in hostile or threatened areas vulnerable but successful attacks broke up governance, aid efforts, and intimidated local populations. This strategy has been most damaging to the Iraqi police force, which remain the weakest element in the security apparatus.

- *Create informal distributed networks for C⁴I–deliberately or accidentally.* Like drug dealers before them, Iraqi insurgent and Islamist extremists have learned enough about communications intelligence (COMINT) and signal intelligence (SIGINT) systems to stop using most vulnerable communications assets and to bypass many—if not most—of the efforts to control cash flow and money transfers.

The use of messengers, direct human contact, coded messages through the Internet, propaganda Web pages, and more random methods of electronic communication are all cases in point. At the broader level, however, insurgents in Iraq seem to have adapted to having cells and elements operate with considerable autonomy and by loosely linking their operations by using the media and reporting on the overall pattern of attacks to help determine the best methods and targets.

Smuggling, drug sales, theft, looting, and direct fund transfers also largely bypass efforts to limit operations through controls on banking systems, charities, and so forth. Under these conditions a lack of central control and cohesive structure may actually be an asset, allowing highly flexible operations with minimal vulnerability to roll up and attack.

The existence of parallel, noncompeting groups of hostile nonstate actors provides similar advantages and has the same impact. The fact that insurgent and Islamist extremist groups operate largely independently and use different tactics and target sets greatly complicates U.S. operations and probably actually increases overall effectiveness.

- *Find street scouts and spotters.* Like many previous insurgent groups, Iraqi hostiles learned to have children, young men, and others use cell phones, signals, and runners to provide tactical scouting, intelligence, and warning in ways that proved very difficult to detect and halt.
- *Make cities and towns urban sanctuaries and defensive morasses.* Iraqi insurgents found that cities with supportive and/or accepting populations can be made into partial sanctuaries and centers for defensive fighting and ambushes and that tactical defeat can normally be dealt with by dispersal and hiding among the civilian population. Such tactics combine well with attacks on local authorities and security forces friendly to the United States, efforts to block nation-building at the local level, and efforts to exploit religion, ethnicity, tribalism, and so forth.
- *Use neighboring states and border areas as partial sanctuaries.* While scarcely a new tactic, Iraqi insurgents have made increased use of cross-border operations and taken advantage of the difficulties in securing the Syrian, Iranian, and Saudi borders. By March 2005, for example, these tactics had created a near sanctuary in the area along the Euphrates River from Hit and Haditha toward Syria and through Ubaydi, Qaim, Karabilah, and Qusaybah to the Syrian border along the road to Abu Kamal.[33] The Vietnamese used the same tactic in Cambodia and Laos, and so have many other insurgent forces. The idea of securing a nation based on securing the territory within its tactical boundaries is often a tactical myth.
- *Create dispersed and rapidly mobile operations and centers, mixed with fixed "die-hard" and "sleeper" installations.* The insurgents rapidly learned not to concentrate operatives and to keep them rapidly mobile. They

mixed these with "die-hard" elements designed to fight and defend them-selves and inflict casualties if attacked and with sleeper cells and stay-behind operations to recover after an area was attacked, captured, and "secured" by Coalition and Iraqi forces.

- *Exploit weaknesses in U.S. human intelligence (HUMINT), battle-damage assessment (BDA), and damage-characterization capabilities.* Iraqi insur-gents and other Islamist extremists learned that U.S. intelligence is opti-mized around characterizing, counting, and targeting things, rather than people, and that the U.S. has poor capability to measure and characterize infantry and insurgent numbers, wounded, and casualties. They exploit these weaknesses in dispersal, in conducting attacks, in concealing the extent of losses, and in manipulating the media by claiming civilian casual-ties and collateral damage.
- *Counter U.S. advantages in intercepting satellite and cellular communica-tions.* Insurgents utilize the text-messaging function of cell phones to com-municate in an effort to avoid electronic eavesdropping by the United States. Insurgents will often use more than one phone to communicate a message, so that those listening in only hear part of the message.
- *Exploit slow Iraqi and U.S. reaction times at the local tactical level, particularly in built-up areas.* Opponents learn to exploit the delays in U.S. response efforts and rigidities in U.S. tactical C^4I behavior to attack quickly and disperse.
- *Exploit fixed Iraqi and U.S. patterns of behavior.* Hostile groups take advan-tage of any tendency to repeat tactics, security, movement patterns, and other behavior, while finding vulnerabilities to attack.
- *Hit at U.S. HUMINT links and translators.* United States dependence on Iraqi translators and intelligence sources is a key area of U.S. vulnerability and one the insurgents have learned to focus on.
- *Use "resurgence" and reinfiltration—dig in, hide, and reemerge.* Insurgents disperse under pressure or when defeat seems likely. They let the United States take an "empty" city or objective and then "resurge" when the U.S. tactical presence declines.
- *Use incident frequencies, distribution of attacks, and tactics that strain or defeat U.S. intelligence, surveillance, and reconnaissance (IS&R) assets and the ability to support Iraqi forces.* There is no question that assets like remotely piloted vehicles (RPVs), aircraft, SIGINT systems, and so forth can provide significant capability *when they are available.* It is unclear whether it is deliberate or not, but the geographic spread and daily incident count in Iraq indicates that insurgent movements and actions often reach numbers too large to cover. In fact, the United States averaged some 1,700 to 2,000 patrols per day during May 2004. While it is nice to talk about "netcentric" warfare, it is a lot harder to get a big enough net.

Insurgents learned that the United States has less ability to track and characterize irregular forces, insurgent/terrorist teams, and urban and dis-persed infantry than forces using mechanized weapons or significant num-bers of vehicles. Blending into the civilian population has worked well for local insurgents and Islamists in both Afghanistan and Iraq, and Iraqi insurgents learned that they can exploit rules of engagement where U.S. and Iraqi government forces do not have soldiers or agents on the ground to perform targeting and "Identification Friend or Foe" (IFF) functions. As valuable as "IS&R" assets are, they do not provide some critical kinds of situational awareness with any reliability.

- *Increase the size and power of IEDs to nullify the advantages of U.S. and Coalition armor.* In two separate instances in early January 2005 IEDs destroyed a Bradley fighting vehicle and an Abrams tank. The two vehicles are among the more heavily armored vehicles in the U.S. arsenal. Prior to the two bombings both the Abrams tank and the Bradley fighting vehicle had proven relatively effective in protecting the troops inside.

- *Choose a vulnerable Iraqi and U.S. force.* Hostile forces aim to deny the U.S. and Iraqi forces a large, cohesive enemy while attacking small or dispersed elements of U.S. and Iraqi forces, facilities, or targets.

- *Counter U.S. intelligence, surveillance, and reconnaissance (IS&R) capabilities by adapting new techniques of communication and interaction.* The steady leakage of details on U.S. and allied intelligence collection methods has led Islamist extremist and terrorist movements to make more use of couriers and direct financial transfer; use electronic communications more safely; screen recruits more carefully; find ways to communicate through the Internet that the United States cannot target; disperse better; and improve their hierarchy and cell structure.

- *Counter U.S. and Iraqi government intelligence, surveillance, and reconnaissance (IS&R) assets with superior human intelligence (HUMINT).* Developments in Iraq indicate that the United States faces a repetition of its experience in Vietnam in the sense that as various insurgent factions organize, they steadily improve their intelligence and penetration of organizations like the CPA, Coalition Joint Task Force 7 (CJTF-7), the Iraqi government and security forces, and the Iraqi factions backing nation-building.

    Like Vietnam, Iraq is a warning that hostile HUMINT sources are often pushed into providing data because of family ties, a fear of being on the losing side, direct and indirect threats, and so forth. In Iraq's case it seems likely that family, clan, and ethnic loyalties have made many supposedly loyal Iraqis become at least part-time sources, and that U.S. vetting will often be little more than either a review of past ties or checks on the validity of data being provided. The end result may be an extremely high degree of transparency on the United States, the Iraqi government, aid, and every other aspect of Iraqi operations. This will often provide excellent targeting data on key U.S. and allied officials, events, and so on. It can include leverage and blackmail and vulnerability data, as well as warning of U.S. and other military operations. Dual loyalty and HUMINT penetration of Iraqi security and military forces may be the rule, rather than the exception.

- *Use the media, infiltrators/sympathizers, and former detainees for counterintelligence.* Constantly monitor the media and Internet for data on U.S. and Iraqi intelligence, targeting, and operational data. Use infiltrators and sympathizers. Debrief released prisoners and detainees to learn what their capture and interrogation reveals about U.S. and Iraqi intelligence efforts.

Iraqi-U.S. Asymmetric Interaction and Noninteroperability

The United States not only initially failed to properly assess the growth of terrorism and insurgency during the first year following the fall of Saddam Hussein, but the insurgency also rose and became steadily more effective. The United States failed to treat the Iraqi forces it was creating as serious partners. It failed to promptly restructure its force goals and training and equipment effort for Iraq military, security, and police forces.

The end result was a growing asymmetry in interoperability between U.S. military forces and the new Iraqi forces as the insurgency took hold. As the data in the following chapters make brutally clear, the United States initially failed to provide minimal facilities and equipment such as body armor, communications, and vehicles. While the U.S. training teams and U.S. commanders in the field made steadily better efforts to organize and train Iraqi forces to protect themselves, the United States as a whole concentrated on manpower numbers and then left Iraqis out in the field to die.

The seriousness of this problem is all too clear when one considers the impact of less serious shortfalls in equipment in U.S. forces. It is clear from the congressional and media reaction to the discovery that the United States was slow to uparmor the Humvees and trucks for its ground forces in December 2004. At the same time, it is striking that the resulting debate over the equipment issued to U.S. and Coalition forces failed to ask what equipment was being provided to Iraqi forces even though they had been a prime target of the insurgents and terrorists since late summer of 2003.

3   Coalition Training and Equipment Efforts

The Failures of 2003

THE COALITION efforts to shape, train, and equip Iraqi military and security forces need to be put in historical perspective. It was not until the spring of 2004 that the effort to create the Iraqi forces that both Iraq and the Coalition needed gained real urgency, and until then no guidance was given to shape the training program to meet the needs that were evolving in the field. For most of the year following Saddam's fall, the broad goal was to spend several years shaping a military designed to defend Iraq's borders. For much of that time the training was of such low priority that it was left to an uncoordinated effort by the Iraqi Ministry of Interior, which lacked U.S. support for more than the creation of regular police forces tailored to deal with civil crime.

This occurred even though it was becoming clearer and clearer that the insurgency was rapidly becoming more serious and that much more effective Iraqi forces would be needed. A General Accountability Office (GAO) report issued in June 2004 summarizes Coalition reporting on the growth of the insurgency, its impact on the nation-building and stability effort, and on the need for more Coalition (and Iraqi) forces as follows:

According to U.N. reports, the security situation in Iraq began to deteriorate in June 2003. Reports from the U.N. Office of the Humanitarian Coordinator for Iraq show that attacks against international organizations and the multinational force began to increase during June and July 2003. The U.N. Secretary General reported that the overall security situation had deteriorated dramatically by the end of August 2003, a month marked by the bombing of the Jordanian embassy on August 7, the bombing of the U.N. headquarters in Baghdad on August 19, and the killing of an important Shi'a leader on August 29.

By September 2003, according to the U.N. Secretary General's report, Iraq had entered a new phase. All international organizations and contractors, as well as Iraqis cooperating with the CPA, were potential targets of deliberate, direct, and hostile attacks. The assessments of contractors and nongovernmental organizations with whom we met generally agreed with the U.N. assessment of these security trends.

Various U.S. and U.N. reports and data indicate that violence escalated sharply against the coalition, Iraqis cooperating with the coalition, international organizations, and international civilian aid groups and contractors in October–November 2003 and again in April–May 2004. CPA data show an extended increase in certain significant insurgent activities during those two periods, with the level of the attacks in April–May 2004 exceeding the level of attacks during October–November 2003. In April 2004, Sunni insurgents fought the multinational force in Fallujah, Ramadi, Samarra, and Tikrit, while a radical Shi'a militia attacked the force in the southern cities of Karbala, Kut, Nassiriyah, Kufa, Najaf, and Basra, as well as in part of Baghdad.

According to CPA data, the number of significant insurgent acts against the coalition declined soon after the early April escalation but then rose again in May, with the number of attacks in May exceeding the number of attacks in April.

DOD [Department of Defense] data on the number of U.S. military personnel killed or wounded due to hostile action in Iraq generally support U.N. and CPA assessments of the security situation since the declared end of major combat operations . . . initial increases in U.S. military casualties in June–July 2003 were followed by much more significant increases in October–November 2003 and April–May 2004. While the number of significant insurgent acts against the coalition increased from April to May, the number of U.S. military casualties declined.

Overall, according to U.N. and U.S. reports, the nature of the attacks against the coalition and its partners changed significantly from the summer of 2003 through the late spring of 2004 in terms of their targets, source, location, sophistication, and effectiveness. In general, the insurgents' targets expanded to cover almost all foreign groups operating in Iraq, whether military or civilian personnel, as well as Iraqi security forces and Iraqi political leaders viewed as collaborating with the occupation. Further, the group of insurgents grew from former regime loyalists to include foreign terrorists, Sunni Islamic extremists, and, most recently, Shi'a radicals. The areas of instability expanded from Baghdad, the Sunni Triangle, and to a lesser extent the Kirkuk and Mosul areas that were already very unstable due to ethnic and political tensions, to include majority Shi'a areas in the south.

According to State Department public opinion polls, the majority of Iraqis remain extremely concerned about the security situation in their country. The State Department reported in early January 2004 that about 62 percent of residents in five Iraqi cities named safety and security as their greatest worry. According to a late January 2004 State Department report, Iraqis tended to fear general street crime and low-grade explosions as the greatest threats to self and family. This poll also showed that most Iraqis see the greatest threat to their country's security to be sectarian or ethnic conflict and large-scale attacks. In a later polling report published in mid-June 2004, the State Department reported that security remained the most urgent issue for residents of five Iraqi cities.

... The Secretary of Defense said in early May 2004 that there will be uncertainty in Iraq and increased attacks against the coalition, Iraqis, and the United States during the period leading up to the elections.

In April and May 2004, the Deputy Secretary of Defense said that the multinational force was engaged in combat and a continuing war in Iraq, rather than peacekeeping as had been expected. The increase in attacks has had a negative impact on the presence and operations of international military and civilian personnel in Iraq. It has led to an increase in U.S. force levels and to a decrease in freedom of movement for international civilians working to rebuild Iraq and assist in its political transition.

As a result of the increase in violence during April 2004, the United States and the United Kingdom decided to increase their overall force levels in the country. The United States decided to maintain a force level of about 138,000 troops until at least the end of 2005, keeping about 33,000 more troops in Iraq as of May 2004 than the 105,000 troops originally planned. On May 24, 2004, the President said that if military commanders determine that they need more troops to fulfill the mission, he would send them. The following week, the United Kingdom announced that it would send an additional 370 troops to southern Iraq in response to the increased violence, bringing its total troop contribution to the multinational force to about 8,900 military personnel. This figure includes 170 engineering personnel who would deploy for 3 months to help fortify U.K. military bases and facilities in Iraq against the increased threat of mortar and rocket attacks.

During April 2004, the United States redeployed forces from Baghdad and northern areas of Iraq to cities in the south that had come under the control of a radical Shi'a militia. The United States did so because Iraqi security forces and at least one contingent of the multinational force would not or could not fight the insurgents. For example, according to a CPA official, Iraqi police in the cities of Karbala, Najaf, and Kut collapsed in April when a radical Shi'a militia overran the cities and took control of police stations. Moreover, according to a USAID report, after heavy fighting in the city of Kut, a non-U.S. contingent of the multinational force withdrew from the city as the militia overran it.

The deteriorating security situation has also adversely affected the operations of civilian organizations in Iraq. The dangerous environment has led many to halt operations completely or to reduce activity by severely restricting staff movement around the country. No systematic data exist on the effect of these restrictions on efforts to assist in Iraq's political transition and reconstruction. Anecdotal evidence suggests, however, that the efforts overall have been scaled back.

In general, international civilian staff have had increasingly little contact with the Iraqi people, and Iraqi staff working for the coalition, including interpreters, have been increasingly threatened for cooperating with foreign organizations. Many important reconstruction efforts had to at least temporarily cease operation. Civilian organizations that continue to operate in the country face increased security measures for their personnel and compounds in the country. The following examples show the effect of the security situation on the operations of the CPA and supporting U.S. agencies, reconstruction contractors, international organizations, and nongovernmental aid organizations.

- Due to the unsafe security environment, the CPA and its supporting U.S. agencies have had difficulty staffing their operations, opening offices through-out the country, and providing protection for U.S. civilian personnel as they travel around the country. U.S. agencies, particularly USAID, had difficulty in attracting and retaining personnel because of security concerns. In addition, ac-cording to a CPA official, as the security situation worsened during 2003, the CPA abandoned plans to fully staff offices throughout Iraq to assist in Iraq's political transition and reconstruction and instead established a much smaller field presence. Further, the CPA established stringent security measures that U.S. government staff had to follow in traveling outside the Green Zone, the coalition's "safe area" in Baghdad, thereby making it difficult for them to move around the country. In late February 2004, the Department of Homeland Security decided to stop sending teams of customs investigators to assist CPA. They could no longer do their jobs because it had become too dangerous for them to move around the country. CPA officials also stated that they were concerned about the safety of their Iraqi employees, particularly their interpret-ers, as insurgents had increasingly targeted them for cooperating with the coalition.

- In an April 17, 2004, document, the CPA administrator stated that lack of security is the key obstacle to reaching reconstruction objectives. Referring to the entire reconstruction program, the administrator stated that a worsened security situation would mean that projects would take longer to complete and that the kinds of projects undertaken and their costs would change to an unknown extent. Our review of selected electricity projects showed that the security situation delayed the implementation of key projects, thereby contrib-uting to the CPA not meeting its objective of providing 6,000 megawatts of electrical generating capacity to the Iraqi people by its original goal of June 1, 2004. In late March 2004, the CPA Inspector General reported that rising security concerns were a significant cost driver for CPA activities and contractor projects, representing at least 10 percent to 15 percent of total costs.

- The United Nations and its programs have faced significant setbacks as a result of the deteriorating security situation. Most importantly, after the attacks on the U.N. headquarters in Baghdad in August and September 2003, the U.N. Secretary General redeployed all U.N. international personnel from Baghdad, Basra, and other area offices to neighboring countries, particularly Jordan and Kuwait, where they have continued to support assistance operations inside Iraq. As of late 2004, the United Nations had not allowed most of its interna-tional personnel to return to Iraq. Although Iraqi staff continued some U.N. programs, the United Nations had to scale down or delay both ongoing activities and new initiatives. The United Nations sent three separate assessment teams to Iraq during the first half of 2004 to assist Iraqis in assessing options for forming an Interim Government and in preparing for national elections. The dangerous security situation forced these teams to restrict their travel around Iraq during the first half of 2004, thereby limiting their interaction with Iraqis during important political discussions about the country's future.

- In discussions during the fall of 2003 and the spring of 2004, nongovernmental organization representatives stated that the deteriorating security situation has forced numerous nongovernmental aid organizations to reduce or shut down operations in Iraq. In response to the dangerous security environment, many nongovernmental organizations and contractors that we interviewed have hired private security to provide protection for their staff and compounds. In addition, one representative emphasized his view that as more international workers leave Iraq, insurgents will increasingly focus their efforts on killing Iraqi nationals who are seen as collaborators. U.N. officials and documents have expressed concern that the lack of security could threaten Iraq's transition toward a democratic government. According to a U.N. assessment, the lack of security may lead to major disturbances that could undermine the administration of the elections, alter the established timetable, and compromise the overall credibility of the process. By mid-April 2004, the multinational force had begun to consider how it could provide security, logistical, and other support for the elections, but the United Nations and others had not yet developed a specific plan for important tasks such as the registration of political parties, voters, and candidates or the number and locations of polling sites.

Since June 2003, the security situation has become more dangerous for international military and civilian personnel operating in Iraq and for Iraqis who work with them. Instead of engaging in post-conflict nation building, the United States and its partners have been rebuilding the country in a wartime environment. They have attempted to combat a growing insurgency through military, economic, and political measures. The deteriorating security situation, however, has generally hindered the implementation of economic reconstruction and political transition efforts.[1]

Planning for the Wrong Forces and the Wrong Mission

In spite of such warnings and the developments discussed in Chapter 2, the Coalition continued to concentrate on providing the wrong forces for the wrong mission. Planning for Iraqi military, security, and police forces still focused more on ensuring that they would not be a challenge to the new democratic Iraq that the CPA expected to create than on creating forces that could be effective in dealing with meaningful threats. Virtually all of those interviewed regarding the effort to shape Iraqi forces during 2003 cite major organizational problems and a lack of meaningful priorities, coordination, and resources. One senior adviser with extensive prior experience in working in such international efforts describes the situation as follows:

The CPA was by some margin the most dysfunctional organization I have ever encountered—and I've worked in the UN! No one could doubt the energy, commitment, and engagement by principals, managers, and workers, but it was sorely lacking in any organizational rigor, central control, and clear lines of authority and responsibility. The vacuums created by CPA dysfunctionality were inevitably filled with bureaucracy, endless committees, the inept, the displaced, and those brought out of retirement. We should not underestimate how much further on we would be in Iraq if we had been organized from the beginning with a reasonably coherent organization managing the postconflict phase and equipped with the right people. This may be a harsh judgment but one that is necessary if we are to avoid making the same mistakes in the future. The CPA was, of course, created in a hurry but only because the realization that the scale and magnitude of the task was beyond a retired three-star general and the ninety days he had predicted he would be on the ground. Some of the consequences, I suspect, were that our engagement with the Iraqis suffered horribly, the info-ops campaign was a near disaster, and the political and military intent were never really synched and then executed in any meaningful sense. Clearly, person-alities played a part in all of this, as did the omnipresent Washington desire for exceptionally long screwdrivers. We all have our views on the policy errors and cock ups—as each have their advocates and antagonists (e.g., disbanding the Iraqi army, extent of de-Ba'athification, enough troops for the job, funding mechanisms, war fighting versus counterinsurgency campaigns, etc.)—but the one thing coherent, well-led organizations can do is retrieve, recover, and stabilize the consequences of poor policy decisions. Poor organizations find this next to impossible and end up living with the legacy rather than addressing the outcome.

It was very apparent that the internal conflict going on between the Depart-ment of Defense and agencies within the Department of State—INL [State De-partment Bureau of International Narcotics and Law Enforcement] in particular had an appalling reputation—and others had a substantial effect on our ability to make progress. Influencing the agencies in Washington in order to achieve success in Baghdad was critical, but throw in the time difference, inexperienced staffers, [and] the sheer weight and magnitude of the challenges being faced and it is of little wonder that for every minor success there were any number of frustrations and inefficiencies that were left unresolved. Interestingly, when al-lowed to fester for a while they inevitably grew in complexity until they attracted attention and then you would begin to get the appropriate attention. This would start with a torrent of e-mail from Washington. That is fine—the key was ensuring that you were not responding to some minor staffer eager for information to feed the machine but to someone who could act on your requirements.

The key lesson has to be that you must take proper consideration of what the most appropriate organization is needed to manage the inherent complexity of somewhere like Iraq. The policy- and decision-making processes need to be put in place, and the functional areas, exact roles, and clear lines of authority need to be established. Considerable frustration was caused by visitors who would come into theater, take a look, identify a problem or two (a particularly easy task in Iraq), and then leave. They would leave the difficult part—identifying, resourcing, and implementing the solution—to others.

The initial goal the CPA set for the Iraqi Army was to create three light motorized divisions (over a period of several years) that were designed for border defense. These were to be built slowly from the ground up and gradually become heavier, mechanized divisions with a vaguely defined longer-term goal of creating six to nine divisions over a period of five years or more.

The police were still treated as a secondary mission with little understanding of the growing scale of crime, much less the problems the police faced in dealing with well-organized terrorism and insurgency. The security and civilian intelligence services were initially seen as a potential political threat and as elements that had to be kept weak and free of any taint of the repression of the past regime. The keys to developing military forces were to keep them subordinate to the new civilian authority and democratic system the United States hoped to create and not repeat the past mistake of creating large, corrupt, expensive, and political military forces.

Time was not yet seen as a critical issue, nor was the need to bring Iraqi forces online with any speed. Unlike the previous Iraqi forces, the new Iraqi military was to be lean with the appropriate leadership and driven by well-trained officers and cadres of noncommissioned officers (NCOs). It was to grow at a pace dictated by manpower quality, and they were to have the incentives, pay, facilities, and the career structure necessary to create a relatively moderate-sized force in a functioning democracy. Furthermore, several members of the Interim Government, including Ahmed Chalabi, continued to oppose an effort to create effective military forces of any kind and continued to make efforts that slowed down the U.S. effort in the months to come.

Providing the Equipment and Training Effort with Too Little, Too Late

The first efforts to create Iraqi military forces began in July–August 2003, and the Coalition formally established the Coalition Military Assistance Training Team (CMATT) in August 2003 and made an initial Iraqi Relief and Reconstruction Fund (IRRF) appropriation in November. This effort was led by Walter Slocombe, who became Iraq's de facto minister of defense, and Major General Paul D. Eaton, who became the commanding general of the Coalition Military Assistance Training Team. General Eaton arrived in Iraq only weeks after the CPA officially disbanded the old Iraqi military forces in May 2003.

The US/MNSTC–I effort relied heavily on training in Jordan and using Jordanian officers. In addition, an NCO academy was set up in Iraq. The goal was to create U.S.-trained and equipped battalions that would become cadres that could train other Iraqi forces. Eventually, three Iraqi light motorized brigades would be created which could grow to three divisions over time. The team on the ground did all it could with the resources and guidance it was given. In practice, however, every aspect of the actual program faced massive political and material problems. There was no plan to build on, and only minimal staff was provided. General Eaton was initially given a team of five and a facility with little equipment and no air-conditioning.

Facilities were also a key problem. As has been noted earlier, the Iraqi barracks and facilities left intact by the fighting were looted, lacked wiring and plumbing, and would not have been acceptable even by the standards of Saddam's conscript forces. Suitable facilities had to be built or reconditioned virtually from scratch, and getting the proper material not only involved formal contracts but then ran into delivery problems compounded by the growing violence, sabotage, and theft in the country. As a result, facilities became the initial limiting factor.

Initial Equipment Difficulties

These problems were compounded by equipment supply difficulties. The United States issued competitive bids for the equipment for the three initial motorized battalions modeled largely on U.S. Army tables of equipment and organization (TO&E). They were to have a mix of shoot, move, and communications capabilities that could grow rapidly to a three-division force and gradually become heavier over time. It should be noted, however, that the request for proposals was geared to providing light forces to screen a border. No attempt was made to develop TO&Es tailored to serious counterinsurgency warfare, and this meant steady follow-on efforts to provide better and heavier equipment in virtually every area.

The winner—the Neur Corporation—was selected in a "blind" evaluation with almost unanimous support. The winning company, however, was said to have ties to a relative of Ahmed Chalabi, and the award was contested. Given the lack of priority for effective Iraqi forces, the award was rescinded, and the contract was then held up. As a result, the U.S. team had to improvise, building on existing contracts and finding any vehicle possible to get the required services and equipment.

Training and Force Development Coordination Problems

Equally significant, the training mission for the army was kept separate from training for the security and police forces. This was done to create new security and police forces that would be typical of those in a Western democracy, but it meant that the training teams and methods for the police did not prepare them for terrorism and insurgency, and much of the recruiting and training mission was left to local authorities. The largest elements of the security forces were created as the Iraqi Civil Defense Corps (ICDC) and Facilities Protection Service (FPS), which were little more than a mix of poorly trained and equipped security guards, locally recruited with minimal regard to qualifications and loyalty and unable to cope with serious criminal activity, much less terrorism and insurgency. The FPS was so unsuited to the mission of defending against insurgency, terrorism, and serious crime that the State Department and Department of Defense stopped counting them as part of Iraqi security forces in September 2004.[2]

Still further problems existed. The interim Iraqi government placed the regular military under the new minister of defense, and the central government controlled security and police forces under the new minister of the interior. There was little coordination and poor cooperation between these ministries, the Ministry of Finance, authorities in the governorates, and local authorities—many of which created their own security and police forces at the local level. Moreover, the U.S. and Coalition efforts to create national forces took place at a point when the CPA was still negotiating to persuade the various Shi'ite and Kurdish factions to integrate their militias into the regular military and security forces and disband the rest—an effort that had real promise under the CPA but was never properly implemented after the transfer of sovereignty in June 2004.

The fact that so little manpower and resources were available for training also meant that much of the mission of creating Iraqi forces also took place at the field level. In practice this meant that each of the five Multinational Force–Iraq (MNF–I) regional commands took a different approach to what each saw as a relatively low priority mission. They shaped Iraqi forces around the needs and perceptions of that command rather than as part of a coordinated plan or one designed to have them eventually take over the security mission, and they located Iraqi forces where it was convenient to the MNF–I command element, rather than deploy them where they were most needed to establish sovereignty and control.

Throughout this period the efforts to shape the Iraqi police forces lagged badly behind the efforts to shape the military forces. A combined assessment of the CPA effort to develop the Iraqi police by the inspector general of the Department of State and the inspector general of the Department of Defense summarizes the nature and impact of the CPA effort as follows:

> Perhaps even more than the military, the Iraqi police during the Saddam Hussein era were perceived to be corrupt and brutal implementers of oppression. Accordingly, an early decision of the CPA was to cashier police officers closely tied to the former regime. Other members of the IPS [Iraqi Police Service] abandoned their duties or were casualties of the conflict. Only about 30,000, mostly low-ranking police remained on duty as a residual force—a number clearly insufficient to enforce law and order even had stability been established. Consistent with the CPA goal of erasing troublesome aspects of the Hussein regime, command and control of the remnants of the police force were decentralized. This further diluted cohesion and effectiveness of the residual force.
>
> In June 2003, the CPA and MOI [Ministry of the Interior] issued a directive that all police officers had to return to work no later than July 3. Those failing to do so were subject to immediate termination. According to International Criminal Investigative Training Assistance Program (ICITAP) officials, about 38,000 had returned to the IPS as of July.
>
> To bolster the force, an additional 30,000 police were recruited by Coalition Joint Task Force 7 (CJTF–7) and the Major Subordinate Commanders (MSCs). The driving objective was to get "boots on the ground." In doing so, the CPA

enunciated minimal requirements for entry into the IPS. Subsequently, to meet MNSTC–I training quotas, two patterns of recruiting evolved. Iraqis did most of the recruiting in the Baghdad area. Coalition forces (working through the major subordinate commands or MSCs) were in charge of recruiting in the rest of the country. Iraqi recruiters appear to have enforced minimum requirements as enunciated by CPA, while the MSCs sent to JIPTC [Jordan International Police Training Center] some recruits who did not meet those minimum standards.

During the time of the CPA, such an approach was both inevitable and, perhaps, appropriate. In the wake of the collapse of the Saddam Hussein regime, no Iraqi policy makers were in a position to make authoritative decisions. The CPA decision to cleanse the political system of Hussein sympathizers—notably, the *"de-Ba'athification"* effort—effectively decapitated the IPS of its standing leadership. Even though some former police officers have been reincorporated into the force, it was necessary to start almost from scratch to build a new police force. The result was a "bottom-up" approach with primary emphasis on minimal basic training.

Overall, there is little consensus on how to train Iraqi police. One exception is the universal agreement that the eight weeks devoted to the basic course is insufficient time to produce a capable policeman. Thus, there is tacit consensus that the training program to date has not created an effective IPS. (There is no consensus on how long a time would be required to achieve the desired results.)

As this assessment was being conducted, MNSTC–I and CPATT [Civilian Police Assistance Training Team] leaders were planning to lengthen the basic training course to 10 weeks. This seems to be an appropriate step, but the IG Team makes no recommendation as to the optimum time required for such training. At the outset of the CPA effort to build IPS capacity, the assumption—even to some extent, the reality—was that training could be molded within a rapidly stabilizing political and security environment. The unexpected virulence and scope of subsequent terrorism and insurgency induced changes in the program, but such modifications have lagged [behind] the "street reality" in Iraq.

Adjustments in the training course have been and are being made. During this assessment, the JIPTC staff completed a CPATT-directed revision of the basic curriculum to include more "hands on," self-protection exercises. Other IPS in-country academies are adopting these changes. IP personnel and MOI officials strongly support the adjustments and the shift in emphasis.

A CPA decision to decentralize command and control of the IPS has had unintended consequences. Decentralization was consistent with the intent to disperse political power. Commendable in concept, the emerging result within the IPS is a pattern of fiefdoms, subject to political machinations. An example of this political maneuvering is the situation of competing chiefs of police in Najaf where one responds to the provincial governor, the other to the MOI.

Pay problems have been an equally troubling result of decentralization. Under the CPA designed system, much of the central government's funding is allocated to the provincial governors. Thereafter, the monies are sub-allocated to respective elements, such as the police. Accordingly, each provincial chief of police controls his share of sub-allotted funds. Allegations of mismanagement and corruption in the disbursement of pay for IPs, equipment purchases, etc., are credible. Recentralization of control is not the total answer to these issues—especially to corruption—but the IG Team concludes that tighter MOI control is desirable.[3]

As is the case with many aspects of Iraqi force development, the mistakes made early in the effort had a major and lingering effect. In some cases, this legacy may take years of additional effort to correct.

Tilting toward Reality

For nearly a year the United States acted as if the insurgency was not nationalist in character, was driven by former regime loyalists and foreign volunteers, and was small and unpopular. It emphasized the foreign threat increasingly after January 2004, although Major General Charles H. Swannack noted that only fifty men out of the 3,800 that the Eighty-second Airborne apprehended in the Sunni Triangle area were foreign. For nearly a year the United States acted as if the threat would go away once the United States and the rest of the MNF–I defeated it and that it could be dealt with without supplying serious aid to Iraq.

It was not until the insurgency gathered serious momentum that the United States began to see the mission of creating effective Iraqi forces as critical to successful nation-building and to the reduction of the U.S. and MNF–I presence in Iraq. The reason for such decisions is illustrated by the level of activity that built up between the spring and fall of 2003. For example, Taskforce Ironhorse of the U.S. Army Fourth Division carried out four major operations between June 8 and November 6. During one such phase, carried out between August 11 and September 6, the unit carried out 182 raids, 11,590 Coalition-only patrols, 2,285 joint patrols, 373 flash checkpoints, and 905 static checkpoints. As of November 6, the unit had carried out a total of 361 raids, 21,877 Coalition-only patrols, 3,504 joint patrols, 2,654 flash checkpoints, and 843 static checkpoints.[4]

Reporting by DIA and MNF–I show that the number of serious violent incidents climbed from none in early May 2003 to over 200 in June, around 500 in July, around 600 in August, 700 in September, and over 1,000 in October and November, before dropping to around 800 between December 2003 and February 2004. They rose back to around 1,000 in March 2004 and then averaged well over 1,500 per month through February 2005. This count only included attacks on Coalition targets and partners—defined as including Coalition targets, Iraqi government officials, Iraqi security forces, infrastructure, and some civilians but not attempts, minor attacks, or criminal activity. The count of attacks on civilians also seems to have been defined in ways that produced a significant undercount.[5]

A U.S. Central Command (USCENTCOM) count of the causes of damage to U.S. facilities from May 2003 to March 2004 further illustrates the escalating methods of violence used: 30.8 percent were caused by bombs or IEDs, 14.3 percent by RPGs and mortars, 10.5 percent by small arms and grenades, 13.1 percent by downed helicopters, and 30.6 percent by accidents and "non-hostile" causes—although many accidents were increasingly the result of speeding through hostile areas to avoid ambushes.[6]

Shifts from October 2003 to Spring 2004

In October 2003, the MNF–I created a four-phase plan that took a more serious approach to creating Iraqi forces. The phases were to:

1. provide mutual support and create the conditions by which the Iraqis could take over;
2. give local Iraqi forces the security responsibility for the surrounding area;
3. slowly increase Iraqi force responsibility to larger and larger geographic regions; and,
4. provide a strategic overview while the Iraqis assumed the national security missions.[7]

The United States decided to triple its planned rate of initial buildup for Iraqi military forces, although the mission of the army still focused primarily on border defense and not on counterinsurgency warfare. This decision was made in November–December 2003 and largely as a result of the steady increase in insurgent attacks. This ongoing increase in the insurgency led to further U.S. action in January 2004, when Major General Karl W. Eikenberry was sent to survey the situation and subsequently recommended possible changes.[8] General Eikenberry did not actually arrive in Iraq, however, until January 2004, and it was only in February 2004, nearly a year after Saddam's fall, that the Eikenberry mission helped give building up Iraqi military forces for the counterinsurgency mission the priority it needed. The assessment in the Eikenberry report also led other aspects of the mission to be greatly expanded and escalated. The United States also acted upon its recommendation that a Civilian Police Assistance Training Team (CPATT) be generated and subordinated with the Coalition Military Assistance Training Team (CMATT) under the umbrella organization that became known as the Office of Security Transition.

As a result, shaping the structure of the police, border forces, and other security forces was finally made part of the U.S. military training and equipment mission, and the necessary emphasis was placed on integrating the development of military, security, and police forces. Up until that time the creation of the police, border forces, and other security forces had remained under the Ministry of the Interior. Much of the effort within the ministry had been left largely to individual programs and uncoordinated efforts—some of them highly regional. There was no real "top-down" direction for the effort until March 2004 when CPATT was created and Commanding General Brigadier Andrew Mackay appointed to command it. His first assessment—as part of what was known as the police working group—set up by General Ricardo Sanchez to try to get concurrent planning ahead of Washington prevarication over the Eikenberry report made for bleak reading.[9] It assessed that the Coalition effort had the following status and issues to confront:

- Strategic failure in delivering an effective police force.
- Emphasis on quantity and not quality, along with the ongoing need to ensure quality over quantity.
- Lack of clarity on definition of an "effective" policeman.
- Need to reverse the situation in time for elections.
- Need to introduce ability to maneuver police forces around Iraq.
- Police and border infrastructure and communications very poor.
- Need to introduce broad range of policing capability/specialist courses.
- Accelerate training output but not at the cost of quality.
- Need to substantially involve Iraqi people to a greater extent.
- Overhaul entire funding/resource situation.
- Build a police counterinsurgency force.
- Substantially reform the Ministry of Interior.
- Ensure CPA conduct justice and prison reform concurrently.

And, Commanding General Brigadier Mackay's assessment reached the following conclusions:

- No centralized coordination or control either within the CPA or the Ministry of the Interior meant that one year had been wasted.
- An absence of overall policy, vision, and real control plagued the situation, and the organizational element of the mission needs urgent attention.
- The effort is running out of time and needs IPS to counter the insurgency and be ready for the elections.
- The supplemental budget needs to be harnessed, as not a single statement of requirement has yet been made.
- Opposition from the CPA, which views this as a civil and not military function, could be expected.

The Washington Problem

The U.S. Congress must accept some blame for failing to create procedures that allow time-critical expenditures on security aid. Yet, as officers like Major General Charles H. Swannack, the commander of the Eighty-second Airborne, pointed out in interviews, the CPA sometimes made it as difficult to use U.S. aid funds to train and equip Iraqi security forces as did the Congress, and commanders sometimes had to use Commander's Emergency Relief Program (CERP) aid when they should have had all the funds they needed.[10]

It is also impossible to ignore the fact that the secretary of defense and the joint chiefs of staff were slow to act on many aspects of the advice of the Coalition training mission, slow to task General Eikenberry, and then slow to act upon his report. Until April 2004 the United States failed to recognize the need to treat the Iraqis as full partners in achieving security in Iraq and to make meaningful efforts to train and equip them effectively to perform counterinsurgency missions and more conventional warfare.

The United States issued National Security Presidential Directive 36 in May 2004. This directive placed the U.S. assistance to Iraqi military and police forces under the control of CENTCOM and gave high-level policy direction to the force development effort. The timing, however, was awkward because the transfer of authority to the Iraqi Interim Government (IIG) was scheduled for June 2004 and was about to create an interregnum of several months in many Iraqi efforts as a new government and new (and inexperienced and sometimes feuding) ministers took over. Moreover, the $1.8 billion in Iraqi Relief and Reconstruction Fund (IRRF) appropriation in November 2003 was not actually allocated to the security sector until the fall of 2004.[11] The situation was then complicated by the transition of power from the CPA to a sovereign interim Iraqi government and the appointment of new Iraqi ministers of defense and of the interior, which became serious sources of disruption and led to coordination problems for several months.

Given this background, it is surprising that General Paul D. Eaton was able to give his successor, Lieutenant General David Petraeus, as good a start and as good a mix of capabilities as he did. By June 2004 the Iraqi Army had many of its initial training facilities and barracks ready and had trained some 1,500 officers for a force of three light divisions, most trained in Jordan. It had also trained some 3,500 NCOs. The problems did not lie with the military or the civilians who were actually trying to build Iraqi forces in the field. They occurred at the highest policy levels.

4 Failing to Deliver an Adequate Training and Equipment Program through the Tenure of the CPA and Mid-2004

THE TRANSFER of power to the Interim Iraqi government (IIG) in June 2004 did succeed in giving added legitimacy and Iraqi leadership to the nation-building effort. At the same time, it created new problems. It brought new ministers of defense and of the interior to office in half-formed offices and disrupted plans to disband the various party militias. Tensions between the new ministers made many problems worse, as did their lack of administrative experience and drive. Moreover, new tensions developed with the Ministry of Finance. These problems were increased by a major turnover in lower-ranking personnel. These problems were particularly serious in the case of the Ministry of the Interior. One of the leaders of the Coalition effort to create effective security and police forces notes:

> Another major weakness of the campaign was the inability to build the necessary institutional capacity.... In 2004 ... there were three ministers of interior. The first barely left a mark. The second, Samir Sumaiday, was outstanding. He immediately set about redesigning the organizational structure of the MoI [Ministry of the Interior], sorted out functional areas of responsibility and created a C2 structure that got away from the Iraqi instinct of trying to ensure that all decision-making was centralized. He was however only there for about 10 or so weeks, and the progress we were beginning to make was astonishing.
>
> He then fell victim to the political maneuvering that occurred within the CPA over the formation of the IIG during the course of the transition at the end of July. Another Sunni minister was put in because it was felt that he had a larger and more substantial political constituency. Unfortunately the pace and progress begun by Sumaiday then ground to a halt and remained so throughout 2004. We all watched the inevitable train crash occurring, but the political imperative won out despite the consequences of a highly dysfunctional Ministry of Interior. Building institutional capacity within the MoI was clearly critical if we were to have a functioning police force a fact lost in the politics of it all.

As for the Coalition effort, the administrative changes were more consistent and positive. Ambassador Paul Bremer and General Sanchez had a poor relationship that seriously hurt civil-military cooperation between the CPA and U.S. Command in Iraq. Interviews and press reports indicate that their successors, Ambassador John Negroponte and General George Casey, developed far better relations, and cooperation in strengthening Iraqi military, security, and police forces improved strikingly when they took over in June 2004.

One press report indicates that they met in Washington in April 2004 to try to avoid the deep tensions and civil-military friction that had affected General Sanchez and Ambassador Bremer. According to this report, they assembled a red team when they arrived in Baghdad which began to meet on June 28, 2004, and which created a four-phase plan based on (1) integrating the political, military, and economic assistance efforts, (2) building up the Iraqi security forces, (3) rebuilding Iraq's ruined economy, and (4) instituting a two-part communications strategy to show that the insurgents could not offer Iraq a meaningful future and to try to alienate the Iraqi people from the insurgents.[1]

At a more formal level the Bush administration made its first real effort to define responsibility for managing the Iraqi force development process, although it did so well over a year after the fall of Saddam Hussein's regime. The United States issued National Security Presidential Directive 36 (NSPD–36) that clearly defined the responsibilities for U.S. government operations in Iraq after the June 28, 2004, termination of the Coalition Provisional Authority (CPA). The key portions of the directive stated,

> Commander, USCENTCOM, under the authority, direction and control of the Secretary of Defense, shall continue to be responsible for U.S. efforts with respect to security and military operations in Iraq.... The Secretary of State shall be responsible for the continuous supervision and general direction of all assistance for Iraq. Commander, USCENTCOM, with the policy guidance of the Chief of Mission, shall direct all United States Government efforts and coordinate international efforts in support of organizing, equipping, and training all Iraqi security forces. At the appropriate time, the Secretary of State and the Secretary of Defense shall jointly decide when these functions shall transfer to a security assistance organization and other appropriate organizations under the authority of the Secretary of State and the Chief of Mission.[2]

To implement NSPD–36, the Department of Defense created the Multinational Security Transition Command–Iraq (MNSTC–I) under the overall direction of Commander, Multinational Force–Iraq (MNF–I). MNF–I's Coalition Military Assistance Training Team (CMATT) was assigned the responsibility of managing the Iraqi Army (IA) training program, which included special forces, the navy, and the air force. The MNF–I's Civilian Police Assistance Training Team (CPATT) was assigned the responsibility of managing the Iraqi Police Service (IPS) training program.[3]

The Period from June 2004 to the Fall of 2004

It is difficult to track just how successful such efforts to restructure the creation of effective Iraqi military, security, and police forces were once the decision was taken to create the kind of forces the new Iraqi government needed. The data that are available, however, strongly argue that changes in U.S. policy did not mean rapid changes in implementation and that the flow of resources remained far too low during much of 2004.

Certainly, the Coalition effort still concentrated more on quantity than quality, and—as it becomes all too clear in later chapters—produced grossly inflated numbers of men and forces that lacked the qualifications, motivation, training, equipment, facilities, leadership, unit continuity and integrity, and follow-on advisory support to be effective. According to Department of Defense updates, Iraqi security forces totaled about 219,000 personnel as of June 18, 2004. These included approximately 7,000 Iraqi armed forces, 36,000 Iraqi Civil Defense Corps (ICDC), 84,000 police officers, 18,000 Department of Border enforcement staff, and 74,000 Facilities Protection Service (FPS) personnel.

The structure of Iraqi forces as of May 2004 is shown in table 4.1, and it is important to note that overwhelming emphasis was still being given on forces with little or no value in counterterrorism, counterinsurgency, and dealing with serious crime. Moreover, only 7,000 men out of 219,000 were in the armed forces (3.2 percent), and 110,000 were in the poorly trained and equipped FPS and ICDC (50 percent). The FPS was so weak and ineffective that it was later dropped from the totals for Iraqi forces. The ICDC was so weak that it was first reorganized into the Iraqi National Guard in June 2003 and when that proved ineffective merged into the Iraqi Army in January 2005.

Progress in Training and Equipping Iraqi Security Forces

The U.S. government has only issued limited data on its efforts to train and equip Iraqi forces during this period. The material available from unclassified U.S. sources during the time of the CPA omits critical details on the nature of the training Iraqis received and provides little data on the portion that actually went through academy and received significant military training. It provides only limited data on the flow of U.S. aid to the Iraqi Army and security forces, and U.S. reports often use unrealistic metrics to report on how the equipment effort actually met Iraqi requirements.

The reporting systems on the overall progress of the U.S. effort in Iraq that the United States adopted after the end of the CPA also disguised the details of many serious problems in the security and aid efforts that were revealed in previous reporting. The reporting no longer distinguished construction and nonconstruction expenditures by category, no longer reported the number of serious incidents occurring by day and week, and began to omit any data on equipment transfers either in terms of absolute numbers or relative to requirements.

TABLE 4.1
Controlling Authority and Mission of Iraqi Security Forces in May 2004

Ministry	Force Element	Mission
Defense	Iraqi Armed Forces	The regular army and other services will provide the military defense of Iraq when fully operational, including defense of the national territory and protection and security of critical installations, facilities, infrastructure, lines of communication and supply, and population.
Defense	Iraqi Civil Defense Corps	The corps will perform security and emergency service that directly supports coalition operations to provide security and stability, complementing the police force but designed to perform operations that exceed the capacity of the police.
Interior	Iraqi Police Service	This service will provide primary civil law enforcement for public safety, security, and order.
Interior	Dept. of Border Enforcement	This department will monitor and control the movement of persons and goods to, from, and across the borders of Iraq. It includes Iraqi Border Police charged with border and customs enforcement and immigration.
Interior	Facilities Protection Service	FPS will guard and secure individual ministry and municipal facilities against vandalism and theft. These guards are hired and equipped by individual ministries and can vary greatly in capability.

Note: According to a CPA official, the Iraqi Armed Forces then included units of the Iraqi Army, Iraqi Naval Infantry, Iraqi Army Aviation, Iraqi Coastal Defense Force, an Iraqi counterterrorism force, and associated headquarters.

Source: U.S. Department of Defense status reports; CPA Orders 22, 26, 27, 28, 67, 73, and General Accountability Office, *Rebuilding Iraq: Resource, Security, Governance, Essential Services, and Oversight Issues*, Washington, D.C., June 2004, GAO-04-902R, p. 55.

U.S. officials and officers justified these shortfalls in reporting in three ways. The first and least convincing explanation was that their mission focused on the future, and past reporting wastes time focusing on the past. The second was that they lacked the resources to provide such reporting—which was tantamount to saying they lack the resources to develop adequate data and trend analysis to manage their programs and ensure they are effective. The more convincing explanation is that the debate in Washington over how many troops are on the ground, equipped, or trained has focused on the wrong issues and misleading numbers. As one senior officer intimately involved with the effort to create Iraqi forces has put it, "The real issue is how many will actually fight, how well they will fight, and who they will fight for."

The end result, however, was that U.S. reporting on the development of Iraqi forces, like U.S. reporting on the insurgency and terrorism, lacked the transparency to provide a clear picture of what was happening and to establish serious credibility. The United States adopted a public-relations approach that seemed to be "no new news but good news."

Yet, the data the Coalition and United States did provide are still adequate to show that there were serious problems in the effort to train and equip the Iraqi security forces through the fall of 2004. The data that describe progress through September 2004 document a major failure on the part of the United States, particularly on the part of the CPA and Department of Defense, to develop effective Iraqi military, security, and police capabilities on a timely basis.

Progress at the Time the CPA Went Out of Business at the End of June 2004: The CPA View

The CPA made the following fourteen claims about its progress in creating security and effective Iraqi forces when it gave sovereignty back to the Iraqi Interim Government in June 2004:

- The Iraqi government announced a new law allowing it to impose emergency security measures to combat terrorism.
- The initial battalion of the Iraq Intervention Force (IIF) deployed into Baghdad at the end of June.
- The IIF was being established, trained, and equipped for urban counterinsurgency operations.
- All three battalions of the first IIF brigade were scheduled ready by the end of July.
- At the end of June, forty-one of forty-five battalions of the Iraqi National Guard (formerly the Iraqi Civil Defense Corps) were manned above 75 percent strength.
- Iraqi forces had begun joint patrols throughout Iraq with Coalition and Iraqi police forces.
- Efforts were under way to recruit six additional 400-man public order battalions as part of the Iraqi Police Service civil intervention force.
- With these additions, the Iraqi Police Service civil intervention force would total nine public order battalions and two counterinsurgency battalions.
- A total of 5,502 new IPS recruits had completed the eight-week training course.
- Five classes—or over 3,411 students—had graduated from the Jordan International Police Training Center.
- Four classes—or 2,091 students—had graduated from the Baghdad Public Safety Academy.
- Approximately 25,000 IPS personnel who served as police under the former regime had completed a three-week Transition Integration Program (TIP) taught by the Coalition.
- IPS officers were also being taught basic criminal investigation, criminal intelligence, and dignitary protection by Coalition advisers.
- The Iraqi Air Force was to be given two Seeker reconnaissance aircraft to conduct surveillance of the borders and oil facilities, and officials were rushing procurement of fourteen more.

None of these claims said anything about force quality, and it is more than a little ironic that Department of Defense public-relations efforts after early 2005 stressed that Iraq had only one deployable battalion in July 2004.

Progress at the Time the CPA Went Out of Business at the End of June 2004: The GAO View

The CPA's reassuring statements contrast sharply with both the historical background provided in previous chapters and the reporting by the General Accountability Office (GAO) during this period, although the GAO analysis was based largely on Multinational Corps–Iraq (MNC–I) reporting. The GAO report only received limited attention at the time, but it remains the most authoritative picture of what was actually happening to Iraqi forces at the time sovereignty was transferred to the Iraqi Interim Government. The GAO report states:

> The multinational force is also organizing, training, equipping, mentoring, and certifying Iraqi security forces so that it can transfer security responsibilities to them and eventually draw down the multinational force. . . . The multinational force's security transition plan calls for a four-phased transfer of security responsibilities from the multinational force. . . .
>
> As of March 26, 2004, Iraq had about 203,000 security personnel of greatly varying capabilities. Of these forces, only the Iraqi Armed Forces are specifically mandated for the military defense of Iraq, while the others are intended exclusively for civil law enforcement and protection duties. However, according to senior DOD [Department of Defense] officials and multinational force documents, these security forces, especially the Iraqi Police Service and Iraqi Civil Defense Corps, were insufficiently trained and equipped for these duties. During the escalation of violence that occurred during April 2004, some of these security forces collapsed. The multinational force has taken action to address training and equipping problems, but it is unclear how this will affect the long-term plan to shift security responsibilities to Iraqi forces.
>
> Since the fall of 2003, the multinational force has developed and refined a plan to transfer security responsibilities to Iraqi security forces in four phases. In October 2003, a multinational force document outlined the security transition concept, including (1) an initial phase, called mutual support, where the multinational force establishes conditions for transferring security responsibilities to Iraqi forces; (2) transition to local control, where Iraqi forces in a local area assume responsibility for security; (3) transition to regional control, where Iraqis are responsible for larger regions; and (4) transition to strategic over watch, where Iraqi forces on a national level are capable of maintaining a secure environment against internal and external threats, with broad monitoring from the multinational force.
>
> Transition through these phases is contingent on decreasing threat capability, increasing Iraqi security capability, and the ability of civil administration to exercise control of Iraqi forces. According to the multinational force document, transferring control for local security to Iraqis should allow the multinational

force to reduce the number of troops devoted to stability operations and reduce the number of forward operating bases. This would allow the multinational force to focus on offensive operations against coalition opponents.

The multinational force began to shift responsibilities to Iraqi security forces in February 2004, earlier than planned, citing the growing capability of these forces. In Baghdad, for example, the coalition forces withdrew to bases outside of the city, giving Iraqi forces greater responsibility for security within the city. According to State Department public-opinion polls published around that time, about 20 percent of Iraqis said that the multinational force was very effective at keeping law and order on the streets, and one-third believed the force was very effective in protecting Iraqis from major threats and civil war. Furthermore, Iraqis preferred that more security responsibilities be transferred to their own police and army. In a later polling report published in mid-June 2004, the State Department said that Iraqis viewed the multinational force as part of the security problem, not the solution. According to the report, Iraqis were confident that Iraqi security forces would be able to maintain security without the multinational force.

Iraqi security forces include more than 200,000 members of the armed forces, police, and other agencies of the Ministry of Interior. These forces have varying missions and capabilities, but most are not trained or equipped to engage well-armed insurgents. The CPA and multinational force reported problems in training and equipping these forces in 2004.... According to senior DOD officials, these forces performed poorly in the crises in Fallujah and southern Iraq in early April 2004.

As of May 2004, the multinational force was responsible for training, equipping, mentoring, and certifying all Iraqi security forces, such as the Iraqi Armed Forces and the Iraqi police. U.N. Security Council Resolution 1546 states that after the transfer of power, Iraqi security forces would fall under the command of appropriate Iraqi ministers, and welcomed the continued development of a security partnership between the sovereign government of Iraq and the multinational force. According to an annex to the resolution, the Iraqi Armed Forces will be responsible to the Chief of Staff and Minister of Defense, while the other security forces will report to the Ministry of the Interior or other government ministers. The resolution states that the government of Iraq has the authority to commit Iraqi security forces to engage in operations with the multinational force. According to the resolution, the multinational force and Iraqi government are developing various coordination mechanisms to achieve unity of command of military operations when Iraqi security forces operate with the multinational force.

The total number of Iraqi security forces as of March 26, 2004, just prior to the insurgent activities of early April, was 203,000—approximately 86 percent of the goal set by the multinational force. Of these forces, the Iraqi Armed Forces is the only force specifically trained and equipped for the defense of Iraqi territory and population. However, in March 2004 this force experienced the greatest shortfall in personnel, with only 8 percent of the troops needed.

Although the other Iraqi security forces existed in greater numbers, they were not intended to fight a pitched battle against well-armed insurgents. Iraqi police officers are tasked solely to uphold general law and order through such activities as performing criminal investigations, arresting suspects, and questioning witnesses. Iraqi Civil Defense Corps soldiers are trained for constabulary duties, such as setting up traffic control checkpoints, patrolling and cordoning off streets, performing crowd control, providing convoy security, and other civil functions. Members of the Facilities Protection Service are trained to guard Iraqi ministry buildings and other fixed sites. According to CPA officials, they are effective exclusively in locations already controlled by local military and law enforcement personnel. For example, according to a CPA official, Facilities Protection Service guards at a fixed site would be overrun by an enemy force that contained more than 10 to 20 insurgents, or one that had numerous heavy weapons, without prompt help from the multinational force.

According to the President, senior DOD officials, and multinational force commanders, Iraqi security forces responded poorly to a series of anti-Coalition attacks in April 2004. In western and central Iraq, insurgents attacked the multinational force in Fallujah, Baghdad, Ar Ramadi, Samarra, and Tikrit, while a radical Shi'a militia launched operations to dislodge multinational forces and occupy cities from Baghdad to Basra in the south. In particular, units of the Iraqi Army, Iraqi Police Service, and the Iraqi Civil Defense Corps refused to engage the enemy.

According to DOD officials, the 2nd Battalion of the Iraqi Armed Forces refused to engage insurgents and support the 1st Marine Expeditionary Force in Fallujah. One problem cited included the belief of the soldiers, reinforced by briefings during their training, that they would never be used as an internal security force. Weak battalion leadership and insufficient or poor equipment were also mentioned as contributing factors. According to a CPA official, Iraqi police forces in Fallujah, Najaf, Karbala, and Kut collapsed. The number of police officers dropped by 2,892 during the week of April 17 to 23, according to the CPA weekly assessment. These declines resulted from officers being killed in the line of duty; sent for retraining and reintegration; or removed from the Iraqi Police Service for actions supporting the insurgency. According to a CPA official and an assessment by the multinational force, the Iraqi Police Service was overwhelmed due to disorganization, insufficient training and equipment, and weak mentoring. However, CPA also said the police forces are civil law enforcement units and are not intended to withstand guerilla attacks. Nonetheless, in other locations they stood up to the attacks. Iraqi Civil Defense Corps units also collapsed during April, with soldiers staying home, declaring a neutral stance, or resigning throughout central and western Iraq. According to the multinational force interim assessment, desertion was most prevalent between April 2 and April 16. During this time, up to 12,000 Iraqi Civil Defense Corps soldiers did not show up for duty.

The assessment also found that Iraqi Civil Defense Corps units were not sufficiently equipped or trained for high-intensity tasks, such as engaging large numbers of insurgents. Furthermore, lack of equipment and poor training resulted in general fear and disillusionment among personnel. Additionally, better-equipped and better-trained battalions in northern and southern Iraq held together during the crises of mid-April, although they did not face the same level of threat. Iraqi Civil Defense Corps soldiers were also susceptible to intimidation or sympathy for anti-coalition fighters. Finally, soldiers were less likely to carry out their duty when their home township was under insurgent pressure, leading to the collective desertion of units from the troubled townships.

The multinational force is taking steps to assess and respond to the various problems of the Iraqi security forces and is considering how these forces can provide security during Iraq's upcoming election process. As of late May 2004, a new team of senior military officers was assessing every unit in the Iraqi security forces. This team will oversee the accelerated training of Iraqi soldiers, police, and other security personnel.

In April 2004, the multinational force began a new reconstitution program for police officers who had deserted in Najaf and Karbala and scheduled senior leadership and additional specialized courses for the end of May. In addition, it planned to begin implementing its equipment distribution plan, define the equipment requirements for the entire Iraqi Police Service and the Department of Border Enforcement, and better inform major subordinate commands about which equipment they would receive and when. Further, the multinational force planned to start institutionalizing a monthly report and certification plan for police stations.

According to a Department of Justice (DOJ) official, in an effort to support the multinational force training program for the Iraqi Police Service, DOJ and its components have developed a number of specialty courses designed to transition the fundamentals of basic training into operational and investigative capacity. The specialty courses are designed to build investigative directorates in the areas of intelligence analysis, counterterrorism, organized crime, basic criminal investigation, post-blast investigations, and fingerprinting. Teams of personnel and experienced contractors from many DOJ components are currently deployed or are preparing to deploy to provide training in support of this initiative.

According to an implementation order published in April 2004, the multinational force is pursuing multiple courses of action to rebuild the Iraqi Civil Defense Corps. It will also develop and rebuild battalions with new equipment scheduled to arrive throughout May 2004. However, a CPA official with access to CPA contracting information stated that Iraqi Civil Defense Corps equipment would probably not make it to Iraq until June or possibly July 2004. The multinational force will also review the criteria for recruitment and possibly change recruiting practices to stop commissioning entire battalions from the same area.

The multinational force also plans to ease de-Ba'athification standards and invite experienced and capable former soldiers and officers to join the Iraqi Civil Defense Corps. The multinational force expects some 4,000 to 5,000 Sunni to be incorporated into the Iraqi Civil Defense Corps in this way. The training program will begin concentrating on developing and mentoring leaders at all levels of the Iraqi Civil Defense Corps. Furthermore, all major subordinate commands will permanently embed training teams within Iraqi Civil Defense Corps battalions. These teams will perform refresher training and mentoring, and provide direction until battalion leadership is fully developed and capable of assuming command.

Given the poor performance of the Iraqi security forces during April 2004, it is unclear what level of security they will be able to provide during the period leading up to Iraq's national elections, which are currently scheduled to be held by the end of January 2005. As of mid-April 2004, the multinational force was considering what sort of security and other support it would provide during the election process. According to a planning document, the extent of this support will depend on the ability of the Iraqis, international organizations, and contractors to provide for security and other support tasks. The document stated that the multinational force expected some areas to be under the local control of the Iraqi security forces by the time elections take place. The document did not acknowledge, however, the poor performance of Iraqi security forces during early April 2004.

Effective Iraqi security forces are critical for transitioning security responsibilities to Iraq. However, Iraqi security forces proved unready to take over security responsibilities from the multinational force, as demonstrated by their collapse during April 2004. Of these forces, only the Iraqi Armed Forces are specifically mandated for the military defense of Iraq, while the others are intended exclusively for civil law enforcement and protection duties. The multinational force identified problems in the training and equipping of the Iraqi forces as reasons for poor performance.

Although the multinational force is beginning to address these problems, it is unclear what impact April's security collapse will have on the plans for transitioning Iraq's security to Iraqi security forces or the extent to which these forces will be capable of providing security during the Iraqi election process. What is clear, however, is that the development of effective Iraqi security forces will continue after the transfer of power to an interim Iraqi government.[4]

Too Little and Too Late in Getting Resources to the Iraqis

It is unclear how serious a problem funding and the ability to actually obligate and spend money was during this period. One legacy of the CPA was that Iraq's total defense budget for 2004 was only $101 million and its justice budget was only $151 million, although Iraq's actual defense budget for 2004 became $450 million. There is, however, an unexplained category called "additional security projects" that was raised from $500 million to $1 billion in March 2004.[5]

Other CPA reporting, including the following examples, also showed how slow the flow of resources to Iraqi forces really was:

- The weekly status reporting issued by the Department of Defense as of July 13, 2004, confirmed the fact that the actual flow of U.S. aid to Iraq and its impact on the Iraqi security still remained almost glacially slow. As of July 13, the United States had only actually spent $220 million out of the $2,976 million apportioned for security under the fiscal year 2004 aid program of $18.4 billion.

- CPA reporting as of June 29, 2004, showed that obligations for nonconstruction security procurement were about 25 percent of goal, and commitments were around 50 percent. The figures for construction tasks were far more favorable and almost totally misleading. They indicated that $749 million was obligated and $1,003 million was committed to meet a goal for July 1, 2004, of $749 million.
- The CPA status report issued on July 6, 2004, showed that obligations for nonconstruction security procurement were about 30 percent of goal on June 30, 2004, and commitments were around 60 percent. The figures for construction tasks were, again, far more favorable but almost totally misleading. They indicated that the $825 million was obligated as of June 30, 2004, and $985 million was committed to meet a goal for July 1, 2004, of only $749 million. Yet virtually every report on Iraqi security efforts indicates that facilities remain grossly inadequate.
- The status reports as of July 13, 2004, were less detailed than previous statements but showed that the CPA 2207 Report called for $3.243 billion in fiscal year 2004 aid funds for construction and nonconstruction projects for security and law enforcement. While $1.507 billion of this total had been obligated, only $220 million had actually been spent. The CPA 2207 Report called for $1.038 billion in fiscal year 2004 aid funds for justice and public safety, but only $300 million had been obligated, and only $14 million had been spent.

Force Status Data

Additional sources of data that the United States made available on the status and readiness of Iraqi forces in the summer of 2004 helped make the list of "achievements" claimed by the CPA less than credible:

- As of June 26, 2004, the U.S. reporting summarized in the final CPA status report showed a net average increase in the number of significant insurgent attacks using improvised explosive devices (IEDs), vehicle-borne IEDs, mortars, rocket-propelled grenades, and improvised rockets over the period since September 2003. They were averaging over forty per day, and the total number of incidents of all kinds was far higher.[6] The United States had reported the capture or killing of many Iraqi foreign and domestic insurgents but no decline in the total number of active insurgents since its first meaningful estimates in July 2003. It could not characterize the leadership or membership of either domestic or foreign insurgent groups with any precision or the level of actual Al Qa'ida central influence and control.
- The Iraqi Interim Government was experiencing serious loyalty and performance problems in critical areas like Baquba in late July. Some reports

indicated the top four security officers in the new government security forces had to be removed during fighting with insurgents during this time.

- The CPA went out of business just as the first battalion of the Iraq National Task Force Division began to deploy to Baghdad and as the new Iraqi government overrode its plans to leave the Iraqi Civil Defense Corps (ICDC) as a largely passive defense force and converted it to a National Guard. The Iraqi police were just beginning to acquire serious counterinsurgency capabilities in the form of nine public order battalions and two counterinsurgency battalions as part of an Iraqi Police Service (IPS) civil intervention force.

- The efforts to create an effective Iraqi Police Service (IPS) remained a near disaster. The 120,000-man force reported in some U.S. documents had at least 25,000 totally unqualified personnel, and training was more of a myth than a reality.[7]

- In early August 2004, defections were reported to remain a major problem, and the police and security forces were reported to be including 30,000 more names on their roles than they could actually account for. The British officer in charge of the Civilian Police Assistance Training Team (CPATT), Brigadier General Andrew Mackay, referred to the fact that many police left without sending in resignations or having their departure reported as "ghosts."[8]

- As of July 30, 2004, the central Iraqi police office dealing with the key problem of kidnapping still had almost no office equipment, no phone of its own, no air-conditioning, no computers, and an authorized staff far too small to do the job. There were forty-two officers assigned to a task that the head of the section estimated required one thousand.[9]

- By June 2004 the new Iraqi Department of Border Enforcement (DBE) was supposed to have a strength of some 18,000. Priority had been given to the police, however, and the DBE only had 255 men who had actually been trained as a rapidly improvised new border patrol academy.[10]

Manpower and Training Status

The CPA never standardized its public reporting on the status of Iraqi training, and its data always implied a much higher level of training than actually took place. A later study by MNSTC–I showed that the CPA reported an increase in total Iraqi security forces (ISF) strength from some 90,000 in October 2003 to roughly 200,000 in January 2004. The CPA continued to report figures of over 200,000 through April 2004, although this was a rough estimate of the total manpower claimed to be "on duty" and had nothing to do with training and equipment—or even audits of actual personnel as distinguished from authorized levels.[11]

The training data on the Iraqi security forces were also altered in ways that disguised the level of training in most services in the CPA reporting issued from April 2004 onward. This was done by implying that training under the Ba'ath regime or limited on-the-job training under the Transition Integration Program (TIP) was adequate. This kind of reporting was so misleading that the entire manpower reporting process had to be restructured after Iraqi forces failed to perform in Fallujah and Sadr City in the spring of 2004, and the MNF–I had to issue a new set of totals based on "trained" manpower in May 2004. This figure was closer to 130,000 than the peak figure the CPA issued in February 2004, which was close to 210,000. It still, however, ignored major quality, vetting, and training problems and the fact that much of the manpower involved was too weakly equipped to carry out anything but the most limited missions.

The end result was yet another reappraisal of such numbers in August 2004. This led the MNSTC–I to create a new category called "trained and equipped." The total for such manpower was only 96,000 in September 2004, a massive contrast to the CPA reporting of over 200,000 some ten months earlier and the peak of some 160,000 to 170,000 reported as "trained" manpower in August 2004.

The Overall Status of Iraqi Security Forces' Manning and Training Efforts

The problems in emphasizing quantity over quality are illustrated by the fact that the final status reports of the CPA used different types of training data for each report. For example, the data issued on June 25, 2004, shows that only 5,857 out of 88,039 Iraqi police had serious academy training, although another 2,387 were in the training pipeline. The CPA report issued on July 6, 2004, did not provide the same detail on training data as in previous reports but did indicate that only 3,411 students had graduated from the Jordanian police academy, and 1,674 students had graduated from the Baghdad Public Safety Academy. Even these students had courses lasting less than a fifth as long as similar training in the United States and Europe. The figures for the Department of Border Enforcement showed that only 255 of the 18,248 officers had postwar academy training with an additional twenty-five in training.[12]

The CPA went out of business before the Iraqi Civil Defense Corps was transformed into the National Guard, but its final reports stated that only 2,362 out of 39,128 men were "in training." It should be noted, however, that the other 36,762 had completed their initial training and were with units conducting follow-on training or security operations with Coalition forces. Some of these Iraqi National Guard (ING) units were among the first the Coalition formed and trained, and some had been training and operating for nearly a year by this time.

The CPA's final report on the status of the Iraqi Army for July 6 showed that 10,222 men were said to be in service of which 2,316 were "in training." The data for the Facilities Protection Service showed an active strength of 74,069. No data were provided on what portions were regarded as trained and only seventy-seven were reported to be "in training." Most of this training, however, was little more than at the "boot camp" or token level. An investigation by the General Accountability Office—based largely on the work of Coalition advisers to the Iraqi police—described it as follows:[13]

The multinational force and CPA had problems training and equipping the Iraqi Police Service and the Iraqi Civil Defense Corps in late March 2004. While some police training occurred at academies in Jordan and Baghdad, according to an official from the State Department Bureau of International Narcotics and Law Enforcement (State/INL), the prevailing security situation has prevented CPA and State/INL police trainers from moving freely across the country and establishing additional training facilities.

As a result, multinational force commanders assumed responsibility for temporary police training in their areas of responsibility. State/INL provided the commanders with a temporary curriculum, the Transition Integration Program. The full curriculum is 108 hours long and provides basic police training in such subjects as basic human rights, firearms familiarization, patrol procedures, and search methods. According to a State Department official, the various major subordinate commanders had wide latitude in terms of training police and did not uniformly adopt the Transition Integration Program. They were free to establish their own curriculum and requirements for police, which varied in depth and scope. Training could last between 3 days and 3 weeks.

According to a State/INL official, some commanders required trainees to undergo class and field training, while other commanders only required officers to wear a uniform. According to a multinational force interim assessment from May 2004, the Iraq Civil Defense Corps also lacked proper training. It stated that investment into training the Iraqi Civil Defense Corps units varied among the multinational divisions and that the units in the western and center-south major subordinate commands in particular were the least prepared for combat. Furthermore, the training was not sufficient for high-intensity tasks.

One CPA official agreed with this, stating that the training for the Iraqi Civil Defense Corps did not prepare it to fight against well-armed insurgents with mortars and rocket-propelled grenades, for example. The assessment also noted that the Iraqi Civil Defense Corps units contained too many inexperienced officers and soldiers.

Progress and Problems in Creating an Effective Police Training Effort

As has been touched upon earlier, the United States created a Civilian Police Assistance Training Team (CPATT) in March 2004 under military command and the Multinational Force–Iraq (MNF–I), the group that later became the Multinational Security Transition Command–Iraq (MNSTC–I). This put the police training and organization effort under a general officer, Brigadier General Andrew Mackay, supported by a civilian deputy from the International Criminal Investigative Training Assistance Program (ICITAP) team of the Department of Justice.

Unlike the team training the military, the CPATT had both civilian and military elements.[14] The Department of Defense now had primary responsibility for security operations in Iraq, including training of security forces, but the Department of State had overall responsibility for security assistance in nation-building operations within the U.S. government.

The State Department Bureau of International Narcotics and Law Enforcement (INL) had the most institutional experience in training police forces and had been tasked with developing an appropriate training program for the Iraqi Police Service for the CPA and before the rise of the insurgency led to need for a military focus on counterinsurgency and the issuing of NSPD–36.[15] As a result, the Department of Defense and the State Department continued to share responsibility for the development of the Iraqi Police Service.

Views differ over how effective these initial efforts were, the scale and nature of the problems involved, and how effective cooperation was between the civilian and military elements of CPATT. Work by Robert M. Perito provides a highly critical picture of the problems in the efforts to create an effective Iraqi Police Service, including the issues of using unqualified personnel and the lack of training.[16]

Moreover, it was not until June 2004 that an MNSTC-I "troop-to-task" study began to define the size and nature of the force that was really required and set a goal of 135,000 men. This was a major increase over the prewar strength of 58,006 men for the IPS authorized for the general director of police under Saddam Hussein, and it rapidly became a moving target as the rise of the insurgency made it clear that more and more specialized elements and security forces were needed.[17]

In practice, terrorism, insurgency, and organized crime had already long made this impractical. Whatever Iraq might have been with proper stability operations and nation-building, it was now a nation involved in low-level insurgency and civil war. The police had to be able to fight to survive—never mind to give ordinary Iraqis security—and had to coordinate their operations with the military. Others feel that the police and security advisory effort was beginning to accomplish what it could in the face of major resource and bureaucratic constraints and laid the groundwork for the more effective efforts that followed. One senior adviser within CPATT provided the following inside view of what was happening at this time, a significantly more positive picture of the progress that began in the spring and summer of 2004:

> ... it took the best part of a year for Washington and CJTF-7 to realize that the planning and progress for security-sector reform (SSR)—as it related to the police—was woefully inadequate and that the limited individual training that had been introduced was not going to produce a police force of any real effectiveness. The counterinsurgency campaign was also beginning to take real shape and there was a realization that decisive remedial action had to be taken if the Iraqi Police and Border Police were going to be built into an effective force.

Additionally US International Police Advisors were deploying into theatre but with no real sense of what their task or purpose would be. The plan was to have 500 of these individuals in theatre and there was a recognition that they could have real value but they would have to be coordinated and commanded by the military within CPATT if they were to be of any enduring utility.

By the time therefore that Eikenberry had visited, compiled his report and the police working group had been put together the counterinsurgency campaign had moved on apace and there was a growing urgency to fulfill the CPATT mission. CPATT were required therefore to bring all of these disparate and different strands together and try and weld it all into a coherent organization that would Organize, Train, Equip and Mentor the Iraqi Police and Border Police.

On the command and control side CG CPATT worked, initially, directly to General Sanchez. General Sanchez, at that point, had not received formal direction from DoD [Department of Defense] to proceed with the setting up of CPATT although it was clearly gathering a head of steam within Washington. The police working group was primarily his means of getting ahead with some concurrent planning ahead of the formal direction arriving. That subsequently arrived in the form of a memo from [Defense Secretary Donald] Rumsfeld that directed that CENTCOM take on the Organize, Train, Equip and Mentor mission for the IPS and Border Police.

With the formal direction received the Command and Control arrangements began to take shape although it was a chaotic and particularly fractious birth. The original plan saw CPATT coming into existence at the beginning of April 2004 but as events unfolded around Iraq it was patently obvious that we should just get on with it and as a result CPATT was formally established on 08 March 2004. CPATT established itself in a former kitchen which crammed in about 10 military and civilian officers. As CPATT expanded we stuck desks into the corridor.

Essentially CMATT was resubordinated from the CPA to CJTF-7 but with its CG being told to form an OSC (Office of Security and Cooperation), which then commanded both CMATT and CPATT. The organizational model had both CPATT and CMATT sharing the same central staff—all of whom were CMATT one day but OSC the next and therefore responsible for CPATT staff functions as well. Numerous frictions were caused by the speed of this re-organization.

CPATT was also in a separate part of the building from CMATT and MG [Major General Paul] Eaton which had its benefits in that we just got on with the Organize, Train, Equip and Mentor mission with minimum interference. Gen Sanchez, to all intent and purposes, continued to have CPATT working directly to him as he really did understand what was required. Another aspect worth highlighting was that the "policy" ownership issue became a real bone of contention without anyone really understanding that there was no "policy." The issue was, of course, military control over a civil function but given the lack of progress it was inevitable that the military would have to take on the task of rebuilding the Iraqi police and border force.

A compromise on policy was eventually hammered out that had the head of CPATT Brigadier General Andrew Mackay reporting to two bosses. The CG of the OSC (eventually to become MNSTC-I with LTG Petraeus arrival in June 2004) and the 3* US civilian head of the MoI within the CPA. The involvement of the latter allowed everyone to state that policy direction of a civil function was coming from a civilian. Not surprisingly none was ever forthcoming—it hadn't up until then—and it was therefore developed by the military and civilian officers within CPATT.

The command and control arrangements were eventually made more coherent with the arrival of LTG [Lieutenant General David] Petraeus who changed the name of the organization to MNSTC-I on transition at the end of July 2004 CJTF/7 itself changed and became MNF-I (Multinational Force—Iraq and took the Corps (MNC-I: Multinational Corps–Iraq) and MNSTC-I under command.

Brigadier General Andrew Mackay reported:

> ... the re-organization and subsequent aligning of functions and responsibility in the creation of CPATT was a particularly brutal and fractious period. It should and could have been avoided but was absolutely necessary if progress in rebuilding the Iraqi Police Force was to be made. Too much time had been lost. Security Sector Reform is, in reality, a nascent concept and one that many people do not understand well yet the lessons from Bosnia, Kosovo and Afghanistan were all ignored or perhaps they were lessons that had never been gathered in the first place. Convincing Washington of the virtues of quality over quantity was not easy either. The statistics being bandied about gave a false impression of what was being achieved. We did try to come up with coherent Measurement of Effectiveness but that system was only maturing as I left. There was too much concentration on the OA (Operational Analysis) effort on intelligence and info ops rather than measuring success and, as a result, were not able to articulate the considerable progress that they were actually making ... on the formation of CPATT my clear intent was to try and have the Iraqi Police and Border Force in some kind of shape to ensure the delivery of the elections in January 2005. This was, I think, achieved but by the skin of our teeth. We managed to get just enough equipment fielded, just enough training conducted, just enough mentoring into the right places and just managed to plug the various organizational or institutional capacity holes in the Ministry of Interior. To be sure the prime deliverer of the elections were the coalition forces but the Iraqi police and border police stood alongside them on election day and should, rightly, take significant credit for being there.

An American expert who participated in a later phase of the CPATT effort made the following points—some of which highlight issues that a report by the inspector generals of the Department of Defense and State Department found had left an important legacy that still had a major impact on the Iraqi police and security services in mid-2005. They note that the Coalition and CPATT were very slow to provide the Iraqi police with the weapons, equipment, and training they needed to operate and survive in a counterinsurgency campaign.

They also highlight tensions between the Department of Defense and State Department, whose merits are hard to judge at a distance but which struck a number of both U.S. and British advisers as significant. The American expert states:

> I started to recommend back in February 2004 that JIPTC [Jordan International Police Training Center] modify its curriculum to place more emphasis on paramilitary training as opposed to women's rights, human rights, etc. That type of training is not unimportant for democratic policing, but it is useless if the policeman is dead. Unfortunately, the police trainers—particularly from Western Europe—were adamant about the need to train Iraqis in community and democratic policing.
>
> When I departed in March 2005, JIPTC still did not provide firearms training to IPS recruits on anything but 9mm pistols—not terribly effective against AKs, RPKs and RPGs. The reason constantly given by JIPTC/INL management as to why the level of firearms training had not been increased was that DOS/DynCorp had contractual issues in getting the berms built to handle the firing of AK-47s. In my view this was inexcusable and reinforced a pattern of significant mismanagement of JIPTC by DOS—instances that I could detail in another venue.
>
> That is not to say ICITAP [International Criminal Investigative Training Assistance Program] was perfect, but they did indeed establish and run the police training through the spring of 2004 with INL [State Department Bureau of International Narcotics and Law Enforcement] providing only funds and DynCorp providing the construction/logistics. In a political move, DOS muscled ICITAP out of the directorship of JIPTC in the spring of 2004.
>
> When the ICITAP director and founder of JIPTC returned to Kosovo, DOS installed their own director ... who so horribly mismanaged JIPTC that the UK was considering pulling their contingent.... [The director] was subsequently relieved—or "promoted" in DOS speak—and a new INL director was installed. LTG [Lieutenant General David] Petraeus had pushed for [the director's] removal and was rebuffed by then-INL director.... Eventually, it took GEN [George] Casey to weigh in to get [the director] removed.
>
> One of the significant lessons that should be learned from this effort is that a lack of unity of command and competing bureaucratic aspirations SIGNIFICANTLY hampered the IPS training and, in my view, cost lives unnecessarily. DOS is not primarily a law enforcement organization and while they contract out for police mentors through INL in various countries, DOJ/ICITAP actually is responsible for police academies. There should only be one agency responsible for law enforcement training and the Department of Justice would seem the logical choice since they maintain far more requisite knowledge in this area. INL is simply an anachronism that seeks to keep DOS "relevant" in areas where they have little expertise. What really needs to happen is a change in the funding authorizations to allow DOJ to directly fund international law enforcement training. At the moment ICITAP is dependent upon funds from INL and so the golden rule is in effect—they who hold the gold, rule.[18]

In any case, the creation of new Iraqi security forces and police forces was anything but ideal. Paramilitary and gendarmerie-like forces were what Iraq really needed, and special elements like the Emergency Response Unit, Civil Intervention Force, and SWAT teams were vital. The Minister of the Interior's creation of a Special Police Commando Unit—led by his cousin, a former Iraqi intelligence officer, and with a large number of members of the Republican Guard—was more questionable, but the unit did have considerable effectiveness.[19]

Manning and Training Issues in Mid-2004

Data provided by the Department of Defense and State Department in June 2004 and other studies, including the following, provide additional insight into what was happening to Iraqi military, security, and police forces as of mid-2004:

- As of June 25, 2004, the CPA reported that only 5,857 out of 88,039 Iraqi police had serious academy training, although another 2,387 were in the training pipeline. No figures were made available for how many could be said to have the necessary equipment, transportation, communications, and facilities. The figures for the Department of Border Enforcement showed that 255 had postwar academy training out of a total of 18,248, and an additional twenty-five were in training.
- Another study of the Iraqi Police Service (IPS) showed a total force of 79,876 as of July 1, 2004, with more than 50,000 untrained, 7,000 academy trained, 18,000 TIP trained, and 450 field trained. The goal was then to create a force of 85,000 by January 1, 2005, with more than 38,000 untrained, 19,000 academy trained, 28,000 TIP trained, and 10,000 field trained. The goal was to create an Emergency Response Unit with high-end SWAT units, public order battalions with maneuver capability, counterinsurgency police regiments, highway patrol units, leadership courses, and a specialist training academy. This same plan called for the completion of the full range of IPS training facilities, including an Iraqi police academy, by July 2005.
- The same report indicates that the Iraqi Border Police (IBP) had 8,200 men with 400 academy trained, and the goal was then to create a force of 8,200 by January 1, 2005, with 1,800 academy trained.
- Brigadier General Andrew Mackay, the commanding general of CPATT, reported that only 87,000 men and women of 120,000 on the payroll could actually be accounted for. Only 6,000 police recruits out of the totals shown had police academy training as of early August 2004, with another 21,000 taking a "three-week" course that was sometimes more than a week shorter. At least 60,000 men were serving in police related functions with no training.[20] The eventual goal was a minimum of eight weeks of training.
- According to Robert M. Perito, even as late as December 2004 the 90,000 men in the Iraqi Police Service (IPS) called "available for duty" included 48,000 rehired officers with no more training than the three-week Transition Integration Program (TIP) training discussed earlier, plus 18,000

rookies trained at the eight-week course in Amman.[21] Other data provided in a background brief to the press indicated that it took until the end of 2004 to train 20,000 police.[22]

- No figures were provided for trained manpower in the new National Guard, although 2,362 out of 39,128 were said to be "in training." The same was true for the Iraqi Army. A total of 10,222 men were said to be in service, of which 2,316 were "in training." The data for the Facilities Protection Service showed an active strength of 74,069. Once again, no data were provided on what portion was regarded as trained, and only seventy-seven were reported to be "in training." The service has since been dropped from the State Department's updates.

- Previous reporting by the CPA showed that the July 13 totals for trained manpower were almost meaningless for the Iraqi National Guard, where figures for most men shown as "trained" actually came from figures for the output of the token training program conducted for the Iraqi Civil Defense Corps—when the force had a different name, role, and mission. For most men involved, the total training program for most new recruits to the National Guard lasted all of two weeks, and the first week is largely orientation. There also were serious problems in paying the National Guard, and skimming off part of their pay was common at the command level. Many of those who were paid got less than $145 a month out of a pay scale that calls for a minimum of $170.

- Training in urban warfare and providing reconnaissance assets and other special equipment were only beginning, and the few meaningful details that have been made public are not reassuring. For example, the CPA reported as it went out of business that it had decided to give the new Iraqi air force two Seeker reconnaissance aircraft to conduct surveillance of the borders and oil facilities and was rushing procurement of fourteen more.

- Brigadier General James Schwitters, the U.S. commander of the Coalition training team assisting the army, stated in early August that only 3,000 of the men in the army could be regarded as trained.[23]

It should be noted that there were special conditions in Iraq that cannot be blamed on the U.S. effort to organize and fund the facility, equipment, and training effort. For example, both the CPA and post-CPA manpower totals were somewhat misleading because some 25 to 33 percent of men were on leave, in training, or absent to deal with family and pay issues at any given time, but this was a fact of life in Iraq. Many Iraqis were in mixed units and had to get home to give their families their pay as well as deal with family issues.

Equipment Issues in Mid-2004

The data the United States provided on the equipment holdings of Iraq's forces reflected continuing problems, although they were no worse than the overall U.S. reporting on every aspect of the aid effort. From the start, the

Department of Defense and CPA failed to provide meaningful metrics of actual progress and success, as distinguished from metrics of money spent, buildings contracted for, peak power generation capacities, and so forth. One of the most glaring of these failures was the inability to provide data on the progress in equipping the Iraqi security forces and giving them proper facilities—a failure matched by what may well have been the most avoidable problem in the early stages of the U.S. aid effort.

Equipment Status under the CPA

According to a multinational force planning document, units were still awaiting basic initial deliveries of uniforms, helmets, body armor, vehicles, radios, AK-47 rifles, RPK machine guns, ammunition, and night-vision equipment.[24] This was a time when a CPA official claimed that most, if not all, of this equipment was currently flowing into the region.

A multinational force assessment noted that Iraqis within the Iraqi Civil Defense Corps felt the multinational force never took them seriously, as exhibited by what they perceived as the broken promises and the lack of trust on the part of the multinational force. Yet, initially these forces were not trained, equipped, or intended for offensive and active counterinsurgency missions. Equipment shortfalls are more than statistics. They are a measure of how many Iraqis were being put into the field without the essential equipment and facilities needed to function and survive.

These problems help explain why the Department of Defense reported the following desertion and manning problems in the Iraqi Civil Defense Corps from April 2 to April 16: Northeastern Iraq, including the cities of Baquba and Tikrit, from about 9,100 to about 6,100, or 30 percent; Baghdad and surrounding area, from about 6,200 to about 3,200, or 49 percent; Central-Southern Iraq, including Karbala, An Najaf, and Al Kut, from about 3,500 to about 2,500, or 30 percent; Multinational Division–Center South Western Iraq, including Fallujah, from about 5,600 to about 1,000, or 82 percent.[25]

The Equipment Effort at the End of the CPA

It is striking that it took the U.S. government until July 13, 2004, to provide reporting on efforts to equip the Iraqi forces in anything approaching a systematic form and that the entire system had to be revised again in August and September of 2004. This new reporting still did not provide any insight into facility problems that were still a critical weakness for virtually every element of the Iraqi security and police forces. The data also had serious category and definition problems that understated the seriousness of the CPA and Coalition Joint Task Force 7 (CJTF-7) failure to provide effective support to the Iraqi police, security forces, and military. The following are some examples:

- The United States reported on requirements in terms of the goals set by the CPA before the transfer of power and not on the new requirements set since April 2004. As a result, they sharply exaggerated the adequacy of the equipment for every element—especially the National Guard, special forces elements, and the police.

- The figures for weapons did not reflect the fact that current plans did not recognize the need for heavier weapons that only became part of the program once the decision was taken to create heavier forces and a mechanized brigade.
- The figures for vehicles were based on very limited requirements and did not reflect the need for armored/protected vehicles. The figures set for the Facilities Protection Service covered a force of security guards with the mission of guarding and securing individual ministry and municipal buildings against theft and vandalism, and counting them sharply understated actual need for any kind of serious counterinsurgency/counterterrorism environment. This became a source of embarrassment in U.S. reporting on Iraqi forces, and they were not counted in the totals after August 2004.[26]
- The figures for communications were generally outdated and did not reflect the understanding that much better systems are needed if the Iraqi forces are to play an active role in counterinsurgency. As a result, some holdings were reported as zero, although limited communications are in place. The Iraqi Special Operations Forces, however, did operate with interim equipment that was adequate and often directly from the Coalition, when operations required it. The U.S. command in Iraq feels its overall effectiveness has not been hampered by a lack of communications equipment during operations, regardless of what the equipment data reflect.

A GAO report issued in June 2004 made the following comments about the equipment effort at this time and again reflected the analyses and complaints of the advisers in the field:

> Providing equipment for Iraqi forces also posed problems. According to DOD [Department of Defense] officials, both the Iraqi Police Service and the Iraqi Civil Defense Corps were poorly equipped in late March 2004 due to significant delays for provisioning all Iraqi security forces. According to CPA, these delays were related to several factors, including delays in contractor delivery and performance, delays in allocating and releasing the funding, and a shortage of experienced contracting officials in Baghdad. The Iraqi Police Service was beset by continued delays in equipment provisioning and a lack of awareness of equipment, funding, and contracting status. According to data from the CPA's Provost Marshal's Office, as of March 28, 2004, the Iraqi Police Service was operating with 41 percent of its required patrol vehicles, 63 percent of its required uniforms, 43 percent of its required pistols, 21 percent of its required hand radios, 7 percent of its required vehicle radios, and 9 percent of its required protective vests.
>
> In March 2004, equipment provisioning for Iraqi Civil Defense Corps was months behind schedule. According to a CPA official, no Iraqi Civil Defense Corps units possessed body armor, and many were using Saddam-era helmets

for protection. According to a multinational force planning document, as of April 23, 2004, units were still awaiting the delivery of uniforms, helmets, body armor, vehicles, radios, AK-47 rifles, RPK machine guns, ammunition, and night vision equipment. A CPA official stated that most, if not all, of this equipment is currently flowing into the region. A multinational force assessment noted that Iraqis within the Iraqi Civil Defense Corps felt the multinational force never took them seriously, as exhibited by what they perceived as the broken promises and the lack of trust of the multinational force.[27]

Another report on the Iraqi Police Service provides more tangible figures. It shows that the IPS needed 3,329 more radios and one hundred more police radio base stations. Plans called for one pick-up truck or SUV per 3.5 officers, but the IPS had 268 out of the 3,356 pick-up trucks needed and twenty-seven out of 305 SUVs. It had one water truck out of twenty required, and one fuel truck out of twenty required. Body armor and basic weapons deliveries were still in progress.

Another measure of the scale of the IPS police equipment effort was that the Coalition had now identified a requirement for 553 police stations, twenty-six headquarters, fifteen training academies, and eighteen joint coordinating centers. The Iraqi Border Police needed eighty-five stations, and there was an additional requirement for eighty-seven customs and training posts. The total facilities cost was now $182 million.

Militia and Civilian Disarmament Issues

The United States and the Coalition made other mistakes during this period, although many of the problems in Iraqi force development at this time were also the result of mistakes and political pressure coming from Iraqi interim officials and leading Iraqi political figures in various exile movements. For much of the first year of the occupation, there was more talk than substantive action about disarming Iraqi civilians and Iraq's Shi'ite and Kurdish militias. It was not until February 2004—five months before it was disbanded—that the CPA really staffed the effort to disarm the major militias that had been key elements of the resistance to Saddam, and it only reached key agreements and began to implement them in May 2004—when it was beginning to go out of business.

According to a GAO report, the CPA developed a transition and reintegration strategy for disbanding or controlling the militias in late May 2004. CPA Order 91, which was issued in early June 2004, was intended to provide legal authority for implementing a transition and reintegration process. It declared militias outside of central government control, declaring them illegal except as provided by the order and law.[28]

The CPA's transition and reintegration strategy took three major approaches to disbanding or controlling militias operating outside the control of Iraq's central government: (1) recruiting militia members into officially recognized Iraqi security forces, (2) retiring some militia members with veterans' benefits, and

(3) reintegrating others into Iraq's civil society and economy through education, training, and job placement.

On June 5, 2004, the CPA announced that nine parties that maintained militias had agreed to develop and implement transition and reintegration plans. The parties were the Kurdistan Democratic Party, Patriotic Union of Kurdistan, Iraqi Islamic Party, Supreme Counsel of the Islamic Revolution in Iraq/Badr Organization, Iraqi National Accord, Iraqi National Congress, Iraqi Hezbollah, Iraqi Communist Party, and Da'wa.

They then included roughly 100,000 former resistance fighters. The key militias involved included the Kurdish Kurdistan Democratic Party (KDP) militia that claimed some 41,000 men, and the Patriotic Union of Kurdistan (PUK) militia that claimed 31,000. Together they were known as the Pesh Merga, and had a nominal strength of some 72,000 men. They also included the Badr Corps with a nominal strength of 16,000 to 16,500 and six other militias: the Iraqi Hezbollah (not affiliated with the Lebanese Hezbollah), the Iraqi Communist Party, the Iraqi National Accord (INA), the Iraqi National Congress (INC), elements of Al Dawa (the Jafri faction), and the Iraqi Islamic Party—the only Sunni militia.

In spite of the short time involved, the CPA was able to get an agreement in early June 2004 from all nine of these militias to disband or integrate into the Iraqi forces. This agreement did not cover all militias. Several smaller militias were not contacted because they were small, difficult to contact, or less important politically. Some militias have decided to continue hostile operations against the Coalition rather than take part in the transition and reintegration process.

The agreement did, however, cover about 100,000 former resistance fighters, with phased draw-down agreements reached with six of the nine militias while the remaining three claimed to have already disbanded their fighting organizations. The CPA estimated that about 90 percent of these individuals would complete the transition and reintegration process by January 2005—the rest would complete the process by October 2005. The CPA estimated that out of this total, about 60 percent of the militia members would transition into Iraqi security services—such as the Iraqi armed forces, Iraqi Police Service, or the internal security forces of the Kurdistan regional government.

The Kurds agreed to transform the Pesh Merga into three elements that would still provide them with some element of security while serving the interest of the government: mountain rangers to guard the borders, a counterterrorism force, and a rapid reaction force. The other militias were to disband and either receive veterans benefits or join the Iraqi military, Civil Defense Corps, or police. CPA Order 91 also established penalties for those who did not implement the agreement, which effectively banned any leaders and political movements that did not participate in the Iraqi political process.

Both the CPA plans and this agreement were coordinated with the Ministry of Defense, the Ministry of the Interior, and Ministerial Committee for National Security. The Ministry of Labor and Social Affairs and other Iraqi agencies (e.g., the Foreign Ministry, the Iraqi Intelligence Agency, and Ministry of Education) came together in a body called the Transition and Reintegration Committee that was to administer the process after the transfer of authority and in fact began to do so in late May of 2004.

The Ministry of Labor and Social Affairs was critical to implementing one of the most innovative elements of the program: treating those in the militias opposing Saddam Hussein as if they were veterans in the Iraqi Army. For example, militias with fifteen years of service became eligible for pensions, and those wounded with disabilities were treated as if they were soldiers. This was to be part of a $205 million program in the Ministry of Labor and Social Affairs to provide a nationwide job training and placement program that included significant funding for veterans and to ease the impact of both employment problems and the tensions growing out of the breakup of Iraq's regular forces.

The CPA developed phased plans to disband the militias (busing was part of the recruiting efforts, primarily of the Iraqi armed forces (IAF)—there was no plan to move militias in mass) and plans to integrate those who wanted to join the Iraqi forces to enter the military, ICDC, and police. Quotas were established by province and city for those who wanted to join the ICDC with broader quotas for the police—largely because the Ministry of the Interior simply did not know the short-term employment needs of local police forces.

The CPA office asked for $9.7 million for a staff of international experts and Iraqis to manage and coordinate this effort. This request was still pending when the CPA disbanded in June, although it had explicit support from the prime minister and the national security adviser. Some progress was made with elements of militias like the Badr Corps—each of the four Arab militias with transition and reintegration plans had a complete schedule for moving their designated members through IAF recruiting and, indeed, had had at least one group of former fighters processed through the recruiting stations in Baghdad, Basra, or Mosul before the CPA went out of business (some, such as the Badr Corps, had several). Such arrangements were not needed for the Pesh Merga, as there were Pesh Merga transition offices (established by the CJTF–7) in Iraqi Kurdistan that assisted with transition efforts there.

There were some weapons recoveries, but they were limited and fell behind the goals originally set. For example, the CPA set a ceiling of $1.5 million for a MANPADS ("manportable" surface to air missiles) weapons buyback program using funds seized from the Iraqi government but only found it useful to commit $610,000 and had only expended $320,000 at the time it ceased to exist.[29] The pattern of attacks as of early August 2004 indicated the program had had little or no impact.

The team the CPA put together was able to achieve a great deal in its negotiations, but the effort began too late to be implemented while the CPA was still in power, and the new Iraqi government failed to implement it. As part of the transfer of power, the Ministry of Defense, the Ministry of the Interior, and the Ministry of Labor and Social Affairs all gained new ministers, and none gave implementing the CPA's plans any serious priority.

The new minister of defense resisted any effort to integrate any militia in a movement with a religious character into the armed forces, and the new minister of finance did not implement the Prime Minister's decision to fund the $9.7 million program recommended under the CPA. Even more seriously, the new minister of the Ministry of Labor and Social Affairs canceled the nationwide job training and placement program, effectively eliminating one of the key aspects of the veterans' program for either the militia personnel who qualified or those in the Iraqi forces under Saddam Hussein.

The situation grew steadily worse as it became clear that Sadr's Mehdi Army posed a threat to the Shi'ite and other militias operating in the South and the East, and the insurgency steadily grew in strength. It became clear that CPA Order 91 was effectively dead and that the Iraqi Interim Government could not afford to take action against leaders and parties simply because they maintained militias. The fighting against Sadr then further reinforced the reluctance of such militias and parties to comply.

As a result, the militias continued to be a serious potential problem and one that became all too apparent in June 2005 when senior ministers endorsed using militias like the Pesh Merga and the Badr Brigade against Sunni insurgents. Ethnic and sectarian militias present a continuing risk that ethnic and sectarian forces could trigger civil fighting. By the early summer of 2005 some Sunni groups were charging that such militias were detaining and killing Sunnis—compounding the risk that the insurgency might take on the form of a more serious civil war.

This situation continues to degenerate, and the militias present a serious problem if the Iraqi political process collapses and Iraq moves toward civil war. The largely ethnic (Kurdish Pesh Merga) and sectarian (various Shi'ite faction) units in the military and security forces are a source of considerable tension when they operate in Sunni and mixed areas and sometimes use excessive force or violate human rights. Ex-militia forces are a major problem in the Shi'ite south. They sometimes bypass or ignore the official police, act as Shi'ite religious enforcers, and clash with other Shi'ite factions. They could help divide Iraqi forces along ethnic and sectarian lines if Iraq's political process fails, and they increase the risk of a serious civil war.

The one positive development since these efforts has been that the near collapse of Sadr's militia, following fighting in the South in late 2004, seems to have removed any immediate threat his militia will pose to the Iraqi government and MNF–I. Unfortunately, efforts to disband and disarm the remaining militias may at best be an administrative fiction until the Kurdish, Shi'ite, and Sunni groups involved become convinced that the new government is legitimate, will serve their interests, and can provide true security.

If these groups should agree to demobilize, the legal basis for such a program remains in place. Moreover, converting a substantial part of the Pesh Merga to a border security force might help deal with the most serious problem Iraq faces, which is to integrate the Kurds into a federal system where they are truly part of an Iraqi nation but still feel secure. Converting and disbanding the Shi'ite militias should also become progressively easier if the Iraqi government demonstrates that the Shi'ite majority has finally achieved a fair share of power and the nation's wealth.

The fact remains, however, that massive amounts of arms will almost certainly continue to be hidden or be readily available, given the number of arms already disbursed among Iraq's population. Moreover, reconstituting or creating new militias will be all too easy if ethnic and sectarian differences become violent, and Lebanon and the Balkans are clear warnings that "national" military, security, and police forces can suddenly fracture along partisan lines and become instruments of civil war.

The HUMINT Problem

The problems in creating effective Iraqi forces greatly complicated the difficulties the United States had in obtaining the intelligence it needed to fight a counterinsurgency campaign. The United States initially tried to use the same technical intelligence means it brought to the theater to deal with Iraq's regular military forces as it did to deal with the rising threat of insurgency and terrorism. While such systems could be adapted to provide information of great value, they could not provide the level of political detail, situational awareness, and other information that could only come from human sources and networking with Iraqis.

The United States then tried to develop effective human intelligence (HUMINT) largely on its own, relying on the interface between Iraqis and U.S. officers and intelligence experts rather than creating a partnership with the Iraqis in which Iraqis played a major role in the intelligence collection and analysis effort. The United States initially tried to create a network of informers and local contacts and carry out analysis on its own, rather than create effective Iraqi intelligence collection and analysis and rely on Iraqis, due to its lack of area and language skills and understanding of local political and tactical conditions. While the situation had improved by mid-2005, Iraqi intelligence was still in its early formative stages. Training and equipment was limited, and senior Iraqi ministers and officials saw the Iraqi effort as weak and badly needing additional U.S. support. Iraqi battalions and field units did seem to be developing better HUMINT and networks of informers, but the overall structure was very weak at the brigade headquarters level and all higher levels.

Iraqi operations had to depend heavily on Coalition input, and effective training was just beginning to be developed and put in place. Deep divisions existed within the new Iraqi government over how much various elements of the new Iraqi intelligence efforts could be trusted. This led to serious tensions over the new national intelligence service, and even ministers in the newly elected government charged that the United States and its Central Intelligence

Agency (CIA) were still controlling the service and would not turn it over to Iraq. The functional problem had become a political one, fueling all of the endemic conspiracy theories about U.S. motives and intentions.

Creating such "partner" organizations is anything but easy and creates a host of political and security problems. At the same time, one of the critical lessons of Vietnam was that the United States and its outside allies simply could not create intelligence networks with the scale and access necessary to substitute for effective national intelligence, security, and police efforts and that language, access, and local expertise are critical elements of HUMINT in dealing with insurgency and terrorism on a national scale. The United States simply did not have the capability in terms of expertise and access to suddenly improvise a largely autonomous HUMINT effort as a substitute for partnership with an intelligence organization run by local allies. It needed Iraqi help and was far too slow to create the kind of help it needed.

5   The Fall of 2004

The Effort to Train Iraqi Military, Security, and Police Forces Slowly Begins to Gather Momentum

AS SUMMER faded into fall, the reorganization of the training and equipment effort that had begun in the spring of 2004 did begin to gather momentum and to have more effect. The Multinational Security Transition Command–Iraq (MNSTC–I) began to get the manning levels it needed to be effective. It also was now organized into two key elements dealing with the military and police forces and with senior U.S. and British commanders. These elements included:[1]

- Military
    - CMATT (Coalition Military Assistance Training Team): CMATT organizes, trains, and equips the Iraqi armed forces (IAF). During operations, it provides ongoing mentoring and advising to Iraqi leaders at all levels of command. It assists the Ministry of Defense leadership in developing accession sources and leadership programs across all services of the Iraqi armed forces. End state is the development of an Iraqi armed forces capable of planning and conducting unilateral operations in order to maintain security within Iraq and defend its sovereignty.
    - JHQ (Joint Headquarters Advisory Support Team): The JHQ mentors and assists the Iraqi Joint Headquarters in order to become capable of exercising effective national command and control of the IAF, contributing to the IAF capability development process, and contributing to improving the internal security situation within Iraq in partnership with Coalition forces.
- Police
    - CPATT (Civilian Police Assistance Training Team): CPATT organizes, trains, equips, and mentors the Iraqi civilian police forces and Department of Border Enforcement forces and monitors, advises,

and certifies the Facilities Protection Service forces in order to develop capable and credible Iraqi security forces.

Creating More Effective Core Forces

Various elements of the Iraqi Army and National Guard were also slowly becoming more active. Small elements of Iraqi combat forces became active in a number of high-threat areas like Samarra, Sadr City, Najaf, Fallujah, and Mosul. The Chronology at the back of this book details the timeline for these operations.

The total number of capable forces remained small, however, and the total manpower in mission-capable units was far lower than figures for total Iraqi security forces (ISF) manpower and training manpower in table 5.1 might indicate. The core force of combat-capable Iraqi units, however, still consisted of only six army and intervention-force battalions with an authorized strength of roughly 700 men each (total of 4,200 men). Six more army and intervention-force battalions were supposed to be ready by the end of October (for a total of 8,400 men), but the State Department Iraqi Military Forces Update report issued as late as November 3, 2004, indicated that only 3,987 army and intervention-force soldiers were active.

Looking back at these data, only six battalions were operational in the fall of 2004, and those had limited combat capabilities and were dependent on U.S. support. Regular army and Iraqi intervention forces reported as fully trained and equipped totaled 6,323, but this figure included several hundred men at the brigade level and higher headquarters and included a number of AWOLs who were subsequently dropped from the rolls, which can be seen in subsequent reports.

Nevertheless, the few combat elements that were given enough training and equipment to make them combat-ready began to play a larger role. More importantly, the Coalition advisory team placed more and more emphasis on leadership and unit integrity and less and less emphasis on sheer numbers. It pressed harder to reward effective leaders and remove weak ones. It also attempted to compensate for the lack of trained units and cadres by stiffening weak units with officers and enlisted men until they could function, rather than on replacing weak units with new units that might be just as weak. This emphasis on leadership and unit integrity is scarcely a new lesson of war fighting but is a critical warning of the dangers of focusing on throughput and end strength, rather than meaningful capability.

Two Iraqi Army battalions, a commando battalion, a counterterrorist force, and two National Guard battalions were active in the fighting in Najaf in October 2003. Approximately 2,000 Iraqis were involved in the operation in Samarra, and another 2,000 Iraqi soldiers fought in Fallujah. These troops still lacked the experience, armor, and heavy weapons to take lead roles in combat without substantial U.S. support, and some elements presented problems, but they steadily improved their performance over time. This core force increased steadily in the fall of 2004, and the groundwork was laid for creating a much larger Iraqi force structure. The Coalition had trained an additional twelve battalions of regular army and intervention forces by the end of December, bringing the total of these battalions to eighteen. In addition, six brigade headquarters and three division headquarters had been formed. Command and control mechanisms within the army had improved with one division establishing a command post in Fallujah to assist in the command and control of Iraqi forces, which were operating under the operational control of the Multinational Force–Iraq. The total number in those eighteen battalions and higher headquarters totaled 9,660, indicating that a number of units were operating at low strength.

The Ministry of Defense implemented a system to recruit and train former army soldiers, and the first replacements from that pool began flowing into units by the last week of December. This proved to be a more viable replacement system but still had serious problems. The goal was to have twenty-seven battalions (18,900 men) ready for the Iraqi elections at the end of January. Due to infrastructure delays at two separate locations, however, the training of five battalions of the regular army was delayed two to four weeks. Five battalions were slated to complete their initial training in February.

The training and equipment effort began to go beyond creating infantry units, and a mechanized brigade was being created. At this point, the unit was planned to consist of fifty T-55 tanks, forty-eight BMP-1s, fifty-seven MTLB armored personnel carriers, and thirty-six Spartans. The unit was titled the First Mechanized Brigade, and 259 soldiers of the first battalion were in training. These men were being trained to handle ten MTLBs in the near future. There were plans for additional battalions, and the MNSTC–I hoped to have one battalion ready for the elections.

Major progress was being made in the construction and repair of military facilities. More than $1 billion had been spent or was under contract in this effort by October 2004. There was a joint command headquarters operating and Iraqi military officials regarded it as a high-status appointment. Five major bases for brigade-size forces, to include three with divisional headquarters, had been built. Police stations were being renovated, and a total of forty-one border forts were completed, including twenty-seven in the north. Roughly 300 were then planned.

The Iraqis had also developed a concept for their own training command, modeled on a NATO-developed design. The goal for the command was to eventually oversee seven basic-training centers, several branch training centers, officer military academies, and other officer professional development schools to include a staff college. While fully implementing this plan was planned to take at least two years, important initial efforts were under way, and the very fact that such a plan existed was a sign of progress.

Manning, Training, and Equipment of the Overall Mix of Iraqi Forces by Major Force Element

Total active strength went down as largely incapable forces were omitted from the count, but the total of forces with meaningful mission capability increased. While the U.S. government continued to provide only limited details as to the progress made in training and equipment and provided no breakdowns on the number and adequacy of bases and facilities, the Department of Defense did report enough data on Iraqi manpower, training, and equipment as of late September 2004 to provide the quantitative breakdown shown in table 5.1.[2]

These data reflected a far greater rate of progress than had existed as late as June 2004, and some $1.8 billion in additional Iraqi Relief and Reconstruction Fund (IRRF) monies were allocated to the security sector in October 2004. At the same time there were still major problems in the Iraqi forces counted in these totals as of September 2004, including the following:

- The manpower totals did not reflect the fact that 25 to 33 percent of men were on leave or in training at any given time. Many men were in units deployed a considerable distance from their homes and had to travel to give their families their pay and deal with family issues.

TABLE 5.1
Iraq Manpower, Training, and Equipment as of September 22, 2004

Service	Manning			Training	
	Required	Actual	Untrained	In Training	Trained
Army	27,0001	2,699	0	7,910	4,789
National Guard	61,904	41,461	0	2,189	39,272
Iraqi Intervention Force	6,584	7,417	0	5,489	1,928
Iraqi Special Ops Forces	1,967	651	0	75	576
Air Force	502	182	0	39	143
Coastal Defense Force	409	412	0	130	282
Total	98,366	62,822	0	15,832	46,990

	Weapons		Vehicles		Communications		Body Armor	
	Required	On-Hand	Required	On-Hand	Required	On-Hand	Required	On-Hand
Army	23,606	15,432	2,298	1,768	3,596	1,021	20,949	6,137
National Guard	68,760	37,636	2,142	727	11,209	427	62,032	23,320
Iraqi Intervention Force	8,850	3,300	583	152	1,789	1,583	6,584	2,741
Iraqi Special Ops Forces	1,898	1,274	180	67	1,212	115	1,620	605
Air Force	383	0	34	4	21	0	502	0
Coastal Defense Force	486	12	15	15	156	1	409	0
Total	103,983	57,654	5,252	2,733	17,983	3,147	92,096	32,803

- Figures for training had a somewhat uncertain meaning since they included all men trained or in training, but their training was sometimes limited or did not prepare them for demanding aspects of their mission. At the same time, U.S. experts involved in the training process felt that the numbers reported as "trained" did indicate that those counted had at least completed their initial training and were equipped sufficiently to conduct security operations. For many of those reported, the level of their actual training also exceeded basic training because of prior experience or experience in the field. Some had already participated in combat, including some National Guard members. Although National Guard initial training is only three weeks, Coalition units were working closely with many National Guard units to develop their capabilities. The short initial training of these units was not, in many cases, a good indicator of their capabilities.
- The total armed forces, however, had only 55 percent of the weapons authorized for their prior force structure, half of the authorized total of 4,421 vehicles, 28 percent of communications, and 46 percent of body armor.
- The weapons data shown only included small arms and light crew served weapons and did not reflect Iraqi and U.S. plans to create heavier forces with armor.
- Some armor was being delivered—including at least thirty-five reconditioned Iraqi tanks, armored fighting vehicles (AFVs), and armored personnel carriers (APCs), and fifty armored cars from the United Arab Emirates (UAE).
- The MNSTC–I had been promised armor for more Iraqi mechanized units from Jordan and the United Arab Emirates that was slowly delivered.
- The Department of Defense's stated totals for communications equipment were misleading because some radios that were on hand were said to be of interim capability only. U.S. advisers feel that civilian and other radios bought as part of the Commander's Emergency Relief Program (CERP) are adequate, and communications are much better than statistics show.

The army had 12,699 "actives" trained or in training out of what was then a 27,000-man authorized force, and its manpower, equipment, and training effort can be summarized as follows:

- Of active strength, 4,789 were defined as trained (three weeks for former military and eight weeks for new recruits; the vast majority went through the eight-week course). This total was roughly 18 percent of authorized strength and 38 percent of men actually on duty.
- Equipment holdings as of mid-September were 65 percent of authorized weapons, 77 percent of vehicles, 29 percent of communications, and 30 percent of body armor.
- Training was sufficiently limited, so new forces normally needed six to eight weeks of working with U.S. forces. There were exceptions in which units were rapidly formed out of experienced army personnel.

- The Iraqi commandos formed by the Ministry of Defense had proven to be a well-trained and effective source of manpower.

The Iraqi National Guard was Iraq's largest force, but most of it was not a "combat-ready" force, even in terms of local security duty. Its status can be summarized as follows:

- It had 41,461 actives. The requirements called for 61,904. Claims that 39,272 were trained and 2,189 were in training ignored the fact that basic training was limited and generally did not prepare most forces for more than limited counterinsurgency and counterterrorism missions. At the same time, follow-on training with Coalition forces did help prepare them for such operations, and many units gained experience by conducting "framework operations," which played a significant role in the counterinsurgency conflict.
- Forty of the forty-four National Guard battalions were operating in some way with Coalition forces throughout the country—although most in very limited security missions. All except those in the Fallujah-Ramadi area were carrying out joint operations with Coalition forces on a daily basis.
- There were some effective, combat-ready elements but only of battalion size or smaller.
- Equipment holdings as of mid-September were 55 percent of authorized weapons, 34 percent of vehicles, 4 percent of communications, and 38 percent of body armor.

The Iraqi Intervention Force was being trained as a counterinsurgency force but was still being formed. It had 7,417 men active for a force with an authorized strength of only 6,584. Its status was as follows:

- The Department of Defense reported that 29 percent (of authorized strength) had been trained in the fourteen-week initial training program.
- Equipment was 37 percent of authorized weapons, 26 percent of vehicles, 86 percent of communications, and 41 percent of body armor, indicating that all of those trained had been equipped.
- The creation of specialized counterterrorism/counterinsurgency elements was under way, and by September some of these units had conducted operations with Coalition forces in Najaf.

Iraqi Special Operations Forces was another specialized counterterrorism/counterinsurgency force whose development was under way. This force was then more combat experienced and proven than any other force in Iraqi service but had 651 men active for a force with an authorized strength of 1,967. The following describes its status:

- The Department of Defense reported that 88 percent of actives had some training and that 29 percent of the fully authorized force was trained and fielded. It stated that the force would grow once the conditions for doing so are in place and properly set.

- Equipment included 67 percent of authorized weapons, 37 percent of vehicles, 10 percent of communications, and 37 percent of body armor, indicating that equipment levels—with the exception of communications—were becoming more sufficient for those who were trained and conducting operations. Interim communications, which often refers to equipment provided by Coalition forces, were available when required.
- The new Civil Intervention Force and Emergency Response Unit, which were other key elements in the counterinsurgency plans developed by Prime Minister Ayad Allawi, were just beginning to form. Both of these forces were conceived by the Coalition between April and June. The Civil Intervention Force had not yet begun training. The Emergency Response Unit had started training with roughly 25 percent of the force having completed initial training and conducting operations.

The Iraqi Air Force and Coastal Defense Force were still only token forces. The Department of Defense reported that the air force then had 0 percent of authorized weapons, 12 percent of vehicles, 0 percent of communications, and 0 percent of body armor.

Equipment Holdings

The data summarized in table 5.1 still revealed massive shortfalls in weapons, vehicles, communications, and body armor relative to the planned requirements. The data showed Iraqi forces only had about 40 percent of their minimum weapons needs, less than one-third of the minimum number of vehicles, about 25 percent of the necessary communications gear, and about 25 percent of the necessary body armor.

At the same time, the data summarized in table 5.1 showed that the mix of weapons, vehicles, and communications equipment authorized in MNSTC–I plans now generally kept pace with the schedule for training and expanding Iraqi security forces. Individuals and units had the equipment they needed to continue their collective (unit-level) training and conduct security operations in an environment where they were needed. The status for the various forces can be summarized as follows:

- The regular military had about two-thirds of the minimum requirements for weapons, about half the necessary vehicles, and one-fifth of the necessary body armor. All of this equipment was new or reconditioned. The Iraqis did complain about the ambulances provided in the fall of 2004, but MNSTC–I has acquired or ordered new ambulances to replace those that were judged unsatisfactory.
- The new Iraqi Intervention Force and Iraqi Special Operations Force were still in development. However, the Iraqi Intervention Force brigade that had completed training was equipped, and the Iraqi special forces soldiers who were conducting actual operations were equipped. Equipment was on

order for the remainder, evident by the fact that all three brigades of the Iraq Intervention Force (IIF) are now trained and equipped.

- The air force and coastal defense force were still hollow forces with little meaningful capability. However, there were equipment plans for both forces, which were developing initial capabilities in September.
- The security forces and police had about 40 percent of their minimum weapons requirements and one-third of their authorized vehicles. They have only about 25 percent of the necessary body armor, and their crippling communications shortfalls are even worse than that of the Iraqi military.

These figures again show that far too many Iraqis were being exposed to insurgent and terrorist attacks without having the weapons and protection they needed to perform their missions and survive. They do reflect some positive trends, but it is not possible to put them in perspective.

Iraqi Minister of Defense Briefing—September 22, 2004

The United States was not the only source of information on the problems in the force development effort. The Iraqi Minister of Defense gave a briefing in Washington on September 22 in which he discussed problems that he perceived in the training and equipment effort. He did note that some $1.7 billion had been spent to augment the Iraqi forces. Additionally, he highlighted the fact that Iraqi pilots were beginning to use two Seeker light reconnaissance aircraft to cover the border areas and that it was the first role the Iraqi Air Force had played.

He also stated, however, that the police and border enforcement forces were corrupt, frequently did not show up for work, and had many loyalty issues. The minister labeled them "70,000 men filled with corruption." He repeated that the Iraqi National Guard and Army had elements with the same problems and that some would be purged due to their loyalty to Sadr or their unwillingness to fight. The minister declared that past training efforts had failed to screen and ensure loyalty.

Furthermore, the minister highlighted the fact that the vehicle pool for the military and security forces consisted mostly of 3,000 vehicles transferred from former civilian ministries like that of agriculture. Problems with equipment extended to the weaponry the Iraqi security forces employed. They lacked armor and heavy weaponry. The minister attributed this largely to the CPA's fear that the weapons would be turned over to hostile forces.

Resources as of September and October

The data on U.S. expenditures to support the force development effort presented in U.S. reporting on the Iraqi Relief and Reconstruction Fund (IRRF) as of October 2004 indicated that the United States had dispersed $798 million for its security and law enforcement program at a rate of only $8 million a week.[3] It should be noted, however, that the lag between the receipt of goods or services and payment for them was sometimes months long and affected the time when the payment actually showed up in the accounting system. These totals also ignore expenditures made under the Development Fund for Iraq (DFI). The true total for such spending was higher because the figures just quoted only cover the fiscal year 2004 program. Some $51.2 million had previously been allocated to the Iraqi Army in PL-108-11 in April 2003. At the urging of the U.S. Embassy, an additional $1,808.6 million out of the fiscal year 2004 total funding for Iraq Infrastructure Reconstruction Program (IIRP) was reprogrammed to "security and law enforcement" in September 2004.

Unfortunately, the way in which the U.S. government reported on such aid expenditures in Iraq continued to make it almost impossible to reconcile the various reports coming out of the Department of Defense and the State Department.[4] For example, the inspector general of the CPA reported on October 30, 2004, that "as of March 2004, the United States had obligated about $58.5 billion to stabilize the security situation in Iraq: About $57.3 billion for the U.S. military operations and $1.2 billion for Iraqi security forces." Embassy and MNSTC-I officials also report that accounting and corruption were serious problems both on a project basis and in areas like the Commander's Emergency Relief Program (CERP).

To put such reports in broader perspective, the original program level for all aspects of publicly identified security expenditures in the $18.4 billion aid program for fiscal year 2004 was $3,235 million. This was raised to a $5,045 million program for the 2004 fiscal year because of reprogramming on September 30, 2004 ($1,808.6 million was reprogrammed to "security and law enforcement").

In any case, these figures illustrate the slow pace of the U.S. effort to create effective Iraqi forces at the time, although they also reflect the disparity between a large Coalition force presence in Iraq and the initial buildup of Iraqi security forces—and the problems in trying to rapidly create effective Iraqi forces in a country with poor infrastructure and limited administrative capabilities and wracked by an insurgency.

6 The Status of Iraqi Forces in November 2004

FURTHER PROGRESS occurred in the late fall and early winter of 2004. Coalition and Iraqi forces showed in November 2004 that they could cooperate in winning major battles. The battle of Fallujah in November 2004 was a particularly striking example of a tactical victory that took place while Iraqi forces were only beginning to deploy significant strength. The battle is reported to have killed some 1,200 insurgents and led to the capture of nearly 2,000— at the cost of fifty-four American and eight Iraqi lives.[1] While Iraqi troops played a limited role in the fighting, they did attack key targets like mosques and fought effectively in the limited engagements where they were employed.

The loss of the city deprived Sunni insurgents and terrorist groups of their major sanctuary inside Iraq. Still, Fallujah remained a troubled city more than six months later. Many of its citizens had not returned. Rebuilding was slow and far behind the original plan to restore the city, and insurgents were still sporadically active. The evacuation of hundreds of thousands of residents had added to hostility against the Coalition and government and had disrupted part of the effort to register Sunni voters before the January 30 election.

At the same time, even the best Iraqi forces were just beginning to develop any real effectiveness, and many continued to have major readiness, leadership, equipment, training, and readiness problems. Corruption and desertions were still major problems, particularly among the various elements of the Iraqi Police Service (IPS). It is also difficult to track overall progress in creating more effective Iraqi forces during the fall and winter of 2004. The data the United States made public on Iraqi force development after September 2004 were cut back to the point where they no longer indicated how quickly the problems in equipment delays reported in early September were being corrected. All detailed equipment delivery data were deleted from the weekly status report.

The same was true of the amount of detail data on trained manpower. Reporting by force element was largely eliminated from public U.S. reporting by the embassy, Department of Defense, and State Department. The only heading in the *Iraq Weekly Status Report* became "trained/on-hand." This figure had more value than previous totals, however, since it reflected the trained manpower that actually remained on duty and avoided the problem of reporting those who were trained and were not on duty for whatever reason.

Numbers of Active, Trained/Equipped/Authorized Iraqi Military, Security, and Police Forces as of Late November 2004

Some useful data were made available by the Multinational Security Transition Command–Iraq (MNSTC–I), although such data still did not provide the level of detail needed to distinguish between the total number of men trained and equipped and the much smaller numbers of men with fully adequate training and equipment for counterinsurgency and combat missions. They also did not provide any detail on the rate of increase in cadres of fully trained officers and noncommissioned officers (NCOs).

The MNSTC–I data that show total Iraqi manpower by force element as of November 18, 2004, are summarized in table 6.1 below.[2]

On Duty versus Trained and Equipped

Graphic comparisons make it easier to understand the level of progress that was now being reported by MNSTC–I. Figure 6.1 shows the numbers of police

TABLE 6.1
Iraqi Military and Security Forces as of November 18, 2004

Force Element	Current Strength	On Duty, Trained, and Equipped	Total Authorized
Police	87,133	47,342	135,000
Special Police Commando Battalions	2,019	900	2,019
Border Enforcement	16,237	14,593	29,360
Highway Patrol	925	370	6,300
Bureau of Dignitary Protection	484	484	500
Emergency Response Force	168	168	270
Civil Intervention Force	1,091	1,091	3,720
National Guard	43,318	41,409	61,904*
Special Operations Force	604	590	1,967
Intervention Force	6,584	1,816	6,859
Army	16,634	4,507	27,000
Air Force	206	167	502
Coastal Defense Force	409	536	582
TOTAL	175,812	113,437	271,681
Military Forces	*(24,437)*	*(7,080)*	*(36,328)*
Security Forces	*(151,375)*	*(106,357)*	*(235,353)*

*Data from MNSTC–I are not clear. Data in parentheses are taken from U.S. Embassy Weekly Status Report of November 3, 2004. Data for National Guard total appears to be only for sixty-five battalions.

and border enforcement personnel on duty and how many of those on duty were reported to be "trained and equipped" as of November 18, 2004. Figure 6.2 shows the numbers of special operations, intervention force, and conventional army troops who were on duty and how many of those on duty were fully trained and equipped as of November 18, 2004.

FIGURE 6.1

Iraqi Security Forces—Manning versus Trained/Equipped as of November 18, 2004

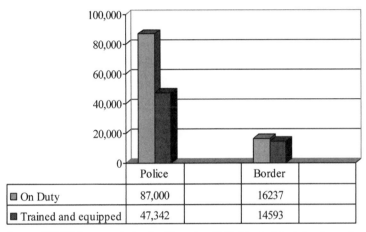

	Police	Border
▨ On Duty	87,000	16237
▪ Trained and equipped	47,342	14593

Source: MNSTC-I answer to inquiry November 2004. "Border" includes the entire Border Enforcement branch.

FIGURE 6.2

Iraqi Armed Forces—Manning versus Trained/Equipped as of November 18, 2004

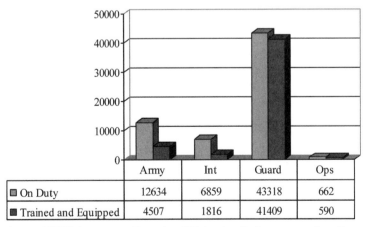

	Army	Int	Guard	Ops
▨ On Duty	12634	6859	43318	662
▪ Trained and Equipped	4507	1816	41409	590

Source: MNSTC-I answer to November 2004 inquiry. "Int" represents the military Intervention Force. "Ops" represents Special Operations Forces.

Lack of Meaningful Equipment Reporting

While data on the overall progress of the equipment effort were limited, MNSTC–I did release a general statement about the equipment delivered to the Iraqi security forces in November 2004. The military reported distributing 5,400 Kalashnikov rifles, 16,000 sets of body armor, 1,900 9-mm pistols, approximately 1,000 machine guns, forty-four armored personnel carriers, and four T-55 tanks. Exactly which forces received what armaments was not made clear.[3]

In another statement on November 13, 2004, MNSTC–I indicated that it had delivered 2,919 AK-47 assault rifles, 4,210 helmets, 107 PKM machine guns, 832 RPK machine guns, 7,850 sets of body armor, 11,000 field jackets, fifty Glock pistols, 100,000 RPK/PKM machine-gun rounds, 2,400 9-mm pistol rounds, 300,000 AK-47 rounds, 600 tactical vests, thirty computers, 300 kneepads, fifty radios, 15,763 pairs of running shoes, twenty holsters, twenty Walther 9-mm pistols, 1,300 army T-shirts, and 19,782 desert-combat uniforms since November 1.[4] These delivery rates were far higher than the rates reported during the spring, summer, and early fall of 2004.

Key Iraqi Force Components

MNSTC–I also provided useful data on Iraq's developing force structure and type of training and equipment in key elements of the emerging Iraqi forces in November 2004, which remained current through late December 2004. The MNSTC–I summarized developments in each of the Iraqi forces as follows:[5]

- The Special Police Commando Battalions represent the Iraqi Ministry of Interior's strike-force capability. The commandos—ultimately to be comprised of six full battalions—are highly vetted Iraqi officers and rank-and-file servicemen largely made up of prior service special forces professionals and other skilled servicemen with specialty unit experience. All members of the unit are chosen based on loyalty to Iraq and its new democratic model. The unit focuses primarily on building raid operations, counterterrorist missions including anti–airplane hijacker, kidnapping, and other similar missions. The force resembles more a paramilitary army-type force, complete with heavy weapons, rocket-propelled grenades, AK-47 assault rifles, mortars, and 9-mm Glock pistols. The commando battalions give the Ministry of the Interior a high-end strike force capability similar to special forces units and quickly stood up to capitalize on previously existing skill sets in Iraq.
- The Iraqi Police Service Emergency Response Unit is an elite 270-man team trained to respond to national-level law enforcement emergencies. Team members undergo a robust eight-week specialized training course spawned from the current wave of anti-Iraqi forces actions. The mission of the emergency response unit is to provide a national, high-end, rapid-response law enforcement tactical unit responsible for high-risk search,

arrest, hostage-rescue, and crisis-response operations. The emergency response unit is the predominant force for national-level incidents calling for a DELTA/SWAT capability and will only be used in extreme situations by local and national authorities.

The $64.5 million effort is part of a larger mission to create nationwide law enforcement and investigative and special operations capability within the Iraqi Ministry of Interior to counter terrorism and large-scale civil disobedience and insurgencies throughout Iraq. The capability will eventually include a counterterrorism investigative unit and special operations unit. Volunteers for the force must first complete the standard eight-week basic-training course or three-week transition-integration program course for prior service officers before entering the specialized emergency response unit training modeled after the U.S. State Department's Anti-Terrorism Assistance and Bureau of Alcohol, Tobacco and Firearms and Explosives' training programs.

Of the total force, 235 eligible candidates received rigorous instruction based on the Anti-Terrorism Assistance Crisis Response Team training program while the balance of thirty-five recruits are part of the Special Operations Explosive Ordinance Team, based on the State Department's antiterrorism assistance explosive incident countermeasures training course. Team members receive instruction on terrorist incidents, kidnappings, hostage negotiations, explosive ordnance, high-risk searches, high-risk assets, weapons of mass destruction, and other national-level law enforcement emergencies. Officers also have an opportunity to receive supplementary training in hostage negotiation, emergency medical procedures, and counterterrorism task-force coordination.

• The Iraqi Intervention Force is the counterinsurgency wing of the Iraqi Army. Ultimately to be comprised of nine battalions organized into three brigades, forces negotiate the standard eight-week basic training all Iraqi soldiers go through learning basic soldiering skills such as weapons, drills, and ceremony. To develop soldier discipline and physical training skills IIF battalions spend several weeks and months after graduation in intensive "military operations in urban terrain" follow-on training—otherwise known as "MOUT" training. During this period soldiers work through instruction in the art of street fighting and building-clearing operations typical of anti-insurgent operations in cities and towns. Units work in close coordination with other Iraqi Army battalions and will be completely stood up to the nine-battalion force by early 2005.

• The Iraqi Special Operations Force—the Iraqi armed forces' high-end strike force resembling U.S. special forces units—continues training and operations in the country with multinational force assistance. Consisting of two trained battalions, including the Thirty-sixth Commando Battalion—an infantry-type strike force—and the Iraqi Counterterrorism Battalion, the

force has been involved in many operations throughout the country fighting anti-Iraqi forces with great distinction while continuing the stand-up
effort of the unit. The force will add a third "support" battalion to its ranks
in the coming months. Training is conducted at an undisclosed location.

"Selection" for the force begins in the Iraqi National Guard and Iraqi
Army units already operating in the country much like typical multinational
special forces' recruiting efforts in their own countries. Outstanding recruits
successfully negotiating the vetting process—including exhaustive background checks, skill evaluations, and unit evaluations along with literacy,
psychological, and physical tests—are run through various team-building
and physical events meant to lean down the recruit pool. The selection
process runs roughly ten to fourteen days.

The Iraqi special forces undergo intense physical training along with
training in land navigation, small-unit tactics, live fire, unconventional
warfare operations, direct-action operations, airmobile operations, counterterrorism, survival, evasion, resistance, and escape. Special forces soldiers
are an army's unconventional warfare experts, possessing a broad range
of operational skills. The unit was formed based on a conversation between
the Prime Minister Ayad Allawi and multinational force personnel to
give the Iraqi armed forces a high-end strike force in its ongoing security
mission against anti-Iraqi forces operating in the country.

- Iraqi Army soldiers negotiate the standard eight weeks of basic training
  including basic soldiering skills instruction in weapons, drills, ceremony, soldier discipline, and physical training. Units negotiate advanced follow-on
  infantry, land navigation, and other operational training after graduation
  and before deployment. The Iraqi Army will ultimately be comprised of
  twenty-seven battalions of infantry—including nine special Iraqi Intervention Force battalions—and three transportation battalions. The army will
  be organized into nine brigades and three divisions. The bulk of the force
  is slated to be in place by early 2005. Plans to create heavier and better
  armored forces are still in flux, but there are now 259 soldiers in the First
  Mechanized Brigade, preparing to train with ten MTLB armored personnel
  carriers. These vehicles were drawn from a pool of over 300 armored
  vehicles, which the Iraqis intend to make ready as the unit grows.

- The Iraqi Coastal Defense Force is the Iraqi armed forces' naval component. Ultimately to number just more than 400 servicemen, the force
  also includes a land-based Coastal Defense Regiment resembling western-
  type "Marine" infantry forces. Land- and sea-based forces negotiate the
  IAF's eight-week basic-training courses before moving on to follow-on
  training and sea training for the boat crews. Boat crews learn the basics
  in seamanship before receiving instruction in advanced seamanship,
  towing, gunnery, sea rescue, chart reading, navigation, antismuggling operations, and rigid inflatable-boat integration and small-boat drill instruction.
  Training is put in the context of a democratically based maritime sea

force. Primary duties include protecting the country's roughly fifty-mile coastline from smuggling and foreign fighter infiltration operations as well as the port assets at Umm Qasr in southern Iraq and oil assets in the Persian Gulf. The force patrols out to the twelve-mile international water boundary in the Persian Gulf with five twenty-seven-meter-long Chinese-made patrol boats and various other support craft.

- The Iraqi Air Force has begun to fly light reconnaissance missions. All Iraqi Air Force pilots and maintenance personnel negotiate comprehensive one- to four-month "conversion courses" largely comprised of familiarization instruction. The Iraqi Air Force is not yet assigned C-130 transport planes but does have plans to obtain them. The training brings air force recruits up to speed on current Iraqi Air Force aircraft and augments prior skills. The air force actively recruits from prior-service personnel pools in the country—officially sending personnel to training after the Iraqi Ministry of Defense's vetting and screening process clears recruits for duty. Training is almost entirely conducted in the United Arab Emirates and Jordan by multinational force partners. After "conversion course" training is completed, trainees go to assigned squadrons in Iraq for follow-on training comprised of advanced instruction and specific operational training. The Iraqi Air Force is initially slated as a six-squadron force of various-make light reconnaissance aircraft and various support aircraft including C-130s and other helicopter craft with operations mainly centered on supporting Iraqi security force operations on the ground, infrastructure reconnaissance, and border-security missions. The majority of the force is scheduled to be operational by the fall of 2005.

Continuing Problems in Training the Police Forces

Progress was still much slower in creating effective police forces than in creating military forces. While some aspects of criminal activity did drop over time, sporadic terrorism and high levels of criminal activity continued to be major problems in the twelve to fourteen governorates where the threat was not high enough to be characterized as an active insurgency.

Warnings in a Senate Staff Report

One of the best insights into these issues is provided in a draft staff report to the U.S. Senate Foreign Relations Committee titled "Iraq—Lessons in Stabilization and Reconstruction, November–December 2004." The report found many of the same problems that the GAO report referenced earlier that had been found in the spring of 2004. It made the following eight key points:

1. *Civilian-Military Structural Gap*: This gap is particularly damaging in the effort to rebuild the Iraqi police and security forces. At the Jordan International Police Training Center (JIPTC) the staff members found

confusion and frustration with the lack of communication and coordination between the civilians and military. The State Department Bureau of International Narcotics and Law Enforcement (State/INL), which funds the U.S. police training assistance programs for the Iraqis, had minimal interaction with the Department of Defense/CENTCOM team that has the policy lead in development of Iraq's police and security forces. Moreover, neither the State Department nor the Department of Defense appears to be in charge of coordinating efforts with the Iraqi Ministry of Interior, which is the "customer" for which the newly trained police forces are produced.

The cadets receive eight weeks of training but leave the academy without a uniform, weapon, or any idea of whether, or where in Iraq, they will be employed. This has provoked questions about the number of Iraqi police actually trained. There also are no minimum standards imposed in vetting cadets or in certifying the capabilities of the newly trained Iraqi police and no identification of cadets who might excel and should be trained further. Civilian contractors who run the academy cannot hire security guards or order the military to provide security escort for the cadets on the return trip across the border to Iraq. Sadly, a number of cadets have been killed on the journey back, victims not only of the insurgents but in some measure of the civilian-military institutional gap.

2. *Confused Roles and Responsibilities*: The Iraqi Ministry of Interior, responsible for Iraq's police forces, has no single U.S. counterpart agency. While there is a U.S. Embassy adviser to the Ministry of Interior, no single U.S. agency appears to have responsibility for the full spectrum of the Iraq police force development. State/INL, the FBI, the Treasury, CENTCOM, and various contractors all have a role. The international police training academy in Jordan is not clearly directed by CENTCOM, although it is run by CENTCOM contractors under the direction of INL with a deputy commander from the Royal Canadian Mounted Police. Moreover, it is unclear which office is responsible for coordinating with other donor nations providing police training such as Germany, the United Arab Emirates, Jordan, Canada, Finland, and Hungary.

3. *Overlapping Funding Sources*: Assistance funding takes a circuitous route from State/INL to CENTCOM to contractors who actually implement the police training program. The police academy was set up under a bilateral agreement between State/INL and the government of Jordan, using Circular 175 authority delegated to INL by the Secretary of State. CENTCOM and the Civilian Police Assistance Training Team (CPATT) in Baghdad are, however, the source of funds for INL support of police training. Funds for 2005 are expected to be provided directly to INL from the Iraqi Relief and Reconstruction Fund (IRRF). Yet some instructors for the academy are apparently under the Department of Justice and

others under the Department of Homeland Security (DHS), including active DHS agents from the border control/customs agency assigned to teach border police. A number of DynCorp private contractors who were supposed to handle follow-on and on-the-job-training in Iraq were diverted to support the training requirements of the police academy. CENT-COM has directed the academy to increase output of Iraqi border police cadets, but there apparently was insufficient funding under the contract for additional staff and insufficient numbers of border police cadets recruited to be trained.

4. *Inadequate Vetting/Quantity vs. Quality*: Staff members were told that anyone in Iraq can be a police cadet. Personnel vetting processes for the police forces are inconsistent and uncoordinated. There are no uniform selection criteria, and potential cadets are usually only subject to minimal screening. Staff members were told that there is no list or database of people eligible for training or trained for the police forces. There is so much pressure to get more Iraqi cadets that the quality of the candidates has been virtually ignored. There are three basic methods for getting Iraqi cadets: (1) accepting those who volunteer, (2) recruiting directly by the military at training centers around the country, and (3) accepting referrals by the chief of police, tribal chief, or other authorities in the provinces. There are no women in the academy classes. All Kurds, Shi'a, and Sunni are trained together, although not all speak Arabic, particularly the Kurds.

   Staff members were told that some cadets arrived at the academy illiterate and with unrealistic expectations. For one class early in the program, out of over 700 former senior Iraqi border control/customs agents nominated by the Ministry of Interior to be trained, 259 were illiterate, lacked basic skills, and/or did not want to stay at the academy. They thought they were going to be in hotels with time to relax in Jordan. The cadets are not allowed to go out of the facility to enter Jordan unless it is work related as an escorted visit. One cadet was over eighty years old. There are an estimated 32,000 Iraqis expected to be trained at the academy by December of 2005. An estimated sixteen countries are providing the training with a total of 322 instructors. Student capacity total for the facility in Jordan in November 2004 was at 3,600, but academy officials indicated they could use more instructors. There are currently an estimated 2.6 instructors per class. An estimated 8,297 police officers had been trained as of November 10, 2004, out of an expected 11,000 goal. The problems have been too few recruits with the right skills as well as recruits who leave for personal or other reasons.

5. *Inadequate Training*: Several officials the staff members talked to expressed concerns about the substance of training provided to the Iraqis and the security and reliability of the police cadets trained. In classes on explosives countermeasures cadets are taught to defuse a bomb by learning how bombs are made. Some expressed fears that insurgents have

infiltrated the cadets and are being taught how to attack better. Thus, there is hesitation on what types of training the Iraqi cadets should receive. At the academy the cadets are not trained on the use of AK-47s, the most common weapons used in Iraq, but on pistols because the facility has constraints on the size of the shooting-range protective barrier. There also are limited amounts of other personnel security-related equipment for training, and staff members were told that equipment ordered has not been delivered for months. After the staff visit a new curriculum with greater emphasis on personnel security was reportedly implemented in December 2004.

The Jordanians provide instructors, language assistance, and a cadet command brigade that implements, mentors, drills, and provides discipline for the cadets. Department of Defense contract instructors could not do all the discipline in Arabic for the cadets, and the Jordanian brigade facilitates training significantly. A senior Jordanian police officer noted that "very few" of the Iraqis selected for training would qualify for police training under the Jordanian system, which involves extensive tests and screening.

6. *Inadequate Follow-up*: Once trained, it is not clear what happens to the graduates. There is no differentiation in cadets who excel to allow them to specialize after they complete the basic course and no team building for units to learn to operate together in the future. Cadets are sent back to Iraq with no job or certainty that they can perform police functions. Iraqi police cadets are given a basic eight-week training course at the police training academy in Jordan but leave there without a uniform, a weapon, other equipment, or any plan for follow-up to ensure they are integrated into and become productive elements of the new Iraqi police force. Those interested in continuing as police officers simply show up at neighborhood or municipal police stations once they return, at which time they may or may not be given work. The contractors hired by the military cannot even hire civilian security guards to protect the cadet graduates returning to Iraq. The day after the staff members' visit to the academy, there were press reports of the kidnapping of between thirty and sixty returning police cadets who had been transported by bus to the border by police academy officials. The academy apparently had requested security escort, but it had been denied reportedly due to operations in Fallujah. Staff members asked but failed to learn from CENTCOM or embassy officials the true fate of these cadets.

7. *Evaluating Improvements in Police Training*: There have been some improvements reported over the past six months. The numbers of police trained reportedly are rising. Some officials indicated cadets are more confident when they leave, but there is no way to evaluate these claims or measure performance. Improvements were not evident from reports of the wholesale disintegration of the Mosul police force in November. State/INL

is trying to develop a follow-on evaluation capability for the police training academy in Jordan and get a better assessment of how many police trained have been hired in each province and their capabilities. The contractors running the police academy, however, are not responsible for such continuity. There also appeared to be no recognition of the need for more consistency between military and civilian police training curriculum in Baghdad and Jordan.

8. *Duplicating Efforts by Civil Defense Force/Civil Intervention Force*: The roles of the new Iraqi Civil Defense Force and new Civil Intervention Force, both under the Ministry of Interior, are not clear. Both units are expected to be more closely related to military units than to civilian police forces. These forces are being established under CENTCOM, but the Department of Defense has not coordinated this effort or integrated it with the civilian police force. State Department personnel recognized that the State Department does not have the experience or expertise to provide aid, training, and equipment for these new forces. The State Department's Office of Diplomatic Security/Antiterrorism Assistance program (DS/ATA) does dignitary protection but has no plan for transitioning this responsibility to the new Iraqi Civil Defense or Civil Intervention Forces or even a clear vision of the objective of these forces. There also is an Emergency Response Unit being trained with both military and civilian applications. It is not clear if the future of these forces will be with the military or if there will be a transition back to civilian oversight. In addition, there are questions about who will fund this organization in the future.

Some of the U.S. and other foreign advisers involved feel this criticism was too demanding. The Civilian Police Assistance Training Team (CPATT) noted that the problems in creating effective police and security forces were, if anything, considerably more challenging at this point than the problems in creating a military force focused purely on military missions. One such adviser put it this way:

The SSR project for the police and border police was the biggest of its kind in the world: Bosnia, Kosovo and Afghanistan all pale into insignificance beside it. The Police in Iraq had been only third or fourth in the pecking order under Saddam and they had all but disappeared, the police stations had all been ransacked and the Ministry of the Interior was dysfunctional to say the least. There was no real capability to speak of and absolutely no ability to maneuver properly trained and equipped police around Iraq.

The IPS [Iraqi Police Service] had 80,000 people in uniform and of those 12–15,000 had received some form of formal training (four weeks). The payroll though had about 120,000 individuals on it. The training program was designed for democratic policing not for counter insurgency operations. The Baghdad Police Academy was to produce 1,000 policemen every other month and another Academy was being built in Jordan, to produce 2,000 every other month. In the midst of this we introduced the "Qualifying Committee" that was essentially a redundancy program aimed at about 30,000 police. We set ourselves the aim of capturing the biometric data of every single police and border officer. We recognized that unless we did so we would never bring the police numbers under control nor would we get the payroll sorted out. We worked out that we needed $60m [million] and went ahead and got it a week before transition.

We had to accelerate the police training program markedly, as well as its recruitment. In addition, we had to accelerate the training program for existing police officers. We had to identify a broad range of specialist courses too (organized crime, forensics, intelligence and so on) as well as trying to shape the Ministry of the Interior—by utilizing the Organize element of the mission—into a more coherent and effective organization. We had to harness what ended up as being a $2 billion funding program and begin the acquisition process.

We had to organize 300 international police advisors (that number rose every month), as well as 80 international police trainers, to act as mentors. Incoming agencies that were going to assist with the specialist training programs—such as the FBI, ATF and DEA had to be harnessed, brought under command of CPATT and pointed in the right direction. We had to look at the Border Police; where we were going to build 100's of border forts and main crossing points and what they would consist of including the necessary technology. We had to look at the 80,000-strong Facilities Protection Service, who were to protect infrastructure and buildings. We had to buy 45,000 AK-47s, 90,000 pistols, 180,000 uniforms, 15,000 vehicles and refurbish 450 police stations.

We also had to factor in 10 percent for losses, which were needed to replace casualties and destroyed infrastructure and equipment. We also had to create some maneuverability into the police force after they proved unable to deploy from Baghdad, following the US recapture of the Najaf police stations. To do this we created nine Public Order Battalions, two Special Police Regiments (equipped with light armor—we just went ahead and purchased STRYKER) a 250-man Emergency Response Unit and a 5,000-strong highway patrol organization.

Interestingly we also got on with what became known as the Baghdad policing plan. The DCG MNF–I essentially got me in told me there was no plan—some 12 months on—for policing in Baghdad and that we needed to come up with one. This did not require professional police officers—we had some very able Iraqi officers who could articulate what was required we just had to write the plan, identify the resources and get on with implementation.

Clearly this all took time.

Few advisers felt, however, that many of the points made in the Senate staff report were not valid at the time. A number of the Iraqis involved also felt such comments provided a good picture of the problems seen from Iraqi side. They point out that if anything, such criticism may have understated some aspects of the problem because the MNF–I only reported on the police trained by the United States and Coalition, and many local police and security forces were locally recruited and not integrated into the national/Coalition effort.

The Critical Importance of Effective Police Forces

These points highlight an issue that some who focus primarily on Iraq's military forces tend to ignore. The insurgency may be the greatest threat to the government, but crime has been, and is, a constant day-to-day threat to ordinary Iraqis even in the more secure provinces. White-collar crime and official corruption threaten their livelihoods. Theft and looting not only threaten their economic well-being but also help cause the breakdown of essential services like water and electric power. Violent crime, kidnappings, and extortion threaten their lives and those of their family members, as well as their economic well-being.

In areas where the insurgency is active crime is often linked to insurgency, and former regime elements in the insurgency have become particularly good at establishing contacts with criminal elements and paying them to carry out acts of crime and sabotage. In the ten to twelve provinces where there is relative safety from insurgent attacks, crime remains endemic and often interacts with local ethnic, sectarian, and tribal violence, as well as police corruption. The failure of the police also encourages local militias and vigilante groups, creating local rivals to the government.

For most Iraqis, as for most human beings throughout the world, governance is measured in terms of the ability to provide security and essential services. Iraqis, however, are particularly sensitive to the problems caused by police corruption and violence after decades under Saddam Hussein and are even more sensitive to the use of military forces in urban areas and civil affairs. Saddam's heritage of using military force to repress the people is particularly important in Shi'ite and Kurdish areas, but almost all Iraqis had reason to fear those elements of the military, like the Special Republican Guard and special security services personnel in military uniforms. The presence of Coalition military as "occupation" forces has compounded these fears and concerns.

As has been discussed earlier, the Coalition's slow beginning ensured the police effort lagged behind the military effort, and the impact lingered through late 2004 and will play out for some years to come. The fact that the following chapters document real progress in this effort does not mean that anyone can ignore the lessons that delayed a critical aspect of Iraqi force development.

As Brigadier General Mackay noted:

> We ... made the big mistake of making the Police a second or even third priority task in the same way that we had done in Bosnia, Kosovo and Afghanistan. As had happened there, a capability gap emerged between the military, who saw policing as "mission creep," and the indigenous forces, who were incapable of doing anything. That vacuum was filled by organized crime, which in turn fuelled the insurgency; insurgents need to be funded from somewhere and organized crime did just that. Our ability to withdraw from theatre is in direct proportion to the effectiveness of the institutions we have built because, in the absence of law and order, the military have to remain in order to provide security.

The creation of effective police forces was never a luxury that could wait on defeating the insurgents. Giving Iraq stability and giving the Iraqi government full legitimacy meant that the Iraqi police had to become as visible as possible—and not the Iraqi military. This meant, however, that Iraqi police forces had to have the paramilitary support necessary to operate in moderate threat areas and the competence necessary to establish the rule of law with proper regard to human rights. The police have to be perceived as relatively honest and effective, reluctant to use violence, and as free of local tribalism and special interests as possible.

As the following chapters show, creating such a force remained a difficult challenge even when far more resources were made available. Progress does not mean miracles. Creating far more effective vetting and training programs cannot suddenly change the police. The police must change their very "culture." They must become proactive, select and promote on the basis of merit, reduce corruption, and respect human rights and the rule of law. This will take time, and there will be some significant police corruption, problems, and abuses for at least the next five years and probably for the next decade. Yet, such progress is vital. Building up the best possible police and security forces—and giving them the training, equipment, and facilities to deal with organized crime and low-level insurgent violence—is critical to Iraq's future.

7   End of 2004 as a Benchmark

Trends in the Progress of Iraqi Security and Military Forces in December 2004

ONE OF THE ongoing problems in assessing the progress in creating Iraqi security forces is that MNF–I, MNSTC–I, and U.S. reporting on these developments has kept changing over time. As has been discussed earlier, the positive side of these changes is that the initial counts of "on-duty" manpower, which exaggerate quantity without regard to quality, were replaced by counts of "trained" manpower after the Eikenberry assessment and desertions in Fallujah and Sadr City in the spring of 2004. These, in turn, were replaced by still more realistic counts of "trained and equipped" manpower in the early fall of 2004, following a new assessment of Iraqi capabilities by MNSTC–I.

None of these methods of counting Iraqi strength reflected combat readiness or mission capability, which is the purpose of creating Iraqi forces. It was not until the spring of 2005 when the MNSTC–I developed still further an Iraqi security force unit capability rating system with four levels of readiness based on personnel, command and control, training, sustainment, equipping, and leadership that either the Coalition or the Iraqi government began to measure mission effectiveness.

Data provided by the MNSTC–I do, however, provide a set of 2004 benchmarks for comparing future progress, although the data cannot be conveniently provided on an exact end-of-year basis because of reporting problems and changes in the categories being reported. If nothing else, such data show that significant changes were occurring in Iraqi efforts and that the force development effort was gathering further momentum by the end of the year.

Manning at the End of 2004: A Statistical "Snapshot"

Figures 7.1 through 7.4 illustrate the status of the Iraqi security and military forces through December 2004. These figures, based on Coalition reporting to the UN Security Council and issued on December 6, provide a better picture of the difference between trained and untrained Iraqi security and military forces than the U.S. State Department's *Iraq Weekly Status Report* issues after September 2004. It should be noted, however, that the numbers for the forces under the Ministry of Interior are generally unreliable, as some data were provided by local chiefs of police, whereas military force numbers were reported by Coalition commanders.

Figure 7.1 shows the numbers of National Guard, army, and special operations forces that trained or were on hand compared to the numbers required in December 2004. Figure 7.2 shows the number of police and border enforcement personnel that were trained or on hand compared to the numbers required. It is important to note that those troops listed as trained/on hand were not all fully trained or equipped. Despite repeated assaults on police stations and National Guard posts and attacks on officers and Guardsmen headed home on leave, the total numbers of police and National Guardsmen had increased slightly. The numbers for the army, special operations, and border enforcement, however, had decreased, as more demanding standards were applied to "trained and equipped" manpower and low-grade manpower was eliminated or deserted. Figures 7.3 and 7.4 show the composition of the Iraqi military and security forces as of December 6, 2004. The military was overwhelmingly dominated by National Guardsmen, while police made up the largest proportion of the

FIGURE 7.1

Iraqi Military Forces Trained/On Hand versus Required as of December 6, 2004

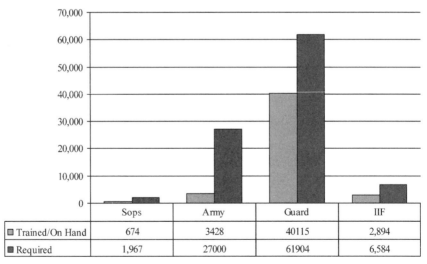

	Sops	Army	Guard	IIF
Trained/On Hand	674	3428	40115	2,894
Required	1,967	27000	61904	6,584

Source: December 6, 2004, report by the United States on behalf of the Multinational Force pursuant to United Nations Security Council Resolution 1546. The "IIF," or Iraqi Intervention Force numbers, are taken from the December 1, 2004, Iraq Weekly Status Update available at www.defendamerica.mil.

FIGURE 7.2

Iraqi Security Forces Trained/On Hand versus Required as of December 6, 2004

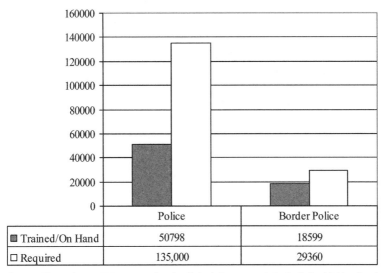

	Police	Border Police
▨ Trained/On Hand	50798	18599
☐ Required	135,000	29360

Source: December 6, 2004, report by the United States on behalf of the Multinational Force pursuant to United Nations Security Council Resolution 1546.

security forces. It takes time to order equipment, receive it, distribute it to large numbers of forces going through training, train units, and to provide bases for units that have completed training. The fact remains, however, that the slow beginnings in trying to create effective Iraqi forces mean that the progress in the manning of both the military and security forces remained well below the required strength necessary to meet the mission need, and similar problems still existed in terms of a force quality.

Manning at the End of 2004: Force Trends

Figures 7.5 through 7.9 expand the end-of-year statistical "snapshot" shown in the previous figures to portray the trends in Iraqi force development. Figure 7.5 shows the levels of manning in both the Iraqi Army and Iraqi National Guard from December 2003 to January 2005. The army's manning levels were erratic throughout 2004. They consistently fell toward the end of 2004 but saw an upsurge to 7,598 in January 2005. What would appear to be a significant drop in the Iraqi Intervention Force's manning levels from January 12 to January 19 is more likely the result of reassigning forces as opposed to desertion or dropout.

The forces listed as part of the IIF on January 12 were redesignated as part of the regular Iraqi Army as of January 19. The National Guard's manning level has remained relatively constant, although it is important to note a decrease in over 6,000 guardsmen between December 2004 and January 2005. The number

FIGURE 7.3
Iraqi Military Forces by Force Element as of December 6, 2004

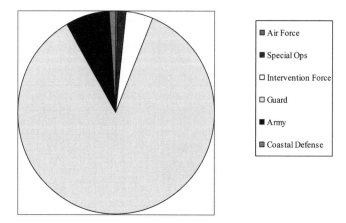

Air Force	Special Ops	Intervention Force	Guard	Army	Coastal Defense
167	674	2062	40115	3428	484

Source: December 6, 2004, report by the United States on behalf of the Multinational Force pursuant
  to United Nations Security Council Resolution 1546.

of trained and equipped soldiers dropped in November but has gone up as
more units have completed their training.

Reports from Fallujah and Samarra continued to indicate that small units
of both the army and National Guard fought well. It also appeared that the
quality of both the guardsmen and soldiers was slowly improving. In one instance on January 18, 2005, four suicide bombs rocked Baghdad within ninety
minutes. Yet, the loss of life was far less than it could have been because of
Iraqi action. Colonel Mike Murray, commander of the U.S. Third Brigade, First
Cavalry, stated that all of the bombers failed to reach their designated targets.
He stated, "Out of four car bombs in Baghdad ... in every case there was an
Iraqi soldier either from the Iraqi Army or the Iraqi National Guard or an Iraqi
policeman that prevented that car bomb from getting to its intended target."[1]
The challenge to retain army soldiers remains a concern.

The levels of manning in both the Iraqi police and Iraqi border enforcement
from December 2003 to January 2005 are shown in figure 7.6. Police manning
levels steadily decreased from the peak in June 2004 (92,227) until late November
2004 when the numbers slowly began increasing once more. The drastic drop
in the numbers of police needs to be kept in perspective. While police units
were frequently overrun, failed to report for duty, or joined the insurgency,

FIGURE 7.4
Iraqi Security Forces by Force Element as of December 6, 2004

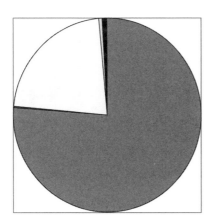 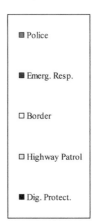

■ Police

■ Emerg. Resp.

☐ Border

☐ Highway Patrol

■ Dig. Protect.

Police	Emergency Response	Border Patrol	Highway Patrol	Dignitary Protection
43627	168	14593	370	484

Source: December 6, 2004, report by the United States on behalf of the Multinational Force pursuant to United Nations Security Council Resolution 1546. These numbers include those on hand. The report to the UN did not include numbers for the Highway Patrol and Dignitary Protection Service. These numbers were taken from the December 1, 2004, Iraq Weekly Status Report available at www.defendamerica.mil. "Emerg. Resp." stands for Emergency Response Unit. "Dig. Protect." stands for the Dignitary Protection Service.

newer reports indicate that some units in Samarra fought tenaciously when attacked. It should be noted that the Justice Department training team has been administering the International Criminal Investigative Training Assistance Program (ICITAP) since May 2003, and it claims that 400 women are employed as police officers in Iraq. The levels in the manning of the border enforcement agency remain erratic and it is unclear how many individuals are actually out on patrol.

Stated manning goals of the Iraqi Army in contrast with the actual manning levels of the army over the previous year are shown in figure 7.7. The manning end goal of the Iraqi Army has steadily dropped since the peak estimation of 40,000 in December 2003. In May 2004 the total required dropped by 5,000, and it dropped by a further 8,000 in July. The drop in the requirements for the army is likely caused by further specialization within the Iraqi military and security forces with regard to missions and roles. The Iraqi Intervention Force and the Iraqi special forces were created as separate entities with specific missions, and the police and National Guard generally confront insurgents with U.S. backing unless they are massed in some large force like in Fallujah. When they are in static positions, the army tends to have a larger role.

FIGURE 7.5

Levels of Iraqi Military Forces over Time, December 2003 to January 2005

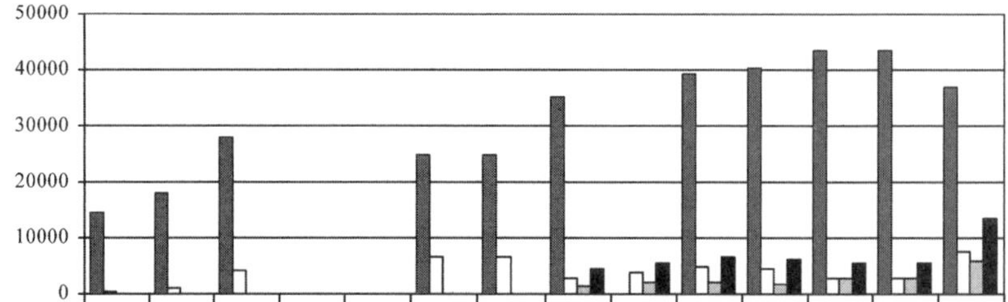

	22-Dec	20-Jan	23-Feb	Mar	Apr	25-May	1-Jun	20-Jul	Aug	27-Sep	27-Oct	24-Nov	1-Dec	19-Jan
■ Guard	14600	17800	27854			24874	24874	35178		39272	40457	43445	43445	36,827
☐ Army	400	1100	4087			6702	6702	2917	3750	4789	4507	2713	2713	7,598
▨ IIF								1473	1928	1928	1794	2894	2894	5,884
■ IIF & Army								4390	5678	6717	6301	5607	5607	13,482

Note: Breakouts of the numbers of National Guard on duty but not trained are not available prior to February 23rd, in May and June, and are not available after September 27th. The Army figures include only those soldiers considered trained and equipped. This figure uses the Iraq Weekly Status Reports released first by the Department of Defense and now the Department of State, available at http://www.defendamerica.mil, as well as information provided by MNSTC-I. For consistency, the figure uses the reports that appear at the end of each month. There are no available numbers for March and April, and only the IIF and Army numbers are available for August. This figure does not include the Iraqi Air Force, Civil Intervention Force, Highway Patrol, or Iraqi Navy.

Figure 7.8 contrasts the manning goals of the Iraqi National Guard with the actual manning levels of the Iraqi National Guard over the last year. Iraqi National Guard requirements increased slightly in May and July 2004 before skyrocketing in September 2004 with an increase of over 20,000 in the end-goal strength as a result of the comprehensive review of Iraqi security force requirements that Ambassador John Negroponte undertook in the fall of 2004.

The National Guard was "merged" with the army on January 6, 2005, in an effort to create a larger, more cohesive, and more effective military force, although experts involved in the U.S. training effort cautioned that it requires synchronization of effort to train, equip, base, and integrate training resources such as trainers and training locations. As one expert put it, "One should not expect a constantly increasing generation of force given the complexity of the task and the requirement to use Coalition forces (i.e., those who sometimes conduct operations) to assist with the training process. The Coalition spent considerable time and effort to improve the capabilities of ING [Iraqi National Guard] battalions, something this report overlooks because it focuses so much on the alleged weakness in the initial training program without any focus on the follow-on training the Coalition provides to ING units. Some 42 battalions of ING are conducting operations at the squad to battalion level (as of early January 2005). They are on the street, and elsewhere, providing security—often

FIGURE 7.6
Iraqi Security Forces over Time, December 2003 to January 2005

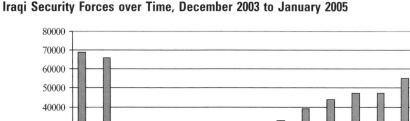

	22-Dec	20-Jan	23-Feb	Mar	Apr	25-May	1-Jun	20-Jul	23-Aug	22-Sep	27-Oct	24-Nov	1-Dec	19-Jan
■ Police	69000	65700	29960			25719	29688	27136	32880	38921	43927	47342	47342	55,05
□ Border Police	12900	20700	18044			17573	17573	18223		16798	14313	14593	14593	14786

Note: There are no data for Iraqi security force levels for March, April, and August 2003. From February 2003 on, the Border Police included the entire manpower for the Department of Border Enforcement. This figure uses the Iraq Weekly Status Reports released by the Department of Defense, available at http://www.defendamerica.mil, as well as data provided by MNSTC-I. For consistency, the figure uses the reports that appear at the end of each month. Gaps in data reflect unavailable numbers. The row for police shows two different types of data: The numbers for police until February 23 reflect police reported as being on duty. The numbers since February 23 reflect the number trained and equipped, and from October 27 the total numbers reflect those trained and equipped either through the eight-week or three-week programs. Thus, the drop in numbers is not as significant as it first appears.

with strong effect. Some units are not as strong as we would like, but others are doing better than expected."

Lastly, figure 7.9 illustrates the stated manning goals of the Iraqi police in contrast to the actual manning levels of the Iraqi police over the last year. Police manning actually exceeded early estimates of the required numbers. Subsequent decreases are, in part, a result of Iraqis taking a larger role in the candidate screening process. The Iraqi Interim Government, while slow to do so, has begun to fire police that fail to show up for work, police that cooperate with insurgents, and police that are blatantly corrupt.

It should also be noted, however, that the insurgent campaign of intimidation and attacks also affected police manning levels. Since October 2004 manning seems to be slowly increasing, but it is nowhere near the estimated 135,000 that are needed. The requirements for police manning increased dramatically in May 2004 and then increased in September 2004 as a result of the review undertaken by Ambassador Negroponte.

Taken together, these figures show trends that reflect progress in strengthening the force elements most critical to giving Iraqi forces the capability to deal with insurgents, terrorists, and serious criminals. They do not show how many

FIGURE 7.7
Trends in Iraqi Army versus Required Total over Time as of January 2005

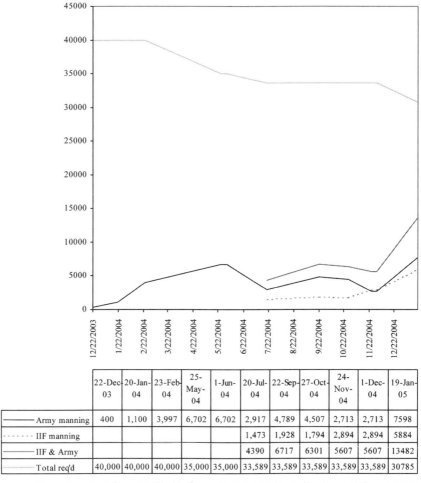

	22-Dec 03	20-Jan- 04	23-Feb- 04	25- May- 04	1-Jun- 04	20-Jul- 04	22-Sep- 04	27-Oct- 04	24- Nov- 04	1-Dec- 04	19-Jan- 05
⎯⎯⎯ Army manning	400	1,100	3,997	6,702	6,702	2,917	4,789	4,507	2,713	2,713	7598
∙∙∙∙∙∙∙ IIF manning						1,473	1,928	1,794	2,894	2,894	5884
⎯⎯⎯ IIF & Army						4390	6717	6301	5607	5607	13482
⎯⎯⎯ Total req'd		40,000	40,000	40,000	35,000	35,000	33,589	33,589	33,589	33,589	33,589	30785

Source: These data come from the Weekly Status Report available at http://www.defenselink.mil/
la/iraq_stat.html, http://www.defendamerica.mil, and inquiries to MNSTC-I. These numbers
include those in training and on hand up until July when numbers indicating those trained/
equipped became available. The graph utilizes the figures available at the end of each
month. Months have been omitted when data were not available. The "total required"
column lists the total number of soldiers required by the Army up until the creation of the
Intervention Force. Following the creation of the Intervention Force, the "total required"
column includes the soldiers needed by the Regular Army and the Intervention Force.

men actually served in units that stood and fought or that had proper training,
equipment, and facilities. They do, however, show that Iraqi forces had come
a long way since June 2004 and that a major effort was now under way to
overcome the legacy of the earlier failures.

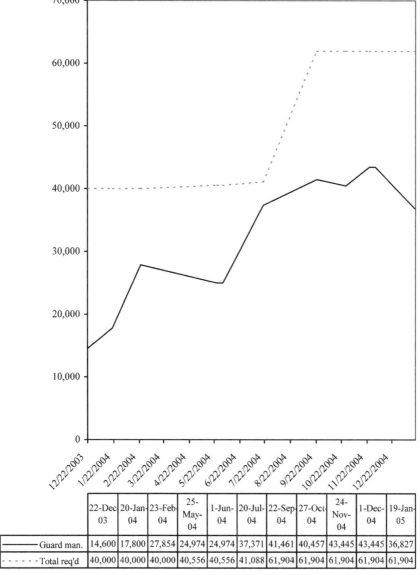

FIGURE 7.8
Trends in Iraqi Guard versus Required Total over Time as of January 2005

	22-Dec 03	20-Jan 04	23-Feb 04	25-May-04	1-Jun-04	20-Jul-04	22-Sep 04	27-Oct 04	24-Nov-04	1-Dec-04	19-Jan 05
—— Guard man.	14,600	17,800	27,854	24,974	24,974	37,371	41,461	40,457	43,445	43,445	36,827
- - - - - Total req'd	40,000	40,000	40,000	40,556	40,556	41,088	61,904	61,904	61,904	61,904	61,904

Source: These data come from the Weekly Status Report available at http://www.defenselink.mil/
la/iraq_stat.html and http://www.defendamerica.mil. This graph includes those in training
and on hand, as breakouts are unavailable. It utilizes the figures available at the end of
each month. Months have been omitted when data were not given.

FIGURE 7.9

Trends in Iraqi Police versus Required Total over Time as of January 2005

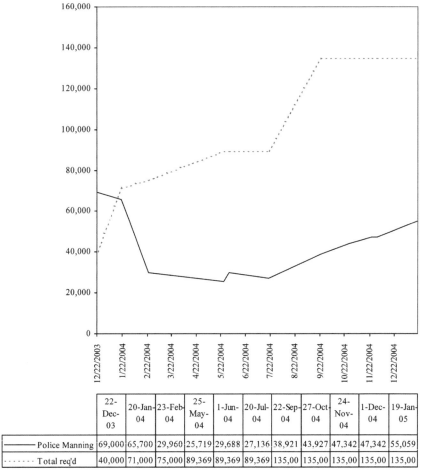

	22-Dec-03	20-Jan-04	23-Feb-04	25-May-04	1-Jun-04	20-Jul-04	22-Sep-04	27-Oct-04	24-Nov-04	1-Dec-04	19-Jan-05
——— Police Manning	69,000	65,700	29,960	25,719	29,688	27,136	38,921	43,927	47,342	47,342	55,059
······· Total req'd	40,000	71,000	75,000	89,369	89,369	89,369	135,00	135,00	135,00	135,00	135,00

Source: Data from the Weekly Status Report available at http://www.defenselink.mil/la/iraq_stat.html, http://www.defendamerica.mil, and data provided by MNSTC-I. The numbers for police up until 23 February reflect police reported as being on duty, not those on duty and trained, as breakouts are unavailable prior to February.

Understanding the Manpower Trend Data

Ironically, some of these trends conceal positive developments that had the effect of cutting total manpower or lowering the rate of manpower increase. Far too many men who lacked the proper physical capabilities, ability to absorb training, and sometimes literacy had been recruited or retained at all ranks during the first year of occupation. Many were poorly vetted or recruited for political purposes. Others were corrupt, failed to lead, or were cowardly. These men now had to be phased out or dismissed, sometimes including senior officers. As a result, the buildup of manpower was in some ways more impressive than the figures shown might imply.

At the same time, these trends in total manpower numbers disguised other significant problems. Recruit quality remained a problem, as did the quality of the output of those training courses that accepted low-grade entrants. Facilities, training, and equipment had improved, but many recruits had limited literacy, no experience with vehicles and modern technology, and little experience with disciplined or structured work experience. The level of education and work experience Iraq had before the Iran-Iraq War was long gone, and even many recruits with military backgrounds under the regime of Saddam Hussein were loosely organized garrison forces conscripted into service and with little meaningful operational experience.

The facts of day-to-day life in Iraq created additional difficulties. Iraqis lived in a social structure and cash economy and one where forces had to visit their families to transfer money and provide services that simply are not as yet available at a local level. Social contact was an important fact of Iraqi life, and families were vulnerable and subject to intimidation in many areas. This often led units to have 10 to 15 percent of their manpower outside the unit. MNSTC–I reported that in an effort to combat the limits of a cash-only economy a fourth company was added to the battalion structure to give increased scheduling flexibility (so that Iraqi soldiers could get the cash home) and to improve readiness.

Motivation remained a major problem. From the start, recruiting relied heavily on the fact so many young men could not find any other job. This inevitably meant much of the recruitment base had a limited incentive to fight or take high risks, and such problems were compounded by the fact that the proper leadership, facilities, equipment, training, and reinforcement capabilities were often lacking. Some insurgents and terrorists may seek martyrdom. When the system fails the man, the man cannot be blamed for failing the system.

The ethnic and religious makeup of the Iraqi military and security forces was an additional concern. The stated MNSTC–I goal was to create an army that is at least 30 percent Sunni Muslims; yet reports indicate that Shi'ites and Kurds did much of the fighting in 2004.[2] The current ethnic and religious mix of the Iraqi forces is unknown because data are not available. But both U.S. advisers and Iraqi officers felt more still has to be done to create religiously and ethnically diverse forces in such a way that no group feels disenfranchised or threatened.

The improvements in the vetting and training problems made in virtually all elements of Iraqi forces in 2004 could only be implemented slowly, and great caution was needed in removing incompetent, incapable, or corrupt personnel. The risk of a political "backlash" in the form of hostility against the Iraqi government or Coalition was all too real, as was the risk of providing new recruits to the insurgency. Changing a manpower "culture" based on favoritism and corruption could not be done quickly, and new retirement and severance payment options had to be developed and implemented. Vetting and training facilities remained limited in size, and in many cases any form of manpower could serve some useful purpose—even if this was a token deterrent or minor security function.

Corruption and favoritism remained a problem, particularly in the police. Incompetent and inactive officers sometimes were left in office until a major scandal or failure occurred. Selection and promotion was still beginning to be carried out on a merit basis and according to the rules, and large numbers of officers and personnel still lacked the kind of training that could change the "culture" of Iraqi forces that had developed under previous regimes. Significant numbers of local police were still appointed outside the new system the Ministry of Interior and MNSTC–I were trying to establish, and CPATT still lacked all of the manpower and resources it needed to be effective.

No amount of vetting and training can substitute for experience in combat or crisis. Large numbers of men were being put into new units without experienced leaders and without any history of unit cohesion. These units lacked cadres of MNSTC–I and MNF–I advisers to help them through the transition and lacked the equipment and support to outmatch the weapons and equipment in the hands of terrorists and insurgents. Police units in particular often had to be deployed in highly vulnerable and poorly protected posts in urban areas. The recruiting, training, and equipping programs were gathering real momentum but did not by themselves produce combat units.

Equipment at the End of 2004

The U.S. weekly status reports on Iraq no longer reported equipment deliveries in terms of total numbers delivered to date or relative to total requirement by the end of 2004. The MNSTC–I did, however, report total equipment deliveries per month. It reported on December 5 that total deliveries for November 2004 included the following:

- Forty-four Panhard M-3 armored personnel carriers, four T-55 heavy tanks, nineteen multipurpose armored vehicles (MTLBs), and four Comp Air 7SL aircraft.
- More than two million RPK/PKM machine gun rounds, 1.2 million 9-mm pistol rounds, 2.8 million AK-47 rounds, 450,000 twelve-gauge shotgun rounds, 999,000 5.6-mm rounds, forty-eight shotguns, 1,000 9-mm pistols, nearly 1,000 PKM and RPK machine guns, 1,150 smoke and riot grenades, 1,900 9-mm Glock pistols, 5,400 AK-47 assault rifles, twenty Walther pistols, seventy-eight rocket-propelled grenade launchers, 16,000 sets of body armor, and 7,400 helmets.
- Two two-ton trucks, fourteen ambulances, ten GAZ heavy transport trucks, fifteen Chevy trucks, four Dodge Durangos, fifty-two Chevy Lumina police sedans.

- Two-hundred vehicle and handheld radios, 150 night-vision goggles, some 11,000 field jackets, 3,000 cold-weather jackets, 2,000 mattresses and beds, 40,000 desert-combat uniforms, 11,000 pairs of running shoes, 300 kneepads, 600 tactical vests, 1,000 holsters, 9,500 T-shirts, 1,200 binoculars, 1,000 handcuff sets, twenty blunt trauma suits, 1,450 compasses, 132 Global Positioning Systems (GPS), 800 "MAG" lights, 750 whistles, 4,150 hats, 344 first aid kits, 2,000 canteens, 1,500 police shirts, and 2,000 police uniforms.[3]

If one looks at total deliveries between July 1 and December 1, 2004, they included more than 69 million rounds of ammunition with another 148 million rounds stored in twelve ammunition sites throughout Iraq. They also included 70,000 pistols, 49,000 AK-47s, 1,700 heavy PKM machine guns, 84,700 sets of body armor, 5,700 vehicles, 54,000 helmets, and 20,000 radios.[4]

What Such Equipment Trend Data Mean

Some of these figures may seem mundane and trivial, but a careful reading shows a more rapid rate of delivery was taking place and that the mix of equipment reflected a considerably better effort to meet the overall needs of Iraqi forces. The problem is that there is no way to relate such data to prior shortfalls, ongoing losses, or total current needs. It is also unclear whether equipment was being provided in the form that gave Iraqis the feeling that they had what they needed to fight and survive and that they would eventually get what they needed to operate as independent forces.

Progress took place in other areas. Some steps could be carried out at very little cost while also boosting Iraqi security and military force confidence. One simple example was that of the ski mask. Providing security and military force members with ski masks allowed them to obscure their identity from insurgents and their sympathizers or informers.[5] Insurgents were less likely to discover the identities of the policemen and soldiers, and insurgents found it harder to intimidate and/or threaten their families, enhancing confidence and effectiveness of Iraqi forces. MNSTC–I reported that as of mid-2005, ski masks were issued to some forces. Likewise, providing Iraqi forces with the tool needed to sight their aging AK-47s helped to improve their shooting accuracy and reduce instances of collateral damage.

On the other hand, this list of deliveries again reveals how lightly armed and equipped most Iraqi forces were at the end of 2004 and raises further questions about the level of equipment shortfalls tolerated during 2003 and the first half of 2004. Iraqi forces were still being created with little more than the most basic equipment.

Americans who evaluate the performance of Iraqi forces at this time and the lessons for future training and support efforts should remember that this was the period when an even more intense U.S. debate began over uparmoring Humvees and trucks and providing heavy armor. Iraqi forces in the field were still being given little or no protection by U.S. and Coalition equipment standards. It was already clear that if Iraqi forces were to stand on their own, demonstrate the true sovereignty and legitimacy of Iraqi forces, and phase out Coalition forces, they must have the equipment to both operate with reasonable safety and decisively outgun and outmaneuver insurgents and terrorists.

Another emerging concern is that weapons supplied to the Iraqi military could be used against Coalition forces, or by the factions in civil fighting, if the Iraqi political process fails. The makeup of the Iraqi military still reveals the fractious nature of the state rather than presents the appearance of a unified *national* force. Forces are primarily Kurds in the north, Sunnis in the west, and Shi'ite in the south. With continuing wrangling over the content of the constitution, with units that are largely ethnic or sectarian, and with divided sectarian and ethnic allegiances among military personnel, the threat of an all-out civil war or military coup remains real and has made the Pentagon increasingly uncertain about equipping the Iraqi military with heavy weaponry. Weapons ending up in the hands of insurgents remains a threat and a concern.

This concern was compounded by the continuing role of ethnic and sectarian militias inside and outside Iraqi forces, the existence of police, and the increasing insurgent efforts to provoke full-scale civil war.

A provision in the Iraqi constitution allowing for regional security forces complicates matters further. Article 9 of the August 28 draft of the constitution holds that "forming military militias outside the framework of the armed forces is banned." However, Article 18 establishes that "the regional government shall be in charge of all that's required for administering the region, especially establishing and regulating internal security forces for the region such as police, security and guards for the region."[6] The evolution and possible expansion of these regional forces are central to U.S. concerns. Heavy weaponry provided to the Iraqi National Army could possibly wind up in the hands of these regional, ethnic, or sectarian forces—forces like the Badr Corps in the south. The stockpiling of U.S.-supplied arms by potentially competing forces could add to sectarian tensions, as well as to the possibility of civil war.[7]

Facilities at the End of 2004

The U.S. State Department reported on the number of reconstruction projects that were under way as of December 2, 2004. The report listed eighty-eight border posts, seventeen police stations, and sixteen military bases for the Iraqi security and military forces being built.[8] Like most U.S. reporting, however, it is impossible to know the extent to which such claims of progress relate to the requirement, how many survive the insurgency, and how many are really adequate once completed. Project reporting that is not related to valid objectives and requirements—and where there is no evaluation of the value of what is delivered—is essentially meaningless. This is important because so many facilities for the police and security forces had been grossly inadequate and underequipped in the past, and many were still extremely vulnerable to insurgent attack and impossible to isolate or protect in the densely populated areas where they are located.

Once again, Iraqi forces suffered from a dual standard. Many were still being deployed without anything approaching the physical security of their Coalition allies. However, regular Army and IIF facilities were becoming better protected, as were many ING and police locations. Some ING were also co-located on Coalition forward-operating bases. Police stations were often difficult to harden due to their physical location relative to other structures and roads in the area, but U.S. experts report that efforts to provide better force protection to police stations were well under way.

Spending at the End of 2004

The Department of Defense weekly status report still showed relatively low levels of fiscal year 2004 aid spending as of December 8, 2004. The total apportionment for security and law enforcement was now shown as $5,045 million. A total of $4,278 million was committed, $2,930 million was obligated, and $961 million had been spent. This was less than 20 percent of the total apportionment months after the 2004 fiscal year ended.[9]

Part of these problems, however, was the result of the way the money was appropriated and allocated. A total of $1,800 million of the $5,045 million was not appropriated until October 2004. MNSTC–I reports that several hundred million of that amount had to be spent in fiscal year 2005 because it was designated for the INL police trainers and advisers. As a result, the amount obligated was adequate relative to the money actually available, and the amount spent was actually 30 percent of the $3,200 billion set aside in the Iraqi Relief and Reconstruction Fund (IRRF).[10]

Operational Readiness at the End of 2004

As might be expected, various insurgent groups made Iraqi forces more and more of a target as Iraqi forces increased in strength and came to play a larger role in securing Iraq. The detailed Chronology at the back of this book shows Iraqi clashes with insurgents since June 2004. It is all too clear that insurgents made steadily greater efforts to prevent and break up the successful development of Iraqi military, security, and police forces. This Chronology also shows that the new and inexperienced Iraqi forces were often vulnerable and lacked the experience to be effective. Military forces do not simply need training and equipment; they need leadership and experience at the unit level and to develop a sense of identity, mutual trust, and unit integrity. This can take years in normal military practice, and U.S. and Western military history is filled with examples of problems that occurred when new units were created without large cadres of proven leaders and other ranks.

The Challenge of Deploying New Forces into Combat

It is scarcely surprising, therefore, that the new Iraqi forces often lacked operational readiness, and there were many occasions on which Iraqi forces failed to perform their missions. These failures were the almost inevitable result of insurgent attacks, a lack of leadership and integrity on the part of some Iraqi officers, and a lack of experience and dedication on the part of Iraqi enlisted men.

The failure of the Iraqi police forces in Mosul during and after the battle of Fallujah in November 2004 was one example of such problems.[11] Nearly 75 percent of some 4,000 Iraqi forces deserted when insurgents attacked on November 12, 2004, in the midst of the U.S.-Iraqi attack on insurgents in Fallujah. The ranks of Iraqi National Guard units dropped from 1,100 to 300 men in a matter of hours, and two companies—some 200 men—abandoned all of their equipment. The 106th Iraqi National Guard Battalion did well, but another battalion virtually disintegrated.[12]

MNSTC–I reported that their commander, Brigadier General Mohammed Keri Barhawi, was wounded twice, attacked many times while serving as the police chief in Mosul, and that his forces only disintegrated after repeated attacks, intimidation, and at times lack of Coalition support. A senior observer commented as follows:

> Opening up two fronts in April 2004 against insurgents in Fallujah and then Moqtada Militia in Baghdad simultaneously was very unfortunate. The new Iraqi Army either fled or rebelled and almost disintegrated overnight—we were far too optimistic and when you look at how their deployment was managed you can only wince. To then allow an inconclusive ending to Fallujah and the obvious festering implications to coalesce which included the ability of insurgents in Fallujah to sustain the overall insurgency campaign was another major error.

There were Iraqi failures to deal with this situation at the command level. General Babakir Shawkat Zebari, the top Iraqi general, refused to admit the scope of the problem at Fallujah. On December 26, 2004, he stated, "Not a single soldier ran away from the battlefield [in Fallujah]. It was not a difficult battle. Fallujah was cleaned and the number of our martyrs [or fatalities] was only seven."[13] To not recognize problems and setbacks within the Iraqi security and military forces compounds the problem by failing to learn from past mistakes. Somewhat similar failures occurred in Samarra, although at a lower level. Some 2,000 Iraqi troops did join the U.S. forces fighting to retake the city in October 2004 but only after some 300 men out of a 750-man battalion deserted before the fighting even began.[14]

Progress in Spite of Setbacks

At the same time, two senior U.S. officers made statements about the level of progress Iraqi forces had achieved by the end of 2004 that help put these problems in a more balanced perspective. In a December 6, 2004, interview Lieutenant General David Petraeus, the commander of MNSTC–I, was questioned about problems in training the Iraqi security and military forces. When pressed as to whether the problem with the security forces was low morale, infiltration, cowardice, leadership, or intimidation, Petraeus replied, "It's probably all of the above."[15] Petraeus made it clear, however, that he felt Iraqi security forces were improving despite setbacks like the dissolution of the Mosul police force in late November. He stated, "This is a rollercoaster that we are riding. You have to realize that every day there are going to be bumps, sometimes explosions, sometimes real plunges, and the idea is to make darn sure you have got your eye on the horizon and you are still climbing with the rollercoaster over time. And I think that's the case."[16]

U.S. General John Abizaid, commander of U.S. Central Command, gave a press conference on December 6, 2004, and highlighted what he considered the achievements and problems within the Iraqi security and military forces. He expressed concern over the level of militant activity and the apparent dissolution of the police force in Mosul. When asked whether the Iraqi forces could assume more of the security missions by the Iraqi national election date, Abizaid replied:

> Iraqi security forces aren't as mature as they need to be for the security environment that's going to exist in the next several months. That doesn't mean that they are not fighting and dying—they are. I think the mid-level chain of command has got to be developed at brigade and division levels in order for the armed forces to develop firmly.
>
> Over time, they will get better. Their equipment is coming in; their organization is developing. I think the Army and National Guard units are going to be challenged over the next several months by an awful lot of fighting. They know it. We know it and what we've got to do is not risk their development by committing them at the wrong time to combat operations.
>
> In places where there is lots of intimidation like Mosul, it's clear that the police are not holding together to the degree we would like them to, so, all these things taken into account make it pretty clear to me that it's a good move for commanders in Iraq to get additional forces to get through the election period. This is the single most important political event that's going to take place in Iraq since its liberation.[17]

General Abizaid's comments came five days after the Iraqi Minister of State for National Security Affairs, Dr. Qassim Dawood, stated that security of the polling centers during the election would be the responsibility of the Iraqi security forces and of Iraqi society more broadly and that the U.S. forces would only be called on if the centers faced a major attack.[18] The U.S. Department of Defense indicated that U.S. troop levels would rise to 150,000 in Iraq to help provide security for the national election.

Abizaid was, however, positive about the progress in creating Iraqi forces and the impact they would have in taking over from U.S. and other Coalition forces:

> It's an intangible action that I'm not so sure I can predict. When do you reach the tipping point where Iraqi security forces are capable of standing alone

without our backup? It will be awhile. I wouldn't want to make a prediction on when that's going to be.

If Iraqi forces are capable of conducting more combat operations independently, the same levels of U.S. forces won't be necessary.

You come to a point where the combat multinational portion of the force becomes secondary to the training effort.[19]

When General Abizaid was asked about the post-election environment in Iraq, he stated, "If the circumstances are such that, as in Afghanistan, the political process leads to better security . . . and if the Iraqi security forces start to gel in terms of leadership and seasoning in important areas around the country—which I think will happen—then we can talk about reshaping [U.S.] forces."[20]

Abizaid made it clear that the goal for U.S. forces would be to take on the training of Iraqi security forces as their main mission with providing general security as a secondary mission, one to be undertaken on a lesser scale and when the Iraqis ask for assistance. He also commented that if Iraqi force development moved to the point where training became the primary mission of the U.S. forces in Iraq, the United States might use less conventional forces and utilize "embedded" trainers and more special operations troops.

Progress in Other Areas

The behavior of Iraqi forces did show that they became more effective when they were given the proper leadership, organization, training, equipment, facilities, and when they had effective backup from the Coalition or other Iraqi security forces. Some fought well in demanding battles and engagements, and even less combat-capable forces like the police seemed to be taking hold in the areas where insurgent and terrorist attacks were less frequent.

The Chronology and various reports from the media and MNSTC–I reflect significant successes and progress in a number of areas between September and December 2004. They were as follows:

- The MNSTC–I began deploying five mobile training teams to each of the MNF–I's six subordinate commands on November 28 to assist in training Iraqi bridge and division senior staff officers. All trainers were formerly instructors at the U.S. Army Command and General Staff College or Combined Arms Service Staff School.
- The Iraqi Army's First Mechanized Brigade received another six T-55 heavy tanks and twenty-seven multipurpose armored vehicles (MTLBs), which are personnel carriers with heavy machine guns, at the Taji military training base north of Baghdad on December 6, 2004. It now has ten T-55s and thirty-seven MTLBs and will be steadily expanding to include refurbished T-72s, which will replace the current T-55s. The brigade is scheduled to be operational by the summer of 2005. The brigade is being built up in three phases of roughly 1,000 men each, drawing on the

manpower in Iraqi armored and mechanized units before the invasion. It will have all the capabilities of a full mechanized brigade, including infantry, armor, artillery, engineers, and logistics and support. The first phase is due to be complete before the end of 2004, the second by February 2005, and the final phase by May or June 2005.

- The United Arab Emirates donated Panhard M-3 armored vehicles to the Iraqi Army (Jordan had previously donated over eighty APCs earlier in the year).
- As of December, MNSTC–I announced the mechanized brigade could grow to a full division. The present force development plans call for three infantry divisions plus various support battalions.
- The Iraqi Army began company-level training with the Egyptian Army's Third Division Northern Command at the Mubarak City training facility near Alexandria.
- Two battalions from the Iraqi Intervention Force conducted operations in Najaf. These same two battalions plus another conducted effective combat operations in Fallujah together with two regular battalions, an Army commando battalion, a police emergency response unit, and Shewani special forces trained by First MEF. These forces constituted 2,700 Iraqis at their peak.
- Iraqi security forces formally assumed local control of security operations in Najaf province on November 30, 2004.
- The army had a total of eighteen battalions (regular army and intervention force) that had completed initial training. Although most of these were not at full strength, many soldiers in these units had fought effectively and were "combat ready," with many being "combat proven." The Ministry of Defense had developed a "direct recruiting" program, whereby it was recruiting and training former soldiers with plans to integrate them into existing units to address manning shortfalls.
- Sixteen National Guard battalions conducted operations effectively at the company level or above with a number conducting operations effectively at the battalion level. Many Iraqi National Guard units conducted combat operations. Current plans are to expand the National Guard from its previous authorized strength of forty-five battalions and six brigades to six division headquarters, twenty-one brigade commanders, and sixty-five battalions.
- National Guard units were slated to begin advanced training in explosive ordnance disposal (EOD) in January 2005 with the goal of creating ten trained companies of fifty men each by the end of 2005.
- Seventy-two men in the special Counterterrorism Task Force of the special forces graduated from a twelve-week training course on December 3, 2004.
- Over 34,000 former police had been trained in the three-week Transition Integration Program. Over 18,000 police had been trained in the eight-week academy program of instruction. The eight-week academies in Jordan,

Baghdad, and other regional academies were graduating nearly 3,000 new police per month and were poised to graduate over 4,000 per month by early March. The eight-week program was being taught at five different locations.

- The Iraqi Police Service graduated 1,423 officers from the eight-week basic police training course at the International Police Training Center in Amman, Jordan, on December 16, 2004, and 140 officers from four advanced courses at the Adnan training facility on December 9. Prior service officers attend a three-week course.
- The eight-week police curriculum had been revised so training would better prepare students for the environment in which they would operate with increased training on survival skills in an insurgency environment, force protection, combatives, and shooting AK-47s as well as pistols. In addition, police stations were being hardened and additional equipment was being issued to police to make them more capable in their operating environment.
- The border forces began to play a more active role. The numbers of trained border enforcement personnel reflect training done by major subordinate commands (divisions). Capabilities among border enforcement personnel varied widely. However, MNSTC–I established a centralized program of instruction for border personnel, presently at the Jordanian Police Academy with Department of Homeland Security instructors. They will move this instruction to Iraq in the near future. In addition, MNSTC–I has started to train some border personnel as units and has deployed a small number of these to the border to conduct operations as units.
- By the end of December the Coalition had trained and equipped six public order battalions and three special police battalions trained to operate with mechanized (wheeled) vehicles.
- MNSTC–I had also helped the Ministry of Interior equip and employ police commando brigades. These newly formed commando units are designed to provide a high-end police and counterinsurgency capability. These battalions successfully conducted offensive operations in Baghdad, Fallujah, Samarra, Mosul, North Babil, and other areas. The Coalition had provided equipment to one full brigade and in mid-December was in the process of equipping a second full brigade, while a battalion of a planned third brigade was being formed. These forces have proved of great significance as have the newly trained public order battalions, three of which had begun operations, and several emergency response units operating effectively at the provincial level.
- The Coalition had also trained, equipped, and helped to employ a small national-level emergency response unit capable of conducting offensive counterinsurgency operations.
- MNSTC–I also began training and equipping provincial level SWAT teams, which will be capable of providing backup support to police when under attack.

- The Iraqi Air Force began to take delivery on light aircraft. These included a total of seven Comp Air 7SL light reconnaissance aircraft, based at the Basra air base by December 2004. The Iraqi Air Force commenced operations August 18, 2004, with the flights of two SB7L-360 Seeker reconnaissance aircraft intended to protect infrastructure facilities and Iraq's borders. The SB7L-360 Seeker is a single-engine, two-man, high-visibility aircraft that is fitted with high-resolution surveillance systems. It is capable of providing live observation feedback to ground forces and also carry digital video-recording hardware and other reconnaissance technology. Their missions are coordinated with Iraqi and Coalition force efforts on the ground and will eventually include operations all over the country.
- The Iraqi Military Academy had started operating again with two pilot classes slated to graduate from two different locations in early January.

This list of developments reflects the growing impact of MNSTC–I's growing emphasis on mission capability, leadership, and the creation of effective unit elements with a matching emphasis on unit integrity during the course of 2004. Force totals are debatable in terms of numbers and misleading as a comprehensive picture of developments in force quality. It is clear from this list of "end of year" accomplishments that Iraqi forces had come a long way since the end of 2003.

8 The Run Up to Elections

Iraqi Security and Military Forces in January 2005

A S MIGHT BE expected, basic force numbers did not change radically between December and January 2005. Iraq did, however, take major steps to restructure its forces like merging the National Guard into the Iraqi Army. Equally significant, this was the period in which Iraq held its first true legislative election in decades. During months leading up to the election, insurgents had made repeated efforts to keep Iraqis from going to the polls and voting. They failed—some 58 percent of registered Iraqis voted on January 30, 2005. This election turnout gave a sense of legitimacy to the Iraqi government, and a combination of a large and visible Iraqi security presence and relative security of most polling places reinforced this position.

An estimated 130,000 Iraqi security forces deployed on Election Day, January 30, 2005. While it was 150,000 Coalition troops that provided the core of the security effort, Iraqi forces did provide the inner two rings of security for over 5,200 polling sites. Not a single polling site was penetrated, and several Iraqi security force (ISF) members gave their lives while stopping suicide bombers on Election Day. The performance of the ISF was particularly striking since there was no approved election security plan until ten days prior to the election. In fact, if some local ISF commanders had not acted to create plans on their own initiative, the operation could not have been nearly so successful.[1]

This lack of violence did, however, lead some U.S. and Iraqi officials and officers to be overly optimistic about the political and military impact of the elections. General John P. Abizaid, commander of U.S. forces in the region, testified before the Senate Armed Services Committee on March 1, 2005. Abizaid rhetorically asked, "Why didn't [the insurgents] put more people in the field [on Election Day]? They threw their whole force at us, and yet they were unable to disturb the elections. I think that the voting in Iraq, the political process that's going on ... have driven those numbers [of insurgents] down."[2]

It was easy to forget that elections are merely the prelude to governance and that all of Iraq's important political problems were still ahead of the new government. It was also easy to forget that part of the reason was that Coalition forces shut down much of the road traffic and movement on Election Day and made security measures more effective. Furthermore, a short-term decline in activity after a surge in such activity before the elections did not mean the insurgents were defeated, and the insurgents soon developed new tactics.

Manning in Levels in January 2005

Figures 8.1 through 8.4 illustrate the status of the Iraqi security and military forces as of January 19, 2005. These graphs are based on the *Iraq Weekly Status Reports* made available by the State Department since September. Figure 8.1 shows the numbers of National Guard, army, intervention force, and special operations forces that are trained or on hand compared to the numbers that are required. Between December 1, 2004, and January 19, 2005, the National Guard suffered fairly substantial manpower losses. That being said, the intervention force has exceeded its goal end-strength, and its numbers increased significantly during the same time period. The first significant troop increase in the new year was the graduation of 670 Iraqi Intervention Force soldiers from the Taji military training base on January 18, 2005. The army experienced moderate growth.

Figure 8.2 shows the number of police and border enforcement personnel that are trained or on hand compared to the numbers that are required. It is important to note that those troops listed as trained/on hand are not all fully

FIGURE 8.1
Iraqi Military Forces Trained/On Hand versus Required as of January 19, 2005

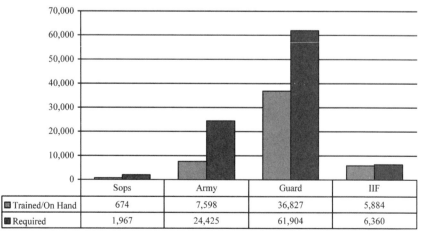

	Sops	Army	Guard	IIF
Trained/On Hand	674	7,598	36,827	5,884
Required	1,967	24,425	61,904	6,360

Source: January 19, 2005, *Iraq Weekly Status Report* available at www.defendamerica.mil. "IIF" stands for the Iraqi Intervention Force.

trained or equipped. Both the police and the border enforcement personnel have been slowly increasing. Figures 8.3 and 8.4 show the composition of the Iraqi military and security forces as of January 19, 2005. The military is still overwhelmingly dominated by national guardsmen, while police make up the largest proportion of the security forces. There has been a fairly significant rise in the number of Iraqi Intervention Force troops.

Total Iraqi Manpower: Debate over Total Numbers

Total Iraqi manning levels became an area of considerable political controversy during this period and a key focus of the Senate confirmation hearings for Condoleezza Rice's nomination as Secretary of State. On January 18, Rice stated that there were 120,000 trained Iraqi troops.[3] Several senators questioned that number, with one Democrat—Senator Joseph Biden—saying that he believed that the number of trained Iraqis was much closer to 4,000.

The truth lay in between, and had little to do with total manpower numbers of any kind. There were certainly far more than 4,000 trained troops equipped for some form of counterinsurgency and counterterrorism mission. The army and the intervention force accounted for more than double that figure. The only way to arrive at an estimate near 4,000 was to only count the Iraqi Army, which had a total of 4,159 men as of January 11, 2005.[4] The Iraqi Civil Intervention Force had another 2,862 men, the Emergency Response Unit had 205, the Bureau of Dignitary Protection had 484, the Iraqi Intervention Force

FIGURE 8.2

Iraqi Security Forces Trained/On Hand versus Required as of January 19, 2005

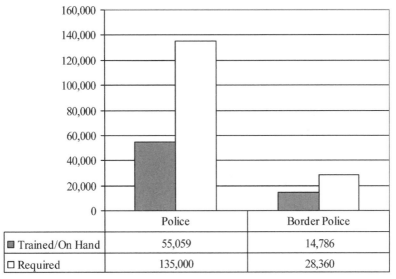

	Police	Border Police
■ Trained/On Hand	55,059	14,786
□ Required	135,000	28,360

Source: January 19, 2005, *Iraq Weekly Status Report* available at www.defendamerica.mil.

FIGURE 8.3
Iraqi Military Forces by Force Element as of January 19, 2005

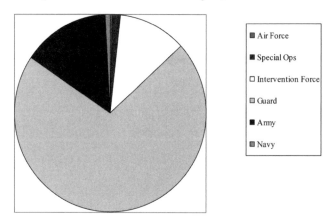

Air Force	Special Ops	Intervention Force	Guard	Army	Navy
145	674	5,884	36,827	7,598	495

Source: January 19, 2005, *Iraq Weekly Status Report* available at www.defendamerica.mil.

had 9,159, and the Special Operations Force had 674. This was a total of 17,000 men and did not count any of the 40,063 men in the National Guard. While the guard was just being integrated into the army on January 6, 2005, it did have a total of nearly forty-five battalions and some had moderate effectiveness. Moreover, even the least trained and lightest Iraqi forces had *some* value in terms of local security, and many could replace Coalition forces in areas like checkpoint duty. The ability to operate directly and independently against insurgent and terrorist forces is only one measure of whether a force is well-enough trained and equipped to play a useful role.

That said, it still was disingenuous to state that there were 120,000 adequately trained and equipped Iraqi troops. If one looks at the numbers provided by the State Department in the *Iraq Weekly Status Report*, one can determine that that figure could only have been arrived at if all of the Iraqi police were considered "troops." That in itself would be an inaccurate designation, as many police received only three weeks of training that did not approach the level of training the army receives. Even if the police *were* counted as "troops," an estimate of 120,000 trained troops failed to take into account the fact that the National Guard had fought erratically at best and been unreliable at worst. MNSTC–I reported that several units in Baghdad, north of Baghdad, and in the Ninewa province performed well. By the end of 2004 there may not even have been the equivalent of 12,000 reliable, well-trained, well-equipped Iraqi troops

FIGURE 8.4
Iraqi Security Forces by Force Element as of January 19, 2005

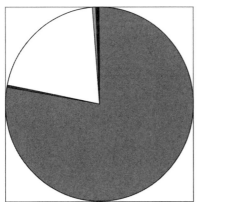
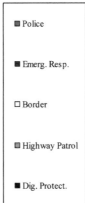

- Police
- Emerg. Resp.
- □ Border
- Highway Patrol
- Dig. Protect.

Police	Emergency Response	Border Patrol	Highway Patrol	Dignitary Protection
55,059	205	14,786	354	484

Source: January 19, 2005, *Iraq Weekly Status Report* available at www.defendamerica.mil. "Emerg. Resp." stands for Emergency Response Unit. "Dig. Protect." stands for the Dignitary Protection Service.

that could engage serious insurgent resistance. There were only one or two battalions with any track record of operating on their own without extensive U.S. support, and Iraq's first mechanized battalion did not become operational until mid-January 2005.[5]

Some reporting coming out of the military provided equally misleading data on the Iraqi order of battle. According to some U.S. military assessments, there were approximately sixty-nine Iraqi Army battalions operating in the country at the end of the year, and the U.S. military hoped to have 130,000 Iraqi forces—not just soldiers but army, guard, police, and so forth—by the January 30 election date.[6]

The embassy report on the end of the year status of Iraqi forces showed, however, that these "army" battalions were largely low-grade National Guard battalions. In fact, the army had a total of twenty-one battalions, many of which were inexperienced and lacking in combat effectiveness, and it did not plan to deploy more than six more battalions before the elections. The army—as distinguished from the National Guard—only built up to around 4,700 men by the end January 2005, and even if the National Guard was counted in the total for the army, the total would be around 45,000 men.[7]

Equipment at the Beginning of 2005

As of January 21, 2005, MNSTC–I reported that individual elements of Iraqi military forces had the following major combat equipment, and it is again interesting to note substantial progress having been made in comparison to the progress achieved in early December:[8]

- The Iraqi Navy had five one-hundred-foot patrol craft and thirty-four smaller boats.
- The Iraqi Air Force maintained three squadrons with nine reconnaissance aircraft and three U.S.-supplied C-130 transport planes. At least two of the reconnaissance planes are Seabird SB7l-360 Seeker aircraft. There is a fourth squadron made up of two UH-1 helicopters. The squadron will receive fourteen more UH-1s as well as four Bell Jet Ranger helicopters and should be operational by the end of January.
- There was now one mechanized battalion with a tank company and transportation battalion. The tanks seem to be T-55s and T-72s. The battalion is listed as operational; the necessary equipment and training to form a full mechanized brigade will be provided by summer 2005.
- Iraq's Mechanized Police Brigade was on patrol with fifty BTR-94 armored vehicles.

These developments reflected further progress toward the heavier forces needed to deal with a serious insurgency but scarcely the kind of progress that could as yet produce the kind of Iraqi forces capable of independent operations and replacing Coalition forces.

Moreover, Iraqi forces had by now cost some $1.71 billion out of the $1.91 billion in ongoing funding for security forces—a high price for such lightly equipped units. (At the same time, only $1,208 million in U.S. fiscal year 2004 Iraqi Relief and Reconstruction Fund II (IRRF) aid for security and law enforcement had so far been dispersed out of a total of $5,045 billion that had been apportioned, although the MNSTC–I reports that disbursement rates were accelerating and that approximately $300 million was disbursed between December 2004 and January 2005.)[9]

Problems with Equipment Procurement within the Iraqi Ministry of Defense

The integrity of the Iraqi Defense Ministry also came into question in two separate incidents. One incident concerned the death of two U.S. contractors and questions over the involved contract. Dale Stoffel, a consultant with CLI USA Inc., had negotiated an agreement with Iraqi officials to repair and renovate a number of Soviet-era armored vehicles, including tanks and armored personnel carriers (APCs). Stoffel became concerned that the officials would not honor the contract or pay him for work already completed. He raised his concerns with the U.S. Department of Defense and the Pennsylvania congressional delegation.[10]

Six days after returning to Iraq, Stoffel and Joseph Wemple were found shot to death ten miles outside of a U.S. military base in Taj. Photos of their possessions were posted on an insurgent Web site. The U.S. Department of Defense launched an investigation, and the Iraqi government denied complicity in the deaths of the two contractors. Whether elements within the Ministry of Defense were involved or not, the story gathered wide U.S. attention and may have discouraged some companies from bidding for contracts in Iraq. Nevertheless, it did not paralyze Iraqi Ministry of Defense procurement activity. In January 2005 Deputy Defense Minister Ziad Cattan signed a $20 million arms deal with the Polish state-owned weapons manufacturer Bumar PHZ.[11]

In the second incident the issue was a sizeable transfer of funds from the Iraqi Central Bank by the Ministry of Defense. Reportedly, $300 million in U.S. currency was removed from the bank and put aboard a plane bound for Lebanon.

Mishal Sarraf, an aide to Iraqi Defense Minister Hazim al-Shalaan, asserted that the money was used to buy armored vehicles for Iraqi personnel, including tanks and APCs. There was no public bidding for the contracts, and the entire Iraqi cabinet did not vote on the deal. Sarraf stated that the arms deal had been approved by the defense minister and by three other senior Iraqi officials, one of whom was Interim Prime Minister Ayad Allawi. The aide further stated that the arms dealers could not be named because it would endanger their lives and that the deal was concluded quickly so as to rush the vehicles to Iraqi forces as speedily as possible.[12] Critics challenged this explanation and leveled charges of corruption. Mowaffak al-Rubaie, then the Iraqi national security adviser, said he was unaware of the deal. He stated, "I am sorry to say that the corruption here is worse now than in the Saddam Hussein era."[13] The director of the Iraq Revenue Watch, Isam al-Khafaji, stated, "That's the tragedy of Iraq: Everyone runs their business like a private fiefdom."[14]

It should be noted that no wrongdoing was confirmed and that the Iraqi government flatly denies any charges of corruption. One of the leading critics of the Ministry of Defense with regard to the arms deal was Ahmed Chalabi, a controversial member of the Iraqi National Congress who was running for a seat in the Iraqi parliament. Chalabi and Defense Minister Shalaan were enemies, and it is possible that the charges are politically motivated. Shalaan vowed to arrest Chalabi and turn him over to Interpol, although nothing actually happened.[15]

Some Iraqi soldiers in the field, however, also complained about the level of funding and equipment that they received from the Ministry of Defense. One Iraqi colonel with the Iraqi Army's 305th "Tiger" Battalion—a unit given control of parts of Baghdad by the United States—stated that the ministry was so disorganized that it did not even know what parts of the city the unit controlled. Furthermore, the colonel stated, his unit received approximately $133 a month, not enough to even supply the unit with paper.[16] How widespread the colonel's complaints about the ministry were among the Iraqi forces was unclear.

Facilities

The Coalition reported that there was roughly $1.91 billion in ongoing construction and reconstruction projects for Iraqi security forces as of January

19, 2005, and over $1.71 billion of that money has already been committed. The projects included four multibrigade installations, hundreds of police stations and border forts, numerous headquarters and barracks, a number of training centers, and many operating bases.

Such plans did, however, present the problem that Iraqi forces were being constantly redeployed to meet changing requirements. There often was little notice of future deployment and facility needs, and in some cases MNSTC–I would get requirements for deployment of a unit such as a 1,200-member special police command with something like a week's notice.[17]

Operational Readiness

As the Chronology shows, Iraqi forces continued to perform erratically and to have operational problems in spite of their performance during the election. Some units had massive desertions or broke under pressure, and this led to further debates in the United States and elsewhere over their current and potential effectiveness. USCENTCOM commander General John Abizaid addressed these ongoing concerns about the Iraqi forces in an interview in late January 2005. He said, "There's this debate, obviously, in Washington going on right now about the failure of Iraqi security forces, and I would say they're far from failure. It's a generational effort. It's not one that's going to happen within the next month. . . . I see failure in some places but more successes than failures. So they'll ultimately be successful."[18]

The Iraqi Army commander, General Babakir Shawkat Zebari, echoed Abizaid's outlook on the progress of Iraqi units in training. He stated, "God willing, during this year, our units will be fully armed, trained and have enough soldiers. After all this is finished, I am very optimistic that the Iraqi Army will be able to protect the territories and border. [If the forces continue to improve] we will be able to protect Iraqi cities and villages within six months."[19] General Babakir also stated at that time that he expected Iraqi forces to number around 150,000 by summer of 2005. He expected that the United States would withdraw its troops from the cities and withdraw to one or two major bases by the end of 2005.[20] Interim Prime Minister Ayad Allawi was more cautious but stated that he had been speaking with U.S. officials in Baghdad about ways to speed up the training and equipping of Iraqi soldiers. He said that such acceleration would allow the Coalition forces to leave slowly, but he reiterated that he would adhere to a "conditions-based withdrawal" as opposed to a "calendar-based withdrawal."[21]

U.S. military officials reported that there were 129,000 Iraqi military and security personnel working with 140,000 election workers and 7,000 candidates to secure the polls during the vote.[22] Although insurgents mounted over 200 attacks and killed forty-four Iraqis during the elections, Iraqi forces are widely regarded as having performed admirably, and 8 million voters were able to cast their ballots. In at least one case an Iraqi guarding a polling station wrestled a suicide bomber away from the site at the cost of his own life. The Iraqi interior minister gave a press conference following the election detailing the reported successes of the Iraqi forces. Three terrorists were captured in Baghdad, three in Kirkuk, seven in Thi-Qar, seven in Wassit, 129 in SaLaden, and thirty-nine in Nineveh. The minister acknowledged that there were seven attacks by insurgents during the election that directly targeted Iraqi police.

In any case, the Iraqi order of battle that could be deployed in independent operations, or in intense clashes, remained a small number of battalions. Even these units generally lacked service support and logistic capabilities, had light weapons and few—if any—armored or heavily protected vehicles. The issue was not one of total manpower, or even how many Iraqi forces could serve some purpose in undemanding duties, it was rather that the functioning order of battle—meaningful units active in the field—still remained small.

Other Force Developments

There were other force developments worth noting. A Department of Defense analysis of the state of Iraqi security forces, current as of January 21, 2004, highlighted the following:

- Operations
  - In 2004 Iraqi forces fought alongside Coalition forces in Najaf, Samarra, Fallujah, Baghdad, North Babil, Mosul, and a host of other locations. In Fallujah alone Iraqi forces had lost eight of their members and had more than forty wounded. Well over a thousand others had now lost their lives.
  - Although Iraqi forces had endured casualties in many of their operations, had been attacked multiple times each day, and had suffered losses through brutal intimidation attacks, there was no shortage of volunteers; in fact, basic-training courses are ongoing for more than 4,400 former soldiers to bring under strength Iraqi regular army and intervention units additional forces.

- Ministry of Defense
  - In January 2005 the Minister of Interior laid out his vision for a "regular police" force of 79,000. These regular police would be supplemented by the specialized police force (i.e., public order battalions (POB) and special police commando units) of 50,000, plus a mechanized brigade of 6,000. Altogether these forces would total 135,000. In contrast MNF–I regarded the POB, commandos, and the mechanized brigade to be additional to the Coalition-proposed regular IPS force of 135,000.[23]
  - In less than a year, Iraqi regular army and intervention forces had grown from one operational battalion to twenty-one battalions, with

six more scheduled to become operational over the next month. With the incorporation of the Iraqi National Guard into the army on Army Day, January 6, the total number of battalions conducting operations was now sixty-eight.

○ Iraq's Muthanna Brigade, originally organized and trained by the Iraqis to provide local security, now had three battalions in operations, including one each in Baghdad, Fallujah, and North Babil, and one more in training.

○ Iraq's Navy was now operational, with five one-hundred-foot patrol craft, thirty-four smaller vessels, and a naval infantry regiment that had recently completed training.

○ Iraq's Air Force had three operational squadrons equipped with nine reconnaissance aircraft that operated day and night and three U.S. C-130 transport aircraft. One more squadron, comprised of two UH-1 helicopters (to be followed by fourteen more and by four Bell Jet Rangers from the United Arab Emirates), was standing up.

○ Iraq's Special Operations Forces now included a counterterrorist force and a commando battalion, each of which has conducted dozens of successful operations.

○ Iraq's first mechanized battalion became operational in mid-January, along with a tank company and a transportation battalion.

○ Iraq's two military academies reopened in mid-October and each graduated a pilot course of new lieutenants, ninety-one total, in early January 2005.

• Ministry of Interior
   ○ The Iraqi Police Service had over 55,000 trained and equipped police officers, up from 26,000 six months ago.

   ○ Five basic police academies were now operational; together, they produced over 3,500 new police officers from the eight-week course each month, a course recently modified to better prepare the new police officers for the challenging environment in which some may serve.

   ○ Iraq's mechanized police brigade recently completed training and began operations in mid-January, using fifty BTR-94 wheeled, armored vehicles.

   ○ Seven police commando battalions were now operational with one more in training and additional battalions planned.

   ○ Six public order battalions were operational with six more planned.

   ○ Iraq's National Police Emergency Response Unit was now operational.

   ○ Iraq's First Special Border Force Battalion was operating on the Syrian border in western Anbar province.

○ Five provincial SWAT teams had been trained, and fifteen more were scheduled for training over the next six months.

The Department of Defense report reflected the usual favorable spin. Nevertheless, a comparison of these milestones with the similar data in the previous chapter reveals improvements over a period of less than two months. It is also clear that the insurgency did not have as much impact on Iraq's elections and political process as the insurgents desired.

9 Iraqi Military and Security Forces in the Spring and Summer of 2005

IRAQI FORCE development remained very much a work in progress during the first eight months of 2005, and events showed how much any success interacted with the course of the insurgency and Iraqi politics. The course of the fighting was far less reassuring from April on than during the period immediately after January 30. As Chapter 11 discusses in detail, the seeming pause in insurgent and terrorist activity after the election was followed by a sharp increase in violence, particularly in major bombings and suicide attacks by Sunni insurgent groups that were clearly targeted at trying to prevent Iraqi Sunnis from joining the government and government forces and at dividing Sunni, Shi'ite, and Kurd. In some cases, this triggered new problems in Iraqi forces and new desertions. By May Arab Sunni Islamist insurgent attacks had driven sectarian and ethnic tensions to new highs and created a growing risk that the struggle between the Arab Sunnis and the Arab Shi'ites, Kurds, and other Iraqi minorities could become a broader form of civil war.

There were serious problems in Iraqi politics and governance that affected the force development effort. The new Iraqi government took nearly two months to agree on a presidency council and prime minister and took from February 1 to May 8 to fully select a cabinet and choose a defense minister. The fifty-five members of the new committee to draft a constitution were not named until May 10 and then included only one Sunni—although the nominal deadline for completing a draft was August 15 and a referendum had to be held by October 15, which could be blocked by a negative vote by two-thirds of the population in any three provinces.[1]

Iraq's already weak governance deteriorated in some areas at both the central and local levels during this interregnum. Tensions grew between the largely excluded Sunnis and the now dominant Shi'ites and Kurds, and there was a surge in the infiltration by foreign Islamist extremists. New problems arose as some of the supporters of the incoming government called for major new purges of the government and the Iraqi security forces to eliminate all "Ba'athists," including many whose only "crime" had been to go along with Saddam Hussein's regime to survive. These problems were exacerbated by the fact that some of the most effective Iraqi units were largely Shi'ite and Sunni in character, including special police and security units in the Ministry of Interior. These units could sometimes be as ruthless as they were effective, and compounded Sunni fears and resentments. The good news was that they helped lead some Sunni clerics and politicians to call for Sunnis to join the armed forces and police. The bad news was that Sunnis began to accuse government forces of excessive force, targeted killings and disappearances, and deliberately attacking Sunni targets.

Top U.S. officials like Secretary of Defense Donald Rumsfeld were concerned enough to come to Iraq to warn against such purges and the risk of broadening ethnic and sectarian conflict and to the stress the need for effective governance. Senior U.S. officers like General George Casey, the U.S. commander in Iraq, warned of the need for effective governance and for inclusion of as many Sunnis as possible. U.S. commanders also made it clear that they felt the insurgency would continue to last for several more years, that developing effective Iraqi forces would take over a year, and that the Multinational Force–Iraq (MNF–I) would probably be needed in significant numbers through 2006.[2]

Nevertheless, the Iraqi force-building effort continued to gather momentum in spite of the problems in governance and the new surge of terrorist and insurgent activity. The following chronology illustrates the kind of day-to-day progress that was now taking place, and it is supplemented by more detail in the Chronology at the back of this book:

> **February 5**: The MNSTC–I direct recruiting replacement graduated its largest class of Iraqi Army recruits to date at An Numaniyah; 2,867 graduated and will serve the Iraqi Army's Third and Fifth Divisions.
> **February 10**: The Iraqi Police Service graduated 272 officers from seven specialty training courses taught at the Adnan training center in Baghdad.
> **February 14**: Reportedly, 10,000 Iraqis arrive at one military base looking to enlist. Half pass the recruiting test.
> **February 17**: A total of 1,491 police officers graduated at the Jordan International Police Training Center. Another 183 graduated from advanced and specialty courses at the Adnan training facility. Also, a contract was signed for six new Iraqi Al Uboor class patrol ships to be built in Iraq by Iraqis, costing $15 million and slated to go in service in six months.
> **February 24**: The Iraqi Police Service this week graduated 1,993 new police officers from basic police training courses in Sulaymaniyah and Baghdad. Also, another 204 graduated from advanced and specialty courses at the Adnan training facility.
> **March 3**: The Iraqi Police Service graduated 292 police officers from advanced and specialty courses at the Adnan training facility, twenty-seven

officers from the special weapons and tactics training course, and seventy-two police officers from the emergency response unit course.

March 10: The Iraqi Police Service graduated eighty-one police officers from advanced and specialty courses at the Adnan training facility.

March 13: More than 2,900 Iraqi soldiers graduated today as part of the direct recruit replacement program at the Iraqi training battalion at Kirkush Military Training Base.

March 16: The Iraqi Police Service graduated 144 new police officers from the Al Kut Regional Training Academy. This was the third class to complete the eight-week training course from the Al Kut facility.

March 22: The military academy at Zahko graduated seventy-three new second lieutenants destined to join the Iraqi Army. Also, the Multinational Security Transition Command–Iraq Civilian Police Assistance Training Team (CPATT) is approaching the halfway point in training and fielding special weapons and tactics teams to each governorate. Seven teams are trained and equipped; two others are currently in training. Also, Iraqi officials state that eighty-five insurgents died earlier in the day when Iraqi commandos, assisted by U.S. air and ground support, overran an insurgent training camp located in swamps near Tharthar Lake in the Sunni Triangle. The commandos were part of the First Police Commando Battalion. The eighty-five dead insurgents were the most killed in any one battle since the offensive against Fallujah.

March 31: The Iraqi Police Service graduated 2,906 new police officers this month from basic police training courses in Baghdad, Sulaymaniyah, Al Kut, Al Asad, and Jordan. They also graduated 159 police officers from advanced and specialty courses at the Adnan training facility.

April 1: An Iraqi flight crew from Squadron 23 of the Iraqi Air Force aboard an Iraqi C-130 transported fifty-one Department of Border Enforcement soldiers from training in the United Arab Emirates and returned them to Iraq on this date. The milestone of this mission was the fact that the Iraqi flight crew prepared the necessary requirements to fly in international airspace and land in a foreign country and performed all of the flight-crew functions.

April 7: The Iraqi Police Service graduated 258 police officers from advanced and specialty courses at the Adnan training facility. Also, 247 recruits picked up graduation certificates from the Iraqi Highway Patrol Academy and headed for new jobs guarding their country's streets and thoroughfares. This was the first class to graduate from the new academy.

April 6: Iraqi soldiers from the 102nd and 112th Battalions, supported by Coalition forces (Task Force 2-8 Field Artillery), captured eighty-one suspected insurgents and insurgent supporters, according to a multinational forces report.

April 11: U.S. soldiers and approximately 500 Iraqi soldiers conducted sweeps dubbed Operation Vanguard Tempest in the Al-Rasheed district in Baghdad. The sweeps netted some sixty-five suspected militants.

April 14: The Iraqi Police Service graduated 260 police officers from advanced and specialty courses at the Adnan training facility.

April 18: Five battalions of roughly 3,500 Iraqi troops responded to insurgent threats and claims of hostage taking by taking control of the city in a four-hour sweep that brought in about forty suspects. The operation by two battalions of police commandos and three public order battalions uncovered several vehicles loaded with explosives and two large weapons caches. No hostages were found.

April 25: Joint Iraqi and U.S. sweeps around Baghdad netted forty-one insurgents and an unspecified quantity of weapons. Ten of the militants are suspects in the shooting down of a civilian MI-8 helicopter.

April 28: The Iraqi Police Service graduated 2,872 police officers in April from basic police training courses in Sulaymaniyah, Basra, Jordan, and Baghdad. Also, the Iraqi Police Service graduated 204 police officers from advanced and specialty courses at the Adnan training facility.

April 29: In Baghdad four suicide car bombers struck in the Azamiyah section of the city. Fifteen Iraqi soldiers died, and thirty were wounded in attacks on an Iraqi army patrol, on a police patrol, and two on barricades close to the headquarters for the Ministry of Interior's special forces.

May 4: The Army of Ansar al-Sunna claimed credit for a suicide bombing in Irbil that targeted an office of the KDP political party where more than 300 people were waiting to get approval to apply for Iraqi security jobs. More than sixty were killed and more than 150 injured by the blast. Reports indicated that the suicide bomber seemed to have mingled among the recruits before detonating his explosives.

May 7: Iraqi soldiers detained twenty-nine suspected insurgents in Abu Dsheer, and soldiers from an Iraqi public order battalion detained forty-four suspected insurgents in Dora.

May 8: In the Rawa area U.S. and Iraqi forces captured fifty-four militants and killed six more in a firefight after information gleaned from a captured Zarqawi aide, Ghassan Muhammad Amin Husayn al-Rawi, directed them to the region. They seized bomb-making material and two large stashes of weapons.

May 9: Iraqi Security Forces conducted two more operations. Iraqi soldiers searched twenty targets and detained forty-seven suspected insurgents in Dora. Iraqi commandos detained another thirty-four suspected insurgents in the Abu Dsheer neighborhood.

May 11: In Hawija, a suicide bomber detonates his explosive vest amongst a crowd that had lined up to join the Iraqi army. The suicide bomber managed to slip by security. Twenty are killed, and another thirty are wounded.

May 12: Reportedly, Polish and Iraqi soldiers seize a cache of weapons and arrest twenty-nine suspected militants in the Wassit province in a mission dubbed "Operation Cobweb." Also, 1,469 police graduated from basic training at centers at Al Hillah and Baghdad. Another 189 police graduated from advanced and specialty courses at the Adnan Training Facility.

May 14: An independently planned and executed cordon and search operation by Iraqi forces led to the capture of twenty-six anti-Iraq forces, according to a multinational forces report. Operation Breadbasket, conducted by the Second Brigade of the Fifth Iraqi Army Division, also netted three regional AIF leaders. Officials said this operation is the most recent example of the growing capability of the Iraqi Army.

May 17: Coalition and Iraqi Security Forces performed cordon and search operations in Heychal Salama resulting in the detainment of 150 suspected anti-Iraq forces, according to a multinational forces report.

While such events are anecdotal, no element of the Iraqi security forces had been overrun since the elections, although more than 175 were killed per month in combat in the late spring. More broadly, major shifts were taking place in the scale of the training and equipment effort and gathering momentum in the deployment of Iraqi forces. Moreover, once it finally took shape, the new Shi'ite and Kurdish-dominated government approached the problem of the insurgency and Iraqi force development with more realism than many initially feared.

Key figures like President Jalal Talibani, Prime Minister Ibrahim al-Jafari, Defense Minister Saadoun al-Dulaimi, and Interior Minister Bayan Baqir Jabr Sulagh al-Zubaydi made it clear that they were committed to taking a strong stand to deal with the insurgency and to creating effective Iraqi forces. The new ministers of defense and interior may have lacked experience but were more committed to practical solutions than most of their predecessors, were more willing to cooperate with each other and other ministers, and accepted the need to give Iraqi force building the time necessary to develop effective and *inclusive* forces. As Ali Dabbagh, a Shi'ite member of the new National Assembly, put it, "It is true the Iraqi security forces are not qualified enough to face these waves of terrorism but with the cooperation of the multinational forces the security situation will improve . . . and we can see it improving now."[3]

Manning Levels of Iraqi Military and Security Forces Following the Election

The manpower data on Iraqi forces shows considerable progress, although such data are not easy to analyze. They do not provide a basis for assessing how many forces were largely Shi'ite or Kurdish and how many were more broadly "national" in character. The reporting format used in the *Iraq Weekly Status Report* changed again in early 2005 and eliminated reporting on the twelve individual military and security force branches in favor of six more general categories. The impact of this new reporting system is shown in figures 9.1 and

FIGURE 9.1

The Development of Trained and Equipped Iraqi Security Forces—Historical Perspective (from MNSTC–I)

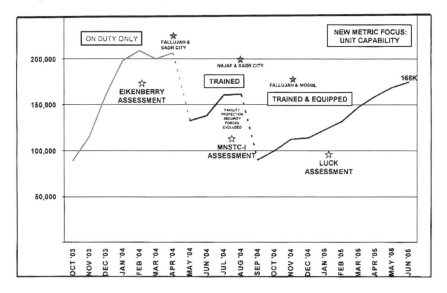

9.2, which compare the resulting manpower totals to the two previous systems used by the CPA and MNF–I.

MNSTC–I sources stated that public reporting continued to evolve to properly reflect the focus of the mission at a given time and explained the shifts shown in figures 9.1 and 9.2 as follows:

> Numbers of "trained and equipped" Iraqi Security Forces have been reported since last August [2004]. This metric represents an evolution in itself. In the early days of ISF [Iraqi security forces] reporting, numbers of forces "on duty" were reported, often without regard for the training or equipment status of that force. At the time, just getting some police visibly onto the streets was deemed critical to public order. After it became apparent that the number of forces on duty wasn't really indicative of their capability, subsequent reports added the training status. In late summer 2004 MNSTC–I started reporting on how many soldiers are both trained and equipped. Then—as now—that is a valuable metric, but must be considered within a broader context. Focus now is shifting to numbers and capabilities of *units*. Standing by themselves, the number of units similarly doesn't tell the whole story of ISF capability. The transition readiness assessment system will help in more accurately defining the capability of the ISF. Transition Teams (assigned to all battalions) will provide solid overall capability assessments of the units already fielded. For security reasons, though, that data—like U.S. readiness reports—will not be publicly provided.

FIGURE 9.2

The Development of Trained and Equipped Iraqi Security Forces (from MNSTC–I)

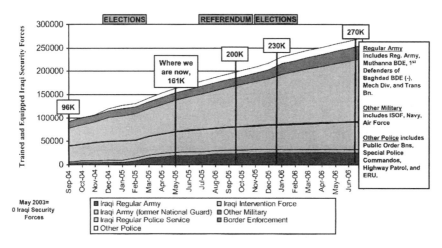

Given this background, the data in figures 9.1 and 9.2 are important for several reasons. They show the problems in the earlier reporting systems, which focused on quantity rather than quality, and produced exaggerated expectations as well as major credibility problems for the CPA and MNF–I. They show a sharp rise in manpower that did have meaningful training and equipment from under 96,000 in August 2004 to 186,000 in June 2005 and over 172,000 in early August 2005. They show the impact of the Eikenberry, MNSTC–I, and Luck assessments on improving the approach to training and equipment of Iraqi forces. They also show a clear plan did exist for expanding the Iraqi manpower pool through July 2006—from 168,000 men in June 2005 to 200,000 in September, 230,000 in December, and 270,000 in July 2006. They show the importance of merging the regular military and National Guard in giving Iraqi military forces the total strength they needed—and need—to be effective. They reflect a balanced emphasis on police and security forces that was becoming significantly more effective than the sheer manpower numbers indicate because many low-quality men were being dropped or retired, while higher-quality manpower was being recruited and trained. And finally, they exclude a major amount of additional manpower with some value in light security missions such as the Facilities Protection Service, Oil Security Service, and Electricity Security Service.

One has only to contrast the figures for "trained and equipped" manpower against the kind of manpower data described in earlier chapters to see that the Iraqi force development program made serious progress just between the beginning of 2005 and the middle of the year. At the same time, figures 9.1 and 9.2 make it equally clear that Iraqi forces still had a long way to go and that much would depend on taking a consistent approach to executing Iraqi force development plans.

Detailed Manpower Trends

The manpower strength of Iraqi forces in the spring of 2005 is shown in more detail in table 9.1, along with the growing strength of Iraqi combat battalions. It should be stressed that the force goals listed as authorized strength represented a moving target and had to change to respond to developments in the insurgency and the actual level of success achieved in creating Iraqi force. The various

TABLE 9.1
Iraqi Active Manning and Force Development Plans in May 2005

Ministry of Defense

Force Element/ Component	Operational as of May 2, 2005		Authorized		Expected 100% Operational Date
	Manpower	Battalions/ Squadrons	Manpower	Battalions/ Squadrons	
Iraqi Army (Combat) Regular and Iraqi Intervention Force	28,215	34	36,315	?	?
Former Iraqi National Guard	39,961	44/–	56,727	62	?
Mechanized/Armor	1,237	1+/–	1,679	3	?
Total	69,114	79/–	94,721	104/–	Sept 05
Special Operations Combat Support, Service Support, and Training Units	3,091	2/–	5,367	4/–	June 05
Iraqi Air Force	183	–/3	453	–/6	Nov 05
Iraqi Navy	521	–/2	582	–/3	TBD
Total	**74,159**	**83/5**	**103,390**	**111/9**	**Nov 05**

Ministry of the Interior

	On Duty As of May 2, 2005	Trained & Equipped	Trained & Equipped As of July 31, 2005	Total Authorized	Expected 100% Operational Date
Police	98,881	57,135	67,500	135,000	Nov 06
Civil Intervention Force Public Order Brigades	5,455	4,181	5,774	4,800	July 05
Eighth Mechanized Brigade	955	955	1,320	1,320	July 05
Special Police Commando Battalions	11,845	8,131	TBD	9,000	Mar 05
Emergency Response Units	216	212	350	401	Dec 05
Border Enforcement	18,779	15,583	19,156	28,360	Aug 06
Highway Patrol	1,464	1,089	2,000	6,300	July 06
Dignitary Protection	500	500	500	500	May 05
Total	**138,085**	**87,786**	**96,600**	**176,881**	**Aug 06**

Source: U.S. Embassy–Baghdad.

totals for "trained and equipped" for different force elements include personnel
with very different levels of training and equipment, and the figures for authorized manpower represent the personnel authorized in May 2005 rather than a
stable end goal.[4] That said, any careful reading of these data and comparison
with the force developments described in previous chapters shows that they
reflect massive progress over the previous year.

Ministry of Defense reporting in May 2005 also reflected progress in developing more effective forces, including the following:

- The data on the Iraqi Army show regular force strength of over 28,000
  men and thirty-four battalions by May 2005 versus one operational battalion in July 2004.
- The Iraqi National Guard was being merged into the army in a way that
  would eventually double its force strength and lay the groundwork for
  creating a national army that could defend the country as well as fight
  insurgents.
- Mechanized forces were active and expanding.
- Special operations forces were rapidly reaching strength of three battalions
  and nearly 2,000 men. These forces were being trained by MNF–I special
  forces and as elite elements with many of the same training programs
  being used in the West.
- The Iraqi Army was beginning to get the mix of combat support, service
  support, logistics, and training it needed to operate independently and as
  a self-sustaining force.
- The Iraqi Air Force was still in formation but expanding to strength of
  six squadrons.
- The Iraqi Navy was awaiting decisions on procuring major patrol boats
  and becoming more than a token force.

Similar trends affected Ministry of Interior forces. The security and special
police forces—some of the most effective units in Iraqi forces—continued to
gather strength. At the same time, a trained regular police force was slowly
beginning to emerge, along with the mix of supporting elements necessary to
deal with an ongoing insurgency, including the following:

- The core "trained and equipped" manpower in the police was now up to
  over 57,000 out of 98,881 on hand and rapidly expanding.
- The Iraqi Civil Intervention Force now had almost all of the manpower
  trained that was needed for its public order brigades and was rapidly
  developing a light mechanized brigade that could deal with insurgent
  attacks.
- Similar progress was taking place in creating the special police command
  brigades and emergency response units (ERU).
- Progress was being made in creating effective border forces.
- The full Dignitary Protection Force was trained, equipped, and active.

If one looks at the overall force strengths in table 9.1, Iraq had a combined total of one hundred operational battalions as of May 2005—eighty in the army and National Guard and twenty in the police—plus the army counterterrorist force and the police emergency response unit. Furthermore, Iraqi manpower and force strength continued to improve through the late spring and summer. By early August the total number of Iraqi military, regular police, and police units that could honestly be described as "trained and equipped" had risen from 96,000 in September 2004 to over 172,000 in early August 2005. The Ministry of Defense forces' portion of this total had reached 78,500 men—with 77,700 in the army, one hundred in the air force, and 700 in the navy. The Ministry of Interior forces totaled 93,800, with 63,500 in the police and highway patrol, and 30,300 in security units and other forces.[5]

Iraqi and MNF–I plans called for total Iraqi manpower to rise to 230,000 forces by the end of December 2005 and 270,000 by mid-2006.[6] This involved maintaining a good balance of military, regular police, and police units. Plans called for about 85,000 military in the Ministry of Defense by December and 145,000 special police and police in the Ministry of Interior. The 85,000 in the military were to include about 83,000 in the army (including the "national" forces originally envisioned, along with the former National Guard, and including combat support, service support, and training units). The remaining manpower was to include the special operations forces and the air force and navy. About 100,000 of the personnel in the Ministry of Interior were to be station/traffic/patrol police; in addition, nearly 20,000 more will be in the special police and the emergency response unit. The rest included the border forces, the highway patrol, and dignitary protection.

By June 2006 the total number of men in Iraqi Security Forces (military, regular police, and police units) was planned to reach approximately 270,000. The Ministry of Defense was to have about 90,000 and the Ministry of Interior about 180,000—provided that there was no change in the currently planned level of regular police. These manpower increases were to lead to continuing increases in the number of combat battalions. In July 2004, just after the Iraqi resumption of sovereignty, neither the Iraqi military nor the Iraqi police had any battalions that could be deployed nationally. Given the plans in early August 2005, the numbers of combat battalions in the Ministry of Defense were total around 106 by December 2005, with slightly under thirty additional battalion equivalents in the Ministry of Interior. In addition, Iraq was to have thirty-five brigade and ten division headquarters providing command and control of Ministry of Defense forces. Of these headquarters elements, some would be relatively mature, but at least a small number of each would still be relatively "young" or inexperienced.

Much of the Iraqi force generation effort was to shift to giving Iraqi combat forces the combat support and combat service support units they need. By December 2006 Iraq planned to field four motorized transportation regiments (working on the goal of one per division). Iraq also planned to generate six bomb disposal companies (with the goal of one per division). In addition, nearly seventy headquarters and service companies were to have been generated (although some equipment shortages will remain). The goal for these headquarters and service companies is one per battalion. By June 2006 the number of Ministry of Defense battalions was planned to reach 114. The number of the Ministry of Interior battalions was to remain unchanged, although their training will have been improved through recently initiated advanced programs.

The Meaning of a Constant Stream of Volunteers

Manpower quality was improving, but there were ongoing questions about motivation and loyalty. Recruiting and retention standards were being raised, as were the standards for promotion. Vetting was being improved overall, although reliable personnel data were often lacking in a war-torn society. In cases like the police, screening examinations adapted from Western police vetting and testing methods were also being applied for the first time in Iraq's history. Recruiting did not become a problem in spite of daily insurgent attacks on Iraqi forces. Insurgents stepped up their attacks on the military and security forces after the election and singled out Shi'ites for attack in events like the religious festivities surrounding the Shi'ite holiday of Ashura. Even so, the U.S. Department of Defense issued an update on February 16, 2005, that stated that between 8,000 and 10,000 Iraqis had shown up at an airfield in southern Iraq to join the army in *one day*.

Both Iraqi and U.S. experts agree that the elections did increase the number of Shi'ite and Kurdish recruits actually supporting the new government. Many of the Iraqis who joined the military, security, and police forces did so because they believed in Iraq's new political process and that Iraqi forces should take over from the Coalition. Much of the total stream of volunteers, however, had little to do with loyalty or patriotism. Serious nationwide unemployment problems continued to exist and pay continued to be a major factor driving such enlistments. Privates in the Iraqi Army earned about $333 a month while corporals could earn approximately $543.[7] These were large salaries for an average Iraqi.

It was also not clear what the end goal of many volunteers was and how strong their ties were to given sects and ethnic groups versus a belief in a unified Iraq. No breakouts are available by sect and ethnic origin, but Kurds were often motivated more to defend "Kurdistan" than Iraq, and Shi'ites to defend Shi'ite power. The number of ex-ethnic and sectarian militia Shi'ites and Kurds who joined some branch of the military, security, and police forces also raised questions about the ultimate loyalty of such volunteers.

The fact that Sunni clerics and politicians began to call for Sunnis to join the Iraqi security forces helped make them more national in terms of composition, but many who joined did so in an effort to counterbalance Shi'ite and Kurdish power. Sunni volunteers seemed to be even more motivated by money than Shi'ite and Kurdish volunteers, and at least some Sunnis left or deserted after getting training and became insurgents. Yet, progress was being made toward creating truly national forces. In the late spring of 2005, three of Iraq's army divisions had a Shi'ite commander, three a Sunni, one a Turcoman, and three a Sunni Kurd. The number of Sunnis volunteering had increased, and officer and NCO training was having some success in creating a leadership core trained as "national" forces.

Equipment Levels

Unclassified U.S. government reporting on the status of plans to equip Iraqi forces continued to be erratic during 2005. The *Iraq Weekly Status Report* continued to lack the detailed breakouts of the equipment effort that were a part of the earlier reporting efforts, and there was no way to relate the data MNSTC-I provided on deliveries to total requirements or requirement by force element.

At the same time, the past reporting of percentages of equipment relative to unit requirements presented problems because there was no definitive ISF structure to which the Iraqis adhered. By the fall of 2004 the Iraqi government had a tendency to create new units that were not part of the regular army force structure, such as the Al Muthanna Brigade or "Defenders of Baghdad," and change the equipment mix.

The regular police still had little equipment standardization and often had serious equipment shortfalls at least through April 2005. Unlike the army and elite security services, the regular police also lacked an efficient system for securing equipment and weapons and tracking actual equipment holdings—including weapons, ammunition, and explosives.[8]

Since there was no force plan agreed to by both the Iraqi government and MNSTC-I, there was no way to hold the Iraqis accountable for adhering to a given force mix.[9] Other MNSTC-I reporting indicated that some 30,000 of the police and security forces in figure 8.4 were not actually trained but were waiting to be trained.

There were continuing reports of inadequate equipment and facilities. For example, Chief of Staff General Richard Myers was told at one police training site in the Jordanian desert during a visit that some recruits use water bottles as simulated weapons during exercises because actual weapons were in short supply.[10] During a visit in June 2005 Iraqis often complained about the flow of equipment, and press reports continued to surface that equipment was being stolen and diverted.

In July 2005 Iraqi Ministry of Defense and U.S. military officials confirmed that they had uncovered a massive scheme to provide Iraqi security forces with substandard equipment that wasted some $300 million over the course of more than a year. According to these officials, at the heart of the scheme was former CPA appointed weapons buyer and former exile Ziad Tareq Cattan. Cattan was supposed to have flown across the globe dispensing money to furnish Iraq's forces with weapons with little oversight. Reports indicate that Cattan frequently charged a 10 percent "finder's fee" for each contract he negotiated and dispersed

TABLE 9.2

Total Equipment Deliveries to Iraqi Forces, July 2004 through May 2005 (as of June 1, 2005)

Type	Ministry of Defense Forces*		Ministry of Interior Forces	Issued in Late Week	Totals
Vehicles	5,665	(1,434)	4,874	114	10,539
Radios	10,537	(6,933)	13,514	0	24,051
PKM Machine Guns	6,595	(2,706)	487	0	7,082
AK-47s	87,740	(36,718)	67,294	3,070	155,034
Pistols	15,160	(6,721)	125,139	6,240	140,239
Ammunition	193,983,724**	(23,431,226)	111,690,813**	3,567,880	305,587,537
Uniforms	280,267	(92,521)	281,301	4,700	561,568
Helmets	87,250	(457,272)	5,633	40	92,883
Body Armor	80,761	(40,903)	87,343	7,410	168,104

* Figures in parentheses show amounts delivered to National Guard before merger with the army.
** Includes 100 million rounds of ammunition pre-positioned in eleven sites in Iraq.
Source: U.S. Embassy–Baghdad.

kickbacks to Iraqi Ministry of Defense buyers, even though the various helicopters, armored personnel carriers, and machine guns he acquired were defective, cheap imitations, or extremely worn. Cattan maintained his innocence and asserted that the Coalition so closely monitored the program that such a high level of corruption would be impossible.[11]

U.S. officials do concede that problems arose because the MNF–I often bought equipment without consulting the Iraqi government or informing it of the details of such purchases. This allowed Ministry of Defense officials to claim that they made purchases out of ignorance, although in most cases such purchase clearly involved serious corruption. Several of the Coalition officials interviewed, however, indicate that the secretary general of the Ministry of Defense in the interim Iraqi government tolerated high levels of corruption and inefficiency and that it was not until the new government took office in April 2005 that serious efforts were made to eliminate gross inefficiency and corruption in areas like military equipment purchases. One example they cited was that the Defense Ministry staff deliberately sabotaged the air-conditioning in the ministry to get kickbacks from the service workers who repaired the equipment.

Nevertheless, the flow of equipment had begun to reach the point where most of the previous shortfalls in basic equipment had been overcome, and some units were getting advanced weapons and equipment. MNSTC–I reporting does provide useful data on total equipment deliveries during the period, as well as weekly reports that show shorter-term deliveries for part of the period. Table 9.2 shows major equipment deliveries between July 2004 and May 2005. Tables 9.3 and 9.4 summarize the unclassified data available on weekly deliveries. Both tables show that most weekly equipment deliveries consisted of relatively light weapons and unarmored vehicles, although Iraqi forces now

TABLE 9.3

Typical Weekly Flows of Equipment Deliveries to All Iraqi Forces, January through March 2005

Type	Week Ending					
	Jan. 8	Jan. 15	Jan. 22	Jan. 29	March 19	March 26
AK-47	2,770	3,459	870	3,310	320	200
RPKs	—	—	—	—	—	—
Sniper rifles	—	—	—	—	—	—
Pistols/handguns	1,500	1,140	437	320	—	330
Grenades	—	—	—	—	—	—
Body armor	3,742	1,000	2,000	5,839	1,250	2,400
Night-vision goggles	—	—	—	—	—	—
Global Positioning Systems	—	—	—	—	—	—
Mobile generators	—	—	—	—	—	—
A-Back scatter	—	—	—	—	—	—
X-Ray vans	—	—	—	—	—	—
Ashok Leylands	—	—	—	—	—	—
Chevy Luminas	—	—	—	—	40	16
Chevy Trailblazers	—	—	—	—	32	62
Chevy LUV trucks	—	—	—	—	—	—
Landcruisers	—	—	—	—	—	—
Nissan pick-up trucks		-	—	—	—	—
Nissan Cabstars	—	—	—	—	34	8
5-ton trucks	—	—	—	—	—	—
21/2-ton trucks	—	—	—	—	19	31
Ambulances	—	—	—	—	—	—
Water trailers	—	—	—	—	—	—
Helmets	10,957	3,659	—	1,213	—	—
PKM machine guns	153	168	—	331	—	—
Up-armored Humvees	—	—	—	—	10	—
Explosive Detector Systems	—	—	—	—	2	—
T-55 recovery vehicles	—	—	—	—	1	—
BMPs	—	—	—	—	28	—
Vehicles (unspecified)	64	61	50	90	—	—
Ammunition (million rounds)	9.5	2.8	3.1	3.1	4.7	.42

Source: Adapted from various editions of the MNSTC–I *Advisor*, data provided by MNSTC–I J–4. Reports did not indicate supplies delivered between February 5 and March 12, 2005.

had extensive communications gear and were getting steadily more sophisticated equipment such as sniper rifles, night-vision goggles, GPS systems, and x-ray vans.

This progress continued into the summer. A report by the Department of Defense in late July described the Iraqi Army equipment effort as follows:

> Equipment shortages have been reduced as equipment procured with U.S.-funded contracts began to flow into Iraq during mid-to-late 2004. The Iraqi Army now has 60 percent of its total authorized equipment, including more than 100 percent of AK-47 requirements. The Iraqi Security Forces Fund (ISFF), as provided for by Public Law 109-13, will further enable MNF–I to meet critical requirements. Furthermore, although there is variance in the rate of absenteeism, AWOL, attrition, and desertion among the Iraqi Army, rates have diminished

TABLE 9.4

Typical Weekly Flows of Equipment Deliveries to All Iraqi Forces, April through May 2005

Type	Week Ending						
	April 2	April 9	April 16	April 23	April 30	May 7	May 14
AK-47	2,610	—	7,272	5,724	1,250	3,400	3,900
RPKs	—	54	118	—	50	—	—
Sniper rifles	—	—	—	—	648	4	—
Pistols/handguns	—	500	11,600	5,760	—	—	—
Grenades	—	—	—	—	—	7,512	4,480
Body armor	7,963	6,460	2,200	5,402	1,799	3,860	2,750
Night-vision goggles	—	600	12	—	—	—	—
Global Positioning Systems	—	−301	—	—	—	—	—
Mobile generators	—	—	—	—	—	4	—
A-Back scatter	—	—	—	—	—	—	—
X-Ray vans	—	—	—	2	—	—	2
Ashok Leylands	—	—	—	18	4	91	15
Chevy Luminas	—	—	126	344	90	33	—
Chevy Trailblazers	26	212	146	250	—	—	50
Chevy LUV trucks	31	523	400	411	240	—	—
Landcruisers	—	—	—	56	—	—	—
Nissan pick-up trucks	4	—	—	—	—	—	—
Nissan Cabstars	23	—	—	—	—	—	—
5-ton trucks	—	—	—	—	—	—	4
21/2-ton trucks	—	—	—	—	57	4	—
Ambulances	—	—	—	—	20	—	—
Water trailers	—	—	—	12	—	—	—
Helmets	—	—	—	—	—	—	—
PKM machine guns	—	—	—	—	—	—	—
Up-armored Humvees	—	—	—	—	—	—	—
Explosive detector systems	—	—	—	—	—	—	—
T-55 Recovery vehicles	—	—	—	—	—	—	—
BMPs	—	—	—	—	—	—	—
Vehicles (unspecified)	—	—	—	—	—	—	—
Ammunition (million rounds)	0.53	0.48	2.5	6.6	21,4	2.9	13.3

Source: Adapted from various editions of the MNSTC–I *Advisor*; data provided by MNSTC–I J–4.

significantly and are now around one percent for some divisions. Still, units that are conducting operations and units that relocate elsewhere in Iraq experience a surge in absenteeism.

U.S.-funded procurement has equipped infantry units primarily with former Warsaw Pact weapons and vehicles. The MOD [Ministry of Defense], using its funds, has also sought U.S.-standard vehicles such as HMMWVs and M-113 armored personnel carriers. Mechanized forces are being trained using T-55 and T-72 tanks, BMP-1s and MTLBs. The ISOF is currently equipped with M4 carbines, M9 pistols, night-vision devices, M24 sniper systems, M240 machine guns, 12 gauge shotguns, 50-caliber machine guns, global positioning systems equipment, and surveillance equipment.

The Iraqi Navy currently has approximately 500 trained sailors on duty. It is equipped with five Predator Class Patrol Boats (PB), 24 Fast Aluminum Boats

(Duel Outboard Engines), 10 rigid-hull inflatable boats, and various small arms and night vision devices. The Iraqi Navy will further equip themselves with six Al Faw Class Patrol Boats (the first of which was delivered in July 2005) and two Off-Shore Support Vessels. With some exceptions, the responsibility for logistical support of the Iraqi Navy has been handed over to the Umm Qasr Base Support Unit (BSU). Maritime and Riverine Advisory Support Team (M&R AST) members provide advice and assistance to both the BSU and the Iraqi Navy Logistics Department in order to cultivate a cooperative working relationship.

The Air Force currently has over 100 personnel and has a fleet of 9 helicopters (4 UH-1H and 5 Jet Ranger), 3 C-130s, and 8 single-engine propeller-driven observation airplanes (6 CompAir turboprop aircraft and 2 Seeker piston aircraft).

The IPS uses a variety of equipment, including Chevy Luv and Nissan pick-up trucks, mid-size SUVs, AK 47s, PKC machine guns, Glock pistols, HF radios, and body armor. The goal is for each police officer and station to be equipped with mission-essential equipment.[12]

The Quality of Equipment Deliveries

Opinions differ of the adequacy of this equipment in giving Iraqi forces the equipment they needed to stand on their own against the best armed insurgents and insurgent ambushes. A number of U.S. advisers, Iraqis, and outside observers feel that the Coalition was far too slow to provide the kind of armor and protected vehicles that Coalition forces had found to be vital for their survival. In fact, Iraqi forces felt so strongly about the need for added armor that some army, National Guard, and elite police elements started reconditioning abandoned armor in various weapons depots or "requisitioned" armor taken from the Iranian exile forces in the Iranian People's Mujahideen.

The MNSTC–I was seeking armor from a variety of sources, including other Arab countries and Eastern European countries that operated the same kinds of Soviet bloc weapons the Iraqis were familiar with and could maintain and sustain. For example, deliveries of Hungarian T-72s were under way to the army, and armored Land Rovers were being delivered to the police.

At the same time, some MNSTC–I experts argue that the lighter equipment shown in tables 9.2 through 9.4 was what the Iraqis needed for most counterinsurgency and counterterrorist missions and what they can actually maintain and support. One MNSTC–I expert put it this way:

> Light forces are often more versatile and essential in a counter-insurgency (assuming they have the right weapons, body armor, Kevlar helmets, etc.), but would also point out that we *are* providing heavy forces to the Iraqis. A mechanized division is already in the military force structure plan and an additional motorized division is being considered. The Iraqi Army already has one armored and one mechanized battalion in operation; another mechanized battalion is in training. The police forces have two mechanized battalions operating under a brigade headquarters; a third battalion is in training. The latter, in fact, will be

provided U.S.-made Armored Security Vehicles, superb wheeled armored vehicles made by Cadillac Gage and used by our own Military Police. In addition,
numerous APCs are now on hand. Up-armored HMMWVs are on order and
other wheeled armored vehicles are either on hand or on order.

A heavier force, whether for force protection or for defense against invasion,
also costs more. The Iraqis can't really afford to purchase, operate and
maintain such a force—even with the multiple billions of dollars we are providing.
Given fiscal constraints that will last for several years, Iraq has to consider
opportunity costs before committing to the addition of more heavy forces. The
Iraqis might decide that the additional motorized division being considered might
better be traded for less-expensive light forces. They could instead decide to
spend that money on much-needed infrastructure protection forces, which may
be even more important strategically.

It should not be expected that the Iraqi military will eventually look like the
American military nor that an American-like military will be needed to defeat
the insurgency.

These views have some validity and do recognize the fact that Iraqi forces did
need protected vehicles. At the same time, they do not refute the fact that
providing nothing but light firepower, and protection in the form of body armor,
has presented significant operating problems for Iraqis who have come up
against well-armed insurgents.

Tables 9.2 through 9.4 also contain a highly diverse mix of civilian vehicles
likely to create future maintenance problems. Certainly, many Iraqi officers feel
their equipment is too light and too vulnerable and see a dual standard in
the Coalition's steady uparmoring of its equipment. This helps explain why
some Iraqi units have taken armor and weapons seized from Iranian People's
Mujahideen (MEK) forces, and others have reconditioned abandoned armor
taken from equipment dumps.

It should also be noted that the quality of the facilities for security force
trainees and fully graduated soldiers remained erratic. While some Iraqi bases
and forts were decently furbished, others remained in an appalling state of
disrepair. For instance, in July 2005 the Fifth Brigade of the Iraqi Army, the unit
tapped to guard the Green Zone, was stationed in a filthy hangar at the Muthanna
airfield with insufficient water supplies for showering, a nonexistent sewage system,
and only occasional electricity. Garbage heaps were abundant, and the conditions
had eroded morale with some Iraqis considering quitting. Other soldiers could
not understand why the United States could not seem to fix what seemed to
be simple problems and viewed the conditions as a sign of disrespect. Fortu-
nately, air-conditioned tents and a row of showers were under construction at
the end of July 2005.[13]

Beginning to Create Logistics and Support Capabilities

Iraqi forces were also beginning to develop the capability to support, maintain, and sustain their equipment. MNF–I and Iraqi forces had created plans to

develop base support units (BSUs) to support the equipment Iraqi forces were getting and create motorized transport units to provide the necessary supplies with both transport assets and the firepower to protect themselves. The latter units—such as the Third Motor Transportation Regiment—were beginning to become active in the spring of 2005, and the plans for BSUs can be summarized as follows:

- Three major BSUs were to be created to cover the entire country, each to support forces within a 200-kilometer radius. These include one at Kasik in the North (turnover date of August 2005), Taji in central Iraq (turnover date of September 2005), and Tallil in the South (turnover date of June 2005).
- Smaller standard BSUs were to be created throughout the country to support operations within a sixty-five-kilometer radius. These included facilities at Kirkuk (turnover date of June 2005), KMTB (turnover date of July 2005), Habbaniyah (turnover date of November 2005), Rustamayiah (turnover date of July 2005), Biap (turnover date of September 2005), Numaniyah (turnover date of May 2005), and Umm Qasr (turnover date of March 2005).

Iraqi forces still had a long way to go before they could provide their combat units, or "teeth," with the proper mix of combat and service support, major combat unit structures and headquarters, logistics, and other facilities. They still tended to be all "teeth" and no "tail." They had, however, now begun the journey and one that offered real hope that they might be able take over much or most of the combat mission from Coalition forces within a few years.

Vetting and Training

Iraqi forces got steadily better vetting and training in 2005. It is unclear exactly how men and women had been screened before the improved vetting process, but MNSTC–I indicated that it could do a better job of checking Iraqi recruits against Ba'ath and other political party records. Iraqis now checked the criminal record of the recruit as well. MNSTC–I sources reported that all Iraqi recruits now underwent basic training in the Iraqi military, and the author's visits to the various training centers involved showed that Iraqis were developing their own training curricula.

There was still some corruption and favoritism in selection of recruits, but much of the problem occurred before actual selection, and the vetting and screening process was becoming more professional once recruits were selected. Military and police units had begun to get serious screening, and police recruits had to pass written screening tests modified from those used by U.S. police forces. MNSTC–I stated, "Training—of all forces, but especially police forces—undergoes constant analysis in light of operational experience. The course length and curriculum of the Transition Integration Program has been standardized in all of the Iraqi police academies. The length of basic training for police recruits has been increased by 25 percent by adding two weeks of regional training on threats and other conditions in the new policeman's area of responsibility. Training at all police schools is now much more likely to be led by an Iraqi and to be "hands on" training instead of simple academic instruction."[14]

MNSTC–I had personnel training the staffs of brigades and divisions as well as Iraqis involved in reconnaissance and surveillance activity. It was deeply engaged in a variety of mentoring programs within ministries and had programs in place for the navy and air force. MNSTC–I was directly involved in training the SWAT teams and other specialized counterinsurgency and protection forces for each province and now offered a variety of police training courses ranging from case management to forensics.

The progress taking place is illustrated by the following milestones:

- A total of 4,516 Iraqi police officers graduated in May from basic courses in Al Kut, Sulaymaniyah, Al Hillah, Jordan, and Baghdad.
- A total of 157 Iraqi officers graduated in May from advanced and specialty courses at the Adnan training facility.
- The first 213 recruits for the Iraqi Navy's direct recruit replacement program (DRR) began training for antiterrorist operations and oil terminal security at the end of May.
- A total of 121 Iraqi police officers graduated in June from advanced and specialty courses at the Adnan training facility. Fifty-eight graduated from a basic criminal investigation course, twenty-nine from a critical incident management course, eighteen from a course on counterterrorism investigations, and sixteen from executive leadership courses.
- As of early June 2005, 32,500 police recruits had completed the eight-week new recruit training program, and 36,000 police with previous training had completed the three-week Transition Integration Program.
- The command of the Kirkuk military training base was transferred from MNSTC–I to Iraqi Brigadier General Abd Zaid.

More generally, the systematic creation of formal training programs for each of the individual elements of Iraqi forces is summarized in table 9.5. By now, the training programs had become large enough in scale and sufficiently institutionalized to have real impact. As table 9.6 shows, these basic-training programs were now supplemented by specialized training programs for each element of the Ministry of Defense and Ministry of Interior forces.

Ministry of Defense Training

By this time Coalition Military Assistance Training Team (CMATT) had all of the advisers it was authorized and was broadening its missions to help the Iraqis make the eventual transfer to Iraqi funding and deal with issues like planning, providing intelligence, and adding the necessary sustainment and support capabilities. Ministry of Defense forces received both general and specialized training: Iraqi Army recruits underwent four weeks of cadre training and eight weeks of basic training.

TABLE 9.5
MNSTC–I Training Program for Iraqi Forces by Force Element

Component	Training
Iraqi Police Service	Former academy graduates: Three-week Transition Integration Program New recruits: Eight-week academy; two-week integration training Mid-careers: Specialized training
Public Order and Mechanized Police	Five-week specialized training
Special Police Commandos	Three-week specialized training
Emergency Response Unit	Four-week basic; four-week advanced specialized training
Department of Border Enforcement	Four-week academy and specialized training
Highway Patrol	Three-week Transition Integration Program training and eight-week academy training
Bureau of Dignitary Protection	Three-week initial training and two- to three-week advanced training Follow-on mentoring by U.S. contractors and Navy SEALs
Iraq Regular Army	Cadre: Four weeks Basic and small unit training: eight weeks (additional skill and collective training varies)
Iraqi National Guard	Basic training: three weeks Collective training: four weeks
Iraqi Intervention Force	Cadre: four weeks Basic/collective training: eight weeks Urban operations training: five weeks
Iraqi Regular Army and Intervention Force	Direct recruit replacement training: three weeks for former soldiers
Iraqi Special Ops Force	Field training provided by U.S. special
Commando Battalion	forces (small-unit tactics and Ranger-type training)
Counterterrorist Task Force	Thirteen-week special operator course
Air Force	Varies by specialty: one to six months
Navy	Eight-week basic, followed by specialized training at Umm Qasr

Source: MNSTC–I, June 2005.

The MNF–I summarized this progress as follows in July 2005:

Training for the individual soldier is divided into two areas: training for new recruits and training for former soldiers. Training for new recruits takes a total of nine weeks and has usually been conducted at the Iraqi Training Brigade (ITB) in Kirkush. Training for former soldiers lasts three to four weeks and has usually been conducted in divisional locations with graduates generally being assigned to the division that trains them. All personnel receive standard infantry-style training; selected soldiers receive specialized training in Army Military Occupational Specialties, such as Signal, Administration, Supply, Armor, Transport, Maintenance and Military Police.

Membership in the Iraqi Special Forces Brigade requires additional training. All Iraqi Special Operations Forces (ISOF) soldiers undergo a three-week Assessment and Selection course. Iraqi Counter Terrorist Forces (ICTF) soldiers receive 12 weeks of training in Jordan on Close Quarters Battle (CQB), Planning, and

TABLE 9.6
Specialty Training Courses

Professional Development and Education	Number
Joint Staff College Instructors	24*
Military Academy Graduates	91
Military Cadets	296*
Contracting Capacity Course	40
Combat Support Courses	**Number**
Intelligence	425
Engineers	85
Signal	20
Military Police	85
Combat Service Support Courses	**Number**
Bomb Disposal	192*
Transportation	813
Maintenance	147
Supply	136
Logistics Officer	50
Medical	20
Administration	20
Instructor Training	301
Air Traffic Controllers	4**
Special Police Courses (through May 31, 2005)	**Number**
Basic Criminal Investigation	1,712
Internal Controls	667
Violent Crimes and Kidnapping	648
Junior, Mid-Level, and Senior Management and Leadership	937
Organized Crime, Drug Enforcement, and Criminal Intelligence	450
Interviews and Interrogations	371
Explosive Hazard Awareness and Post-blast Investigation	262
Interrogation Techniques	22*
Counterterrorism Investigations	136
Critical Incident Management and Incident Command System	470
SWAT (13 of 20 teams)	360
Dignitary Protection, Motorcade Escorts, and Site Security	1,067

* In training.
** On-the-job training.
Source: MNSTC–I, June 2005.

Leadership before they conduct Direct Action missions. ISOF soldiers undergo rigorous training emphasizing small unit tactics, counterterrorism, and unit self-reliance. Improved qualification and vetting standards minimize absenteeism and the risk of insurgent infiltration. The Brigade's chain of command and officer cadre are assessed as being very effective. ISOF elements have been conducting operations for the past year. They have played crucial roles in major combat operations along side of, and sometimes independently of, Coalition forces.

A small number of Army personnel attend advanced training with NATO and U.S. Army schools.

MNF–I has also implemented, in partnership with the MOD [Ministry of Defense], a program to embed Military Transition Teams at the battalion, brigade, and division level. These teams provide Transition Readiness Assessments (TRAs) to MNC–I identifying areas of progress and shortcomings, ultimately leading to those individual units being ready to assume independent control of their area of responsibility. These assessments take into account a variety of criteria similar to but not identical to what the U.S. Army uses to evaluate its units' operational readiness focused on personnel, command and control, training, sustainment/logistics, equipment, and leadership.

It is useful to place these readiness assessments in perspective. The first Iraqi Army infantry battalions finished basic training in early 2004 and were immediately required in combat without complete equipment. They had inadequate time to develop unit cohesiveness, staff proficiency, and a leadership chain of command that is fundamental to a military unit. Ministry of Defense forces did not perform well in Fallujah–several battalions collapsed. Absent-without-leave (AWOL) rates among regular army units were in double digits and remained so for the rest of the year.

Although such problems have not been entirely solved, they have been addressed in large measure because of the ability to put to good use the security sector funding from the Iraq Reconstruction and Relief Fund (IRRF) as provided for by Public Law 108-106. Equipment shortages have been reduced as equipment procured with U.S.-funded contracts began to flow into Iraq during mid-to-late 2004.[15]

The Iraqi Intervention Force (IIF) received the same training as the Iraqi Army with an additional five weeks of urban operations training. Former soldiers who sought enlistment in the army of IIF underwent three weeks of direct replacement training, followed by unit training. The Iraqi National Guard (ING) had previously been trained largely by the major subordinate commanders (MSC), and the training of the ING varied by unit but now was being integrated into the army training program.[16]

The Iraqi Special Operations Forces was divided into the Commando Battalion and the Counter Terrorist Task Force. The Commando Battalion was trained in small-unit tactics and experiences other training similar to U.S. Rangers. This training was administered by U.S. special forces and included advanced training in facilities like "shoot rooms." The Counter Terrorist Task Force was specially selected and assessed and then subjected to a thirteen-week special operator course. Air Force training varied by specialty anywhere from one to six months. Some of this training (the C-130 crews) was done in the United States. The navy recruits underwent eight weeks of basic training and were then relocated to Umm Qasr for specialized training.[17]

MNSTC–I's overall training concept had advanced to the point where it could stress "total force development" for the leadership of the Iraqi armed forces with a clear career path for training both officers and NCOs.

- Basic officer training took place in a twelve-month program at the Iraqi Military Academy at Zahko, using a program Iraqi officers had adapted from the one British forces used at Sandhurst. Promotion led to training at a company commander's course, which was to go into operation in October 2005. The next promotion meant attending a Junior Staff College that was to open in September and then attendance at a Senior Staff College that was to open that same month. Promotion to top ranks meant attending a national defense college, which was to open in 2006.

- The NCO training program was in development, but former Iraqi NCOs underwent a three-week general training course, followed by three to six weeks of branch training. Promotion then involved a four-week squad leader course and a platoon sergeant course that was to open in August 2005. An eight- to twelve-week first sergeant's course was to open in 2006, followed a four- to eight-week warrant officer and sergeant major course at a new academy scheduled to open in March 2006.

These programs would take years to fully train the leadership of Iraqi forces, and many officers and NCOs would serve for sometime without such training, but the very fact such a program existed and had started to operate showed significant progress.

Ministry of Interior Training

The vetting and training of the Iraqi Police Service (IPS) continued to lag behind that of the military, in part because of a slower start and more constant changes and in part because of a lag of resources. In spite of efforts to strengthen the Civilian Police Assistance Training Team (CPATT), it only had about 70 percent of the advisers it was authorized in June 2005 and had staffing problems in getting civilian and other experts in key areas like intelligence, budgeting, manpower, and plans.

A report by the inspector generals of the State Department and of the Department of Defense found the following continuing problems in the vetting and training effort as of the end of April 2005. While such problems are scarcely unexpected given the heritage of Saddam Hussein and the mistakes made by the CPA, they provide an important set of insights into the practical problems that occur in trying simultaneously to create a force and fight a war and the lessons that should be learned for the future. The report states:

> Much of the planning and execution of the IPS training program has been done by Coalition military leaders without sufficient input from Iraqi officials. One high-ranking official in CPATT told the IG Team that "... until recently, Iraqi views were given absolutely no consideration. They [the Iraqis] still do not have a deciding vote." Another stated, "We are not learning our lessons. We still develop great ideas and plans, and then lay them on Iraqis."
>
> During the time of the CPA, such an approach was both inevitable and, perhaps, appropriate. In the wake of the collapse of the Saddam Hussein regime, no Iraqi policy makers were in a position to make authoritative decisions.
>
> Overall, there is little consensus on how to train Iraqi police. One exception is the universal agreement that the eight weeks devoted to the basic course

is insufficient time to produce a capable policeman. Thus, there is tacit consensus that the training program to date has not created an effective IPS. (There is no consensus on how long a time would be required to achieve the desired results.)

The eight-week training course yields a maximum 320 hours of training time. To accommodate an increase in the hours spent on counter-insurgency training and self-defense skills without increasing overall course length, some class room subjects were eliminated, while other subjects were reduced. Courses on democratic policing principles are critically important to the mission and should not be eliminated or reduced.

Currently, the basic course does not include night training. As the Coalition adapts its training plan to deal with the insurgency, it must prepare the IPS to conduct operations in the dark. The enemy is using the cover of darkness to plant improvised explosive devices and conduct other night time operations. Experts agree that police tactics, patrolling, and intelligence gathering activities during day light hours are markedly different than the tactics employed at night.

The Team observed a lack of discipline among the basic recruits at several of the training sites. This was not the case at those facilities conducting specialized training for the Emergency Response Unit (ERU) and the Public Order Brigades (POB). As practiced in the specialized training programs, the use of properly trained Iraqi drill instructors would facilitate discipline and help to create a sense of esprit-de-corps among the cadets. While it is recognized that Iraqis are family and tribal oriented, the training programs must foster a sense of esprit-de-corps and teach teamwork.

As this assessment was being conducted, MNSTC–I and CPATT leaders were planning to lengthen the basic training course to 10 weeks. . . . At the outset of the CPA effort to build IPS capacity, the assumption—even to some extent, the reality—was that training could be molded within a rapidly stabilizing political and security environment. The unexpected virulence and scope of subsequent terrorism and insurgency induced changes in the program, but such modifications have lagged [behind] the "street reality" in Iraq.

Adjustments in the training course have been and are being made. During this assessment, the JIPTC [Jordan International Police Training Center] staff completed a CPATT-directed revision of the basic curriculum to include more "hands on," self-protection exercises. Other IPS in-country academies are adopting these changes. IP personnel and MOI [Ministry of Interior] officials strongly support the adjustments and the shift in emphasis.

. . . trainees allegedly have been selected more on a basis of favoritism than on capability or potential.

In the Baghdad area, applicants learn of recruitment via word of mouth. In light of the relatively good pay prospects, this simple system attracts more than enough applicants. Many simply show up at police stations or at the Baghdad Police College (BPC). The IG Team observed recruiting and selection (a sequentially seamless process) at the BPC. After passing through elemental security screening, aspirants are admitted into the walled facility on a first-come, first-served basis. If, as frequently is the case, more show up than can be processed on a given day, identifying data is taken on those who are turned away. They are given numbers (again, in order of their place in the line) and told when to return to be among those first admitted.

Once admitted to the facility, the process is very basic. On entry into a classroom setting, each applicant is given an identifying number that corresponds to his or her file. The first step is a timed written test, designed and administered by an American contractor. Iraqis proctor the test. Results are machine graded in the presence of an IPS official. Since responding to questions involves understanding the written material, the test presumably establishes basic literacy of the person being examined. Applicants who do not achieve the minimal threshold score are called forward by number, courteously escorted off the premises, and dismissed.

A second stage in the process consists of an interview and physical examination. At BPC, the processing observed by the IG Team covered all of the minimum standards prescribed by the CPA.

The physical exam appears especially cursory. At the time of the IG Team's observation, most applicants appeared to be in their late teens to early 20's and fully functional without any physical handicaps. However, a physician stated he did not have sufficient time to complete a thorough medical examination of so many applicants in such a short time (70 students on the day in question). Consequently, the examination consisted of completing a medical history questionnaire, checking applicants' eyes for squinting, and verifying a steady pulse. The doctor then pronounced the applicant fit or unfit. There was no testing to determine physical stamina, dental review, or body checks for even readily detectable identification marks such as scars or tattoos. The doctor also told the IG Team that a considerable number of students appeared to suffer some form of mental problems, hard to diagnose during the interview process. Elsewhere in the country, MSCs recruit and select candidates to fill available training slots as directed in a monthly "fragmentary order" (FRAGO). The MSCs use various recruiting tools including recommendations from the command's recruiting unit, IPLOs, serving IPS personnel, and from other reliable sources in a given community. These Coalition recruiters are encouraged to accept all recruits who are sponsored by local officials.

Despite the written test, attrition statistics show that illiterates make it into basic training. Less frequent are cases of those with easily detectable physical or mental impairment. Some cadets clearly are older than the established age limits. . . . Occasionally, trainees are separated when information is revealed about past criminal behavior or allegations of involvement with the insurgency. Other common causes for dismissal from training are infractions of discipline, illness or inability to adjust (normally homesickness). The team was advised at JIPTC that a surprising number of students arrive with drugs that are confiscated during in-processing. These instances support a widely shared perception that screening of IP candidates is at best superficial, sometimes inconsistent.

To date, all those going to JIPTC for basic training have been recruited and selected by the MSCs. Even though the processes used by the MSCs theoretically are the same as those used by the Iraqi recruiters, the MOI apparently does not have a sense of commitment to those trainees who enter training via the MSC route.

Many police chiefs and their deputies are accustomed to the IPS culture that prevailed during the Saddam Hussein era. Old habits and methods (e.g., reliance on forced confessions, taking the initiative only when directed, and rigid delineation of responsibilities) work against effective and efficient policing.

The need for attention to these aspects is self-evident. In instances where good leadership is present (often provided by Coalition military personnel or International Police Liaison Officers (IPLOs)), IPs perform satisfactorily and stand their ground in the face of attacks. The absence of such leaders correlates closely with instances in which IP stations have been overrun, often with shocking casualties among ill-prepared and ill-led policemen.

Senior IP officers interviewed by the IG Team were outspoken in identifying insufficient numbers (and quality) of officers as a major weakness within the IPS. They urged restoration of the former "police college" system, preferably with a three-year curriculum, such as that at the Baghdad Police College (BPC) that predated the Saddam Hussein era. MNSTC–I and CPATT are moving ahead to restart officer training at the BPC, although present plans are for a six-month course rather than the more extended course favored by the Iraqis. In a free-form discussion with the Chargé d'Affaires, IPLOs were equally vocal in identifying leadership development as a major weakness in the present training program.

Critics within CPATT and among some instructors assert that the MOI's selection of Candidates (for advanced training) appears to be based more on cronyism and loyalties than on merit. For some attendees, the courses are regarded as a reward, not as a serious professional commitment. The IPS major general at Adnan Palace is among those who urge incorporation of more rigorous testing as courses progress. He believes that is the only way to get and keep the students' attention.

Inducting criminals into the IPS is a continual concern. Even more troubling is infiltration by intending terrorists or insurgents. There is sufficient evidence to conclude that such persons indeed are among the ranks of the IPS. This underscores the need for the most rigorous possible review of each applicant's records. To gain an understanding of the vetting process, the IG Team met with Iraqi police cadets and instructors, International Police Trainers (IPT) at various police training academies, officials of the MOI and Coalition authorities. All Iraqis interviewed suggested that vetting performed by Coalition forces is not as thorough as what could be done by the MOI. The IG Team was told that, especially early in 2003, only a cursory background check, if even that, was conducted before policemen were trained or entered the force.

In terms of policy, several IPS interviewees expressed reservations about aspects of Coalition vetting. For example, they contended that no Iraqi would recruit or employ a candidate who had tattoos. In their culture body tattoos are indicative of a person who has a criminal record or at least a propensity to violate societal norms. Likewise, the longer-term prospects for female members of the IP are problematic. In some areas, notably in Kurdistan, women are accepted members in both the police and military. In most other regions, it is likely that female IPs will be relegated to supporting roles, at best as administrative staff.

It is widely contended that the vetting process is stymied by the lack or inaccessibility of personnel or police records. As with recruiting and selection of trainees, vetting is especially difficult if carried out by non-Iraqis. Indeed, the Coalition's ability to conduct thorough background checks on IPS personnel is severely limited. Use of polygraph techniques is impracticable, given the numbers of candidates to be processed. Effective communications across language and cultural barriers is an issue too.[18]

These comments must be kept in perspective. The report also found that real progress was being made, that Iraqi forces were becoming more effective, and that the Iraqi Ministry of Interior was taking over more and more of the burden of planning and managing the development and training of the Iraqi police and security services. It also found that the CPATT now was strong enough to have a major impact and was working closely with the new minister of interior and his staff.

The training program had reached the point where large numbers of Ministry of Interior forces now had serious training. While the program still had defects, the Iraqi Police Service did give new recruits eight weeks of serious training at the police academy, and the program involved significant counterinsurgency training. Those officers who served and continue to serve received specialized training and sustainment training. Advanced police training took place at the Adnan Palace Complex, where specialized police training had been taking place since mid-2004 and is administered by a wide range of U.S. law enforcement agencies. There were over 500 individuals from the Coalition training Iraqi police officers. A little less than half of these trainers worked from the JIPTC in Amman, Jordan, while the rest operated directly in Iraq. Civil Intervention Force recruits underwent five weeks of specialized training, while the special police commandos got three weeks of specialized training.

Moreover, as the report by the inspector generals notes, a major effort was under way to train those Iraqi police officers with past service who had been retained by the new government:

> One of the challenges of building a viable police force was to retain the veteran policemen who served during the Saddam Hussein era. This group must be retrained with the objective of instilling modern police techniques, respect for human rights, and democratic policing principles. To achieve this goal, CPATT implemented an in-service training program called the Transition Integration Program (TIP). The program also incorporates attention to applicable Iraqi criminal law and procedures to be observed for arrest and detention. Additionally, the TIP was designed to accomplish several other key tasks:
>
> • Identify existing IPS personnel who were academically, intellectually, or morally unsuitable;

- Identify potential leaders within the IPS; and
- Identify potential IPS instructors and field training officers.

TIP training takes place at Coalition forward operating bases (FOBs) and at some of the regional academies. The course is three weeks long and covers 126 hours of instruction. Course subjects include: (1) the philosophy and role of the IPS, (2) prohibitions against torture, (3) police ethics and values, and (4) the code of conduct. About one third of the course time is devoted to firearms instruction on 9mm and AK–47 weaponry.

As of late April this year, 35,526 IPS veterans had completed the TIP program. The program, however, is not without its critics. For example, the Chief of Police at al-Hillah would like to replace the three week TIP course with a longer in-service course that would encompass map reading, hostage rescue, night tactics, etc. As in the case of basic training, the argument is for hands-on training as opposed to the more theoretical approach of the present TIP program.

... the TIP program is a worthwhile and value-added endeavor. By definition, TIP training is for in-service IPs, and satisfies one of the MOI's [Ministry of Interior's] objectives. Many policemen who have attended the course appear to be well motivated and dedicated to the concept of a rule of law regime at the service of Iraqi citizens. The TIP training imparts skills directly relevant to those objectives.[19]

Members of the Emergency Response Unit got eight weeks of specialized training with follow-on mentoring by Coalition advisers. The recruits for the Department of Border Enforcement received four weeks training at the academy along with specialized training. The highway patrol officers underwent three weeks of TIP training and eight weeks of academy training. Lastly, the Bureau of Dignitary Protection's training program consisted of three weeks of initial training, two to three weeks of advanced training, and final follow-on mentoring by U.S. contractors and Navy SEALs.[20]

Table 9.7 shows the overall pattern of these efforts as of the end of May 2005. There is no doubt that they did not approach the level of training in Western security and police forces, that many training programs would have been longer if the police were not under so much pressure from the insurgency, and that gaps still remained in the effort. At the same time, it is clear that CPATT had made massive progress since the spring of 2004 and done so in the face of considerable obstacles, and many of the problems the inspector generals of the State Department and of the Department of Defense had found in April 2005 were already being addressed at that time, and substantial further improvement had been made by the summer of 2005.[21]

The MNF–I summarized the level of police and security force vetting and training in late July as follows:

Training—of all forces, but especially police forces—undergoes constant analysis in light of operational experience. The course length and curriculum of the Transition Integration Program has been standardized in all of the Iraqi

TABLE 9.7
Training at Police Academies as of May 29, 2005

Eight-Week Academies	Total Trained
Baghdad Police College	12,391
Jordan International Police Training Center	17,138
Sulaymaniyah	1,571
Al Kut	334
Al Asad	127
Kirkuk	0
Al Hillah	517
Basra	452
Mosul	2,457
Total	**34,987**
TIP Academies	**Total Trained**
MND–Baghdad (Karada)	1,609
MND–CS	
(Karbala/Babil/Al Hillah/Babylon)	6,301
MND–SE	
(Basra/Diwaniyah)	7,465
MNF–W	
(Al Quadisiyah)	4,868
MNF–W	4,268
MND-CN	
(Kirkuk/Tikrit/As Sulaymaniyah)	11,291
Total	**35,802**

Source: MNSTC–I, CPATT, June 2005.

police academies. The length of basic training for police recruits has been increased by 25% by adding two weeks of regional training on threats and other conditions in the new policeman's area of responsibility. Training at all police schools is now much more likely to be led by an Iraqi and to be "hands on" training instead of simple academic instruction.

Some 62,000 trained police were on duty as of late June 2005. To date, over 35,000 police recruits have completed the 8-week basic police classroom training, and more than 35,500 veteran police have received the 3-week Transition Integration Program (TIP) training. Over 13,500 police personnel have completed specialized training, such as fingerprinting, explosive ordnance disposal, investigations, and counterterrorism. New police academy graduates do not receive the originally envisioned field training by International Police Liaison Officers (IPLOs) due to the current security situation, so new police receive informal mentoring from veteran Iraqi police.

Police are recruited through a combination of methods depending on the stability of the province in which they live. In stable provinces, recruiting is done by MOI [Ministry of Interior], community leaders, IPLOs, and Multinational Force Major Subordinate Commands (MSCs). In areas where insurgents are more active, the MSCs play a larger role in recruitment. The Iraqi police advertise for recruits via radio, posters, police stations, and employment centers. Most recruiting is done from the local population, with the goal of matching the ethnic composition of the local area; however, all police must commit to serving any-where in the nation if necessary.

Police recruits undergo a physical fitness test, medical examination and back-ground check; increasingly, more sophisticated vetting tools are being developed and employed. Vetting is performed by the MSCs and, on a more limited basis, by an assessment tool developed by a MNSTC–I contractor that screens for literacy, cognitive, and suitability characteristics.

MSCs have increasingly engaged Iraqi Police Service Chiefs in the review of the police candidate rosters. The MOI and MNSTC–I's Coalition Police Assis-tance Training Team (CPATT) are working closely together to conduct training and deploy IPS in-processing teams (vetting teams). These in-processing teams will deploy to Al Kut, Basra, Al Hillah, and Mosul police academies. This pro-cess should be complete by November 2005, and thereafter police candidates will be vetted by MOI. The MOI Qualifying Committee has received information on 120,000 MOI employees, and a final screening process has been completed on 90,000 of them. The work of the Qualifying Committee to weed out "ghost employees" (who are being paid but not working) and other police who do not meet minimal standards is ongoing.

The rate of absenteeism, AWOL, attrition, and desertion in the IPS varies by province. Most police units have experienced a decrease in absenteeism as the number of trained police has increased. The exact extent of insurgent infiltration is unknown. Effectiveness of the Iraqi police officer cadres and the chain of command varies by province and the experience level of the chain of command. The P3 teams are focusing their efforts on developing capability at the provincial police headquarters and MOI in a top-down approach.[22]

Embedded Advisory Teams: The Importance of the Luck Mission

A major advance in training took place in Iraq's forces once they were deployed. The United States began to embed large training teams in each Iraqi unit until it demonstrated it could stand on its own. This reform seems to have been at least partly a result of the review of U.S. strategy and operations in Iraq made by retired four-star General Gary Luck in January 2005.

The Department of Defense stated at the time that the purpose of General Luck's mission was "to provide some assessment of how we're doing" in training and fielding Iraqi security units.[23] Other reports have suggested that Luck's mandate may have been far more wide-ranging, extending to an evaluation of the entire U.S. strategy in Iraq. Other reports indicate that by late 2004, the United States was also seeking to find some way to largely extract U.S. forces from the counterinsurgency mission by the end of 2005 or early 2006, but the Defense Department has denied this.[24]

In her Senate confirmation testimony, Condoleezza Rice described General Luck's mission and the progress of Iraqi security forces as follows: "We think that, among those people, there clearly continue to be questions about on-duty time, that is, people who don't report for duty. And so this is being looked at. We are trying to provide for some of these units mentors who can help, trying to provide leadership from the Iraqis themselves that can help these people. But this is the reason Gary Luck has gone out, at Secretary Rumsfeld's direction, to take a hard look at the training program to see what General Petraeus . . . what he's been able to achieve; to work with the Iraqis to address some of these problems of leadership and morale and desertion in the armed forces and in the police forces; and to look at some of the equipping of the police forces."[25]

The full results of the Luck mission have not been made public. Reports and interviews indicate, however, that General Luck was satisfied with the progress Lieutenant General Petraeus had made, and his report focused on providing teams of Coalition advisors to train and fight with new Iraqi units as they deployed. One unidentified defense official was quoted as saying, "Luck's assessment in general is that he feels the commanders have a plan, Petraeus is having an impact, and these forces have a good crack at becoming more and more capable over time."[26] At the same time, the Luck mission emphasized the need to go beyond formal training and equipment programs and to put an Iraqi face on the security and military missions and to embed U.S. training elements in the new Iraqi forces to help them as they build up the leadership experience and unity integrity necessary to operate effectively on their own.

The result was a plan for utilizing embedded U.S. troops as "advisers," as opposed to having entire U.S. units jointly patrolling with Iraqi troops, an approach likely to lower the U.S. profile and quell a degree of the anti-American sentiment. At the same time, such advisers would have the ability to call for U.S. air support and backup forces and would have access to U.S. intelligence.

An early report on the Luck mission in the *New York Times* summarized its conclusions as follows:

> Luck . . . endorses a plan by American commanders in Iraq to shift the military's main mission after the Jan. 30 elections from fighting the insurgency to training Iraq's military and police forces to take over those security and combat duties and become more self-reliant, eventually allowing American forces to withdraw. . . . The aim would be to double or even triple the number of trainers now at work with Iraqi security forces, up to as many as 8,000 or 10,000, though General Luck has not mentioned a specific number. A senior defense official who has been briefed on General Luck's initial conclusions and recommendations said the plan would draw on a mix of officers and senior enlisted troops from Army and Marine units already in Iraq.
>
> Many commanders say that providing more trainers is meant to bolster the Iraqi will to fight, help train officers who would lead, curb desertion and provide Iraqi forces with the confidence that American units would back them up—in some cases fighting alongside them if needed, military and Pentagon officials said. Two American advisers have died fighting with Iraqi units. But the training would follow a step-by-step approach that would take months if not years, proceeding at different paces in different parts of the country, depending on the troops' performance. American forces would work closely with

Iraqis in the most dangerous parts of the country, but would still take the lead combat role there.[27]

The development of Iraqi forces has since reflected a major effort to provide such training and in-unit or "embedded" U.S. cadres. General John Abizaid indicated in an interview in late January 2005 that he felt that close relationships between U.S. forces and indigenous troops made efforts in Afghanistan more successful than those in Iraq. He commented that embedded advisers could foster a similar relationship, likely improving efforts to strengthen Iraq forces.

The program did begin awkwardly. The Iraqis were not consulted when MNF–I and MNSTC–I came up with advisory teams and requested forces in December and January. When they did discuss the program with the Iraqi minister of defense and minister of the interior, the minister of defense accepted the program, but the minister of the interior initially balked. It took some persuasion to get him to agree to a test case with four police stations.[28]

One problem was finding enough advisers. An army reserve unit from Rochester, New York, the 98th Training Division, had been the main body from which advisers have been drawn.[29] Reportedly, as of February 24, 2005, there were forty-five training teams assisting Iraqi units and advising their leaders.[30] The actual quality of the training, however, has differed significantly by trainer and adviser. According to some reports, Iraqi units trained by the Vinnell Corporation and the U.S. National Guard have been less effective than forces trained by the U.S. Army Special Forces. However, U.S. sources reported in mid-April 2005 that there were already some 2,000 U.S. military advisers working directly with Iraqi forces.[31]

In March 2005, U.S. officials were still engaged in determining the number of embedded American advisers needed to improve Iraqi leadership and overall capabilities. General Abizaid stated that that decision lay with Secretary of Defense Rumsfeld. Referring to the numbers of advisers needed in Iraq, Abizaid commented, "We're trying to figure out how much augmentation will be required."[32] Since that time, however, the number of advisers has steadily increased, and this has led to changes in the way the Coalition manages the advisory effort. In March 2005 the Multinational Corps–Iraq (MNC–I, the operational headquarters under Multinational Force–Iraq, MNF–I) became responsible for all operations, and all Iraqi Army units were placed under their tactical control. In addition, the Coalition transition (advisory) teams that worked with those units were almost all placed under corps control as well. This was always the case with former ING units, but now the transition teams in regular army and intervention-force units were largely placed under the control of the corps.

The MNSTC–I essentially became an assistant, albeit a very major one, to the Iraqi Joint HQs and Ministry of Defense for fulfilling the role of "force provider." Its function became to recruit, train, equip, base, and sustain. As a result, it did not get operational reports on the units once they completed their training and started to conduct operations or closely track when and where

TABLE 9.8
Transition-Team Training Model

CONUS	Kuwait	Taji	Camp Victory	Link-up with MSCs and Iraqi Units
10–45 days + travel	10 days + travel	10 days	2–5 days	First 24 hours:
Individual Tasks: • Weapons • Commo • HMMWV • Combat Lifesaver	Live-Fire Training: • Convoy • TCP/ECP	General officer and senior Iraqi briefings	Warlock installation and training	Specific tactical situation
Team Building	Individual Equipment Issue	Situation briefings	Make-up training	Security measures and support procedures
Iraqi METL Tasks: • MOUT • ECP/TCP	Acclimatization	Interaction with Iraqi units and transition teams in the field	Team planning & prep	Status of Iraqi unit
Cultural Orientation	Cultural Orientation	Linkup with sponsors, interpreters Cultural Orientation Draw, test, prepare team equipment		First week: Joint training plan

Source: MNSTC–I, CMATT, June 2005.

they are assuming battle space. That was MNC–I's responsibility. It did receive information from MNC–I on their manning, equipment, and basing status in order to assist the joint headquarters (JHQ) in addressing the needs of these units.

MNF–I and MNSTC–I have worked together with the Ministry of Defense and Ministry of Interior to implement the program at all levels of Iraqi force development. They use a system where MNSTC–I shapes the training effort and creation of new unit elements and then transfers them to MNF–I operational command. Once the units become active they get embedded Coalition advisory teams as they actually become operational that stay until the unit demonstrates it has effective leadership and unit cohesion in actually performing its mission. The desired training levels before and at the time of this transition are shown in table 9.8.

By the early summer of 2005, virtually all Iraqi Army units and advanced Ministry of Interior units had at least ten-man teams of Coalition advisers. There were still serious shortages in the number of advisers assigned to support units and headquarters units and to Ministry of Defense and Ministry of Interior officials at every level down, but combat and major support units not only had the training teams they needed but a partner unit of Coalition forces to work with until they were capable of independent operations.[33]

The Department of Defense described the military training effort that resulted as follows in late July 2005:

MNF–I has implemented a structured training and assessment process for Iraqi Military Forces. Training for the individual soldier is divided into two areas: training for new recruits and training for former soldiers. Training for new recruits takes a total of nine weeks and has usually been conducted at the Iraqi Training Brigade (ITB) in Kirkush. Training for former soldiers lasts three to four weeks and has usually been conducted in divisional locations with graduates generally being assigned to the division that trains them. All personnel receive standard infantry-style training; selected soldiers receive specialized training in Army Military Occupational Specialties, such as Signal, Administration, Supply, Armor, Transport, Maintenance and Military Police.

Membership in the Iraqi Special Forces Brigade requires additional training. All Iraqi Special Operations Forces (ISOF) soldiers undergo a three-week Assessment and Selection course. Iraqi Counter Terrorist Forces (ICTF) soldiers receive 12 weeks of training in Jordan on Close Quarters Battle (CQB), Planning, and Leadership before they conduct Direct Action missions. ISOF soldiers undergo rigorous training emphasizing small unit tactics, counterterrorism, and unit self-reliance. Improved qualification and vetting standards minimize absenteeism and the risk of insurgent infiltration. The Brigade's chain of command and officer cadre are assessed as being very effective. ISOF elements have been conducting operations for the past year. They have played crucial roles in major combat operations along side of, and sometimes independently of, Coalition forces.

A small number of Army personnel attend advanced training with NATO and U.S. Army schools.

MNF-I has also implemented, in partnership with the MOD [Ministry of Defense], a program to embed Military Transition Teams at the battalion, brigade, and division level. These teams provide Transition Readiness Assessments (TRAs) to MNC-I identifying areas of progress and shortcomings, ultimately leading to those individual units being ready to assume independent control of their area of responsibility. These assessments take into account a variety of criteria similar to but not identical to what the U.S. Army uses to evaluate its units' operational readiness focused on personnel, command and control, training, sustainment/logistics, equipment, and leadership.[34]

New Iraqi units were being deployed into the field with stronger cadres of Coalition advisers, including teams that average at least ten men per battalion, brigade and division headquarters, special force elements, and combat support, service support, and logistic units. Such advisory teams stay until such units demonstrate they have the leadership and committed manpower to operate on their own. Military commanders called this development "a sea change in methods."[35] It builds on the lessons learned in Afghanistan and addresses the problems caused by the lack of mid-level Iraqi leadership in all elements of Iraq's forces, the lack of a history of unit integrity and morale, and the lack of experience at all levels in creating an effective team and fighting force.[36]

In contrast, efforts to provide such teams for regular police force units lagged in spite of major efforts by CPATT, largely due to a lack of resources and problems in support from agencies in the United States such as the Department of Homeland Security, but many regular police units either had such teams or were acquiring them. Once again, the report by the inspector general of the State Department and inspector general of the Department of Defense provide important insights into the level of progress in April 2005 that are supported by interviews with CPATT advisers and others who served in Iraq:

> A strong mentoring program is integral to the concept of training Iraqi police. Initially, this was to be the function of IPLO [international police liaison officers] field training officers, each working closely with a small number of policemen who had received basic training. This concept would mirror a model that worked satisfactorily in Bosnia and Kosovo. INL contracted with DynCorp to provide the IPLOs. The first 24-member contingent arrived in Iraq during November 2003. Most IPLOs are retired policemen. By March 2005, this number had risen to about 500.... INL has proposed funding for an additional 400 IPLOs. In actuality, the mentoring program in Iraq has not materialized as planned. The security situation is so precarious that any post-training mentoring is, at best, intermittent. There have been periods during which the IPLOs were unable to move beyond the confines of their quarters. Consequently, IPLO interaction with Iraqi policemen is largely with instructors/supervisors at the BPC and regional academies or during periodic visits to police stations.

> To accomplish the latter, the IPLOs must rely on Coalition military forces for transportation and security. The military police (MP), who provide that logistical assistance, act as additional mentors once on site. As the security situation has evolved, so has the work of the IPLOs. IPLOs now devote much of their time and attention to assessing police stations and units. There, the IPLOs gather data on equipment status and availability, discipline problems, and reports of incidents involving the IPS. This is documented in Police Station Monthly Reports (PSMR), which are derived from the Facility Assessment Forms prepared by MPs and IPLOs. In theory, this information will enable the MOI to more effectively manage both personnel and material resources of the IPS.

> Lines of authority and responsibility for mentoring are not well defined. As the contract administrator, INL has administrative responsibility for the IPLO program. This includes providing life support (e.g., food and lodging, basic security, etc.). CPATT provides operational control. However, Coalition military officials tend to rely on MPs for the mentoring function. Consequently, the IPLOs are sometimes underutilized.[37]

The problems involved in embedding sufficient advisers in the police are illustrated by the fact the number of IPLOs assigned by districted to each region as of May 1, 2005. Region I–Baghdad (98), Region II–Tikrit (94), Region III–Mosul (30), Region IV–Ramadi (34), Region V–Babylon (43), Region VI–Basra (24), with the CPATT command staff (9), National Assets Bureau (75), Administrative Bureau (26), and various other areas (63). It is, however, important to note that the IPLOs ran even higher risks than the advisers embedded in regular Iraqi Army and security units. For example, on March 9, 2005, a massive suicide truck bomb targeted the al-Sadeer Hotel in Baghdad. Thirty-five IPLOs were injured; the most serious casualty was the loss of an eye.[38]

It is unclear how much progress had been made by the summer of 2005, but the Department of Defense described the process in these areas as follows in late July 2005: "Police Partnership Program (P3) teams are partnered at the provincial levels with the police to help identify areas of progress and shortcomings to determine when these forces will be able to assume independent control of their area of responsibility. In lieu of the TRA, police partnership assessments look at factors that are more tailored to the tasks of a police force. More than half of provincial police headquarters currently are assessed to have control in their province."[39] This focus on embedding advisory cadres to develop effective leadership and unit integrity formal training is a key lesson of the MNF–I and MNSTC–I effort. It reflects an underlying reality of military history that transcends cultures and the conditions of particular wars. Soldiers, security personnel, and police are not cars or transistor radios. They cannot be turned out of training centers like a product. They must either be transitioned into effective and proven units or transitioned into some structure that can substitute for that leadership and experience.

Regardless of the quality of training and equipment and the political and ideological conditions shaping a war, men who are thrust into combat or high-risk operations only function well if they have proven leaders they feel that they can trust. Their primary motivation also ultimately comes to be how they feel about the other men in their units, how important the approval of their peers is in crisis and combat, and how confident they are that their unit will do everything possible to support and protect them.

Force Developments

Many of the more detailed aspects of Iraqi force development also showed an increased rate of progress. The MNSTC–I reported on the status of Iraqi force developments as of March 12, 2005, noted:

> On 1 July 2004, for example, there was one "deployable" or "national" battalion available to the Iraqi Ministries of Interior and Defense (i.e., a unit that could be moved to a trouble spot anywhere in the country). Now there are 52 such battalions and 96 battalions conducting operations in total, in addition to regular police, border guards, and other security force elements. All told, there are more than 142,000 trained and equipped Iraqi police, soldiers, sailors, and airmen.

A large portion of these fifty-two battalions did consist of National Guard units that had been merged into the Army in January, and which had originally been formed for the local mission of supporting the police within a given province. These units now had a national mission as part of the army, and the early results were mixed. When National Guard units had previously told they were going to Fallujah in November 2004, AWOL rates then climbed to 70 percent in some units.[40]

Nevertheless, the increase in trained and equipped manpower continued at a rapid rate throughout the rest of the spring and summer. By the end of July 2005, the number had risen to 172,300 with 78,500 military and 93,800 police and security forces. The military now included 77,700 army, 100 air force, and 700 navy. The regular police and highway patrol totaled 63,500, and the security forces totaled 30,300.[41]

Ongoing Force Developments

The MNC–I submitted a report to the United Nations on April 10, 2005, pursuant to UN Security Council Resolution 1546. This report provided data submitted by MNSTC–I as of May 14, 2005.[42] Coupled with other reports from the Iraqi government, Iraqi force developments had reached the following status as of early August 2005:

- Operations
    - Iraq was now operating its own joint command centers and was bringing modern computerized operations centers into operation in areas like Baghdad. The Ministry of Defense and Ministry of Interior developed and operated a joint command center during Operation Lightning.
- Ministry of Defense
    - Iraqi forces now operated a full command and staff structure. The chief of staff of the Iraqi armed forces was a four-star officer, General Babakir Shawkat Zebari. He had a three-star deputy, Lieutenant General Nasier Al Abadi. There were three joint commands: training command, support command, and special operations command, headed by Brigadier General Najh Hashim. There were also three single-service commands: army commander (Lieutenant General Abdul Qadr), navy commander (Commander Muhammad Jawad), and air force commander (Major General Kamal Abdul-Sattar Barzanjy). The joint staff include personnel (M1), intelligence (M2), operations (M3) logistics (M4), plans (M5), communications (M6), training (M7), and comptroller (M8). There were two major special staff divisions: staff judge advocate and surgeon general.
    - The Iraqi ground forces headquarters was opened in a ribbon-cutting ceremony in Baghdad on May 15, 2005, by General Abdul Qadir Jassim, Iraqi ground forces commander.
    - Concerning Iraqi Regular Army and Intervention Forces, with the incorporation of the Iraqi National Guard into the Army, the total number of battalions conducting operations was now eighty. The Iraqi Army had gone from one battalion in July 2004 to twenty-seven battalions of infantry in January, which included nine special Iraqi Intervention Force battalions and three transportation battalions. The total rose to thirty-seven battalions in June with four

more in formation. In addition, forty-three National Guard battalions were being merged into the army, and these forces were undergoing a major upgrading in terms of vetting and retention, training, and equipment. As is discussed in table 9.11, Iraqi military forces now had a detailed order of battle with clear force goals.

- The merger of the Iraqi Army and National Guard had created a ten-division order of battle, and as is shown in table 9.11, overall manning of the combat elements of this force was now relatively high. As shown in this table, Iraqi military forces now had a detailed order of battle with clear force goals. The final brigade of the three division regular army graduated on April 20 and brought the number of operational combat brigades to ninety-nine.

- Iraq's first mechanized battalion became operational in mid-January, along with a tank company and a transportation battalion; the remaining elements of a mechanized brigade were being trained and equipped by summer. The First Mechanized Battalion, First Iraqi Army Brigade began operations in the Abu Ghraib area south of Baghdad, and an Iraqi mechanized unit began joint duty with U.S. armored forces in providing security for movement through insurgent areas in late April 2005.

- MNSTC–I was working to complete the Second Mechanized Infantry Battalion of the First Mechanized Brigade, which was to be equipped with BMPs by the summer of 2005. The rest of the armored division was projected to be trained and equipped by the end of 2005, and another mechanized division with wheeled armored vehicles was planned for 2006. Other units were acquiring light-armored vehicles from the United Arab Emirates, Jordan, Eastern Europe, and other services. The equipment confiscated from the Iranian People's Mujahideen (MEK) was being made available to Iraqi units, and some units were getting armor from the various equipment dumps left over from the war. Iraqi units had ceased to wait and had begun to improvise.

- The Iraqi Seventh Division was being readied for deployment in the West. It was being deployed because the locally recruited National Guard units would or could not deal with the insurgency. The end result has been to disband all of the existing units in Al Anbar, make the former "Defenders of Baghdad" into the First Brigade, and create two new brigades for a force designed to deal with the most hostile area in Iraq.

- The Iraqi Intervention Force (IIF) was becoming the counterinsurgency wing of the Iraqi Army. It had been organized after the fighting in Fallujah and designed to defeat anti-Iraqi forces in Iraq with primary focus on urban areas and to assist in the restoration of a secure and stable environment in which Ministry of Interior security forces can maintain law and order. It was organized as the First Division and was ultimately to be comprised of nine infantry battalions and three armored battalions, organized into three brigades, and to acquire a full range of support units. Its armored forces had BMPs taken from MEK units and were to acquire some seventy-seven refurbished T-72s provided by Hungary.

The division became operational in January and had a total of 170 U.S. advisers embedded by June. Its forces negotiated the standard eight-week basic training all Iraqi Soldiers go through to learn basic soldiering skills such as weapons, drill and ceremony, soldier discipline, and physical-training skills. After graduation, IIF battalions spent several weeks and months in intensive "military operations in urban terrain" (MOUT) follow-on training. In this period soldiers worked through instruction in the art of street fighting and building-clearing operations typical to anti-insurgent operations in cities and towns. Units worked in close coordination with other Iraqi Army battalions and were scheduled to a completely stood-up nine-battalion force during 2005.

o   Iraq's Special Operations Forces included a Counter-Terrorist Force and a Commando Battalion, each of which had conducted dozens of successful operations. The unit was formed based on a conversation between the Prime Minister Ayad Allawi and multinational force personnel to give the Iraqi armed forces a high-end strike force in its ongoing security mission against anti-Iraqi forces operating in the country.

Special forces soldiers were the army's unconventional warfare experts, possessing a broad range of operational skills. The forces consisted of two trained battalions, including the Thirty-sixth Commando Battalion—an infantry-type strike force—and the Iraqi Counterterrorism Battalion. The force had now been involved in many operations throughout the country fighting anti-Iraqi forces with great distinction while continuing the stand-up effort of the unit. The force was to add a third "support" battalion to its ranks in the coming months.

The Iraqi Special Operations Force continued training and operations in the country with multinational force assistance. Training was conducted at an undisclosed location. Selection for the force began in the Iraqi National Guard and Iraqi Army units already operating in the country. During the ten- to fourteen-day selection process, recruits negotiated exhaustive background checks, evaluations, and literacy, psychological, and physical tests and were run through various team-building and physical events meant to reduce the pool of recruits. The Iraqi special forces underwent intense physical, land navigation, small-unit tactics, live-fire, unconventional warfare operations, direct-action operations, airmobile operations, counterterrorism, survival, evasion, resistance, and escape training.

○ One motorized transport regiment was already in service, and plans exist to create a motorized transport regiment for each division. This was part of an overall plan to fully staff divisional and brigade headquarters, add combat and service support units, and give Iraqi units the ability to operate independently in the field and end their dependence on base support and Coalition forces for such operations.

○ Other new forces completed their training and would be ready to assume full-time duty between the end of March and June 2005. These included three more Iraqi Army battalions and several former Iraqi National Guard battalions.

○ The Ministry of Defense was seeking to create sixteen new infrastructure—or oil security battalions—with an authorized strength of 727 men each, the strength of other army battalions. These strategic infrastructure battalions (SIBs) were being created to defend pipelines and other oil infrastructure at the direction of Deputy Prime Minister Ahmed Chalabi. They were a response to the fact that the oil infrastructure in the Kirkuk–Bayji area alone had been struck fourteen times between March and June 2005.

Four battalions already existed but lacked manpower, training, and equipment. The others were to be formed by local/direct recruiting, and given suitable vehicles, AK-47s and light machine guns, GPS, night-vision goggles, radios, and other necessary equipment. Chalabi had approved a $35 million, three-month plan to train the necessary trainers and equip the first four SIB battalions. Part of the plan was to bring the personnel into the military, but the $35 million did not cover the same equipment as the regular army. The plan called for training the first four battalions starting in mid-July and going on through October and to assess funding needs for the remaining battalions.

○ Iraq's 600-man navy operated with five 100-foot patrol craft, thirty-four smaller vessels, and a naval infantry regiment that recently completed training. The force also included a land-based Coastal Defense Regiment with an active strength of one hundred men and building up to a strength of 300. The U.S. Department of Defense described the Iraqi Navy's progress as follows in late July 2005:

> The Iraqi Navy is currently executing operational missions that include border and waterway protection from smuggling and infiltration and site protection of port and oil assets in the Persian Gulf. The force patrols out to the 12-mile international water boundary in the Persian Gulf using 27-meter patrol boats, rigid-hull inflatable boats, and other

support vessels. The Iraqi Navy currently has approximately 500 trained sailors on duty. It is equipped with five Predator Class Patrol Boats (PB), 24 Fast Aluminum Boats (Duel Outboard Engines), 10 rigid-hull inflatable boats, and various small arms and night vision devices. The Iraqi Navy will further equip themselves with six Al Faw Class Patrol Boats (the first of which was delivered in July 2005) and two Off-Shore Support Vessels. With some exceptions, the responsibility for logistical support of the Iraqi Navy has been handed over to the Umm Qasr Base Support Unit (BSU). Maritime and Riverine Advisory Support Team (M&R AST) members provide advice and assistance to both the BSU and the Iraqi Navy Logistics Department in order to cultivate a cooperative working relationship. It is anticipated (based on progression along the CTF-58 assessment program) that the Iraqi Navy will assume point defense responsibilities of the oil terminals by September 30, 2005. Assumption of the waterside mission (the afloat defensive screen) is dependent on the acquisition and initial operational readiness of the six Al Faw class.

The Iraqi Navy Training Department currently conducts all of its own training, assisted by the M&R AST. All members of the Iraqi Navy received their initial training in Kirkush. Following basic training, they were trained on mission-focused technical skill sets: ship handling, marlin spike seamanship, navigation, engineering, weapons handling, small boat operations, shipboard damage control, etc.[43]

In June, the Iraqi Navy began interoperability training with their Predator patrol boats and an amphibious transport ship. The Iraqi Navy signed the Iraqi Navy Transition Roadmap on the USS *Normandy*. The roadmap lays out plans to develop the Iraqi Navy to defend its coastal waters, to give it the capability to perform integrated sea operations, shore support, boarding-and-search operations, point-of-defense of oil terminals, and an overall command and sustainment program.

○ Iraq's Air Force had three operational squadrons. One additional squadron was stood up in late January/early February. It had nine reconnaissance aircraft, a helicopter squadron, and three C-130 transport aircraft. All Iraqi Air Force pilots and maintenance personnel negotiated comprehensive one- to four-month "conversion courses" largely comprised of familiarization instruction. The training brings air force recruits up to speed on current Iraqi Air Force aircraft as well as serving to augment prior skills.

The air force actively recruited from prior-service personnel pools in the country—officially sending personnel to training after the Iraqi Ministry of Defense's vetting and screening process clears recruits for duty. Training was almost entirely conducted in the United Arab Emirates and Jordan by multinational force partners. After "conversion course" training was completed, trainees went to assigned squadrons in Iraq for follow-on training comprised of advanced instruction and specific operational training.

The Iraqi Air Force was initially slated to be a six-squadron force of various-make light reconnaissance aircraft and various support aircraft, including C-130 transport planes and other helicopter craft with operations mainly centered on supporting Iraqi security forces' operations on the ground, infrastructure reconnaissance, and border-security missions. The majority of the force was scheduled to be operational by fall 2005.

The U.S. Department of Defense described the Iraqi Air Force's progress as follows in late July 2005: "Like the Army and the Navy, the Iraqi Air Force is conducting operational missions while equipping and training. The Iraqi Air Force's counterinsurgency missions focus on aerial observation/surveillance and air transportation. The Air Force currently has over 100 personnel and has a fleet of 9 helicopters (4 UH-1H and 5 Jet Ranger), 3 C-130s, and 8 single-engine propeller-driven observation airplanes (6 CompAir turboprop aircraft and 2 Seeker piston aircraft). There are 19 Iraqi C-130 personnel currently being trained in the United States. Language training and flight training are being conducted at Al Ali Air Base. Crews have previously trained in Jordan on the UH-1H and Seeker."[44]

- Command centers were being created for the Ministry of Defense, the Ministry of Interior, and joint operations.
- Iraq's two military academies reopened in mid-October and each graduated a pilot course of new lieutenants, a total of ninety-one, in early January 2005. The new year-long military academy course was under way based on an Iraqi modification of the course at Sandhurst. Britain had taken the lead in shaping the program at the academy, and Italy was taking the lead in creating staff colleges. A senior command defense college was being developed.

- Ministry of Interior
  - Five basic police academies were operational; together, they produced over 3,500 new police officers from the eight-week course each month, a course recently modified to better prepare the new police officers for the challenging environment in which some may serve. Several other regional academies were under construction.
  - Police operations were being steadily modified to deal with the insurgent threat. Suicide bombings and other attacks had led to a steady rise in the number of AK-47s and PKM machine guns issued to the police and increases in the issue of body armor.
  - Iraq's Mechanized Police Brigade had completed training and began operations in mid-January, using fifty BTR-94 wheeled, armored

vehicles. One additional mechanized police battalion was in training. The Eighth Mechanized Police Brigade (MPB) was a paramilitary, counterinsurgency Iraqi police unit that would deploy to high-risk areas using light-armored personnel carriers. The MPB was planned to comprise three battalions.

The MPB was planned to be able to deploy as a company, battalion, or even a brigade-level force. The brigade will be stationed in central Iraq. The Russian-made personnel carriers, known as BTRs, were used to transport Iraqi security forces across Iraq. With a three-man crew, each carrier was capable of transporting up to ten officers. The BTR has twin 23-mm cannons and a 7.62-mm machine gun.

The MPB could serve as outer cordon security for military and other strike missions. The BTRs provided the members of the Eighth MPB safe transport to high-risk areas with lethal fire power capability.

○ Iraqi police mechanized units were starting to receive delivery of armored security vehicles and began training with them in mid-March 2005. Logistics units at the division level and a brigade each for logistics, signals, MPs, and engineering were scheduled to stand up by 2006.[45] Vehicle plans included a battalion of Cadillac Gage ASD armored security vehicles and two battalions of BTR-94s, and a range of additional procurements were under study. According to MNSTC–I, uparmored HMMWVs were on order as of summer 2005.

○ Within the Civil Intervention Force (CIF) there were three main elements as of July 2005: the Emergency Response Unit (ERU), the Eighth Mechanized Police, and the Public Order Brigade (POB).

Each type of CIF received different training. The ERU personnel received a four-week basic and four-week advanced crisis-response training (CRT) course. Selected individuals went through a five-week explosive ordnance disposal (EOD) training course. The Eighth Mechanized Brigade received a six-week training course. Selected personnel attend an operator and maintenance course at Taji for the armored security vehicles. Lastly, the POB receives a six-week training course at the Numaniyah training base.

The CIF used a variety of equipment: Chevy Luv pick-up trucks, mid-size SUVs, Nissan pick-up trucks, AK-47 assault rifles, PKC light machine guns, Glock pistols, HF radios, and body armor. The Eighth Mechanized Brigade uses BTR armored personnel carriers with 23-mm cannons. Each battalion and member is currently equipped with all mission-essential equipment.

The Special Police Transition Teams (SPTTs) embedded with the Eighth Mechanized Brigade and the battalions of the Public Order Brigade submitted a TRA at least monthly on the same areas as do the army military transition teams. The SPTTs focused their efforts on mentoring the cadres with the least experience. Most recruiting is done from the local population with the goal of matching the ethnic composition of the unit with that of the area in which it is deployed.

The first three public order battalions were brought into the ISF without CPATT-developed training. The fourth public order battalion completed training last month. Each battalion was equipped with all mission-essential equipment. These units were to be fully trained and equipped by the fall of 2005. Notably, the ERU has a miniscule AWOL/attrition rate. The Eighth Mechanized Brigade has a moderate rate, and the public order battalions experience AWOL and attrition rates that are inversely proportional to their pay and training. Candidates for CIF are recruited from the surrounding police stations and provinces.

As with other police units, the exact extent of insurgent infiltration is unknown. A vetting process is used to screen out foreign elements. The effectiveness of the Iraqi police officer cadres and the chain of command varies by province and the experience level of the chain of command.

○ Nine police commando battalions were operational. The special police commando battalions represented the Iraqi Ministry of Interior's strike-force capability similar to special forces units. The commandos were highly vetted Iraqi officers and rank-and-file servicemen largely made up of prior service special forces professionals and other skilled servicemen with specialty unit experience. While some reports stated that "all members of the unit were chosen based on loyalty to Iraq and its new democratic model," it initially was largely Shi'ite and was often criticized for excessive force in dealing with Sunnis.

The police commando force was, however, being expanded to develop a strength of twenty-seven battalions with four more battalions in training. The units focused primarily on building raid operations, counterterrorist missions including anti–airplane hijacker, kidnapping, and other similar missions. The force resembled a paramilitary army-type force complete with heavy weapons, rocket-propelled grenades, AK-47 assault rifles, mortars, and 9-mm Glock pistols.

○ Nine public order battalions were operational, and three were commencing training.

○ Iraq's National Police Emergency Response Unit was operational, and its elements had conducted operations in Baghdad, Fallujah, and Mosul. The $64.5 million effort funded an elite 270-man team that could respond to national-level law enforcement emergencies, countering terrorism, large-scale civil disobedience, and insurgencies throughout Iraq. It was to eventually include a counterterrorism investigative unit and special operations unit.

It is interesting to note that the report on the Iraqi police and security services by the inspector general of the State Department and inspector general of the Department of Defense provides a different view of this force from the MNF–I:

> The ERU is a Coalition-initiated capability that has not been sanctioned or supported by the Iraqi government. As a result ERU members are not on the MOI [Ministry of Interior] payroll, nor do they have police credentials or weapons authorization cards. There are currently three ERU companies, with a fourth serving as a headquarters company. Despite non-sponsorship by the MOI, elements of the ERU have successfully participated in several high-level missions with remarkable results. Like the POBs, the ERU companies train and deploy as a unit. Camaraderie, morale, and esprit-de-corps are high, despite severe pay issues. Nevertheless, given the lack of sponsorship, attrition is a problem.
>
> The ERU units have no element responsible for gathering, analyzing and disseminating intelligence. Students interviewed by the IG Team stated that the ERU relies on US Special Forces for operational intelligence. This intelligence data is filtered through the MOI, an unwieldy and time consuming process. Formal sponsorship and integration of the ERU within existing IPS structures would serve to alleviate this problem.[46]

- Iraq's First Special Border Force Battalion was operating on the Syrian border in western Anbar province; the Second Battalion completed training in early February and has begun its deployments, and a third completed training in March.
- Five provincial SWAT (special weapons and training) teams had been trained, and fifteen more were scheduled for training over the next six months. These provincial SWAT teams have been formed by some governors and provincial police chiefs. In addition to standard police basic training, the provincial SWAT teams receive four weeks of training consisting of human relations and police conduct, firearms training (with AK-47 assault rifles and Glock pistols), mechanical breaching (e.g., multiple entry, multiple rooms), and specialty training—sniper training, offensive driving, intelligence, and surveillance. Recruits are drawn from existing IPS officers selected by IPLOs assigned to the province of origin. These forces mainly use Chevy Luv pickups, AK-47s, and Glock pistols. These forces are first trained to a basic level and are receiving additional practical skills training. Currently, new SWAT personnel are recruited only as replacements for existing SWAT teams. An increase in specialized training is required. The provincial SWAT team assessments are included with the provincial police Transition Readiness Assessments (TRAs).
- The provincial emergency battalion units are formed by the local chiefs of police without Coalition forces' involvement. To date, CPATT has not conducted training for these units and has not provided

equipment or supplies. If these units join a recognized Ministry of Interior unit, then they would receive full training and supplies.

○ The Iraqi Highway Patrol (IHP) had about 1,400 members trained and on duty in late July 2005. IHP officers attend a twenty-one-day training program that covers basic policing, driving skills, convoy escort, and weapons qualification with pistol, rifle, and machine gun.

IHP officers used a variety of equipment: Chevy Luv pick-up trucks, mid-size SUVs, Nissan pick-up trucks, AK-47 assault rifles, PKC machine guns, Glock pistols, HF radios, and body armor. The IHP did not have a TRA at this time. The goal for recruiting was a minimum of 300 cadets monthly until a force of 6,300 was built. All IHP patrolpersons and officers graduated from the four-week IHP academy. The equipment goal was for each patrolperson and station to be equipped with mission-essential equipment. The IHP began working with the U.S. Military Police Brigade in Baghdad in July 2005 to develop individual and squad skills and defined goals.

• Other
   ○ Members of the NATO Training Mission–Iraq were now helping to advise and train the Iraqi staffs of the National Joint Operations Center, the Ministry of Defense Operations Center, and the Ministry of Interior Operations Center, as well as the Armed Forces Joint Headquarters and Ministry of Defense.
   ○ NATO trainers were also assisting the cadre of the Iraqi Military Academy, and NATO trainers will help Iraq reestablish its staff college and war college in 2005. A number of NATO nations were already providing equipment for Iraqi security forces and training opportunities in NATO countries with many additional offers extant.
   ○ The Bureau of Dignitary Protection (BDP) safeguarded high-level government officials and visiting dignitaries. The Ministry of Interior does not recognize the BDP. As of April 2005, 395 candidates had completed training. There is no requirement for members of the BDP to be policemen or to have previously received basic police training. BDP agents have no arrest powers, nor do they carry police credentials or weapons' permits. Students undergoing BDP training generally are selected from the guarded dignitary's family and/or tribe. Based on this selection criterion, many of the trained BDP personnel were replaced after the April 2005 change in government leadership. Incumbents to office selected their own trusted agents and relatives to serve in this capacity.[47]

Near-Term Goals

No decisions had been made about the longer-term structure of Iraqi forces and how it should eventually be transformed from a counterinsurgency force to a national defense force. These include key decisions as to the extent to which it should establish more heavy armored forces and a large air force or navy.

MNSTC–I experts cautioned against investing in heavier forces before it was clear they were needed. An MNSTC–I adviser put it this way: "A heavier force, whether for force protection or for defense against invasion, also costs more. The Iraqis can't really afford to purchase, operate, and maintain such a force—even with the multiple billions of dollars we are providing. Given fiscal constraints that will last for several years, Iraq has to consider opportunity costs before committing to the addition of more heavy forces. The Iraqis might decide that the additional motorized division being considered might better be traded for less-expensive light forces. They could instead decide to spend that money on much-needed infrastructure protection forces, which may be even more important strategically."[48] The new minister of defense agreed with many of these comments, and it was clear that the future financing of Iraq's forces had become a serious consideration in making such choices.

In other areas, Iraq and the MNF–I set the following near-term goals and priorities:[49]

- Better intelligence
- Improving the institutional capability of the Ministry of Defense and Ministry of the Interior
- Strengthening the police
- Improving border defense and security
- Creating an effective army command structure
- Strengthening national counterterrorist forces
- Transitioning detainee operations to Iraq
- Securing the national electrical and oil infrastructure
- Integrating Iraqi counterinsurgency planning and execution
- Force protection
- Establishing a process of continuous transition from Coalition to Iraqi forces

The Iraqi government and MNF–I were now focusing on both creating the kind of balanced Iraqi forces that could stand on their own in fighting the insurgency and transitioning operations from Coalition to Iraqi forces. The command guidance that emerged out of these priorities was to build an army, not just combat battalions, with suitable logistics and institutional training. It was to finish manning, training, equipping, and basing the Seventh Division (two brigades and a division headquarters), standardize the various infantry battalions, create new forward operating bases in the West and Northwest, add special forces as enablers, and fund infrastructure security requirements.

The Iraqi government and MNF–I also sought to fund new reconnaissance aircraft, develop better support for the emergency response units, man existing public order battalions at 750 men each, and improve existing forces while new elements were being generated. Special emphasis was being put on improving combat service support functions by adding motorized transport regiments and standardizing headquarters and service companies. Divisional signal companies were being developed, as were intelligence, surveillance, and reconnaissance (IS&R) capabilities.

One other change that illustrated the growing role of the Iraqi government in shaping Iraqi force plans and force development was a new set of goals for the Iraqi police service, although such plans were scarcely without problems:

> As Iraqi officials articulate positions on IPS [Iraqi Police Service] issues, an emerging concept is the development of a "third force"—a capability between orthodox police and internal security military units. Consistent with this objective, the MOI [Ministry of Interior] enthusiastically embraces the preparation of the Public Order Brigades (POB). An MOI initiative, Special Police Commando Units and an IPS mechanized brigade are now operative. CPATT conceived the POB program and is engaged in training the Special Police Commandos.
>
> At the same time, the MOI has not claimed ownership of the CPATT-trained Emergency Response Unit (ERU), the Bureau of Dignitary Protection (BDP), or even the SWAT teams that have performed well in operations in Mosul and elsewhere. MOI attitudes relative to these units are reflected in frequent failure to pay IPs serving in those units. The IG Team concludes that, as the Iraqis eventually assume responsibility for IPS training, the status of these Coalition-conceived units may languish.[50]

Operational Readiness

As has been touched upon earlier, there was a slow increase in the level of Iraqi military, security, and elite police unit activity during the spring and summer of 2005 and improvements in areas like intelligence and counter-IED operations.[51] Many of these activities are listed in the Chronology. At the same time, there were still significant problems with the new combat elements of various forces, and readiness and desertions remained serious issues.

Concerns over Iraqi Progress Following the Election

In testimony before the Senate on February 3, 2005, Deputy Defense Secretary Paul D. Wolfowitz acknowledged that many new Iraqi soldiers had failed to return to their posts after going home to deliver paychecks. He stated that Iraqi Army units were experiencing absentee rates of up to 40 percent and that 1,342 Iraqi soldiers and police had died since June 2004.[52] The problem of recruits going home with their paychecks had not been anticipated in the original timelines in the training plan and delayed some training schedules dramatically.[53] In the same hearing, Chairman of the Joint Chiefs of Staff, General Richard Myers, estimated that approximately 40,000 of the reported 136,000 members of the Iraqi military and security forces were trained and equipped to "go anywhere and take on any threat" in Iraq. The rest, he acknowledged, were not yet ready for duties beyond policing calm parts of southern Iraq.

General John Abizaid, commander of CENTCOM, highlighted a different concern over the Iraqi military leadership. He stated, "There's a shortage of trained officers that will respect the government, be loyal to the government and support the government over the long term."[54] Lieutenant General David Petraeus stated, "In an Iraqi unit, the leader is really of paramount importance. He sets the tone for an organization. There is really a premium on finding, investing in and strengthening good leaders."[55] These warnings reflected the fact that some Iraqi unit leaders continued to be reluctant or unwilling to lead their unit into the field. In other cases, they deployed but acted like autocrats instead of leaders. Soldiers were sent on personal errands for the unit leader. Other Iraqi commanders take the view that the soldiers have to like the commander and be cajoled into accepting and completing missions. These views frustrated the U.S. advisers and mentors who train these leaders.

The often rigid, hierarchical nature of the Iraqi chain of command presented another problem in creating effective leaders. Junior officers who exhibited promising initiative and leadership could be frustrated by the failure of higher-ups to delegate authority. Patrols and simple tasks could not be performed without the explicit order of the unit commander. U.S. advisers worried that such an atmosphere would discourage the best soldiers and possible leaders from staying with the Iraqi military.[56] They saw efforts to train junior officers in initiative and "leading forward" as critical, as well as efforts to create a Western-style force of well-trained and effective NCOs, but they worried about the scale and continuity of such Iraqi efforts to change the "culture" of Iraq's forces.

In spite of major Iraqi and Coalition efforts to create mixed or "national units," observers were concerned that much of the officer corps remained more loyal to region, tribe, religion, or ethnic group than to the country. This presented the risk of separatism in the case of the Kurds and dominance in the case of the Shi'ites. Both U.S. experts and senior policy officials were concerned that the Shi'ite majority would purge Iraqi forces and the Ministries of Defense and Interior. One U.S. official in Baghdad reported that Shi'ites were indeed "clearing out political undesirables from the police and army." To what degree this is happening and whether it is widespread is unclear, but such actions would only push more armed men toward the insurgency.

The commander of MNF–I, General George W. Casey, highlighted four continuing problems in his testimony before the Senate Armed Services Committee on March 1, 2005. He pointed to the following challenges:[57]

- Providing the training, equipment, and sustainability to Iraqi forces while their force structure is in the midst of serious changes
- Developing Iraqi forces without a system that measures their capabilities
- Enhancing loyalty and developing effective leadership in the Iraqi chain of command
- Creating police who can do their job in a violent atmosphere while respecting the rule of law

Despite these challenges, USCENTCOM commander General John P. Abizaid expressed optimism about the ultimate success of the force-building effort in March 2005. He stated that "They [Iraqi forces] will get better and I think in 2005 will take on the majority of the tasks."[58]

Increasing Deployment and Activity

In spite of the problems in the their overall readiness, Iraqi forces continued to intensify their military raids, and the number of active Iraqi units actually deployed and fighting the insurgent forces slowly continued to grow. A combination of Coalition and Iraqi raids led to significant insurgent casualties and captures and to the deaths or capture of many mid-level fighters and some high-level insurgent leaders, although most of the wanted insurgents remained elusive.[59]

HUMINT slowly improved, with growing support from Iraqi forces, and the capture of insurgents and terrorists helped provide additional information—as did the capture of many of their records, diaries, and computers. U.S.-run detention centers were nearing capacity. In January 2005 the number of captured insurgents reached the highest levels since March 2004. The United States had roughly 7,900 "security detainees" in captivity in January 2005. The total then increased by another 20 percent to 11,350 by early May. Major General William H. Bradenburg, commander of U.S. detention operations in Iraq, declared that U.S. and Iraqi forces were arresting an average of fifty suspected insurgents every day, with the 2005 average approaching seventy arrests per day.[60]

Press sources on such developments are uncertain and sometimes conflicting, but they report that responsibility for providing security in parts of Baghdad began to be turned over to Iraqi forces in late February 2005 and in earnest in March 2005. The 305th "Tiger" Battalion of the Iraqi Army appears to have been the first unit to assume security responsibilities in parts of Baghdad in February.

In March it was joined by the Fortieth Iraqi Army Brigade, bringing the total number of neighborhoods in Baghdad in Iraqi Army hands to ten, including the violent Adhamiya neighborhood and Haifa Street. The commander of Iraqi forces in Baghdad, General Mudhir Mawla, stated, "These operations now are being planned and conducted 100 percent by the Iraqi forces."[61] General Mawla recognized the significance of the gradual transfer, stating, "The plan depends on the success of the Fortieth Brigade in Baghdad. If we succeed in controlling Baghdad, then there will be no need for the presence of U.S. forces. They will have bases outside of Baghdad."[62]

The mixed character of Iraqi performance was indicated by the fact that the United States could deploy a former Iraqi National Guard unit like the 302nd Battalion to the troubled, Sadr-dominated Haifa Road area in Baghdad and plans to deploy a force of some 10,000 Iraqis in Baghdad by late 2005 in an effort to replace U.S. troops. The 1,000 men in the 302nd had also taken twenty-six casualties in fifteen months of fighting—a higher rate than most U.S. units.

The 302nd was also one of the units that now had a twenty-five- to seventy-five-man U.S. advisory team embedded in the unit and was a demonstration of the effectiveness of having U.S. forces help Iraqi units make the transition to full combat effectiveness in the field—a shift in U.S. training efforts that took place early in 2005 and which is described in more detail in the final chapter of this analysis. One special feature of this effort was deploying a team of U.S. special forces to train a thirty-man strike platoon in raids, targeting reconnaissance and undercover intelligence.[63]

At the same time, another such unit—the 305th battalion—that was deployed to Baghdad in May 2005 had lost 50 percent of its original strength to desertions since being formed in late 2003 and had lost dozens more as it moved toward deployment. Its marksmanship and fire discipline remained terrible (soldiers would "cook" an entire magazine in a single poorly aimed burst), and its members tended to "huddle," rather than actively patrol.

The Iraqi Army deployed units to real missions in increasing numbers, and by April it had two areas of operation (AORs) of its own in Mosul and the Haifa Road area in Baghdad. The units performed well in providing security before the elections and in Mosul afterward, although Iraqi battalions operated in areas near U.S. battalions. Even in this case, however, two battalion commanders had to be replaced in Mosul and one company commander after he hid from an angry crowd on election day.[64]

Iraq also began to conduct independent operations in moderate- to high-threat areas like the greater Baghdad area. The Iraqi Interior and Defense Ministries announced on May 26 that they had launched a joint action dubbed "Operation Lightning" involving more than 40,000 Iraqi security forces in Baghdad. The troops, who manned 675 mobile checkpoints and mounted sweeps throughout the city, moved to gain control of all of the roads in and out of the city. The U.S. military reported that Operation Lightning led to a 38 percent reduction in vehicle-borne bombs exploding and a 23 percent increase in such bombs being detected prior to detonation. The operation decreased improvised explosive device (IED) detonations by 10 percent, and the number of coordinated or elaborate attacks against Coalition and Iraqi forces fell by 18 percent.

Other major Iraqi operations included the following:

- Iraqi forces rehearsed, planned, and executed an infiltration and raid entirely on their own southeast of Mosul that yielded intelligence used to capture six insurgent suspects on May 26.
- At the end of May, U.S. chairman of the Joint Chiefs of Staff, General Richard Myers, stated on NBC's *Today Show* that Iraqi Security Forces were conducting five operations completely on their own and without Coalition support.

- Coalition forces and Iraqi Security Forces uncovered approximately fifty insurgent weapons and ammunition caches in seventy-two hours in the Al Anbar province in early June. North of Karmah, the joint operation uncovered a series of bunkers that contained weapons, ammunition, night-vision goggles, uniforms, cell phones, and living quarters. Reportedly, detainees and local residents provided tips that led to the successful raids.
- In June Iraqi and Coalition forces captured insurgent leader Mullah Mahdi in Mosul after a brief gun battle. Mahdi is believed to be linked to Ansar al-Sunna and to the Syrian intelligence service. According to Iraqi Major General Khalil Ahmed al-Obeidi, "He [Mahdi] was wanted for almost all car bombs, assassinations of high officials, beheadings of Iraqi policemen and soldiers, and for launching attacks against multinational forces."[65] Despite Obeidi's statements, the exact extent of Mahdi's role in the insurgency is unclear.

At the same time, the government made efforts to persuade Sunni insurgent groups to give up their support for the insurgency and join Iraq's new political process. The details of these talks are unclear. In a typical press report on such activity, Aiham Alsammarae—a former electricity minister under the Interim Government—claimed that he had been in contact with the leaders of the insurgent groups, the Islamic Army in Iraq and the Mujahideen Army. Alsammarae claimed that he had met with the groups' leaderships approximately ten times in four months and that the leaders were ready to enter into negotiations with the Iraqi government and the United States. The Iraqi government had not been contacted by Alsammarae and neither had the MNF–I forces.[66] It is clear, however, that progress was slow and limited.

The New Force Evaluation Matrix

The fact that virtually all active Iraqi units could take over some kind of useful mission by the summer of 2005 did not mean they had the readiness to take over most missions or that more than a small portion could perform demanding missions. The vast majority of Iraqi military, security, and police units only had the readiness to perform limited security missions.

Iraq's evolving structure was still a very mixed force. Some units performed well. Others were developing the leadership and sense of unit cohesion and integrity needed to become effective—although often only with a major stiffening of U.S. advisers and by a replacement policy that constantly fed in new officers and other ranks until the unit actually held together. However, there were still many cases in which new—and sometimes previously effective—police and other units refused to fight, huddled in defensive positions, or had serious desertion rates. Corruption, nepotism, political favoritism, false manpower reports, and false activity reports continued to be serious problems—something that was inevitable in trying to develop security and police forces in a foreign culture and in a country that was governed in a corrupt manner for decades.

Iraqi forces had, however, advanced to the point where readiness could be judged in terms of unit mission capability and not broad factors like "trained and equipped." The Iraqi Army and National Guard, security services, and police were now being rated at a battalion or other individual unit by a new evaluation matrix developed by the MNSTC–I. This matrix was developed by a combination of Iraqi brigade and battalion commanders and their U.S. advisers and looked at factors like manning levels, equipment levels, training, command and control, leadership, and logistics.

As has been touched upon earlier, this matrix was called the Transition Readiness Assessment (TRA). The assessment of operational units conducted through Multinational Corps–Iraq (MNC–I) Coalition military transition teams embedded at the battalion, brigade, and division level units for the Iraqi Army, special police transition teams (SPTTs) with the Ministry of Interior's special police commando battalions and civil intervention forces, and partnership at the provincial level with Iraqi police forces.[67]

As table 9.9 shows, the TRAs rated Iraqi units as having one of four levels of mission capability. This ranking system differed by force type and evolved over time. For example, in July 2005 the assessments of military units took into account a variety of criteria similar to–but not identical to–the criteria the U.S. Army used to evaluate its units' operational readiness. They focused on factors like personnel, command and control, training, sustainment/logistics, equipment, and leadership.

Overall, operational Iraqi Army units were assessed and categorized as belonging to one of four levels–level one being able to operate independent of Coalition forces and level four being incapable of operations–per table 9.9.[68] The results of this readiness system are classified because MNF–I feels that too much detail would effectively target the less ready units for insurgent attack and deprive them of some of their value as a deterrent and in performing less demanding missions. This is a major consideration since units belonging to levels one, two, and three can and are all performing some useful mission, even if most units cannot stand alone.

Reports on its outcome have, however, been issued in various "blogs" and press reports. According to some press reports, the Iraqi Army and National

TABLE 9.9
Iraqi Transition Readiness Assessment

Level 1	*Fully Capable*: A level one unit is fully capable of planning, executing, and sustaining independent counterinsurgency operations.
Level 2	*Capable*: A level two unit is capable of planning, executing, and sustaining counterinsurgency operations with Coalition support.
Level 3	*Partially Capable*: A level three unit is partially capable of conducting counterinsurgency operations in conjunction with Coalition units.
Level 4	*Incapable*: A level four unit is forming and/or incapable of conducting counterinsurgency operations.

Source: MNF–I, June 2005.

Guard had a total of eighty-one battalions by late May 2005, but a new evaluation matrix developed by the MNSTC–I only rated three battalions at the top
level of readiness and capability, and this did not mean they were capable of
independent operations. Only one of twenty-six brigade headquarters had such
a rating. If one included all of the special police battalions, the press reported
that the total force rose from eighty-one battalions to 101, but the number rated
in the top category only rose from three to five. The United States had concluded that it needed to make further major increases in the number of U.S.
advisory or "transition teams" embedded in Iraqi units and was seeking to
rapidly deploy 2,500 more men by mid-June.[69]

For reasons touched upon earlier, the new rating system found that Iraqi
units were particularly weak in logistics, because they were being rushed into
combat readiness, lacking support personnel like truck drivers, supply clerks,
medics, and engineers. Instead of the nearly fifty-fifty tooth-to-tail ratio in U.S.
forces, only 4,000 of the 75,800 men in rated units were performing support
function. As a result, equipment still tended to mysteriously disappear, the
manpower rolls sometimes had phantom soldiers, and maintenance and support
were provided largely by U.S. forces. This helps explain why the Iraqi government and MNF–I planned to convert one out of five companies in each Iraqi
battalion—some 140 men each—into service support units, to create separate
transportation regiments and a brigade, and to set up ten maintenance and
supply bases across Iraq.[70]

MNSTC–I experts summarized the status of Iraqi forces in mid-June as
follows: no special police units were rated "fully capable" and less than a
handful of army units. Some 40 percent of the special police units were rated
"capable" and 20 percent of army units. Some 40 percent of the special police
units were rated "partially capable" and 45 percent of army units. Less than
10 percent of the special police units were rated "incapable" and less than 20
percent of army units.

Once again, the system was slower in ranking the regular police than the
military and security forces. Only a small fraction of Iraq's 940 police stations
had been assessed using the new system as of May 1, 2005.[71] The new
readiness system was, however, being steadily expanded to cover the police,
and the MNF–I described the effort as follows in late July 2005:[72]

> MOI [Ministry of Interior] Civil Intervention Forces (CIF), Emergency Re-
> sponse Units (ERU), and Special Police Commando Battalions are evaluated using
> a Transition Readiness Assessments (TRAs) process that is similar to that used
> for MOD [Ministry of Defense] forces. MNC–I Special Police Transition Teams
> (SPTTs) are embedded with the MOI's Special Police Commando battalions and
> CIF. The SPTT criteria are similar to those of the MOD forces. Police Partnership
> Program (P3) teams are partnered at the provincial levels with the police to
> help identify areas of progress and shortcomings to determine when these forces
> will be able to assume independent control of their area of responsibility. In lieu
> of the TRA, police partnership assessments look at factors that are more tailored

to the tasks of a police force. More than half of provincial police headquarters currently are assessed to have control in their province.

Progress in reaching the highest levels of readiness continued to be slow through the fall of 2005, but more than sixty army/National Guard combat battalions could perform some role as "partially capable" forces by early August 2005, and more than twenty combat battalions were "capable." In the case of special police forces—which included the public order battalions, mechanized battalions, special police commando battalions, and emergency response units—there were roughly twenty-eight battalion equivalents authorized and twenty-one actually operational. Some ten each of these twenty-one battalions were "partially capable" or "fully capable." Iraq was a long way from having a perfect force but a much longer way from the strength of a single active battalion in July 2004.

U.S. vice-chairman of the Joint Chiefs of Staff, General Peter Pace, spoke as follows about the ability of Iraqi security forces to conduct counterinsurgency operations on their own. At a Senate Armed Services Committee hearing in June 2005, General Pace stated:

> Only a small number of Iraqi Security Forces are taking on the insurgents and terrorists by themselves. Approximately one-third of their army battalions are capable of planning, executing, and sustaining counterinsurgency operations with Coalition support. Approximately two-thirds of their army battalions and one-half of their police battalions are partially capable of conducting counterinsurgency operations in conjunction with Coalition units. Approximately one-half of their police battalions are forming and not yet capable of conducting operations. The majority of Iraqi Security Forces are engaged in operations against the insurgency with varying degrees of cooperation and support from Coalition forces. Many of these units have performed superbly in conducting operations against the enemy, and their operational capability is continuing to improve.[73]

The focus of Iraqi and MNF–I efforts had, however, shifted from force formation to force effectiveness, and by mid-2005 MNSTC–I's goal was to "graduate" most remaining units from basic/small-unit training at level three ("fighting alongside" coalition forces) by the end of 2005 through mid-2006. Their progression to level two or level one will follow on varying timelines. Some "graduated" units may still be assessed as level four (forming), but they should be the exception.

Manpower Relative to Force Structure as Another Measure of the Readiness of Iraqi Forces

Other forms of MNF–I reporting provide additional insights into Iraqi progress in achieving readiness. Table 9.10 shows the manpower in the Iraqi military force structure as of the end of June 2005. Three things are striking about the data in this table. The first is the clear emergence of a ten-division Iraqi force structure in the army and of clearly defined unit elements in the air force and navy. Readiness is not simply a matter of unit capability; it is a matter of developing a force structure that is large enough to be effective. The second is the high manning levels in many units. There were many battalion and other force elements still badly under strength, but other units were overmanned. Iraqi forces were slowly coming together. Third, while some 10 to 20 percent of Iraqi manpower was still on leave/pass status, the percentages that were actually absent without leave (AWOL) were now relatively low. In short, the basic structure to bring Iraqi military forces to a higher level of readiness was now in place.

Problems and Progress in the Iraqi Police

For reasons discussed throughout this analysis reports on the progress of the Iraqi police continued to be considerably more mixed than reports on the Iraqi Army and Security Forces and varied sharply according to unit and the specific mission involved. The largely Iraqi-created special police commandos, for example, got high praise for their aggressiveness, effectiveness, and discipline. The 5,000-man force was formed by former Minister of Interior Falah al-Naqib with the help of his senior U.S. adviser Steve Casteel, a former DEA official with extensive experience with narcoterrorism in Latin America. It was led by Adnan Thabit, a former "Ba'athist," and performed well in Mosul, Ramadi, Baghdad, and Samarra, and acquired a reputation for its toughness, although not for its gentleness and respect for human rights.[74]

In Baghdad special police commandos under the command of Brigadier General Rashid Flaieh became embroiled in a controversy surrounding the deaths of ten Sunni suspects in July 2005. Flaieh's commandos received fire from insurgents near Amariya. Though several of the commandos were injured, they returned fire and then pursued the fleeing gunmen. When General Flaieh took his wounded to the Noor Hospital, close to Abu Ghraib, an area known for its support of the insurgency, he was informed that several militants were being treated inside. According to General Flaieh, his men recognized ten of those who had attacked them, restrained them, and put them into an "armored van."[75]

It remains unclear whether the commandos were from the First Brigade as alleged by doctors or whether they were members of a paramilitary force called the special security force, as General Flaieh maintains. The suspects were locked in the van for two hours, according to the general, but witnesses said it was more like twelve hours. When the van was opened up, all ten Sunnis, all members of the Zobaas and Dulaimi tribes known to be involved in the insurgency, had suffocated. According to doctors who examined the bodies, the victims' bodies indicated that they had been subjected to electrical shock and cable beatings. General Flaieh denied that the suspects had been tortured and asserted that they had suffocated in the van due to a faulty air conditioner.[76] Virtually all of the details of the encounter were disputed by doctors, witnesses, and other policemen.

TABLE 9.10
Iraqi Military Force Structure and Manpower Readiness (as of June 24, 2005)

Force/Unit Element and Location	Authorized	Actual Assigned	Percent Manned	AWOL
I. Total Forces				
Iraqi Army				
Iraqi Intervention Force (IIF)	9,819	9,989	102	2
Regular Army (does not include ING)	40,783	42,237	104	2
Iraqi Army (former Iraqi National Guard)	42,547	31,666	74	2
Iraqi Special Operations Force (ISOF)	1,967	1,031	52	3
Army: RA, IIF, IA	92,074	81,992	89	2
Army: RA, IIF, IA, ISOF	94,041	83,030	88	2
Iraqi Navy (IQN)	631	763	121	1
Iraqi Air Force (IQAF)	695	256	37	0
II. Iraqi Army				
Headquarters/Training/Trans				
Joint Forces Headquarters	505	292	58	0
Iraqi Military Academy Ar Rustamayiah (IMAR)	238	78	33	0
Zahko Military Academy	N/A	26	—	0
First Training Battalion (Taji)	240	763	318	0
First Transportation Regiment (Taji)	765	908	119	1
Second Transportation Regiment (An Numaniyah)	765	738	96	2
Third Transportation Regiment (Al Kisik)	765	510	67	0
First Engineer Regiment	184	181	98	1
Iraqi Army Force Structure				
First Division Total	9,645	9,572	99	2
First Division (IIF) HQ (Baghdad–Taji)	225	963	428	1
First Division 1 BDE (IIF) (Baghdad–Al Rustamayiah)	174	303	174	1
First Division 2 BDE (IIF) (Fallujah)	174	356	205	8
First Division 3 BDE (IIF) (Mosul–Ghabat)	174	319	183	1
First Division 4 BDE (IIF) (Fallujah)	174	398	229	9
Second Division Total	9,645	9,875	102	1
Second Division HQ (Mosul–Al Kindi)	225	0	0	—
Second Division 1 BDE (Irbil–Kesenzan)	174	0	0	—
Second Division 2 BDE 1 BN (Mosul–Al Kindi)	727	1,160	160	0
Second Division 3 BDE (Mosul–Al Kindi)	174	534	307	0
Second Division 4 BDE (Dahuk–Fenfil Camp)	174	941	541	4
Third Division Total	7,290	8,078	111	5
Third Division HQ (Al Kisik)	225	371	165	0
Third Division 1 BDE (Tal Afar)	174	414	238	7
Third Division 2 BDE (Al Kisik)	174	342	197	11
Third Division 3 BDE (Al Kisik)	174	240	138	0
Fourth Division Total	8,744	8,089	93	1
Fourth Division HQ (Toahs Kharmato)	225	197	88	—
Fourth Division 1 BDE 1 BN (Tikrit)	727	574	79	0
Fourth Division 2 BDE (Kirkuk)	174	0	0	—
Fourth Division 3 BDE (Sulaymaniyah)	174	172	99	0
Fifth Division Total	8,017	9,168	114	2
Fifth Division HQ (Kirkush)	225	312	139	0
Fifth Division 1 BDE (Kirkush)	174	469	270	1
Fifth Division 2 BDE (Baquba)	174	237	136	0
Fifth Division 3 BDE (An Numaniyah)	174	290	167	0

(Continued)

TABLE 9.10
Continued

Force/Unit Element and Location	Authorized	Actual Assigned	Percent Manned	AWOL
Sixth Division Total	15,635	14,436	92	3
Sixth Division HQ (Baghdad Protection Division)	225	652	290	1
Sixth Division 1 BDE (Baghdad)	174	190	109	0
Sixth Division 2 BDE (Baghdad)	174	204	117	0
Sixth Division 3 BDE (Baghdad)	174	211	121	0
Sixth Division 4 BDE (Baghdad)	174	211	121	0
Sixth Division 5 BDE (Baghdad)	174	0	0	—
Seventh Division Total	7,290	2,487	34	0
Seventh Division Div HQ	225	0	0	—
Seventh Division 1 BDE (Martyr Monument)	174	320	184	0
Seventh Division 2 BDE (Fallujah)	174	0	0	—
Seventh Division 3 BDE (Ramadi)	727	0	0	—
Eighth Division Total	6,563	6,751	103	1
Eighth Division HQ	225	176	78	0
Eighth Division 1 BDE (Diwaniyah)	174	105	60	0
Eighth Division 2 BDE (Hilla)	174	101	58	0
Eighth Division 3 BDE (Kut)	174	104	60	0
Ninth Division Total	4,868	2,524	52	2
Ninth Division (Tadji)	96	0	0	—
Ninth Division 1 Mech BDE	96	345	359	0
Ninth Division 2 Armored BDE	96	0	0	—
Ninth Division 3 Mech BDE	96	0	0	—
Tenth Division Total	8,191	5,468	67	1
Tenth Division HQ (Basra)	225	169	75	2
Tenth Division 1 BDE (Basra)	174	345	198	1
Tenth Division 2 BDE (Al Samawah)	174	160	92	0
Tenth Division 3 BDE (Al Nasiriyah/Oor camp)	174	114	66	0
Tenth Division 4 BDE (Al Betairah Airport)	174	129	74	0
Iraqi Special Operations Forces				
SOF HQ	143	33	23	0
Thirty-sixth Battalion	829	602	73	4
Iraqi C Task Force	451	290	64	0
Recce Company	190	49	26	0
SPT	354	64	53	3
III. Iraqi Navy				
Iraqi Navy Force Structure				
Iraqi Navy HQ	92	380	413	1
Iraqi Navy (Seamen)	231	191	83	0
Iraqi Navy (Infantry)	308	192	62	2
IV. Iraqi Air Force				
Iraqi Air Force Structure Air Force HQ	49	17	35	0
Third Squadron VIP	74	24	32	0
Twenty-third Squadron Transport	144	113	78	0
Seventieth Squadron Recce	84	36	43	0
Twelfth Squadron Jet Ranger	66	13	20	0
Fourth Squadron Helo	97	0	0	—
Second Squadron Helo	97	53	55	0
Ninety-sixth Squadron Recce	84	0	0	—

Source: MNF–I.

Doctors at the al Yarmouk Hospital went on strike in July 2005 in protest over rough treatment at the hands of the Iraqi Army. According to medical staff, soldiers entered the hospital with their weapons—an action forbidden by a government order signed by Barham Saleh—pulled blankets off women patients, and insulted the overnight doctor. The doctors demanded that the soldiers apologize to the doctor, that security be provided for all of the hospital's doctors, and that the Ministries of Defense and Interior should rigidly enforce the prohibition of weapons in hospitals.

Iraqi Interior Minister Bayan Jabr responded to charges of detainee abuse by Iraqi soldiers in July by reiterating the fact that he had strengthened the office of the inspector general (IG). Jabr stated that he had empowered the IG to investigate human rights abuses and allegations of corruption. The IG was given the ability to bring charges against individuals involved in human-rights abuses and instances of corruption. Lastly, the IG was instructed to inform the interior minister of all such cases. Jabr pointed out that the ministry had arrested individuals within the ministry who were found to have been involved in such instances.

The danger, however, is that if such incidents are repeated, the forces of the Ministries of Interior and Defense, largely composed of Shi'ites and some Saddam-era soldiers, will fail to attract Sunni support and rather be seen as an instrument of oppression rather than an example of the rule of law. The goal is to create a force that reinforces the law and elicits respect from the Iraqi people, not an apparatus reminiscent of Saddam's police state.

There were also reports of the slow rebuilding of Iraqi police units in Mosul and in its approaches like the town of Qayyarah on the Tigris and along the main Mosul-to-Baghdad highway. The area had become a major trouble spot after insurgents fled the battle of Fallujah, and police in the area had suddenly deserted in numbers that cut their strength from 2,000 to fifty. By April 2005, however, many units were up to strength and the police were actively patrolling the area.[77]

General Abizaid and four other high-ranking U.S. officers gave briefings in late May 2005 that made it clear that they felt the police had fallen behind the regular military forces, and this meant army units and elite units had to be used for security duties, rather than replacing Coalition forces in combat. They took an unusually public stance on the issue, and some warned that it would "take years" to make such Iraqi forces effective and deal with the insurgency. They also stated that these problems with the police were a key reason why Iraqi forces could not participate actively in Operation Matador in April, the largest Marine offensive since Fallujah and a key effort to secure main routes from Syria and the Syrian border area. They claimed the lack of troops was also a reason so many insurgents were able to disperse.[78]

At the same time, some of these problems had occurred because the police took the brunt of insurgent attacks, largely because they were more exposed and more vulnerable. According to Pentagon sources, the police took the vast majority of the 1,850 casualties in Iraqi forces that Department of Defense sources had counted as of mid-May 2005.[79] Given the lack of training, equipment, facilities, and leadership they began with, it is not surprising that there were many cases in which police units had high desertion rates, huddled in their headquarters, or did not perform their duties. There were also cases where they performed actions like torturing three Shi'ite militiamen in their custody to death.[80]

The problems in the police were compounded by the lack of a retirement system under Saddam Hussein's government that meant older police, and even their widows, were carried as active to give them some income. Selection and promotion by favoritism and bribe taking had become part of the police culture, as had passively waiting for complaints from victims and then taking money from both the accused and complainant. The lack of a fully staffed financial management, manpower, planning, and financial control structure in the Ministry of the Interior also added to these problems.

By the early fall of 2005, however, things had made some limited improvement. The Ministry of Defense was now gradually beginning to take shape as a functioning ministry with key staff elements like an inspector general. As has been shown earlier, most serious equipment problems had been corrected, although problems existed in the way the inventory was distributed. Tables 9.5 through 9.7 have already shown the improvement in training. "Trained and equipped" manpower exceeded 91,000 in the early summer (including 58,764 police, 5,136 in the civil intervention force, 8,131 police commandos, 205 in the central emergency response unit, 1,118 highway patrol, and 500 dignitary protection), and a tentative force goal of 135,000 men had been established. These figures did not include any men from the older Iraqi Civil Defense Force, or any of the 74,400 men still assigned to the remnants of the relatively low-grade Facilities Protection Service.

The Iraqi Special Police Force had made progress toward reaching a strength of some 56,000 men, although serious questions remained about how broadly based its leadership and manpower were and how many Sunnis were included. As of October 1, 2004, there were three police commando battalions, no public order battalions, and no mechanized police battalions; this gave the Iraqi Special Police Force a total strength of only three battalions, none of which were rated as operational. All were deployed at Ar Rustamayiah in the greater Baghdad area. As of May 30, 2004, the *operational strength* of the Iraqi Special Police Force included nine police commando battalions, twelve public order battalions, two mechanized police battalions, and four special border forces; this gave the Iraqi Special Police a total operational strength of twenty-seven battalions. In addition, four more battalions were in training, including three police commando battalions and one mechanized police battalion. There were also twenty-seven SWAT teams with an average of twenty-seven men each. Forces were now deployed in the Mosul area, active in the greater Baghdad area, operating in Fallujah and Ar Ramadi, deployed at An Numaniyah and Scania, and beginning to deploy in the west in Al Anbar.

The Special Police Forces had developed a clear command structure under Major General Adnan Thabit, and the mechanized battalions were being organized into the Eighth Mechanized Police Brigade. Police training was now supported by regional academies in Iraq, in addition to the training center in Jordan. Regional academies now existed in Adnon, Mosul, and Sulaymaniyah in the north; A Asad, Taji, Baghdad, Hilla, and Kut in the Center; and Basra in the south. These efforts were backed by the same new "top-down" approach to embedding trainers and partners in both the Ministry of Interior and active regular police operations that was now being used in the military and special police. The previous training effort had been restructured to create both a Police Partnership Program (Ministry of Interior) and an integrated Police Partnership Program (provincial), called the P3(P), to work with the force in each province.

The teams in the Ministry of Interior provide a core of trainers to help the minister become more functional. The provincial or P3(P) teams were designed to give the police in each province a steadily higher degree of independence and eventually create the conditions for the disengagement of provincial Coalition forces. P3(P) teams with a nominal strength of ten men, covering the full range of necessary expertise in an integrated team, were being deployed to assist senior Iraqi police and act as partners in staffing provincial headquarters. A total of nineteen teams had been set up by June 2005, although the majority were still in the process of acquiring the necessary manpower. These teams operated from forward operating bases near the headquarters and helped police leaders deal with key problems such as logistics, intelligence, financial accounting and contracts, budget planning and management, special police operations, counterinsurgency, and communications. By June 2005 there were over 480 such advisers active in the field. The goal was to maintain 500 posts and build toward 600, while developing an effective liaison between their efforts and the work of Coalition forces.[81]

This improvement in training was accompanied by some improvement in leadership. Much of the old order at the top was gone, and many new leaders were men who had come from the army and who had strongly opposed the old system. By June 2005, seventeen of the eighteen provincial chiefs were ex-military. A major crimes unit was being established that actually investigated, rather than simply put people in jail. Police elements were slowly being rebuilt in cities like Fallujah, Mosul, Ramadi, and Baiji using manpower that was take from outside the region and less subject to influence and intimidation. Efforts were under way to reduce favoritism, provide proper pay, eliminate corruption, and provide the kind of entry- and lower-level training that had been totally missing in the regular police force under Saddam Hussein. While illiteracy had not been eliminated, it was being reduced. The Iraqi people were coming into stations in larger numbers, providing more intelligence and using telephone tip-lines. The result was a major improvement in regular police capabilities in fourteen of Iraq's eighteen provinces.

The CPATT and Ministry of Interior also had developed reporting systems designed to measure the readiness of the regular police and their levels of manning and equipment similar to those used for military units. These included detailed monthly police station reports, which covered manning, training, readiness, and equipment. Personnel quality was surveyed in depth, including activities like prisoner rights, human rights, and property accountability. These were used to develop summaries of police activity by province. For example, the report on police stations in Baghdad province for May 2005 scored leadership at 51 percent, station manning at 72 percent, personnel status at 92 percent, training at 75 percent, effectiveness at 74 percent, force protection at 74 percent, equipment at 86 percent, and facilities at 86 percent. Detailed assessments were made within each category, and the reports include data on crime rates and detainees. There had been eighty-six insurgent attacks on stations in Baghdad province in May; 102 police were killed in action and 257 were wounded, and the stations held 689 detainees, 56 percent of which were rated as nonviolent.[82]

These provincial reports include detailed equipment counts and comparisons against authorized holdings, analysis of force-protection systems, percentage data on the adequacy of training by rank, analyses of intelligence capabilities, and analysis of financial management capabilities. There was also an independent assessment by the provincial chief of police. Each province was then rated according to the same four levels of readiness used for the military and special police units.[83] This system was still in the process of implementation in the early summer of 2005, but it again showed that major progress had been made and that a serious attempt to establish real-world readiness standards was under way.

The Iraqi Border Forces

The Iraqi Border Police were still a largely hollow force as of the early summer of 2005, but serious efforts were under way to increase their numbers, improve their training and equipment, give them better facilities, and create a new chain of forts along the Iraqi-Syrian border. A tentative force goal of some 40,000 men was shown on their organizational charts, but the border enforcement forces had only 15,583 actives, and the Iraqi Bureau of Dignitary Protection (BDP) only had 500 men assigned for an authorized strength of 2,760.[84]

While Muhammed Sabr in the Iraqi Department of Border Enforcement called his men "desert wolves," this scarcely seemed to be the case. Interviews and press reports indicated their performance was weak on the Jordanian, Saudi, and Iranian borders and very weak on the Syrian border. One press report indicated that some border forts had lost some 80 percent of their manning, lacked weapons, furniture, and even uniforms. Some had been looted and others destroyed by insurgents. Of the thirty-two border forts originally planned for Al Anbar province, many had not been completed, others were abandoned, and many were badly understaffed. Trucks (and men) routinely entered Iraq illegally for small bribes.[85]

The Department of Defense touched on some of these problems in its July 2005 reporting on the force:

> To date, more than 15,500 Border Police have been trained. The Border Police receive training in small unit patrolling, vehicle search, personnel search, rights of the individual, life saving, Iraqi Border Law, handling of detainees, and weapons. Border police equipment includes Chevy Luv pick-up trucks, mid-size SUVs, Nissan pick-up trucks, AK-47s, PKC machine guns, Glock pistols, HF radios, and body armor.
>
> Currently, the ISF [Iraqi security forces] do not have a system in place to track the Border Police's readiness and capabilities. The goal is for each member and station to be equipped with mission-essential equipment. No estimate exists on the percentage of desertion and absenteeism, although we know that the Border Police has experienced a significant rate of attrition. The extent of insurgent infiltration varies by province. In some areas of the border, there appears to be a high level of insurgent infiltration.
>
> The effectiveness of the Border Police officer cadres and the chain of command varies widely but is generally moderate to low. An effort has been ongoing to energize the Border Police leadership and recruit for the Border Police Academy.[86]

The border forces were, however, beginning to get the training they needed. Border forts and facilities were largely complete in the eastern border area with Iran, and facilities and equipment were being improved in the North and South. While any such plans had to be tentative, the strength of the border defense force battalions had already risen sharply and plans for further expansion were under way. These plans are shown in table 9.11. Iraq was increasing the number of regional headquarters from five to eight and planned to establish sixteen regional brigade headquarters to provide better coordination and direction. It had created a central headquarters and training academy and three regional training academies.[87]

The MNC–I, MNSTC–I, and Ministry of Defense were working to help Iraq regain control of its borders in the tough spots, primarily the border with Syria,

TABLE 9.11
Iraq Border Defense Battalion Deployments

Border Defense Battalions by Region	Actual March 2005	Planned Additional Units		
		July 2005	Jan 2006	August 2006
Syrian border	4–5	4	2	2
Jordanian border	2	—	—	1
Saudi border	7	—	1	1
Kuwaiti border	2–3	—	—	1
Iranian border	12–13	—	3	8
Turkish border	7–8	—	—	1
Total additional	N/A	4	10	24
Total active at time shown	36	40	46	60

as soon as possible. This effort was in its early stages, but reconstruction of the border forts in those areas, generation of additional border guards, generation of additional Iraqi Army units, and support for the ports of entry where Department of Homeland Security border support teams now provided some support were all under way. Iraq's First Special Border Force Battalion was operating on the Syrian border in western Anbar province by the summer of 2005. The Second Battalion completed training in early February and has begun its deployments, and a third completed training in March. Construction on new facilities in the West was under way.

Border transition teams were to begin linking up with Iraqi Border Guard units in August and September and were already in Iraq and completing their final preparations. This, too, was a large and complex effort but was at least under way and may help reduce the number of foreign suicide bombers and movement of funds and leaders. It will also have an impact on smuggling, which saps some of Iraq's economic power. It will, however, require additional equipment and technology, such as backscatter x-ray machines, which are already finding contraband at the ports of entry, and the PISCES system, which requires significant database development to be effective in the mid-term. Construction on new facilities in the West was under way. In short, the border forces still had a long way to go, but the situation was getting better.

The Issue of Financing

By the summer of 2005, Iraqi forces had grown to the point where financing was beginning to be a major issue, particularly to those Iraqi officials who were concerned with how the Iraqi forces should be shaped and self-financed once the insurgency was largely over. By mid-May of 2005, some $6.21 billion had already been made available for Iraqi force development, of which only $1 billion had come from Iraqi funding and $5.21 billion from U.S. appropriated funds. Some $5.41 billion of this funding was to be executed in programs run by MNSTC–I. The accounting for these funds was anything but neat, but table 9.12 shows where the money went in broad terms and what the key priorities were during the initial stages of Iraqi force development.

In terms of ongoing funding priorities, money had to be allocated to projects like creating a standardized battalion table of organization and equipment (TO&E), fielding a mechanized division and motorized division, creating a Fourth Special Police Commando brigade, and enabling Iraqi Army units to occupy uncovered Coalition bases. The MNF–I had also worked with the Ministries of Defense and Interior to identify some $5.7 billion in proposed funding, including $2.6 billion for the Ministry of Defense, $1.4 billion for the Ministry of Interior, $1.1 billion for construction, and $180 million for quick reaction forces. In addition, $409 million was to be diverted to such projects as the Jordan training center ($99 million), improving army operations and maintenance ($210 million), and tier one personal-security detachments ($100 million).

TABLE 9.12

Allocation of U.S. Aid Funding to Iraqi Forces (in millions of U.S. dollars funded as of May 15, 2005)

Category	Initial IRRF $3.2 Billion in FY04 Supplemental	IRRF Reallocation $1.8 Billion In Reprogramming
Iraqi Army Forces	1,600	—
Special Forces	—	67
Iraqi National Guard	241	84
Basing	—	320
Quick Reaction Force	—	80
Iraqi Police Service	1,040	—
Jordan training, International Police Advisers	600	—
Specialized Police training, Adnon Palace	200	—
Specialized Police infrastructure	—	50
Public training and facilities	161	81
BDP/ERU expansion; additional 45,000 IPS officers	—	500
Construction	—	166
Border Enforcement (DBE)	280	—
DBE Border Forts	—	64
Additional 20,000 DBE officers	—	127
Facilities Protection Service (FPS)	73	—

Source: MNSTC–I, Iraqi security forces fund requirements review, May 15, 2005.

Key Ministry of Defense proposals included thirty-nine projects. These included completing the First Mechanized Division; adding a motorized division; adding sustainment, including seven base units and a vehicle maintenance contract; buying more tactical communications equipment; and funding branch schools. They also included funding for more support units such as three division-level signal companies; three intelligence, surveillance, and reconnaissance (IS&R) companies; nine military police (MP) companies; and five motorized rifle regiments. It is notable that at this point funds were limited enough that they could not buy five divisions worth of tactical communications equipment, support companies for some battalions, eighteen oil security battalions, and an additional motor transport regiment.

Key Ministry of Interior proposals included forty-three projects. These included life-support systems, equipping and training six police commando battalions, equipment and training for more personnel for public order battalions, secure communications for major headquarters, training funding, and maintenance contracts for a variety of systems. Funds were too limited to buy full equipment and training for the Department of Border Enforcement, an information technology (IT) systems architecture for the ministry, equipment to expand the highway patrol, equipment for two more public order brigades, equipment and training for fifteen police commando battalions, UHF/HF radios, and expansion of the Mosul academy. In addition, there were some fifty detailed construction projects for various elements of the military, security, and police forces.

Such detail may seem relatively mundane until it is realized how important it is in creating balanced force quality in both the military and police services and in the capability to transition from Coalition to Iraqi forces over time. The very fact that such financing plans existed and were prioritized within each ministry also represented a major advance over the previous year.

At the same time, the Ministries of Defense and Interior still faced major problems in terms of planning and managing their resources. Both ministries had several problems in common. The overall structure of financial planning and management in each ministry was weak, and the departments designed to control the flow of money had limited effectiveness. Coordination with the MNF–I and MNSTC–I was poor, and in critical areas like equipment purchases there was little coordination. MNSTC–I could place one set of orders based on its force plans, and various elements of the Ministries of Defense and Interior placed orders for different force plans on their own. The Ministry of Finance exercised little control, and there was little coordination of the Coalition aid effort and the Iraqi budget at the planning level and at any detailed level of fiscal control and responsibility. The July 2005 report of the inspector generals of the State Department and Department of Defense illustrates the practical impact of some of these problems on the Iraqi police services, but such problems affected both the Ministry of Defense and Ministry of Interior and every element of the Iraqi forces:

> On the resource front, an immediate issue is the MOI [Ministry of Interior] budget. For FY05 (January 1–December 31, 2005), the MOI budget is adequate to fund salaries of 128,000 employees.
>
> Some time before this fieldwork, then IIG [Iraqi Interim Government] Prime Minister [Ayad] Allawi approved funding for 156,000. The Council of Ministers did not ratify this decision; hence, the Minister of Finance did not fund MOI's increased requirement. Meanwhile, present MOI personnel (both IPs [Iraqi Police] and staff, the latter predominantly at MOI headquarters in Baghdad) number about 170,000. By training additional IPs, CPATT [Civilian Police Assistance Training Team] effectively exacerbates the budget shortfall.
>
> A factor in the MOI's financial capability to sustain the growing IPS [Iraqi Police Service] force is the considerable, though undetermined, number of "ghost" employees on the ministry's roster. Although not productively engaged in the MOI's structure, these persons are, nonetheless, on the payroll. Some encumber sinecures for family or tribal members.
>
> Others are retired personnel who draw salaries in a socio-economic system without adequate—or any—pensions.
>
> It is conceivable that the Iraqi transitional government (ITG) may allocate additional fiscal year 2005 funds to the Ministry of Interior. Absent such action, some Coalition officials opine that capital development funds could be shifted within the ministry's budget to cover salary shortfalls, although the deputy minister states categorically that shifting resources between funding "chapters" is not possible. One senior Coalition official posits that, contingent on Congressional

approval of the DoD [Department of Defense] supplemental legislation and the requested $5.7 billion additional training fund, the United States may be able to cover the prospective MOI budget deficit relative to IPS salaries. At best, this would be a stopgap measure. More importantly, the IG Team believes any such action would establish an unfortunate financial and political precedent.

The Coalition IPS training program is capital intensive. Thus far, the U.S. Government has spent about $190 million in building or renovating training facilities both at JIPTC and inside Iraq. By and large, the Coalition created the facilities. The MOI will inherit them. The Deputy Minister of Interior (Finance) told the IG Team that the "MOI has no funding in the Ministry's FY05 budget for police academies." Thus, the Coalition will bear the full cost of operating and maintaining these facilities. Yet to be determined are the costs for out-year operation and maintenance (O&M) and the MOI's determination and ability to shoulder those costs.[88]

Corruption remained a major problem, particularly in the equipment and purchasing sections of the Ministry of Defense, although the new government had made a major effort to clean up this aspect of the ministry's operations and find more honest officials. The hiring of manpower within the services and the ministries often far exceeded authorized levels, a problem compounded by phantom appointments, favoritism, and nepotism. In short, the progress in force development outpaced the ability to plan and allocate resources—a problem that promised to be far more serious in the future as expenditures within the Ministries of Defense and Interior put more and more strain on the budget and the Coalition spent available aid funds.

It was also clear that these problems would create problems for the Iraqi government as it took over full responsibility from the MNF–I and MNSTC–I. The Iraqi government would have to exercise far tighter control over planning, costs, and expenditures to keep the cost of Iraqi forces within its budget. Aid would almost certainly diminish, while competing civil needs would take on higher priority as security improved. Iraq would also have to make hard choices in funding forces capable of defending its borders against potential foreign threat, as distinguished from forces focused on counterinsurgency. As was the case in virtually every aspect of Iraqi force development, "progress" was very different from "success" or "victory."

10 The Iraqi View of Iraq's Emerging Forces

IRAQI OFFICIALS and officers provide an important additional perspective on the development of Iraqi forces. While there is no way to conduct a systematic survey of Iraqi officials and officers, e-mails, and visits, but discussions from late 2004 through the spring and summer of 2005 showed that such officials and officers had a good picture of the problems involved, readily acknowledged that Iraqi forces still had a long way to go, and accepted the seriousness of the challenges they had to meet. With some exceptions senior Iraqi officials and officers understood the risks imposed by Iraq's ethnic and sectarian divisions; the election of a new, inexperienced, and Shi'ite-dominated government; the uncertainties in being dependent on a U.S.-dominated MNSTC–I aid program, and the problems of having to persuade the United States to provide the aid and equipment necessary to create truly independent Iraqi forces that could stand on their own. Furthermore, top officials in the newly elected government made these positions public from the point they first took office and consistently supported these positions through the summer of 2005, in spite of a series of bloody bombings designed to drive Iraq toward ethnic and sectarian conflict.

Iraqi Prime Minister Ibrahim al-Jafari gave a speech at the end of May in which he expressed what he considered to be "Iraq's three pivots to security." First, Jafari stated that Iraq would seek to improve the capabilities of the Iraqi security forces through training, delivery of equipment, and improving readiness. Second, the prime minister stated that preventing terrorists from infiltrating Iraq and the necessary coordination with bordering states was another priority. Thirdly, Jafari stated that many attacks had been stopped by tips provided by Iraqi citizens, and he encouraged them to continue to report such activity.

Iraqi Foreign Minister Hoshyar Zebari went before the UN Security Council to formally ask that the MNF–I remain in Iraq. He stated, "We look forward to the day when our forces are able to assume full responsibility for maintaining our national security at which time there will be no need for the engagement of the MNF. Until then, we need the continued presence of the MNF in Iraq."[1]

Both the Minister of Defense and Minister of Interior continued to stress the importance of developing forces that would maintain a rule of law, and respect for human rights—even in the face of a major counterinsurgency campaign. They also stressed the need to fight corruption and change the past culture of Iraq's military and police forces to stress professionalism and promotion by merit.[2]

One example of such efforts is the statement that the minister of defense, Dr. Saadoun al-Dulaimi, made to an international forum in Brussels in July 2005:

> ... it is not sufficient just to have successful and effective law enforcement forces. These forces must also be truly representative of all the peoples of Iraq. For Iraq to succeed in moving forward its law enforcement staff, police, military and civilian, must put aside their sectarian and ethnic prejudices and work for the best interests of Iraq as a whole. In this regard, I am determined to work with the new government to keep politics out of defense and security matters. Moreover, law enforcement more than anywhere else needs expertise from all quarters. There are many, including some police and military officers from the former regime whose hands are not stained with blood, who are already working against the terrorists and who, as individuals, have an important role to play in the new Iraq. We welcome them with open arms. There is, however, no room for tribal militia or special units in the modern, professional security forces that we are now building.[3]

Senior Iraqi officials also continued to pursue policies of restraint and inclusiveness throughout the summer, not only in the face of continued provocation from Islamist extremist terrorists but also in the face of all of the problems in creating a constitutional process and effective governance in the face of great Sunni uncertainty and sometimes resistance to a political process that they had failed to join before the election.

Force Development Principles and Strategy

Iraqi officers stressed that Iraqi forces had to develop in ways that were both inclusive of all the sectarian and ethnic factions in Iraq and compatible with the emergence of an Iraqi democracy. The official position was that this meant force development on the basis of the following six principles:

- Democracy
- Civilian control of the military
- Transparency
- Rule of law
- Responsibility and accountability
- Equality and justice among religions

The reality was that Iraqis fully understood how difficult this would be—particularly in the middle of a major counterinsurgency campaign and with many ethnic and sectarian differences. Many also privately added three other principles: unity, anticorruption, and effectiveness.

Developing Effective Ministries and "Governance"

Iraqi officials at many levels made it clear that Iraq was still in the process of developing an effective Ministry of Defense and Ministry of Interior and anything approaching a coordinated national security structure at the top. The development of effective structures to manage police and internal security forces at the governorate and local level was seen as even more of a work in progress. They estimated that it would take all of 2005 and most of 2006 to develop a stable and more comprehensive overall structure for handling the "governance" aspects of Iraq's military, security, and police forces.

Iraqi officials and officers felt that the three months of transition it took to form a new government between January 30, 2005, and April–May 2005 had created much the same turbulence and uncertainty as had occurred when ministers had changed with the return to sovereignty in June 2004, although many were pleased with the choices of new ministers and saw them as improvements over their predecessors. They also felt that the effort to create a new constitution and the transition to yet another new Iraqi government in late 2005 or early 2006 would create turbulence under the best of circumstances. They noted that the three-month delay in forming a new government after the January 30, 2005, election left the Ministries of Defense and Interior without fully effective direction during this period, and they worried that ethnic and sectarian divisions within the new elected government might create a series of problems indefinitely into the future. They made it clear that even Iraqis actively involved in the process of Iraqi politics, governance, and force building could not predict how new governments would behave over the course of 2005–2006 or how the constitutional process and the success or failure of efforts at political inclusion will change Iraqi security policy.

Many of these concerns were resolved by the spring and summer of 2005. Iraqi officials and officers generally gave high marks to the new government and the new ministers of defense and interior. They felt both were more concerned with "hands-on" efforts to make their ministries more effective and eliminate corruption. However, some were now deeply concerned about the risk that the tensions between Sunni and Shi'ite—and the desire of the new Shi'ite-dominated government to "purge" even officials and officers with low-level ties to the Ba'ath and Saddam Hussein's government—could potentially cripple Iraqi force development.[4] The seriousness of such concerns was confirmed by warnings against such purges by top U.S. officials and a sudden visit to Baghdad by U.S. Secretary of Defense Donald Rumsfeld to talk to Iraq's new president, Jalal Talibani, Prime Minister Ibrahim Jafari, and other top officials.[5]

Moving toward Iraqi Control of the Force Development Effort

Iraqi officials and officers acknowledged the limits to their ability to plan and manage Iraq's force development in any orderly way under the CPA and interim Iraqi government. At least as of the spring of 2005, Iraqi officials and officers had never had a clear basis for force planning that could be tied to a real-world budget and no way to predict the level and flow of U.S. and other MNSTC–I aid. They also understood that even if the course of the insurgency was predictable, Iraqi military and security developments would have to be very much a matter of improvisation and uncertainty.

At the same time, they stated that cooperation among the ministries had improved since the January 30 election and felt this would continue if there were no purges of existing staffs on sectarian and ethnic lines. They noted that communications were better, and there was more experience in day-to-day coordination. They felt Iraqi government relations with the United States and other MNF–I elements were good and noted that the Iraqi government now had a national security coordination committee scheduled to meet twice a week, as well as a higher level joint coordination group at the minister–deputy minister level. They also felt that the key ministries involved in national security were gradually acquiring experienced civilian personnel, adequate facilities and equipment, and adequate communications.

Moreover, even those Sunnis taking part in the constitutional process remained dissatisfied as of the fall of 2005, as Shi'ite and Kurdish representatives to the drafting committee attempted to push through a version of the document that the Sunnis objected to on several grounds. On August 28, 2005, Sunni Arab negotiators, in a joint statement by the fifteen-member Sunni panel, rejected the Iraqi draft constitution and asked the Arab League and the United Nations to intervene. Chief among Sunni objections to the document was the issue of a federal Iraq, which Sunnis believe would deprive the west of oil revenues, and exclusionary references to the Ba'ath Party, which many Sunnis see as an attempt to codify their political disenfranchisement. Another issue was the document's failure to enshrine Iraq's identity as "Arab." However, as of September 14, 2005, Shi'ites and Kurds agreed to amend the constitution as it goes to UN print to cite Iraq as a founding member of the Arab League, a nod to Sunni demands for national ethnic identity. Federalism clauses, however, were not removed, thus preserving Shi'ite and Kurd regional options.[6]

While they felt progress was slower in creating effective coordination and cooperation at the governorate and local level—and presented major problems in many areas and in key cities like Basra—Iraqis saw some improvement in these areas as well. They felt that local elections on January 30 had helped in some areas, although they felt such developments depended a great deal on the province and city.

Developing an Iraqi Force Plan

Iraqi officials stated that the interim Iraqi government had developed the outline of a national strategy for the next five to seven years during the period between June 2004 and the January 2005 election. This strategy was based on the following four elements:

- Threat analysis
- Analysis of the interests of neighboring states, other nations, and the international community and the resulting diplomatic and security requirements
- Strategy needed to develop armed forces and security forces and the resulting requirements in terms of force size and equipment
- Economic and social strategy

The details of this plan underwent major changes after the new government took office in April 2005. Many of the detailed force goals that the new government worked out with the MNF–I and MNSTC–I have been described in the previous chapter, and the Iraqi minister of defense described the following major challenges in July 2005:[7]

- Corruption and growing criminality
- Foreign insurgents and anti-Iraqi terrorists trying to destabilize the country
- Intelligence, particularly overcoming poor analysis and assessment capability
- Institutional capacity, including leadership and professional skills
- Filling out the force structure with combat support and combat service support units
- Strengthening border security—with a total of 3,631 kilometers of external borders
- Undertaking the infrastructure security mission
- Logistics and sustainment, particularly in the medium and long term, as a major concern
- Rebuilding the navy, air force, and special operations forces
- Continuous Iraqi armed forces transition, particularly the issue of the full integration of former National Guard units into the regular army, the issue of militias, and the whole issue of establishing a sustainable cycle of training and exercises without assistance

Discussions with top-level officials and officers made it clear that they were well aware of the force development problems described in previous chapters, and they showed a great deal of frankness and objectivity in discussing the difficulties they faced.

The minister of the interior focused heavily on corruption, changing the culture of the police, the need to train forces in human rights and the rule of law, and the need to provide more training in the field for forces already in service. He was particularly concerned with the regular police service and the additional forces recruited at the local level that had not been through MNSTC–I training. At the same time, Iraqi officials and officers were aware that sectarian and ethnic tensions could still tear the government apart, that nothing was stable in terms of current force plans, and that they had little ability to plan in terms of known budgets and levels of aid. They also realized they remained dependent on the United States and MNSTC–I for many aspects of funding and support.

On the one hand, they saw the need for longer-term planning and realized that the new government still had to develop the staffs and capability to make its own force development plans, deal with budget and resource issues, and plan and conduct operations. On the other hand, many felt that dependence on the Coalition, the uncertainties of Iraqi politics, and the changing dynamics of the insurgency placed severe limits on what the government could do before a new government was elected in late 2005 or early 2006.

Iraqi Intelligence

Iraqis understood that their present intelligence capabilities were limited, and they remained dependent on the United States and MNF–I except at the local level or in the case of small-unit operations in areas where units developed HUMINT contacts of their own.[8] They acknowledged that they were penetrated by hostile agents and that this was likely to continue until the new government acquired far more popular legitimacy and Sunnis and Iraqi Islamists gave it more support—a matter that might well take years. They acknowledged that current Iraqi counterintelligence capabilities were inadequate, and that vetting was often cursory and uncertain. Like senior U.S. officers in Iraq, they acknowledged that the government and all elements of Iraqi forces were heavily penetrated by supporters of various insurgent groups, and that insurgent HUMINT was still much better than that of either Coalition or Iraqi forces.[9]

Iraqi officers and officials did feel, however, that Iraq was beginning to develop effective human intelligence capabilities. These intelligence capabilities were divided into three major groups: military intelligence in the Ministry of Defense, the Police Intelligence Directorate in the Ministry of the Interior, and the Iraqi National Intelligence Services in the Prime Minister's office.

Military intelligence was headed by the director general of intelligence and security. This office was being developed as a key priority, and the minister of defense acknowledged in July 2005 that it "is still in its early stages of formation. It needs to better focus its efforts on 'hot spots' to achieve best effect. But it also needs secure nationwide communications and better training and equipment. There is a particular need for short-term improvements in its analytical and assessment staff and, in the longer-term, for bilateral arrangements to enable the exchange of intelligence products with our friends and allies."[10]

Iraq hoped for extensive further training help from the intelligence sections of NATO countries. More broadly, both actionable operational intelligence and counterintelligence were seen as key priorities at every level, and Iraqi officers and officials make it clear that "good intelligence is more important than good weapons." The Ministry of Interior had also created a special intelligence section to support "quick intervention" operations and was attempting to improve intelligence and counterintelligence efforts in the field at the level of the security and police services.

There was, however, considerable debate within the new Iraqi government over one aspect of Iraqi intelligence. While military and counterinsurgency intelligence flowed to Iraqi forces from the United States and MNF-I and they received human intelligence at the tactical level in return, Iraqi national intelligence had been formed with the support of the CIA, which attempted to keep its operations compartmented away from the newly elected government. According to press reports, the CIA refused to hand over control of this part of Iraq's Intelligence Service, and the head of the Iraqi Intelligence Service that the CIA had chosen at the time of the CPA continued to report to the CIA.

The history of this problem began when the CPA transferred sovereignty in June 2004. According to the press report, what was then the CMAD—the Collection, Management, and Analysis Directorate—was split with roughly half the agents going to the new Ministry of Interior and the rest to work on military intelligence in the Ministry of Defense. Both of these intelligence departments were led by Kurds with pro-U.S. backgrounds who now reported to the Iraqi prime minister.

However, a key group of CMAD operatives was recruited into a third Iraqi intelligence agency, which became the secret police force or Mukhabarat. Its Iraqi director was Mohammed Abdullah Shahwani, a Sunni general whose sons had been executed after his involvement in a failed coup against Saddam Hussein in the mid-1990s. Reports indicate that Shahwani's top deputy was a Kurd, and Shi'ites made up only 12 percent of the force.

Also, the CIA took the national intelligence archives of the past year and kept them in their headquarters in Baghdad where they could not be accessed by the new government. CIA officials stated on background that they did so because it had evidence of Iranian attempts to penetrate Iraqi intelligence using the two strongest Shi'ite parties in the new government: SCIRI and Dawa, the party headed by Iraqi Prime Minister Ibrahim al-Jafari. Members of those parties claimed the real reason was that the CIA was preventing them from knowing about U.S. intelligence collection on them before the election.

Hadi al Ameri, the commander of the Badr Brigade, formerly the armed wing of the Supreme Council for the Islamic Revolution in Iraq, echoed such claims. SCIRI, claimed that the Iraqi Intelligence Service "is not working for the Iraqi government—it's working for the CIA. . . . I prefer to call it the American Intelligence of Iraq, not the Iraqi Intelligence Service. . . . If they insist on keeping it to themselves, we'll have to form another one." Laith Kubba, Jafari's adviser and spokesman, was reported as saying that the prime minister wanted to take on a bigger role in antiterrorism efforts but was impaired by the lack of a reliable, skilled Iraqi police force and military. Kubba said, "The prime minister is very clear in his philosophy on governmental sovereignty and the will of the Iraqi people. He knows all these institutions must be brought under Iraqi

law and the Iraqi parliament . . . but he's a realist and he is also aware that
Iraq today faces a huge challenge with these attacks. . . . In the interim period
he has to make do with whatever he has at his disposal."

These press reports seem to be generally accurate and illustrated both
the continuing problems Iraqis have with ethnic and sectarian divisions and the
inevitable tensions between a truly sovereign Iraqi government and the United
States or any other power operating on its soil.

Manpower Issues Affecting Force Development

In spite of calls for further purges by some Shi'ite groups, Iraqi officers and
officials felt that the problems of de-Ba'athification had been largely overcome
and that the Ministry of Defense and armed forces were now open to all except
hardliners and extremists. Although there were some cases of clear ethnic or
sectarian differences, most Iraqi officers and officials felt that that a deliberate
effort should continue to be made to create a "national force" that included
Shi'ites, Sunnis, Kurds, and other minorities. They also stated that de-Ba'athification should not be applied in ways that prevented the recruitment of qualified
Sunni officers and other ranks or men from military and other forces who were
not directly involved in the repressive and violent acts of Saddam Hussein's regime.

The Shi'ites and Kurds who commented on Iraqi force developments generally accepted the fact ex-Ba'athist officers and noncommissioned officers should
play a critical role in every branch of the military, security, and police services;
that many should be Sunni; and that the Ministries of Defense and Interior
had to recruit as many experienced personnel as possible, also essential to creating
effective Iraqi forces on anything approaching a timely basis. Only a few Shi'ites and
Kurds talked about revenge or taking new steps to exclude Sunnis.[11] Sunnis were
generally more worried about the future and purges of the armed forces and
government. Few, however, felt this would halt progress or divide the country.
Many felt that more secular and more national governments and political parties
were needed, but serving Sunni officers and officials were not pessimistic.

At the same time, Iraqis made it clear that no one really knew what mix of
different sects and ethnic groups existed in each force element and how much
of the evolving Iraqi force had been truly "national" in the sense of mixing
such groups. The goal seems to consistently have been to limit the creation of
tribal, sectarian, and ethnic forces in the regular military and elite security
forces, but many units still became largely ethnic, particularly in the police and
National Guard. Iraqi officers and officials understood that they still had to deal
with many other serious problems in the composition of some existing forces.
Recruiting and composition of National Guard and police units had been local
in the past, sometimes with little vetting other than the support of some
local chief or political figure. This had often led to politically appointed leaders
with little real capability and forces lacking the will, physical condition, and/
or literacy to be effective.

Iraqi officials and officers clearly wanted this situation to change and noted that Iraq's various forces are being purged of low-grade and suspect manpower, which is being retired or paid to leave. This process was still under way, however, and Iraqis noted that there was still a strong tendency to politicize senior appointments and to fail to remove incompetent and corrupt officials and officers for political reasons or because of family and ethnic ties.

Some Iraqi officers pointed out that force development had constantly been affected by the lack of security and Iraq's lack of economic development. One noted that personnel from other areas did not know the ground and local condition, stood out in Iraq's highly localized society, and were vulnerable for these reasons. At the same time, local personnel had been subject to pressure or attacks on their families from local insurgents who almost immediately learned their functions and either attacked them or sought to use them for intelligence and infiltration. The fact that many Iraqis had been driven to volunteer out of economic pressure and desperation often produced recruits with little real motive to fight.

Pay and leave presented additional problems. Bases and caserns generally did not provide family housing, and this left families vulnerable. Many felt Iraqi personnel had to visit their families for social reasons and provide their pay in cash, and this meant that a high percentage of forces were constantly on leave. They were also worried that recruits and actives who went on leave have been vulnerable to pressure and intimidation. The lack of protected vehicles, uncertain discipline in taking leave, and a lack of experience made new volunteers especially vulnerable. One Iraqi official noted that even though he was senior enough so that his family could be housed safely in a government area, he had reservations about what would happen to the rest of his extended family. He left his family in place and concealed his duties from everyone in his hometown except family members and close friends.

Iraqi officials and officers did, however, seem to feel that many of these conditions would be temporary, and such threats would ease in late 2005 and during 2006. Like U.S. officers, they noted the value of "critical mass." As more and more trained and equipped Iraqi forces come online, they felt the government would be able to establish a steadily better structure for force protection and a steadily better overall climate of security. Many also felt that if currently hostile Iraqi Sunnis could be included in the government, the remaining native insurgents and all outside insurgents would become more isolated, and the areas in which they could operate would become steadily more limited. In short, they are optimistic enough to feel that time was on their side, and the insurgents will be much less effective in attacking Iraqi forces once they reach the numbers, quality, and experience planned for late 2005 and 2006.

Creating an Effective Iraqi Training Structure

Iraqi officers and officials often said that they were proud of what had been accomplished to date but acknowledged that training, equipment, and creating combat-ready forces remained serious problems that would take years to fully solve. In interviews early in 2005 they cited the fact that serious training efforts are "only ten months old" and noted that even when trainees complete their training they still need leadership, experience, unit cohesion, and the support of experienced personnel. These conditions were only beginning to exist in the various Iraqi forces in mid-2005.

Iraqi officers also understood that current training periods were generally too short. Those involved in Iraqi force development were also far less likely to praise the competence of the men trained under Saddam's regime than Iraqis with no practical experience. They had seen how serious the training problem really was even with Iraqis who had years of service under the Ba'ath regime. The Minister of Defense noted some of these points in a formal speech in July 2005:

> In training and equipping battalions to meet the imperative of counterinsurgency and antiterrorism operations, we must not forget the need to build armed forces that can in the long run sustain themselves. This means that we have to start to turn our attention to a whole range of issues from institution building, particularly leadership and command, to specialist skills such as personnel, finance, acquisition, and contracting.
>
> The current training and equipment plan for our armed forces addresses only our short-term needs. As part of the longer-term objective to build a sustainable force that meets the whole of the defense requirement there is a need for an ongoing program of continuous training and exercises. The staff college at Al-Rustamiyah will, with NATO's much appreciated support, provide a superb environment for young officers to learn their trade. It will serve our needs for many years to come. There is, however, a similar need with regard to a continuous program of all-arms training for soldiers and NCOs and, in due course, for more advanced training and for an annual program of exercises (including joint and combined exercises.[12]

Iraqi officials and officers noted, however, that Iraq did not have time to train its military, security, and police forces under ideal conditions in wartime, and that in-unit training could be more useful in any case. They felt that basic training was useful largely in instilling discipline and fundamentals, but that Iraqi military, security, and police forces in the field were constantly being forced to adapt to changes in insurgent and criminal behavior and found that this required them to "learn and relearn" from field experience and to meet real-world local conditions. One officer commented that "our tactical conditions and training need to change constantly in terms of detailed requirements, sometimes in ways that mean training has to be revised on a monthly basis. One real problem that we all have is that much of our training—under Saddam and now—is for fighting conventional forces. We are only gradually developing effective training for counterterrorism and counterinsurgency."

Iraqi recognition of the need for experienced cadres of leaders was a key reason Iraqi officers generally welcomed having experienced U.S. and

MNSTC–I officers embedded in new Iraqi units until such units developed the leadership and experience to act on their own (Iraqi officers did, however, express concern that U.S. officers and personnel who lack area skills and experience in working with Iraqis are often impatient and overly demanding and tend to bully the Iraqis they are supposed to inspire and train).

Facilities and equipment were seen as continuing problems, although more so by the officers and officials in the forces under the Ministry of Interior. Effective forces require training, leadership, and unit cohesion, but they also require adequate equipment, secure facilities, and facilities in the right areas. Improvements were taking place in the three latter areas, but Iraqis felt such progress lagged badly behind requirements. They cautioned that all of the elements of force quality had to be brought into balance for each element of the military, security, and police services training efforts to be effective.

At the same time, Iraqi officials believed that real progress had been made in creating the kind of training organization and facilities that Iraqis needed. They felt the facilities for effective basic training were now in place, and that training time and training in more advanced skills could be expanded as force levels became more adequate and the immediate demand for personnel was less critical. Iraqi officers pointed out that academies for more advanced training existed at the joint headquarters level. Past academies in Irbil and Sulaymaniyah were back online and had been modernized, and a new academy in Baghdad was coming online. A former regime training center in Tikrit had been reopened, initially with MNSTC–I support but then with Iraqi training cadres. Iraq was beginning to create the kind of high-level training facilities it needed at the ministry level and planned to create a staff college, war college, and center for national security studies. Much depended, however, on getting support from MNSTC–I, NATO countries, and other outside support.

Iraqi officers and officials were not in a rush to eliminate all outside training and advisers—in fact, they welcomed most offers of training from new countries and most signs of outside support. They welcomed the help they have had from Egypt, the United Arab Emirates, and Jordan in addition to the MNSTC–I countries and hoped for new training contributions from Germany, Italy, Norway, and France. MNSTC–I reported that "NATO provides a valuable function in screening (with their Iraqi counterparts) offers of training and donations of equipment. Some training offers have been refused, primarily for political reasons." They felt such multinational contributions were highly useful in spite of the potential problems in different training methods and interoperability. They did, however, recognize the need for standardization and coordination of training efforts over time and wanted to take over the overall leadership and organization of training as soon as possible.

While Iraqis did not use the term as such, they also noted that as Iraqi forces expanded to reach significant levels of capability, they would acquire the "critical mass" necessary to provide a far more effective overall training and leadership structure, less pressure and more time for training, and be able to take over far more of the mission from the United States and MNSTC-I. Iraqi officials and officers hoped for such "full capability" in 2006, and President Talibani talked about 2007 early in his time in office, but Iraqis acknowledge they will need MNSTC-I aid and support in training, equipment, and other areas through 2010.

The Iraqi View of Force Development

Iraqi officials and officers discussed Iraqi force developments in general terms and did not provide detailed numbers or force descriptions. They saw Iraqi forces as in a constant state of development. They felt that it is unfair to judge such forces and their progress at this time, given the history of problems in Iraqi force development, but that many past problems were being rapidly overcome and most of the remaining problems will be overcome during the course of the coming year.

They questioned the value of the search in the United States for the exact total manpower in "effective" Iraqi forces and for exactly how many Iraqi forces were properly trained and equipped and could engage the insurgents. They pointed out that no Iraqi forces as yet had all of the strength in terms of armor, firepower, and support necessary to engage in main force combat without U.S. support. They pointed out that Iraqi forces differed sharply in capability not only by force element but also in terms of experience, capability, and leadership at the battalion level within each different branch of the Iraqi military, security, and police forces.

At the same time, Iraqi officials and officers pointed out that virtually every element of the military, security, and police forces could already perform some useful function in terms of improving security, although often in ways subject to very sharp limits. They felt that the situation was improving steadily as new and better trained/equipped Iraqi forces come online, as Iraqi forces become better organized and manpower is better selected, and as Iraqi officers and other ranks gain experience. From their perspective the issue was not whether the glass is two-thirds empty or one-third full, it was how rapidly it is filling.

They also pointed out that fully effective Iraqi forces with enough armor and/or counterinsurgency equipment to operate offensively against insurgent forces without extensive MNSTC–I support were just coming online. As one Iraqi put it, "What do you want to count and what tasks do you want to judge it by? Why do you want to count what we are rather than what we are becoming?" Iraqi officials and officers felt that they could not form stable force plans at this time. They felt that their force goals had to be in flux and that equipment, deployment, and facility plans were almost certain to change. They understood the volatility of the Iraqi political climate, as well as the inability to predict their budgets and the level of MNSTC–I aid.

Iraqis also believed that some of the major challenges they faced at the ministry, service, and unit levels were to create an effective and cohesive C^4I system (command, control, communications, computers, and intelligence); to create an effective intelligence system that could properly be integrated into Iraq's developing command, control, communications, and computer capabilities; and to provide the combat, service, and logistic support necessary to allow Iraqi forces to operate as full independent forces.

The Army

Iraqis felt that the Iraqi Army had advanced to the point where the chief of staff's office had an operating formal structure with deputy chiefs of staff for operations, administration, and training. Iraqi officers saw a number of major challenges in the development of the army. One was to give it the training and equipment necessary to operate as a fully independent force and eventually replace MNF–I forces. A second was the need to redeploy army units away from caserns and locations chosen for MNF–I convenience and security so the Iraqi armed forces can meet Iraqi government priorities and needs. The third was to create a more stable plan for force expansion—one that takes into account the problems created by the merger of the army and National Guard.

They also noted in July 2005 that the Ministry of Defense intended to create the command, control, communications, and combat support and service support forces to allow Iraqi military forces to operate as fully independent forces. This means creating the following additional forces over the coming eighteen months:

- Three division-level signal companies
- Ten engineer companies
- Three intelligence, surveillance, and reconnaissance companies
- Ten military police companies
- Five motor transport regiments
- A support company for each battalion (administration, maintenance, stores and supplies, and medical)

Merging the National Guard into the Army

Iraqis understood that merging the National Guard into the army in early 2005 presented problems. The National Guard was the successor to a low-grade force called the Iraqi Civil Defense Corps (ICDC), which was recruited and vetted largely on a local level for glorified security-guard duty. Training and equipment was limited; leadership often owed more to politics and regional needs than effectiveness; and much of the National Guard's manpower lacked the necessary physical condition, education, and loyalty.

The National Guard had had six divisions of three brigades each with three battalions of three to four companies each—most only had light infantry weapons. There were no mortars, although the guard was authorized to maintain thirty-two heavy machine guns per battalion, an increase in authorization by twenty-four guns. However, it is still not clear how many heavy machine guns are actually in the field. This made the guard a large force on paper, but most had serious—if not crippling—force-quality problems when it had to be used in offensive operations.

Iraqis commented that the ICDC/National Guard was created on the basis that each of the five MNC–I commands or regions essentially created a separate force, largely on the basis of recruiting by local leaders. Each MNC–I originally created National Guard companies at the MNC–I brigade level without any headquarters and with very limited basic training. This produced rapid force expansion but without force quality. Iraqis noted, however, that the National Guard was slowly being purged of its low-quality leadership and manpower—which has been retired or paid to leave. Changes had also begun to take place in equipment, selection, training, and organization. It was initially organized largely at the company level. This was later expanded to battalions that became very large, sometimes reaching 1,000 men—a size too large to be effective.

Iraqis understood that the guard would need major reorganization, more training, and better equipment. Iraqi officers could not, however, provide a clear plan for what the guard would become as it is merged with the army. Nevertheless, as one Iraqi Army officer put it, even the weakest National Guard units could still be used for a wide range of security duties like manning checkpoints and providing area security in low- to medium-threat areas until their manning, equipment, and training improved.

The Air Force

Iraq was just beginning to develop an air force, and Iraqis were fully aware of the limits to its effectiveness. The minister of defense noted in July that "the Iraqi Air Force is woefully inadequate to support a highly mobile modern army. There is an urgent need for (1) helicopter lift capability to enable rapid ground-force deployment in support of the counterterrorism mission, (2) medium-transport flight, including for safe transport of VIPs, senior officers, and journalists across Iraq, (3) airborne reconnaissance and surveillance capability to support a range of missions including counterinsurgency, border security, and infrastructure security, and (4) specialist staff training."[13] He also warned that "the maintenance and long-term sustainment costs of helicopters and fixed-wing aircraft can be very substantial and must form a part of any donation or, in the longer-term, assisted purchase if we are to make effective use of such capability. There is a real danger that inappropriate donations will either bankrupt the Ministry of Defense or sit unused."

The air force did, however, now have a major general in command and a functioning headquarters and staff. It is acquiring C-130s for "strategic mobility" and helicopters for transport, support, reconnaissance, and combat support missions. Helicopter gunships will be its initial combat weapon. It does not yet have clear force plans or plans to acquire modern fixed-wing combat aircraft.

Navy/Coast Guard

The Iraqi Navy was just becoming a light coastal defense force. Its naval infantry battalion was being trained for point defense of oil platforms—a key mission in securing oil exports.

Ministry of the Interior Forces

There was obvious rivalry and tension between the Iraqis serving in the Ministry of Defense and those in the Ministry of the Interior at the time of the Iraqi Interim Government, but cooperation did seem to be improving before the election. Once the elections took place and the new government was formed, Iraqis felt the new ministers made a much better effort to cooperate than their predecessors.

In general, Ministry of Interior officials and officers expressed many of the same concerns about the quality of the Iraqi security forces and police discussed in previous chapters. While things were improving, they felt locally recruited police still had low overall recruiting and training standards, were often corrupt, and could do little more than passively man police stations and carry out minimal police duties in relatively secure areas. The regular police were seen as slowly improving in such areas but as generally ineffective in dealing with levels of crime that are a major security problem in areas where insurgents have little capability and impact. They acknowledged that local and sectarian or ethnic militias were often the de facto police in high-crime areas.

They also noted, however, that the Ministry of the Interior had created elite units that were carefully selected and trained, mobile, had adequate communications, and were working directly under the Ministry of the Interior. Such forces had elements in Baghdad and every governorate by the spring of 2005. They felt the Iraqi special police commandos, public order battalions, the police mechanized brigade, and emergency response unit were all emerging as effective paramilitary units with the training, leadership, and equipment to provide security in medium- to high-threat areas. Iraqi traffic, immigration, and civil defense police were also felt to be getting better selection, leadership, training, and equipment.

Opinions were divided about the border police. Some felt they were slowly improving and now had better facilities, protection, and equipment. Other Iraqis felt they were still very weak and prone to desert or become inactive under limited pressure and that it would be at least several years before the force could correct its leadership, selection, training, and equipment problems.

Iraqis Do Not See the Past as the Defining Prologue to the Future

In spite of all the problems and uncertainties they faced, Iraqi officials and officers remained relatively optimistic about the future. Iraqi officials and officers felt that progress is now certain to be made if the new Iraqi government shows suitable leadership, cohesion, and inclusiveness and did not purge the developing Iraqi force structure. All wanted Iraq to take over planning and management of the Iraqi force development effort as soon as possible, but they exhibited little belief in the kind of conspiracy theories that blamed the United States and MNSTC–I for deliberately keeping Iraqi forces weak and seeking a permanent occupation. If anything, Iraqi officials and officers were more worried that the United States and MNF–I might not provide the continuing support they need. While some felt Iraqi forces might be able to largely stand on their own against the insurgents by the end of 2006, they also felt that they would still need support from U.S. armor, artillery, air, special forces, and intelligence. Some felt that a major U.S. and MNSTC–I advisory, training, equipment, and aid effort will be needed through 2010.

Iraqi officials and officers had considerable confidence in the United States, British, and other MNSTC–I officers involved in helping Iraq to train and organize Iraqi forces. Iraqi officials and officers felt that most of the MNF–I and MNSTC–I teams they work with did have Iraqi interests at heart, and they felt the training effort was getting steadily better. None expected to get Western standards of advanced equipment and technology versus the kind of equipment better suited to Iraq. They also welcomed the recommendation of the Luck mission to insert U.S. officers and NCOs into Iraqi units to provide leadership and unit cohesion and combat training as an essential next step in creating a transition to effective and independent Iraqi forces.

This does not mean that Iraqi officials and officers did not feel that changes were needed in the current MNF–I and MNSTC–I plans for Iraqi force development. There were serious criticisms of the MNF–I and MNSTC–I effort. Iraqis were particularly critical of the level of equipment they are getting and do see Iraqis as being treated by a "dual standard" that has left Iraqi forces much more vulnerable than U.S. and MNF–I forces. Several saw the following seven changes as necessary:

1. Developing and implementing plans more quickly to create Iraqi forces that are equipped and deployed to stand on their own.
2. Developing common plans with the United States and MNSTC–I to phase down the role of MNF–I forces according to common criteria and in ways in which both sides have the same expectations, allowing Iraqis to predict the future level of MNSTC–I aid and remaining capability.
3. Developing mid-term plans to create forces with enough support and heavy land and air weapons to eventually replace all MNF–I forces other than those remaining in an advisory and training role.
4. Taking over the planning and command and control of operations at the local, then provincial, and then national level.
5. Taking over the planning and management of the way in which aid funds and assistance were used so that Iraqis could integrate the aid and advisory effort into the overall operations of the Ministry of Defense and Ministry of Interior and Iraqi national budget.

6. Shifting the planning and management of the overall training effort into Iraqi hands and relying on Iraqi trainers and Iraqi-developed course plans.
7. Taking over the planning and management of the procurement and facility development effort and having the MNF–I and MNSTC–I respond to Iraqi plans, rather than develop plans for Iraq.

Iraqis also noted that some of the U.S. and MNF–I combat forces they worked with had inadequate training for working with foreign forces. The felt some of their advisers rotated too quickly to acquire and exploit the expertise they needed to work with Iraqis in the field, lacked adequate indoctrination into the current strengths and weaknesses of Iraqi forces, and sometimes treated them unfairly and not as partners—or as partners who had to take over the lead role as soon as possible.[14]

11 The Evolving Nature of the Insurgency and the Risk of Sectarian and Ethnic Conflict

THE DEVELOPMENT of Iraqi forces is only one side of the story. If Iraqi forces are to be successful, they must deal with the fact that the insurgent and terrorist threat in Iraq remains all too real, continues to evolve in response to the changes in Iraqi and Coalition forces, and has elements that are doing their utmost to provoke a large-scale civil war. As of September 19, 2005, the United States had suffered 1,899 killed, of which 1,479 had been killed in hostile action, and well over 14,000 Americans had been wounded. Coalition allies had lost 197 lives, and estimates of killed Iraqi Security Forces totaled 3,194.[1] Approximately 23,589–26,705 Iraqi civilians and 66 international media workers had been killed as of August 31, 2005.[2]

The insurgency does not have a single face. Iraq faces a wide mix of active and potential threats, and the task that Iraqi military, security, and police forces face is anything but easy. It is still far from clear whether a combination of Coalition and Iraqi government forces will be able to decisively defeat the various insurgent groups, and as the insurgency has developed, there have been growing Sunni Islamist efforts to create a major conflict between the Sunnis and the Shi'ites and Kurds.

An Unstable Mix of Threats

Iraq's forces must deal with a complex mix of threats—only some of which have as yet come into play. The Sunni elements of the insurgency involve a wide range of disparate Iraqi and foreign groups and mixes of secular and Islamic extremist factions. There are elements tied to former Ba'athist officials and to Iraqi and Sunni nationalists. There are elements composed of native Iraqi Sunni Islamists, groups with outside leadership and links to Al Qa'ida, and foreign volunteers with little real structure—some of whom seem to be seeking Islamic martyrdom rather than clearly defined political goals. Tribal and clan elements play a role at the local level, creating additional patterns of loyalty that cut across ideology or political goals. The stated objectives of various groups range from a return of some form of Ba'athist-like regime to the creation of an extremist Sunni Islamic state, with many Iraqi Sunnis acting as much out of anger and fear as toward any clearly articulated goals.

The various insurgent and terrorist groups often cooperate, although there are indications of divisions between the more Ba'athist-oriented Iraqi Sunni groups and some of the Sunni Islamic extremist groups with outside ties or direction. At least some Sunni groups are willing to consider negotiating with the new government, while Islamist extremist groups are not. This had led to threats and some violence between various Sunni factions.[3]

There have also been growing reports of Iraqi Sunni executions of foreign Sunni Islamic extremists since November 2004.[4] One notable event took place on August 13, when Sunni Iraqis in Ramadi took up arms against Abu Musab Zarqawi's forces in defense of their Shi'ite neighbors. The fighting came on the heels of a proclamation by Zarqawi that Ramadi's 3,000 Shi'ites leave the city of some 200,000 residents. The order was given in retaliation for supposed expulsions of Sunni minorities by Shi'ite militias in the mostly Shi'ite south of Iraq. Yet in Ramadi, members of the Sunni Dulaimi tribe formed security cordons around Shi'ite homes and fought Zarqawi's men with grenade launchers and automatic weapons. All told, five foreign fighters and two local tribal fighters were killed.[5]

At the same time, there is the constant threat that Sunni Arab extremists will provoke something approaching a full-scale civil war. They have stepped up suicide and other attacks on Shi'ites and Kurds, and many of these attacks have clearly been designed to block efforts at including Sunnis in the government and to try to provoke Shi'ites and Kurds into reprisals that will make a stable national government impossible to achieve. The very success of the January 30 elections changed the strategy and tactics of such religious extremists, and it is clear they will do everything possible to block the acceptance of the draft of the constitution, Iraqi Sunnis from entering the government, and the elections scheduled for the end of 2005.

There is also the risk of factional fighting within the Shi'ites, and between Iraq's Arabs and Kurds. Serious divisions exist between the more secular and more religious Shi'ites over how religious a new Iraqi state should be, and conflicts also exist within Shi'ite religious factions. Figures like the Moqtada al-Sadr raise the risk of renewed Shi'ite insurgent movements, and tensions between Arabs and Kurds have long been near the flashpoint in Kirkuk and present serious problems in Mosul.

Iraq's neighbors have conflicting interests and play a role in the insurgency. Syria has supported and tolerated Sunni Islamist infiltrations and has allowed ex-Ba'athists to operate from Syria. Turkey is primarily interested in ensuring Iraq's Kurds do not become an example to Turkey's Kurdish dissidents. Iran has its own interests in supporting Iraq's Islamic Shi'ites, creating an ally, and ending American "encirclement." The Arab states of the Persian Gulf and Middle East do not want a Shi'ite-dominated Iraq and fear a Shi'ite "crescent" of Lebanon, Syria, Iraq, and Iran.

The Uncertain Cycles and Patterns in the Insurgency

Complex insurgencies involve patterns that can play out over years and sometimes decades. It is easy to claim trends toward "victory," but it is generally far more difficult to make them valid or real. For example, the Iraqi Interim Government (IIG) claimed in early 2005 that some sixteen of Iraq's eighteen provinces were secure, which was clearly untrue. There was a significant level of security in ten to twelve provinces, and the United States and IIG had won significant victories in Najaf and Fallujah in 2004, but the insurgency was clearly not defeated or incapable of attacks in supposedly safe Shi'ite and Kurdish areas.

Similarly, Coalition and Iraqi success in preventing insurgent attacks on polling places during the January 30 election did not mean that there were not several hundred attempted attacks and actual attacks before the election. Nor did they prevent a new round of attacks and acts of terrorism after the election. The United States lost twenty-four men and sixty were wounded in one attack on a mess tent in Mosul on December 21, 2004.[6] Some sixty-eight Iraqis were killed in attacks in Karbala and Najaf a few days earlier, and some 175 were wounded.[7]

Vice Admiral Lowell E. Jacoby, director of the Defense Intelligence Agency, summarized the state of the insurgency as follows in February 2005:

> The insurgency in Iraq has grown in size and complexity over the past year. Attacks numbered approximately twenty-five per day one year ago. Today, they average in the sixties. Insurgents have demonstrated their ability to increase attacks around key events such as the Iraqi Interim Government (IIG) transfer of power, Ramadan, and the recent election. Attacks on Iraq's Election Day reached approximately 300, double the previous one-day high of approximately 150 reached during last year's Ramadan.
>
> The pattern of attacks remains the same as last year. Approximately 80 percent of all attacks occur in Sunni-dominated central Iraq. The Kurdish north and Shi'a South remain relatively calm. Coalition forces continue to be the primary targets. Iraqi security forces and Iraqi Interim Government (IIG) officials are attacked to intimidate the Iraqi people and undermine control and legitimacy. Attacks against foreign nationals are intended to intimidate nongovernmental organizations and contractors and inhibit reconstruction and recovery. Attacks against the country's infrastructure, especially electricity and the oil industry, are intended to stall economic recovery, increase popular discontent, and further undermine support for the IIG and Coalition.
>
> Recent polls show confidence in the Iraqi Interim Government remains high in Kurdish communities and low in Sunni areas. Large majorities across all groups opposed attacks on Iraqi security forces and Iraqi and foreign civilians.

Majorities of all groups placed great importance in the election. Sunni concern over election security likely explains the relatively poor showing by the Sunni electorate in comparison with the Shi'a and Kurdish groups. Confidence in Coalition forces is low. Most Iraqis see them as occupiers and a major cause of the insurgency.

We believe Sunni Arabs, dominated by Ba'athist and former regime elements (FRE), comprise the core of the insurgency. Ba'athist/FRE and Sunni Arab networks are likely collaborating, providing funds and guidance across family, tribal, religious, and peer group lines. Some coordination between Sunni and Shi'a groups is also likely.

Militant Shi'a elements, including those associated with Muqtada al Sadr, have periodically fought the Coalition. Following the latest round of fighting last August and September, we judge Sadr's forces are rearming, reorganizing, and training. Sadr is keeping his options open to either participate in the political process or employ his forces. Shi'a militants will remain a significant threat to the political process, and fractures within the Shi'a community are a concern.

Jihadists, such as al-Qa'ida operative Abu Musab al Zarqawi, are responsible for many high-profile attacks. While Jihadist activity accounts for only a fraction of the overall violence, the strategic and symbolic nature of their attacks, combined with effective information operations, has a disproportionate impact.

Foreign fighters are a small component of the insurgency and comprise a very small percentage of all detainees. Syrian, Saudi, Egyptian, Jordanian, and Iranian nationals make up the majority of foreign fighters. Fighters, arms, and other supplies continue to enter Iraq from virtually all of its neighbors despite increased border security.

Insurgent groups will continue to use violence to attempt to protect Sunni Arab interests, regain dominance, provoke civil war, and/or serve the interests of Neo-Salafi Sunni extremism. Subversion and infiltration of emerging government institutions, security, and intelligence services will be a major problem for the new government. Jihadists will continue to attack in Iraq in pursuit of their long-term goals. Challenges to reconstruction, economic development, and employment will continue. The keys to success will remain improving security with an Iraqi lead, rebuilding the civil infrastructure and economy, and creating a political process that all major ethnic and sectarian groups see as legitimate.[8]

Uncertain Claims That the Insurgency Is Losing Ground

Jacoby's statement provided an excellent overview at the time it was made but did not anticipate the level of Sunni Islamic extremism that was to follow and a shift in targeting by Sunni Islamic extremists to attack Iraqi targets in an attempt to provoke a civil war. Several senior U.S. officers went even further and claimed that the insurgency was losing ground after the election.

On February 17, 2005, U.S. Secretary of Defense Donald Rumsfeld told the Senate Armed Service Committee that classified estimates on the size of the insurgency were not static but rather "a moving target." In the same session General Richard B. Myers, chairman of the Joint Chiefs of Staff, also avoided hard numbers but described the insurgency as having limited capabilities, meaning that the insurgency can mount only around fifty to sixty attacks on any given day. Lieutenant General John F. Sattler, the head of the USMC Expeditionary Force, claimed in March that insurgent attacks were averaging only ten per day with two producing significant casualties versus the twenty-five per day with five producing significant casualties before the battle of Fallujah in November 2000.

General George W. Casey, commander of MNF–I, consistently had warned that the insurgency would take years to fully defeat but stated on March 9, 2005, that "the level of attacks, the level of violence has dropped off significantly since the [Iraqi] elections."[9] U.S. Chief of Staff General Myers claimed that same week that the number of attacks had fallen to forty to fifty per day, far fewer than before the elections but roughly the same as in March 2004.[10] The Iraqi interim minister of interior, Falah al-Naqib, also made such claims. So did Lieutenant General Sir John Kiszeley, then the British commander in Iraq.[11]

As is the case with many other types of official U.S. reporting on Iraq, however, such claims were not supported with the detail and transparency necessary to establish their credibility. The United States ceased to provide detailed unclassified data on the types of insurgent attacks or their locations in the summer of 2004. The private organizations that try to do this produce interesting results but results that are often suspect. U.S. official sources did say the following about the status prior to the Iraqi election:[12]

- Some forty to sixty towns and cities have been the scene of attacks each week since late August. Many are outside the Sunni Triangle and Al Anbar province.
- The most violent city in terms of number of major incidents has been Baghdad with twenty to forty attacks a week.
- Mosul is second with four to thirteen major attacks per week.
- The level of attacks in Basra has been relatively low by comparison, but peaks of seven attacks per week have occurred in Basra and its environs.

In contrast, they stated the following about the time shortly after the Iraqi election:

- Attacks against U.S. soldiers per day have fallen to between forty and fifty. U.S. officials state that this is approximately half the level of one year previously.
- Approximately half of the attacks that do occur cause no casualties or property damage.

Uncertain Trends in the Numbers

Such estimates of the patterns in the insurgency reflect problems that have been typical of the U.S. and British official reporting on the insurgency and which make it difficult to analyze its intensity and predict trends. The counts quoted by senior U.S. officials focused on attacks directed at U.S. and Iraqi government targets rather than all attacks and did not include all attempts and minor incidents. They also did not include Iraqi criminal activity or sabotage, and the Iraqi Ministry of Defense and Ministry of Interior had stopped all meaningful reporting in these areas in the summer of 2004.

Unclassified work by Defense Intelligence Agency (DIA) and MNF–I showing the approximate number of total attacks per month from June 2003 to February 2005 is summarized in figure 11.1. These data reflected patterns typical of the cyclical variations in modern insurgencies.[13] The same is true of the trend data on U.S. casualties shown in figure 11.2, and it is clear from a comparison of the data in these two figures that the patterns in the insurgency are highly cyclical, and there is only an uncertain correlation between incident counts and casualty counts, and even accurate incident counts would be only the crudest possible indication of the patterns in insurgency without a much wider range of comparative metrics.

FIGURE 11.1
Approximate Number of Major Attacks per Month, June 2003 through February 2005

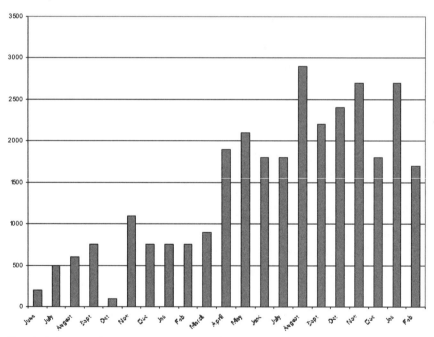

Note: Includes approximate number of attacks on Coaliation, Iraqi security forces, Iraqi government officials, civilians, and infrastructure.

Source: Adapted from the DIA and MNF-I data presented in Joseph A. Christoff, *Rebuilding Iraq: Preliminary Observations on Challenges in Transferring Security Responsibilities to Iraqi Military and Police*, Government Accountability Office (GAO) GAO-05-431IT, March 14, 2005, p. 10.

FIGURE 11.2
Approximate Number of U.S. Killed and Wounded, March 2003 through December 2004

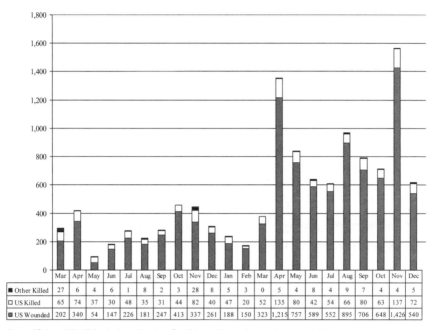

	Mar	Apr	May	Jun	Jul	Aug	Sep	Oct	Nov	Dec	Jan	Feb	Mar	Apr	May	Jun	Jul	Aug	Sep	Oct	Nov	Dec
■ Other Killed	27	6	4	6	1	8	2	3	28	8	5	3	0	5	4	8	4	9	7	4	4	5
□ US Killed	65	74	37	30	48	35	31	44	82	40	47	20	52	135	80	42	54	66	80	63	137	72
▨ US Wounded	202	340	54	147	226	181	247	413	337	261	188	150	323	1,215	757	589	552	895	706	648	1,426	540

Note: "Other Killed" includes all other Coalition military forces but no civilians and no Iraqis.
Source: Adapted from data provided by U.S. Department of Defense, www.defenselink.org, and the Iraq
   Coalition Casualty Count, http://icasualties.org/oif/, accessed July 18, 2005.

Other reporting gave strong indications that insurgent activity had surged
before the elections and then temporarily eased back rather than diminished in
any lasting way. An internal U.S. Army analysis in April also calculated that
the apparent shift was more a shift in focus to more vulnerable non-U.S. targets
than an actual drop in incidents.[14] Similarly, a study by the National Intelligence
Council in the CIA that was leaked to *Newsweek* concluded that U.S. government reporting had so many conflicting sources and methods of analysis that the
resulting metrics could not be trusted and that there was inadequate evidence to
support any conclusions about whether the insurgents were being defeated.[15]
   The DIA figures and Coalition casualty data were skewed in favor of counts
of attacks on Coalition forces and undercounted attacks on Iraqi civilians and
some aspects of Iraqi officials, military, and police. One of the tragedies of Iraq
is that as part of its effort to "spin" reporting on the war in favorable directions,
the Department of Defense has never publicly attempted to count Iraqi casualties of any kind or treat the casualties of Iraqi military and police as those of
partners whose sacrifice deserves recognition.

The MNF–I and MNSTC–I do report that they keep track of Iraqi casualties and cited a total of 2,000 Iraqi police casualties in reporting in June 2000, but they generally do not disclose such numbers. One MNSTC–I expert stated, "Data on Iraqi casualties are collected by the Coalition, but public distribution of information about this topic should remain the purview of the Iraqi government. They have more visibility over the issue, could be more accurate in reporting, and are the appropriate authority to discuss the meaning."[16]

Coalition counts also have undercounted major acts of sabotage. Like most such partial counts, this disguised important shifts in the patterns in insurgency. As the Chronology in the back of this book shows, insurgents also shifted from U.S. and Coalition targets to Iraqi government, Kurdish, and Shi'ite targets, and the major incidents came to include a far more bloody series of suicide bombings.

As a result, it is not surprising that there was a major resurgence in insurgent and terrorist activity in the months that followed and as a new Iraqi government finally completed its selection process in late April and early May 2005. An independent count of Iraqi military and police casualties showed that some 1,300 had been killed between the fall of Saddam Hussein in April 2003 and the end of 2004 but that an increase in insurgent activity and a new focus on Iraqi forces resulted in 109 killed in January 2005, 103 in February, 200 in March, 200 in April, and 110 in the first week of May. This was a total of roughly 1,200 killed in the first six months of 2005, raising the total to over 2,400 killed—scarcely a decline in insurgent activity.[17] In contrast, the MNF–I reported that "more than 2,000" Iraqi security forces personnel had been killed by the end of July 2005.[18]

Since that time, the frequency and intensity of attacks have continued to fluctuate with no evidence the insurgency is getting significantly better or worse. U.S. and Iraqi officials and officers continued to make contradictory claims, but both U.S. and Iraqi forces took the insurgency seriously enough to launch major new campaigns and to plan for a new surge of attacks during the constitutional referendum and the December 2005 elections.

The Iraqi government has been reluctant to release casualty data, perhaps because it fears this could show its weaknesses and discourage recruiting. The Ministry of Defense did report, however, that eighty-five Iraqi soldiers were killed in May, compared with forty in April, an increase of 75 percent. At least seventy-nine soldiers were wounded in May, compared with sixty-three in April. The Ministry of Interior reported that 151 Iraqi police were killed in May, compared with eighty-six in April, an increase of 75 percent. At least 325 policemen were wounded in May, compared with 131 in April. The Ministry of Health reported that 434 civilians were killed in May, compared with 299 in April, and that 775 civilians were wounded, compared with 598 the previous month.[19]

The number of car bombings rose from sixty-five in February 2005 to 135 in April, and the total number of major attacks per day rose from thirty to forty in February and March to seventy in April and May. The intensity of the attacks also increased as more suicide bombings took place by Islamist extremists—many conducted by young men from countries like Libya, Saudi Arabia, and the Sudan who infiltrated from across the Syrian border. The number of major attacks involving suicide bombers rose from 25 percent in February to a little over 50 percent in April. There were sixty-nine suicide bombings in April 2005, more than in the entire period from the fall of Saddam Hussein to the transfer of power in June 2004. In May some ninety suicide bombings were the primary cause of some 750 casualties that month.[20] The annual pattern was equally serious. If one only counts car bombings, there had been more than 482 successful bombings in the year since the handover of power on June 26, 2004, killing at least 2,176 people and wounding at least 5,536.[21]

While the insurgents focused more on Iraqi targets, and increasingly on Shi'ite and Kurdish targets that might help provoke a major civil war, the attacks on MNF–I forces climbed from forty a day in March to fifty-five in April, far below the peak of 130 a day before the January 30, 2005, elections—but scarcely reassuring.[22] The good news for the United States was that only 146 Americans died during the three-month period from February 1 to April 30, 2005, versus 315 in the previous three-month period.[23]

The difficulty in analyzing the patterns in a constantly changing situation is illustrated by another surge in activity that took place as the new government was appointed. The Iraqi government announced most of its appointments on April 28, 2005—some three months after the election and months after the supposed deadline for doing so. In the week that followed (April 28 to May 6), there were ten major suicide bombings and thirty-five major attacks. Insurgents killed more than 270 Iraqi civilians, and at least fourteen bodies that may have been from previous attacks were found in a Baghdad garbage dump. Many of the attacks were against Iraqi forces and recruits, and the intensity of the attacks is indicated by the fact that a suicide bomber from the Army of Ansar al-Sunna killed more than sixty people in the Kurdish city of Irbil in northern Iraq in a single attack.[24] For the first time, in April more than 50 percent of the car bombings were suicide attacks.[25]

During the same period, eighty more bodies had been found floating in the Tigris, and nineteen more were discovered in a soccer stadium.[26] The total number of U.S. forces killed now totaled 1,593 (1,216 killed in hostile action), and 12,243 had been wounded. Some 180 allied military and eighty-six U.S. civilians had been killed, and unofficial estimates put the number of Iraqi dead at least 21,450 to 24,325.[27]

These developments led some U.S. officers and officials to claim that the insurgents were lashing out because they had taken so many casualties that they were desperate and/or to say that the successful car bombings by Islamic extremists had little strategic meaning since they alienated the Iraqi people and could easily be carried out by a small number of largely foreign volunteers who were not representative of Iraqi Sunnis. Such arguments could not be disproved or proved, but they were made at a time the U.S. Marines found it necessary to conduct a major offensive along the Euphrates from Haditha to the Syrian border, the largest offensive since the attack on Fallujah. U.S. forces also had to launch another major operation to secure the area south and west of Baghdad and follow them up with a series of major campaigns around Mosuf and in western Iraq during this summer and fall.[28] Such operations have had to be followed up again and again, largely because many of the insurgents can disperse the moment they come under pressure, and the Coalition and Iraqi forces both lacked the manpower to occupy high-threat areas and the requisite Coalition or Iraqi government teams to back up tactical victories with civic-action programs and efforts to establish effective governance.

As of the early summer of 2005, insurgents and terrorists continued to try to strip the new government of its perceived legitimacy. In spite of MNF–I estimates that some 1,000 to 3,000 insurgents were being killed and captured each month, attacks on Iraqi security forces and government officials contin-ued, and the number of suicide bombings continued to mount. There were twenty-one car bombings in Baghdad alone during the first two weeks of May and 126 in the eighty days before May 18. This compared with twenty-five during all of 2005. Daily attacks had averaged thirty to forty a day in February but were at least seventy a day in June.[29]

Additionally, insurgents continued attacks designed to disrupt supplies of water, electricity, crude oil, gasoline, and heating oil, particularly to Baghdad. This shift in attack patterns indicated that insurgents were carrying out a sophis-ticated plan to sabotage government services, hoping to convince residents that the government cannot provide for its people. Because of the technological expertise involved in these attacks, some experts believed that former Hussein-era officials were still aiding the sabotage efforts—although others felt that by this time there was a large pool of such expertise in the various insurgent forces.[30]

In June 2005 the Iraqi Ministry of Interior released new figures on Iraqi civilian and security force casualties. The ministry found that Iraqi civilians and police officers died at a rate of about 800 a month from August 2004 until May 2005. Reportedly, insurgents killed 8,175 Iraqis during that time.[31] Figures were not available for the months prior to August 2004, and no breakdowns of the data were made available. This gap in the data may be partly explained by the fact that until summer 2004 casualty information was gathered by the Ministry of Health and relied on information provided by hospitals and morgues.[32] Yet, reli-ance on hospitals and morgues alone to count deaths provides a low figure for approximate deaths. Certainly not every dead body is taken to the hospital or morgue, and certain groups of Iraqis probably avoid the hospitals altogether. In the summer of 2004 the Ministry of Interior took over the responsibility of counting the number of Iraqis killed. The Health Ministry did provide a breakdown of Iraqi deaths by province from early November 2004 until early April 2005, but this count relied on its traditional method of gathering data from morgues and hospitals. The ministry noted that during this period the following had occured:[33]

- Thirty-two percent of the 3,853 deaths accounted for by the ministry occurred in Baghdad.

- Al Anbar witnessed the second highest number of deaths.
- Najaf had the third highest number of deaths.
- Children represented 211 out of the 3,853 deaths.
- The highest death rates per capita were in Al Anbar, followed by Najaf and Diyala.
- The ministry recorded 15,517 wounded of which men made up 91 percent.

Iraqi Interior Minister Bayan Jabr stated in June 2005 that insurgents had killed approximately 12,000 Iraqis since the Coalition invasion, an average of 500 a month as reported by the *New York Times*.

A group called the Iraq Body Count (IBC), in conjunction with the Oxford Research Group, released a study of Iraqi casualties since the Coalition invasion. The study concluded that approximately 25,000 Iraqi civilians were killed in 2003 and 2004 with about a third having been killed by Coalition troops. These figures may be as good an estimate as is now possible, but the study relied on casualty reports made available on 152 selected Web sites and did not try to verify the sites' sources. Some of the sites are relatively unknown and are of uncertain reliability. It also is not clear how strenuously the IBC has tried to sift military casualties from civilian casualties. Impinging the credibility of the IBC's figures further is the fact that it is an avowed antiwar group.[34]

Senior U.S. officers like General John Abizaid gave far more cautious briefings in May than officers had given in February and talked about years of combat.[35] The U.S. chairman of the Joint Chiefs of Staff, General Richard Myers, stated in late May that while the levels of insurgent attacks had decreased, their lethality had increased.[36] The only good news was that there was no significant Shi'ite anti-Coalition or government insurgent activity since Sadr's militia ceased to actively try to occupy cities and shrines in the South after its defeat in the summer and fall of 2004—although Sadr had rebuilt at least part of his organization and did support anti-Coalition demonstrations after the January 2005 election.

The Limits to the Insurgency

The insurgency in Iraq has not been a national insurgency. Iraqi Kurds have never supported it, and only small numbers of Shi'ites have ever taken an active role. It has been driven by a relatively small part of Iraq's population concentrated in part of the country, and a group of foreign volunteers and extremists, which may have been around 1,000 men and did not seem likely to exceed 3,000 as of September 2005.

Although there are no accurate census data, the Arab Sunni population only seems to be around 15 to 20 percent of Iraq's total population, and only 6 to 8 percent of Iraq's total population is located in the areas most hostile to the Coalition and the Iraqi government. Moreover, if one looks at the total population of all the scattered cities and areas where insurgents and terrorists largely dominate, it does not exceed 6 to 9 percent of Iraq's total population. Furthermore, the insurgency has not been dominated by foreign fighters. Brigadier General John Custer, director of intelligence for USCENTCOM, addressed the primacy of the foreign fighter myth in summer 2005. He stated, "When you take a look at who we have killed, who we have captured, who we have in detention, it is 95 percent, at least, Iraqi-Sunni-Arab, and if you look at the Zarqawi network you will find that it's vastly Iraqi."[37]

General John Abizaid, commander of the U.S. Central Command, said that the four provinces with particularly difficult security situations are in western Baghdad, Al Anbar, Nineveh, and Saahuddin.[38] Yet even in these areas where insurgents have significant local influence, much of the population is divided, and only limited areas have normally been under active insurgent control. Many Iraqis do passively support the insurgency—and provide political support for attacks on Coalition forces. One Coalition private poll, conducted in February 2005, showed that as many as 45 percent of the Iraqi Arabs polled supported attacks on Coalition forces, while only 15 percent strongly supported the Coalition. Out of those native Sunni Iraqis who supported the insurgency, however, most only provided sympathy or passive support. And, as has been touched upon earlier, there are clear signs that even Iraqi Sunnis who do support the insurrection sometimes actively oppose the actions of outside Islamist extremists and terrorists.

There have also been indicators that some formerly hostile Sunnis are moving toward participation in the government and the evolving Iraqi political process. The negotiations between anti-government Sunnis and Iraqi officials stepped up after the January 30, 2005, elections. While most Sunnis boycotted the elections, the elections were successful enough in legitimizing majority Shi'ite rule and in including the Kurds to show some Sunni-continued opposition could simply end in isolation and a loss of wealth and power. As is discussed in more detail shortly, a total of sixty-four Sunni clerics signed a fatwa legitimizing Sunni participation in the Iraqi military, security forces, and police forces on April 8, 2005. Sunni sermons included similar themes and effectively stated that violence against the Iraqi forces was wrong.[39]

These security problems are compounded by the fact that NGOs, national and international aid organizations, and Iraqi and outside investors generally judge Iraq by its most threatened areas, not the ten to twelve provinces that are relatively safe. It is also impossible to predict when new forms of ethnic and sectarian fighting may take place, and crime, corruption, and bureaucratic delays can paralyze legitimate activity while encouraging profiteering and exploitation. Governance is also often weak or ineffective at the provincial and local levels. As a result, the flow of civil and economic aid and investment to even the most secure areas remains extremely low. This compounds the government's problems in establishing its legitimacy and security and attracting Sunnis in high-threat areas.

The Continuing Threat

The Iraqi government and Coalition face at least several years of continuing threat. Insurgent attacks continue in Baghdad, Mosul, Karbala, and Najaf. The Sunni Triangle, the area along the Tigris, and the "Triangle of Death" south of Baghdad all continue to be areas of intense Sunni insurgent activity, and the stability of Shi'ite and Kurdish areas remains uncertain.

Estimates of the Size of Threat Forces

Estimates of the number of insurgents have varied widely ever since the struggle first became serious in August 2003. Much depends on the definition of insurgent and the level of activity and dedication involved, and virtually everyone who issues such estimates admits they are little more than sophisticated "guesstimates." A few outlying estimates have been as low as 3,500 full-time actives making up the "core" forces. Most U.S. military estimates range between 8,000 and 18,000, perhaps reaching over 20,000 when the ranks swell for major operations. Iraqi intelligence officials, on the other hand, have sometimes issued figures for the total number of Iraqi sympathizers and insurgents as high as 200,000 with a core of anywhere between 15,000 and 40,000 fighters and another 160,000 supporters. *Newsweek* quotes U.S. sources as putting the total of insurgents at 12,000 to 20,000 in late June 2005. Another U.S. expert is quoted as saying it had some 1,000 foreign jihadists, 500 Iraqi jihadists, 15,000 to 30,000 former regime elements, and some 400,000 auxiliaries and support personnel.[40]

The true figure may well fall somewhere in this range of different figures, but the exact number is also largely irrelevant. The real issue is whether the insurgency enjoys enough popular sympathy among Sunnis and others to continue to fight and whether the violence of Sunni Islamist extremist groups can paralyze efforts at inclusiveness and national unity—or even trigger civil war. In practice, suicide bombings by small groups of such extremists may be far more dangerous than the lower levels of violence by larger mainstream Ba'athist or Sunni groups.

Political developments also affect the cycles and nature of the insurgency. Some experts believe the January 30, 2005, elections led some of the native Iraqi insurgents to be more willing to consider negotiating with the government and playing a role in the political process, while events inside and outside Iraq led Al Qa'ida and other Islamist extremist groups to see Iraq more and more as a center of their operations both because of the possibility of "defeating" the United States and because it was one of the few theaters of operations that had significant public support in the Arab world.[41]

Iraq faces two more elections during 2005—a constitutional referendum scheduled for October and a full national election for the end of the year. The insurgents have shown they have every incentive to create as much political turmoil as possible, they continue their attacks on the Iraqi government, economy, intelligentsia, security forces, and the Coalition, and they provoke civil war.

Comparisons of Threat and Iraqi Forces

There is no way to quantify how the development of Iraqi military, security, and police forces has kept pace with the development of effective Iraqi government forces. There are also no meaningful comparative casualty estimates, although MNSTC–I has issued reports of over 1,000 dead in the various elements of Iraqi forces, and one U.S. commander has talked about 15,000 insurgent and terrorist casualties.[42]

In any case, numerical comparisons are largely pointless. The ratio of security forces to insurgents sometimes has to reach levels of 12 to 1 through 30 to 1 in order to provide security in a given area, if there is no political solution to the problems that create the insurgency or active presence by the government. In other cases, a small number of security forces can decapitate a movement or cell and end it. Intangibles like the battle for political perceptions and "hearts and minds" are often far more critical than the numbers of insurgents and defenders.

As Chapter 2 has shown, threat forces have evolved, as well as Iraqi military, security, and police forces. The insurgents and terrorists have grown in capability and size, although serious fighting in Fallujah, Mosul, and Samarra may have reduced their capabilities toward the end of the year. The insurgents have also learned a great deal about how to use their weapons, build more sophisticated IEDs, plan attacks and ambushes, improve their security, and locate and attack targets that are both soft and that produce political and media impact. Insurgents deployed six suicide bombers with explosive belts in February 2005 alone, indicating that insurgents are learning ways to get around security restrictions that make car bombings more difficult.[43]

The Meaning of Coalition Victories and Insurgent Defeats

Insurgents have suffered a series of significant and continuing tactical defeats since early 2004, notably in cities like Najaf, Baghdad, Samarra, Fallujah, and Mosul but also increasingly in the "Triangle of Death," Sunni Triangle, western Iraq and Iraqi-Syrian border areas. Nevertheless, Iraqi government and U.S. attempts to root out the insurgency have so far had limited impact. While some U.S. officers have talked about the battle of Fallujah in November 2004 as a "tipping point," many U.S. experts were cautious even at the time. They felt the insurgents did lose a key sanctuary, suffered more than 1,000 killed, and lost significant numbers of prisoners and detainees. They also lost some significant leaders and cadres. Many insurgents and insurgent leaders seem to have left Fallujah before the fighting, however, and many others escaped.

No province has been safe from occasional attack, and the frequency and intensity of attacks have been only part of the story. Various insurgent groups were still able to attack in other areas like Mosul, Ramadi, Samarra, Baquba, Balad, Baiji, Tal Afar, and Hawija during the fighting in Fallujah and seem to have planned to disperse and to shift their operations before the fighting in Fallujah began.[44] The fighting in Mosul was particularly severe after the battle of Fallujah, and the U.S. military reported a total of 130 to 140 attacks and incidents a day.[45] While the Coalition and Iraqi forces did capture large numbers of weapons and supplies, few experts—if any—felt that the insurgents faced any near-term supply problems given the numbers of weapons looted from Iraq's vast arms depots during and after the fighting that brought down Saddam Hussein.

The battles that have followed during the course of 2005 have been less concentrated and less intensive but almost continuous—mixed with raids, captures, and the sudden "swarming" of known and suspected insurgent headquarters and operational areas. They have also involved continuing kidnappings and assassinations and exceptionally bloody suicide bombings of Shi'ites and Kurds—designed to provoke a civil war. While neither MNSTC-I nor the Iraqi government have provided counts of insurgents killed and wounded, the figures almost certainly exceed 10,000 between May 2003 and May 2005 and could be substantially higher.

The U.S. Marine Corps launched its largest offensive in the Syrian border area and hostile areas along the main route from Syria to Iraq in April 2005. This Operation Matador and a series of follow-up attacks by Marine, U.S., and Iraqi forces in western Iraq again showed that the insurgents could not survive if they stood and fought but could always disperse and survive.[46] Iraqi forces only played a limited support role in these battles but did deploy in greater strength in other areas. These included a major 40,000-man Iraqi security operation called Operation Lightning in the greater Baghdad area in June 2005. This operation too had its successes but again could not destroy insurgent activity in any given area on a lasting basis.

In spite of such new offensives, Sunni insurgent groups remained active in Sunni-populated areas like the Sunni Triangle, the Al Anbar province to the west of Baghdad, and the so-called Triangle of Death to the southeast of Baghdad. As a result, four of Iraq's provinces continued to have a major insurgency threat and a major insurgent presence. Sunni insurgents have repeatedly shown since the battle of Fallujah that they can strike in ethnically mixed and Shi'ite-dominated cities like Baghdad, Tal Afar, Mosul, and Basra and occasionally in Kurdish areas.[47]

General Casey stated in March 2005 that insurgents operating from the Sunni areas had enough manpower, weaponry, ammunition, and money to launch between fifty and sixty attacks a day.[48] Casey did, however, point to the arrest of several suspected terrorist leaders. Although the terrorists retained enough ammunition and arms to continue fighting for years, the general maintained that the capture of certain leaders had degraded the insurgents' abilities to fashion IEDs, the deadliest weapon confronting U.S. troops.

U.S. and Iraqi efforts to thwart individual insurgent attacks—while tireless— have also sometimes been hollow victories. As one U.S. Marine specializing in counterinsurgency in Iraq recently noted, "Seizing the components of suicide bombs (or IED-making material) is like making drug seizures, comforting, but ultimately pointless. There will always be more. Both sides are still escalating to nowhere." The fact also remains that securing Coalition areas and forces often simply drives insurgents and terrorists to attack Iraqis. There has been continuing sabotage of key targets like Iraq's oil facilities and a constant campaign of intimidation, disappearances, and "mystery killings." Even cities that were supposedly liberated before the battle of Fallujah, like Samarra, have been the source of enough continuing attacks to force the redeployment of large numbers of Iraqi security and police forces and elements of key U.S. counterinsurgency units like Task Force 1-26.[49]

The Dominant Role of Iraqi Sunni Arab Insurgents

A violent split between the Arab Shi'ites and Kurds remains possible, as do such splits within the major Shi'ite factions inside and outside the government. Barring such divisions, however, the insurgency will remain largely Iraqi and Sunni dominated. CENTCOM estimated in the summer of 2005 that 90 percent of the insurgency was Iraqi and Sunni, with a maximum of 10 percent foreign contribution to insurgent manpower.[50] While relatively small, this foreign element is recognized as almost exclusively Sunni, a particularly violent segment of the insurgency, and ideologically driven by Neo-Salafi extremism. Likewise, the foreign element is seen as an important source of money and material support to the insurgency, as is discussed in detail in Chapter 12.

In August 2005, for example, Saudi authorities announced that they had seized 682 Iraqis who tried to infiltrate Saudi territory in the first six months of 2005. Interior Ministry spokesman Brigadier General Mansour Turki stated that new security measures were being taken along the border with Iraq, including the erection of sand barricades, the deployment of heat sensors and cameras, and round-the-clock patrols. Still, according to Turki, the problem remaining is a lack of security measures on the Iraqi side.[51] Aside from an 800-kilometer border with Saudi Arabia, porous borders with Jordan and Syria remain liabilities in combating foreign assistance to Iraq's Sunni insurgency.

Some thirty-five Sunni Arab "groups" have made some kind of public announcement of their existence or claimed responsibility for terrorist or insurgent attacks—although many may be little more than cells and some may be efforts to shift the blame for attacks or make the insurgent movement seem larger than it is.[52] Some may be little more than tribal or clan groupings, since many elements of the Sunni insurgency have strong tribal affiliations or cells. An overwhelming majority of those captured or killed have been Iraqi Sunnis, as well as about 90 to 95 percent of those detained.

The Sunni insurgents are divided into a complex mix of Sunni nationalists, pro-Ba'ath/ex-regime, Sunni Iraqi Islamists, outside Islamic extremists, foreign volunteers with no clear alignment, and paid or politically motivated criminals. Some are organized so that their cadres are in relatively small cells, some as small as two or three men. These cells can recruit or call in larger teams, but the loss of even a significant number of such cells may not cripple a given group, and several Sunni groups operate in most areas. Others seem to operate as much larger but normally dispersed groups capable of coming together for operations of as many as thirty to fifty men.

The main Sunni insurgent groups are concentrated in cities like Mosul and Baghdad; in Sunni-populated areas like the Sunni Triangle, the Al Anbar province to the west of Baghdad, and the so-called Triangle of Death to the southeast of Baghdad; and in Sunni areas near the Iraqi and Turkish borders. As a result, four of Iraq's provinces have both a major insurgency threat and a major insurgent presence.

Al Anbar is both Iraq's largest province (roughly the size of Belgium) and one of its least populated—roughly a million people out of Iraq's 27 million. It is at least 90 percent Sunni Arab, offers a route to a potential sanctuary in Syria, and has borders with Jordan and Saudi Arabia. Aside from Fallujah, the area immediately surrounding the Euphrates and its agricultural areas have become a key operating area for insurgents. So have the towns along its border with Syria and the road to Syria, and insurgents take advantage of the desert and rough terrain for smuggling and dispersal. While it has some major cities, it has long been a tribal area where the government has exercised limited control. It is scarcely surprising that it has become a center of the Sunni insurgency, and some estimates indicate that 500 of the 1,630 U.S. servicemen killed in Iraq during the war up to June 2, 2005, died in Al Anbar. It is one of the few areas where insurgents have openly occupied towns and set up checkpoints, and large numbers of Jordanian truck drivers have been killed on the road from Amman in an effort to break up lines of supply.[53]

They have not, however, established long-term control over "safe havens" from which to operate. Sunni insurgents have exerted considerable sway—at various points—in Fallujah, Rawa, Anna, Haditha, Ramadi, Rutbah, Qaim, Ubaydi, Karabilah, Haqliniyah, Barwanah, Tal Afar, and others. However, Coalition assaults have largely disrupted continuous control.

In early September 2005, U.S. and Iraqi forces began "Operation Restoring Rights" on the insurgent stronghold of Tal Afar. It was the largest to-date urban assault since Fallujah. Troops faced little resistance, suspecting that most insurgents fled the city during the pre-assault evacuation of civilians. The following are developments in the fight for Tal Afar as of the fall of 2005:

- One hundred fifty-seven terrorists were killed; 291 others were arrested. On the other hand, one Iraqi serviceman was killed plus six civilians.
- In the al-Sarai district of Tal Afar, explosives were planted in most of the houses, which led to the destruction of ten to twelve houses in the area.
- Around ten to twelve houses have been destroyed because of the explosives planted in them by the terrorists. Dozens of other houses were destroyed

in the last three months during combat operations. U.S. $10,000–15,000 will be paid to the families who lost their homes.

- Twenty trucks of supplies have arrived in Tal Afar from Baghdad. Ten ambulances were sent from Mosul to the nearby town. About 1,000 tents have been provided for the refugees who fled their town of Tal Afar, and seven medical facilities have been set up on the outskirts of the northern town.
- The Iraqi government has said it will deploy peacekeeping forces into the town of Tal Afar after the combat operations in the region are over. In addition to that, 1,000 residents of the town will be trained to maintain security in the long run. The tribes based in the area will also play a major role in maintaining security and stability.[54]

Sunni insurgents have repeatedly shown since the battle of Fallujah, however, that they can strike in ethnically mixed and Shi'ite-dominated cities like Baghdad, Mosul, and Basra in spite of such U.S. and Iraqi offensives. The road from Baghdad to the international airport outside the city remains a high-threat area and has become a symbol of the Coalition and government's problems in bringing security to Iraq. Iraqis have come to call it "Death Street," and the Coalition calls it "IED Alley." The threat in Sunni neighborhoods like Amariya, Hamra, Jihad, and Qaddisyaa is bad enough that senior officials bypass it in helicopters, and regular convoys of armored buses called "Rhinos" have become the only relatively secure way to travel by land.[55]

More broadly, insurgents continue to operate in the Kurdish and more secure Shi'ite areas. Islamist extremists use bombings and other large attacks to fuel a constant feeling of insecurity and to try to divide Iraqis along ethnic and sectarian lines. No province is safe from occasional attack, and attacks are only part of the story. Sabotage, politically oriented crime, and intimidation are all important weapons in the insurgent arsenal.

Ba'athists, Ex-Regime Loyalists, and/or "Sunni Nationalists"

Iraq's Arab Sunnis are only beginning to forge new political identities out of the power vacuum left by Saddam Hussein's dictatorship. It is important to note that while most of Iraq's ruling elite during Saddam Hussein's decades of dictatorship were Sunni, the top elite came from a small portion of Sunnis, many with family backgrounds in what were originally rural military families. The top elite had strong ties not only to Saddam's extended family but to Tikritis in general and the al-Bu Nasir tribe and its Bejat clan and Majid family.[56] The vast majority of Sunnis got little special benefit from Saddam Hussein's rule, and many Sunnis suffered from his oppression in the same way as other Iraqis.

Most Sunni Arabs, like most Shi'ite Arabs, favored a strong, unified Iraqi state during 2003–2004, when public opinion polls covering broad areas were still possible. Like Iraq's Arab Shi'ites, polls show that Iraqi Sunnis are generally religious and see Islam as a key aspect of their lives, but they do not favor a theocratic state. Sunni efforts to create a new political identity include the minority that has participated in the new government and political process, many who boycott it, and political parties like the Muslim Brotherhood and Iraq Islamic Party. They also include clerical bodies like the Association of Islamic Scholars, which is headed by Dr. Muthanna Harith al-Dhari–an Egyptian-educated Islamic scholar. The Association of Islamic Scholars claims to represent some 6,000 mosques, or 80 percent of the total. There is no way to validate such claims.[57]

The Sunnis' self-imposed exclusion from the electoral and constitutional process before the January 30, 2005, elections backfired for a Sunni population that saw the political future of the country unfolding without its input in the summer and fall of 2005. Sunni leaders threatened that a constitution forced through without the consent and consideration of the Sunni population would result in a stepped-up Sunni insurgency.

In summer 2005 a former Iraqi electricity minister, Iyham al-Samarri, announced that he had established a sort of communication organization through which the various insurgent groups could convey their views and concerns to both the elected Iraqi government and the Coalition.[58] It became clear, however, that al-Samarri had a questionable past and a controversial tenure as electricity minister. Furthermore, it could not be substantiated that al-Samarri had had any contact with any insurgents as he claimed. Not long after he claimed this ability to speak on behalf of the insurgents, militant groups criticized him via the Web. They asserted that he did not speak for them and that he was "spreading lies." A week later, an Internet statement appeared stating that the Army of the Mujahideen and the Islamic Army in Iraq had appointed a spokesman, Ibrahim Youssef al-Shammari, to speak on behalf of the two insurgent groups. His identity was confirmed on Web sites linked to the two militant organizations.[59]

The furor over who did and did not speak for the various groups within the insurgency led analysts to suggest that perhaps some of the militants were moving to form political wings.[60] It remained unclear whether such wings would seek to formally run in the elections to come, or whether they would seek to simply put forward cogent demands and expectations.

Ba'athists, Non-Ba'athists, or Semi-Ba'athists?

U.S. analysts–like those in the CIA–acknowledge that Ba'athist and ex-regime loyalists represent only a part of the insurgency, although they have played a key role in leadership, organization, and financing. The largest elements of the insurgency appear to be newly radicalized Iraqi Sunnis. According to the CIA reports, the Sunni loss of power, prestige, and economic influence is a key factor, as is unemployment and a loss of personal status. Direct and disguised unemployment among young Sunni men has been 40 to 60 percent in many areas ever since the fall of Saddam Hussein. Many insurgents are motivated by tribal or family grievances, nationalism, and religious duty. Others are motivated by the U.S. occupation—particularly those who have lost a loved one fighting U.S. forces—and the political and economic turmoil that accompanied the occupation.[61]

Moqtada al-Sadr has been publicly supportive of the political process in Iraq, and he has urged Shi'ites to avoid sectarian fighting with the Sunni population. Yet the strength of his militia remains a concern. The Sadr Organization and other organized religious groups have been accused of political assassinations and kidnappings, as have Kurdish forces in the north. Sadr's Mehdi Army maintains omniscience in certain areas such as Basra that creates an environment of fear according to local accounts.[62]

Another challenge is presented by uniformed, government-sponsored police and security forces who use their power to express loyalties to religious parties or political factions. In August 2005, Basra Police Chief Hassam Sawadi said that he had lost control of over three-quarters of his police force and that men in his ranks were using their power to assassinate opponents.[63] Reports indicate that government police and military forces in the Kurdish north are similarly using their power to intimidate Sunnis through abductions and assassinations. Such activity poses the threat of deepening regional fissures. Likewise, the misuse of power by Coalition-sponsored forces could possibly deepen resentment toward Coalition forces, particularly among the Sunni population.

This does not mean that ex-Ba'athists do not play a critical role. The Ba'ath Party did not dissolve when the CPA formally abolished it in May 2003. It reorganized with a new structure, established a new politburo in 2004, and at least some elements operated from a de facto sanctuary in Syria.[64] At the same time, many full-time and part-time Iraqi members' groups associated with the Ba'ath are linked more by tribe, family, and locality than any sense of Ba'ath political identity. Many of the Sunni insurgent groups or cells that are not Islamist extremist groups, or associated with them, may get money or some degree of leadership from the Ba'athist structures that have emerged since the fall of Saddam Hussein, but they have no meaningful ties to or family linkage to former Ba'ath groups or to former members of Saddam Hussein's government and the Ba'ath regime. It is generally misleading to call them "former regime loyalists" (FRLs) or "former regime elements" (FREs). They are rather Sunni nationalists involved in a struggle for current power. This has allowed the insurgency to broaden its base and establish ties to Islamic groups as well.

Other Iraqi-dominated Sunni insurgent groups have a significant degree of independence from the former Ba'ath leadership, although it is clear that many cooperate in at least some operations and that many of the elements with at least some ties to ex-supporters of Saddam Hussein's regime have some degree of central leadership and coordination. U.S. experts talk of informal networks, using tools like the Internet to coordinate operations and exchange data on tactics, targets, and operations. There is evidence of such exchanges between cells in Iraq and outside groups, including those in Syria and Afghanistan. Insurgent groups also use the media to get near real-time information on what other groups and cells are doing and to find out what tactics produce the maximum political and media impact.

In short, it is unclear how much influence various "Ba'athist" groups have. However, both U.S. and Iraqi Interim Government officials—such as the MNF–I commander General Casey and Iraqi Defense Minister Hazim al-Shalaan—believe that Ba'ath leaders in Syria coordinate with at least some of the Ba'ath sympathizers. The office of the Iraqi prime minister also called for the arrest of the following six senior members of the former regime in March 2005:[65]

- Izzat Ibrahim al-Duri (believed to be the leader of the New Regional Command and New Ba'ath Party)
- Muhammed Younis al-Ahmad (financial facilitator and operational leader of the New Regional Command and New Ba'ath Party)
- Rashid Ta'an Kazim (Central Ba'ath Party regional chairman in Al Anbar province)
- Abd Al-Baqi Abd Al-Karim Al-Abdallah Al-Sa'adun (recruiter and financier of terrorist activity in eastern and central Iraq)
- Aham Hasan Kaka al-Ubaydi (a former intelligence officer now associated with Ansar al-Islam)
- Fadhil Ibrahim Mahmud al-Mashadani, also known as Abu Huda (top member of the New Ba'ath Party and a key financier of insurgent and terrorist activity)

Ba'athist elements benefit from the fact that they still have access to some of the former regime's money and that they began to organize—at least at a crude level—before the invasion began and have since steadily tightened up their organization and purged suspect members. According to one report, they held a major meeting at Al Hasaka in April or May of 2004 to tighten up their structure. Field leaders reportedly include Mohammed Younis al-Ahmad, a former aide to Saddam Hussein, and Ibrahim Sabawi, Hussein's half-brother and a former security director. They also benefit from the fact that some elements of the leadership of the Iraqi Fifth Corps are still in Mosul, and Syria has provided a covert sanctuary for at least some Iraq Ba'athist leaders.[66]

The relations between such mainstream Iraqi Sunni insurgent groups and the smaller Islamic extremist groups are mixed. In some cases, MNF–I and U.S. officials see evidence that secular Sunni groups and even Hussein loyalists were cooperating with extreme Islamists. In Mosul Ba'athists worked with Salafists to attack American troops and derail the election process.[67] While the two groups have conflicting visions and aspirations for Iraq's future—and sometimes feud or even kill each other—their short-term goals are largely the same: instability and insecurity, breaking up the new Iraqi government and depriving it of popular legitimacy, keeping Iraqi forces from becoming effective, and driving the U.S. and MNF–I forces out of Iraq.

Guesstimates and the "Numbers Game"

As has already been discussed, there are no reliable estimates of the numbers of the various types of Sunni insurgents or breakdowns of their strength by motivation and group. There also are no recent polls that provide a clear picture of how many Iraqi Arab Sunnis support the insurgents, although some ABC News polls indicated that the number was well over 33 percent by the spring of 2004. Many members of the Sunni clergy have become steadily more supportive of the insurgency since that time, and battles like Fallujah have inevitably helped to polarize Sunni opinion.

U.S. officials kept repeating the estimate of total insurgent strength of 5,000 from roughly the fall of 2003 through the summer of 2004. In October they raised their estimates to a range of 12,000 to 16,000 but have never defined how many are hard-core and full-time and how many are part-time. As has been discussed earlier, estimates as divergent as 3,500 and 400,000 were being cited in the spring and early summer of 2005.[68]

U.S. and Iraqi official experts would be the first to indicate that any such numbers were little more than "guesstimates." They have been consistently careful to note that they are uncertain as to whether the numbers are increasing or decreasing with time as a result of U.S. and Iraqi operations versus increases in political and other tensions that lead Iraqi Arab Sunnis to join the insurgents. There is no evidence that the number of insurgents is declining as a result of Coalition and Iraqi attacks to date. U.S. experts stated in the spring of 2005 that they had no evidence of a decline in insurgent numbers in spite of large numbers killed and captured since the summer of 2004.

Once again, the numerical strength of the insurgents is only part of the issue. Insurgent cadres have also steadily become more experienced, adapting tactics and methods of attack as fast as the Coalition can counter them. Coalition troops reported that insurgents in Fallujah utilized an improved RPG in efforts to counter armored vehicles. The fighting from September to November 2004 has shown they are developing networks with some form of central command, planning, and financing.

The Crime Problem

At least some elements in the Sunni insurgency work with criminal elements looting and sabotage campaigns. These clearly involve some native and foreign Sunni Islamist extremists—particularly in areas like kidnappings—but the alliances Ba'athists and Sunni nationalists have with criminal groups seem to be much stronger. They also seem to dominate the cases where tribal groups mix insurgents and criminals. The insurgents and their criminal allies understand the limits of the Coalition's ability to cover the given areas and the Coalition's vulnerabilities. Many patterns of Coalition, Iraqi government, and Iraqi forces activity are easily observed and have become predictable. Bases can often be observed and are vulnerable to rocket and mortar attacks at their entrances and along their supply lines. There are many soft and relatively small isolated facilities.

The crime problem also affects Iraqi popular confidence in the government and its popular legitimacy. Far more Iraqis face day-to-day threats from criminals than from terrorists and insurgents, although there is no area totally free from the risk of attack. If Iraqis are to trust their new government, if insurgents are to be deprived of recruits and proxies, and if Iraq is to move toward economic development and recovery, the crime problem must be solved at the same time the insurgents and terrorists are being defeated. This is a key priority in terms of Iraqi force development because it means effective regular policy is critical and must have the same emphasis as developing military and security forces.

The Intelligence and Security Problem

Ba'athists and Sunni nationalists and Sunni Islamist extremists all pose acute security and counterintelligence problems for MNF–I and Iraqi forces. As has been touched upon in previous chapters, the insurgents have good sources within the Iraqi Interim Government and forces, Iraqi society, and sometimes in local U.S. and Coalition commands. This is inevitable, and little can be done to stop it. Iraq simply lacks the resources and data to properly vet all of the people it recruits. Many Iraqis only work for the government or in the Iraqi forces because they cannot find other employment. They may, in fact, quietly sympathize with the insurgents. Workers in U.S. and government facilities and in various aid and construction projects are even harder to vet. Men who do support the government are vulnerable to threats against their families, kidnappings, and actual murders of friends and relatives.

U.S., allied, and Iraqi human intelligence is improving, but Coalition efforts are badly hurt by high turnover and rotations. Most Iraqi networks serving the United States in hostile areas have serious quality and loyalty problems, while others either use their positions to settle scores or misinform Coalition troops. Iraqi intelligence is just beginning to take shape and has only limited coverage of Sunni areas. Training and equipment have improved significantly in the last six months, and Iraqi units do seem to be able to get better input from the local population, but the training and organization of effective Iraqi intelligence and counterintelligence efforts will take at least until the end of 2005 and probably well into 2006.

Coalition and Iraqi government vulnerability is unavoidable to some extent. Aid projects are easy to infiltrate and to target when nearing completion. NGO or contractor headquarters are easily observable targets. Infrastructure and energy facilities are typical targets that have long lines of pipes or wires and many vulnerable links. The media has to be careful and defensive, as do emergency workers and medical teams. Any nation is inevitably filled with soft or vulnerable targets that insurgents can choose at will, and experienced insurgents and terrorists will always target these vulnerabilities.

Inclusion versus Exclusion

In theory, the various Sunni insurgent groups are more capable of paralyzing progress and fighting a long war of attrition than of actually defeating an Iraqi government that is dominated by a cohesive Shi'ite majority and maintains good relations with the Kurds. Regardless of who is doing the counting, the total for active and passive native Iraqi Sunni insurgents still leaves them a small minority of Iraq's population. Unless the Iraqi government divides or collapses, they cannot bring back Arab Sunni minority rule or the Ba'ath; they cannot regain the level of power, wealth, and influence they once had. They cannot reestablish the form of largely secular rule that existed under Saddam Hussein or reestablish Iraq as a country that most Arabs see as Sunni.

Richard Armitage, the former U.S. deputy secretary of state, commented on the insurgency and its lack of realistic political goals as follows: "In Algeria, the so-called insurgents, or in Vietnam, the so-called insurgents, they had ... a program and a positive view.... In Iraq that's lacking; ... they only have fear to offer. They only have terror to offer. This is why they're so brutal in their intimidation."[69]

At the same time, the various Sunni insurgent elements are becoming better trained and organized and may still be able to establish themselves as *the* dominant political and military force within the Sunni community—particularly if Iraq's Arab Shi'ites and Kurds mishandle the situation or react to the growing provocation of bloody suicide attacks and other killings by Neo-Salafi extremists.[70] They can try to present themselves as the only legitimate alternative to the occupation, even if they fail to provide a popular agenda. This means they can survive and endure as long as the government is too weak to occupy the insurgency dominated areas—and as long as the large majority of Sunnis in given areas does not see a clear incentive to join the government and Iraq's political process.

Yet, an understanding of these same political and military realities may eventually drive many Sunni insurgents to join the nonviolent political process in Iraq if the Shi'ite and Kurds elements that now dominate the government and political process act to include them and provide suitable incentives. Such shifts are likely to be slow and limited in scope. Historically, most insurgent groups have a much better vision of what they oppose than what they are for, and they have limited interest in pragmatic "realpolitik." Most Sunni groups are still committed to doing everything—and sometimes anything—they can to drive the Coalition out and break up the peaceful political process almost regardless of the damage done to Iraq and to Sunni areas.

Much will depend on just how willing Iraqi Shi'ites and Kurds are to forget the past, not overreact to Sunni Islamist and other attacks designed to divide and splinter the country, and to continue to offer Iraqi Sunnis a fair share of wealth and power. Iraq's president and prime minister have both done this. The search for a Sunni minister of defense examined some ten candidates before choosing Sadun al-Dulaimi in early May 2003 and was a key factor delaying the creation of a new government. At the same time, other Shi'ites and Kurds have called for the systematic purging of all Sunnis with ties to the Ba'ath, including many in the Iraqi forces, and unexplained raids have taken place on Sunni political groups involved in trying to negotiate with the government.[71]

Islamist Groups and Outside Volunteers

Other key insurgent elements include Arab and Islamist groups with signifi-cant numbers of foreign volunteers, as well as Iraqi Islamist extremists. These include groups like the one led by Abu Musab al-Zarqawi, first known as al-Tawhid wal-Jihad or Unity and Holy War, now known as Tandhim Qa'idat al-Jihan fi Bilad al-Rafidayn or Al Qa'ida of Jihad Organization in the Land of Two Rivers.[72] The other easily identifiable group is the offshoot of Ansar al-Islam or Protectors of Islam, an Islamist group created in the Kurdish regions in September 2001, called Ansar al-Sunna or Protectors of the Sunna Faith. Ansar suffered a joint attack from Kurdish and U.S. forces in March 2003, forcing many of its fighters to scatter, possibly to Iran, before several allegedly settled in Mosul. Other groups and their area of operation include the following: (1) Al-Muqawama al-'Iraqiya al-Wataniya al-Islamiya, Fayaliq Thawrat 1920 or the Iraqi National Islamic Resistance, the 1920 Brigades in West Baghdad, Ninewa, Diyala, and Anbar and (2) Al-Jibha al-Wataniya litahrial-'Iraq or the National Front for the Liberation of Iraq, which seems to be an umbrella for groups of Islamists and nationalists, namely the Islamic Army of Iraq, the Army of Mohammad, the Iraqi Resistance Front, the Iraqi Liberation Army, and the Awakening and Holy War, operating in Fallujah, Samarra, and Basra.[73]

There seem to be no clear limits to the willingness of some of the more extreme Sunni Arab insurgent elements to escalate, even if this means trying to drive the nation into a civil war they cannot win. Some are likely to escalate even further as their situation becomes more threatened. It seems almost certain that many cadres and leaders of such groups and cells cannot be persuaded, only defeated. Some non-Islamist extremist groups will remain alienated almost regardless of what the government and other Sunnis do and will move on to join the most extreme Islamist movements.

It is unlikely that such groups make up more than 10 percent of the insurgent force and may make up around 5 percent. While the number of foreign volun-teers has increased with time and estimates now range up to 3,000, it is also important to point out that as of June 2005 they made up less than 600 of some 14,000 detainees. Coalition experts also estimated that they made up less than 5 percent of insurgent casualties and detainees to date.[74] Nevertheless, they may be the most dangerous element in the insurgency since they have increas-ingly tried to provoke a civil war between Iraq's Arab Sunnis and its Arab Shi'ites, Kurds, and other minorities. In June 2005, U.S. Lieutenant General John Vines, commanding general of Coalition forces in Iraq, identified the foreign fighters as the most violent group in Iraq's ongoing insurgency. According to Vines, insurgent activity among Iraqis was being driven by money, not ideology, and foreign jihadists were using their financial resources to get Iraqis to attack other Iraqis.[75]

Foreign Sunni Islamist extremist volunteers seem to have carried out most of the suicide car and pedestrian bombings since 2003. These are among some of the bloodiest and most-publicized insurgent attacks. One U.S. defense official estimated that as of July 2005, Iraqis had directly carried out less than 10 percent of more than 500 suicide bombings.[76] These attacks also accelerated sharply in the spring and summer of 2005; the Associated Press counted at least 213 suicide attacks as of July. Don Alston, a U.S. Air Force general and MNF–I spokesperson, stated, "The foreign fighters are the ones most often behind the wheel of suicide car bombs, or most often behind any suicide situation." And General Abizaid stated that the Coalition had seen a rise in suicide bombers coming from North Africa, particularly Algeria, Tunisia, and Morocco.[77]

What is not clear is the extent to which the fact young men are recruited from countries in North Africa, the Sudan, Syria, Saudi Arabia, and other countries means that Islamist extremist organizations are dominated by foreign fighters. Recruiting outsiders as cannon fodder or "martyrs" has become all too easy in a region where religious extremists have learned how to exploit religious feelings; it does not mean that those directing the effort and carrying out the support activities are not Iraqis or that such movements and activities do not have substantial Iraqi support.

The U.S. State Department Assessment of Zarqawi

The U.S. State Department's "Country Reports on Terrorism" described the overall level of such terrorist activity in Iraq at the end of 2004 and the role of key Islamist groups as follows:

> Iraq remains the central battleground in the global war on terrorism. Former regime elements as well as foreign fighters and Islamic extremists continued to conduct terrorist attacks against civilians and non-combatants. These elements also conducted numerous insurgent attacks against Coalition and Iraqi Security Forces, which often had devastating effects on Iraqi civilians and significantly damaged the country's economic infrastructure.
>
> Jordanian-born Abu Mus'ab al-Zarqawi and his organization emerged in 2004 to play a leading role in terrorist activities in Iraq. In October, the U.S. government designated Zarqawi's group, Jama'at al Tawhid wa'al-Jihad, as a Foreign Terrorist Organization (FTO). In December, the designation was amended to include the group's new name Tanzim Qa'idat al-Jihad fi Bilad al-Rafidayn (or "The al-Qa'ida Jihad Organization in the Land of the Two Rivers") and other aliases following the "merger" between Zarqawi and Osama bin Laden's al-Qa'ida organization. Zarqawi announced the merger in October, and in December, bin Laden endorsed Zarqawi as his official emissary in Iraq. Zarqawi's group

claimed credit for a number of attacks targeting Coalition and Iraqi forces, as well as civilians, including the October massacre of forty-nine unarmed, out-of-uniform Iraqi National Guard recruits. Attacks that killed civilians include the March 2004 bombing of the Mount Lebanon Hotel, killing seven and injuring over thirty, and a December 24 suicide bombing using a fuel tanker that killed nine and wounded nineteen in the al-Mansur district of Baghdad.

In February 2004, Zarqawi called for a "sectarian war" in Iraq. He and his organization sought to create a rift between Shi'a and Sunnis through several large terror attacks against Iraqi Shi'a. In March 2004, Zarqawi claimed credit for simultaneous bomb attacks in Baghdad and Karbala that killed over 180 pilgrims as they celebrated the Shi'a festival of Ashura. In December, Zarqawi also claimed credit for a suicide attack at the offices of Abdel Aziz al-Hakim, leader of the Supreme Council for the Islamic Revolution in Iraq (SCIRI), one of Iraq's largest Shi'a parties, which killed fifteen and wounded over fifty.

Zarqawi has denied responsibility for another significant attack that same month in Karbala and Najaf, two of Shi'a Islam's most holy cities, which killed Iraqi civilians and wounded more than 120. Terrorists operating in Iraq used kidnapping and targeted assassinations to intimidate Iraqis and third-country nationals working in Iraq as civilian contractors. Nearly sixty noncombatant Americans died in terrorist incidents in Iraq in 2004. Other American noncombatants were killed in attacks on Coalition military facilities or convoys. In June, Zarqawi claimed credit for the car bomb that killed the chairman of the Coalition-appointed Iraqi Governing Council. In April, an American civilian was kidnapped and later beheaded. One month later, a video of his beheading was posted on an al-Qa'ida-associated Web site. Analysts believe that Zarqawi himself killed the American as well as a Korean hostage, kidnapped in June. Zarqawi took direct credit for the September kidnapping and murder of two American civilians and later their British engineer co-worker, and the October murder of a Japanese citizen.

In August, the Kurdish terrorist group Ansar al-Sunna claimed responsibility for the kidnapping and killing of twelve Nepalese construction workers, followed by the murder of two Turkish citizens in September. Many other foreign civilians have been kidnapped. Some have been killed, others released, some remain in their kidnappers' hands, and the fate of others, such as the director of CARE, is unknown.

Other terrorist groups were active in Iraq. Ansar al-Sunna, believed to be an offshoot of the Ansar al-Islam group founded in Iraq in September 2001, first came to be known in April 2003 after issuing a statement on the Internet. In February 2004, Ansar al-Sunna claimed responsibility for bomb attacks on the offices of two Kurdish political parties in Irbil, which killed 109 Iraqi civilians. The Islamic Army in Iraq has also claimed responsibility for terrorist actions. Approximately 3,800 disarmed persons remained resident at the former Mujahideen-e Khalq (MeK) military base at Camp Ashraf; the MeK is a designated U.S. Foreign Terrorist Organization (FTO). More than 400 members renounced membership in the organization in 2004. Forty-one additional defectors elected to return to Iran, and another 200 were awaiting ICRC assistance for voluntary repatriation to Iran at the end of the year. PKK/KADEK/Kongra Gel, a designated foreign terrorist group, maintains an estimated 3,000 to 3,500 armed militants in northern Iraq, according to Turkish Government sources and NGOs. In the summer of 2004, PKK/KADEK/Kongra Gel renounced its self-proclaimed ceasefire and threatened to renew its separatist struggle in both Turkey's southeast and urban centers. Turkish press subsequently reported multiple incidents in the southeast of PKK/KADEK/Kongra Gel terrorist actions or clashes between Turkish security forces and PKK/KADEK/Kongra Gel militants.[78]

The State Department report also provided the following more detailed description of the role of Ansar al-Islam (AI), also known as Ansar al-Sunnah Partisans of Islam, Helpers of Islam, Kurdish Taliban:

> Ansar al-Islam (AI) is a radical Islamist group of Iraqi Kurds and Arabs who have vowed to establish an independent Islamic state in Iraq. The group was formed in December 2001. In the fall of 2003, a statement was issued calling all jihadists in Iraq to unite under the name Ansar al-Sunnah (AS). Since that time, it is likely that AI has posted all claims of attack under the name AS. AI is closely allied with al-Qa'ida and Abu Mus'ab al-Zarqawi's group, Tanzim Qa'idat al-Jihad fi Bilad al-Rafidayn (QJBR) in Iraq. Some members of AI trained in al-Qa'ida camps in Afghanistan, and the group provided safe haven to al-Qa'ida fighters before Operation Iraqi Freedom (OIF). Since OIF, AI has become one of the leading groups engaged in anti-Coalition attacks in Iraq and has developed a robust propaganda campaign.
>
> AI continues to conduct attacks against Coalition forces, Iraqi government officials and security forces, and ethnic Iraqi groups and political parties. AI members have been implicated in assassinations and assassination attempts against Patriotic Union of Kurdistan (PUK) officials and Coalition forces, and also work closely with both al-Qa'ida operatives and associates in QJBR. AI has also claimed responsibility for many high-profile attacks, including the simultaneous suicide bombings of the PUK and Kurdistan Democratic Party (KDP) party offices in Ibril on February 1, 2004, and the bombing of the U.S. military dining facility in Mosul on December 21, 2004.
>
> Its strength is approximately 500 to 1,000 members, its location and area of operation is primarily central and northern Iraq.... The group receives funding, training, equipment, and combat support from al-Qa'ida, QJBR, and other international jihadist backers throughout the world. AI also has operational and logistic support cells in Europe.[79]

Zarqawi Operations in 2005

Views have differed sharply over the size of Zarqawi's movement, the depth of its ties to Bin Laden and Al Qa'ida, how many of its current "fighters" are Iraqi versus non-Iraqi, and how many other Islamist extremist groups exist and how independent they are of Zarqawi and Al Qa'ida. A number of groups claim affiliation with Zarqawi, but it is unknown how closely tied many of these groups are to Zarqawi. It is likely that some of them either only claim him as an inspiration or operate as almost totally independent groups and cells. This seems to include a number of elements organized along tribal lines.

At the same time, forces with ties to Zarqawi have been capable of large offensive operations like the spring 2005 attack on the Abu Ghraib prison, and many of the insurgent forces the U.S. Marine Corps fought in its offensive along the Euphrates and near the Syrian border in May 2005 either had ties to Zarqawi or were part of mixes of Zarqawi loyalists and other Iraqi Sunni insurgents.

In the spring of 2004, U.S. officials estimated that there might be a core strength of fewer than 1,000 foreign fighters in Iraq or as many as 2,000. However, some MNSTC–I and Iraqi experts felt that so many volunteers were coming in across the Syrian and other borders that the total was rapidly increasing.[80] A few press estimates went as high as 10,000 before the fighting in Fallujah, but seemed to be sharply exaggerated. It seems more likely that Zarqawi's movement now consists of a series of cells with a limited central organization. They probably total less than 2,000 full- and part-time men—including both Iraqis and foreigners—and probably with a core strength of no more than several hundred.

Zarqawi does seem to have been able to recruit more and more outside volunteers after the fighting in Fallujah and substantially more volunteers for suicide bombings after the January 30, 2005, elections brought a Shi'ite and Kurdish dominated government to power. It is not clear whether this is sharply strengthening his movement or simply helped to cope with the constant attrition caused by MNF–I and Iraqi attacks. The problem of infiltration, however, was serious enough to make improving border security a top Coalition and Iraqi government priority in January and February 2005 and a factor in a major Marine offensive in the Syrian border area in May 2005.[81]

While U.S. claims about the importance of the killings and captures of Zarqawi's senior lieutenants have sometimes seemed exaggerated—as do claims to have nearly killed or captured Zarqawi—there were real successes. On January 10, 2005, then Prime Minister Allawi announced that Izz al-Din Al-Majid, a chief Zarqawi financier, was arrested in Fallujah in early December 2004. Al-Majid had more than $35 million in his bank accounts and controlled $2 billion to $7 billion of former regime assets stolen from Iraqi government accounts. His objective, according to interrogators, was to unite the insurgent groups Ansar al-Sunna, Jaysh Muhammad, and the Islamic Resistance Army. Since that time, the appendix to this report shows that MNF–I forces have killed or captured many other such senior cadres.

In July 2005 U.S. chairman of the Joint Chiefs of Staff General Richard Myers announced that the Coalition had captured a long sought after battlefield commander, Abu 'Abd-al-Aziz. According to the U.S. military, al-Aziz had led a foreign fighter cell in Fallujah up until the United States took control of the city. Fleeing the city, al-Aziz apparently came to Baghdad and earned the moniker "the Amir of Baghdad" among fellow insurgents.[82] Later that month, the U.S.

military announced the capture of what was described as an Al Qa'ida commander and close confidant to Zarqawi. Khamis Farhan Khalaf Abd al-Fahdawi,
or Abu Seba, was captured with approximately thirty other terrorist suspects.
It is believed that Seba played a role in the murder of Egypt's ambassador and in
the attacks on Pakistan's and Bahrain's envoys. An Internet posting purportedly
written by Zarqawi's group claimed that Seba was a low-level leader of a cell
in Baghdad and that the U.S. forces were inventing ranks to portray an image
of success in taking down the terrorist networks.[83]

Not long after, an Egyptian insurgent named Hamdi Tantawi was captured
by Iraqi police in the town of Yusufiyah, along with weaponry, computers,
and money. It is believed that Tantawi financed insurgent operations and
allegedly was a lieutenant to Ayman al-Zawahiri, the second most recognized international Al Qa'ida figure behind Osama Bin Laden. Further details were
unavailable, and it is unclear whether Tantawi was operating independently or
coordinating with Zawahiri and/or Zarqawi. If he was as close to Zawahiri as
suggested by the press reports, it would suggest that the coordination between
the old guard Al Qa'ida leadership and the Al Qa'ida in Iraq group is far
closer than previously thought. It would also suggest that Bin Laden and
Zawahiri are perhaps not as hard pressed and on the run along the Afghan
border with Pakistan as has largely been assumed.

Zarqawi and Suicide Bombings and Volunteers

Any list of Zarqawi's operations remains speculative, although news agencies
have tried to compile summaries of Zarqawi's operations. See table 11.1 below
for one of the more comprehensive lists.[84]

Certainly, the importance of such Islamist extremist elements is not determined by their numbers. They tend to conduct the bloodiest attacks, do the most
to try to divide Iraq along ethnic and sectarian lines, and create a series of
high-profile bombings and atrocities, which captures media and public attention
both inside and outside Iraq. For example, some 400 people were killed in suicide
bombings in Iraq during the first two weeks of May 2005, many in bombings by
Sunni extremist groups clearly targeting Shi'ites and Kurds and doing so during
a key period of transition to the new government elected on January 30. Most
of the suicide bombers in Iraq seem to have been foreign jihadists recruited by
Islamic extremist movements and Islamists in other countries and sent to Iraq
with the goal of seeking "Islamic" martyrdom. Islamist extremist Web sites have
become filled with the claimed biographies of such martyrs.[85] Experts differ
over just how many such suicide bombers exist and where they come from.
Reuven Paz calculated in March 2005 that some 200 suicide bombers could be
documented and that 154 had been killed in the previous six months. He estimated
that 61 percent were Saudi and 25 percent were Iraqi, Kuwaiti, and Syrian. Nawaf
Obaid found forty-seven Saudi suicide bombers in Saudi media records in May
2005 and estimated the total number of Saudi insurgents in the hundreds. Evan

TABLE 11.1
Speculative List of Zarqawi Operations

Date	Attack	Number Killed	Statement Date/Format
8/19/03	Suicide car bombing UN headquarters in Baghdad	At least 17	Audio, April 6, 2004
8/29/03	A car bomb explodes outside Iraq's holiest Shi'ite shrine in Najaf	Hakim killed plus at least 82 others	Audio, April 6, 2004
10/26/03	Missiles launched from improvised launcher system hit Al Rashid Hotel, while Paul Wolfowitz is visiting	1	Audio, April 6, 2004
11/12/03	Suicide truck bomb kills Italians based in Al Nasiriyah	26	Audio, April 6, 2004
12/27/03	Series of car bomb, mortar, and machine-gun attacks on Coalition forces in Karbala	19	Audio, April 6, 2004
1/24/04	American forces on the Al Khalidiya bridge, IED	3	Audio, April 6, 2004
1/28/04	Suicide bombing—CIA in Al Shahin hotel and the Presidential Palace in Baghdad	4	Audio, April 6, 2004
2/18/04	Suicide attacks on Polish forces in Al Hillah	13	Audio, April 6, 2004
3/17/04	Mount Lebanon hotel, car bomb (unclear whether bomber was killed)	27	Audio, April 6, 2004
4/24/04	Suicide bombers crash into oil stations in port in Basra	3	Web statement, April 25, 2004
4/29/04	U.S. soldiers killed when car bomb detonates south of Baghdad—responsibility for attack was claimed, stating that seventy soldiers were allegedly killed	10	Web statement, May 2, 2004
4/30/04	Unconfirmed attack, no news reports confirm attack that Web site alleges took place, stating that fifty-one soldiers were killed when someone named Abu Al Walid Al Tunesi (the Tunisian) carried out a suicide attack against five army vehicles each carrying fifteen soldiers in the Al Youssefeya neighborhood south of Baghdad	—	Web statement, May 2, 2004
5/2/04	Mortar attack in Ramadi area kills U.S. Marines	6	Web statement, May 1, 2004
5/2/04	Suicide bomber detonates car at the edge of the Green Zone at the U.S. headquarters	6	Web statement, May 6, 2004

(Continued)

TABLE 11.1

Continued

Date	Attack	Number Killed	Statement Date/Format
5/11/04	Beheading of Nick Berg	1	Video, May 11, 2004
5/13/04	Unconfirmed suicide attack on a U.S. patrol in al Taji area in northern Baghdad	—	Web statement, May 13, 2004
5/18/04	Suicide car bomb explodes near U.S. headquarters, killing Izzedine Salim, at that time head of IGC, and several others	7	Web statement, May 17, 2004
5/22/04	A suicide attacker exploded a car bomb outside the home of a deputy interior minister, killing at least three police and one civilian	4 (plus suicide bombers)	Web statement, May 22, 2004
6/5/04	Ambush along road to Baghdad airport kills two Americans and two Poles working for Blackwater USA security company	4	—
6/6/04	Twin car bombings outside former Iraqi air base used by U.S. Army just north of Baghdad	9	Web site claims responsibility
6/14/04	Car bomb attack on vehicle convoy in Baghdad kills thirteen, including three GE employees	13	Web site allegedly written by "military wing of Monotheism and Jihad," also believed to be led by Zarqawi, claims responsibility
6/17/04	Two car bombs in northern Baghdad kill 41 Iraqis	41	Web statement, June 17, 2004, claims responsibility
6/22/04	Beheading of South Korean hostage	1	Video, June 22, 2004
6/24/04	Forty-four killed in Mosul in attacks that included a series of car bombs	See below	Web statement, June 24, 2004, claims five attacks on police stations in Mosul
6/24/04	Assault on Iraqi security forces in Baquba	See below	Web statement, June 24, 2004, claims two attacks in Baquba

Date	Event	Casualties	Notes
6/24/04	Assault on Iraqi security forces in Ramadi	See below	Web statement, June 24, 2004, claims one attack in Ramadi
6/24/04	Assault on Iraqi security forces in Baghdad	Total of approximately 100 killed in series of attacks on 6/24/04	Web statement, June 24, 2004, claims one attack in Baghdad
7/8/04	Mortar attack in Samarra	1 Iraqi, 5 Americans	Web statement, July 11, 2004
Early July 2004	Claims attack outside Prime Minister Ayad Allawi's home	—	Web statement, July 14, 2004
7/13/04	Beheading of Bulgarian hostage	1	Video statement, aired on al Jazeera
7/17/04	Suicide bomber hits motorcade of Iraqi Justice Minister Malek Dohan al-Hasan	3 Iraqi guards, 2 civilians	Web statement
7/18/04	Defense Ministry official Issam Jassem Qassim was shot dead outside his home by three gunmen	1	Unclear whether Zarqawi claimed responsibility for attacks—note that over the last month several Iraqi bureaucrats have been killed, and it is unclear whether Zarqawi's group is responsible for all
7/19/04	Suicide car bombing blows up fuel tanker near Baghdad police station	10 killed, 62 wounded	Unclear if Zarqawi responsible
8/1/04	Car bomb blasts outside five Iraqi Churches	At least 15	Iraq accuses Zarqawi of attacks
8/11/04	A Web site carried a one-person video claiming to show militants beheading a "CIA agent" in Iraq (CIA said that it was unaware of it being anyone in the organization)	—	A Web site used by Islamic militants
8/16/04	Egyptian hostage beheading	1	Unconfirmed according to Egyptian Foreign Minister
8/24/04	Assassination bid on Iraq's interim environment minister, Mishkat al-Moumin	—	Zarqawi's group claimed
9/06/04	Zarqawi escapes U.S.-led ambush near Fallujah	—	Confirmed by United States
9/07/04	Car bombing kills seven U.S. soldiers and three Iraqi national guards	10	Zarqawi claims attack on tape received by AFP

(Continued)

TABLE 11.1
Continued

Date	Attack	Number Killed	Statement Date/Format
9/12/04	Zarqawi speaks on audiotape for forty-five minutes about humiliating the American Coalition forces, referring to the fighting in Najaf and the Sunni Triangle	—	Confirmed by CIA
9/14/04	Car bombing outside Baghdad's main police headquarters; several hours later, twelve policemen and their driver are killed in drive-by shooting	At least 47 killed, 114 wounded	Claimed by Zarqawi, al Tawhid
9/16/04	Kidnapping of two American nationals, Eugene Armstrong and Jack Hensley, and one British national, Kenneth Bigley	3	Claimed by Zarqawi, confirmed by United States
9/20/04	Beheading of American hostage, Eugene Armstrong	1	Video, September 20, 2004, claimed by Zarqawi, al Tawhid; confirmed by CIA
9/21/04	Beheading of American hostage, Jack Hensley	1	Claimed by Zarqawi on Iraqi TV and Web site; confirmed by United States
9/30/04	Three car bombs explode	At least 51 killed, more than 130 wounded	Zarqawi's group claims responsibility
10/24/04	Forty-four Iraqi soldiers executed by shots to the head	At least 44 killed	Zarqawi's group claims responsibility via the Internet
12/3/04	Gunmen storm police station, killing sixteen officers; car bomb exploded during clash between Iraqi security forces and rebels	30 killed (16 were police)	Zarqawi claims responsibility
12/13/04	Suicide car bombing at checkpoint	6 killed, 19 injured	Zarqawi's group claims responsibility, according to a statement posted on an Islamic Web site regularly used by militants
12/19/04	Car bombs explode through funeral procession in Karbala	60 killed	Zarqawi's group claims responsibility
12/29/04	Assassination attempt against Abdel Aziz Al-Hakim, Iraq's largest Shiite Muslim party	15 killed, 50 wounded	Zarqawi's group claims responsibility by a statement posted on an Internet Web site

Date	Event	Casualties	Responsibility
1/1/05	Video released on Islamist Web site shows five Iraqi security officers being shot to death by militants	5 killed	Zarqawi's group claims responsibility via a posted message
1/4/05	Assassination of Governor Ali Al-Haidari	7 killed (6 were his bodyguards)	Zarqawi group claims responsibility in a message posted on a Web site
1/21/05	Attempt to bomb Australian embassy in Baghdad	2 killed	Zarqawi claims responsibility
2/28/05	A suicide car bomber strikes a crowd of police and Iraqi National Guard recruits in Hillah	125	Zarqawi group claims responsibility
4/19/05	Suicide bomber drives his car in the Adhamiyah district	4 killed, 31 wounded	Zarqawi
5/7/05	Two explosives-laden cars hit a U.S. security company envoy in Baghdad	At least 22 people	Zarqawi group claims responsibility
May 2005	There have been at least twenty-two car bombings in Baghdad since the new government took office at the beginning of May. This month alone has seen a series of attacks across Iraq that have claimed the lives of nearly 500 people, marking one of the deadliest periods since the fall of Baghdad in 2003.	Up to 500 throughout the month	Mix of Zarqawi's and other radical Islamist groups

Source: Brinda Adhikari, ABC News. Table does not include all hostage executions.

271

F. Kohlmann found 235 suicide bombers named on Web sites since the summer of 2005 and estimated that more than 50 percent were Saudi.[86]

Whatever the numbers of such recruits may be, Saudi officials and counterterrorist experts are deeply concerned about the fact that some clerics and Islamic organizations recruit young Saudis for Islamist extremist organizations and infiltrate them into Iraq through countries like Syria. Such efforts are scattered and individual, rather than tied to movements like Al Qa'ida in visible ways, and can bypass the Saudi counterterrorist structure, which is focused on internal security. They do, however, end up using young Saudis as tools in suicide bombings, have involved infiltrations across the Saudi border, and present the problem of a whole new generation of young Saudis being trained as Islamic extremists and jihadists outside the country. The problem is also scarcely unique to Saudi Arabia and presents the same problem to other Sunni Islamic countries. Interviews with top U.S. and Iraqi officials and commanders in June 2005 indicated that such jihadists actually came from many countries including other Persian Gulf countries, North Africa, Syria, the Sudan, and Central Asia. Such Iraqis singled out Syria as the major problem. None singled out Saudi Arabia or Iran.

Many lower-level Islamist/extremist volunteers are not trained or skilled fighters. They come from a wide range of countries, often with little or no training, and the overwhelming majority has only a limited history of affiliation with any organized Islamist or extremist group.[87] The actual movements, however, do have a large percentage of Iraqi and foreign fighters who are considerably better organized, well armed, and capable of effective ambushes and attacks. These more experienced jihadists have shown they can fight hard and are sometimes willing to stand and die in ways that force MNF–I and Iraqi troops into intense firefights and clashes.

Zarqawi and "Weapons of Mass Media"

Zarqawi's movement has been extremely effective at striking at targets with high media and political impact, particularly in the form of suicide bombings and beheadings.[88] In the summer of 2005, Zarqawi's group attacked several Muslim diplomats in an effort to stymie relations between the new Iraqi government and foreign governments. Egypt's Ihab Sherif, tapped to become the first Arab ambassador to Iraq, was kidnapped and then killed by the Jordanian terrorist's Al Qa'ida movement. An Internet statement released by the group suggested that he might have been beheaded and stated that he had been killed for Egypt's recognition of the Iraqi government, for the country's fostering of disbelief in Islam, for "waging war against Muslims" by cracking down on Islamist groups like the Muslim Brotherhood, and by sending an ambassador to Iraq at U.S. Secretary of State Condoleezza Rice's bidding.[89]

Soon afterward, Pakistani Ambassador Mohammed Younis Khan and Bahraini Chargé d'Affaires Hassan Malallah Ansari were targeted by Zarqawi's group. In separate attacks, both Khan's and Ansari's convoys were hit with gunfire in what were described as attempted kidnappings. Ansari suffered a minor gunshot wound, and Pakistan quickly relocated Khan to Jordan. Not long after, two of Algeria's diplomats to the new Iraqi government were kidnapped in Baghdad and later killed.

Although some of Zarqawi's deputies have been apprehended, and the Syrians delivered up Saddam Hussein's brother-in-law, much of the group's leadership has survived U.S. and Iraqi assaults. U.S. officials believe the insurgent leadership is so well informed by its intelligence network that it can stay ahead of U.S. and Iraqi forces, fleeing towns before Coalition forces arrive and slipping in and out of the country.[90]

Ironically, jihadist Web sites often list complaints detailing a lack of press coverage for some of their attacks.[91] The militant groups have largely been viewed as very successful manipulators of Arab and Western media outlets, able to tailor their attacks for maximum media coverage and psychological effect. The proliferation of groups could be an indication that there has developed competition for press coverage, media exhaustion, or of a reduced capacity of the insurgents to launch attacks that grab headlines.

Zarqawi's Al Qa'ida in Mesopotamia group started an online Internet magazine entitled Zurwat al Sanam in an effort to wage a more effective propaganda and recruiting campaign. This effort has been mirrored by other insurgent groups on the Web, and some analysts believe that it is a defensive tactic to counter the perceived inroads made by the January 30 elections and the capture of important terrorist lieutenants in the months that followed.[92] A group allied to Zarqawi issued a statement on the Internet in May 2005 claiming that he had been injured during an exchange with Iraqi troops. The group affirmed that he was alive and well, but the information could not be independently verified.

Zarqawi's Al Qa'ida in Iraq group took their attempted manipulation of the news media to new heights in June 2005. In an Internet statement the organization severely criticized the al Jazeera satellite television station for what it called impartial reporting. It claimed that al Jazeera, long criticized by U.S. officials, had "sided" with the United States over Iraq.

Zarqawi Ties to Bin Laden and Outside Sunni Islamist Groups

The Zarqawi group has strengthened its ties to outside terrorist groups. In October 2004, Zarqawi publicly pledged allegiance to Bin Laden and changed the name of his organization from al-Tawhid wal-Jihad (Unity and Holy War) to Al Qa'ida in the Land of the Two Rivers.[93] While there is no evidence that the two men have ever met or even directly communicated, Bin Laden issued a statement in December 2004 confirming Zarqawi as the "Emir" of Al Qa'ida in Iraq.

Movements like the Army of Ansar al-Sunna, which claimed responsibility for the attack on the U.S. mess tent in Mosul in December 2004 and for many other suicide attacks, seem to have a mix of links to Zarqawi and possibly Al Qa'ida. They seem to be largely Iraqi, but their mix of Sunnis and Kurds is uncertain, as is the extent to which the group and its cells are at least partly a legacy of Ansar al-Islam—an active Islamist group that reportedly provided sanctuary for Zarqawi before the war. In November 2004 Ansar al-Sunna claimed that it had twice collaborated with Zarqawi's group and another group known as the Islamic Army in Iraq.

In February 2005 a leaked U.S. intelligence memo indicated that an intercepted communication, reportedly from Bin Laden to Zarqawi, encouraged Iraqi insurgents to attack the American homeland.[94] Even so, U.S. intelligence analysts view bin Laden and Zarqawi as separate operators, and it remains unclear as to what—if any—organizational or financial support Bin Laden provides Zarqawi's organization.[95]

Another "Zarqawi letter," written on April 27, 2005, by one of his associates (Abu Asim al Qusayami al Yemeni), seemed to reflect Zarqawi's complaints about the failure of some of his volunteers to martyr themselves, typical of the kind of complaints and calls for more support that he has used both to try to lever more support from Bin Laden and gain more support from Arabs outside Iraq.[96] Some analysts believe that Bin Laden made a strategic error by declaring Zarqawi the "emir" for operations in Iraq. Iraqis are deeply distrusting of outsiders and in particular neighbors in the region. Bin Laden's declaration could be seen by Iraqis in highly nationalistic terms as a Saudi ordering a Jordanian to kill Iraqis. These analysts believe that this will motivate those Iraqis who were previously unsure of whether to offer their support to the elected government.

Zarqawi appears to have made some efforts to remake his organization's reputation to reduce tensions with Iraqi Sunnis and possibly Iraqi Shi'ites as well. The Web site pronouncements claimed that the group had tried to avoid Muslim casualties with the notable exception being the Iraq military and security forces. They quickly denounced attacks on civilians like the massive suicide car bombing in Hilla in March 2005.[97] Zarqawi has, however, advocated attacks on Shi'ites and said he views them as apostates. It was clear that many bloody suicide bombings and other attacks had support from elements loyal to Zarqawi and that many were sectarian attacks on Shi'ites or ethnic attacks on Kurds. It is now unclear whether any Shi'ite element, including many of Sadr's supporters, are willing to cooperate with such Sunni extremist groups.

A tape attributed to Zarqawi in May 2005 was anything but reticent.[98] In the one hour and fourteen minute tape he explained why Muslim civilians were being killed in his attacks and justified the killing on the basis of research by "Abu Abdullah al Muhajer." He claimed that many operations were canceled because they were going to kill large numbers of Muslims, but mistakes were made and "we have no choice. . . . It's impossible to fight the infidels without killing some Muslims." He stated that Muslims were killed on 9/11 and in

Riyadh, Nairobi, Tanzania, and if these were considered illegitimate, then it would mean stopping jihad in every place.

He said that Iraq's geography made direct combat with the enemy difficult, and the only way to intensify combat was suicide operations. He compared Iraq to Afghanistan with its mountains and to Chechnya where there were woods and said it was easier for the "mujaheddin" to have a safe place to hide and plan after fighting with the enemy. He stated that it was difficult for the "mujaheddin" to move in Iraq because of the checkpoints and the U.S. bases; therefore suicide operations are easy to carry out and to effectively force the enemy to leave the cities for places where it would be easier to shoot them. "These operations are our weapon. . . . If we stop them jihad will be weaker. . . . If the enemy gets full control of Baghdad it will implement its plan and control the whole nation. The whole world saw what they did in Abu Ghraib, Camp Bucca, and prisons in Qut, Najaf and Karbala . . . that's when they did not have full control, so what would happen if they do?"

He heavily attacked Iraq's Shi'ites and Shi'ites in general. He said his group never attacked other sects in Iraq who are not considered Muslims but fought the Shi'ites because they assist the enemy and are traitors. According to Zarqawi, the Shi'ites pretend they care about civilian casualties. He mentioned operations carried out by Failaq Badr (with dates, locations, numbers of people killed) during the 1980s and 1990s. He also claimed there was a plan to eliminate the Sunnis in Iraq and that Sunni mosques were being handed over to Shi'ites and that Sunni clerics, teachers, doctors, and experts were being killed. He claimed that Sunni women were being kidnapped and that Shi'ite police participated in raping women at Abu Ghraib.

He claimed there were problems at Iraqi government–run prisons in Iraq, including one in Qut, which he said was being run by Iranian intelligence, and a prison in Hilla run by a Shi'ite major general called Qays, who "cuts Muslims' bodies and rapes women." He mentioned a specific story where Qays threatened to rape the wife of one of the fighters (evidently Major General Qays Hamza, chief of Al Hillah police). He says his fighters tried to kill Qays but he survived. (There was a Web statement dated March 30 about a suicide bombing in Hilla that targeted Major General Qays).[99]

Another tape–attributed to Zarqawi–aired on July 6, 2005. In the tape Zarqawi reaffirms that targeting Iraqis is legitimate, and he dubs the Iraqi security forces apostates. He calls on Iraqi clerics who disapprove of targeting Iraqis to reconsider their views. The Jordanian asserts in the message that the United States went to war with Iraq in order to advance Israel's interests and refers to the conflict in Iraq as a "quagmire." He declares that the United States will soon invade the lands of Sham (Greater Syria) on the pretext of stopping insurgent infiltration and that this had not yet happened due to the ferocity of the militant attacks. He also announced the creation of a new brigade charged with killing the members of the Failaq Brigade, a Shi'ite militia. Zarqawi also asserts that many Iraqi females have come to him asking to be dispatched on suicide missions. He uses this to try and shame Iraqi males into seeking suicide missions and to try and convince their wives and girlfriends into shaming them into such missions.[100] According to some U.S. experts Zarqawi circulated a tape openly calling for civil war against Shi'ites in September 2005.

Zarqawi has long been identified with the militant Islamist preacher Isam Mohammed al-Barqawi or Abu Mohammed al-Maqdisi, with whom Zarqawi shared a cell block in a Jordanian prison in the mid-1990s. Zarqawi has referred to al-Barqawi as his "sheik," and the preacher is considered the spiritual guide of the terrorist, as well as many other militants.[101] A statement posted on an Islamist Web site in summer 2005, allegedly written by Zarqawi, revealed a strained relationship between the two extremists.

Al-Barqawi was interviewed on al Jazeera satellite television saying that the suicide bombings in Iraq had killed too many Iraqis and that the militants should not target Shi'ite Muslims. Zarqawi's statement addressed the interview, questioning al-Barqawi's statements and imploring the preacher to not "turn against the Mujahideen."[102] If authentic, the posting seems likely to confirm what Zarqawi's letter to Bin Laden suggested: that the font of support Zarqawi expected to come forth in Iraq and the Middle East has yet to materialize on the scale he envisioned.

Zarqawi and Syria

Experts differ in opinion as to how much of Zarqawi's operations have taken place in Syria and with Syrian tolerance. There are reports that Zarqawi and top lieutenants met in Syria in the spring of 2005, but these have not been confirmed by U.S. officials. In fact, U.S. intelligence assessments expressed doubt in June 2005 that Zarqawi had crossed into Syria earlier in the year, stating that such an event was inconsistent with Syrian, and Zarqawi's, pattern of behavior. U.S., British, and Iraqi experts do believe, however, that a substantial number of recruits pass through Syria with Syrian tolerance or deliberate indifference—if not active support.[103]

Sunni Iraqi Nationalist versus Sunni Islamic Extremist, or De Facto Cooperation?

In August 2005, U.S. Major General Douglas Lute predicted that Zarqawi would move his base of operations to the Horn of Africa as Coalition pressure in Iraq continued to hamper his ability to operate effectively in the region. Zarqawi's organization sustained significant losses during its activity in Iraq, and Lute cited Yemen, Somalia, Sudan, and Ethiopia as possible safe havens for terrorists in the near future. Somalia has already been infiltrated by Islamist elements, and a 900-strong U.S. force in Djibouti is trying to preclude further infiltration of the Horn of Africa at its tip. U.S. troops are also training Ethiopian and Eritrean forces, but vast ungoverned areas in the region are thought to provide an attractive re-basing solution should the Arab Peninsula become too problematic for certain terrorist organizations.[104]

Opinions differ sharply as to whether the different Sunni elements that make up the insurgency are dividing or coalescing. Many analysts suggest that Ba'athists and their former adversaries, such as the Salafists and the Kurds, are finding a common cause with foreign fighters.[105] Yet, there are also reports of fighting between the more secular native Sunni insurgents and Sunni Islamic extremists and some executions of such extremists by the more secular groups. The level of communication and cooperation between the various movements remains unclear.

The inability to characterize many Islamist movements—and the fact that successful suicide bombings and other attacks can have a major political and media impact even if they serve little clear military purpose—illustrates the fact that outside threats must be measured in terms of effectiveness and not numbers. In practice, the insurgents can choose the place and time of the attack, focus on targets with key political and media impact, and have an effect even if they fail to achieve the purpose of their attack but create visible explosions or kill innocent civilians.

In contrast, the insurgents often have excellent intelligence from sources within the Iraqi government, Iraqi forces, the Iraqis supporting Coalition forces and government activities, and Iraqi industry. This enables them to locate soft targets, hit at key points in terms of Iraq's economy and aid projects, and time their attacks to points of exceptional vulnerability. In practice, it also allows them to pick weak and vulnerable elements of the Iraqi military, security, and police forces and often produce significant casualties. At the same time, in many areas they can use intimidation, threats, kidnappings, and selective murders and assassinations to paralyze or undercut Iraqi units. This means a comparatively small number of core insurgents can bypass or attack the developing Iraqi forces with considerable success.

Like the Iraqi Sunni Arab insurgents, outside groups have improved their ability to take advantage of the fact that media coverage of the fighting, particularly by Arab satellite television, provides a real-time picture of what tactics and weapons work, what strikes have most media and political impact, and often what targets are vulnerable. This "Al Jazeera Effect" substitutes for many elements of a C^4I system. At the same time, confronting this confusing array of threats is made more difficult without general Iraqi loyalty and stand-alone Iraqi forces. These groups pose a special threat because they have no clear boundaries that limit them to Iraq and so few restraints and limits on the kinds of violence they use. In their eyes, Iraq is a theater of operation for far broader causes. Their core beliefs are based on a vision of Sunni Islam that rejects Shi'ites and even rejects Sunnis who dissent from the extremists.

So far, such groups have generally been careful to avoid any open claims to a split with Iraqis Shi'ites, and some cooperated with Sadr and his militia. They have, however, carried out mass attacks and bombings on Shi'ites, and they have repeatedly shown that they place few—if any—limits on the means of violence against those they regard as enemies of Islam. If anything, they ultimately gain the most if the Sunni and Shi'ite worlds divide, if Iraq becomes the continuing scene of violence between the United States and Arabs, if United States forces remain tied down, and if their actions create as much regional instability as possible. This helps explain why Sunni insurgent movements, and particularly Islamist extremists, made Iraq's political process a primary target before and after the January 30, 2005, elections. Insurgents feared that a relatively secure and successful election would cement Shi'ite dominance in Iraq and would signal the demise of both the Islamist and Ba'athist visions for the future of Iraq.

On December 29, 2004, Ansar al-Sunna declared, "All polling stations and those in them will be targets for our brave soldiers."[106] Similarly, the Islamic Army in Iraq warned in mid-January 2005, "Do not allow polling stations in your neighborhood because they put your lives in danger. Do not also interfere with the employees who work in these voting centers, as they will be killed. Keep away from these places as they will be attacked." On January 23, 2005, Zarqawi released an audiotape saying, "We have declared an all-out war on this evil principle of democracy and those who follow this wrong ideology."[107]

Another disturbing aspect of this extremism is that it increasingly accuses the United States of "dehumanizing" Muslims, Arabs, and Iraqis by its invasion of Afghanistan and Iraq and actions in the war on terrorism. It cites episodes like the very real American abuses of Iraqi prisoners at Abu Ghraib, and U.S. strategic writing on the use of precision weapons and the use of specialized nuclear weapons like "bunker busters." The corollary of this argument is that Islamic extremists are justified in turn in "dehumanizing" Americans and all of their allies and in using tactics such as high-casualty attacks like suicide bombings and the use of chemical and biological weapons. This again ignores all of the core teachings of Islam to justify virtually any act of violence, no matter how extreme.[108]

The Uncertain Status of the Shi'ites

Public opinion polls show that Arab Shi'ites, like Arab Sunnis, favor a unified Iraq and a strong central government. Such polls also show that Iraqi Shi'ites tend to be highly religious—more so in terms of their support for recognition that Iraq should be an "Islamic state" than Sunnis—but do not favor a theocratic state or anything approaching the present state in Iran. With the possible exception of Sadr, leading Iraqi clerics do not support anything approaching Iran's concept of a supreme leader, and key figures like the Grand Ayatollah Sistani strongly oppose direct clerical participation in the government or politics.

Key Shi'ite political parties like Al Dawa and SCIRI have a strong religious character but are largely secular in their goals and actions. Although Al Dawa and SCIRI operated in Iran from 1980 onward, they remain Iraqi nationalists, and their "gratitude" to Iran is often limited—particularly because of Iran's history of treating them on an opportunistic basis. Members of Al Dawa can privately be sharply critical of Iran, and members of both parties resent past pressure to recognize the authority of Iran's supreme leader.

The risk of a major civil war in Iraq seems limited, but it cannot be dismissed. Iraqi Arab Shi'ites resent the U.S. presence, but most seem to realize that the fact that they make up 60 percent of the population will give them political dominance if Iraq is secure enough that its new political system divides up power according to the size of given factions. Not all recognize the need to forgive their past treatment, to include Sunnis in the government and military, or to resist the continuing provocation of Sunni extremist attacks.

The Role of Moqtada al-Sadr

Moqtada al-Sadr now seems to be committed to participating in Iraq's political process and to opposing any split between Arab Sunni and Arab Shi'ite. His Mehdi (Mahdi) Army did, however, present a serious threat to Coalition and government forces in Najaf, in Sadr City in Baghdad, and in other Shi'ite areas in the South during much of the summer and early fall of 2004. U.S. officials indicated that U.S. forces faced up to 160 attacks per week in Sadr City between August and September 2004 of varying severity.

The various battles and political compromises that led Sadr to turn away from armed struggle in the late fall and early winter of 2004 seem to have changed this situation significantly. U.S. officials indicated that the number of attacks had dropped significantly to between zero and five a week in early 2005, and they remained at this level through May 2005. More important, Sadr joined the Shi'ite coalition in the election campaign and his supporters play a role in the new National Assembly and government.

General John Abizaid remarked in March 2005, however, "we have not seen the end of Muqtada Sadr's challenge."[109] Although Iraqi government forces have been able to move into the area, Sadr's movement still plays a major political role in Sadr City in Baghdad and remains active in poorer Shi'ite areas throughout the country.

Sadr's supporters sponsored demonstrations calling for U.S. forces to leave Iraq in April 2005, and top Sadr aides in his Independent National Bloc issued warnings to Ibrahim Jafari, then the prime minister designate, that he must pay more attention to these demands or that the Sadr faction might leave the United Iraqi Alliance and become an active part of the opposition. The group also demanded the release of some 200 Sadr actives arrested during earlier fighting and that all criminal charges against Sadr be dropped.[110]

Sadr was able to exploit the political weakness and divisions of other Shi'ite movements in the South and their lack of ability to govern, as well as the fact that other hard-line Islamist movements won significant numbers of seats in local governments in key areas like Basra.[111] In summer 2005 Sadr attempted to collect 1 million signatures on a petition that asked the Coalition to leave Iraq in what appeared to be his burgeoning attempts to recast himself as a major political force within Iraq. Sadr's Council for Vice and Virtue launched at least one attack on secular students in Basra for having a mixed picnic.[112]

Sadr revived the Mehdi (Mahdi) Army, which was again beginning to be openly active in parts of southern Iraq such as Basra, Amarah, and Nasiriyah, and still had cells in Najaf and Kut as well. While some U.S. official sources stated the army was relatively weak, it began to hold parades again, and while only limited numbers of arms were displayed, it was clear that such weapons were still available in the places where they had been hidden during the fighting the previous year.[113] By the late spring of 2005, the Mehdi (Mahdi) Army seemed to be the largest independent force in Basra, played a major role in policing Amarah, and had effectively struck a bargain with the government police in Nasiriyah that allowed it to play a major role. Unlike most militias, it also had the active participation of Shi'ite clergy, mostly "activists" who strongly supported Sadr. One reason for the rebirth was the lack of effective action by the government. For example, the government police in Nasiriyah had 5,500 men but was 2,500 men short of its goal.[114]

The Role of Other Shi'ite Factions

The Supreme Council for the Islamic Revolution in Iraq (SCIRI) and the faction of Abdul Aziz al-Hakim also still have large militia elements and ones Sunni groups have sometimes accused of committing atrocities against them. Al Dawa, the Badr Corps, and the Iraqi Hezbollah remain potential security problems, and Sunnis feel particularly threatened by the Badr Corps. Broader tensions exist between Sunni and Shi'ite. Both Iraq's Sunni interim president, Ghazi al-Yawar, and King Abdullah of Jordan sounded warnings about the risks of Shi'ite dominance in the January 30, 2005, elections and possible Iranian influence.[115] These warnings may well be exaggerated. Iraqi Shi'ites are Iraqi nationalists, not tools of Iran, and neither Iraqi Shi'ite clerics—aside from the Sadr faction—nor most of the Shi'ite population support a clerical role in politics. Yet, no one can predict how stable Iraq's political structure will be in spite of the January 30, 2005, election.

Shi'ite and Kurdish militias pose a risk of a different kind. Sunnis accuse them of killings, intimidation, and a host of other crimes, while Shi'ites and Kurds see them as a potential source of aid in fighting the insurgency. This issue acquired new urgency in early June 2005 when Prime Minster Jafari held a press conference in which he lauded the Kurdish Pesh Merga and the Badr Organization, formerly the Badr Brigade. The Iraqi President and Kurd, Jalal Talibani, joined the prime minister as well as the founder of the Badr Organization and SCIRI head, Abdul Aziz al-Hakim, at Hakim's headquarters to celebrate the anniversary of the founding of the Badr group.[116]

The president applauded what he, and presumably Jafari, viewed as the militias' positive contributions to Iraq. Talibani stated, "[The Badr Organization] and the Pesh Merga are wanted and are important to fulfilling this sacred task, to establishing a democratic, federal and independent Iraq."[117] Addressing a variety of allegations against the two militias, Talibani remarked, "It [Badr

Organization] is a patriotic group that works for Iraq's interest and it will not be dragged into sectarian or any other kind of struggle."[118] Jafari went on to dub the Badr Organization a "shield" protecting Iraq.

The difficulty is that such militias were supposed to be abolished under the guidelines set out in the Interim Government. Iraqi officials state that they are nominally under the control of the Ministry of Defense and the Ministry of Interior, although the Kurds have long vowed to maintain the independence of the Pesh Merga as a means to defend their autonomous area.

Further, questions remain about the Badr Organization, which has been vehemently condemned by many Sunnis. The Badr Organization and its precursor, the Badr Brigade, was created by SCIRI and trained by the Iranian military. What influence the Iranians may have over the Badr is unclear. Once more, Sunnis assert that the Badr are the ones responsible for the targeting and assassination of a number of senior Sunni clerics, many from the Muslim Scholars' Board. Although this cannot be definitively refuted, the Coalition has yet to find evidence of such activity on part of the Badr Organization. Making matters worse, the Sunnis opposed the appointment of Bayan Jabr as Minister of Interior, claiming that as a member of SCIRI, he was a pawn of the Iranians and that the ministry's "wolf brigade," led by Abdul Waleed, was responsible for some of the assassinations of Sunni figures.[119] Yet again, the Coalition has failed to find any evidence to support such claims.

While it is far from clear whether the Badr Corps or even Shi'ites are to blame, some Sunnis also feel that the Badr Corps has been responsible for targeting Sunni leaders and figures, killing them and dumping their bodies. Baghdad's central morgue began to detect such killings shortly after the new government was formed on April 28, 2005, and claimed that at least thirty cases had been found by late June. The killers were said to have seized some victims wearing police uniforms—which can be bought cheaply in much of Iraq—but also to have had Toyotas and Glock pistols, which are more difficult to obtain. There have also been mass abductions and killings of ordinary Sunnis, like fourteen Sunni farmers who were taken from a Baghdad vegetable market on May 5, 2005. It is possible that insurgents have done this to try to foment sectarian tension, but revenge killings and intimidation are at least possible.[120]

Although it would certainly hamstring the new Iraqi government to alienate these militias, maintaining their full structure and chain of command within the Iraqi security forces increases the chances that those units will continue to maintain ultimate allegiance to the leadership of the Badr or the Kurds. Thus, the security forces could be divided by factions, decreasing their effectiveness and leading to the disintegration of Iraqi forces if Iraq were to descend into full-scale civil war.

Insurgent Pressure to Move toward Civil War

While the election turnout initially dealt an apparent blow to the Sunni insurrection, much of the post-election insurgent activity has been directly

targeted at Shi'ite clergy and political leaders, Shi'ite civilians, and Shi'ite institutions. Attacks have also been targeted for key Shi'ite holidays like the
February 19, Ashura holiday. While most Shi'ite leaders strongly resisted any
calls for reprisals against Sunnis, other Shi'ites called for such action, and there
do seem to have been Shi'ite killings of Sunni clergy and civilians.[121]

On August 31, nearly 1,000 Shi'ite pilgrims were killed in a stampede in
Baghdad. The pilgrims were crossing the al-Aima bridge en route to the shrine
of Moussa al-Kadhim when rumors began to spread that there were Sunni
suicide bombers in their midst. The resulting panic ended in 953 Shi'ites dead,
according to the Iraqi Interior Ministry. Moqtada al-Sadr vowed vengeance
against Sunnis, who he believed organized the pandemonium. Later in a sermon,
Sadr spoke out against the Coalition's presence in Iraq, as it hampered a sectarian war, which he asserted had already begun.[122] This sermon placed in question
the Mehdi Army's uneasy truce with Coalition troops. Prior to the stampede,
Moqtada al-Sadr had publicly opposed Shi'ite participation in sectarian warfare.

On September 14, Iraq's Al Qa'ida leader and Sunni insurgent Abu Musab
al-Zarqawi declared a war on Shi'ite Muslims in Iraq. The declaration was made
through an audio file on the Internet. According to the recording, the declaration
came in response to the recent joint U.S.-Iraqi offensive on the town of Tal Afar,
a Sunni insurgent stronghold. Zarqawi referred to the assault as an "organized
sectarian war." Earlier that day, the Sunni-Muslim Al Qa'ida said in an Internet
posting that it was waging a nationwide suicide bombing campaign to avenge
the military offensive against Sunni rebels in Tal Afar. Pursuant to this proclamation, Baghdad erupted in violence:

- *September 14, 2005.* At least 167 people die and more than 570 are injured
  as more than a dozen bombs explode throughout Baghdad. This day marks
  the single worst day of killing to hit the capital since the U.S.-led invasion
  of March 2003.
    - A suicide bomber in a car blew himself up in Baghdad, killing eleven
      people who lined up to refill gas canisters, police said. The blast
      in northern Baghdad, which also wounded fourteen, came hours
      after what appeared to be a series of coordinated blasts, including
      one that killed at least 114 people.
    - Gunmen wearing military uniforms surrounded the village of Taaji
      north of Baghdad and executed seventeen men, police said. The
      dead were members of the Tameem tribe, al-Hayali said. The
      gunmen looted the village before leaving.
    - Vehicle-borne improvised explosive device (VBIED) exploded in the
      Uruba Square in the Zahra district of northwest Baghdad. The terror-
      ist attack killed at least seventy-five Iraqi civilians and wounded more
      than 130. The wounded were evacuated to the Al-Shulla Hospital in
      central Baghdad where another suicide VBIED detonated, causing
      more civilian casualties.

- ○ Suicide car bomb attack in Kadimiya in the market area. At least 80 killed, 150+ injured. North of center of Baghdad.
- ○ Task Force Baghdad Unit reported striking a VBIED in west Baghdad. The soldiers established a cordon and began searching the area for triggermen. Several Iraqi civilians were wounded in the attack. There were no U.S. casualties.
- ○ VBIED detonated on a U.S. convoy in east Baghdad. The suicide bomber was reportedly driving against traffic before detonating on the convoy. Two U.S. soldiers received non-life-threatening wounds in the attack. Ten minutes later, a suicide VBIED detonated near a U.S. convoy in southeast Baghdad with no injuries to U.S. personnel or damage to equipment.
- ○ VBIED attack against U.S. forces in central Baghdad failed when the terrorist struck an M1 Abrams tank but did not detonate his explosives. The tank crew reported the driver was still alive and trapped inside the vehicle with a 155-millimeter round. The Task Force Baghdad Unit secured the site and called for assistance from an explosive ordnance disposal team.

- • *September 15, 2005.* Suicide bombers continued to strike Baghdad, killing at least thirty-one people, twenty-three of them Iraqi police and Interior Ministry commandos.
  - ○ A suicide bomber killed fifteen police commandos in the Dora district of Baghdad, police said. Five civilians were also killed. The blast wounded twenty-one people. Hours later, two more bombs detonated in the same area. Ten more policemen died in the explosion and ensuing gun battle with insurgents.
  - ○ Two police officers were killed and two wounded in Kirkuk.
  - ○ Three civilians were killed in an attack on a Ministry of Defense bus in the east of Baghdad.
  - ○ Three bodies of people who had been shot dead were found in the Shula district of Baghdad, police said.
  - ○ Three bodies were found in the New Baghdad district. Police said they had been shot dead.
  - ○ Three Shi'ite pilgrims heading to the southern city of Kerbala for a religious event were killed by gunmen in northern Baghdad.
  - ○ Three workers were killed and a dozen wounded in east Baghdad in a drive-by shooting by unidentified gunmen. The attack occurred in an area where laborers gather each day for work.

Some top leaders also called for bringing key militias like the Shi'ite Badr Corps and Kurdish Pesh Merga actively into the struggle. Some U.S. officials, however, were optimistic in the summer of 2005. Brigadier General John Custer stated, "The incredible violence that the Shi'a community has endured over last year leads me to believe that they are smart enough and understanding of the big picture enough to back away from civil war at all costs. The specter of the dark cloud of civil war has moved away. It is much less evident than it was last year."[123]

Shi'ite splits are possible, as are sectarian and ethnic splits. Moreover, few Shi'ites can forget that Sadr is believed to have been responsible for the assassination of Al Khoi right after the fall of Saddam Hussein and for the killing of Mohammed Bakr al-Hakim, Abdul Aziz al-Hakim's brother, in August 2003.

Basra had effectively been taken over by a local government after the January 30, 2005, election that was much more of a Shi'ite fundamentalist government than the mainstream of Al Dawa or SCIRI. The local police were intimidated or pushed aside by such elements in May, and Shi'ite militia joined the police and took over. While some of those accused of being involved—such as police chief Lieutenant Colonel Salam Badran—were affiliated with SCIRI in the past, most such "Islamists" seem more fundamentalist than SCIRI's leadership. There have been reports of threats, beatings, and killings affecting liquor stores, male doctors who treat women, and even barbers cutting hair in "non-Islamic" ways. Individuals in plain clothes have also made threats and put pressure on local businesses. Even if such cases do not divide Iraq's Arab Shi'ites—and serious issues do exist about how "Islamic" the future government should be in Shi'ite terms and who should rule—they may well cause even greater fear among Sunnis and increase the risk of civil conflict.[124]

Divisions among Shi'ite groups could put new burdens on Iraq's forces and/or potentially paralyze or divide key elements of the government. It is not clear whether Sadr and other Shi'ite elements will hold together or whether other splits will not occur during 2005. Iraq must deal with forging and approving a constitution and with moving toward general elections at the end of the year without any clear picture of what political leaders, political parties, and power-sharing arrangements will emerge in the process. The risk also exists that the Kurds and Shi'ites might split in ways that could lead to civil conflict or that Shi'ite politics may begin to react far more violently to Sunni insurgent bombings and attacks, striking back at the Sunnis rather than seeking to include them.

Shi'ite political leaders have generally been careful to avoid this so far, but the preaching in mosques has become more polarized, and popular tension is growing. Attacks like the bombings in Karbala and Najaf on December 20, 2004, have been followed up by many similar anti-Shi'ite attacks since the elections. At least some Sunni Arab and Islamist extremist insurgents are certain to continue to try to provoke a sectarian Sunni versus Shi'ite rift using any means possible, no matter how bloody and violent.

The Kurds and Other Minorities

The Kurds represent a faction that is now considerably more powerful relative to other Iraqi factions in military and security terms than their 15 percent of the population. Iraqi security and stability depends on finding a power-sharing arrangement that gives the Kurds incentives to be part of the political process just as much as it does on developing such arrangements for the Arab Sunnis. There is no basic political or economic reason such a compromise cannot be found. Unfortunately, however, Iraq has a long history of not finding such compromises on a lasting basis, and Saddam Hussein's legacy left many areas where Kurds were forcibly expelled and Sunni Arabs and minorities were given their homes and property.

The two major Kurdish parties, the Kurdish Democratic Party (KDP), headed by Masoud Barzani, and the Patriotic Union of Kurdistan, headed by Jalal Talibani, retain powerful militias, known collectively as the Pesh Merga. Their current strength is difficult to estimate, and some elements are either operating in Iraqi forces or have been trained by U.S. advisers. The Iraqi Kurds could probably assemble a force in excess of 10,000 fighters—albeit of very different levels of training and equipment.

There are serious tensions between the Kurds, the Turcomans, and Assyrian Christians, as well as between Kurds and Arabs. At a local level there are many small tribal elements as well as numerous "bodyguards" and long histories of tensions and feuds. Even if Iraq never divides along national fracture lines, some form of regional or local violence is all too possible. Tension between the Kurds and Iraqi Arabs and other minorities has been particularly critical in areas like Kirkuk and Mosul.

The Kurds claim territory claimed by other Iraqi ethnic groups and demand the return of property they assert was seized by Saddam Hussein during his various efforts at ethnic cleansing from 1975 to 2003. The future of Kirkuk and the northern oil fields around it is the subject of considerable local and national political controversy between the Kurds and other Iraqis. The Kurds claim that over 220,000 Kurds were driven out of their homes by Saddam Hussein in the 1970s and fighting in the Gulf War and that over 120,000 Arabs were imported into "Kurdish territory." The Kurds see control of Kirkuk as their one chance to have territorial control over a major portion of Iraq's oil reserves, but Kirkuk is now roughly 35 percent Kurd, 35 percent Arab, 26 percent Turcoman, and 4 percent from other groups. This makes any such solution almost impossible unless it is violent.

There has also been some armed violence between Kurds, Arabs, and Turcomans, as well as struggles over "soft" ethnic cleansing in the North, and there may well be more violence in the future. Many experts feel that the only reason Kirkuk has been relatively peaceful and still has something approaching a representative government is that the Kurds have not been strong enough relative to the other factions in the city to impose their will by intimidation or force.

According to U.S. government documents and interviews with Turcoman families, Kurdish security forces abducted hundred of Turcomans from Kirkuk in the spring and summer months of 2005 and put them in prisons deep within acknowledged Kurdish territory.[125] This was an apparent bid to create an overwhelming Kurdish majority in order to lend greater legitimacy to the Kurds claim on Kirkuk.

The Kurds also face the problem that at present they have no control over Iraq's oil resources or revenues and no access to any port or lines of communication that are not subject to Iraqi, Turkish, or Iranian interdiction. They also have a very uncertain economic future since they have lost the guaranteed stream of revenue provided by the UN Oil-for-Food program; Iraq can now export oil through the Gulf and reopen pipelines to Syria as a substitute for pipelines through Turkey; and there is far less incentive to smuggle through Kurdish areas now that trade is open on Iraq's borders. The Kurds also face the problem that Iran, Syria, and Turkey all have Kurdish minorities that have sought independence in the past, and any form of Iraqi Kurdish autonomy or independence is seen as a threat.

Kurdish unity is always problematic. The Kurds have a saying that "the Kurds have no friends." History shows that this saying should be "the Kurds have no friends, including the Kurds." The Barzani and Talibani factions have fought on several occasions, and there was a state of civil war between them during 1993–1995. Patriotic Union of Kurdistan (PUK) forces were able to take control of Irbil in 1994 and put an end to the first attempt to create a unified and elected government that began in 1992. Barzani's Kurdish Democratic Party (KDP) collaborated with Saddam Hussein in 1995 when Hussein sent a full corps of troops into Irbil and other parts of the area occupied by Talibani. Tens of thousands of Kurds and anti-Saddam activists fled the area, and the United States did not succeed in brokering a settlement between the two factions until 1998.[126] The present marriage of convenience between the KDP and PUK has not unified the Kurdish-controlled provinces in the North. There were minor clashes between their supporters in 1995, and these political divisions could create future problems for both Kurdish political unity and any agreement on some form of autonomy.

Other Kurdish actions have exacerbated ethnic tension in a struggle for the control of Kirkuk. There are reports that the KDP and PUK systematically kidnapped hundreds of Arabs and Turcomans from the city and transported them to prisons in established Kurdish territory.[127] This activity allegedly spread to Mosul as well. While some of the abductions had occurred in 2004, reports indicated that there was a renewed effort following the January 30 elections that solidified the two parties' primacy in the Kurdish areas. According to a leaked State Department cable in mid-June 2005, the abducted were taken to KDP and PUK intelligence–run prisons in Irbil and Sulaymaniyah without the knowledge of the Iraqi Ministry of Defense or the Ministry of Interior–but sometimes with U.S. knowledge. In fact, the emergency services unit, a special Kirkuk force within the police, was both closely tied to the U.S. military and implicated in many of the abductions, along with the Asayesh Kurdish intelligence service.[128] It should be noted that the head of the emergency services unit is a former PUK fighter.

Kirkuk province's Kurdish governor, Abdul Rahman Mustafa, stated that the allegations were false. However, the State Department cable indicated that the U.S. 116th Brigade Combat Team had known about the activity and had asked the Kurdish parties to stop.[129] According to Kirkuk's chief of police, General Turhan Yusuf Abdel-Rahman, 40 percent of his 6,120 officers probably assisted in the abductions despite his orders, and they followed the directives of the KDP and PUK instead. Abdel-Rahman stated, "The main problem is that the loyalty to the police is to the parties and not the police force. They'll obey the parties' orders and disobey us."[130] According to Abdel-Rahman, the provincial police director, Sherko Shakir Hakim, refused to retire as ordered by the government in Baghdad once he was assured that the KDP and PUK would continue to pay him if he stayed on. The various factions in Kirkuk do seem to have agreed on a compromise local government in June 2005, but the city continues to present a serious risk of future conflict.

All these problems are compounded by the rebirth of Kurdish insurgency in Turkey and acute Turkish pressure on the Iraqi government, Iraqi Kurds, and MNSTC–I both to deny Turkish Kurdish insurgents a sanctuary and to set any example that would encourage Kurdish separatism in Turkey. The Turkish Kurdish Worker Party (PKK) is a movement that has often used northern Iraq as a sanctuary and which led to several major division-sized Turkish military movements into the area under Saddam Hussein. While estimates are uncertain, some 6,000 PKK forces seemed to be in Iraq in the spring of 2005 with another 2,000 across the border.[131] These same factors help explain why Turkey has actively supported Iraq's small Turcoman minority in its power struggles with Iraq's Kurds.

Insurgent activity in the Kurdish areas was particularly intense in the city of Irbil, which has been the site of several suicide bombings. In summer 2005, Kurdish security officials and the KDP intelligence service announced the arrest of approximately six insurgent suspects who, the authorities believe, came from six separate and previously unheard of militant organizations. The head of the Irbil security police, Abdulla Ali, stated that there was evidence that the groups had links to international terror groups, established jihadi groups in Iraq like Ansar al-Sunna, and even links to intelligence services from nearby countries.[132] This evidence was not made public, but the Kurdish authorities stated that it appeared as though various groups were working together and that, to the anger and disappointment of the Kurdish authorities, local Kurds were assisting them.

The Role of Crime and Criminals

The vast majority of Iraqi criminals have limited or no ties to the insurgents, although some are clearly "for hire" in terms of what they target or in being willing to take pay for sabotage or acts of violence that help create a climate of violence in given areas. Many U.S. and Iraqi intelligence officers believe that some criminal networks are heavily under the influence of various former regime elements or are dominated by them and that some elements of organized crime do help the insurgency. The U.S. Defense Intelligence Agency stated in

July 2005 that some aspect of insurgent financing was derived from kidnapping for ransom, drug trafficking, robbery, theft, extortion, smuggling, and the counterfeiting of goods and currency.[133] Furthermore, at least some Shi'ite criminal groups use the insurgency or Sunnis as a cover for their activities.

Like most aspects of the insurgency, it is difficult to know the strength of criminal elements and the extent to which they are or are not tied to insurgent groups. The collapse of Saddam's regime, massive unemployment, the disbanding of a wide range of military and security elements, the destruction of Iraq's military industries, de-Ba'athification, and sheer opportunism have all combined to make organized and violent crime an endemic part of Iraqi society, even in many areas where the insurgents have little real strength. They also are a powerful force behind local vigilante and militia efforts that at least indirectly challenge the legitimacy of the central government.

Crime also has the impact of sabotage even when there is no deliberate intent to support the insurgency. It adds to the image of ineffective governance by acts like wire and equipment thefts that limit the government's ability to distribute electric power. It deprives the government of oil revenues through oil thefts and adds to Iraq's fuel problems by the endemic theft of gasoline. While most kidnappings are almost certainly decoupled from any political motive, some may have been done for hire at the bidding of various insurgent groups. At best, the end result is a climate of cumulative violence with some elements of Sunni versus Shi'ite tension. At worst, crime vastly compounds the government's and Coalition's security problems, offers insurgent groups yet another kind of informal network, helps block investment and development, compounds the problem of hiring security forces, and undermines legitimacy.

The fact that the Ministry of Interior stopped reporting meaningful crime statistics in mid-2004 makes trend analysis almost impossible. The same is true of the casualties involved. The Ministry of Health reported in the spring of 2005 that some 5,158 Iraqis had died from all forms of criminal and insurgent activities during the last six months of 2004, but most experts felt such reporting might only include about half the real total. The Baghdad Central Morgue counted 8,035 deaths from unnatural causes in Baghdad alone in 2004, a major increase from 6,012 in 2003 and a figure that compared with 1,800 in 2002—the last year of Saddam Hussein's rule. The morgue reported that 60 percent of those killed were killed by gunshot wounds and were unrelated to the insurgency and were largely a combination of crime, tribal vendettas, vengeance killings, and mercenary kidnappings.[134]

Other Forms of Financing the Insurgency

Analysts believe that elements of Saddam Hussein's regime sought refuge in the United Arab Emirates, Jordan, Iran, Saudi Arabia, and Syria at various points before, during, and after major combat operations in Iraq. Those elements were then able to establish a financial base from which to send funds to the insurgents on the ground.

A senior intelligence officer in the U.S. Defense Intelligence Agency (DIA), Caleb Temple, testified before the House Armed Services Subcommittee on Terrorism, Unconventional Threats, and Capabilities and the House Financial Services Subcommittee on Oversight and Investigations. Temple stated that the insurgents' financiers had the connections and enough money to fund their activities, perhaps even increase the violence, for some time. He stated:

> We believe terrorist and insurgent expenses are moderate and pose little significant restraints to armed groups in Iraq. In particular, arms and munitions costs are minimal—leaving us to judge that the bulk of the money likely goes toward international and local travel, food, and lodging of fighters and families of dead fighters; bribery and payoffs of government officials, families, and clans; and possibly into the personal coffers of critical middlemen and prominent terrorist leaders.[135]

Temple and Acting Assistant Treasury Secretary Daniel Glaser asserted that various criminal activities as well as certain Islamic charities also contributed to the flow of funds to insurgents in Iraq. Vital to strangling the insurgency, Temple stated, was the ability to staunch the flow of money. He asserted, "Drying up money and stopping its movement degrades terrorist and insurgent operations. It hinders recruitment and impedes couriers, disrupts procurement of bomb components, and creates uncertainty in the minds of suicide bombers regarding whether their families will receive promised compensation."[136]

In July 28, 2005, testimony before the House Armed Services Committee, Glaser listed some of the most common methods of funding the insurgency:[137]

- Funds provided by charities, Iraqi expatriates, and other deep-pocket donors, primarily in the Gulf, but also in Syria, Lebanon, Jordan, Iran, and Europe.
- Criminal activities, such as kidnapping for ransom, possible narcotics trafficking, robbery, theft, extortion, smuggling, and counterfeiting (goods and currency).

Glaser also reviewed some of the efforts underway to help stanch these cash flows:

- Since March 2003, the U.S. government has focused on the need to locate, freeze, and repatriate Iraqi assets from around the world, as well as to find cash and other assets within Iraq that were stolen and hidden by former regime elements.
- In May 2003, the UN Security Council adopted UNSCR 1483, which calls on UN member states to identify, freeze, and transfer to the Development Fund for Iraq (DFI) assets of senior officials of the former Iraqi regime and their immediate family members, including entities owned or controlled by them or by persons acting on their behalf. The president subsequently issued Executive Order (E.O.) 13315, which authorizes the secretary of the treasury to freeze the assets of former regime elements. To date, under

E.O. 13315, the Department of the Treasury has designated scores of Iraq-related entities and individuals (including fifty-five senior Iraqi officials who were named by the president in issuing E.O. 13315 and forty-seven administrative or "derivative" designations). The U.S. government, in turn, submits these names to the United Nations for listing by the UN 1518 Committee under UNSCR 1483.

- Only a week ago, the Department of the Treasury designated six of Saddam Hussein's nephews (sons of Saddam's half brother and former presidential advisor Sabawi Ibrahim Hasan Al-Tikriti), and we understand that their names have now been accepted at the United Nations. Four of the designated individuals provided financial support (and in some cases, weapons and explosives) to Iraqi insurgents. Similarly, on June 17, 2005, we designated Muhammad Yunis Ahmad for providing funding, leadership, and support from his base in Syria to several insurgent groups that are conducting attacks in Iraq.

- On June 9, 2005, we also designated two associated Syrian individuals, General Zuhayr Shalish and Asif Shalish and a related asset, the Syria-based SES International Corporation for their support to senior officials of the former Iraqi regime. SES also acted as false end-user for the former Iraqi regime and facilitated Iraq's procurement of illicit military goods in contravention of UN sanctions.

- Just as there is a UN Security Council Resolution requiring countries to freeze the assets of former Iraqi regime elements, so too are there UN Security Council Resolutions requiring countries to freeze the assets of individuals and entities related to Al Qa'ida, Usama bin Laden, and the Taliban (UNSCR 1267) and other global terrorist groups (UNSCR 1373). The United States implements its obligations under these resolutions through E.O. 13224. To date, the Treasury Department has designated over 400 individuals and entities under E.O. 13224. These actions include individuals and entities tied to jihadist insurgency groups: Sulayman Khalid Darwish (January 25, 2005) (Syria-based Zarqawi supporter/financier), also designated by the UN, pursuant to UNSCR 1267; Syria joined the United States in co-designating Darwish at the United Nations.

- U.S. outreach efforts to countries in the Gulf region are manifold, both bilaterally and multilaterally. For example, just this calendar year I have personally traveled to Saudi Arabia, Bahrain, and Kuwait, and have led the U.S. delegation to the Middle East/North Africa Financial Action Task Force (MENA FATF)—a new multilateral body that works to ensure the implementation of comprehensive anti-money laundering and counterterrorist financing systems throughout the region. Launched in November 2004, this fourteen-member body held its first plenary session in Bahrain in April 2005 and is preparing for its second plenary session in September of this year, currently scheduled to take place in Beirut. This body has the potential to be effective in persuading its members to implement systems to freeze assets in a timely and effective manner.

- We also have extensive outreach efforts to Europe—most prominently the U.S.–EU Counter-Terrorist Financing Working Group, chaired by Assistant Secretary of State Anthony Wayne. Through this and other mechanisms, we are working to ensure the effective and aggressive implementation of targeted financial sanctions throughout Europe.
- The full range of U.S. efforts against terrorist financing are coordinated by the Terrorist Financing Policy Coordination Committee (PCC), which is chaired by Deputy National Security Advisor Juan Zarate and includes representatives from the Departments of the Treasury, State, Justice, and Defense, as well as representatives from the law enforcement and intelligence communities.

The Problem of Syria

Foreign countries also play a role. Both senior U.S. and Iraqi officials feel that Syria may overtly agree to try to halt any support of the insurgency through Syria but allows Islamic extremist groups to recruit young men, have them come to Syria, and then cross the border into Iraq—where substantial numbers have become suicide bombers. They also feel Syria has allowed senior ex-Ba'athist cadres to operate from Syria, helping to direct the Sunni insurgency. As has been touched upon earlier, these seem to include top-level officials under Saddam Hussein such as Izzat Ibrahim al-Duri, one of Saddam Hussein's vice presidents.

General George Casey, the commander of the MNF-I, is a U.S. officer who has been careful not to exaggerate the threat of foreign interference. Nevertheless, Casey has warned that Syria has allowed Iraqi supporters of Saddam Hussein to provide money, supplies, and direction to Sunni insurgents and continues to be a serious source of infiltration by foreign volunteers.[138] General Casey highlighted Syria's complicity in this regard when testifying before the Senate Armed Services Committee on March 8, 2005. He stated: "There are former regime leaders who come and go from Syria, who operate out of Syria, and they do planning, and they provide resources to the insurgency in Iraq. I have no hard evidence that the Syrian government is actually complicit with those people, but we certainly have evidence that people at low levels with the Syrian government know that they're there and what they're up to."[139]

The U.S. State Department spokesman described Syria's role as follows in the late spring of 2005:

> I think that what we've seen, again, are some efforts, but it certainly isn't enough. We do believe the Syrians can do more. We do believe there's more they can do along the border to tighten controls.
>
> We do believe that there's more that they can do to deal with the regime elements that are operating out of Syria itself and are supporting or encouraging the insurgents there.
>
> And so, again, it's not simply a matter of them not being able to take the actions, at least from our perspective. Part of it is an unwillingness to take the actions that we know are necessary and they know are necessary.[140]

In late February 2005 the Baghdad television station al-Iraqiya aired taped confessions of several alleged insurgents who were captured in Iraq. Many of the men from Sudan, Egypt, and Iraq claimed that they were trained in Syria— at least three believed that they were trained, controlled, and paid by Syrian intelligence officials. They were instructed to kidnap, behead, and assassinate Iraqi security forces. The majority of the men expressed remorse for their actions and said they were driven almost exclusively by monetary rewards; there was almost no mention of religious or nationalistic motivation. Syria has repeatedly and emphatically denied that it supports or harbors any persons involved in the insurgency in Iraq. After months of American pressure and accusations, however, Syrian authorities delivered a group suspected of supporting the insurgency from Syria to Iraqi officials in February 2005. Among the captives handed over was Sabawi Ibrahim Hassan, Saddam Hussein's half-brother and a leading financier for the insurgency. Syria's Foreign Minister, Farouk al-Sharaa, stated that Syria was doing all that it could but that it needed equipment tailored to policing the borders, such as night-vision goggles.[141]

There have also been reports that Zarqawi obtains most of his new young volunteers through Syria and that they are recruited and transited in ways that have to be known to Syrian intelligence. There have also been media reports that Zarqawi's top lieutenants, and perhaps Zarqawi himself, have met in Syria for planning sessions.[142] These reports were called into question by U.S. intelligence assessments in June 2005.

U.S. officials and commanders, as well as Iraqi officials, acknowledge that Syria has made some efforts to improve its border security and reduce infiltration. In summer 2005 Syrian security forces fought suspected militants, possibly former bodyguards of Saddam Hussein, for two days near Qassioun Mountain, and a sweep of the border area with Lebanon led to the arrest of some thirty-four suspected militants. In a high-profile case, Syria arrested a man and his brother's wife whom they accused of facilitating militants' passage into Iraq. The woman admitted on Al Arabiya satellite television that the brothers had crossed into Iraq to join Saddam Hussein's Fedayeen prior to the Coalition invasion.[143]

U.S. Central Command director of intelligence, Brigadier General John Custer, acknowledged in July 2005 the moves that Syria had made as well as the problems in patrolling the border. Custer stated that Syria had bolstered the forces along the eastern border with units relocated from Lebanon. In comments that went against other intelligence officials had provided, Custer stated, "I think Syria is intent on assisting the United States in Iraq. . . . [I have] no information, intelligence, or anything credible [that Syria] is involved or facilitating in any way [the flow of insurgents into Iraq]. . . . Could they do more? Yes. Are they doing more? Yes. They are working very hard. As troops have been pulled out of Lebanon, we've seen some of those troops go to the border. I am convinced that they are not only doing it along the border but are arresting people as they transit."[144]

The British military attaché in Damascus, Colonel Julian Lyne-Pirkis, inspected the Syrian efforts at the border and agreed with Custer's assessment. Custer suggested that the border interacted with a tradition of lawlessness and lack of Syrian ability to create a greater impression of Syrian complicity than there actually was. He stated, "It's not a question of intent—it's simply capacity and capability. You've got a 600-kilometer border there, some of the toughest desert, and you have a thousand-year-old culture of smuggling. Smuggling men now is no different than smuggling men a thousand years ago. It's all a smuggling economy."[145] Syria faces problems because its border forces are relatively weak, they lack training and equipment, and much of the border is only demarcated by an earthen berm. At the same time, many feel Syria deliberately turns a blind eye toward many operations and the large number of Islamist extremist volunteers crossing the border.

Also crossing the border are unknown sums of cash by method of cash couriers. Because Iraq's formal financial system is still maturing, and because porous borders allow for the easy transfer of money carried across by human mules, this is an effective and preferred method for financing the insurgency from abroad. Syria is a particular concern in this regard, as identified by Daniel L. Glaser, acting assistant secretary, Office of Terrorist Financing and Financial Crimes, U.S. Department of the Treasury, in July before the House Armed Services Committee. Through various sanctions programs, the Treasury Department has targeted Syrian individuals, entities, and officials for a range of issues, including harboring assets of the former Iraqi regime, interfering in Lebanon, inadequately policing the flow of cash across its borders, and failing to implement money laundering and terrorist financing controls.[146]

On September 12, 2005, in a State Department briefing, U.S. Ambassador to Iraq Zalmay Khalilizad said that Syria is the "number one offender" in the Middle East region working to impede the success of Iraq. Khalilizad said Syria is knowingly allowing terrorists to use its territory for training exercises and permitting them to transit across Syria into Iraq and kill Iraqis.[147] This followed the September 10, 2005, announcement by Iraqi Interior Minister Bayan Jabor that Iraq would close its border with Syria at the Rabiah crossing point near the city of Mosul, beginning September 11 until further notice.

Some analysts have suggested that the regime in Damascus may view the insurgency in Iraq as a means to "export" their own Islamist extremists who might otherwise take aim at Assad's secular regime (led by an Allawite minority). However, such a view, analysts say, is extremely nearsighted, as it is quite possible that extremists in Iraq could return the very way that they came and cross back into Syria, bringing practical guerilla warfare experience with them much like the Mujahideen who fought in the Afghan War brought back to their countries of origin. Such hardened and trained militants could then pose a very serious threat to the ruling regime. As one commentator stated, "They [militants and Syria] may have slept in the same bed to fight the Americans, but what's important for Al Qa'ida is that it has entered the bedroom [Syria] and secured a foothold there."[148]

Indeed, such views were supported by classified CIA and U.S. State Department studies in summer 2005. Analysts referred to the return of experienced and trained militants to their country of origin or a third-party country as "bleed out" or "terrorist dispersal."[149] The studies sought to compare the returning Mujahideen from Afghanistan to those who fought in Iraq. Like Syria, those countries could be threatened by the fighters who return with advanced warfare skills.[150] A Marine Corps spokesperson pointed out that if nothing else, certain techniques such as the use of IEDs had already been transferred from Iraq to combat zones like Afghanistan. Experts, however, point to the fact that while the Afghan War attracted thousands of foreign fighters, Iraq has yet to do so, meaning that the potential number of returning veterans would be much less.[151]

Saudi Interior Minister Prince Nayef echoed the conclusions of the CIA and State Department studies, pointing out that many of the terrorists who operated in Saudi Arabia from May 2003 on were either veterans of the Soviet conflict in Afghanistan or had trained in the camps that operated until Operation Enduring Freedom eliminated them. Nayef and other Saudi officials believe that the Saudis who return from the conflict in Iraq will have skills that are even more lethal than those exhibited by the Afghan War veterans. Nayef stated, "We expect the worst from those who went to Iraq. They will be worse, and we will be ready for them."[152]

In a speech before the UN Security Council in May 2005, Iraqi Foreign Minister Hoshyar Zebari asked that Iraq's neighboring states do more to prevent terrorists from crossing into Iraq. Syria figured prominently in his speech, in which he acknowledged the efforts by the government but implored the regime to make greater efforts. Zebari stated, "We have learned recently that Syria has stopped more than a thousand foreign fighters from entering Iraq from Syria. We welcome this action but note that it confirms our long-held view that Syria has been one of the main transit routes for foreign terrorists as well as for remnants of the previous regime."[153] Reportedly, another Iraqi official handed a list over to the Syrians that contained the names, addresses, and specific roles in planning attacks in Iraq of individuals living in Damascus. According to the Iraqi official, the Syrians ignored the list.[154]

One senior U.S. intelligence official echoed the foreign minister, stating, "There's no question that Syrian territory plays a significant role with regard to how outside figures [move] into the insurgency in Iraq. The problems with the regime are a mixture of willingness and capability."[155] A *Washington Post* article that ran in early summer 2005 featured an interview with a pro-claimed insurgent sympathizer/organizer within Syria. The man, Abu Ibrahim, made several claims about the insurgency and its relation to Syria. He dubbed Syria a "hub" for organizing insurgents and claimed that when the United States pressured the Syrian government in late 2004, men like him were taken into custody by Syrian agents only to be released several days later.[156]

He openly admitted to ferrying men, weapons, and money into Iraq, himself possibly fighting on one occasion, and stated that he was routinely tailed by Syrian agents, but that they did not interfere with his activities. Ibrahim stated that in the early days of the war, Syrian border guards waved busloads of would-be insurgents through checkpoints and into Iraq.[157] He claimed that he had seen a rise in the number of Saudis coming to Syria to be transported to Iraq to join the insurgency. Purportedly, Ibrahim and others were inspired by a radical Syrian preacher named Abu Qaqaa. When he asked a sheik why the Syrian government had not arrested them for their activities, "he would tell us it was because we weren't saying anything against the government, that we were focusing on the common enemy, America and Israel, that beards and epaulets were in one trench together."[158] Although it may be impossible to verify Abu Ibrahim's claims, they do not appear to differ greatly from the public statements and assessments of the U.S. military and intelligence community.

Iraqi Interior Minister Bayan Jabr repeated the prime minister's call to neighboring countries in July 2005. Jabr met with the interior ministers from Syria, Jordan, Kuwait, Iran, Egypt, and Saudi Arabia in Istanbul and reiterated that the Iraqi government wanted the neighboring countries to do more to staunch the flow of weapons and insurgents into Iraq.[159] The ministers released a communiqué that condemned the murder of Egypt's ambassador, pledged to prevent terrorists from using their territories as bases and recruitment centers for terrorists, and called for the rapid exchange of information on terror suspects and their movements. Jabr, commenting before meeting with the ministers, stated, "I will say clearly in my speech about the countries—maybe without names but they know themselves—the countries who support directly or indirectly the insurgents. I will talk to these countries to stop these activities and to cut short these terrorists."[160]

In July 2005 the U.S. Treasury Department announced that information obtained from Saddam Hussein's half-brother and former adviser, Sabawi Ibrahim Hasan al-Tikriti, indicated that Tikriti's four sons were responsible for supplying money, arms, explosives, and other means of support to the insurgents in Iraq from bases in Syria. Reportedly, Tikriti supplied street addresses for each of his sons. One son, Omar, is suspected of being behind several of the attacks on U.S. forces in Mosul.[161] The U.S. Treasury Department eventually blocked the assets of six of Saddam Hussein's nephews. Stuart Levey, the U.S. Treasury's Undersecretary for Terrorism and Financial Intelligence stated, "This action targets the money flows of former regime elements actively supporting attacks against Coalition forces and the Iraqi people."[162] Acting Assistant Treasury Secretary Daniel Glaser asserted that cash couriers from the region, Syria in particular, were the primary method for funneling money to insurgents. He stated that large sums belonging to former Iraqi officials who are now in Syria, or who are now controlled by Syria, are responsible for much of the financing.[163]

U.S. officials commented that as of summer 2005, some intelligence showed that Syrians were providing weapons, training, money, and perhaps even "barracks-like housing" for volunteers who had made their way from Yemen, Morocco, Saudi Arabia, and elsewhere. Furthermore, the intelligence indicated that the makeshift staging areas for militants preparing to cross the border into Iraq had become more complex.[164] A series of *Financial Times* interviews with would-be militants and their families during the summer of 2005 revealed the extent to which Syria might be aiding the insurgency. A mother of one fighter stated, "... you go to a mosque to make initial contact. Then you are sent to a private home and from there for a week's intensive training inside Syria."[165] The militants who were interviewed claimed that they were trained in remote Syrian territory, close to the Iraqi border, with a focus on how to use Kalashnikovs, RPGs, and remote detonators. The fighters claimed that some attacks were even planned from Syrian territory.[166]

Iraqi Prime Minister Ibrahim Jafari and U.S. Secretary of State Condoleezza Rice both made it clear in mid-2005 that they felt that Syria continued to allow both Iraqi Ba'athist and Islamist extremist elements to operate inside Syria and across the Syrian-Iraqi border.[167] U.S. Lieutenant General John Vines estimated in summer 2005 that about 150 fighters crossed into Iraq from Syria each month.[168] This presented problems for both Iraqi and Coalition forces because Iraq had comparatively few border posts, and many isolated posts had been attacked, and some had been destroyed or abandoned.[169] A major effort was underway to rebuild them and strengthen the Iraqi border forces, but it has made limited progress so far, and the morale and effectiveness of these border forces are often still low.

The border area around Huasaybah (Qusaybah) in Iraq has long been a center for smuggling and criminal activity. Two Muslim tribes in the area—the Mahalowis and Salmanis—have long controlled illegal trade across the border and seem to permit insurgent activity with at least Syrian tolerance. The Iraqi government also proved unable to secure the area. A 400-man Iraqi unit sent in to try to secure Huasaybah in March 2000 virtually collapsed and was forced to hide out in a local phosphate plant.[170]

The entire route along the Euphrates from Hit and Haditha to Ubaydi, Qaim, Karbilah, Qusaybah, and Abu Kamal in Syria has also been a center and partial sanctuary for insurgent forces and a conduit for volunteers and supplies coming in from Syria. By the spring of 2005 it became so serious a center for some of the insurgents who fled from the fighting in Ramadi and Fallujah that the U.S. Marine Corps launched its largest offensive since Fallujah against insurgent forces in the area, sometimes meeting stiff resistance from both Iraqi Sunni insurgents and Sunni Islamic extremist groups.[171]

At the same time, the insurgents do not need major shipments of arms, virtually anyone can go in and out moving money and small critical supplies, and volunteers can simply enter as ordinary visitors without equipment. U.S. Customs and border protection (US CBP) officers are working to train their Iraqi counterparts and have had moderate success in detaining potential insurgents and arms suppliers and in breaking up smuggling rings. Another US CBP team of officers and border agents was deployed in Iraq on February 1, 2005, to assist further in the training of Iraqis. This may help, but Iraq's border-security forces have so far been some of its most ineffective units. Many of its new forts are abandoned, and other units that have remained exhibit minimal activity. Yet, even if Iraq's border forces were ready and its neighbors actively helped, border security would still be a problem.

This illustrates a general problem for both Iraq and its neighbors. Iraq's borders total 3,650 kilometers in length. Its border with Iran is 1,458 kilometers, with Jordan 181 kilometers, with Kuwait 240 kilometers, with Saudi Arabia 814 kilometers, with Syria 605 kilometers, and with Turkey 352 kilometers. Most of these borders are desert, desolate territory, easily navigable water barriers, or mountains. Even Iraq's small fifty-eight-kilometer coastline is in an area with considerable small craft and shipping traffic, which presents security problems.

It is also important to note that Syria plays a role in dealing with some of Iraq's Shi'ites as well as its Sunnis. While it may tolerate and encourage former Iraqi Ba'athist operations in Syria and transit by Islamist extremists, Syria also maintains ties to elements of formerly Iranian-backed Iraqi Shi'ite groups like the Supreme Council for the Islamic Revolution in Iraq (SCIRI), Al Dawa, and Al-Dawa-Tanzim al-Iraq that it first developed during the Iran-Iraq War. Syria has an Alawite-led regime that is more Shi'ite than Sunni, and while it sees its support of Sunni insurgents as a way of weakening the potential threat from a U.S. presence in Syria, it also maintains ties to Shi'ite factions as well.

The Problem of Iran

The role Iran plays in the Iraqi insurgency is highly controversial. Iran certainly has an active presence in Iraq and has ties to several key Shi'ite political parties. These include key elements in the Shi'ite-based United Iraqi Alliance (UIA) that emerged as Iraq's most important political coalition in the January 2005 elections: the Supreme Council for the Islamic Revolution in Iraq (SCIRI), Al Dawa, and Al-Dawa-Tanzim al-Iraq. The Revolutionary Guard and Iranian intelligence have been active in southern Iraq since the early 1980s, as well as in other areas. They almost certainly have a network of active agents in Iraq at present.

Prime Minister Allawi repeatedly expressed his concern over Iran's actions during 2004 and early 2005, as did other senior officials in the interim Iraqi government. Some senior Iraqi Interim Government officials clearly see Iran as a direct and immediate threat.

Iraqi interim Defense Minister Hazim al-Shalaan claimed in July 2004 that Iran remained his country's "first enemy," supporting "terrorism and bringing enemies into Iraq. . . . I've seen clear interference in Iraqi issues by Iran. . . . Iran interferes in order to kill democracy." A few months later Shalaan—a secular Shi'ite who is one of Iran's most outspoken critics in Iraq—added that the Iranians "are fighting us because we want to build freedom and democracy, and they want to build an Islamic dictatorship and have turbaned clerics to rule in Iraq."[172] Shalaan made the following points in a briefing on September 22, 2004:

- Iranian intervention and support of Sadr pose major threats; and some infiltration has taken place across the Syria border.
- Iran is behind Sadr. It uses Iranian pilgrims and sends arms, money, and drugs across the border.
- Iraq must have strong border defense forces. "If doors and windows are empty, no amount of cleaning will ever get rid of the dust."

In a study of Iran's role in Iraq, the International Crisis Group noted that an Iranian cleric and close associate of Ayatollah Sistani warned in November 2004 that "Iran's policy in Iraq is 100 percent wrong. In trying to keep the Americans busy they have furthered the suffering of ordinary Iraqis. . . . We are not asking them to help the Americans, but what they are doing is not in the interests of the Iraqi people; it is making things worse. We [Iranians] have lost the trust of the Iraqi people [*Mardom-e Aragh az dast dadeem*]."[173]

In contrast, King Abdullah of Jordan has made a wide range of charges about Iranian interference in Iraq and went so far as to charge during the period before the Iraqi election that Iran was attempting to rig Iraq's election with up to 1 million false registrations. He has since talked about the risk of an Iraqi-Syrian-Lebanese "axis" or "crescent."

In an unusual interview aired on Iraqi TV on January 14, 2005, Muayed Al-Nasseri, commander of Saddam Hussein's "Army of Muhammad," claimed that his group regularly received arms and money from both Syria and Iran. "Many factions of the resistance are receiving aid from the neighboring countries," he said. "We got aid primarily from Iran."[174] It should be noted, however, that Iran has repeatedly denied these charges. Moreover, most of the U.S. and Iraqi officials interviewed during 2004 and through mid-2005 viewed claims that Iran was an active supporter of the Sunni insurgency or playing a currently hostile role in Iraq with skepticism. Senior ministers in Iraq's newly elected government—some Sunni—largely discounted Iran as an immediate threat. American experts seem more concerned with the potential role Iran could play in any Iraqi civil conflict, or once a Shi'ite political majority takes office, than with direct Iranian support of a Shi'ite insurgency.

As General George Casey put it, "I don't see substantial Iranian influence on this particular government that will be elected in January. I see Iran as more of a longer-term threat to Iraqi security . . . a long-term threat to stability in Iraq. If you look on the other side, I think Syria is a short-term threat, because of the support they provide to Ba'athist leaders operating inside and outside of Iraq."[175]

Many of the Iraqi exile groups and militia members who lived in Iran before the fall of Saddam Hussein were never particularly grateful to Iran during the time they had to remain in exile and are not pro-Iranian now. The Ayatollah Sistani, Iraq's pre-eminent Shi'ite religious leader—as well as virtually all of the influential Iraqi clergy except Sadr—is a quietest who opposes the idea that religious figures should play a direct role in politics. Moreover, the Grand Ayatollah Sistani has rejected the religious legitimacy of a *velayat-e faqih* or supreme religious leader like Iran's Khameni. The major Iraqi Shi'ite parties that did operate in Iran before Saddam's fall did endorse the idea of a *velayat-e faqih* while they were dependent on Iran but have since taken the position that Iraq should not be a theocratic state, much less under the control of a *velayat-e faqih.*

The analysis of the International Crisis Group and of many U.S. experts in and outside Iraq interviewed for this analysis do not support the existence of any major Iranian effort to destabilize or control Iraq through June 2005.[176] However, the present and future uncertainties surrounding Iran's role, however, can scarcely be ignored. Iran does seem to have tolerated an Al Qa'ida presence in Iran, or at least transit through the country, as a means of putting pressure on the United States, in spite of Al Qa'ida's distinctly uncertain tolerance of Shi'ism. Iran may have been active in supporting groups like Al Ansar in the past, or at least turning a blind eye, and may allow cross-border infiltration in Iraq's Kurdish region now. In July 2005 Kurdish intelligence officials asserted that Ansar was based primarily in Iran and that attacks in the Kurdish areas could only have occurred with Iranian support. According to an Iraqi Kurdish reporter, the Iranian cities of Mahabad and Saqqiz are centers where Ansar recruited among the Iranian Kurds. Such claims cannot be independently verified.

Iran has not been, and never will be, passive in dealing with Iraq. For example, it sent a top-level official, Kamal Kharrazi, to Iraq on May 17, 2005—only forty-eight hours after U.S. Secretary of State Condoleezza Rice had left the country. Kharrazi met with Prime Minister Jafari and Foreign Minister Hoshyar Zebari. He also met with other top officials and key members of the Shi'ite parties, and his visit was at a minimum a demonstration of Iran's influence in an Iraq governed by a Shi'ite majority, even though some key Iraqi Shi'a parties like Al Dawa have scarcely been strong supporters of Iran. Kharrazi also gave an important message at his press conference, "... the party that will leave Iraq is the United States because it will eventually withdraw ... but the party that will live with the Iraqis is Iran because it is a neighbor to Iraq."[177]

In summer 2005, the Iraqi and Iranian ministers of defense, Sadun al-Dulaimi and Admiral Ali Shamkhani, met and concluded a five-point military agreement. The meeting, however, produced conflicting statements as to what had been agreed upon. The Iranian minister asserted that as part of the deal Iran would train a number of Iraqi troops. His Iraqi counterpart, Dulaimi, however, stated that the Iraqi government was satisfied with the Coalition efforts and that Iran would not be training Iraqi troops. Iran would, however, be providing $1 billion in aide that would go toward reconstruction. Dulaimi conceded that some would go to the Ministry of Defense.[178]

Iran faces a dilemma. It needs U.S. support for Iraq to help it deal with the insurgency and provide economic aid. Yet, it fears the U.S. presence in Iraq and the risk of being "encircled" by the U.S. presence in Iraq, Afghanistan, and the Persian Gulf. Iranian officials have threatened to destabilize Iraq if the United States brings military pressure against Iran because of its activities in nuclear proliferation. A split in Iraq's government could lead some Shi'ite factions to actively turn to Iran for support, and the divisions in Iran's government create the ongoing risk that hard-line elements might intervene in Iraq even if its government did not fully support such action. At this point in time, however, these seem to be risks rather than present realities.

The Problem of Turkey

The Kurdish issue in northern Iraq has two major implications for Turkey. First, Ankara is concerned about activities of Kurdish separatist groups in northern Iraq, whose chief objective is an independent Kurdistan in and around Turkey. Turkey is engaging in heavy diplomacy with both the U.S. and Iraqi administrations to crack down on these organizations and eliminate the Kurdish rebels who are launching attacks into Turkish territory. This long-standing concern is the primary reason for the presence of Turkish intelligence and military units in northern Iraq since the Gulf operation.

In summer 2005, Kurdish PKK rebels launched a series of attacks on Turkish forces allegedly from bases in northern Iraq. In two months more than fifty Turkish security forces were killed in attacks, mostly in the form of planted IEDs, a weapon utilized widely by Iraqi insurgents. In July 2005 the Turkish prime minister threatened cross-border action against the rebels if the attacks did not stop, although such action is generally regarded as extremely provocative and even illegal. Recep Tayyip Erdogan stated, however, that "there are certain things that international law allows. When necessary, one can carry out cross-border operations. I hope that such a need will not emerge."[179]

Perhaps exacerbating the debate about cross-border operations were the conflicting reports that the United States, which considers the PKK a terrorist organization, had ordered the military to capture the organization's leaders. A member of the Turkish military claimed that the United States had agreed to seize the leaders while U.S. military spokesmen were unaware of such an agreement. The official U.S. position seemed to be that the United States opposed any cross-border action as an infringement on sovereignty and likely to incite further violence between the Kurds and the various sects opposed to their independence or autonomy. Furthermore, the United States made it clear that any discussion of the PKK should center on the Iraqi government. The U.S. chairman of the Joint Chiefs of Staff, General Richard Myers, stated, "I think the difference now is that they [Turkey] are dealing with a sovereign Iraqi government, and a lot of these discussions will have to occur between Turkey and Iraq, not between Turkey and the United States."[180]

Second, Turkey has consistently opposed strong autonomy for a Kurdish zone within Iraq out of the fear that it would create unrest and aspirations for independence among Turkey's own Kurdish population. Given the rich water supplies in the Kurdish-populated regions of Turkey and the colossal irrigation project (the Southeast Anatolian Project) that Turkey invested in for over four decades, an autonomous Turkish Kurdistan is out of the question for Turkish policymakers.

Despite the present tension in U.S. and Turkish ties and Turkey's relations with Iraq, Turkey is significantly involved in postwar reconstruction in Iraq. Turkey also offered to assist with the training of Iraqi police forces. The most recent example of Turkish effort to help the creation of a stable and unified Iraq was the meeting held in April 2005 in Istanbul where all Iraq's neighbors, Egypt, and Bahrain convened to address issues related to cross-border insurgency and terrorist infiltration.

The Problem of Jordan

Jordan shares a border with Iraq, and some analysts believe that a limited number of insurgents may cross into Iraq from that border. Most Arab Jordanians are very much opposed to the rise of a Shi'ite-dominated Iraq. The Jordanian government, however, has trained a good number of the Iraqi security forces and is very much concerned with extreme Islamist elements within its own territory. In spring 2004 a plot to create a massive chemical-laced explosion over Amman by radical Islamists was uncovered and disrupted by the Jordanian security forces. There is little-to-no evidence that the Jordanians are either actively helping any insurgents or turning a blind eye to them.

On August 19, 2005, Katyusha rockets were fired at two U.S. warships in Jordan's Red Sea Aqaba port. The rockets missed the ship, one hitting a warehouse and killing a Jordanian soldier. Another exploded near a Jordanian hospital, resulting in no casualties, and a third landed outside of Eliat airport in neighboring Israel but did not explode. The Iraqi branch of Al Qa'ida, linked to Jordanian Abu Masab al-Zarqawi, claimed responsibility for the failed attack. On August 23, Jordanian officials arrested a Syrian man, Mohammed Hassan Abdullah al-Sihly, who they accused of carrying out the attack, although police claimed that three accomplices slipped across the border into Iraq.[181] Jordanian Interior Minister Awni Yirfas reported that his government was in close contact with Iraqi authorities to capture the men.[182]

A Jordanian, Raad Mansour al-Banna, is the main suspect in a suicide bombing of a police recruitment site in Hilla in February 2005, considered the single deadliest attack, in which 125 people were killed.[183] On August 21, 2005, Laith Kubba, spokesman for Prime Minister Ibrahim al-Jafari, accused Jordan of allowing the family of Saddam Hussein to finance the insurgent campaign in Iraq in an effort to reestablish the Ba'ath Party in that country.[184]

While commentators focus on the fact that Abu Musab al-Zarqawi is himself a Jordanian, it should be noted that the Jordanian government has sentenced

Zarqawi to death in absentia. Though there may be some Jordanians involved in the insurgency, Jordan has been very cooperative in its efforts to train Iraqi police and to monitor its borders.

In summer 2005 Jordanian forces broke up an alleged recruitment ring in Amman. According to the main defendant, Zaid Horani, he and several other Jordanians crossed into Syria and boarded buses in Damascus, Syria, that were bound for Iraq as the Coalition forces invaded. Horani apparently returned home and helped to organize a recruitment pipeline for Jordanians interested in joining the insurgency in Iraq. Figuring prominently in the case was a Syrian, Abu al-Janna, who was allegedly the point of contact in Iraq for the Jordanians. Al-Janna is reportedly a central figure in the regional terror network.[185]

A Jordanian, Raad Mansour al-Banna, is the main suspect in a suicide bombing of a police recruitment site in Hilla in February 2005, considered the single deadliest attack, in which 125 people were killed.[186] Commentators point out that Abu Musab al-Zarqawi is himself a Jordanian. It should be noted, however, that the Jordanian government sentenced Zarqawi to death in abstentia and that although there may be some Jordanians involved in the insurgency, Jordan has been very cooperative in its efforts to train Iraqi police and to monitor its borders.

Iraqi Views of the Threat

There is no single Iraqi view of any major issue that affects Iraq. Iraqis disagree on details regarding almost all of the issues covered in this analysis and sometimes presented very different views of how seriously they took the threat from Syria and Iran, how and whether they quantified various threat forces, and how seriously they saw given extremist, terrorist, and insurgent elements. There was also no agreement on whether the threat was getting better or worse, although most felt the election was a major step forward and that insurgent attacks were less successful than they feared. Like the United States and MNSTC–I, they see the following four major threats:

- *Zarqawi and outside Islamist extremist organization fighters*: These are mostly foreign Arabs. One cannot quantify this threat, but numbers are small and probably well under 1,000. The problem is that their methods of attack have great impact.
- *Former regime elements (FREs)*: Large numbers and a mix of true supporters of the Ba'ath, alienated Sunnis, paid volunteers, temporary recruits, and other Iraqis make up the FREs. There is no way to quantify them, but some feel it is in the 15,000 to 30,000 level depending on how one estimates full-time ands part-time fighters.
- *Iraqi Native Islamist Extremist Organization fighters*: A small and just emerging group, one cannot quantify its members, but numbers are small and probably well under 500. The problem is their methods of attack can be a mirror image of outside extremists and have great impact.

- *Organized crime*: The major source of violence and insecurity in at least twelve of the eighteen governorates, organized crime often seems to cooperate with terrorists and insurgents. Many different levels of seriousness exist, but numbers are very high, as is impact.

Some Iraqis—particularly Sunnis—feel elements of various militias are becoming a problem. Some accuse the Shi'ite militias of atrocities against Sunnis, and Arabs accuse the Pesh Merga of supporting ethnic cleansing in the North, although the details are unclear. Iraqi officials feel MNSTC–I estimates of the insurgent threat are misleading because they seem to only include hardcore insurgents. They also feel that the minister of defense was generally correct in including some 200,000 sympathizers in one guess at the threat. He stated, "It does no one any good to deny the insurgents have major public support, particularly in Sunni areas. Our political problem is much more important than our military one."

Inclusion versus Conflict

Civil war is not a risk; it is an ongoing reality. The question is just how intensive it will become. The insurgency has gradually created a low-level civil war, and Sunni Islamist extremists have made a concerted effort to drive it toward a broader Sunni versus Shi'ite conflict. Much of the future nature of the insurgency in Iraq depends on the wisdom and pragmatism of Iraq's present and emerging political leaders over the course of 2005 through 2007. This will be especially true before, during, and after the effort to create a new constitution, the referendum to follow, and the full-scale election now scheduled for December 2005.

Iraqi and U.S. policymakers clearly understand the issues and risks involved. U.S. and other MNSTC–I officials pressed hard for "inclusion" before the elections and for Iraqi government contacts and negotiations with the so-called "rejectionist" elements among Iraq Sunni Arabs after the elections. In addition to the visits by Secretary of Defense Rumsfeld discussed earlier, U.S. Deputy Secretary of State Robert Zoellick visited Iraq after the election and in May. Secretary of State Condoleezza Rice visited Iraq on May 16, 2005—again to deliver the message that the government must be inclusive, avoid purges of the civil service and Iraqi forces, and develop the existing Iraqi force structure as rapidly as possible. Senior U.S. officers have delivered the same message, as has the U.S. Embassy team.

Shi'ite Resistance to Sectarian Conflict

So far, Iraq's Arab Shi'ite leaders have resisted polarization along ethnic and sectarian lines. Key religious leaders as diverse as the Grand Ayatollah Ali al Sistani and Abdel Aziz al-Hakim have been strong voices calling for inclusion and opposing any general reprisals against Iraq's Sunnis. Iraq's new president and prime minister both stressed a strategy of inclusion and amnesty upon taking office.[187] Iraqi officials have also continued to negotiate with those who boy-cotted the elections—and some have joined the new political structure and been included in writing the constitution.

Forming the new Iraqi cabinet presented serious problems, however, in part because so many Sunnis chose not to participate in the political process before the January 30 election. Some new officials have also been a source of tension. The new minister of interior, Bayan Jabr, had some Sunni figures call for his removal because they felt he was tied to SCIRI's Badr Corps, which they blamed for attacks on Sunnis. The new cabinet did, however, include seven Sunnis. Iraq's new minister of defense, Sadun al-Dulaimi, was chosen after a long political struggle to find a Sunni with real political credentials who was accept-able to Iraq's Shi'ites and Kurds. Dulaimi was a former officer with training as a sociologist. He became an exile during the Iran-Iraq War and had been sentenced to death in absentia by Saddam Hussein. He had returned to Iraq after Saddam's fall and had set up the Baghdad-based Iraq Center for Research and Strategic Studies, which conducted a number of Iraq's public opinion surveys.

While some Sunnis charged that Dulaimi did not have the political weight to be a serious leader, he was the member of the government who announced on May 16, 2005, that Iraqi forces would stop raiding Sunni mosques and "terrifying worshipers."[188] He was also a man that many of his subordinates came to respect, although some still continued to fear a Shi'ite purge of Sunni workers in the ministry. Other key Sunnis included Abid Mutlak al-Jubouri, one of three deputy prime ministers, and Osama al-Najafi, as minister of industry.

So far, Iraq's Arab Shi'ite leaders have resisted polarization along ethnic and sectarian lines. This has included key religious leaders as diverse as the Grand Ayatollah Ali al Sistani and Abdel Aziz al-Hakim. Moreover, the role of Moqtada al-Sadr has been much more uncertain. On August 24, 2005, seven people died in an attack on Sadr's office in Najaf, which led to unrest among Shi'ite populations there and in other cities. Sadr called for calm and continued his insistence on nonreprisal. Sadr sided with anti-federalist Sunni leaders during the Iraq constitution process.[189] This was largely regarded as an effort to prevent steps toward the dissolving of the Iraqi state, and thus a positive move. Sadr has supported Shi'ite political involvement in the new government, although many fear the brand of government that he wishes to see imposed. His organization has close ties with the Shi'ite Supreme Council for the Islamic Revolution, the largest Shi'ite political party.

Sadr's militia began playing a role in the intra-sect Shi'ite power struggle as early as October 13, 2003, when al-Sadr's men attacked supporters of moderate Shi'ite Grand Ayatollah Ali al-Sistani near the Imam Hussein shrine.[190] And while Sadr has urged his followers not to be drawn into sectarian fighting, in the summer of 2005 his organization was accused of a rash of political assassina-tions and kidnappings in the Shi'ite south. Sadr's political ambitions were made clear early, with continued appeals or demands to Coalition forces to leave Iraq and allow for the establishment of an Islamic regime.

The Uncertain Role of Iraq's Sunnis

As has been noted earlier, there were growing signs of tension and sometimes clashes between Iraqi Sunnis and foreign-led Sunni Islamist extremist groups in the spring of 2005. Even hard-line voices also have shown a deep concern for national unity. In late May Harith al Dhari, a senior Sunni imam who ignited sectarian tensions when he blamed the Badr Corps for killings of Sunnis, condemned the killing of a prominent Shi'ite cleric.[191]

In early April 2005 many of the native Iraqi Sunni clerics in the Association of Muslim Scholars reversed their previous condemnation of Sunni Iraqis who joined the security forces. Ahmed Abdul Ghafour al-Samarrai, a leading cleric in the organization, gave a Friday sermon encouraging Iraqi Sunnis to join the army and police, to prevent Iraq from falling into "the hands of those who have caused chaos, destruction, and violated the sanctities."[192] A total of sixty-four Sunni native Iraqi imams and religious scholars signed the fatwa that al-Samarrai wrote, including such leading previously hard-line imams as Ahmed Hassan al-Taha of Baghdad.[193]

Sunni groups like the National Dialogue Council, a body composed of thirty-one Sunni groups—and Sunni political figures in the government like Adnan Dulaimi—have long pushed for inclusion. Sunni Islamist extremism and sectarian violence have pushed other Sunni leaders in this direction as well. On May 21, over 1,000 Sunni Arab clerics, political figures, and tribal leaders declared an end to their boycott of the government-oriented political system and said they were uniting in a Sunni bloc and wanted to actively participate in the drafting of the constitution. This included both moderate and hard-line members of the Iraqi Islamic Party and Association of Muslim Scholars.

There are only seventeen Sunni members of the 275-person National Assembly. No one knows how a Shi'ite majority will behave or govern. There have been unexplained Iraqi security raids on seemingly peaceful Sunni political groups like the Dialogue Council. Some Sunnis have also charged that government forces have deliberately raided their mosques, mistreated prisoners, and may have executed Sunni civilians. At the same time, Sunnis have been unrealistically demanding and deeply divided over how to deal with any movement toward inclusion.

The Sunni clerics in the Association of Muslim Scholars who urged their followers to join the Iraqi forces did so in an ambiguous fatwa, stating that the "new army and police are empty of good people, and we need to supply them. . . . Because the police and army are a safeguard for the whole nation, not a militia for any special part, we have issued this fatwa calling on our people to join the army and police."[194] This was a far cry from reports in September 2004 that indicated that the association's spokesperson, the son of the president of the association, supported the targeting of what he termed "collaborators."[195]

An investigation by the *New York Times* raised serious questions as to whether the Dialogue Council's leaders were prepared to accept an Iraq that was not Sunni ruled. The *New York Times* found that the council's conservative Islamic secretary general, Fakhri al-Qaisi, felt that Shi'ites were only 30 percent of the population and not 60 percent and argued that Sunni Arabs were closer to 40 percent than 20 percent. He also reacted to the raid on the council's office by saying that the council was interested in negotiation but that "I think it's a scheme to wipe us out, destroy us," he said. "Their slogans about democracy are all but lies."[196]

According to the *New York Times*, he said that vice president Sheik Ghazi al-Yawar, the highest-ranking Sunni in the government, ". . . hasn't protected his friends or cooperated sincerely with us in the council." He described the new minister of defense, Sadun al-Dulaimi, as a "double agent." Saleh Mutlak, another council member, charged that the leaders of the military wing of Supreme Council for the Islamic Revolution in Iraq (SCIRI), one of the two leading Shi'ite religious parties, had been a major obstacle in the negotiations with the new government. He also said that Prime Minister Jafari was half-hearted: "We could not reach anything with him," he said. "He speaks in a vague way. He never comes to the point."

While this was only one report at a time of considerable tension, interviews with Iraqis revealed the same Sunni claims about demographics and attitudes toward the elections. It is also clear that some senior figures in both SCIRI and Prime Minister Jafari's Al Dawa party believe in purging the new government of Ba'athists and setting very demanding requirements for any inclusion. These do seem to include Abdul Aziz al-Hakim, the leader of SCIRI who is not in the government but is a key voice in Shi'ite politics.

The initial group of fifty-five members of the legislature chosen to draft the new constitution on May 10, 2005, included twenty-eight Shi'ites from Prime Minister Jafari's United Iraqi Alliance, fifteen Kurds from the Kurdish Alliance, eight members from former Prime Minister Ayad Allawi's Shi'ite-dominated alliance, and one each to a Communist, a Turcoman, a Christian, and one Sunni Arab. At U.S. urging, the government offered on May 26, 2005, to add fifteen more Sunni seats to the 101 seats in the Constitutional Commission actually doing the draft, which would have given Sunnis a total of seventeen seats or nearly 20 percent of the total.[197]

Underlying these negotiations were the fears that the option to delay the writing of the constitution by six months might be invoked and that either that event or the insistence of the negotiators at the constitutional committee on a certain number of seats for Sunni Arabs deemed unacceptable by Sunni negotiators might precipitate a withdrawal of Sunni participation in the writing of the constitution and the loss of an opportunity to sap some support among the Arab Sunni community for the insurgency. Jafari, however, said that he would not seek to invoke the extension.

Adnan Dulaimi, head of the Sunni affairs department within the new Iraqi government and a Sunni himself, brought up the specter of such a Sunni rejection. "If they don't agree at the end [to twenty-five Sunni Arab seats], we'll withdraw from the process of writing the constitution. We will never accept the thirteen [additional plus the two we have] seats they want to give us. In the referendum, if they don't agree to our demands, we'll call on three provinces to reject the constitution."[198]

Other Sunni politicians and negotiators, however, suggested that the problem would not be as intractable as indicated by Dulaimi. Naseer Ani, a Sunni directly involved in the negotiations, stated, "We insist on the number, but it is politics—everything is possible."[199] Reportedly, 1,000 Sunni scholars, politicians, and eminent figures met at the end of May to discuss the community's political role. In early June Iraqi politicians were mulling over the possibility of expanding the committee to sixty-nine members so that they could accept the twenty-five-seat Sunni demand. In mid-June the constitutional committee offered to give the Sunnis ten advisers on the committee but no more than the fifteen full members. The Sunni delegation to the committee agreed to the arrangement but stressed its dissatisfaction with the number of voting members it had. Key Sunni factions seem to have reluctantly agreed to such a compromise in June 2005.

Many issues still remain, however, regarding the role Sunnis will play in the constitutional process and the election that will follow and how much popular support any Sunnis who do participate will get; their inclusion remains at risk. It is also clear that any failure at inclusion that was recognized as valid by a broad majority of Iraqi Sunnis could have a critical impact on both the short- and long-term stability of Iraq and the pace of the insurgency. The new constitution can be vetoed if a two-thirds majority of voters in Iraq's eighteen provinces decide to vote against it. Sunnis dominate Al Anbar province and have large majorities in the Salahuddin and Nineveh provinces. The effort to draft a constitution was also on a tight schedule.

The draft was to be approved by a fifty-five-person committee of the National Assembly, then by the 275-member National Assembly by August 15, and then accepted in a national referendum by October 15. A one-week extension was then voted through on August 15. With August 22 came another extension of the process. On August 28, the Shi'ite and Kurd representatives of Parliament used their vast majority to approve a version of the bill that the Sunnis quickly and publicly rejected. Discreet negotiations continued in an attempt to appease Sunni concerns, but a manageable solution was never met. On September 6, Bahaa al-Araji, a leading Shi'ite on the committee, announced that the talks had ended and that the constitution would be printed in the form in which it was passed in the National Assembly the week prior.[200] This set the stage for the October 15, 2005, constitutional referendum. Even as the constitution made its way to the UN printer in mid-September, discussion and amendment continued to unfold.

The key issues for Iraqi success in fighting the insurgency are whether large numbers of Sunnis who are now neutral or passively hostile toward the Iraqi Interim Government can be persuaded to join in the political process and whether some form of stable new balance of power can be found that will make

Sunnis accept a political process dominated by the Shi'ites and in which the Kurds and other minorities also play a role proportionate to their size. There cannot be an end to the Sunni insurgency without a political solution that the vast majority of Sunnis at least tolerate and hopefully support.

At the same time, the Iraqi government must show it can actually govern at the local and regional level. The Iraqi military, security, and police forces must reach a level of critical mass where they are large enough to serve the country and large enough to take over most of the burden of maintaining security from the United States. They must be effective enough to show that the new Iraqi government is not only legitimate in terms of politics but in terms of force. Political legitimacy is essential to good government, but no government can govern that lacks the force to ensure the security of its population and deal with insurgent and terrorist threats.

There also will almost certainly be at least another year of intensive fighting against Islamist and extremist elements that will reject inclusion in the political process almost regardless of what political system emerges during the coming elections. There are only three ways to deal with Iraq's most hard-line elements: kill them, imprison them, or drive them out of the country. There is a very real war to fight, and it is still unclear when or if Iraqi forces will really be ready to fight it with anything like the total numbers required.

No one who has dealt with Arab Iraqis can be unaware of the fact that most think of themselves as Iraqis and nationalists and not just as Sunnis and Shi'ites. Insurgency can turn into a broader civil war, however, and the future inclusiveness of the Iraqi government is anything but clear in a climate in which Iraq is just beginning to develop political leaders and parties.

Insurgency and the Effectiveness and Visibility of Iraqi Military, Security, and Police Forces

Finally, much depends on Coalition and Iraqi success in creating effective Iraqi forces that are the visible element of security operations that Sunnis and other Iraqis see on a day-to-day basis. The lack of highly visible Iraqi forces and the fact that U.S. occupiers have both won virtually every past victory and still dominate most security activity have so far tended to sustain the image of a nation where fighting is done by foreigners, non-Muslims, and occupiers.

Many Coalition and Iraqi Interim Government tactical victories have also produced a costly political and military backlash. Even successful military engagements can lead to the creation of as many new insurgents as they kill or capture. The lack of popular support means that many existing insurgents disperse with their weapons or bury their weapons and supplies for later retrieval.

To return to points made earlier, many Iraqis see U.S. and Coalition-dominated military actions as actions by "occupier" forces; they are a source of constant propaganda and fuel conspiracy theories. Real and imagined civilian casualties, collateral damage, and the impact on civilians and shrines that these engagements cause remain a constant problem. All of these points reinforce the need to create larger and more effective Iraqi forces as soon as possible and to give them full force protection and counterinsurgency capability.

At the same time, Iraqis also do not want their own military constantly visible in the streets, or militias and other unofficial forces that often support hardline interpretations of Islam and/or enforce their own selfish interest. Most ordinary Iraqis also see crime as much more of a day-to-day threat than insurgents. As a result, the efforts of the Iraqi government and MNSTC-I to create effective police and security forces in parallel with creating effective military forces are absolutely critical to nation-building, political legitimacy, effective government, and the effort to eventually create a true civil society. This raises serious issues about how the new Iraqi military, security, and police force treat their own population. One of Jalal Talibani's first acts in becoming Iraq's new president in April 2005 was to offer an amnesty to Iraqi Sunni insurgents. This followed up on a more limited offer of insurgent amnesty by then Prime Minister Ayad Allawi in 2004. Such acts of political inclusion are as critical to Iraqi success in defeating the insurgents as the effectiveness of Iraqi forces.[201]

There are indications, however, that some Iraqi forces—including commando units—continue to use far more brutal methods in searching for, interrogating, and dealing with other Iraqis than Coalition forces are permitted to use.[202] These abuses include their treatment of Iraqi detainees. Moreover, there are indications that some Coalition forces encourage Iraqi forces to do this and use them as proxies for actions they are not allowed to take. At a minimum, U.S. and other Coalition forces operating with Iraqi units sometimes stand by and allow such activities to take place.[203] Such actions are particularly divisive when largely Kurdish or Shi'ite units operate in Sunni areas.

U.S. State Department human-rights reporting notes that Iraqi forces must operate in a climate of extraordinary violence and extremism on the part of their opponents and make protecting Iraqi civilians their primary mission. It also, however, sounds an important warning about the Iraqi police, security, and National Guard actions through December 31, 2005:

> With the ongoing insurgency limiting access to information, a number of instances in the Report have been difficult to verify. However, there were reports of arbitrary deprivation of life, torture, impunity, and poor prison conditions— particularly in pretrial detention facilities—and arbitrary arrest and detention. There remained unresolved problems relating to the large number of Internally Displaced Persons (IDPs). Corruption at all levels of the Government remained a problem. Some aspects of the judicial system were dysfunctional, and there were reports that the judiciary was subject to external influence. The exercise of labor rights remained limited, largely due to violence, unemployment, and mal-adapted organizational structures and laws; however, with international assistance, some progress was underway at year's end.

... With the ongoing insurgency, there was a climate of extreme violence in which persons were killed for political and other reasons. There were occasional reports of killings particularly at the local level by the Government or its agents, which may have been politically motivated. In early December, Basra police reported that officers in the Internal Affairs Unit were involved in the killings of 10 members of the Ba'ath Party. Basra police also reported that the same Internal Affairs Unit officers were involved in the killings of a mother and daughter accused of engaging in prostitution. The Basra Chief of Intelligence was removed from his position as a result of the accusations; however, he retained command of the Internal Affairs Unit. An MOI [Ministry of Interior] investigation into the Basra allegations was ongoing at year's end. Other instances reflected arbitrary actions by government agents. For example, on October 16, Baghdad police arrested, interrogated, and killed 12 kidnappers of 3 police officers.

... The TAL expressly prohibits torture in all its forms under all circumstances, as well as cruel, inhuman, or degrading treatment.

According to Human Rights Watch (HRW), during this reporting period, torture and ill treatment of detainees by police was commonplace. In interviews with 90 prisoners conducted from August to October, 72 claimed that they had been tortured or mistreated. The reported abuses included some instances of beatings with cables and hosepipes, electric shocks to their earlobes and genitals, food and water deprivation, and overcrowding in standing room only cells.

Additionally, HRW reported that specialized agencies, including the Major Crimes Unit, Criminal Intelligence, Internal Affairs and possibly the Intelligence Service, were responsible for pretrial irregularities, such as arrest without warrant, lengthy periods of detention before referral to an investigative judge, and the denial of contact with family and legal counsel. Although detainees were primarily criminal suspects, they also included others, such as members of the Mahdi Militia and juveniles, who sometimes were caught in arrest sweeps.

There were instances of illegal treatment of detainees. For example, on November 1, Baghdad police arrested two Coalition Force citizen interpreters on charges involving the illegal use of small arms. After their arrest, police bound the detainees' arms behind them, pulling them upward with a rope and cutting off their circulation. This treatment was followed by beatings over a 48-hour period with a steel cable, in an effort to make the detainees confess. Both interpreters required medical treatment after their release to Coalition Forces. No further information on the incident was available at year's end. In another case, the Commission on Public Integrity (CPI) gathered enough evidence to prosecute police officers in Baghdad who were systematically raping and torturing female detainees. Two of the officers received prison sentences; four others were demoted and reassigned.

There were also allegations that local police sometimes used excessive force against both citizens and foreigners. On November 28, a foreign national reported that police beat him at a police station in Kufa. According to the victim, he witnessed police beating detainees at a police station while he was filing a claim on another matter. When he questioned the treatment of the detainees, he was beaten and detained for 4 hours.

A number of complaints about Iraqi National Guard (ING) abuses surfaced during the year. For example, in November, the ING raided a house in southern Baghdad and arrested four alleged insurgents. The family was evicted, and the ING burnt the house. In another incident, a doctor at the al-Kindi hospital in Baghdad said that the ING had tried to force him to treat one of their colleagues before other more serious cases. When he refused, they beat him. There also were many reported instances of ING looting and burning houses in Fallujah in November.

According to an ING official, disciplinary procedures were in place to deal with the mistreatment of citizens and a number of members of the ING were fired during the year for violations.

There were numerous reports and direct evidence that insurgents employed multiple forms of torture and inhumane treatment against their victims.... Although there was significant improvement in Iraqi Corrections Service (ICS) prison conditions following the fall of the former regime, in many instances the facilities did not meet international penal standards. According to the Government, it generally permitted visits by independent human rights observers. In August, the International Committee of the Red Cross (ICRC) visited ICS facilities. The Ministry of Human Rights established a permanent office at the Abu Ghraib prison. HRW visited some ICS facilities.

After the fall of the former regime, prison functions were consolidated into the Ministry of Justice, and the ICS was transferred from the Ministry of Labor and Social Affairs to the Ministry of Justice. According to the Government, ICS confined civilians under the rule of law, and a valid confinement order from a judge was required. Confinement was not connected with military intelligence operations nor was there any contact with military confinement functions.

... Allegations of inmate abuse by ICS Officers continued, although fewer than in the previous year. The ICS Internal Affairs Division claimed it conducted investigations of all detected or reported cases and that appropriate corrective action was taken if an allegation was verified. Although fewer than 10 cases were investigated between July and December, an individual with access to human rights complaints alleged that hundreds of cases were pending, accusing ICS officers of abuse and torture of detainees and prisoners, including women. No further information was available at year's end.

... At year's end, ICS was investigating eight cases in which inmates alleged police predetention abuse and torture. Overcrowding was a problem. Inmate disturbances and riots reduced available prison beds by approximately one-third, and pretrial detention facilities were often overcrowded. The insurrections in Sadr City and later in Najaf created additional overcrowding in detention facilities.

... Detainees were generally retained in custody pending the outcome of a criminal investigation. Individuals were generally arrested openly and warrants were issued only with sufficient evidence, although, there were numerous reports of arbitrary arrest and detention.

There were no publicized cases of criminal proceedings brought against members of the security forces in connection with alleged violations of these rights, nor were there publicly known measures adopted to prevent recurrence.

Due to the insurgency, high-crime rates, and limited police training, innocent persons were sometimes arrested and detained erroneously.

... The MOI's responsibilities extended only to internal security. MOI commands a number of uniformed forces, including the Iraqi Police Service (IPS) and Department of Border Enforcement. The MOI also has criminal and domestic intelligence capabilities and regulates all domestic and foreign private security companies operating in the country. The MOI also has authority over the Civil Defense Directorate, the firefighters and emergency response organization, and the Facilities Protection Service shielding strategic infrastructure, government buildings, and cultural and educational assets.

... In the aftermath of the fall of the former regime, a police presence temporarily vanished, except in the Kurdish North. Police equipment was stolen. After April 2003, a large recruitment and training program was established, including hiring former police officers.

During the year, various specialized units were created, including an Emergency Response Unit (with capabilities similar to a SWAT team) and Public Order Battalions that perform riot control functions, as well as specialized counterinsurgency units.

More than any other group, the police have been a target of terrorist attacks. Over 1,500 IPS personnel have been killed between April 2003 and year's end. Additionally, pervasive lawlessness has led to an increase in violent and organized crime, particularly related to kidnappings.

... There was a widespread perception that police made false arrests to extort money. Some police officers did not present defendants to magistrates and held them in detention cells until their families paid bribes for their release. In the Central Criminal Court in Baghdad, the time between arrest and arraignment was often in excess of 30 days, despite the 24-hour requirement.

There were organized police abuses. For example, on September 4, approximately 150 police, none of whom had uniforms or badges, surrounded the Iraqi Institute of Peace (IIP), which is associated with the International Center for Reconciliation of the Coventry Cathedral, in response to an alert that a prominent former regime figure might be inside the Cathedral. Four individuals identified themselves as MOI officials but did not show badges. Armed men, some with heavy weapons, broke down the doors and ransacked the IIP building, stealing phones and money. The incident ended with no serious injuries but without judicial follow-up.

On August 16, a ministry, reportedly wishing to occupy the real property used by a political party, caused party members to be arrested and detained for almost 60 days without charges. During their detention, a habeas corpus writ from the Chief Investigative Judge of the Central Criminal Court was ignored. The minister involved also refused to appear before the judge to explain his ministry's actions. The political party members were eventually released; however, the property involved remained under the control of the ministry at year's end.

... Reportedly, coerced confessions and interrogation continued to be the favored method of investigation by police. According to one government official, hundreds of cases were pending at year's end alleging torture. There have been several arrests, and both criminal and administrative punishments were handed out to police in cases where allegations of torture were substantiated.

Additionally, corruption continued to be a problem with the police. The CPI was investigating cases of police abuse involving unlawful arrests, beatings, and the theft of valuables from the homes of persons who were detained; however, the police often continued to use the methods employed by the previous regime. In addition to the CPI, several other mechanisms were put into place to address this problem, including an internal affairs capability, mentoring, and training programs that focus on accountability.

. . . Efforts to increase the capacity and effectiveness of the police were ongoing; however, there was little indication that the IIG took sufficient steps to address this problem adequately or to reinforce publicly the message that there will be no climate of impunity.

Because of arbitrary arrest and detention practices, some prisoners were held in incommunicado detention.

. . . Lengthy pretrial detention continued to be a significant problem due to backlogs in the judiciary and slow processing of criminal investigations. Approximately 3,000 inmates were in pretrial detention, and 1,000 were held post-trial.

. . . Corruption remained a problem in the criminal justice. In the fall, the MOI referred allegations of misconduct involving a judge to the COJ. The allegations concerned professional misconduct, including bribery. At year's end, this case was still pending.[204]

A report by the inspector general of the State Department and the inspector general of the Department of Defense noted the following as of late April 2005: "The International Police Liaison Officers' (IPLOs) daily reports chronicle disturbing accounts of instances in which IPS personnel are not professional in the performance of their duties. There are frequent reports of breakdowns in discipline, feuds among police units, and prisoner abuse. In the absence of viable tracking systems, the IG Team is not able to determine whether or to what degree Coalition-trained police may be perpetrators of such actions. The failure to impose proper discipline rests with IPS leaders (some of whom have been directly, even violently, involved in the unseemly questionable incidents). The examples set by poor leaders for Coalition-trained personnel (mostly new recruits) bode ill."[205]

The Coalition, U.S., and MNSTC–I efforts to give the new Iraqi military, security, and police forces human-rights training and the kind of respect for the rule of law necessary to win hearts and minds are vital to success. The same is true of NATO training efforts and those of other countries.[206] There is no question, however, that such training is not always successful and that Islamist suicide bombings and atrocities sometimes provoke Iraqi forces to extremes.[207] There are also controversial units like the 5,000-man special police commando that are Iraqi recruited and trained. While such units are often highly effective, they have not been models of respect for human rights.[208]

Counterinsurgency and counterterrorist operations are necessarily brutal and violent; war is war. They also, however, are battles for the hearts and minds of both the people where the war is fought and of the enemy. The effectiveness of Iraqi forces is heavily dependent on their winning such support and not mirroring the actions of Saddam Hussein's forces and regime. As similar U.S. errors at the Abu Ghraib prison compound demonstrated all too clearly, excessive force and interrogation methods quickly become counterproductive and self-defeating even if they produce short-term results. The political dimension and impact of military, security, and police operations is not one that either Coalition or Iraqi commanders and forces can afford to ignore, even in the heat of battle. The primary purpose of Iraqi operations is to reforge a nation; not defeat an enemy.

12 Building the Future

THERE IS no easy conclusion to this analysis, and the situation is very much in flux. Iraq is making progress in creating effective forces, and it has strong MNF-I and MNSTC-I support. The Coalition continues to strengthen such efforts, and groups like NATO are making important new contributions. The fact remains, however, that Iraq, the United States, and other members of the Coalition face serious challenges in overcoming the legacy of past neglect and failure.

The steady evolution of the insurgency is a major threat and one that presents a serious challenge to the effort to create effective Iraqi forces. Iraq's political process could fail and lead to intense sectarian conflict between Iraqi Arab Shi'ite and Iraqi Arab Sunni. It faces a serious threat from outside Sunni Islamists and remains divided between Arabs, Kurds, and other minorities. There is a real risk that such tensions and clashes can escalate to a serious civil war.

Political, economic, and social progress present equally important challenges. Iraq is at best "a work in progress," and it is unclear when, if ever, it can meet the five tests of "victory" outlined at the beginning of this analysis:

- Establishing a pluralistic Iraqi government capable of both governing and providing security to the people of Iraq and finding a new balance of political power acceptable to Arab Shi'ites, Arab Sunnis, the Kurds, Turcomans, and other minorities—this means effective governance at the local, regional, and national level.
- Creating effective Iraqi military, security, and police forces capable of bringing security to the entire country, of eventually replacing all Coalition forces, and capable of conducting effective operations while winning the support of the vast majority of the Iraqi people.

- Providing effective aid, debt and reparations relief, and Iraqi economic reform efforts that—coupled with effective security—move the nation onto the path to stable economic development where wealth and economic growth are distributed in ways that meet the needs of all of Iraq's people.
- Developing a new national consensus that legitimizes Iraq's post–Saddam Hussein government and social structure and that can find a "golden mean" between the different goals and expectations of its different ethnic and religious elements.
- Finding a new balance of relationships with Iraq's neighbors that will ensure that they do not threaten Iraq or interfere in its affairs, while making it clear that Iraq no longer poses a threat to any neighboring state.

Defining "Victory" and "Defeat"

This analysis documents positive trends, but also shows that Iraq, the United States and its allies, and the world can "lose" the struggle in Iraq as well as win it. Such a defeat is not *probable*, but it is *possible*. There is no one variable that could produce such a "defeat," and there are no agreed definitions of what "victory" and "defeat" mean. The previous chapters have shown, however, that a "defeat" could take the following forms:

- A war of attrition whose costs and casualties eventually mean that the Bush administration loses the public and congressional support necessary to go on fighting.
- The open failure of U.S. efforts to create effective Iraqi military, security, and police forces and any ability to phase down the U.S. and multinational force presence at an acceptable rate.
- A large-scale Iraqi civil war in which some combination of Arab Sunni versus Arab Shi'ite, Arab versus Kurd, secularist versus theocrat, or a struggle for authoritarian rule make continuing the Coalition presence purposeless or untenable.
- The collapse of effective Iraqi governance because of divisions between Shi'ite, Sunni, and Kurd.
- The creation of a religious state without the pluralism and tolerance critical to a U.S. definition of victory.
- The creation of open or de facto divisions in Iraq that ally the Iraqi Shi'ites with Iran and create the equivalent of a Shi'ite crescent divided from the Sunni part of the Arab and Islamic world.
- The continued failure of U.S. aid and Iraqi economic development to meet the needs and expectations of the people and the destabilizing impact of long-term, large-scale unemployment.
- The failure to meet popular expectations regarding personal security, reductions in crime, and the availability of key services like water and electricity, education, and medical care.

- Demands by an Iraqi government that U.S. forces leave on less-than-friendly terms.
- Domestic U.S. political conditions that lead to the enforcement of some "exit strategy" that makes the United States leave before a stable Iraq can be created.
- The isolation of the United States from its regional and other allies, most remaining members of the Coalition, and the support or tolerance of the United Nations.

The variables in this list are interactive and can combine in a wide range of ways to produce different real-world scenarios for "defeat." Furthermore, the cases on this list are simply the key candidates; there are many more scenarios that might occur.

"Winning" is equally hard to define. Iraq will be unstable for at least the next five to ten years, and what appears to be "victory" could become a "defeat" if later political and economic upheavals create a hostile regime, chaotic country, or state with a theocratic or strong-man regime so far from democracy that it made the current fight futile. The most likely "best case" outcome is now the kind of "victory" that produces an unstable, partially dependent state with a unified and pluralistic regime but one that is scarcely an American client.

In any case, Iraq, the Coalition, and friendly outside states can only succeed if they recognize that the level of progress required to produce any meaningful definition of "success" or "victory" in all of the necessary areas will be a matter of years, if not a decade. No matter how impatient policymakers may be, history still takes time. It is certain that there will be reversals, even if the ultimate result is success.

The Broader Context of Success: A Nation for Iraqis and by Iraqis

Nation-building in Iraq involves a mix of requirements and risks that progresses in each area and is interactive with progress in the others. This has particular importance for an assessment of Iraqi military, security, and police forces. Even the most effective defeat of terrorists, insurgents, and large-scale criminal violence cannot be a substitute for a pluralist government, a new national consensus, economic progress and development, and stable foreign relations. At the same time, no combination of successes in these other areas of progress will be adequate without security. Indeed, security is the precondition for most other forms of success.

No analysis of Iraqi force developments can ignore the fact that there is a long list of political, military, and economic uncertainties beyond the process of Iraqi force development that will shape the outcome of the insurgency and the success of the force building effort. Iraqi internal politics are a major uncertainty, and it is too soon to predict how well Iraqi forces can or cannot supplement and eventually replace Coalition forces. The nation-building aspects of the "war after the war" remain a struggle in progress, and there still is no way to know whether the light at the end of the tunnel is daylight or an oncoming train.

Victory or defeat will ultimately be determined by the Iraqi political process and has become an Iraqi responsibility. Counterterrorism and counterinsurgency require political and economic, as well as military, solutions. At least as much depends on Iraqi capability to build on the foundation provided by outside aid and to create the right kind of political and economic context for military success. Serious problems have emerged from the inability of the Iraqi government to follow-up on U.S. and Iraqi military and security efforts and to establish effective governance at both the central government level and in the field.

Iraqis must work out a form of power sharing that can include Arab Shi'ites, Arab Sunnis, Kurds, Turcomans, and Iraq's smaller minorities. The politics of ethnic and sectarian tension and rivalry cannot be resolved by force in any stable or lasting way. Only the Iraqis can bridge the gaps between Sunni and Shi'ite, Arab and Kurd, and various Shi'ite factions. Only Iraqis can find the proper way of sharing the nation's oil wealth and find the right balance between a secular and religious state.

Economic progress is now slow, unemployment is extremely high, and this affects security as well. Dollars can have as much impact on this kind of struggle as bullets. The reprogramming of U.S. aid to serve military and security interests in 2004 has made a vital start, but it is still unclear whether a broader plan exists to recast the U.S. economic aid effort to achieve the security and stability that is a critical precondition to longer-term aid efforts. As was noted in Chapter 2, the increase in the insurgency raised the security costs of USAID funded aid projects from 4.2 percent of the total cost from March 2003 to February 2004 to 22 percent during the final nine months of 2004, and the total "security surcharge" reached 50 percent in some areas by April 2005.[1]

Iraqi Sovereignty Means Iraqi Responsibility

Much of the burden of success will and must fall on the new Iraqi government. Many key challenges are already clearly the province of Iraqis and the new Iraqi government. It is the Iraqis who must now come to grips with the following broad challenges in nation-building:

- Deal with the transition to yet another new government between late 2005 and mid-2006, possibly with new sets of ministers of defense and interior and different political leadership and goals.
- Adapt to any new laws, mandates, federalism, and sharing of national revenues growing out of the creation of a new constitution.
- Cope with ethnic and religious tensions.
- Find ways to integrate militia elements into the regular forces/police forces and have the rest go back to civilian life; implement the now largely abandoned CPA plan.
- Find some way to get stable and predictable budgets and levels of aid; negotiate at least a predictable level of medium-term aid.
- Create fully effective ministries, limit corruption, and purge low-quality and passive leaders, officials, and officers.

Iraqi Responsibility for Taking Over the Security Mission

Outside powers can only do so much. Iraqi ability to create an inclusive political structure, find an Iraqi solution to pluralism and "federalism," and establish effective governance is now up to the Iraqis. The most the United States, other nations, the United Nations, and the international community can do is to provide aid and advice. At the same time, the ability of Iraqi forces to replace U.S. and other Coalition forces will be an increasing test of the perceived legitimacy of the Iraqi government.

Elections may be a noble luxury, but day-to-day security and governance are essential to survival. Accordingly, the ability and willingness of Iraqi forces to increasingly stand on their own in meeting these latter challenges is a *sine qua non* for success in nation-building.

Iraqis must take over responsibility for meeting the following challenges in the security dimension:

- Cope with aggressive insurgent and extremist attacks and efforts to split Arab Sunnis, Arab Shi'ites, Kurds, and other minorities.
- Implement a force development plan for the armed forces and manage the integration of the army and National Guard.
- Create effective intelligence, counterintelligence, and C^4I (command, control, communications, computers, and intelligence) capabilities.
- Develop and implement plans to acquire more adequate equipment, force protection, and facilities.
- Begin a systematic transition to forces that can operate without MNSTC-I support.
- Redeploy Iraqi forces to meet Iraqi, rather than MNF–I, needs.
- Restructure, train/retrain, and purge the police forces to make them both effective crime fighters and an aid in counterinsurgency and counterterrorism.

According to MNSTC-I, Iraqis have begun to do so. A report by an MNSTC–I expert states, "At least since the Iraqi government assumed sovereignty late last June, they have exercised as much influence in the decision to use Iraqi forces in the counterinsurgency as has been exercised by Coalition leaders. This is not an attempt to shift any "blame" to the Iraqis; it is simply an attempt to say that both Iraqi and Coalition forces have been involved in making tough decisions."[2]

It is also clear, however, that Iraq has at best only made a beginning. While the Iraqi performance in operations since Operation Lightning has been increasingly reassuring, it will be well into 2006 and probably well into 2007 before Iraq has all of the security capabilities it needs in these areas and their effectiveness will depend upon the success and inclusiveness of Iraqi politics.

On September 6, 2005, the U.S. military pulled hundreds of troops out of the southern city of Najaf, transferring control to the Iraqi military. The city was the site of clashes between U.S. forces and Moqtada al-Sadr's Shi'ite Mehdi Army in August 2004. And in August 2005, tensions surged again when clashes erupted between Sadr's men and Iraqi Interior Ministry forces seen as loyal to a rival Shi'ite bloc, the Supreme Council for the Islamic Revolution in Iraq. Nineteen died in those battles. The Iraqi force replacing the departing U.S. troops is composed primarily of Shi'ite Muslims.[3]

On September 15, 2005, Mowaffak al-Rubaie, who chairs the committee responsible for security transfers to Iraqi forces, said that Iraqi troops were soon expected to take control of Karbala, Samawa, and Nasiriyah as well. He further suggested that the gradual process of handing over such urban areas to Iraqi control would allow for U.S. troops to begin exiting the country.[4]

Creating Effective Iraqi Military, Security, and Police Forces

Even if Iraq can deal with all of its other problems, there is no promise that efforts to create effective Iraqi forces will succeed. Serious problems remain in every aspect of the Iraqi force development program, and the effort to create effective Iraqi forces may well fail—particularly if Iraq's Sunnis cannot be integrated successfully into its government, economy, and forces; if major friction takes place between Shi'ite and Kurd; or if the Shi'ites should divide and armed factions like Sadr's militia again become active. Yet, the more one considers the history of the efforts to create effective Iraqi military, security, and police forces described in this report, the more it is clear that by pursuing the right program consistently and with the right resources the Coalition can still succeed in solving the security aspects of the nation-building problem in Iraq.

The previous analysis shows that the United States has corrected many aspects of its initial mistakes. The key questions from a policy viewpoint are now whether the United States and its allies are moving quickly enough to create forces that can provide real security and deal with the insurgency problem in time to meet the needs and expectations of the Iraqi people. No one can argue that Iraqi forces will be ready to deal with every aspect of the current threat posed by insurgency and terrorism in the near future.

Iraqi forces will remain a fraction of what is needed through at least mid-2005 and probably deep into 2006. Many critical elements of Iraqi Army, security forces, and police development may not be complete by the end of 2007—and this assumes a high degree of continuity and consistency in Iraqi force development efforts, and a move toward united national forces, rather than ethnic and sectarian divisions. Iraqi forces will not have airpower, significant armor, or modern intelligence, surveillance, and reconnaissance (IS&R) support for years to come. Creating Iraqi forces that can be fully effective in both dealing with continued insurgency and terrorism and capable of defending Iraq against any active threat from its neighbors will not be a matter of sudden "tipping points," it will be a process involving "tipping years."

All of these points reinforce the need to create larger, more effective, and "National" Iraqi forces that mix ethnic and sectarian manpower as soon as possible, and to give them full force protection and counterinsurgency capability. Yet, there will be serious trade-offs in Iraqi force quality if the training, force building, and equipment effort is rushed. The end result could be a failed force.

Both the Coalition and Iraqis must continue to find ways to work together to find the fastest pace at which new Iraqi forces can be developed without losing their effectiveness in the process. At the same time, the United States and its allies must work out longer-term plans and force goals with the new Iraqi government to scale up a larger training and equipment program that can both give Iraq the forces it needs to stand alone as a truly sovereign nation and also be affordable and self-financed in future years.

The Future Role of the United States and Coalition—and of U.S. and Coalition Forces

Allied support for a long Coalition presence has never been strong, and U.S. popular support and congressional support is waning. According to a poll conducted by *Newsweek* in early August 2005, only 26 percent of Americans said they supported keeping large numbers of U.S. military personnel in Iraq for as long as it takes to achieve U.S. goals there; 38 percent said they would support keeping troops there less than a year; 13 percent said one to two years; and 12 percent said that troops should be brought home now.[5] This type of political pressure at home forced the issue of troop withdrawal to the fore.

Any U.S. plans for troop reductions are, however, anything but concrete. In a classified briefing to senior Pentagon officials in July, top American Middle East Commander General John Abizaid outlined a plan that would gradually reduce American forces in Iraq by perhaps 20,000 to 30,000 troops by spring 2006. However, General Abizaid also warned that it is possible the Pentagon might have to keep the current levels of about 138,000 American soldiers in Iraq throughout 2006, if security and political trends are unfavorable for a withdrawal.

Plans called for an increase of U.S. troop presence to 160,000, up from 138,000, during the period before the December 15, 2005, elections. This would be a temporary measure to secure the elections. That number would gradually decline back down to 138,000 troops initially, and then by another 20,000 or 30,000 troops by late spring of 2006, according to senior Pentagon officials.[6] However, no set timetable for withdrawal had yet been established.[7]

On August 20, 2005, U.S. Army Chief of Staff Peter Schoomaker indicated that the United States may have to keep over 100,000 troops in Iraq into 2009. On September 12, 2005, Iraqi President Jalal Talabani said that the United States could withdraw 40,000 to 50,000 troops by the end of the year, declaring there were enough Iraqi forces trained and ready to begin assuming control in cities throughout the country. Talabani said the number of "well-trained" Iraqi security forces stood at 60,000 and would reach 100,000 by the end of the year. All told, there are about 190,000 Iraqis enlisted in the military or local security forces.[8]

Meanwhile, the air mission in Iraq has become a study in contrast between the heft of U.S. support and the meager reality of Iraqi air capabilities. In September 2005, Iraq's Air Force consisted of thirty-eight aircraft, including three C-130E transports, sixteen UH-1 Huey helicopters, and two Australian SB7L-360 Seeker propeller aircraft. At this time, the U.S. Air Force was doing all of the reconnaissance, all of the close air and light attack support, and is using its C-17 and C-130s to transport Iraqi troops. CENTCOM Tactical Air Commander Lieutenant General Walter Buchanan—who commands about 330 air force, navy, and Coalition aircraft in the Persian Gulf—predicted in September that the United States could continue to fly missions against insurgents in Iraq for another five years. His inside estimate for a viable Iraqi Air Force was three years, with the caveat that five was more likely. The air force has more than 205 aircraft in the region, including more than thirty-five F-16 fighters, more than twenty B-52 bombers and A-10 Warthog ground attack craft, over thirty-five reconnaissance and intelligence craft, and over fifty-five transports. The navy supplies an additional 127 aircraft.[9]

Whatever the United States and its allies do, they must not ignore that, although Iraq must take over responsibility for Iraq, that fact in no way means that the United States and its allies are free of future responsibility to Iraq and to the Iraqi people. This is particularly true of the United States. Regardless of how well the United States can maintain the Coalition or broaden the international effort to support Iraq through the United Nations and measures like contact groups, the U.S.-led invasion has left it with a deep moral and ethical responsibility, and it still has much to do.

Iraqi success will depend on U.S. and Coalition willingness to provide sustained military support and a broad-based aid program for at least several more years. The United States also cannot plan now for withdrawal or some fixed ceiling to its military effort. There may be periods like the elections scheduled for the end of 2005 when new surges of U.S. and other Coalition troops are necessary.

The fact that Iraq must take over responsibility for Iraq in no way means that the United States and its allies are free of future responsibility to Iraq and to the Iraqi people. This is particularly true of the United States. Regardless of how well the United States can maintain the Coalition or broaden the international effort to support Iraq through the United Nations and measures like contact groups, the U.S.-led invasion has left it with a deep moral and ethical responsibility, and it still has much to do.

Iraqi success will depend on United States and Coalition willingness to provide sustained military support and a broad-based aid program for at least several more years. The United States also cannot plan now for withdrawal or some fixed ceiling to its military effort. There may be periods like the elections scheduled for the end of 2005 when new surges of U.S. and other Coalition troops are necessary.

Foreign Troops and Iraqi Legitimacy

The answer cannot be adding more U.S. and other Coalition troops as a substitute for effective Iraqi forces. Temporary surges and reinforcements to U.S. and British forces may be necessary, but they are at best a short-term expedient and one that inevitably will have political costs that offset their military impact.

There are no clear sources of significant forces from other countries. It would take very large forces to make a difference, and foreign countries will be reluctant to deploy troops to remote areas. Moreover, small, isolated deployments would rapidly become targets, while staying in large bases would be pointless. As various Coalition partners end their role in Iraq, some say they will be willing to turn their forces from combat to training. It may be realistic to preserve some contributions that are now planned to decline, but it is unrealistic to assume that any such forces would not go to "hot spots" like the border.

The nature of both the insurgency in Iraq and Iraqi politics make it all too clear that only Iraqi forces can minimize the anger and resentment at U.S. forces, give the emerging Iraqi government legitimacy, and support efforts to make that government and the Iraqi political system more inclusive. Even the segments of Iraqi society that tolerate Coalition forces as a necessity today want them out as quickly as is practical.

Even the best possible new elections, restructuring of the government, and efforts to create a constitution cannot by themselves make the new Iraqi government legitimate in Iraqi eyes unless that government provides security with Iraqi forces. Iraqis need to be seen as steadily taking over the security role by their countrymen, the region, and the world. Poll after poll has shown that Iraqis see physical security as one of the most important single issues in their lives, generally followed by economic and educational security. The same polls show that they want Coalition forces to leave as soon as possible—and often long before Iraqi forces can be ready.

The visible presence of U.S. and Coalition forces must decrease over time— not increase—and any sustained deployment of thousands of additional U.S. or other foreign troops can only make the Iraqi government less legitimate. At the same time, no amount of improvement in U.S. intelligence and area expertise can substitute for effective Iraqi support. As one U.S. major general noted in March 2005, "The real things that are so absolutely critical in the fight we're in today on the streets of Baghdad is an understanding of the city, an understanding of the culture, and the ability to speak the language, and Iraqi forces bring that to the street."[10]

General George Casey, the top U.S. commander in Iraq, spoke to this point in late January 2005. He stated: "Can I sit here and look you in the eye and say that the Iraqi security forces, guaranteed 100 percent, are going to be able to defeat this insurgency themselves? Of course not.... [But] we cannot stay here forever in the numbers that we are here now; I firmly believe that. The Iraqis have to take ownership of this."[11] The presence of more U.S. and other

Coalition military personnel in Iraq without the consummate area skills, experience, specialized abilities, and the ability to provide effective training can only be counterproductive. The more untrained and inexperienced forces on the street or in contact with Iraqis, the greater the hostility of the Iraqi people and the greater the likelihood of a tactical error that inflames the populace.

The Broader Question of American "Overstretch"

It is also important to note that the United States is exhausting its ability to create, rotate, and retain the skilled forces that actually help in combat and specialized missions. The United States will soon have rotated 1 million men and women through Iraq—including those rotated more than once.

This does not mean there is not a medium- to long-term case for a larger worldwide pool of U.S. forces. This would ease the strain of rotations and combat duties on the existing number of actives and reservists. A strong case can already be made for the ongoing efforts to reorganize the U.S. Army to create more combat units available for rapid deployment and for reorganizing all U.S. forces in terms of training and structure to support asymmetric warfare, armed nation-building, and stability operations.

Major increases in end-strength, however, take years to pay off before they can provide the kind of forces needed in Iraq, and one cannot in any way get around the fact that Americans are seen as occupiers more than as allies and that Iraqis will become increasingly hostile until Iraqi forces largely replace at least the visible day-to-day presence of U.S. security forces and can take the lead in combat operations.

NATO, UN, and Regional Forces Are at Best a Temporary Expedient

The search to broaden international support for Iraqi nation-building is important both to meet Iraq's needs and establish the legitimacy of Iraq's new government. It is not a way to achieve a successful "exit strategy" for either Iraq or the United States. It is all too easy to try to shift the burden of creating effective Iraqi forces and creating security in Iraq to other nations or to international organizations.

It is certainly desirable to seek such aid to supplement the role that the United States and other MNSTC–I states must play and to "internationalize" the nation-building effort in Iraq at the political and economic level. The fact that more U.S. forces are not a substitute for Iraqi forces, however, does not mean that the United States can find substitutes for the U.S. forces that Iraq still needs.

The Role of NATO and European States

The effort to create effective Iraqi forces is one that the United States can only delegate in limited ways. NATO can play a significant role in some critical aspects of training and has already begun to do so. There is no practical chance, however, of significant numbers of additional European or NATO combat forces being added to the equation despite French concerns that the presence of NATO military trainers would open the door to combat troops.

The U.S. Department of Defense announced on September 22, 2004, that NATO would provide further training to Iraqi security forces at the request of the Iraqi Interim Government. The training began with the creation of a permanent training center at Ar Rustamayiah to train mid-level and senior security personnel. NATO "dual-hatted" U.S. Lieutenant General David Petraeus to lead this effort, as well as the MNSTC–I, and there has since been real progress.

NATO began its first eight-week training program for Iraqi security personnel on October 2, 2004. The course took place at the Joint Warfare Center in Norway and currently involves the training of nineteen mid- and upper-level Iraqi officials from the military, Ministry of Defense, and Ministry of Interior.

On October 4, 2004, General James Jones, NATO's top commander, announced that up to 3,000 NATO troops could be involved in the training of the Iraqi security forces. The trainers, however, were unlikely to arrive prior to the Iraqi elections. Five days later, NATO committed to sending 300 trainers but not until the end of the year. This agreement was formalized on December 9, 2004, with Poland, Hungary, and the Netherlands agreeing to send military trainers. France, Belgium, Greece, Spain, and Luxembourg refused to send any trainers to Iraq. This 300-man team will slowly create academies in Baghdad and Zahko near Turkey. This effort should strengthen the inchoate staff and war colleges. Staff college instructors were scheduled to begin training in late April 2005.

On February 22, 2005, each NATO member country pledged to contribute to the training effort. At this point sixteen NATO countries had troops on the ground in Iraq and almost all of them had senior officers involved at the NATO training mission in Baghdad. France agreed to provide money for one of the trust funds being established for the Iraqi military and security forces. The NATO Joint Warfare Center in Stavanger, Norway, also had begun to train Iraqi leaders, and the second course began in March 2005.[12]

Overall, NATO announced its intention to train 1,000 Iraqi officers by the end of 2005. NATO also renewed its pledge to open a military training academy at Ar Rustamayiah on the outskirts of Baghdad. NATO indicated that it would continue its training efforts in Norway and at the NATO defense college outside of Rome. NATO seemed responsive to a call earlier in February for more trainers and more funds, particularly for the creation of the Training, Education, and Doctrine Center by Lieutenant General Petraeus.

Germany, France, Belgium, Spain, and Greece continued to refuse to train Iraqi soldiers in Iraq but agreed to do so elsewhere. Belgium already trains Iraqis at a facility in the United Arab Emirates while France agreed to train troops in France. Lieutenant General Petraeus indicated in early February 2005 that NATO equipment contributions had been significant and were important to the continuing effort. NATO delivered some 9,000 weapons in time for the January 30 elections. Hungary agreed to donate seventy-seven T-72 tanks to the Iraqi military, although the details concerning shipment, who would pay for the shipment, and the date of delivery all remained unclear.[13] Such donations often create the problem that countries willing to donate equipment will not provide support or sustainment and that donations of different types of equipment force the creation of separate maintenance and support cycles.

NATO's most serious contribution, however, may be the creation of Iraqi staff colleges and advanced training efforts for Iraqi officers in Iraq. MNSTC–I described these contributions by NATO as follows in mid-2005:

> Although currently composed of only 116 personnel, the NATO Training Mission–Iraq (NTM–I) provides significant contributions to the mission of training and equipping the Iraqi armed forces. Perhaps because so many of its personnel are senior officers, their contribution is far beyond that expected from such a small organization. One of its most valuable is helping with development of the institutional capacity—the professional military education underpinnings—of the Iraqi armed forces. Both junior and senior staff college classes will start this fall in Ar Rustimiyah because of NTM–I leadership.
>
> Iraqi officers manning the national, military, and MOI [Ministry of Interior] operations centers have received the benefit of NATO-provided information technology education, other training, and mentorship in actual operations. In the longer term NTM–I will start war college classes next year, will probably take over assistance at the military academy and will eventually produce something roughly equivalent to U.S. TRADOC [U.S. Army Training and Doctrine Command]. Another important line of operation for NTM–I is coordination of foreign equipment donations and out-of-country training offers, a task that is of great consequence to the overall training and equipping effort.[14]

NATO is now in the process of creating a full National Defense College, and such an effort will be critical to creating the kind of modern military elite Iraq will need in the future.

There are also limits to the amount of training Iraqis require outside Iraq. As of August 2005, Iraq had at least ten major training facilities, the better part of a training brigade, special-skill training elements/schools, and countless ranges, shooting houses, and other training facilities—and it prefers to train its troops at home, as it's cheaper, done by Iraqis, and avoids expensive/dangerous movements. There already were typically well over 3,200 Iraqis out of country in training at any given time. Iraqis are taking advantage of training offers that are fully funded and provide the training they really want and can't do for themselves yet (such as the German training of Iraqi engineer unit cadre and trainers, who now train Iraqis at Tadji in the United Arab Emirates). They have other individuals all over the world in short and long courses. But the movement of large elements is costly, difficult, and time-consuming for the Iraqis.

Limited additional increases might be possible, but the results might outweigh any benefits in terms of problems in interoperability and men simply seeking good foreign assignments. Any apparent cost savings would probably be mythical in the case of Egypt or Jordan; they would end up being paid for by other aspects of U.S. foreign aid.

The United Nations and International Community

The world would be a better place if commentators and analysts stopped talking in vague terms about the "international community." In practice, the real-world "international community" that can participate in nation-building consists of a relatively small number of organizations and NGOs with limited and overcommitted resources. Calling for the "international community" to substitute for U.S. action or the action of any other country is meaningless unless that call can be tied to the identification of specific organizations and specific resources that can credibly be allocated to a given task or mission.

In the case of Iraqi security, the United Nations has no military forces and is unable to recruit new forces at a scale that could begin to replace U.S. and British forces. The United Nations as a whole lacks the support needed for such a mission, and it has no readiness to become involved in a counterinsurgency campaign. Moreover, Iraqis do not want to replace one set of "occupiers" with another.

The United Nations could, however, perform missions that do not fall within the core competencies of Coalition military forces, like delivering humanitarian aid. These could include missions affecting aspects of civilian life varying from providing electricity and water to basic education. Incorporating the United Nations in humanitarian settlement and assistance would also minimize the friction between Iraqi citizens who require the provision of basic services and Coalition forces who lack the expertise, time, and resources to create and maintain them. The United Nations and international organizations did play an important role from May to August 2003 when significant humanitarian activity by international organizations in Iraq took place.

The key problem is security. Insurgents have already driven the United Nations and most NGOs out of Iraq once. Other recent experiences in international operations indicate that the vulnerability of UN workers to attacks is an obstacle that will have to be resolved if the United Nations and NGOs are to function in environments where there is a significant terrorist threat or any faction that feels it can gain from attacking such "easy" targets.

The question is whether any "blue helmet" approach to security is practical and/or whether the U.S. military structure can be made more interoperable with nonmilitary international actors in conflict zones. The contributions of international organizations to postconflict settlements should not be abandoned in Iraq or any other troubled region. Their experience and efficiency in humanitarian aid make them a significant asset that should be seen as a supplement to military operations and not as an additional weight on them.

General John M. Shalikashvili, the former chairman of the U.S. Joint Chiefs of Staff, recognized the need for good cooperation as he said, "What's the relationship between a just-arrived military force and the NGO and PVO [private voluntary organization] that might have been working in a crisis-torn area all along? What we have is a partnership. If you are successful, they are successful; and if they are successful, you are successful. We need each other."

The Unified Task Force (UNITAF) in Somalia, the Civil Military Operations Centre for Rwanda, and NATO-led Implementation Force (IFOR–Operation Joint Endeavour) also provide examples of constructive cooperation between international armed forces and the United Nations. The most relevant and recent case for such cooperation is the joint effort under the International Security Assistance Force (ISAF). ISAF witnessed substantial collaboration between the United Nations and military forces, both at strategic and operational levels.

Clearly there are differences between these UN-mandated military operations and the U.S.-led Coalition operations in Iraq. However, if the goal is to maximize the utility of military forces and achieve the highest level of consequence management and humanitarian assistance, then the U.S. military should develop ways to integrate interoperability with international aid organizations into military strategy. Efforts such as NGO- and military-sponsored seminars and military training exercises such as Prairie Warrior at the Command and General Staff College and Purple Hope at the Joint Forces Staff College should be expanded in number and content. More joint training is essential for improved mutual understanding between these two entities to increase effectiveness of complex military interventions.

The Potential Role of Regional Forces

Neighboring countries are not a solution. They cannot provide the necessary combat-ready forces in a sustainable form. The presence of neighboring countries' troops would present serious internal political liabilities. Troops from Iran could inflame the Shi'ite issue, Saudi Arabia is dealing with its own bout of insurgents, Syria would present Sunni and Ba'ath Party conflicts, Turkey would be problematic due to the Kurdish question, and Jordan is already doing what it can without openly supporting the United States and inviting internal turmoil given the Israeli-Palestinian conflict.

Even if the Iraqi political repercussions were less severe, other Arab and Islamic forces cannot deploy with the necessary speed and also lack the ability to sustain their forces in the field. Once more, such efforts would inevitably be seen as efforts to bail the United States out of a war that had no public supporters. The domestic outcry within these countries would be intense, to say the least.

Ongoing Changes in U.S. Force Development Strategy

Any effort to address the future changes that need to be made in the U.S. effort to create effective Iraqi forces must take account of the progress MNSTC–I has already made and the ongoing changes the United States is already considering. For all its initial mistakes, the U.S.-led effort has steadily improved and adapted, and further improvements seem to be under way.

One of these changes is the growing emphasis on creating effective Iraqi forces, rather than direct Coalition defeat of the insurgents, touched upon in previous chapters. MNSTC–I envisions that the Iraqi security forces will gradually be weaned off direct U.S. support. According to MNSTC–I, "Through Coalition mentorship and assistance, the ISF eventually get to the point where they only need *support* from Coalition forces, then to the point where they can conduct operations *independent* of Coalition forces. MNF–I's training and readiness system will measure just where ISF units fall on that readiness spectrum."[15] Another change is the understanding that no training program, no matter how good, can make up for a lack of experienced leaders and proven units and combat teams. Training, equipment, and facilities are vital; they also are not enough.

Seeking Success Rather Than an "Exit Strategy"—Changing the Main Mission of U.S. Forces

It can be dangerous to talk of "exit strategies." The term "exit strategy" has become a synonym for finding some reason for withdrawal, rather than a strategy for some form of victory. Far too often, it is tied to calendar deadlines that have nothing to do with whether the time is right for withdrawal and to a political effort to disguise defeat. At this writing the conditions in Iraq not only do not justify such an approach, it would be a betrayal of Iraqis who still have the chance to create the conditions for a far better Iraq than existed under Saddam Hussein.

It is clear, however, that the United States has changed its strategy to focus on creating effective Iraqi forces as both a key to some form of "victory" and to eventually reducing the U.S. and Coalition presence in Iraq as Iraqi forces take over the security mission. Lieutenant General John R. Vines, the commander of the Eighteenth Airborne Corps, made this point shortly after he assumed command of U.S. ground forces in Iraq in February 2005. In an interview Vines asserted that the main mission for the U.S. military following the January 30 elections is to train Iraqi military and security forces. To this end Vines suggested that up to 10,000 U.S. military advisers could be assigned to Iraqi military and police units.[16] It is important to note that the number of advisers suggested by Vines is higher than what was previously reported.[17]

The commander of U.S. forces in northern Iraq, Brigadier General Carter Ham, stated that, "The shifting of emphasis to developing Iraqi security forces as the first priority seems right. Shifting primary responsibility for conduct of counter-insurgency operations to Iraqi forces is necessary and proper."[18] It has since become all too clear, however, that no valid timetable can be established for reductions in Coalition forces until Iraqi forces are available in much larger numbers and the trends in their performance is clear. In fact, reports of such timetables have led to a wide range of contradictory reports and to more specula-tion than insight.

For example, U.S. Defense Secretary Donald Rumsfeld noted in March 2005 that the U.S. presence in Iraq was dropping from a peak of 152,000 at the time of the election to around 135,000, and Iraqi forces were expected to rise from 145,000 to around 200,000 by the end of 2005—although he was careful to note that U.S. forces might have to build up to over 150,000 again to secure Iraq's next election, which was then scheduled for December 2005.[19]

U.S. officers gave lower numbers in April 2005, stating that U.S. strength might drop from elements of seventeen brigades and 142,000 personnel that month to thirteen brigades and 105,000 personnel by early 2006.[20] At the same time, *Jane's Defense Weekly* reported that the United States had adopted a three-phase strategy developed by General George Casey, the commander of MNF–I, to pave the way for major drawdowns in U.S. force by the end of 2005. While many of the details and deadlines in the *Jane's Defense Weekly* article are as suspect as most media reporting on such plans, the broad outlines of the article are still of interest:[21]

- Phase one, which was said to have begun on April 15, 2005, and which was to be completed by August, was said to focus on manning, training, and equipping individual Iraqi Army units at the individual and platoon levels to create Iraqi units capable of operating as independent platoons with minimal U.S. supervision and transitioning to having the Ministry of Defense pay Iraqi troops.
- Phase two was to partner each Iraqi Army battalion with two company-sized U.S. Army units to give Iraqi Army battalions the capability to operate independently at the battalion level by October 2005.
- Phase three involved having Iraqi Army battalions certified by their part-nered U.S. advisers as being capable of battalion-sized operations and being assigned specific battle spaces occupied by U.S. units. U.S. company-sized units were to provide a quick response force through December 2005. Each battalion was to have a U.S. military transition team of roughly sixty men with a major or senior captain and experienced NCOs to help prepare the Iraqi unit.

New reports about such plans also emerged during the summer of 2005. In early July 2005, a British newspaper printed a classified British government study signed by Defense Secretary John Reid on the feasibility of drawing down British troop strength from 8,500 to 3,000 by the middle of 2006. The memo stated that the British perceived that the U.S. military was hoping that they could reduce their troop presence and hand over security responsibilities for fourteen of the eighteen provinces to the Iraqis by early 2006.[22]

President Bush continued to reiterate that the United States had a "success strategy" and not an "exit strategy," would not set a timetable for withdrawal, and that U.S. soldiers would "stand down as Iraqi soldiers stood up."

On July 27, 2005, General Casey stated, "I do believe that if the political process continues to go positively and if the development of the security forces continues to go as it is going, we'll still be able to take some very substantial reductions in the spring and summer of next year." Casey also said that while car bomb attacks had reached a peak of 143 in May, they had since declined. Casey also said that "the level of attacks they've been able to generate has not increased substantially here over what we've seen in the last year.... This insurgency is not progressing ... what you are seeing is a change in tactics to more violent, more visible attacks against civilians, and that is a no-win strategy for the insurgency."[23]

That same day Iraqi Prime Minister Ibrahim al-Jafari said that the departure of U.S. forces should take place as quickly as possible, but that while "we desire speed," this should depend on how quickly Iraq could train, equip, and field its own soldiers and police to take over security duties. "We do not want to be surprised," he added. It is important to note that such statements do not attempt to set deadlines or specify the rate and level of Coalition withdrawal. This reflects the reality that any such "plans" should depend on how quickly Iraqi forces become effective and how quickly the insurgency fades. U.S. officers in the field also tend to be less optimistic about such deadlines than politicians and reports in the media and cite problems in the Iraqi police training effort and delays in deploying Iraqi forces into combat, which they feel are likely to lead to delays in any such transition.[24]

Regardless of the form it takes, the transition will not be easy. In addition to Iraqi politics and military success, much depends on the future quality of the advisers the Coalition embeds in Iraqi troops, security, and police units—the latter of which still had shortages of advisers in mid-2005. There is a need for better language and area skills, and providing advisers with the proper training and combat background has proved to be a serious problem. It is unclear how many advisers will come from forces not yet deployed in Iraq. Some of the estimated 10,000 soldiers could be part of an increase in U.S. personnel levels, although a substantial part of U.S. forces in Iraq could be shifted to take on the training and support role within U.S. forces.[25]

The Search for "Critical Mass"

One key uncertainty is when Iraqi forces will achieve "critical mass" in terms of their ability to take over key missions and replace MNF-I forces. As of early 2005, the Iraqis took part in about 1,200 patrols a week with U.S. forces, while U.S.-led Coalition forces lead 12,000 patrols a week.[26] These figures are changing because the U.S. Department of Defense wants the Iraqis to assume the bulk of those patrols as quickly as possible, but Iraqi forces continue to have major problems with leadership, desertions, and effectiveness.

Lieutenant General Petraeus gave the following assessment of Iraqi forces in early May 2005:

> With hindsight, we apparently reached the "critical mass" point (i.e., the point at which the combination of rebuilt infrastructure—especially for training

and bases, equipment, Iraqi trainers, Iraqi leaders, and life support, etc., all supported generation/training of forces at multiple locations simultaneously) in late January, it appears, and the chain reaction since then has been substantial.

As an example, three divisions that were struggling in terms of strength back in November due to casualties, intimidation, etc., are now at 88 percent, 102 percent, and 102 percent respectively, with the former headed to 100 percent in the next couple of weeks (based on recruits/former soldiers already completing training) and the latter two headed to 110 percent in the week ahead (based on former soldiers/recruits that have already completed training). And the one at 88 percent would be over 100 percent had the authorization not changed (from three line companies per battalion to four).

There is still a huge amount of work to be done and daily drama in a host of areas, but the ISF is hanging tough and steadily getting stronger. Have scrubbed numbers hard by the way, taking some 8,000 out of the police trained/ equipped numbers (in provinces hit hardest during tough times in October– January) over the past four months (since we ID'd to the GAO [General Account- ability Office] the challenges in personnel accountability with regular police), and still the numbers of MOI [Ministry of Interior] trained/equipped have grown steadily.[27]

It may well be mid-2006 at the earliest, however, before it is really clear whether Iraqi forces can reach the level of "critical mass" where they become effective enough to take over virtually all of the missions in dealing with the insurgency. Serious problems may remain in the quality of the police force and our depen- dence on largely Shi'ite or Kurdish units, and in the existence of independent militias and local forces. Much will depend on the economic and political situation and the speed at which Iraqi forces are given the armor, airpower, firepower, and sustainability to operate without American support.

Maintaining an Emphasis on Force Quality

The Coalition must continue to focus on the quality of the Iraqi troops as opposed to just the pure numbers of Iraqi troops in uniform. While it is im- portant for the Iraqi forces to continue to grow in size, the soldiers must be able and willing to effectively stand and fight. U.S. Secretary of Defense Donald Rumsfeld highlighted this focus in his testimony before the Senate Armed Ser- vice Committee on February 17, 2005. He stated, "Beyond numbers, it seems to me the capability is what really is important. And capability is a function . . . partly of numbers, to be sure, but it's also of training, equipment, leadership, mobility, sustainability, access to intelligence, experience."[28]

The Coalition has given more priority to developing new ways to better determine the capabilities of the Iraqi units in development, and initial efforts have now been implemented. Lieutenant General Petraeus made this point in an interview in February 2005. He said, "We are going to have to move to a way where we can start tracking the capability."[29] Far more needs to be done, however, and suggestions like developing the equivalent of the U.S. Mission

Essential Tasks Lists (METLs)—a common measurement used in the United States to judge performance and identify key tasks for training—had not been implemented as of June 2005.

Keeping the Police Effort in Balance

As the previous chapters have shown, the Coalition and Iraqi government must give a high priority to the development of both military forces and effective security and police forces. It is tempting to focus on the insurgents, but the present effort is the correct one. Effective police and security forces are critical to day-to-day security against both insurgents and criminals and to giving the Iraqi government the public face of legitimacy—something that extended deployments of Iraqi military forces simply cannot accomplish. The MNSTC–I advisory effort has also been limited in this area. As of May 2005, MNSTC–I J-5 (future plans) had a staff of fifteen but only one person detailed to work with the police force.[30] Many elements of the Iraqi police also needed more expert civilian advisers and civilian agencies like the Department of Homeland Security, which often gave such efforts low priority and left key training elements undermanned.

It is hardly surprising, therefore, that senior officers like General John Abizaid warned during a speech in Washington on May 18, 2005, that Iraqi police units were not cohesive enough to mount an effective challenge to insurgents, which would allow American forces to begin phasing out of the fighting. Abizaid warned that the Iraqi forces had fallen "behind" in developing the capability to shoulder a major role in combat, and he blamed a tendency among Iraqi police to operate as individuals rather than in cohesive units as both a major part of the problem and as a factor making them more vulnerable to intimidation. He said, "The police and the Ministry of the Interior ... are ... behind in terms of sophistication, chain of command, cohesion of leadership. ... It delays the Ministry of Defense forces going out and doing the internal security mission and that keeps American embedded trainers and embedded transition teams in the field longer."[31]

These problems can easily become much more severe in late 2005, and during 2006, as Iraq struggles to decide on a constitution, elect yet another new government, and then actually try to govern in the face of sectarian and ethnic differences, and insurgent efforts to provoke civil war. This is also an area where Coalition and other foreign forces are even less able to substitute for Iraqi forces than in the case of the military. Effective training and advisory efforts are critical, particularly in ensuring that the police become a competent proactive and investigative force, rather than a passive presence. Outside aid and advice is necessary to create effective command and communication links, reduce corruption, and train the kind of gendarmerie forces that can deal with insurgent attacks without repeating the violence and repression used by Saddam's security forces.

The CPATT [Civilian Police Assistance Training Team] has made major progress and has developed plans to provide the support Iraqi police forces need. Yet, it is still unclear whether a similar program to embed Coalition advisers and forces in the Iraqi police in the field will be put fully in place. This is a significant problem as the Iraqi police are under constant harassment and intimidation, and units have completely dissolved in Samarra and Mosul when put under pressure.

The Need to Provide All the Necessary Support and Resources

The United States has every possible incentive to create effective Iraqi military, security, and police forces. This is the only practical way to "win" in Iraq, cut the size of U.S. commitments, and establish a government the Iraqis see as legitimate. The United States certainly understands this at the command level in Iraq and in MNSTC–I and seems to now understand it at the policy and command level in Washington as well.

What is not clear is whether all the necessary resources are really being provided and whether a comprehensive and realistic plan exists in Washington to ensure that Iraqi military, security, and police forces develop as they should. General Gary Luck's plan to strengthen Iraqi forces with American advisers is a useful step but only if it leads to Iraqi forces that become fully independent and can replace U.S. and other Coalition forces.

As yet, there is no public plan that shows that the United States will give Iraqi forces the heavier equipment they need to fight and survive, the facilities they need to be protected, the communications required, or any of the other essential tools that will create truly independent and self-sufficient forces. Experts may argue over how much armor and heavy weapons are needed and their priority relative to improvement in support and logistics capabilities. There is also the risk the coalition could end up arming forces that will fight each other in a civil war. However, such a plan is critical to an effective Coalition strategy and plan for Iraq and to maintaining Iraqi confidence in the Coalition.

Problems still exist in the coordination of the State Department and the Department of Defense efforts, particularly in their operations in Washington, and these problems are compounded by uncertain support from other civilian agencies. These problems have had a particularly important impact on the development of the police force, both in terms of trainers, mentors, and field advisers. There has been an excessive emphasis on coordination, reporting, and committee meetings in Washington to handle functions that should be under a clear single line of authority in the U.S. country team in Iraq with equally clear lines of authority for other Coalition partners and the Iraq government. By and large, this exists at the military level, but it is significantly less effective at the level of regular and elite police forces.

The Problem of Affordability, National Defense, and Transfer to the Iraqi Government

In an ideal world, the United States, the Coalition, and the Iraqi government would not have to look beyond the immediate need to defeat the insurgency.

Wars don't occur in ideal worlds, however, and mid- and long-term force development issues cannot be ignored. Unless the United States is prepared to provide a series of massive new aid programs and maintain a major presence in Iraq for far longer than either Iraqis or Americans want, there is an immediate need for much more detailed plans and programs to eventually turn all of the force development and training effort over to the Iraqi government. In practice, this means having the Iraqi Ministry of Defense and Ministry of Interior take over as many present MNF–I and MNSTC–I efforts as quickly as possible and letting Iraqis take over responsibility for longer-term planning even before it can manage such programs.

Near-, mid-, and long-term affordability are already major issues. Iraq does not have the income to pay for the force posture that it and the Coalition are creating. Investment for counterinsurgency equipment and forces must come at the cost of not investing in the kind of military forces needed to defend Iraq's borders and the kind of police and security forces best suited to peacetime. This means hard trade-offs have to be made between existing and future missions, and cost-containment and affordability are already major issues for every aspect of force development.

More generally, the Iraqi people and Iraqi politicians need to understand that security too has become an Iraqi responsibility. The United States and its allies may still provide advisory teams and aid for years to come, and the United States and Britain may offer some kind of "over-the-horizon" guarantees, but Iraq's stability and inclusiveness depend heavily on the perception that Iraq will be truly sovereign, foreign combat troops will leave, there will be no permanent bases, and that Iraqi forces will eventually be able to deal with threats or military pressure from nations like Syria, Turkey, and Iran.

The Need for an Integrated Strategy

Iraq, the Coalition, and the United States not only need a workable strategy and plan for the development of Iraqi forces that can operate independently and replace U.S. and other Coalition forces as soon as is feasible but they need one that is integrated into an overall plan for every aspect of military, advisory, and aid activity in Iraq. This need for a coherent stability and nation-building strategy and detailed plans to implement it is a key lesson of the U.S. experience in both Afghanistan and Iraq. No one can ignore the ad hoc nature of dealing with the day-to-day changes imposed by the reality of war, but this is no rationale for failing to tie all U.S. government efforts together around some common interagency effort and maintain a focus on a common plan and strategy.

It is interesting to note in this light that some of those working at the MNF–I and MNSTC–I contrast the fact that detailed transition and force development plans were created for Afghanistan, against the fact that the MNF–I was slow to create a detailed plan and strategy. One former MNSTC–I staff officer put it this way—although it is important to note his impressions are dated and MNSTC–I now has such plans:

> There is no plan at MNSTC–I for the development of Iraqi security forces. While training and equipping are ongoing, they are ad hoc in a sense. We have timelines for how quickly we expect forces to be ready, we have PowerPoint briefings galore, we have ideas being implemented, but those are not based on any sort of plan. At no point has MNSTC–I sat down and identified a desired end state, a basic set of assumptions, possible complications and constraints, or any of the other things that happen during a planning process.... MNSTC–I J-5 (Future Plans) was overmanned and it would not have taken any additional resources to develop a plan for the command.... LTG [Lieutenant General David] Petraeus was aware that a plan would be helpful, as he told the director of J-5 ... in December 2004 to "get out of the weeds" and start thinking long-term (J-5's primary function was instead preparing briefings).

> In January 2005, three days before GEN [General Gary] Luck arrived, [we were] told to start developing a plan for the command ... [and] started on a "mission analysis," which is the first step in planning. In February ... another team start[ed] again using a different methodology ... a third mission analysis was done and was presented ... in April, but nothing had been done with it yet. Bare in mind, this is only the first step.

> Of course ... having a plan on the shelf [does not] guarantee success, [and no] military command will be able to strictly follow a plan. However, going through the planning process allows you to ask the questions you need to ask and identify potential pitfalls in advance so you can find ways to work around them. When things change and you have to adjust, at least you have something to adjust rather than shooting from the hip every time something unexpected happens. Also, a command plan would help get all of the J-sections, as well as CMATT [Coalition Military Assistance Training Team], CPATT, and JHQ-AST onto the same sheet of music instead of each going in their own direction. MNSTC–I does not have any sort of common vision regarding its mission.

Integrating a Political, Economic, and Security Strategy

At the same time, an integrated strategy cannot simply be a U.S. or Coalition strategy. A successful U.S. and Coalition strategy must be tied to a strategy that either is developed in coordination with the Iraqi government or developed by it. The time has passed when, if ever, the United States and MNSTC–I could impose order on Iraq. Iraqi decisions will now determine Iraq's fate, and only Iraqis can forge political unity or federalism, establish effective governance, establish effective Iraqi forces and security, and move Iraq back toward economic development.

It is again critical to note that mid- and long-term success in creating effective Iraqi forces requires integrated economic, political, and security development. Any data on the Iraqi economy are extremely uncertain and virtually impossible to relate to different parts of the country, given age groups and ethnic and sectarian factions. Some data are heavily biased by wartime profiteering and the flood of aid money. Others are almost certainly far too pessimistic.

A survey for the UN Development Program (UNDP), "Iraq Living Conditions Survey 2004," does however provide some important insights. The document is based on questioning more than 21,600 households in May 2004.[32] While some of the methodology was uncertain, it found that some 24,000 Iraqis had died as a result of the invasion and its aftermath, although the total could have been between 18,000 and 29,000. About 12 percent of those were under age eighteen.[33]

Some 85 percent of households complained of electricity cuts, and 29 percent relied on generators. Only 54 percent of Iraqi families had clean water. Only 37 percent were connected to a sewage network, compared with 75 percent in the 1980s. These figures were very similar to estimates provided by Iraqi officials in February 2005, although many felt the situation had deteriorated during the course of the year, and the data for these areas in Chapter 2 supports their views.

The report also claimed that the number of Iraqi mothers who die in labor had reached ninety-three in every 100,000 births, compared with fourteen in Jordan and thirty-two in Saudi Arabia, although much of this problem and the others the survey found were the result of previous wars and the actions of the previous regime. The survey also found that 6 percent of Iraqis lived in war-damaged homes. It found the average annual per capita household income was only $255 in 2003 and dropped to $144 in the first half of 2004. Some 23 percent of Iraqi children were said to be chronically malnourished, and there was only 79 percent enrollment in primary schools.

The UNDP estimates that Iraq has a very young population. Nearly 40 percent of the 27 million Iraqis are under the age of fifteen years, and the mean age in Iraq is an incredible low of 23.8 years. The UNDP survey of Iraqi living conditions carried out in 2004 also indicated that the average dependency ratio in Iraq was 73.97 percent. This meant that seven out of ten Iraqis are dependent on the earnings of the other three, who are overwhelmingly young Iraqi men. While young Iraqi men are the population who are mostly depended upon, the unemployment rate among them is officially 33.4 percent. The figure reaches "an astonishing level of 37.2 percent for young men with secondary or higher education."[34] This could be increasingly alarming when one factors in the underestimation of official figures.

The frustration caused by increasing levels of national unemployment was compounded by the CPA's decision to lay off a considerable number of government workers in 2003–2004. According to analysts at the Federal Reserve Bank of Boston, the CPA fired 500,000 Iraqis who were state employees and an additional 25,000 to 30,000 who were former Ba'athists.[35] This indicates that during its time the CPA laid off 8 percent of the active Iraqi workforce. The number of Iraqis it employed, on the other hand, is ambiguous; yet the fact remains that none of the employment targets set by the U.S. administration or the CPA were actually fulfilled. Therefore, there is broad consensus that the

Coalition policies were not effective at reducing the overall level of unemployment in the country, and some experts argue that it even worsened the situation.

A new, less-sweeping UNDP survey conducted in May 2005 found the following key results:[36]

- 78 percent of households in the country had an unreliable electricity supply; in Baghdad the figure rises to 92 percent.
- 37 percent of urban households and only 4 percent of rural ones had a sewage connection.
- 61 percent of Iraqi households had access to a safe and stable drinking-water supply, but 28 percent of these experienced daily problems with that supply.
- 5 percent of households had been damaged by military activity; the figure rises to 8 percent in the north of the country.
- Only 52 percent of urban households were accessible by paved road; the figure dropped to one in ten in rural areas.
- 31 percent of males over age fifteen were unemployed.
- Almost 25 percent of children between the ages of six months and five years suffered from malnutrition.
- More young people today were illiterate in Iraq than in previous generations.
- Just 83 percent of boys and 79 percent of girls of school age were enrolled in primary school.

Other economic and infrastructure problems continue to hinder progress in Iraq. While no reliable unemployment figures exist in Iraq, it seems almost certain that real and disguised unemployment was above 30 percent for young men in Shi'ite areas in the summer of 2005 and 40 to 60 percent in most Sunni urban areas and towns. The Iraqi water system was at an unacceptable level at the time of the U.S.-led Coalition's invasion, and that level has deteriorated by an additional 50 percent in most governorates across Iraq as of July 2005. Sanitation infrastructure is at a considerably worse status than that of water. Only 9 percent of the urban population outside of Baghdad is served by a sewage system, while the rural areas and the North do not have piped sewage systems at all. Lack of a sanitation system is becoming a serious environmental and health concern.

According to the United Nations/World Bank needs assessment report of October 2003, none of the sewage treatment plans were operational, and 50 percent of the generated wastewater (i.e., raw sewage) in Iraq was being discharged to rivers and waterways, which was consequently used as drinking water by an overwhelming majority of Iraqis who do not have access to potable water. The status as of July 2005 remained largely unchanged, as USAID reports on the progress of the sewage system indicated as follows: "[USAID is] expanding and rehabilitating one water treatment plant and constructing another to increase capacity by approximately 120 million gallons per day; rehabilitating sewage treatment plants. The sewage treatment system in Baghdad ... will be restored to almost 100 percent capacity, serving 80 percent of Baghdad's population."[37] There is no date for the completion of the only sewage treatment project in progress.

These economic problems are reinforced by the mismanagement of Iraq's economic development. Direct subsidies for the Public Distribution System (formerly known as the Food Baskets), refined oil products (i.e., fuel, kerosene, diesel and gas), and the indirect subsidies for electricity, water, and agricultural inputs incur heavy burdens on the economy. The cost of direct subsidies is more than 10.2 billion Iraqi dinars (ID) in the public budget in 2005, its share of the GDP being more than 37 percent.[38] Lack of refinery capacity causes Iraq to import 80 percent of its liquefied petroleum gas (LPG), 74 percent of its gasoline, 49 percent of its kerosene, and 46 percent of its diesel, the same as prewar levels.[39] These imports and the subsidies associated cost the Iraqi economy hundreds of millions of dollars; yet U.S. reconstruction efforts have largely bypassed the development of refineries and hence not decreased the amount of imports.

Lack of strategic planning is all too evident. A July 2005 State Department report stated that projects on "facility assessment" of oil and gas fields have been awarded.[40] The fact that such projects were still just beginning in mid-2005 indicates that the actual conditions of Iraq's biggest oil fields were still unknown, and assessments had yet to be conducted in spite of the fact that Iraq's economy was in urgent need of major oil field rehabilitation to reach the planned level of exports. The oil sector is also a critical example of the need to integrate Iraqi political development, force development, and economic development. Oil revenues will constitute more than 90 percent of Iraq's national income for 2005, 2006, and 2007—and possibly the foreseeable future. The current Iraqi budget fiscal projections are based on treating Iraqi oil revenues as national income. Yet, the Shi'ite majority and Kurdish minority are both seeking to decentralize the allocation of oil revenues and reduce the central government's role and authority over oil money.

No U.S., Coalition, or Iraqi strategy and approach to nation-building or security can survive Iraq dividing along ethnic and sectarian lines or continued economic failures and a lack of day-to-day personal security. It cannot survive mistakes like failing to create an inclusive government or purging the Iraqi forces and civil service of everyone suspected of being a "Ba'athist." Iraq cannot survive on the basis of a foreign vision of the future; it can only survive if Iraqis have the vision to create the future they need.

The Economic Aid Dimension

Iraq can only deal with these problems over the next three to five years if it gets large amounts of continuing economic aid. The many failures in the U.S. and Coalition effort to create effective Iraqi forces documented in the earlier chapters of this book have at least been largely overcome, but the same cannot be said of the aid effort. The initial ideological bias of the CPA and the illusion

TABLE 12.1

The Flow of U.S. Iraqi Relief and Reconstruction Fund (IRRF) I and II Aid, as of June 22, 2005 (in millions of U.S. dollars)

Sector	2207 Report	Apportion	Committed Current	Obligated Current	Disbursed Current
Security and Law Enforcement	5,035.6	5,035.6	4,913.9	4,434.8	2,690.5
Electricity Sector	4,308.2	4,057.6	3,700.4	2,666.8	1,241.4
Oil Infrastructure	1,723	1,723	1,609.4	1,101	347.6
Justice, Public Safety, and Civil Society	1,224.2	1,224.2	1,105.1	902.1	337.2
Democracy	905.4	905.3	886	852	442.2
Education, Refugees, Human Rights, and Governance	363	363	306.8	285.2	103.1
Roads, Bridges, and Construction	355.2	355.2	329.3	193.7	104.4
Health Care	786	786	717.9	570.2	123.1
Transportation and Communications	509	508.5	479.8	379.1	104.7
Water Resources and Sanitation	2,156.7	1,829.2	1,753.9	1,293.9	203.4
Private Sector Development	860.3	840.3	833.5	817.4	460.3
Administration Expense (USAID, State)	213.0	29.0	29.0	29.0	29.0
TOTAL	**18,439.5**	**17,656.9**	**16,665**	**13,525.2**	**6,186.9**
IRRF 2 Construction	—	10,409.9	9,798.6	7,482.1	2,822.5
IRRF 2 Nonconstruction	—	6,341.7	5,980.4	5,191.1	2,922.3
IRRF 2 Democracy	—	905.3	886.0	852	442.2
IRRF 1 Subtotal	2,473.3	2,473.3	2,473.3	2,473.3	2,150
Grand Total IRRF 1 and 2	**20,912.8**	**2,473.3**	**19,138.3**	**15,998.5**	**2,150**

Source: *Iraq Weekly Status Report*, June 24, 2005, figure 4.0. Section 2207 is from the U.S. State Department's "Report on Iraq Relief and Reconstruction."

that the United States had the competence to create a new Iraqi economy out of the mess left by Saddam Hussein in a country his wars had effectively bankrupted in 1984 are only part of the story.

In broad terms the United States simply did not know what to do or how to go beyond classic project aid in dealing with insurgency. The reprogramming of aid to meet short-term goals—adding dollars to bullets—had to be forced on the system largely by the U.S. Embassy team in Baghdad and the U.S. military. USAID and the U.S. Department of Defense proved incapable of conducting effective surveys of requirements, establishing valid contracts, administering contracts, ensuring that projects could be carried out in threatened areas, and assessing success and failure with any objectivity.

As table 12.1 shows, spending lagged far behind the rates needed to have an impact. Reprogramming has led to accelerated spending in the security and law enforcement areas, but the spend-out rate on the electricity sector, oil infrastructure, justice and civil society, democracy, education and governance, health care, transportation, and water resources has been dismal.

While the reprogramming of aid to meet short-term security needs has served a vital purpose in substituting dollars for bullets—and some projects have been successful—far too much money has been spent and is being spent on U.S.-conceived efforts that pour money into U.S. and foreign contracts, spend money outside Iraq or on overhead and security, and do not lead Iraq toward effective economic development. This spending has failed to create jobs and investment activity that has a meaningful macroeconomic scale or that will act to meet the needs of key sectors and governorates. The USAID and Department of Defense aid planning and contracting effort is a self-inflicted wound that needs to be replaced by Iraqi planning and management as soon as possible. Reliance on U.S. contractors and non-Iraqi contractors compounded the security problems and wasted vast amounts of money that never reached Iraqis or improved their lives. While some contractors showed courage and dedication, many simply took the money and "hid" in secure areas, and corruption was endemic in many aspects of the aid effort.

At this point in time it is too late to fix the U.S. management and planning structure that has wasted so much of the past aid effort, and there is no meaningful chance of obtaining the level of outside aid from other donors necessary to substitute for U.S. funds. What is needed is the same kind of effort for aid that has gone into creating effective Iraqi forces. It is to let the Iraqi government make its own plans, manage its own efforts on Iraqi terms, and spend the money in Iraq. The U.S. Embassy team should certainly vet each project, insist on suitable reporting and accounting, and blow the whistle on corruption. It is brutally clear, however, that the talent to plan and manage an effective effort simply does not exist in Washington, and outsiders may be able to advise in transforming the kind of "command kleptocracy" that existed under Saddam Hussein but do not have the skills necessary to run that transformation themselves.

"Tipping Years" versus "Tipping Points": Opportunities and Recommendations for Changes in U.S. Policy and Actions

Given this background, it is possible to make several more general recommendations for U.S. policy and action over the coming years. There is no magic way to predict the future or set deadlines, but it is also clear that 2005–2007 will be critical "tipping years."

Some of these recommendations are already being implemented, and the issue is sustainment and reinforcement of such action. Others may be in the process of implementation, although at least one former member of the MNSTC–I stated in May 2005 that "MNSTC–I has not developed a plan for creating Iraqi security forces. There are ideas being put into play, there are timelines, and there are plenty of PowerPoint presentations, but there has been no planning process or 'road map' for creating forces."

Many of the details of Coalition and U.S. plans to create effective Iraqi forces remain classified. However, if Iraqi military, security, and police forces are to be created at anything like the levels of strength and competence that are required, the United States needs to take—or reinforce—the steps highlighted below.

U.S. and Coalition Policy Priorities

- Give helping the Iraqi political and governance effort all the support possible and push for inclusiveness and national unity. No success in security is meaningful without success in politics and governance.
- Accept the fact that success in Iraq is also dependent on the ability to create effective counterinsurgency forces in the Iraqi police and military forces as soon as possible, and that this is a top priority mission. U.S. and other Coalition forces can win every clash and encounter and still decisively lose the war after the war.
- Make it fully clear to the Iraqi people and the world that the United States and its allies recognize that Iraqis must replace U.S. and Coalition forces in "visibility" and eventually take over almost all missions.
- Keep reiterating that the United States and its key allies will set no deadlines for withdrawal—or fixed limits on its military effort—and will support Iraq until it is ready to take over the mission and the insurgents are largely defeated.
- Fully implement plans to strengthen Iraqi forces with large numbers of U.S. transition teams as soon as possible, but clearly plan to phase out the teams and eliminate Iraqi dependence on them as soon as is practicable.
- Keep constant pressure on the Iraqi government to improve its effectiveness at the central, regional, and local level in supporting Iraqi forces and in providing aid and governance efforts that match the deployment and mission priorities of the security and police forces. (This is an area where the rest of the U.S. government truly needs to help, particularly with developing the ministerial capabilities needed to complement U.S. successes with the military and police.)
- Push the Iraqi government toward unified and timely action toward promoting competence and removing incompetent personnel.
- Make the supporting economic aid effort as relevant to the counterinsurgency campaign as possible, and link it to the development of Iraqi government and security activity effort in the field. The aid effort must become vastly more effective in insurgent and high-threat areas. One of the most senior officers pointed out as early as mid-2003 that "dollars are more effective than bullets. Physical security is only a prelude to economic security."
- Take a much harder look at the problems in Iraqi governance at the central, regional, and local levels. Force the issue in ensuring suitable Iraqi government coordination, responsiveness, and action. Tie aid carefully to the reality of Iraqi government civil efforts to put government in the field, and follow-up military action with effective governance.
- Make it clear that the United States and Britain will not maintain postinsurgency bases in Iraq and that the forces will stay only as long as the Iraqi government requests and needs their support.
- Accept the need for a true partnership with the Iraqis, and give them the lead and ability to take command decisions at the national, regional,

and local levels as soon as they are ready. Make nation-building real. Some work is already being done with this with the provincial support teams and the provincial reconstruction and development councils.

- Accept the reality that the United States cannot find proxies to do its work for it. NATO may provide helpful aid in training but will not provide major aid or training on the required scale. Other countries may provide politically useful contingents, but U.S., British, and Iraqi forces must take all major action. Continue efforts to build Coalition support, but don't provoke needless confrontations with allies or other countries over levels of troops and training aid that the United States simply will not get. Concentrate on the mission at hand.[41]

Priorities for Iraqi Force Development

- Continue pressure on the Iraqi government to be as inclusive as possible in every activity, to find some inclusive and federal approach to draft the new constitution, to keep the Iraqi forces and civil service "national" and avoid purges of any kind, and do everything possible to avoid the risk of escalating to civil war.
- Prepare and execute a transition plan to help the new Iraqi government that will emerge out of the coming constitutional referendum, and the election that will follow, understand the true security priorities in the country, and ensure it acts as effectively as possible in developing effective governance and efforts to create Iraqi forces. Create an effective transition plan to help the government elected in the December 2005 elections.
- Resist U.S. and Iraqi government efforts to rush force development in ways that emphasize quantity over quality, and continue the focus on leadership, creating effective units, and ensuring that training and equipment are adequate to the task.
- Continue efforts to ensure that the ethnic and religious makeup of all facets of the Iraqi military and security forces become more ethnically and religiously diverse to prevent any one group or religion from feeling persecuted by the rest.
- Continue the development of Iraqi military and police forces that can stand on their own and largely or fully replace Coalition forces as independent units. In particular, continue development of the combat support and combat service support forces that will enable Iraqi operations following the departure of Coalition forces, including transportation, supply, military intelligence, military police, and so forth. Give Iraqi military and police forces the equipment and facilities they need to take on insurgents without U.S. or other support and reinforcement.
- Ensure that the "defeat" of criminal elements receives high priority. Make creating an effective police and security presence in Iraqi-populated areas a critical part of the effort to develop effective governance.

- Pay careful attention to the integration of the former Iraqi National Guard into the Iraqi Army. Careless integration risks creating a force that is larger but not effective. This cannot be dealt with by treating the merger simply as a name change.
- Focus on the importance of political security. Security for both Iraqi governance and Iraqi elections must come as soon and as much as possible from Iraqi forces. Iraqi forces will not be ready to undertake such missions throughout the country through the end of 2005, probably well into 2006, and possibly well into 2007. However, they are able now to have local and regional impact. Wherever they are operating, they must be given the highest possible visibility in the roles where they are most needed. Careful planning will let them contribute significantly to the success of the constitutional referendum in October and to the national election at the end of 2005.
- Create command, communications, and intelligence systems that can tie together the Iraqi, U.S., and British efforts and that will give the new Iraqi government and forces the capability they will need once the United States leaves.
- Carefully review U.S. military doctrine and guidance in the field to ensure that Iraqi forces get full force protection from U.S. commanders and suitable support and that U.S. forces actively work with and encourage Iraqi units as they develop and deploy.
- Further develop the Iraqis' ability to engage in public affairs and strategic communications. Make sure that Iraqi information is briefed by Iraqis and not by Coalition spokespeople.
- Reexamine the present equipment and facilities program to see if it will give all elements of Iraqi forces the level of weapons, communications, protection, and armor necessary to function effectively in a terrorist/insurgent environment. Ensure a proper match between training, equipment, facilities, and U.S. support in force protection.
- Encourage the Iraqi government to provide reporting on Iraqi casualties, and provide U.S. reporting on Iraqi casualties and not simply U.S. and Coalition forces. Fully report on the Iraqi as well as the U.S. role in press reports and briefings. Treat the Iraqis as true partners and give their sacrifices the recognition they deserve.

The Need for Focused Public Diplomacy

It is not enough to do the right things; the United States must also be seen to do the right things. This means that the United States and its allies not only need to develop a comprehensive strategy for Iraq that ties together all of the efforts to improve Iraqi forces described above but also a strategy that can publicly and convincingly show Iraq, the region, and the world that the United States is committed to the kind of political, economic, and security development that the Iraqi people want and need.

U.S. public diplomacy tends to be vague and unfocused and make broad ideological statements based on American values. It tends to deal in slogans and be "ethnocentric," to put it mildly. What Iraqis need is something very different. They need confidence that the United States now has plans to respond to what they want. They need to see that the United States is tangibly committed to achieving success in Iraq and not an "exit strategy" or the kind of continuing presence that serves American and not Iraqi interests.

This means issuing public U.S. plans for continued economic and security aid that clearly give the Iraqi government decision-making authority and administrative and execution authority wherever possible. It means a commitment to expanding the role of the United Nations and other countries where possible and to working with key allies in some form of contact group. It also means providing benchmarks and reports on progress that show Iraqis a convincing and honest picture of what the United States has done and is doing—not the kind of shallow "spin" that dominates far too much of what the U.S. government says in public.

One key to communicating such a strategy is to have such a meaningful plan and to implement it. Another is frankness and depth. There is also a need to have a strategy that focuses on the fact that Iraqi, regional, and global perceptions of the U.S. and Coalition invasion of Iraq will not ultimately be based on why it invaded or what it does while it is in Iraq but rather on how it leaves and what it leaves behind.

Another key to success is to have a public strategy that formally commits the United States in ways that at least defuse many of the conspiracy theories that still shape Iraqi public opinion and the private views of many senior Iraqi officials and officers. The United States can scarcely address every conspiracy theory: their number is legion and constantly growing. It can and must address the ones that really matter.

There are three essential elements that U.S. and Coalition public diplomacy must have in order to be convincing:

- Make it unambiguously clear that the United States fully respects Iraqi sovereignty and that it will leave if any freely elected Iraqi government asks it to leave or will alter its role and presence in accordance with Iraqi views.
- Make it equally clear that the United States has no intention to dominate or exploit any part of the Iraqi economy and will support Iraqis in renovating and expanding their petroleum industry in accordance with Iraqi plans and on the basis of supporting Iraqi exports on a globally competitive basis that maximizes revenues to Iraq.
- Finally, make it clear that the United States will phase down troops as soon as the Iraqi government finds this desirable and will sustain the kind of advisory and aid mission necessary to rebuild Iraqi forces to the point where they can independently defend Iraq but will not seek permanent military bases in Iraq.

This latter point is not a casual issue. Nothing could be worse than rushing out before Iraq's forces are ready except trying to maintain bases in a country with Iraq's past and where the people do not want them. Virtually from the start of the U.S. invasion, Iraqis have been deeply concerned about "permanent bases." Yet even some of the most senior Iraqi officials and officers have privately expressed the view that the United States was seeking to create some eighteen such bases. Many Iraqis still feel that the United States is seeking permanent bases at such complexes as those at Taji where most Iraqi security forces receive training, Camp Victory at Baghdad International Airport, and Balad Air Base and Logistics Support Area in Anaconda north of Baghdad.

Iraqis held these views even though the United States has sought to eventually move toward a position of "strategic overwatch" in Kuwait. The United States already gave up thirteen of the 119 facilities and bases it occupied at the start of the year. It hoped to consolidate its operations in the 106 bases and facilities still scattered throughout Iraq to four major air bases, as part of its broader effort to shift the security mission to Iraqi forces and lower the visibility of the U.S. presence. These bases included Irbil or Qayyarah in the North, Al Asad in the West, Balad in the center, and Tallil in the South.[42]

The Need for Metrics, Credibility, and Transparency

The United States—particularly the Department of Defense—needs to address another set of related issues. The reporting coming out of Iraq since the fall of 2004 is more reassuring than the reporting that preceded it. The fact remains, however, that the MNF–I and the United States have not provided enough data to allow the media, analysts, and public to draw clear conclusions about the level of progress that is being made and establish the kind of credibility necessary to win sustained U.S., allied, Iraqi, and foreign support.

While the trends in Iraqi forces since the fall of 2004 are positive, the steady cutbacks and censorship of U.S. reporting have made it impossible for anyone other than experts to find the facts. U.S. officials and officers often complain about the fact that the media does not give them sufficient credibility, but the other side of the coin is that they have not provided enough transparency and hard facts to earn such trust.

U.S. Secretary of Defense Donald Rumsfeld has taken issue with complaints over the reporting of the progress of the Iraqi security forces. He has stated, "It is flat wrong to say that anyone is misleading anyone, because they are not. We are providing the best data anyone has in the world to Congress on a regular basis every week."[43] Rumsfeld did not, however, address the long chain of evidence provided in this analysis that a great deal of official reporting has not been objective or complete in the past. Some aspects of Coalition reporting have also gotten worse—not better—with time. This is all too apparent in comparing the Iraq weekly status sheets released by the State Department from January

19 to February 9, 2005. The January sheet lists the manning numbers for twelve different branches of the military and security forces. It also illustrates those considered trained against the eventual number required. The February sheet, however, lists the manning numbers for only six far more general categories and stresses the overall number of trained Iraqi forces.

Breakdowns for each branch showing those Iraqis that have been trained versus the end-manning requirement for each branch have been eliminated. In another case, the MNF–I continued to report that there were forty-six National Guard brigades when there were only forty-two because officers felt any reduction in numbers would lead to more publicity about failures in the program.

The MNF–I and MNSTC–I do provide a great deal of useful data. The problem is that it is too hard to find and often buried in the kind of reporting that provides nothing but good news in ways that talk down to the reader. The present lack of information would also be less disturbing if the United States had shown earlier that it was providing all of the resources to create effective Iraqi forces, if it did not so consistently downplay the size of the insurgent threat, if it had not set a "dual standard" that helped make Iraqi forces vulnerable and increased Iraqi casualties, and if it had not provided more data earlier in the fighting. It is also unconvincing to argue that such data are not available or are particularly difficult to process in an era of advanced information technology.

A Shifting Department of Defense Interest in Metrics

The U.S. Department of Defense announced in April 2005 that it had created an "Iraq room" to analyze the data being provided on Iraq, develop suitable metrics and reporting systems, and provide the information to Secretary of Defense Donald Rumsfeld.[44] On the military side these metrics included such measurements as casualties and insurgent attacks. Analysts look at the number of arrests, detainees' identities and roles in the insurgency, and the locations. On the civil side they included such metrics as the pace of construction projects for schools, clinics, electrical grids, and manufacturing plants. They also look at political developments.

In an article in the *Washington Times*, a senior Pentagon official is quoted as saying, "The secretary is big on metrics. . . . He's a metrics kind of guy. He believes you cannot tell how you are doing unless you are taking measurements." Another department official was quoted as saying, "It's kind of a fusion center with a lot of policy analysts who sift through an enormous amount of data and information that's coming in from commanders."[45]

Given this background, it is clear the United States should be able to provide almost all of the data it needs to establish more credible reporting without security becoming a concern. The U.S. government needs to provide the following information on the Iraqi military, security, and police forces to show it has corrected the grave mistakes it made during the first year of the occupation and that the effort to create such forces has the necessary resources and is gathering the proper momentum:

- Plan for force development with well-defined goals and milestones
- Breakdowns of the frequency, location, and character of insurgent attacks and incidents
- Reporting on Iraqi casualties and losses
- Meaningful data on the training levels of Iraqi forces and the size of combat-capable elements
- Updates on the equipment of Iraqi forces
- Data on the adequacy of the facility effort
- Accurate data on the status of Iraqi combat activity
- Summary reporting on Iraqi desertions and defections and abandonments
- Meaningful data on the actual funding of the Iraqi security effort

The Need for Public Transparency

It will not, however, be enough to simply provide more data. As has been discussed earlier, official reviews of the data the Department of Defense has used have raised questions about its accuracy. For example, a U.S. Army analysis in April calculated that an apparent decline in the number of attacks the United States was counting was more a shift in focus to more vulnerable non-U.S. targets than an actual drop in incidents.[46] Similarly, a study by the National Intelligence Council in the CIA found that U.S. government reporting had so many conflicting sources and methods of analysis that the resulting metrics could not be trusted and that there was inadequate evidence to support any conclusions about whether the insurgents were being defeated.[47]

The United States is fond of calling for more transparency on the part of other governments, but it sometimes forgets that transparency is also a matter of providing depth, honesty, and objectivity. The United States needs to do the following:

- Start talking honestly about the threat. Admit the scale of Iraqi Sunni insurgency efforts. Be honest about the scale and nature of the foreign threat and the complex mix of groups involved rather than placing too much emphasis on Al Qa'ida. Provide objective reporting on the role of outside powers like Iran and Syria—without exaggeration.
- Provide public and honest weekly reporting. Use transparency to force the issues so no one can delay or hide a future lack of progress. Prove to the Iraqi people, the American people, and Congress that there is real and not simply cosmetic success.
- Provide honest data on the Iraqi training effort that distinguishes serious training from token training.

- Provide similar data on facilities and equipment. Map the areas where such aid has been fully provided and where Iraqi forces have taken over the mission. Substitute frankness and transparency for propaganda.
- Force accountability on the system. Demand that all contract terms be met, make it clear that contract disputes will not be tolerated, and take the trouble to fire any U.S. military and federal employees who delay contract and aid efforts.
- Above all, report on the situation in the form of benchmarks in achieving the kind of integrated plan discussed earlier.
- Show there is a real plan that ties together the political, military, economic/ aid, and public diplomacy efforts.
- Be honest when setbacks occur and about trend lines. Tie the sacrifices in blood and dollars to an in-depth effort to show there is a plan for success and whether it is or is not working.

The Tet Offensive Syndrome

Any U.S. approach to these issues should remember the lessons of the Tet Offensive and more broadly Vietnam, as well as American reversals in Lebanon and Somalia. The enemies of the United States clearly recognize that a strategy of attrition is often the key to defeating the United States in grand strategic terms even if the United States can win every military battle. If the American people are to "stay the course," they need to be prepared for the realities of just how long such missions take and their real-world costs. Americans are not inherently casualty and cost adverse, but they must believe that the mission is worth the cost, that victory is possible, and that they are being told the truth.

The current approach to public affairs and the media in the U.S. government and military is far too often to offer the reassuring spin of the day: to "cherry pick" the good news, exaggerate it, and understate or omit bad news and uncertainty. The result is cumulatively to deprive U.S. officials and the U.S. military of their credibility and to make the media hostile or critical whenever it does not have direct contact with forces in the field and is not able to make its own judgments. It is also to cumulatively build up distrust in the American people, as real-world events play out over time in far less reassuring ways.

Successful propaganda cannot ultimately be based on a "liar's contest," even when the lies are lies of omission. Like leadership, it must consist in educating people in the truth and in the validity of the mission and the means being used to achieve it. There is also a long history in the U.S. government and U.S. military of cases where such liar's contests do more to blind those telling the lies to the reality of the situation than they do to sustain political and public support. In short, transparency, the truth, education, and leadership are the medium- and long-term keys to success, and short-term spin artistry can easily become the prelude to failure.

The Broader Lessons for U.S. Policy and Planning

Finally, the United States has broader lessons to learn from Iraq about stability operations, nation-building, counterinsurgency, counterterrorism, force transformation, and the need to create effective local allies.

It is difficult to review the data without concluding that the United States failed the Iraqi people and the Iraqi forces it was trying to create for more than a year. These failures were partly failures driven by inexperience and by the wrong kinds of planning and doctrine.

The Need for Accurate Grand Strategic Assessment

The United States committed a grand strategic error of monumental proportions in misjudging the political conditions, economic conditions, structure of governance, and popular support of an outside invasion and occupation. It did not understand the country it invaded or occupied. A full and realistic grand strategic understanding of the conditions of war, the nature of the opponent and allies, and the need to create an effective peace should always be an essential precondition for going to war.

The United States proved incapable of performing such an assessment in this case. Worse, it both lacked pragmatism and realism in its effort to make such assessments, and both its senior civilian policymakers and its highest-level commanders confused war fighting with grand strategy. This vastly increased the risk of unrest and insurgency and vastly complicated the task of creating effective Iraqi forces. Worse, these problems were compounded by a kind of cultural arrogance that tacitly assumed U.S. values and perceptions not only were correct but also would become Iraqi perceptions. The United States went to war without understanding or giving importance to the value of the society it intended to liberate and transform.

Nation-Building as a Critical Element of War Fighting

The United States was unprepared for nation-building and made no prewar commitment to perform it. Even if it had understood conditions in Iraq, it was not ready to take on the necessary commitment of nation-building until this was forced upon it by events, and it then clearly lacked the talent, interagency structures, and experience to perform such tasks efficiently. It was not prepared to deal with the problems of ensuring the stability and security of Iraq as it advanced into the country and failed to secure its process of governance as Saddam Hussein's regime fell.

The U.S. military was unprepared at the senior command level for counterinsurgency and especially for serious partnership and interoperability with the new Iraqi forces it was seeking to create. It was slow to recognize the need for training personnel and slow to actually assign them. In mid-2005, key advisory staffs in the Ministry of Defense and Ministry of Interior remained undermanned. The personnel departments of the U.S. military services failed to recognize the need for such assignments and the skills needed and failed to perform their mission on a timely and efficient basis.

More generally, the U.S. military failed to see the need to create specialist areas where advisers would deploy for long tours, gain expertise, preserve continuity, and maintain the personal relationships critical to working with their Iraqi counterparts. The system was not broken; it simply could not work. What was needed was the following:

- Far more ability to deploy far more military specialists in civil-military and counterinsurgency operations with suitable language and area skills.
- The ability to extend critical tours for the duration so that U.S. troops acquire real operational expertise and establish stable and lasting personal relations with Iraqis.
- The ability to supplement the U.S. military with large numbers of skilled and highly motivated civilian counterparts to handle the wide range of civil missions in the field that are now badly undermanned or handled by the U.S. military.

The civil side of the advisory effort was organized around creating the wrong kind of police forces for a kind of nation-building that could only take place in a far more permissive environment. Creating effective police and security forces for high-risk environments is a mission for which the State Department and USAID were unprepared and which should have been part of an integrated effort linking the creation of effective military, security, and police forces. More generally, many—if not most—of the personnel involved in planning and contracting for the economic aid effort had little understanding of the practical urgencies of stability operations or ability to deal with the exigencies of terrorism and insurgency.

The resulting problems were compounded by political screening of many appointees during the time of the CPA, particularly those assigned to work with the Ministry of the Interior. Recruiting of personnel with military and security expertise, Arabic language skills, and expertise on Iraq ranged from poor to outright failure. In the case of the Ministry of Interior, key civilian advisers still had no military experience, counterinsurgency expertise, and area and language skills as of mid-2005.

It is far from clear if any of the efforts made to create improved U.S. capabilities to date have served any useful purpose. The creation of a new office for this mission in the State Department ignores the need for proven competence and essentially creates a large interagency committee with no one in authority. It ignores the dismal performance of USAID and the Department of Defense in planning, executing, and assessing virtually every aspect of the aid process in Iraq and the massive problems that occurred because of overdependence on U.S. and foreign contractors. The United States did not demonstrate it had a coordination problem; it demonstrated that it had a fundamental competence problem. There is a clear need for a presidential commission to assess what went wrong with the aid programs in Iraq and whether fundamental changes are needed in the leadership, mission, and structure of USAID and every aspect of the U.S. aid program that would be involved in stability operations and nation-building.

More broadly, the widespread military complaints in Iraq that they had no civilian counterpart seem all too valid. They are matched by the feeling of many career and contract State Department personnel who actually serve in Iraq in high-risk posts that the Foreign Service as a whole has become risk averse to the point of cowardice. The burden of risk taking has fallen on far too few dedicated personnel and is matched outside Iraq by a "fortress embassy" mentality that sometimes emphasizes security over the need to take necessary risks. There seems to be a basic need to reappraise recruiting and retention for the Foreign Service and to aggressively "select out" officers who are not willing to take reasonable risks in performance tasks like nation-building and stability operations.

At the same time, the bureaucratic resistance of other departments and agencies to devoting assets and personnel to such missions, to accepting tours long enough to matter, and to encouraging the best rather than the unnecessary to accept assignments is also a major problem. It seems very likely that only the National Security Council (NSC) can force the level of action and coordination required and timely and effective agency action.

Undervaluing Local Military, Security, and Police Forces and Their Role in Shaping Legitimacy and Popular Support

No one who has talked to the U.S. advisers who served in the field from the earliest days of the advisory mission to the present can have anything other than respect for what they tried to do and for their deep concern for the forces they were training. The advisory teams saw the Iraqis as both partners and as people.

At higher levels, however, the U.S. government and the U.S. military were slow to react for nearly a year, focusing on U.S. forces and U.S. priorities. The end result was that the United States effectively exploited a situation in which Iraqis had no economic choice other than to volunteer, and the United States sent them unprepared into the field. The fact that these forces then experienced failure after failure was inevitable, and the fact that some died as a result of U.S. incompetence and neglect was reprehensible. The men did not fail the system; the system failed the men.

The history of the U.S. effort to create Iraqi forces is also a warning that Americans at every level need to think about what alliance and interoperability really mean in creating allied forces for this kind of nation-building and warfare. Iraq is only one example of how vital a role such forces must play in many forms of asymmetric warfare. What is equally clear is that Americans must understand that they have a moral and ethical responsibility to the forces they are creating and are not simply creating a useful expedient. The only truly important force numbers in this report count people—not things or dollars.

Accepting the Need for Adequate U.S. Deployments and the Risk of Overstretch

The United States must decide what overall strategy it intends to pursue in any future cases in which stability operations and nation-building become a key part of the mission if it is to avoid overcommitting its forces and the risk of defeat and failure. It should consider the following scenarios and examples:

- If the United States does plan to change nations by force and do so without massive native or Coalition support, it needs a fundamentally different force posture. The Iran-invasion scenario is a case in point.
- If the United States intends to work with a local ally and have the ally assume the burden, then it needs to plan accordingly. The Korea scenario is an example.
- If the United States intends to fight a regional war without using force to change the regime, the nation-building and stability burden does not exist. The Taiwan Straits are this kind of scenario. In an era of asymmetric wars, however, it may be more the exception than the rule.
- If the United States only intends to conduct nation-building and stability operations in small, weak nations, it still will need specially trained and equipped forces, the ability to conduct stability operations, and the ability to train effective local forces. Afghanistan is a case in point.

What the United States cannot afford is to repeat a strategy of denial—rejecting the nation-building and stability missions and the need to act immediately to create effective local forces until such actions are forced upon it. Quite aside from the costs in the scenario involved, such policies are virtually certain to "stretch" a major part of U.S. forces and/or make the United States vulnerable to other threats. The United States must also be ready in more than military terms. It must create the civilian components and interagency progress necessary to place the burden on a government-wide basis.

Finally, the administration and Congress must insist that U.S. policies and plans for armed intervention include an explicit assessment of the costs and risks of nation-building and stability operations and that there be detailed operational plans from conflict preparation to final termination. The United States' failure to do this in Iraq—particularly after the lessons of Vietnam, Lebanon, Somalia, the Balkans, and Afghanistan—has had a bitter cost to Iraq, the United States, and its allies. Any further repetition would be simply inexcusable. This kind of failure must never happen again.

Chronology of Events Involving Iraqi Security Forces

2003

May 23 Paul Bremer issues Order No. 2, the Dissolution of Entities, dissolving the old Iraqi armed forces.

September 12 U.S. troops of the Eighty-second Airborne Division accidentally kill ten Iraqi policemen in the city of Fallujah. Fallujah's residents promise a wave of violence against U.S. troops.

October Estimates indicate that the Iraqi security forces will number some 170,000.

October 9 A car laden with explosives slams into a Baghdad police station. Ten Iraqis are killed.

October 27 The headquarters of the Red Crescent and three Baghdad police stations are hit in the same day by four coordinated suicide bombs. Forty-three die, and more than 200 are wounded in the bloodiest day since the fall of Saddam Hussein's government.

November Estimates for the necessary manning of the Iraqi Civil Defense Corps (ICDC) rise from 25,000 to 40,000 troops. Estimates for the necessary manning of the border police rise from 11,800 to 25,700.

November 4 U.S. Secretary of Defense Donald Rumsfeld states that over 100,000 Iraqi security forces have been trained.

December 14 Seventeen Iraqis are killed when a suicide car bomber runs into a police station near Baghdad.

2004

January 25 Iraqi policemen in Ramadi are attacked on two separate occasions. Seven Iraqi police die.

January 31 Nine Iraqis are killed and forty-three others wounded when a suicide bomber runs his car into a police station in Mosul.

February 10 Fifty-five Iraqis are killed and approximately sixty-five are wounded when a car bomb explodes outside a police station in Iskandariya. Many of the dead were applying for jobs as policemen. When Ahmed Ibrahim, the Iraqi police chief, arrives, the gathered crowd nearly riots while chanting anti-American slogans.

February 11 A gathering of Iraqi Army recruits is attacked in central Baghdad by a suicide car bomber. Forty-seven are killed and at least fifty more wounded.

February 14 Approximately seventy insurgents stage a daring raid on the headquarters of both the police and the Iraqi Civil Defense Corps in Fallujah in a bid to free many of their cohorts. Up to seventy prisoners escape, and a number are seen fleeing with the insurgents. Fifteen policemen and four Lebanese and Iranian insurgents are killed.

February 23 A car bomb detonates outside of a Kirkuk police station, killing at least ten and wounding more than thirty-five Iraqis.

March 9 Two American officials from the Coalition Provisional Authority (CPA) and their Iraqi translator are killed intentionally by Iraqi policemen seventy miles south of Baghdad. These are the first American civilian deaths in Iraq.

March 23 In Kirkuk and Hilla, eleven Iraqi policemen are shot and killed in two separate attacks.

April Available Iraqi Army forces drop from 5,600 to 2,400. The available civil defense forces drop from 34,700 to 23,100.

April 5 U.S. Marines lay siege to Fallujah following the murder of four American security contractors in the city and desecration of their bodies. Several Iraqi battalions refuse to fight in either Fallujah or Sadr City.

April 21 Several suicide bombs explode outside of a number of police facilities in the area of Basra. Crowds assault the Coalition forces, trying to reach the wounded with stones. At least sixty-eight are killed by the bombs.

April 30 The siege of Fallujah ends at the urging of Iraqi politicians. The Fallujah Brigade, a cobbled-together militia led by former Iraqi Army officers, is formed to rid the city of foreign fighters.

May 7 Four Iraqi police officers are killed when their squad car is ambushed by insurgents in Mosul.

June 6 A police station and military base in the Baghdad area are bombed—twenty-one Iraqis are killed in the attacks.

June 10 The Moqtada al-Sadr's Mehdi Army takes control of a Najaf police station in direct violation of the ceasefire agreement between Sadr and the United States. Sadr's forces free the prisoners and loot the station.

June 14 Multiple suicide bombings aimed at Iraqi police kill dozens of civilians in Baghdad.

June 17 Forty-one are killed and approximately 142 are injured when suicide car bombers detonate outside a military recruitment center and a city council building in Baghdad.

June 24 Sunni insurgents launch a series of coordinated attacks on Iraqi security forces in Fallujah, Baghdad, Mosul, Ramadi, and Baquba. At least seventy Iraqis are killed.

July The Iraqi Civil Defense Corps (ICDC) disbands and is replaced by the Iraqi National Guard (ING). The Iraqi Intervention Force (IIF) is established with an end-manning goal of 6,600. The Special Operations Force is established with an end-manning goal of 1,600 troops. The Coastal Defense Force is established with an end-manning goal of 400, as is the Air Corps with an end-manning goal of 500.

July 16 Australia deploys the Iraqi Army training team, consisting of fifty soldiers with the task of training a full brigade of Iraqi soldiers.

July 28 A car bomb kills seventy Iraqis outside of a police recruiting center in Baquba.

August U.S. Marines arrest the Al Anbar province's police chief on charges of corruption.

August 3 Insurgent attacks in Baquba, Baghdad, and the Al Anbar province kill six U.S. troops and approximately three Iraqi national guardsmen.

September Iraqi Prime Minister Ayad Allawi and U.S. President George W. Bush both state that there are 100,000 fully trained and equipped Iraqis providing security in Iraq. NATO ambassadors agree to send 200 trainers to help rebuild the Iraqi Army. The First Infantry Division arrests a senior commander of the Diyala province's Iraqi National Guard, alleging that he maintained ties to insurgents. The end-manning goal of the Iraqi National Guard increases from 41,000 to 61,900 and the end-manning goal for border enforcement from 16,300 to 32,000. The end-manning goal for the Iraqi police increases from 90,000 to 135,000.

September 6 Seven U.S. soldiers and three Iraqi soldiers are killed by a car bomb outside of Fallujah.

September 10 The Fallujah Brigade disbands without having secured the city. A small riot breaks out as people leave a mosque. Iraqi police fire into the crowd, killing two people and injuring five. Aides to al-Sadr claim that the dead and injured were unarmed.

September 14 Twelve policemen are killed in Baquba by a drive-by shooter. Forty-seven Iraqis are killed and 114 are wounded by a car bomb outside a military recruitment area. The recruits were forced to stand outside blast-absorbing concrete barriers. The ensuing crowd curses the United States and blames U.S. warplanes for the attack. Elements associated with Abu Musab al-Zarqawi claim credit for both attacks.

September 17 Thirteen are killed by a suicide car bomb near a police checkpoint in Baghdad.

September 18 A suicide car bomb kills nineteen and wounds sixty-seven in Kirkuk. The bomber targeted a crowd of young men seeking employment with the Iraqi National Guard.

September 19 A car bomb aimed at a joint Iraqi–U.S. patrol near Samarra kills one Iraqi soldier, one Iraqi civilian, and wounds seven others.

September 21 An insurgent abandons a car loaded with explosives near the Iraqi National Guard recruiting center in the Jamiya neighborhood of western Baghdad. No one was hurt.

September 22 The Iraqi National Guard center in the Jamiya neighborhood of western Baghdad is hit by a suicide car bomb that kills at least eleven and wounds an unknown number. Recruits gathered around the center are apparently the target.

September 23 U.S. Secretary of Defense Donald Rumsfeld testifies that since May 1, 2003, 721 Iraqi personnel have died providing their country with security.

September 25 Seven Iraqi National Guard applicants die in the Jamiya neighborhood of western Baghdad at the hands of insurgents. A U.S. Army soldier faces twenty-five years in jail for his part in the death of an Iraqi national guardsmen in Adwar in May. An Iraqi police captain, Salman Turki al-Shamani, is killed by insurgents near Baquba.

September 26 Two suicide car bombers try to drive into a base used by U.S. Marines and the Iraqi National Guard in Karmah near Fallujah. When challenged, they detonate the cars. No injuries are reported.

October The Iraqi Highway Patrol and the Dignitary Protection Service are established with end-manning goals of 1,500 and 500 men, respectively.

October 1 Three thousand U.S. and 2,000 Iraqi forces launch an assault on the approximately 500 militants controlling the city of Samarra, an area sixty miles north of Fallujah. Estimates now indicate that the Iraqi security forces will need to number some 346,700 men, double the estimate from October 2003.

October 4 General James Jones, NATO's commander, announces that up to 3,000 NATO troops could be involved in the training of Iraqi security forces. U.S. and Iraqi forces take Samarra, killing one hundred militants. Iraqi units fight with distinction and capture twenty-four suspected foreign fighters. Three car bombs—two in Baghdad and one in western Iraq—kill at least twenty-six people and wound more than one hundred others. Iraqi security forces fight a gun battle in downtown Baghdad after one of the blasts. One of the suicide bombers rams a recruiting center for Iraqi plainclothes policemen.

October 5 An estimated 3,000 U.S. and Iraqi troops begin a campaign designed to wrest control of insurgent-held areas of the Babil province. Iraqi special forces play a prominent role in the subsequent raids.

October 6 A suicide bomber drives an explosives-laden vehicle into an Iraqi checkpoint at the Iraqi National Guard encampment near Anah, 160 miles northwest of Baghdad. Approximately 1,200 members of the 202nd Iraqi National Guard, Seventh Army Battalion, and First Ministry of Interior Commando Battalion are designated to stay in Samarra. The governor pledges to send 1,500 additional police officers.

October 9 Eleven Iraqi national guardsmen are killed and six others injured during an insurgent attack on the National Guard compound located in Karabilah near the Syrian border. NATO declares its commitment to sending 300 military trainers to Iraq after stiff resistance, especially from France. The program is unlikely to be in place before the end of the year.

October 10 Iraqi national guardsmen assist in a border operation that results in the deaths of two insurgents or smugglers. At least ten Iraqis die in explosions near the oil ministry and police academy.

October 12 In Ramadi a joint force of U.S. and Iraqi troops arrests a Sunni cleric, Sheik Abdul Aleem Saidy, and his son. Iraqi police in Sadr City continue buying heavy weapons from al-Sadr's militia forces.

October 15 A suicide car bomber narrowly misses a unit of Iraqi police on patrol, killing ten bystanders.

October 19 Four Iraqi national guardsmen are killed and eighty are injured in a mortar attack eighty miles north of Baghdad. Insurgents unsuccessfully try to assassinate Colonel Mohammed Essa Baher, the commander of the 507th Iraqi National Guard Battalion. Baher had identified a financier, allegedly a part of the al-Zarqawi terror network, the day before the attack.

October 23 Three minibuses filled with forty-nine Iraqi recruits for the Sixteenth Iraqi Army Battalion, Seventh Army Brigade, are ambushed by insurgents dressed as Iraqi police. All forty-nine recruits and three accompanying civilians are killed. The ambush takes place as the recruits leave a training base in Kirkush, fifteen miles from the Iranian border and northeast of Baghdad. This is the single most deadly insurgent ambush to date. At least four Iraqi national guardsmen are killed by a car bomb at a checkpoint south of Samarra. Another car bomb kills between ten and sixteen Iraqi policemen at a checkpoint outside of the Marine base in Al Asad in the Anbar province.

October 25 An Iraqi national security aide declares that up to 5 percent of Iraq's security forces are most likely infiltrated by insurgents.

October 26 Prime Minister Allawi blames the United States and its Coalition allies for the massacre of the forty-nine Iraqi Army recruits. Iraq's Interior Minister, Falah al-Naqib, announces a new campaign to rid the police force of corrupt and ineffective members. A militant group, the Army of Ansar al-Sunna, claims responsibility for the murder of eleven Iraqi national guardsmen it had captured on the road between Hilla and Baghdad.

October 28 Two senior Iraqi police officers are killed near Latifiya, south of Baghdad, allegedly by the Army of Ansar al-Sunna.

October 30 Iraqi police officers allegedly fired indiscriminately on civilians after an attack on an American convoy south of Baghdad. Reportedly, the police direct their fire on three minibuses and three vans, killing fourteen and wounding ten.

November 2 A car bomb intended for an Iraqi security convoy kills four Iraqi civilians and wounds twelve Iraqi national guardsmen in Mosul. NATO begins its first eight-week training course for security personnel at its joint warfare center in Norway. Nineteen mid- to high-level officials from the Iraqi military, Ministry of Defense, and the Ministry of Interior attend.

November 3 Three decapitated bodies of Iraqi national guardsmen are found underneath the Fourteenth of July Bridge in Baghdad. A group calling itself the Brigades of the Iraqi Honorables claims responsibility for killing the three men. Ansar al-Sunna posts pictures of another decapitation on the Internet, claiming that the victim is Major Hussein Shanoun, an officer in the new Iraqi Army.

November 6 More than fifteen Iraqi police officers are killed by a series of closely coordinated assaults against police stations in Samarra. In addition, an Iraqi National Guard commander, Abdel Razeq Shaker Garmali, is among those killed in Samarra.

November 7 Insurgents launch an attack against a police station in the town of Haditha, taking twenty-one policemen hostage. The insurgents kill all of them execution-style. In another attack on a police station in the town of Haqlaniya, insurgents kill the head of security in western Iraq, Brigadier Shaher al-Jughaifi. Unknown gunmen kill Iraqi police Colonel Abdul Adim Abed in the Mualmeen neighborhood of Baquba. The director of security in Sulaymaniyah, Brigadier Sarkout Hassan Jalal, claims that Islamic militants regularly smuggle recruits from Iran into Iraq and on to Fallujah and other "hot spots." The Iraqi government declares a state of emergency for sixty days with the exception of the northern Kurdish regions. The declaration coincides with the beginning stages of an assault on the restive city of Fallujah. Iraqi commandos from the Thirty-sixth Iraqi Commando Battalion, supported by U.S. Marines, take control of Fallujah's main hospital just prior to the declaration.

November 8 The battle for Fallujah begins. Approximately 10,000 U.S. troops and 2,000 Iraqi forces confront 3,000 to 5,000 insurgents. Iraqi commandos seize a hospital and a railway station. The hospital is the focal point of erroneous casualty reports following the first assault on Fallujah.

November 9 Two police stations in Baquba are attacked. One police officer is killed, and eight are wounded. Reportedly, the police stand their ground and fight well. Elsewhere, a suicide car bomb strikes an Iraqi National Guard base north of Kirkuk, killing at least three. Prime Minister Allawi visits Camp Fallujah and gives a speech in front of the assembled Iraqi forces. The prime minister's speech is met with praise and cheers.

November 10 Insurgents loot and strip an Iraqi National Guard base in the town of Hammam al-Alil. The National Guard battalion stationed there falls apart when attacked, leaving the base, armory and all, to the militants. Two members of the Iraqi security forces are reported killed in action in Fallujah. Prime Minister Allawi places Major General Abdul Qadir Mohammed Jassim, the Iraqi ground forces commander in Fallujah, in control of the western Anbar province until a civilian authority can be appointed. In Fallujah, the First Battalion, First Brigade of the Iraqi Intervention Force begins operations against the insurgents in Fallujah on its own and controls one part of the city by itself. The Second Battalion, First Brigade aids U.S. forces in bringing the Hydra Mosque under control. The Fourth Battalion, First Brigade, and the Iraqi Police Service's Emergency Response Unit see action. The Fifth Battalion, Third Brigade helps U.S. forces subdue insurgents in the Al Tawfiq Mosque. The Sixth Battalion, Third Brigade mans vehicle checkpoints with U.S. forces in the heart of Fallujah.

November 11 An Iraqi police vehicle and an American convoy are attacked by a suicide car bomber in central Baghdad. Nineteen people are killed. In Mosul reports indicate that insurgents openly roam the streets and repeatedly attack police stations and government facilities. The insurgents, numbering between 400 and 500, split into groups of fifteen to twenty to carry out attacks. Several police stations are burned to the ground despite pleas from imams via mosque loudspeakers. Insurgents seize control of six to seven police stations for the better part of an hour. When they are repelled, the fighters seize vehicles, weapons, body armor, radios, and uniforms. One senior police officer, the brother of Mosul's police chief, is shot dead in his front yard. Fighters attack the Iraq Media Network. Brigadier General Carter Ham, commander of Task Force Olympia, states that he has never seen the level of command and control exhibited by the insurgents prior to this date. Ten Iraqi National Guard troops die in the fighting. In response, U.S. soldiers and members of the Iraqi National Guard raid southern portions of the city. In Fallujah U.S. and Iraqi forces seize control of 70 percent of the city. A total of nine Iraqi security force members are wounded.

November 12 The First Battalion of the new Iraqi Army encounters stiff resistance in the Jolan section of Fallujah. Brigadier Abdul Hussain Mahmoud Badar arrives in the Maysan province to take command of the Iraqi National Guard's Seventy-third Brigade. Badar flees the same day, having been verbally threatened by individuals who claim to be actively involved in the insurgency.

November 13 Iraqi Interim Prime Minister Allawi declares Fallujah liberated. Insurgents launch two attacks on an Iraqi National Guard base near Mosul, killing two guardsmen and wounding twenty-one.

November 14 A total of six Iraqi military personnel are reported killed and more than forty wounded in the fighting in Fallujah. Reports indicate that Iraqis are taking over the screening process for police recruits and are firing thousands for incompetence or inaction. Iraqi sources state that such incompetence or corruption in the police led to the death of the forty-nine recruits last month. Reports indicate the firing of the police chiefs in both Samarra and Mosul, following waves of insurgent attacks. The same reports state that Iraqi military officials have raised the recruiting age from seventeen to twenty, require a letter of approval from a local community council for each recruit, require that recruits have a family member in the service to be eligible, and order that committees will be sent to recruits' neighborhoods to investigate their morality.

November 15 Insurgents attack two police stations in Baquba. Elements are believed to have belonged to Saddam Hussein's intelligence apparatus. It appears that there are a few foreign fighters, mostly Syrians, mixed in. Fighting continues in Mosul. The Iraqi interior minister reports that in one unidentified Iraqi city a wounded Iraqi police officer was taken from his bed, dismembered, and that his remains were strung up in the city square.

November 16 Militants fight with national guardsmen from the Patriotic Union of Kurdistan in the northern Mosul neighborhood of al-Ta'mim. Three guardsmen are hurt and at least two insurgents are killed. U.S. officials state that between 1,000 and 2,000 insurgents have been killed in Fallujah and an additional 1,000 detained.

November 17 Brigadier General Carter Ham states that Mosul is back under U.S. and Iraqi control. Insurgents fire mortar rounds on the al-Ahrar police station within the city. The Iraqi Ministry of Interior states that it is investigating reports that thirty-one security force recruits may have been kidnapped in Rutbah. The Iraqi police in Karbala indicated that they believed that they may have been taken. NATO unanimously agrees to increase the number of military trainers in Iraq from sixty-five to approximately 400. These trainers require around 1,600 supporting staff and will not serve in a combat role. Reports indicate that new personnel will be in place in the next six weeks.

November 18 Militants detonate a car bomb in Baghdad outside the emergency Yarmouk police station in the west of the city. Two civilians die. Reports indicate that insurgents in Baghdad are lining one particular street with police uniforms in an effort to intimidate future recruits. Shelling and sporadic fighting continues in the southern outskirts of Fallujah. In Mosul a mortar attack in the western portion of the city wounds five Iraqi soldiers. Iraqi commandos, backed by U.S. troops, prepare to storm rebel-held parts of the city. Two Iraqi National Guard officers are publicly beheaded in the city by a group claiming allegiance to Abu Musab al-Zarqawi.

November 19 A suicide car bomber rams an Iraqi police checkpoint in Maysalon Square in eastern Baghdad. The attack kills five police officers and wounds four others. Elsewhere in Baghdad, worshipers outside a mosque protest the assault on Fallujah. Some of the protestors fire on Iraqi national guardsmen who subsequently return fire. A police convoy traveling through the city is hit by a suicide car bomber, killing one policeman and a bystander and wounding five others. In Fallujah the commander of the First Marine Expeditionary Force states that the assault had "broken the back of the insurgents" in the city. He reports that fifty-one U.S. troops and eight Iraqi troops had been killed and that an additional 425 U.S. troops and forty-three Iraqi troops were wounded. He states that approximately 1,200 insurgents were killed, twenty-five to thirty civilians were being treated for injuries, and that he knew of no civilian deaths caused by the fighting. Insurgents attack a police station in Muqdidiya with mortars, killing a police officer. In Mosul reports indicate that residents are growing uneasy with the presence of Kurdish national guardsmen in the city.

November 20 Unidentified assailants kill an Iraqi National Guard recruit in a drive-by shooting near Baquba. He was on his way to a training center when he was attacked. Iraqis find the bodies of eight Iraqi policemen some fifteen miles west of Mosul. U.S. forces reportedly detain three Iraqi national guardsmen who were working for the insurgency. Reports indicate that approximately fifteen Iraqi Army troops were killed in the last twenty-four to thirty-six hours.

November 21 Militants attack a convoy ferrying Iraqi national guardsmen in Ramadi. The insurgents kill nine guardsmen and wound an additional seventeen. In Mosul U.S. troops discover the bodies of nine Iraqi soldiers who had been shot execution-style. Attackers kill the police chief and his driver in the town of Khalis. An Internet statement from a group purportedly affiliated with Abu Musab al-Zarqawi appears, claiming that the group had killed seventeen Iraqi national guardsmen from Kisik.

November 23 Approximately 5,000 U.S., British, and Iraqi troops launch an offensive dubbed Plymouth Rock in locales south of Baghdad in an effort to pacify the restive area. Reports indicate that the main elements involved are Iraqi SWAT forces supported by the Twenty-fourth Marine Expeditionary Unit. The campaign begins with early morning raids in the town of Jabella in the Babil province, which net thirty-two suspected militants. Elsewhere, interim Defense Minister Hazim al-Shalaan tells reporters that he cannot provide safety for voters or candidates in the upcoming election. He states that Iraqis don't understand elections and that they are not aware of the candidates. Shalaan accuses a "vile coalition" within Interim Prime Minister Allawi's government of obstructing the flow of funds to former soldiers' pensions and to the new Iraqi Army. In Baghdad insurgents attack the deputy chief of Baghdad's major crime unit, Colonel Ziyaa Hamed's, car. In Baquba gunmen attack a convoy carrying Iraqi security forces, killing three of them. U.S. Secretary of Defense Rumsfeld states in a press briefing that, although Iraqi forces took part in a supporting role, they performed well in recent operations in Fallujah.

November 24 Iraqi Interim Prime Minister Allawi attends the graduation of 2,500 troops of the Iraqi Intervention Force at the Numaniyah military base near Kut, southeast of Baghdad. The graduates will form the Second Brigade of the Iraqi Intervention Force and are specially trained in counterinsurgency tactics. U.S. Lieutenant General

David Petraeus states that they will be operational within two weeks and that the Third Brigade should be ready by the end of December. In Mosul militants attack Iraqi General Rashid Flaieh, the head of the Iraqi commando unit in the city. Flaieh is unhurt.

November 25 U.S. troops and Iraqi national guardsmen launch raids on suspect buildings in the west side of Mosul. Reports indicate that some eleven dead Iraqi soldiers were found in and around Mosul. They were bound and shot in the back of the head. Iraqi Minister of State Qassim Dawood states in a press conference that Colonel Fawas Armoot was chosen as Ramadi's police chief. Dawood declares that soldiers in Fallujah have discovered a rudimentary chemical- and biological-weapons facility that was being run by insurgents. The minister states that Iraqi police have captured five foreign terrorists—Libyan, Tunisian, and Syrian—trying to cross the border into Iraq.

November 26 U.S. troops and Iraqi national guardsmen continue to conduct operations in Mosul. The forces raid one mosque run by an imam who is suspected of being an insurgent leader. The Iraqis perform well, although they encounter no enemy fire. Two executed Iraqi soldiers are dumped at a busy traffic circle in downtown Mosul. U.S. forces believe that soldiers are being kidnapped at taxi stands when they return home on leave.

November 27 Three Iraqi police officers die in a bombing attack. The location of the attack remains unclear.

November 28 Iraqi police detain two men and a vehicle packed with explosives in the Al-Jadriya neighborhood of Baghdad. In Baquba militants fire mortars at the Al-Wahda police station, wounding a police officer. Militants storm a police station in Samarra, stealing several police vehicles and looting the armory. Iraqi police fail to confront them. U.S. and Iraqi forces launch land and amphibious raids to the south of Baghdad, killing seventeen militants and capturing thirty-two. In Basra British and Iraqi troops surround the headquarters of the southern regional Iraqi National Guard after Brigadier General Diaa al-Kadhimi refused to step down as commander in favor of Salah al-Maliki.

November 29 A car bomb near Ramadi explodes, killing four Iraqi police officers and wounding three others. Three Iraqi national guardsmen are injured as well. In a separate attack in Baghdadi, 120 miles northwest of Baghdad, a suicide bomber detonates his car at a police checkpoint, killing seven Iraqi police and national guardsmen. The blast injures an additional nine security personnel. Brigadier General Kadhimi continues his standoff in Basra. Reports indicate that at least fifty pro Interim Government or security force personnel have been killed in Mosul in the last ten days. The police chief states that no police are on active patrol because the city remains too dangerous. The United States and the Iraqi National Guard strike a deal with Mosul police to move back into several of the police stations that were seized or looted during the beginning of the Fallujah campaign. The police agree to man some of the more dangerous stations by mid-December. Reports indicate that Iraqi security forces have abandoned Tal Afar. The governor of Najaf, Adnan al-Zurufi, announces that his security chief has been arrested by police in connection with a plot to assassinate the governor and several other top regional officials.

November 30 In the Babil province south of Baghdad, Iraqi and U.S. forces capture fourteen suspected militants and discover three arms caches. Near Iskandariya, the Iraqi SWAT team and the Iraqi specialized forces capture several high-value suspects in separate operations. In Najaf the Eleventh U.S. Marine Expeditionary Unit commander declares that Iraqi security forces have formally assumed control of the entire province and have the ability to conduct limited operations on their own.

December 2 Iraqi National Security Minister Qassim Dawood states that securing the polling centers for the Iraqi election will be left to the Iraqi security forces and Iraqi society as a whole. He declares that U.S. forces will only be called upon if a polling center faces a major insurgent attack.

December 3 Gunmen shoot and kill sixteen Shi'ite Iraqi police officers, laying siege to a police station in the Baghdad neighborhood of Sayidiya. Sources believe that the area harbors militants who fled Fallujah prior to the U.S. and Iraqi attack on the city. In a separate attack at the other end of the city, insurgents ram a suicide car bomb into a crowd outside of a Shi'ite mosque, close to a nearby police station. Fourteen die and a gun battle ensues between the Iraqi police and the insurgents who fire on the police station. In Mosul three police stations are attacked, although no immediate casualty reports are available. An Iraqi National Guard captain is assassinated in Karbala.

December 4 A suicide car bomber kills at least eighteen Kurdish militiamen when he rams his car into their bus in Mosul. More than sixteen are wounded. Another suicide bomber rams a police station in Baghdad near the Green Zone, the Coalition's safe area in Baghdad. The attack kills eight officers and wounds more than thirty-eight. Gunmen attack a police station in the Ghazaliya neighborhood in Baghdad. Another police station is attacked by militants in Samarra. Both attacks are repulsed, with two officers wounded in Samarra.

December 5 Insurgents ram a suicide car bomb into an Iraqi National Guard checkpoint near Bayji and follow the explosion with small-arms fire. Three guardsmen are killed, and eighteen are wounded. In Samarra gunmen attack an Iraqi Army patrol, killing one soldier and wounding four. Two Iraqi national guardsmen are killed and four are wounded in Latifiya in an insurgent attack.

December 6 A statement from the U.S. Customs and border protection officers and their Iraqi counterparts indicates that they caught more than forty terrorists arming insurgents within Iraq. The statement reveals that the officers, working closely with Iraqis, broke up an Iraqi smuggling ring.

December 7 A roadside bomb explodes south of Baghdad, killing three Iraqi national guardsmen and wounding eleven. General John Abizaid, commander of U.S. Central Command (USCENTCOM), declares that the Iraqi security and military forces are behind schedule in their training. He states that the indigenous forces will not be able to secure the country for the January election and that more U.S. troops will be needed temporarily. He suggests that there would be more embedded U.S. trainers and that more special operations forces might need to be created.

December 8 The home of Samarra's police chief is attacked by insurgents. Reportedly, the police chief resigned following the attack. Unconfirmed reports state that a police station within the city was overrun by insurgents. In Ramadi militants detonate a bomb near a police station. No injuries are reported. One Iraqi policeman claims that half of Ramadi's policemen had failed to report for duty because of threats and intimidation.

December 9 NATO formally agrees to increase its training staff in Baghdad from sixty officers to 300. Poland, Hungary, and the Netherlands agree to contribute forces. France, Germany, Belgium, Greece, Spain, and Luxembourg refuse. German Foreign Minister Joschka Fischer states adamantly that no Germans will go to Iraq. A U.S.-backed Iraqi National Guard patrol is ambushed in Mosul. The casualties are uncertain though it is believed that at least one guardsman is killed.

December 10 Militants try to attack an Iraqi National Guard patrol in Samarra with mortars. The attack leaves the guardsmen unscathed but kills two civilians. In Baquba four Iraqi national guardsmen are injured when a roadside bomb explodes by their patrol car. Insurgents attack them with small arms after the explosion.

December 11 Insurgents ambush a police patrol car on a road between Baiji and Tikrit. Two officers die and three are wounded. One of those killed is reportedly Brigadier General Razzaq Karim Mahmud, a senior police commander. In the town of Hit, militants attack a minibus carrying a contingent of Iraqi national guardsmen. Seven guardsmen are killed.

December 12 Reports indicate that more than 160 bodies, many members of the Iraqi National Guard, have been found in and around Mosul since November 12. South of Baghdad seventy-two suspected militants are seized by U.S. Marines and Iraqi security forces near the Euphrates River. Insurgents attack a police station near Mahmudiya. Iraqi national guardsmen and Iraqi police successfully repel the attackers and suffer no losses. They uncover a car bomb across the street from the station, and U.S. forces detonate it. Officials attribute recent success by Iraqi forces in the area to the removal of a senior National Guard officer in November who, it was discovered, had been supplying insurgents with information. He was directly implicated in the murders of twelve Iraqi national guardsmen.

December 14 In central Baghdad a suicide bomber detonates a bomb at an entrance to the Green Zone. Three Iraqi national guardsmen die, and twelve people are wounded. The bombing is the second attack on the same entrance in two days and comes a day and a year after Saddam Hussein's capture. Abu Musab al-Zarqawi's Al Qa'ida in Iraq group claims responsibility for both attacks. U.S. and Iraqi forces continue to fight insurgents in northern Mosul and in the western Anbar province. Two Iraqi national guardsmen are killed and five wounded in a battle with insurgents near Dijail. In Samarra Iraqi police report that three children were killed in the crossfire during a firefight between U.S. forces and Iraqi forces and insurgents.

December 16 A roadside bomb explodes in western Baghdad, killing three Iraqi national guardsmen. Iraqi Minister of Defense Hazim Al-Shaalan orders the Iraqi forces to secure the churches and places of worship for the coming holiday.

December 18 Militants in Samarra fire mortar rounds at an election office located in a youth center. One Iraqi dies, and eight others are evacuated to a hospital by members of the Iraqi National Guard who respond to the attack. Elsewhere in Samarra, Iraqi commandos seize bomb-making material and take into custody three insurgents during a raid. In Mosul Iraqi national guardsmen engage militants in a gun battle in the western part of the city, killing three insurgents.

December 20 A driver throws a hand grenade at a police station in Karbala. No injuries are reported, and the driver is arrested.

December 21 A suicide bomber detonates his explosives at a U.S. military base mess tent near Mosul, killing twenty-two and wounding seventy-two more. The attack hits a dining hall where U.S. soldiers, Iraqi national guardsmen, and Iraqi civilians are having lunch. Three Iraqi security forces personnel are killed. The suicide bomber is believed to be a Saudi allied with Abu Musab al-Zarqawi named Abu Omar al-Mosuli, and apparently he had acquired an Iraqi military uniform. After the attack indigenous insurgent groups claim that the suicide bomber was not affiliated with al-Zarqawi and was a native Iraqi. Najaf's police chief, Ghalib al-Jazairi, states that an Iraqi in custody confessed to having received training in a camp in Syria under the supervision of a Syrian military officer. The Iraqi reportedly took part in a bombing in Najaf in early December that killed fifty-four people. Syria denies having trained any insurgents.

December 23 One hundred and forty-one Iraqi police officers graduate from six specialty training courses given at the Adnan training center. The one- to two-week courses are designed to bolster the regular eight-week training courses and focus particularly on basic criminal investigation, supervision, executive leadership, and kidnapping/hostage rescue.

December 25 In Mosul a roadside bomb explodes, destroying an Iraqi National Guard bus. Five guardsmen die, and three are wounded. Reportedly, Iraqi civilians threw rocks at the burning vehicle after the attack.

December 26 Colonel Yassin Ibrahim Jawad, a high-ranking police officer, is killed in southern Baghdad. General Babakir Shawkat Zebari states that the bombing of the mess tent in Mosul was not perpetrated by a member of the Iraqi military or security forces. He further states that President Bush's criticisms of Iraqi forces, primarily that some would not fight and that some had deserted, were erroneous.

December 28 Insurgents attack and destroy the Um Kashifa police station near Tikrit. Twelve Iraqi police officers are killed. In a separate attack near Tikrit, militants attack a police checkpoint, killing one officer and wounding two others. Police checkpoints south of Tikrit are attacked, killing five Iraqi police officers and wounding three more. Thirteen Iraqi police officers are shot execution-style at one of the stations. U.S. Major Neal O'Brien, spokesman for the First Infantry Division, states that despite the attack, the Iraqi security forces in Tikrit are performing quite well. One soldier cites nearly two-and-a-half months of relative quiet in the city as proof. An Iraqi employed at the city hall states that twenty-five members of the Iraqi National Guard resigned after the attacks. An elaborate ambush on Iraqi National Guard troops takes place south of Baquba. It starts with a roadside bomb that wounds three Iraqi national guardsmen near the Maffrak traffic circle in the Mualemeen neighborhood. A second roadside bomb is found and a disposal team comes to remove it. A suicide car bomber then drives through the security cordon, killing a civilian and twenty-six others. Insurgents in Baghdad detonate a car bomb near the home of Major General Moudher al-Mula, an Iraqi National Guard commander, in an assassination attempt. He escapes unhurt, although several bystanders are killed. In a separate attack in the western Baghdad district of Ghaziliya, insurgents lure Iraqi police officers into an explosive-laden home and then blow up the house, killing seven police officers and wounding two others. In Mosul militants fire from a mosque at a joint U.S.-Iraqi military patrol, wounding one Iraqi national guardsman. Near Samarra, five Ministry of Interior commandos are wounded by an improvised explosive device (IED).

December 29 Iraqi Defense Minister Hazim al-Shalaan announces that the Iraqi National Guard will be incorporated into the Iraqi Army on January 6, 2005, the anniversary of Army Day. He states that forces totaling a division in size will all be graduating on that day. An Iraqi official states that Iraqi security forces have captured a key member of Abu Musab al-Zarqawi's organization in the city of Mosul. Abu Marwan allegedly directed attacks in the city and was responsible for purchasing weapons and training the various terrorist cells.

December 31 Five Iraqi national guardsmen are wounded near Baiji when a car bomb explodes near their patrol vehicle. Two civilians are killed.

2005

January 1 Militants claiming loyalty to Abu Musab al-Zarqawi release a video showing the execution of five Iraqis believed to be Iraqi border guards. The insurgents warn that the same fate will befall any Iraqis who join the military and security services.

January 2 Twenty-two Iraqi national guardsmen die north of Baghdad in the city of Balad when their bus is hit with a car bomb. Four Iraqi police officers die in an ambush in Samarra, and another is wounded. Insurgents shoot and kill the police chief in the town of Jebala. Reports indicate more than 1,000 Iraqi military and security force members have died since September.

January 3 A car bomb detonates outside Iraqi Interim Prime Minister Allawi's political party headquarters, killing three police officers. Four Iraqi national guardsmen die in a suicide car bomb explosion in Dijail, near the site of the bombing of the Iraqi National Guard bus the previous day. In Tal Afar one Iraqi police officer dies and two are injured when an explosion occurs while they investigate a decapitated body. Insurgents had booby-trapped the body with explosives. Six Iraqi national guardsmen die in Tikrit when two roadside bombs explode. In Baiji insurgents kill a police major and captain in a drive-by shooting.

January 4 Iraqi police backed by U.S. forces conduct a large raid in Diali. Iraq forces claim to have captured "an important terrorist." Some suggest that it is Abu Musab al-Zarqawi, but U.S. forces fervently deny this. In Baghdad a suicide truck bomb explodes, killing eight Iraqi police commandos while wounding at least sixty other people. Near Baquba three Iraqi national guardsmen die in a bomb attack.

January 5 At least two newly graduated Iraqi police are killed when a suicide car bomber rams his vehicle into a crowd of people. At least eight other people are killed and forty-four wounded. Insurgents kill Colonel Khalefeh Ali Hassan, security chief for Iraq's Independent Election Commission, in a drive-by shooting in Diyala province. A suicide car bomber tries to strike a joint U.S.-Iraqi military convoy in western Baghdad but succeeds only in killing Iraqi civilians.

January 6 Iraq celebrates Army Day, the eighty-fourth anniversary of the founding of the army in 1921.

January 8 In Ramadi Colonel Jassim al-Kharbeet, a member of the police force, is killed by gunmen. In the Anbar province Brigadier Abid Ahmed al-Assafi is assassinated by militants.

January 10 General Amer Nayef, the deputy police chief of Baghdad, and his son, Lieutenant Khaled Amer, are assassinated by insurgents in the al Dora neighborhood of southern Baghdad. Also in the southern part of the city, a suicide bomber rams his vehicle into the main gate of the al-Mada'en police station, killing three Iraqi police officers. Reports indicate that the attacker's car was painted to resemble a police car or might have in fact been a stolen one. In Samarra the city's deputy police chief, Brigadier Mohammed Mudhafar Al-Badri, is killed in a drive-by shooting. A suicide car bomber detonates his vehicle in front of the entrance to an Iraqi security forces base in Rubai'a, 105 miles northwest of Mosul. Four Iraqi security personnel die. In Basra a suicide bomber attacks a police station. In a coordinated attack another bomber targets a police internal affairs office in Basra. The ensuing blasts kill only the bombers.

January 11 Insurgents detonate a car bomb near a police station in Tikrit. Six Iraqi policemen die. In Mosul insurgents attack a U.S.-Iraqi convoy delivering heaters and supplies to a nearby school. The attackers detonate a car bomb close to the convoy and fire weapons from a mosque. Three Iraqi soldiers die, and six are wounded.

January 12 In Mosul militants detonate a car bomb next to an Iraqi National Guard patrol. The attack kills two guardsmen and wounds two more. An Iraqi soldier discovers a weapons cache in Kadasia while on joint patrol with U.S. soldiers. The uncovered munitions would have provided enough explosives for thirty-five IEDs.

January 13 Insurgents in Baquba detonate a roadside bomb as an Iraqi police patrol passes. Six officers are wounded and one dies. Militants kill an Iraqi National Guard captain in Qaim.

January 14 Thirty-eight Iraqi prisoners escape from the Abu Ghraib prison. Iraqi guards almost immediately recapture ten of the detainees. The prisoners managed to loosen their bonds and overpower the nearby police and guards, fatally shooting one police officer. The Iraqi authorities set up checkpoints in the Sa'alam neighborhood of western Baghdad to try and apprehend the prisoners. It is believed that two Egyptians are among the escaped. Reportedly, Iraqi police officers may have facilitated their escape as the prisoners were moved at night and with little security—conditions that are extremely unusual. Three Kurdish troops die fighting against insurgents alongside Iraqi National Guard forces in Mosul. Militants detonate a car bomb outside a Shi'ite mosque in Khan Bani Saad. Four Iraqi policemen die in the blast along with three civilians. A bus carrying fifteen Iraqi national guardsmen on their way to a U.S. base is ambushed near the western city of Hit. The guardsmen are abducted by unknown assailants, and the bus is burned. Iraqi soldiers and multinational forces arrest two suspected insurgents and uncover a bomb-making plant during a raid in Duluiyah. The raid uncovers 500 kilograms of ammonium nitrate and fifty-five gallons of diesel fuel, ingredients used in the powerful car bombs made by insurgents.

January 16 Gunmen assassinate an Iraqi police captain and two government auditors in Kut. Militants dressed in Iraqi police uniforms open fire on Shi'ite political candidate Salama Khafaji's car in central Baghdad. She is unharmed, and the attackers flee. The Iraqi Defense Ministry releases a statement declaring that Iraqi forces killed thirty-five insurgents near Fallujah over the weekend. An Iraqi National Guard commander in Baquba states that a majority of the city will go to the polls to vote in the January 30 elections. Approximately 900 Iraqi soldiers assigned to the Eighth Brigade, Third Division graduate from basic military training. The soldiers were trained at the Al Kisik military training base and will join the Third Division in pre-election patrols in the Ninewa province.

January 17 In Buhruz insurgents ambush a bus carrying Iraqi soldiers with rifles and rocket-propelled grenades, killing at least seven soldiers. In Baiji a suicide car bomber rams a checkpoint. Seven Iraqi police officers die. Reportedly, guerillas attack Iraqi police stations in Sharqat and Dawr. A spokesman for Interim Prime Minister Allawi states that a man, Izz al-Din Al-Majid, captured in early December by Iraqi security forces was trying to unify Ansar al-Sunna, Jaysh Muhammad, and the Islamic Resistance Army, three insurgent groups.

January 18 Four suicide car bombs explode in Baghdad within ninety minutes. Abu Musab al-Zarqawi claims credit for all four bombs. One bomber detonates a vehicle near the al-Alahi hospital in central Baghdad, killing five Iraqi policemen. Another bomber targets a control point south of the Baghdad International Airport. Two Iraqi security guards die, and three are wounded. Reportedly, another bomb was headed for an army garrison, and the final bomb was destined for a bank where police officers tend to congregate. Colonel Mike Murray, commander of the U.S. Third Brigade, First Calvary states that all four bombers failed to reach their intended targets because of the efforts of the Iraqi military and security forces. Twelve miles north of Hilla, insurgents detonate a car bomb, killing one Iraqi policeman and wounding two others. In Tikrit militants launch several attacks, which kill five Iraqi policemen and wound four others. Another Iraqi policeman dies near Baquba, and three more are wounded during a mortar attack on a police station. The 204th Iraqi Army battalion conducts several raids that net Hashum Mehdi Hussein Al Tai and Ahsan Abd Ali Khadhim Al Obaydi in Khalis. Reportedly, the two men were the primary leaders of the Khalis insurgency. Six hundred and seventy Iraqi Intervention Force (IIF) soldiers graduate from training at the Taji military training base. Interim Prime Minister Allawi states that he has been talking to U.S. commanders in the field about ways to speed up the training and equipping of Iraqi soldiers. In her confirmation testimony before the U.S. Senate Foreign Relations Committee, former National Security Adviser and future Secretary of State Condoleezza Rice states that there are 120,000 fully trained and equipped Iraqi soldiers.

January 20 An Iraqi police official estimates that 250 suicide attackers with 150 car bombs are prepared to strike during the Iraqi elections. His estimate was based on a series of interrogations of captured insurgents. Militants try to seize the Al Salam Hospital in Mosul, but Iraqi forces prevent them from doing so. Hospital workers and patients flee the scene.

January 21 Insurgents lob grenades at an Iraqi police river patrol in northern Baghdad. Four officers are injured. In Hit fifteen militants storm a police station, order the Iraqi policemen out, steal their equipment and two police cars, and then blow up the building. No officers are injured. Iraqi Intervention Force soldiers repel insurgent attacks on the Mosul train station. Reports indicate that $300 million in American currency was taken from Iraq's Central Bank and put on a plane for Lebanon earlier in January. Critics claim that there is no indication why this money was sent and for what purpose. Aides to Iraqi Defense Minister Hazim al-Shalaan state that the money was rushed to arms dealers in an effort to quickly supply Iraqi forces with the equipment needed to fight the insurgency. The aides refuse to list the names of the dealers, citing concerns for the dealers' safety. Iraq's national security adviser was unaware of the transfer, and it is unclear whether the money came from Iraqi or American sources.

January 22 Gunmen ambush and kill Muwthana Salman, an Iraqi intelligence officer, in Baquba. U.S. military and Iraqi police forces arrest one of the top insurgent suspects. Retired four-star U.S. Army General Gary E. Luck, sent by the Pentagon two weeks earlier to assess the training efforts in Iraq, states that the United States must speed up the training process while bolstering the Iraqi security and military forces.

January 23 An insurgent group led by Abu Musab al-Zarqawi posts a video on the Internet showing an Iraqi National Guard colonel being shot in the head. The colonel had been kidnapped in Mosul. Reports indicate that the United States may be attempting to bring back much of Saddam's former army in an effort to bolster the fledgling Iraqi military and security forces.

January 24 The Iraqi Ministry of Interior announces that it has made several significant arrests of insurgents in and around Ramadi. Among them is Abu Omar al-Kurdi, the man Iraqi government officials claim was behind 75 percent of the car bombs in Baghdad in 2003. The Iraqi government states that he is a top bomb maker and recruiter and was one of Abu Musab al-Zarqawi's top men in the Baghdad area. General Babakir Shawkat Zebari, head of the Iraqi military, states that he foresees Iraqi military and security forces numbering 150,000 by summer 2005. Additionally, he foresees U.S. troops pulling out of the cities and operating only one or two major bases by the end of 2005.

January 25 Four Iraqi policemen from the Muthanna station are gunned down in the Rashad neighborhood of Baghdad by insurgents. Reportedly, the gunmen pointedly asked if the individuals were police before they start firing. Elsewhere in Baghdad, a police colonel and his five-year-old daughter are shot to death while driving. In the southeastern portion of the city, gun battles between insurgents and Iraqi police kill three officers.

January 26 Two car bombs target Iraqi security and military forces. One bomb explodes outside of a police station in the town of Riyadh, killing three Iraqi police. Insurgents detonate the second bomb outside of the mayor's office in the same town. Two Iraqi soldiers die. In Baquba militants launch assaults on the offices of the Kurdish Democratic Party and the Iraqi Patriotic Gathering Alliance. The resulting battle kills one Iraqi policeman.

January 27 In Sinjar, seventeen miles southwest of Mosul, a suicide tractor bomber detonates his vehicle outside of the offices of the Kurdish Democratic Party. Four Iraqi soldiers and a guard die in the explosion. Nine soldiers and three guards are wounded. In Baquba a suicide car bomber detonates his vehicle as an Iraqi police convoy passes by the Diyala provincial governor's office. An Iraqi police lieutenant dies in the attack, and three other officers are wounded. The bombing takes place at the same time the governor was expected to arrive for a Peace Day meeting. The meeting was aimed at bringing together Ba'ath figures, insurgents, and interim political figures to discuss options for making the elections peaceful and successful. The governor is unhurt. Militants launch rockets at the home of Deputy Interior Minister for Police Affairs, Major General Hikmat Moussa. No one is hurt by the attack. Insurgents detonate a roadside bomb targeting Iraqi police on patrol near the Al-Sha'ab Stadium in the eastern part of Baghdad. The explosion fails to injure anyone. Commander of the Iraqi Army, General Babakir Shawkat Zebari, states that if the Iraqi military and security forces continue to improve, he believes that they will be able to protect major Iraqi urban areas in six months.

January 28 A suicide car bomber detonates his vehicle outside of the al Dora police station in southern Baghdad, killing four people and wounding two more.

January 30 The Iraqi elections take place. Forty-four people are killed in insurgent attacks, but the number of casualties and attacks is far below the expected number. One Iraqi policeman, Abdul Amir, is killed in Baghdad when a suicide bomber walks up to him outside of a polling station and detonates his explosives. Reportedly, Amir wrapped his arms around the bomber and dragged him away from the polling station before he could utilize his explosives.

January 31 Deputy Prime Minister Barham Saleh announces that the Iraqi government has arrested Anab Mohammed Hamid al-Qas, reportedly an Iraqi military adviser to Abu Musab al-Zarqawi who ranked third in his organization and who helped finance attacks in Baghdad.

February 1 The United States deploys another customs and border protection team in Iraq to help secure its borders.

February 2 Militants stop a convoy of Iraqi army recruits near Kirkuk and force twelve of them to lie in the street. The gunmen shoot the recruits and then run their bodies over.

February 3 Five police and one national guardsman are killed in an insurgent attack on a road south of Baghdad. Chairman of the Joint Chiefs of Staff, General Richard B. Myers, states that 40,000 of the reported 136,000 Iraqi security forces are adequately trained and equipped to go almost anywhere and confront almost any threat. The rest, he stated, are only fit for policing the calmer parts of southern Iraq. Deputy Secretary of Defense Paul D. Wolfowitz testifies that Iraqi units experience up to 40 percent absenteeism and that 1,342 Iraqi police and soldiers had died since June 2004.

February 5 In Basra a roadside bomb explodes, killing four Iraqi national guardsmen on patrol. Two Iraqi soldiers die in an explosion in Samarra. An insurgent group posts a video on the Internet depicting the murder of seven Iraqi national guardsmen.

February 6 Gunmen attack a police station in Mahawil. Fourteen insurgents, five Iraqi national guardsmen, and seventeen Iraqi police die. Iraqi security forces announce that they had captured Khamis Masin Farhan, a former Iraqi general, on December 20 in Baiji. Iraqi officials maintain that he assisted in a number of insurgent attacks.

February 7 Iraqi police officers and national guardsmen note an increase in tips from the general public concerning the insurgency in the week following the election.

February 8 In Baquba a car bomb explodes outside of the provincial police headquarters, killing fifteen recruits and wounding seventeen more. In Mosul a suicide bomber detonates his explosives inside the grounds of the Jumhouri Teaching Hospital. Twelve Iraqi policemen die, and four others are wounded. Witnesses say the bomber called police over to him prior to detonating his explosives. A group affiliated with Abu Musab al-Zarqawi claims credit for the hospital bombing.

February 9 A suicide bomber in Baghdad detonates his explosives in the middle of a crowd outside of the Iraqi National Guard headquarters at the Muthanna airfield. Twenty-two people die, and thirty are wounded. Three police officers die in Baghdad during a firefight in the Ghazaliya neighborhood. Iraqi security forces claim that they have captured a militant involved in beheadings in and around Mosul.

February 10 Four Iraqi policemen die in Samarra when a roadside bomb explodes. A police colonel, Riad Al-Yawi, attached to the Oil Ministry is abducted by gunmen loyal to Abu Musab al-Zarqawi in southern Baghdad. Police and insurgents wage a fierce battle in the town of Salman Pak, southeast of Baghdad. Ten policemen and twenty insurgents are killed. At least sixty-five policemen are wounded. Police capture two Saudis and three Iranians. An Iraqi army driver is shot dead in Balad.

February 11 Four bodies, believed to be Iraqi policemen, are found in Haswa, south of Baghdad. In Baquba a police officer dies in a drive-by shooting.

February 12 A suicide car bomb targeting an Iraqi National Guard patrol detonates, killing thirteen and wounding forty in Balad Ruz. It fails to injure any guardsmen. A group affiliated with Abu Musab al-Zarqawi claims credit for the attack. In Mosul the bodies of six Iraqi national guardsmen and six Kurdish security guards are dumped in separate parts of the city.

February 13 Iraqi troops recover the bodies of three U.S. servicemen killed in a Humvee accident at the Isaki Canal. They weld a tool themselves to recover the bodies and brave freezing water temperatures.

February 14 Reportedly, 10,000 Iraqis arrive at one military base looking to enlist. Half pass the recruiting test.

February 15 Iraqi officials state that Iraqi security forces had captured two brothers who served as Iraqi intelligence agents in the Hussein regime. Sabah Nouri Milhim and Riyah Nouri Milhim were captured sometime in January and are suspected of training, supplying, and financing insurgents in Fallujah and Baghdad. It is believed that they had a large role in the countless attacks on Iraqi security forces in Baghdad.

February 17 In Samarra four Iraqi police officers die in two separate attacks. One attack was reportedly an unsuccessful assassination attempt on a police captain. In Baghdad a suicide bomber kills an Iraqi national guardsman. In a later attack guardsmen shoot and kill another would-be suicide bomber before he can detonate his explosive vest. The attacks occur in the Mansour district. Elsewhere in Baghdad, Ghazi Houshi, an Interior Ministry intelligence officer, is gunned down in the Dawra neighborhood. In Baquba gunmen fire on an Iraqi police patrol, killing one officer. Two insurgents die in the fight. In Mosul a police station is fired upon, wounding the commander and killing his driver. The Jordan International Police Training Center (JIPTC) graduates another 1,491 police officers. Another 183 graduated from advanced and specialty courses at the Adnan training facility. Also, a contract is signed for six new Iraqi Al Uboor class patrol ships to be built in Iraq by Iraqis, costing $15 million and scheduled to be in service in six months.

February 18 Gunmen in Diyala assassinate an Iraqi National Guard officer and four civilians. The Najaf city police chief, Ghalib al-Jazairi, a visible opponent of the insurgency, states that his two sons, members of the police force, had been kidnapped and murdered in Karbala. He states that he is worried that his force has been infiltrated by insurgents. The responsibility for providing security in several parts of Baghdad is turned over to the Iraqi 305th "Tiger" unit.

February 19 In Baquba a car bomb detonates at the National Guard headquarters, killing one guardsman.

February 20 U.S. and Iraqi security forces launch simultaneous raids and set up checkpoints in the cities of Ramadi, Hit, and Haditha. The Iraqi National Guard reports that nine men were arrested for connections to Abu Musab al-Zarqawi. A U.S.

Marine Corps spokesman states that while some of the insurgents in Ramadi had come from Fallujah prior to the assault on the city, most were common criminals. U.S. soldiers and Iraqi police detain seventeen suspected insurgents and seize weapons in a raid in Baghdad. The Iraqi Interim Government reports that an Iraqi battalion had captured Jaffa Sadaq Fette, the leader of a one-hundred-man cell who profited by transporting Iraqis out of the country for insurgency training and then transporting them back in. He was captured February 3 in Balad; 267 Iraqi police begin patrols in Samarra to try to quell the restive city.

February 21 A suicide bomber drove his vehicle into a crowd of people gathered outside the Interior Ministry's Rangers Battalion headquarters in the Qadisiriyah neighborhood of Baghdad. Trainees and volunteers finish a drill as he strikes. At least two die and seven are wounded. Iraqis say that it is the third or fourth time that crowds have been targeted outside the complex.

February 22 In western Baghdad Iraqi police shoot and kill an insurgent attempting to plant an IED near a Shi'ite mosque. The incident occurs in the Ghazaliya neighborhood.

February 24 Insurgents detonate a suicide car bomb at the police headquarters in Tikrit. Ten Iraqis are killed, and thirty-five more are injured. The bomber wore a police uniform, indicating either that it was stolen, sold on the black market, or that the bomber had infiltrated the force. In Qaim four Iraqi national guardsmen are killed by two roadside bombs. In Kirkuk a roadside bomb kills two policemen and injures three. Khattab Omar Arif, the leader of the city's emergency police, states that the bomb was intended for him and instead killed the men guarding him. The Iraq Police Service (IPS) this week graduated 1,993 new police officers from basic police training courses in Sulaymaniyah and Baghdad. Also, another 204 graduated from advanced and specialty courses at the Adnan training facility.

February 26 In Nibai one Iraqi Army soldier is shot dead, and an Iraqi policeman is killed in Baquba.

February 27 In the Musayyib district insurgents try and disrupt an Iraqi Army raid with a car bomb. One Iraqi soldier is killed, and three are wounded. Twelve suspects are captured.

February 28 Insurgents launch the single deadliest attack to date, detonating a suicide car bomb outside of a Hilla city government office where police recruits were waiting to get physicals. The explosion kills at least 127 and wounds more than 150. A separate car bomb explodes in Musayyib—no details are available. In Mosul a firefight between insurgents and Iraqi commandos leaves four civilians dead, and a group of insurgents blow themselves up after they are chased down and surrounded by Kurdish forces and Iraqi police. In Baghdad Iraqi soldiers fight a contingent of Sudanese militants following an attack on an army convoy. The battle takes place in the al-Battaween district. Twenty-two militants are detained, and at least two are killed.

March 2 A suicide car bomber detonates his vehicle near an army recruiting center in the Salihiya neighborhood of Baghdad. Six soldiers die, and twenty-eight are wounded by the blast. This is the third time the center has been targeted in a year. The third attack produced the fewest casualties, and it is believed that the blast walls were successful in protecting the site. A second car bomb explodes two hours later in the Jadriya neighborhood of the city. The second blast targeted an Iraqi military convoy, killing seven and injuring two.

March 3 Colonel Mou'ness Saeed, chief of the al-Mouqdad station in Kirkuk, narrowly dodges an assassination attempt. Gunmen target him in a drive-by shooting, but he escapes unharmed. Insurgents detonate two car bombs near the Ministry of Interior in Baghdad, killing five police officers and wounding seven others. In Baquba a suicide car bomber targets the chief of the emergency police in the Diyala province, Mudhafar Shahab Jiburi. The bomber detonates his vehicle outside the headquarters of the Iraqi emergency police, killing one person and wounding twelve others. Jiburi escapes unharmed. A previously unheard of Iraqi insurgent group, the SaLaden Al Ayobi Brigades of the Islamic Front of Iraqi Resistance (JAME), pledges to stop targeting Iraqi security forces and civilians and to concentrate on U.S. forces. The Iraqi Police Service graduated 292 police officers from advanced and specialty courses at the Adnan training facility, twenty-seven officers from the special weapons and tactics training course, and seventy-two police officers from the emergency response unit.

March 4 Colonel Ghaib Hadab Zarib, the al-Budair police chief, is shot to death outside his home by gunmen. U.S. Army officials announce that Corporal Dustin Berg, an Indiana national guardsman, will be court-martialed for the November 2003 murder of Iraqi police officer Hussein Kamel Hadi Dawood Dubeidi. Fifteen decapitated bodies are found in an old military base between Latifiya and Karbala. The dead include women and children. It is believed that the men were part of a group of Iraqi soldiers kidnapped some time ago.

March 6 Reports indicate that most of the violent neighborhoods in Baghdad, including the Adhamiya neighborhood and Haifa Street, have been turned over to Iraqi forces in the weeks following the election. A reported ten neighborhoods are in the care of the Iraqi Army's Fortieth Brigade. The Iraqi forces hope to control all of the city by December 2005.

March 7 Militants bomb the Balad house of Mohammed Jasim, a major in the Iraqi National Guard, killing his family. Jasim claimed credit for capturing or killing most of the insurgents who had been neutralized in the area. Two Sudanese men were taken into custody for questioning in connection with the attack. In Baquba insurgents launch an elaborate attack on an Iraqi Army checkpoint. Eight cars pull over, and fifty masked militants leap out and open fire on the checkpoint. The attackers withdrew, and the Iraqi forces took their comrades to the hospital. On the way an explosion, believed to be a suicide bomber, rocks the hospital convoy. Officials believe that the attacks were coordinated. Six soldiers, two policemen, and two civilians are killed, and twenty-three people are wounded. A group affiliated with Abu Musab al-Zarqawi claims credit for the attacks.

March 9 Insurgents park a garbage truck packed with explosives close to the Sadr Hotel in central Baghdad. A firefight breaks out between the hotel's armed guards and the insurgents minutes before the truck is detonated. An Iraqi police officer is killed, and more than forty other people are wounded. A group affiliated with Abu Musab al-Zarqawi claims credit. In Basra insurgents detonate a roadside bomb while an Iraqi police convoy passes. Two police officers are killed and five more wounded in the attack. In Habbaniyah, a town within the Sunni Triangle, a suicide bomber drives his car into an Iraqi Army base. The driver is believed to be Sudanese. The bomb kills two officers, a civilian, and wounds fifteen people. Twenty bodies are found near Qaim, close to the Syrian border. It is unclear if the men were Iraqi soldiers or policemen. Investigators believe the killings occurred on March 5, toward the end of the Marine-led Operation River Blitz, which focused on the towns of Ramadi, Hit, Haditha, and Qaim. In al-Habbaniyah a suicide car bomber attacks a joint U.S.-Iraqi checkpoint on the road to a U.S. military base. No casualties were confirmed. Shoqayer Fareed Sheet, a former Iraqi police lieutenant, confessed to a special Iraqi antiterrorism unit, al-Theeb (the wolf), that he had tortured and killed 113 Iraqi police officers, Iraqi soldiers, and Iraqi civilians and had provided Iraqi Sunni insurgents with information.

March 10 In southeastern Baghdad gunmen attack and critically wound an Iraqi Interior Ministry police official, General Abdul Karim Raheem, while he is in his car. Colonel

Aiyad Abdul Razaq, who was driving to work in the same general part of Baghdad, is shot to death. He was the chief deputy of the Jisdiala police station. In central Baghdad the chief of the al-Salihiya police station, Colonel Hamad Ubeyis, is shot to death in his squad car. Shoqayer Fareed Sheet leads al-Theeb to a mass grave at the Wadi Egab Cemetery where thirty-one bodies, believed to be members of the Iraqi security forces, are found. In Baghdad gunmen kill a top police official, Lieutenant Colonel Ahmed Obais, who was being driven to work by a driver and his bodyguard.

March 12 Militants ambush three Iraqi policemen in Mosul's Sukar district. The officers were driving to a friend's funeral. All three were shot to death.

March 13 More than 2,900 Iraqi soldiers graduate as part of the direct recruit replacement program at the Iraqi Training Battalion at Kirkush military training base.

March 14 Ramzi Hashim, a Mosul man, is arrested by the Najaf police. Police chief Ghalib al-Jazairi states that they captured him in a hotel plotting a major attack. The police believe that he was involved in the August 2003 bombing at the Imam Ali Mosque that killed SCIRI head Ayatollah Mohammed Baqr al-Hakim. Iraqi officials announce that they have in their custody Marwan Taher Abdulrasheed and Abdulla Maher Abdulrasheed. The two men were arrested in Tikrit on February 8. Marwan is a former Saddam bodyguard, and officials believe that Abdulla was helping to fund the insurgency.

March 15 A car bomb in Baghdad wounds an Iraqi policeman. No further details are reported.

March 16 In Baquba a car bomb is detonated by insurgents at a checkpoint manned by Iraqi Army soldiers, killing two soldiers and wounding five more.

March 20 A suicide bomber walks into police headquarters in Mosul and detonates his explosives. Two people are killed, including Walid Kashmoula, the chief of Mosul's anticorruption operations. Three Iraqi police officers are wounded when a roadside bomb explodes in Kirkuk. In Baquba gunmen open fire on a police station, killing four Iraqi officers and wounding two others.

March 21 Insurgents try to assassinate Mosul's provincial police chief. The attack is a failure, and seventeen militants die. No Iraqi security force casualties are reported.

March 22 Iraqi officials state that eighty-five insurgents died earlier in the day when Iraqi commandos, assisted by U.S. air and ground support, overran an insurgent training camp located in swamps near Tharthar Lake in the Sunni Triangle. The commandos were part of the First Police Commando Battalion. The eighty-five insurgents were the most killed in any one battle since the offensive against Fallujah. Among the dead insurgents were Iraqis, Sudanese, Algerians, Moroccans, and others. Seven Iraqi commandos were killed, and five were wounded. Reportedly, the camp was part of the Islamic Army of Tikrit, which in an unusual act distributed leaflets announcing that they had sustained eleven casualties in the assault in the swamps. Insurgents attack Iraqi soldiers in Kirkuk, but according to Iraqi officials, they fight them off. No casualties are reported. The military academy at Zahko graduated seventy-three new second lieutenants destined to join the Iraqi Army. Also, the Multinational Security Transition Command–Iraq (MNSTC–I) Civilian Police Assistance Training Team (CPATT) is approaching the halfway point in training and fielding special weapons and tactics (SWAT) teams to each governorate. Seven teams are trained and equipped; two others are currently in training.

March 23 U.S. and Iraqi forces conduct raids south of Mosul near Tal Afar. Iraqi officials announce that Iraqi security forces had disrupted a plot to attack the National Assembly the previous week during its meeting in the Green Zone.

March 24 Eleven Iraqi policemen of the Second Iraqi Special Police Commando Unit are killed when a suicide car bomber detonates his vehicle at a checkpoint in

Ramadi. In Mosul Iraqi police mistake three Iraqi Army officers and two Iraqi police officers for insurgents. They open fire, killing all five men. U.S. and Iraqi forces continue raids near Tal Afar, seizing thirteen suspected insurgents and several weapons. Militants shoot and kill the commander of an Iraqi Army brigade in Basra, Major General Salman Muhammad, as he drives from a friend's funeral in Baghdad.

March 25 Reports cast doubt on the Iraqi claim that police commandos killed eighty-five insurgents in March 22's major raid. Exact casualties remain unknown, but U.S. and Iraqi officials assert that the Iraqis, in their first major lead operation, performed well. A suicide car bomber detonates his vehicle in Iskandariya close to an Iraqi Army convoy. Four soldiers die, and nine soldiers and civilians are wounded. In Fallujah U.S. and Iraqi forces impose a curfew after an Iraqi policeman is shot to death. Reports today indicate that Iraqi commandos admitted that the attack on the terrorist training camp in the swamps on March 22 was not as successful as it first seemed. Most of the insurgent casualties reported were caused by American helicopter gunships. Iraqi commandos confirmed that the dead insurgents were mostly foreign Arabs. A Filipino and an Algerian were found among the dead, allegedly along with Chechens, Saudis, and Afghans.

March 27 A militant group claiming to be Abu Musab al-Zarqawi's Al Qa'ida in Iraq releases a video depicting the apparent shooting death of an alleged employee of the Ministry of Interior. The murdered man identifies himself as Colonel Ryadh Katie Olyway just before he dies. An Iraqi ministry official confirms that a Colonel Olyway worked for both the Ministry of Interior and the Oil Ministry but could not verify the identity of the man in the video. Guards outside of the Ministry of Science and Technology in Baghdad open fire on protesters who were demanding better pay. One protester is killed.

March 28 Militants detonate a roadside bomb near an Iraqi police patrol in southwestern Baghdad. Three police are wounded, and one is killed. The chief of the Balat al-Shouhada police station in southeastern Baghdad, Colonel Abdul Kahrim Fahad, is gunned down while being driven to work.

March 31 Joint Iraqi and U.S. raids in Mosul and Tal Afar begin. In Tuz Khurmatu insurgents detonate a car bomb at an Iraqi Army checkpoint designed to protect visitors to a Shi'ite shrine. Several civilians die, and eight Iraqi soldiers are wounded. The Iraqi Police Service graduated 2,906 new police officers this month from basic police training courses in Baghdad, Sulaymaniyah, Al Kut, Al Asad, and Jordan. They also graduated 159 police officers from advanced and specialty courses at the Adnan training facility.

April 1 In Balad Ruz an Interior Ministry commando is killed during a raid in the Daniya section of the city. Elsewhere in the city, police chief Colonel Hatem Rashid Mohammed is killed by insurgents while getting into his vehicle. Joint Iraqi and U.S. raids continue in Mosul and Tal Afar. Raids have netted eight insurgent suspects and multiple weapons. At a Baghdad mosque a group of sixty-four Sunni Arab imams and religious scholars issue an edict encouraging Sunni Arabs to join the Iraqi Army and police. The edict was signed by Ahmed Hassan al-Taha, an imam who has been a strong critic of the occupation, but not Harith al-Dari, the leader of the association of Muslim scholars. An Iraqi flight crew from Squadron 23 of the Iraqi Air Force aboard an Iraqi C-130 transported fifty-one Department of Border Enforcement (DBE) soldiers from training in the United Arab Emirates and returned them to Iraq. The milestone of this mission was the fact that the Iraqi flight crew prepared the necessary requirements to fly in international airspace, land in a foreign country, and performed all of the flight-crew functions.

April 2 In a bold attack between forty and sixty insurgents launch an attack on the Abu Ghraib prison from all sides, utilizing car bombs, mortars, RPGs, and small arms. The insurgents attack the part of the prison controlled by the Iraqi security forces in an apparent attempt to free an unknown quantity of prisoners. U.S. forces call in reinforcements and repel the attack which lasts for approximately forty-five minutes. In Khan Bani Saad insurgents detonate a car bomb at a police station, killing five, including three policemen, and wounding three more Iraqi police.

April 3 The body of a Kurdish police officer who had been shot to death is found in Mosul.

April 4 During a joint search operation, Iraqi forces are attacked by insurgents in Diyala province. U.S. air and ground assets from the U.S. Army's Forty-second Infantry Division move in to help once they are attacked. One Iraqi soldier is killed during the hour-long battle.

April 5 General Jalal Mohammed Salah, commander of an Interior Ministry mechanized armored brigade, is kidnapped in Baghdad. In Amiriya on Baghdad's western outskirts, insurgents detonate a car bomb as an Iraqi military convoy passes by. No military casualties are reported, but several civilians are hurt. In Tal Afar a bus filled with about fifty Iraqi soldiers is hit by an explosion from a roadside bomb. Three Iraqi soldiers are killed, and more than forty-four are wounded. The soldiers were on their way to distribute pay to their families. Reportedly, Iraqi soldiers believe that the attackers knew they were coming. Several trucks with mounted machine guns were protecting the bus before the explosion.

April 7 Iraq's president, Jalal Talibani, takes office and offers an amnesty to insurgents, possibly even insurgents who have killed Iraqi security force members. The amnesty is seen as much broader than the one posed by the former interim prime minister, Ayad Allawi. In Mosul insurgents launch a bomb attack on an Iraqi Army patrol. Three soldiers are killed and twenty more wounded. The patrol issues a statement claiming to have captured seven attackers. In Basra Major Mahmoud Hassan al-Yassiri, an Iraqi Army officer, is killed when gunmen burst into a restaurant where he is eating with a colleague and shoot him in the head. The Iraqi Police Service graduated 258 police officers from advanced and specialty courses at the Adnan training facility. Also, 247 recruits pick up graduation certificates from the Iraqi Highway Patrol Academy and head for new jobs guarding their country's streets and thoroughfares. This was the first class to graduate from the new academy.

April 9 In Mosul an insurgent car bomb kills two Iraqi policemen. Press reports indicate that claims of abuse had been lodged against members of Iraq's security forces by other Iraqis.

April 11 U.S. soldiers and approximately 500 Iraqi soldiers conduct sweeps dubbed Operation Vanguard Tempest in the Al-Rasheed district in Baghdad. The sweeps net some sixty-five suspected militants. The district is suspected to be a hub of insurgent activity.

April 12 The Iraqi government claims that it has captured Fadhil Ibrahim Mahmud al-Mashadani. Mashadani reportedly aided insurgent attacks and was a high-ranking Ba'athist in the Saddam Hussein regime. The Iraqi government had posted a $200,000 reward for information leading to his capture. In Baghdad Major General Tareq al-Baldawi, the deputy interior minister, is attacked in the Hay al-Adel district. He escapes unhurt. U.S. Secretary of Defense Rumsfeld visits Iraq and states that the United States will not leave until the Iraqi security forces are capable assuming full control of the country.

April 13 Insurgents in Kirkuk detonate a bomb close to twelve Iraqi security force members who are defusing a roadside bomb. All twelve are killed. In Baghdad gunmen attack Colonel Naji Hussein, a Ministry of Interior official, as he drives through the al Dora district. He is wounded by small-arms fire.

April 14 U.S. soldiers and Iraqi soldiers arrest seventeen suspected insurgents in western Baghdad and seize weapons, U.S. currency, and bomb-making materials. Insurgents detonate two car bombs nearly simultaneously near an Iraqi police convoy. Most of the casualties are civilians. The exact number of hurt or killed Iraqi police is unknown. Approximately two hours later, U.S. and Iraqi forces destroy a follow-on car bomb near the same site. Elsewhere in the city, gunmen kill First Lieutenant Firas Hussein while on his way in to work. He was reportedly working for Iraq's intelligence service. In Mahawil a suicide bomber detonates a briefcase full of explosives in a market. Four Iraqi policemen die, and several civilians are wounded. In Kirkuk militants assault the Al-Adala police station, killing three Iraqi policemen and wounding two others. In Baquba Iraqi forces take into custody twenty-seven suspected militants.

April 15 Insurgents attack an Iraqi military convoy in Baghdad. Exact casualties are unknown. In the city's Talbiya district, a roadside bomb detonates near an Iraqi Army convoy, killing one civilian and wounding three others. Reports indicate that fifty Shi'ite prisoners may have been taken by Sunni militants demanding that all Sh'ites evacuate the town of Madain. Civilians are reported fleeing the area.

April 16 Reports indicate that the kidnapping in Madain may be a response to an earlier kidnapping of twenty Sunnis from a nearby town. In Baquba insurgents bomb a restaurant. Ten police officers are killed. In Kirkuk militants shoot and kill a policeman and an Iraqi Army officer. Near Hilla a suicide car bomber plows into an Iraqi police patrol, killing four officers.

April 18 Iraqi security forces, numbering some 2,000 police and soldiers and reinforced by U.S. helicopters, receive a tip that leads them to a weapons cache. They arrest several suspected militants and uncover a bomb-making plant and a firing range. Ten insurgents wearing Iraqi military uniforms appear at Lieutenant General Adnan Qaragholi's home. When invited inside, they shoot and kill Qaragholi, an adviser to the interim defense minister, and his son, Iraqi Army Captain Alaa al-Din. The insurgents left their uniforms at the scene of the shooting. The public information officer for the Iraqi police in Mosul, Brigadier General Younis Mohammad Sulaiman, is killed by gunmen on his way to work. Iraqi security forces take control of Madain City, finding no Shi'ite hostages or prisoners. They arrest ten suspects and seize an unknown quantity of weapons. The Shi'ite bloc that forms the majority in the new Iraqi government announces plans to pursue a drastic purge of Ba'athists in the Iraqi security and military forces. U.S. and Iraqi officials state that this policy could do much to damage the forces that have been created and send many of the best intelligence and military officers over to the insurgency.

April 19 A suicide car bomber detonates his vehicle, a green Kia minibus, near a group of Iraqi security forces and recruits at the Adhamiya Palace in Baghdad. Two Iraqi Army soldiers and two recruits are killed. Eight soldiers are wounded, and approximately thirty recruits are hurt. Major General Adnan Thabit reportedly suggests that the incident in Madain had more to do with local tribal politics than anything else. He suggests further that the media and several political parties turned the incident into a crisis. In Basra two Iraqi policemen are killed and six hurt by the detonation of a roadside bomb.

April 20 Fifty bodies are found in the Tigris River. Some Iraqis believe that these bodies are the hostages who were reportedly taken in Madain, yet Riadh Sakhi, a police officer, states that it appeared as though several of the victims, which included two school girls, had been in the water for weeks and may have washed up as a result of the spring thaw. Reportedly, Iraqi President Jalal Talibani claims to have the names of both the kidnapped and those who committed the crime in Madain. Reports indicate that the bodies of nineteen Iraqi national guardsmen are found in a soccer stadium in Haditha. The men were part of a six minibus convoy headed to Haditha on April 19 to check reports of armed militants. When ambushed, four buses managed to escape, but two were left behind. The Iraqis who escaped returned to the site with U.S. reinforcements but found nothing. Reportedly, the Iraqis in the six minibuses were badly outgunned by the insurgents who were armed with grenade launchers. The guardsmen who were left behind were taken hostage and then executed. In Ramadi two suicide car bombers detonate their vehicles in the center of the city, close to an Iraqi checkpoint. The attackers failed to injure anyone. In Sadr City, militants kill police officer Ali Talib in a drive-by shooting. Elsewhere in Baghdad, a roadside bomb kills an Iraqi policeman and injures two others.

April 22 The prison director for the Nineveh province, Colonel Khalid Najim Abdallah, is killed in Mosul by insurgents who stop his car.

April 23 Reportedly, insurgents detonate a car bomb near an Iraqi National Guard convoy as it passes the village of Zaydan, close to Abu Ghraib prison. Nine soldiers are killed, and twenty more are injured. Three hundred and fourteen Iraqi Army soldiers graduate in Tikrit. In an attack on a joint U.S.-Iraqi convoy traveling a street close to the road to Baghdad International Airport, a suicide bomber wounds seven Iraqi soldiers and three U.S. soldiers. A roadside bomb in Yusufiyah kills an Iraq national guardsman. Three Iraqi soldiers are wounded by an IED that strikes their convoy in Mosul.

April 24 Militants detonate two car bombs at the checkpoint entrance to the Iraqi Police Academy in Tikrit. Six police are killed with an additional thirty-five wounded. Most of the wounded were Iraqi police.

April 25 Joint Iraqi and U.S. sweeps around Baghdad forty-one insurgents and an unspecified quantity of weapons. Ten of the militants are suspects in the shooting down of a civilian MI-8 helicopter.

April 26 The staff judge advocate team from the U.S. Third Infantry Division begins providing human-rights training to the First Iraqi Army Brigade.

April 28 In Basra Iraqi soldiers apprehend six insurgents armed with explosives and various weapons. Militants detonate a bomb in a heavily populated part of east Baghdad as police officers in two pick-up trucks drove by. Two officers die, and two more are wounded. Elsewhere in Baghdad, a Ministry of Interior official, Lieutenant Colonel Alaa Khalil Ibrahim, is shot dead on his way into work. The Iraqi Police Service graduated 2,872 police officers in April from basic police training courses in Sulaymaniyah, Basra, Jordan and Baghdad. Also, the Iraqi Police Service graduated 204 police officers from advanced and specialty courses at the Adnan training facility.

April 29 Iraqi police successfully prevent three suicide bomber attacks near Salman Pak. One police officer is killed, and five others are wounded. In the al Dora district of Baghdad, Iraqi officers safely detonate an IED near the al Dora police station. In Baghdad four suicide car bombers strike in the Azamiyah section of the city. Fifteen Iraqi soldiers die, and thirty are wounded in attacks on an Iraqi Army patrol, on a police patrol, and two on barricades close to the headquarters for the Interior Ministry's special forces. All told, more than ten car bombs explode in Iraq on this date; yet reports indicate that most of the bombers were unable to reach their intended targets. In a separate attack in the city, militants shoot at a police patrol, wounding one officer. Not far from Basra, an IED detonates near an Iraqi border guard patrol, killing one Iraqi soldier and wounding two others.

April 30 Militants shoot at an Iraqi police patrol in Mosul, wounding two officers.

May 1 Following a suicide bomb targeting the funeral gathering of Kurdish Democratic Party official Sayid Ahmed Wahab in Tal Afar, U.S. and Iraqi forces clash with insurgents. No casualties are reported. In the Nahrwan area of Baghdad, six Iraqi policemen are killed in an insurgent ambush on their checkpoint. Several of the eighteen militants are killed as well.

May 2 Insurgents target an Iraqi commando convoy in the al-Huriyah neighborhood of Baghdad. Two commandos are wounded and the commander of Baghdad's commandos, Major General Rasheed Aflayeh, escapes unharmed. In the Zayouna neighborhood, a car bomb explodes close to an Iraqi police patrol, killing two officers. Insurgents detonate a car bomb near an Iraqi Army convoy in the al-Tarmiyah portion of the city, wounding an Iraqi soldier and a police officer. In the southeastern Baghdad neighborhood of Ar Rustamayiah, thirty insurgents attack an Iraqi police checkpoint. Five police officers and an unknown number of insurgents die. A suicide bomber detonates his truck at a checkpoint south of the city. The blast kills eight soldiers and wounds twenty more.

May 3 An Iraqi soldier and policeman die in firefights in Baghdad. In the western portion of the city, three roadside bombs explode close to Iraqi police patrols, hurting four officers. In Ramadi a joint Iraqi-U.S. checkpoint comes under fire from insurgents. Twelve militants are killed, and two Iraqi soldiers are wounded. In Samarra militants shoot and kill three Iraqi policemen following a series of police raids on suspected insurgent-held areas. In Shurgat an Iraqi soldier is killed. No details are released.

May 4 The Army of Ansar al-Sunna claims credit for a suicide bombing in Irbil that targets an office of the KDP political party where more than 300 people were waiting to get approval to apply for Iraqi security jobs. More than sixty are killed and more than 150 injured by the blast. Reports indicate that the suicide bomber seems to have mingled among the recruits before detonating his explosives. Ansar al-Sunna had struck recruits previously in Irbil in February 2004. In Baghdad a car bomb explodes in the Dora area, killing nine Iraqi soldiers and wounding three others.

May 5 Nine Iraqi police officers die in insurgent ambushes on what appears to have been a convoy. Six die in the Sayidiya district and three close to Sayidiya Square. A suicide bomber detonates his vehicle outside of the frequently attacked army recruiting station outside the Muthanna airfield in Baghdad. Thirteen Iraqi soldiers die, and seven are wounded. Major General Salman Hikmat Moussa, an Interior Ministry official, escapes a suicide bomber who detonates his vehicle outside of his home in western Baghdad. One Iraqi police officer dies in the attack, and six others are wounded. Reports released today indicate that Iraqi security forces had captured Ayman Sabawi, an alleged supporter of the insurgency and half brother of Saddam Hussein, in Tikrit.

May 6 In northeastern Tikrit a suicide bomber rams a forty-five-person bus carrying Iraqi police officers to work. Seven officers die, and three are wounded. Lieutenant General Naiser Abadi, deputy chief of staff for Iraq's armed forces, states that he doubts the rumors that Abu Musab al-Zarqawi was injured and recovering in a Ramadi hospital are true. U.S. forces reportedly were investigating the rumors.

May 7 Iraqi soldiers detained twenty-nine suspected insurgents in Abu Dsheer and soldiers from an Iraqi public order battalion detained forty-four suspected insurgents in Dora.

May 8 In the Rawa area U.S. and Iraqi forces capture fifty-four militants and kill six more in a firefight after information gleaned from a captured al-Zarqawi aide, Ghassan Muhammad Amin Husayn al-Rawi, directs them to the region. They seize bomb-making material and two large stashes of weapons. The U.S. military reports that Iraqi forces captured Ammar al-Zubaydi, an alleged aide to Abu Musab al-Zarqawi, on May 5. Reportedly, Zubaydi is responsible for multiple bombing attacks, including a number of attacks in Baghdad on April 29 and the April attack on the Abu Ghraib prison. Those attacks killed twenty-three Iraqi troops and wounded thirty-one. Press releases state that he was planning to assassinate a senior Iraqi official, that he had stolen hundreds of rockets and cases of ammunition from facilities in Yusufiyah in 2003, and that he had helped Abu Omar al-Kurdi, another suspected al-Zarqawi aide captured in December.

May 9 Two Iraqi policemen are killed and six are wounded when a suicide car bomber detonates his vehicle at a police checkpoint in southern Baghdad. Reports state that militants had detonated 135 car bombs in April, more than any other month since the invasion. The same reports indicate that Iraqi police had seized ten vehicles in ten days packed with explosives that were to be used in bombings.

May 11 In Hawija a suicide bomber detonates his explosive vest among a crowd that had lined up to join the Iraqi Army. The suicide bomber managed to slip by security. Twenty are killed, and another thirty are wounded. In Baghdad insurgents detonate a car bomb outside of a police station in the al Dora neighborhood, killing civilians and wounding eight Iraqi police officers. In a separate car bomb attack on an emergency police patrol, four police officers are injured. The attack occurs at Jordan Square in the Yarmuk area of the city. In Jamiya insurgents attack an Iraqi Army patrol, killing three Iraqi soldiers. A suicide bomber detonates his vehicle near a police station in the Dawra area, killing civilians but no Iraqi policemen. In the Mansour district, militants gun down two police officers.

May 12 Iraqi Army Brigadier General Ayad Imad Mahdi is shot to death by gunmen as he drives to work in western Baghdad. An Iraqi Interior Ministry employee, Colonel Jamal Ahmed Hussein, is killed on his way to work in the al-Amin neighborhood. Reportedly, Polish and Iraqi forces seize a cache of weapons and arrest twenty-nine suspected militants in the Wasit province in a mission dubbed Operation Cobweb.

May 13 Reports released by the Iraqi government state that Iraqi forces had captured Saif Aldin Mustafa Nuaimi and Abdul Qadir Ashur Jaburi, two men allegedly affiliated with Abu Musab al-Zarqawi's organization, on April 15. Jaburi, Nuaimi's father, is accused of raising money for al-Zarqawi's group while Nuaimi is an alleged bomb maker. In Baghdad's Adil district, gunmen open fire on an Iraqi police patrol, killing two policemen and wounding three more. In Baquba insurgents detonate a car bomb, killing two Iraqi national guardsmen and wounding five more.

May 14 The bodies of ten Iraqi soldiers are found in western Ramadi. Two Iraqi police officers are killed in a clash in Samarra. Iraqi Army soldiers detained fifty-eight suspects in Miqdadiya.

May 15 In Iskandariya Iraqi police find eleven bodies, four of which had been beheaded. At least three of the dead are Iraqi soldiers. A suicide car bomber detonates his vehicle next to an Iraqi police patrol in Baghdad, killing four people. It is not clear how many officers are killed or wounded. Militants throw grenades at an Iraqi police convoy in the western part of the city, killing one officer.

May 16 In Baghdad an unidentified Iraqi general working for the Defense Ministry escapes an assassination attempt when his guards open fire on a car that pulls up next to his. The vehicle was flush with weaponry. Elsewhere in the city, Defense Minister Sadun al-Dulaimi announces that, due to complaints over Iraqi security force raids by Iraqi citizens, Iraqi forces would no longer be able to raid mosques and places of worship. Insurgents detonate a car bomb in a market within the city. When Iraqi troops investigate, militants detonate a follow-on car bomb, killing nine Iraqi soldiers. Unidentified Iraqis dressed as Iraqi Army soldiers bind, blindfold, and shoot eight civilians in the Al-Sha'ab area of Baghdad. Four more are found in the Ur neighborhood close to a mosque. In Baquba insurgents detonate a roadside bomb, killing five Iraqi soldiers and wounding seven more. Iraqi officials announce that they captured a Mosul-based bomb maker, Salim Yussef Ghafif Huseyn, last week.

May 17 An Interior Ministry official, Brigadier General Ibrahim Khammas, head of criminal intelligence, is killed by gunmen in a drive-by shooting as he leaves for work.

Coalition and Iraqi security forces (ISF) performed cordon and search operations in Heychal Salama resulting in the detainment of 150 suspected anti-Iraq forces, according to a multinational forces report.

May 18 A U.S. military official states that 126 car bombs had been detonated or disarmed since February 27, 2005. Iraqi forces are attacked in central Baghdad. They return fire, killing four militants. Further details are unavailable.

May 19 Reports indicate that the U.S. First Cavalry Division had received over one hundred allegations of abuse by Iraqi military forces by the time they left Iraq in February, spanning back six months.

May 21 Reports indicate that at least three Iraqi policemen are killed overnight.

May 22 Iraqi Army and Ministry of Interior forces, in conjunction with Coalition troops, conduct a series of raids in the Abu Ghraib district, termed Operation Squeeze Play, capturing a number of suspected insurgents. The Iraqi units involved include two battalions from the Third Brigade, Sixth Iraqi Army Division, two battalions from the First Brigade, First Iraqi Intervention Force, and three battalions from the Second Brigade special police commandos.

May 23 In Mosul a member of the Iraqi security forces dies when the bomb he was attempting to diffuse detonates. Operation Squeeze Play continues with Iraqi and Coalition forces having netted some 400 suspects. Militants detonate a car bomb in north Baghdad next to a café popular with Iraqi police. Five people are killed, although it was not immediately clear if any were police officers. Major General Wael Rubaei, an Iraqi security official, is shot to death as he drives into work in Baghdad. In the largest combined action to date, Iraqi and U.S. troops sweep the area near Abu Ghraib prison and the road to Baghdad's airport. Three hundred people are detained. A famous Iraqi police commando, Abdul Waleed, appears on Iraqi state television in a music video and threatens to cut off the arms of insurgents.

May 25 One thousand Iraqi and U.S. troops begin an offensive as a follow-up to Operation Matador in the Anbar province. This Operation New Market uncovers a weapons cache and a clash between U.S. Marines and insurgents. Iraqi Defense Ministry officials announce the capture of an associate of Abu Musab al-Zarqawi in Baquba. Captured on May 24, Iraqi forces describe him as al-Zarqawi's "secretary." In the Baghdad neighborhood of al Dora, insurgents detonate a car bomb that kills eight police commandos.

May 26 Iraqi Interior Minister Bayan Jabr announces that insurgent leader Abu Musab al-Zarqawi had been wounded in an assault. Jabr announces that 40,000 Iraqi security forces will be stationed in Baghdad to help root out insurgents. In western Baghdad, a suicide taxi bomber kills two police officers.

May 28 Two suicide car bombers detonate their vehicles at a checkpoint in the city of Sinjar. Four Iraqi soldiers die, and thirty-five people are wounded.

May 29 Operation New Market ends. A total of twelve insurgents were killed, and thirty were detained. Numerous weapons were seized, including 300 82-mm high-explosive mortars. Operation Lightning, a sweep against insurgents in Baghdad using between 13,000 and 20,000 Iraqi forces and 7,000 U.S. forces, begins.

May 30 In Hilla police commandos demonstrate in front of the Interior Ministry. The ministry discovered that the units had formed unofficially and then had forged documents in an attempt to appear to be government sanctioned. During the demonstration, a suicide bomber mingles with the crowd and then detonates his explosives. When the crowd begins to run, a second bomber runs with them and then detonates his explosives. Thirty-one are killed and 108 wounded. A provincial police chief, Major General Qais Hamza, vows revenge for the bombings. An Iraqi Air Force plane crashes in the Diyala province, killing an Iraqi aviator and a U.S. pilot.

May 31 Operation Lightning captures sixty-five suspected insurgents and kills twelve.

June 1 Near Buhriz a suicide bomber detonates his explosives at a checkpoint, killing two Iraqi soldiers.

June 2 Iraqi Interior Minister Bayan Jabr announces that Operation Lightning has brought control of all roads into and out of Baghdad under Iraqi control. Jabr states that 700 suspected insurgents had been detained and that twenty-eight had been killed. The Interior Ministry releases figures that show that insurgents killed twenty Iraqi civilians a day on average over the past year and a half. Approximately 12,000 civilians were killed by insurgents over the time period. In Mosul two motorcycles rigged with bombs explode next to a coffee shop known to be frequented by police officers and close to a police station. Five people die, and it is not immediately apparent if any were police officers. A suicide car bomber detonates his explosives next to a convoy carrying the deputy chief of the provincial council, Hussein Alwan al-Tamimi, in Baquba, killing him and wounding four police officers. Abu Musab al-Zarqawi's Al Qa'ida in Mesopotamia claims credit for the attack. In Mahmudiya militants attack a police patrol, injuring one policeman. One hundred and twenty-one police officers graduate from advanced specialty courses at the Adnan training facility. The courses included basic criminal investigations, critical incident management, counterterrorism investigations, and executive leadership. Command of the Kirkuk military training base is formally transferred from MNSTC–I to Iraqi Brigadier General Abd Zaid. The Iraqi Navy begins its direct recruit replacement program.

June 4 Iraqi and U.S. forces arrest a man dubbed Mullah Mahdi in Mosul, along with his brother and three other men. Iraqi officials state that Mahdi had links to Ansar al-Sunna and Syria's intelligence service. The same officials claim that he was responsible for all of the major attacks, assassinations, and beheadings of Iraqi security forces in the area.

June 6 A suicide car bomber detonates his vehicle close to an Iraqi Army checkpoint near al-Daira. Six Iraqi soldiers are wounded in the attack. In the Amil neighborhood, a suicide bomber drives his vehicle into a former factory that had been converted to an Iraqi security forces base. Lacking concrete barriers, the attacker managed to get inside the facility and kill approximately three police, although estimates varied.

June 7 The Iraqi Army and U.S. troops launch an offensive in the city of Tal Afar to eradicate insurgent activity in the area. Twenty-three suspected insurgents are captured. Reportedly, the city is believed to house foreign fighters who have come across the nearby border with Syria. Reports differed over whether town elders requested the operation or whether the operation had been planned for some time. Three car bombs are detonated in and around Hawija within minutes of one another, killing eight Iraqi soldiers. Two Iraqi police officers are wounded by a car bomb in Baghdad. In a separate car bomb attack in the capital city, insurgents attempt to target a police convoy but kill mostly civilians. One police officer dies. Police in Musayyib raid an insurgent hideout in Jurf al-Sakhr and seize a cache of weapons. U.S. and Iraqi forces begin a joint assault in Tal Afar.

June 8 Iraqi Prime Minister Ibrahim al-Jafari and President Jalal Talibani meet with the founder of the political party that founded the Badr Brigade. Both Talibani and Jafari hail the Badr Brigade and the Kurdish Pesh Merga as indespensible and legitimate forces. In Baghdad an Iraqi commando is killed and an Iraqi police officer wounded in two separate drive-by shootings.

June 12 Al Qa'ida in Iraq claims to have captured and then executed twenty-one Iraqi soldiers outside of Qaim. Although the bodies were found, the Iraqi Ministry of Defense denies that any soldiers were missing. Militants attack the home of Iraqi Army General Rashid Flaieh, where the funeral for the mother of a top security official was being held in Baghdad. Thirteen people are wounded.

June 13 In Tikrit a suicide car bomber attacks an Iraqi police patrol, killing two officers and wounding four. Two Iraqi police officers die in Samarra when a suicide car bomber detonates close to a joint U.S.-Iraqi military patrol. Three more die in the city when insurgents detonate two bombs close to their barracks, drawing them out, at which point they open fire on them.

June 14 Militants launch a coordinated attack on a Kaanan police station using mortars and a car bomb. An unknown number of Iraqi police and soldiers are among the nine dead.

June 15 More than twenty-six Iraqi soldiers die and many more are wounded when a suicide bomber dressed in an Iraqi Army uniform detonates his explosives in a military mess tent in Khalis. Iraqi security forces announce the capture of Abid Dawoud Salman, a former Iraqi general, and his son Salman, a former captain, in Khaldiyah. According to Iraqi officials, Salman was an important military adviser to Abu Musab al-Zarqawi.

June 16 A suicide bomber rams an Iraqi police convoy on the road to Baghdad's airport, killing eight officers and wounding twenty-five.

June 17 Operation Spear begins in the Anbar province in an attempt to disrupt insurgent activity.

June 18 Operation Dagger begins as a complement to Operation Spear in the Anbar province.

June 19 A suicide bomber with an explosive vest targets a restaurant just outside of the Green Zone in Baghdad. The ensuing explosion kills between two and seven Iraqi police officers. A group claiming fealty to Abu Musab al-Zarqawi claims responsibility on the Internet. In the northern part of the capital a suicide car bomber sidles up to a police convoy and detonates his vehicle, wounding two people. In Tikrit a suicide bomber wearing an Iraqi police uniform drives up to the gate of a U.S. military base and detonates vehicle, killing two Iraqi soldiers.

June 20 In Irbil a suicide car bomber rams a group of traffic cops gathered for roll call outside of their headquarters. The ensuing explosion kills twenty traffic policemen and wounds one hundred. Insurgents launch a coordinated attack on a U.S. military convoy and then an attack on the Baya police station in southwestern Baghdad, utilizing small arms, two suicide car bombs, RPGs, and mortars. Approximately eight policemen are killed, and twenty-three are wounded. One Iraqi soldier dies. Operations Spear and Dagger have resulted in sixty insurgent deaths and the capture of approximately one hundred militants. One thousand U.S. and Iraqi soldiers are involved in the two operations. In the Mansour district, militants detonate a roadside bomb, killing four Iraqi police. A gunfight erupts between police and insurgents, and one policeman dies. Fifteen are wounded. In Nisoor Square, two car bombs detonate close to a police commando station, but there are no casualties. Near Tuz Khurmatu, insurgents detonate a roadside bomb as an Iraqi Army convoy passes, killing three soldiers and wounding two more.

June 21 Iraqi and U.S. troops begin pulling out of Karabilah near the Syrian border, following the conclusion of Operation Spear. Several car bomb workshops were uncovered, one insurgent was captured, and an estimated forty-seven were killed. Insurgents had been harassing the town and had set up roadblocks. In Tuz Khurmatu, Iraqi security forces reportedly prevent a suicide bomber from carrying out an attack, and the Defense Ministry announced that eleven weapons caches had been uncovered around the country. In Al Habibiya citizens inform an Iraqi Army patrol of a stockpile of arms in a nearby sewer. Iraqi security forces uncover RPGs and rounds.

June 22 A suicide car bomber detonates his explosives next to an Iraqi Army patrol in the Ameriyah neighborhood of western Baghdad. No Iraqi soldiers are killed, although the attack kills four civilians. Militants detonate a roadside bomb close to an Iraqi police patrol and special operations unit. The attack near Madain kills two policemen and wounds two more officers.

June 23 In Baghdad a suicide bomber attacks an Iraqi police patrol near a gas station in the north-central part of the city. Three police officers are killed. Three more are killed in a suicide bombing in the Karada area of the city near an old mall.

June 25 In Samarra five cars loaded with insurgents run interference for a suicide car bomber as he rams his vehicle into the wall outside of Lieutenant Muthana al-Shaker's home. Al-Shaker is a member of the police special forces in Samarra. The attack kills multiple civilians but fails to injure al-Shaker. Two insurgents attempting to plant a follow-on bomb for emergency services and police outside of his home accidentally set the device off, killing themselves. In Kirkuk insurgents strap an explosive belt to a dog and detonate it when the dog wanders near Iraqi security forces. One officer is injured.

June 26 In Mosul Iraqi security forces are targeted by al-Zarqawi's Al Qa'ida. One suicide truck bomber rams a police station, killing ten policemen. In the parking lot of an Iraqi Army base on the fringe of the city, another suicide bomber detonates his explosives. Sixteen people are killed, most of them civilians, but reports indicate some security forces personnel are among the dead. A third Mosul suicide bomber walks into the Jumhouri Teaching Hospital, detonating his explosives in a room used by Iraqi policemen charged with guarding the hospital. Five policemen are killed, including several who were sleeping. A total of sixteen policemen are wounded in the attacks. Minister of Defense Sadun al-Dulaimi states that it is necessary to open a dialog with the armed insurgent groups who wish to join the political process. In Sadiyah militants kill six Iraqi soldiers outside of their base. In Baghdad Al Qa'ida in Iraq claims credit for the shooting death of police Colonel Riyad Abdul Karim, an assistant district police director of emergency services, in the eastern portion of the city. In the Amin neighborhood, Iraqi police seize 500 antipersonnel mines, sixty RPG rounds, several mortar rounds, and arrest seven suspected insurgents. Shortly after the raid Iraqi police from the First Battalion, Second Iraqi Army Brigade discover a car bomb and called in experts to diffuse it.

Notes

Introduction

1. For a broader discussion of these issues, see W. Andrew Terrill, *Strategic Implications of Intercommunal Warfare in Iraq*, Carlisle, Strategic Studies Institute, U.S. Army War College, February 2005.

2. For many of the problems involved, see Robert M. Perito, "The Coalition Provisional Authority's Experience with Public Security in Iraq," Washington, U.S. Institute of Peace, Special Report 137, April 2005.

Chapter 1

1. Statement of Joseph A. Christoff, "Rebuilding Iraq: Preliminary Observations on Challenges in Transferring Security Responsibilities to Iraqi Military and Police," General Accountability Office, Washington, D.C., March 14, 2005, GAO-05-431T, p. 1. Christoff is the director of international affairs and trade at the Government Accountability Office.

2. CNN.com, "Rumsfeld: Insurgency Slows Progress," http://www.cnn.com/2005/world/meast/03/20/Iraq.anniversay/index\.html.

3. Based on a slide show provided by Zogby International in March 2004.

4. David Charter, "Most Iraqis Say Life Is Good Now, Poll Finds," *London Times*, March 17, 2004.

5. Cesar G. Soriano and Steven Komarow, "Polls: Iraqis Out of Patience," *USA Today*, April 29, 2004, p. 1.

6. Results taken from a summary provided by the Independent Republican Institute (IRI), "Survey of Iraqi Public Opinion," February 27–March 5, 2005.

7. Dexter Filkins, "Demonstrators in Iraq Demand that U.S. Leave," *New York Times*, April 10, 2005; Anthony Shadid, "Tens of Thousands of Iraqis Demand U.S. Withdrawal," *Washington Post*, April 10, 2005, p. A25.

8. Results taken from a summary provided by the Independent Republican Institute (IRI), "Survey of Iraqi Public Opinion," February 27–March 5, 2005.

9. MNSCT–I response to inquiry.

10. Statement of Joseph A. Christoff, "Rebuilding Iraq: Preliminary Observations on Challenges in Transferring Security Responsibilities to Iraqi Military and Police," General Accountability Office, Washington, D.C., March 14, 2005, GAO-05-431T, p. 1.

11. Paul Bremer, "The Right Call," *Wall Street Journal*, January 12, 2005, p. A10.

12. Transcript of December 21, 2004, interview with Deputy Secretary of State Richard L. Armitage with pan-Arab print reporters, issued by the office of the spokesman, p. 13.

13. For broad reporting on the Iraqi police, see the Coalition Provisional Authority–Interior Ministry report, "Iraq Police: An Assessment of the Present and Recommendations for the Future," Baghdad, Iraq, May 30, 2003, and the following reports from the General Accountability Office, Washington, D.C.: GAO-03-792R, "Rebuilding Iraq," May 15, 2003; GAO-04-0746R, "Iraq's Transitional Law," May 25, 2004; GAO-04-902R, "Rebuilding Iraq: Resource, Security, Governance, Essential Services, and Oversight Issues," June 28, 2004; GAO-05-431T, "Rebuilding Iraq: Preliminary Observations on Challenges in Transferring Security Responsibilities to Iraqi Military and Police," March 14, 2005. GAO reports can be accessed at http://www.gao.gov.

14. Report by the offices of inspector generals of the State Department and Department of Defense, July 25, 2005, http://oig.state.gov/documents/organization/50145.pdf, pp. 9, 55.

15. Statement of Joseph A. Christoff, "Rebuilding Iraq: Preliminary Observations on Challenges in Transferring Security Responsibilities to Iraqi Military and Police," General Accountability Office, Washington, D.C., March 14, 2005, GAO-05-43IT, p. 4.

16. Report by the offices of inspector generals of the State Department and Department of Defense, July 25, 2005, http://oig.state.gov/documents/organization/50145.pdf, pp. 9, 19, 24, and 55.

17. Report by the offices of inspector generals of the State Department and Department of Defense, July 25, 2005, http://oig.state.gov/documents/organization/50145.pdf, p. 24.

18. Statement of Joseph A. Christoff, "Rebuilding Iraq: Preliminary Observations on Challenges in Transferring Security Responsibilities to Iraqi Military and Police," General Accountability Office, Washington, D.C., March 14, 2005, GAO-05-43IT, p. 4.

19. Robert M. Perito, "The Coalition Provisional Authority's Experience with Public Security in Iraq," Washington, D.C., U.S. Institute of Peace, Special Report 137, April 2005, pp. 6–7.

20. Ibid.

21. See also Nancy A. Youssef, "Iraqi Civilian Casualties Mounting," *Knight Ridder*, September 25, 2004.

22. These comments again rely heavily on the work by Robert M. Perito with some additional points based on interviews.

23. Full credit should be given to the research and analysis by Robert M. Perito.

24. For a summary historical perspective, see Ian F. Beckett, "Insurgency in Iraq: A Historical Perspective," Carlisle, Strategic Studies Institute, U.S. Army War College, January 2005.

Chapter 2

1. Quoted in Amy S. Klamper, "Former Iraq Administrator Sees Decades-Long U.S. Military Presence," *Government Executive*, February 6, 2004, http://www.govexec.com.

2. Ellen Knickmeyer, "Insurgents Down Helicopter Near Iraqi Capital," *Washington Post*, April 22, 2005, p. A1; *Washington Post*, May 10, 2005, p. A1; Raheem Salman and Patrick J. McDonnel, "Many Corpses by Few Details," *Los Angeles Times*, April 22, 2005, p. 1.

3. Ellen Knickmeyer and Caryle Murphy, "Sectarian Strike Rises in Iraq as Dozens of Bodies Found," *Washington Post*, April 21, 2005, p. A17; Ashraf Khalil, "Bomb Attacks Persis in Iraq," *Los Angeles Times*, May 2, 2005, p. 1.

4. Warzer Jaff and Ricard A. Oppel, "Northern Iraq," *New York Times*, May 4, 2005.

5. Sheik Qassim Gharawi, a supporter of the Grand Ayatollah Sistani, and Hamid Mukhlis Dulemi of the Sunni Muslim Scholars Group were killed on the same day, May 16, 2005. Ashraf Khalil and Patrick J. McDonnell, "Iraq Violence Taking a Sectarian Shift," *Los Angeles*

Times, May 16, 2005, p. 1; Mona Mahmoud, "Two Sunni Clerics Found Dead; Shi'ite Religious Leader Killed," *USA Today*, May 18, 2005, p. 5.

6. For a broader discussion, see Gal Luft, "Pipeline Sabotage Is Terrorist's Weapon of Choice," *IAGS Energy*, April 1, 2005. The impact of this activity is regularly reflected in the histograms in the U.S. Department of Defense's *Iraq Weekly Status Report*. For example, the April 27, 2005, edition shows that electric power generation remained far below the U.S. goal and usually below the prewar level from January 1, 2004, to April 21, 2005.

7. U.S. Department of Defense, *Iraq Weekly Status Report*, April 27, 2005.

8. Rick Jervis, "Security Costs Drain Funds for Water Projects," *USA Today*, April 21, 2005, p. 8.

9. Yochi J. Dreazen, "Security Remains Main Hurdle to Iraq Rebuilding," *Wall Street Journal*, May 9, 2005, p. 4.

10. Tony Capaccio, "Contractors in Iraq Not Targeted," May 10, 2005, http://www.bloomberg.com.

11. Edward Wong, "At Least Twenty U.S. Troops Wounded," *New York Times*, April 3, 2005.

12. Ellen Knickmeyer, "Zarqawi Said to be Behind Iraq Raid," *Washington Post*, April 5, 2005, p. A1.

13. Daniel Williams and Ann Scott Tryson, "Italy Disputes U.S. Report on Agent's Death," *Washington Post*, May 3, 2005, p. 16.

14. Sharon Behn, "Terrorists Will Keep Targeting Foreigners," *Washington Times*, May 6, 2005, p. 1.

15. For typical reporting, see Jill Carroll, "Iraq's Rising Industry: Domestic Kidnapping," *Christian Science Monitor*, April 22, 2005; Monte Morin, "Crime as Lethal as Insurgency in Iraq," *Los Angeles Times*, March 20 , 2005, p. A1; Sabrina Tavernise, "Iraq's Violence Sweeps away all Norms," *New York Times*, May 6, 2005, p. 1; Solomon More, "A Nation's Unnoticed Abductees," *Los Angeles Times*, May 6, 2005.

16. U.S. State Department, "Iraq," *Country Reports on Human Rights, 2004*, http://www.state.gov/g/drl/rls/hrrpt/2004/41722.htm.

17. John Ward Anderson, "A Gruesome Find, with a Difference," *Washington Post*, March 19, 2005, p. A16.

18. Elliot Blair Smith, "Insurgents' Smallest Weapons Pose Greatest Threat to Troops," *USA Today*, April 12, 2005, p. 11.

19. Bradley Graham and Dana Priest, "Insurgents Using U.S. Techniques," *Washington Post*, May 3, 2005, p. A15.

20. Megan Scully, "Hunting for Solutions to IEDs," *Defense News*, September 27, 2004, p. 22.

21. John Hendren, "Bombs Spur Drive for Vehicle Harder Than a Humvee," *Los Angeles Times*, May 6, 2005.

22. Julian B. Barnes, "Beating the Roadside bombers," *US News and World Report*, May 9, 2005.

23. Mark Washburn, "Iraq's Insurgents Build Bigger, Better Bombs," *Miami Herald*, June 10, 2005.

24. Steve Fainaru, "Large Blast Hits Bus Carrying Iraqi Soldiers," *Washington Post*, April 6, 2005, p. A16.

25. Ellen Knickmeyer, "Insurgents Attack U.S. Base in Iraq," *Washington Post*, April 12, 2005, p. A15.

26. Greg Grant, "Death Toll Sparks U.S. Debate on Origin of IED Expertise in Iraq," *Defense News*, August 15, 2005, p. 13.

27. Ibid.

28. Michael E. O'Hanlon and Nina Kamp, "Iraq Index: Tracking Variables of Reconstruction & Security in Post-Saddam Iraq," August 22, 2005, http://www.brookings.edu/iraqindex.

29. Dexter Filkins, "3 Sunni Election Workers Seized and Killed in Mosul," *New York Times*, August 20, 2005, http://www.nytimes.com/2005/08/20/international/middleeast/20iraq.html.

30. The first such kill was a U.S. helicopter on April 21, 2005. Ellen Knickmeyer, "Insurgents Down Helicopter near Iraqi Captial," *Washington Post*, April 22, 2005, p. A1.

31. Bing West and Owen West, "A Thin Blue Line: Why Iraqi Cops Are Struggling," October 7, 2004, http://www.westwrite.com, accessed on May 10, 2005, and distributed by Major Sheils as "Iraqi Insurgent Sniper.

32. See the translation of sniper data on the proinsurgency militant Web site at "Training," U.S. Department of Defense background paper, May 17, 2005.

33. See Ellen Knickmeyer, "They Came Here to Die," *Washington Post*, May 11, 2005, p. A1.

Chapter 3

1. General Accountability Office, *Rebuilding Iraq: Resource, Security, Governance, Essential Services, and Oversight Issues*, Washington, D.C., June 2004, GAO-04-902R, pp. 43–53.

2. Statement of Joseph A. Christoff, "Rebuilding Iraq: Preliminary Observations on Challenges in Transferring Security Responsibilities to Iraqi Military and Police," General Accountability Office, Washington, D.C., March 14, 2005, GAO-05-43IT, p. 4.

3. Report by the office of inspector generals of the Department of State and the Department of Defense, July 25, 2005, http://oig.state.gov/documents/organization/50145.pdf, pp. 11–12, 16, 19.

4. Ian F. Beckett, "Insurgency in Iraq: A Historical Perspective," Carlisle, Strategic Studies Institute, U.S. Army War College, January 2005, p. 14.

5. Statement of Joseph A. Christoff, "Rebuilding Iraq: Preliminary Observations on Challenges in Transferring Security Responsibilities to Iraqi Military and Police," General Accountability Office, Washington, D.C., March 14, 2005, GAO-05-43IT, p.10.

6. Ian F. Beckett, "Insurgency in Iraq: A Historical Perspective," Carlisle, Strategic Studies Institute, U.S. Army War College, January 2005, p. 8.

7. Statement of Joseph A. Christoff, "Rebuilding Iraq: Preliminary Observations on Challenges in Transferring Security Responsibilities to Iraqi Military and Police," submitted to the U.S. House of Representatives Subcommittee on National Security, Emerging Threats, and International Relations on March 14, 2005, p. 4.

8. Donald Rumsfeld, Department of Defense news transcript, February 3, 2005.

9. Presentation to CG CJTF-7 on March 7, 2004.

10. Sharon Behn, "General Assails CPA Bureaucracy as Unresponsive," *Washington Times*, July 1, 2004, p. 12.

11. Interview, June 2, 2004.

Chapter 4

1. Albert Eisele, "A Second Triangle is Built in Iraq," *The Hill*, April 5, 2005, p. 1.

2. Report by the offices of inspector generals of the Department of Defense and the State Department, July 25, 2005, http://oig.state.gov/documents/organization/50145.pdf, p. 1.

3. Ibid., pp. 1–2. After reorganization the structure looked like this: CMATT reported to the MNSTC–I; MNSTC–I and MNC–I reported to MNF-I.

4. General Accountability Office, *Rebuilding Iraq: Resource, Security, Governance, Essential Services, and Oversight Issues*, Washington, D.C., June 2004, GAO-04-902R, pp. 54–70.

5. Coalition Provisional Authority, "Working Papers: Iraq Status," July 13, 2004, p. 15. The budget data imply but do not explicitly state that such "projects" are actually operating expenses.

6. Yochi J. Dreazen, "For Many Iraqis, A New Daily Fear: Wave of Kidnapping," *Wall Street Journal*, July 22, 2004, p. 1.

7. Robert M. Perito, "The Coalition Provisional Authority's Experience with Public Security in Iraq," Washington, D.C., U.S. Institute of Peace Special Report 137, April 2005, pp. 6–7.

8. Doug Struck, "Iraqi Security Has Come Far, with Far to Go," *Washington Post*, August 1, 2004, p. A18.

9. Yochi J. Dreazen, "For Many Iraqis, A New Daily Fear: Wave of Kidnapping," *Wall Street Journal*, July 22, 2004, p. 1.

10. Robert M. Perito, "The Coalition Provisional Authority's Experience with Public Security in Iraq," Washington, D.C., U.S. Institute of Peace Special Report 137, April 2005, pp. 6–7.

11. Multinational Security Transition Command–Iraq (MNSTC–I) chart entitled "Historical Perspective on ISF Reporting," Baghdad, Iraq, June 2005.

12. Whatever the mistakes of the CPA, the status of the effort to create effective Iraqi forces became progressively more uncertain after the transfer of sovereignty. The totals issued by the U.S. government as of July 13, 2004, suddenly began to count both manpower fully trained in academies or with full military training and manpower in the rushed programs that can be a matter of days or a few weeks as being part of the same total.

The United States stopped issuing meaningful public information on the equipment and training effort, and cut the content of the *Iraq Weekly Status Report* to the point where it had limited value without providing meaningful data at the MNSTC–I Web site (http//:www.mnstci.iraq.centcom.mil). The end result is that there is no way to relate what was happening to a meaningful picture of actual requirements, and the measures of accomplishment that were provided became the kind of empty, self-congratulatory statements typical of public-relations exercises.

As for total manning and equipment levels, the United States initially provided reasonably detailed data on progress in training and equipping Iraqi forces. As time went on, however, such breakouts were eliminated from public U.S. reporting from the embassy, Department of Defense, and State Department. The only heading in the *Weekly Status Report* became "Trained/On-Hand," a heading that seems almost deliberately misleading since it is really just total active strength without the slightest regard to training.

The new figures for trained manpower overstated the training levels for the police and for the border service (DBE) and ignored the fact that the Facilities Protection Service training program has virtually no training at all. At the end of the day, a far less honest reporting system was established, and one that exaggerated the actual level of training.

13. General Accountability Office, *Rebuilding Iraq: Resource, Security, Governance, Essential Services, and Oversight Issues*, Washington, D.C., June 2004, GAO-04-902R, pp. 50–70.

14. Report by the offices of the inspector generals of the Department of Defense and State Department, July 25, 2005, http://oig.state.gov/documents/organization/50145.pdf, pp. 1–2.

15. The full text of NSPD-36 can be found in the report by the offices of the inspector generals of the Department of Defense and the State Department, July 25, 2005, http://oig.state.gov/documents/organization/50145.pdf, pp. 63–65.

16. Robert M. Perito, "The Coalition Provisional Authority's Experience with Public Security in Iraq," Washington, D.C., U.S. Institute of Peace Special Report 137, April 2005, pp. 6–7.

17. Report by the offices of the inspector generals of Department of Defense and the State Department, July 25, 2005, http://oig.state.gov/documents/organization/50145.pdf, p. 9.

18. E-mail to the author by a U.S. official, July 27, 2005.

19. See Robert M. Perito, "The Coalition Provisional Authority's Experience with Public Security in Iraq," Washington, D.C., U.S. Institute of Peace Special Report 137, April 2005, pp. 12–13.

20. Doug Struck, "Iraqi Security Has Come Far, with Far to Go," *Washington Post*, August 1, 2004, p. A18.

21. Robert M. Perito, "The Coalition Provisional Authority's Experience with Public Security in Iraq," Washington, D.C., U.S. Institute of Peace Special Report 137, April 2005, pp. 6–7.

22. Carol J. Williams, "Iraqis More Eager to Help Police," *Los Angeles Times*, July 23, 2004.

23. Doug Struck, "Iraqi Security Has Come Far, with Far to Go," *Washington Post*, August 1, 2004, p. A18.

24. Based on detailed delivery data as of April 23, 2004.

25. Figures taken from the *Iraq Weekly Status Report* for this period and from an interview with an official in OSD (Public Affairs).

26. Statement of Joseph A. Christoff, "Rebuilding Iraq: Preliminary Observations on Challenges in Transferring Security Responsibilities to Iraqi Military and Police," General Accountability Office, Washington, D.C., March 14, 2005, GAO-05-43IT, p. 4.

27. See General Accountability Office, *Rebuilding Iraq: Resource, Security, Governance, Essential Services, and Oversight Issues*, Washington, D.C., June 2004, GAO-04-902R, pp. 50–62.

28. This history and text is based on materials provided in interviews and modified from General Accountability Office, *Rebuilding Iraq: Resource, Security, Governance, Essential Services, and Oversight Issues*, Washington, D.C., June 2004, GAO-04-902R, pp. 63–71.

29. Office of the inspector general, Coalition Provisional Authority, "July 30, 2004, Report to Congress," Appendix, Table E.1.

Chapter 5

1. See http://www.mnstci.iraq.centcom.mil/mission.htm.

2. U.S. Department of Defense, *Iraq Weekly Status Report*, September 22, 2004.

3. The money allocated to total obligations had only put $2,325 million into the start of the pipeline. Office of the inspector general, Coalition Provisional Authority, "Report to Congress," October 30, 2004, p. 59.

4. The Department of Defense Office of the Inspector General (OIG) for inspections and policy is about to begin a joint project with the State Department. OIG is to cover all phases of the training effort for the Iraqi police forces. This should be extended to cover Iraqi military and security forces.

Chapter 6

1. "Telling the Fallujah Story to the World," IMEF and MNC-I Effects Exploitation Team, November 20, 2004 (third cut); Bill Gertz, "Foreign Terrorists in Fallujah," *Washington Times*, December 14, 2004, p. 3.

2. U.S. Department of Defense, *Iraq Weekly Status Report*, November 3, 2004, and information provided from MNSTC–I.

3. Karl Vick, "Insurgents Kill Seventeen Iraqi Civilians; U.S. Army Site Targeted; Soldiers, Guardsmen Slain Elsewhere," *Washington Post*, December 6, 2004, p. A18.

4. U.S. Central Command (USCENTCOM), news release, November 13, 2004.

5. See http://www.mnstci.iraq.centcom.mil/facts_troops.htm, accessed November 11, 2004, and December 18, 2004.

Chapter 7

1. Quoted in "Wave of Suicide Blasts Kills at Least Twenty-five," http://www.cnn.com, January 19, 2005.

2. Rowan Scarborough, "Sunni Role in Military in Iraq Falls Short of Goal," *Washington Times*, January 24, 2005, p. 1.

3. See http://www.mnstci.iraq.centcom.mil/press.htm, May 12, 2004.

4. U.S. Embassy in Iraq, Iraq Year in Review, 2004 Fact Sheet, "Iraqi Security Forces–3."

5. Dan Murphy, "Iraqi Police Take Brunt of Attacks," *Christian Science Monitor*, January 11, 2005.

6. Text of the Draft of the Iraqi Constitution, August 30, 2005, translated from the Arabic by the Associated Press.

7. Craig S. Smith, "Big Guns for Iraq? Not So Fast," *New York Times*, August 28, 2005, section 4, p. 1, column 4.

8. See http://usinfo.state.gov/mena/middle_east_north_africa/new_iraq.html.

9. U.S. Department of Defense, *Iraq Weekly Status Report*, Iraq Weekly Update-20041208.pdf.

10. Multinational Security Transition Command–Iraq (MNSTC–I) response to inquiry.

11. Anthony Shadid, "Troops Move to Quell Insurgency in Mosul," *Washington Post*, November 17, 2004, p. 1.

12. Tom Squitieri and C. Mark Brinkley, "Long Way to Go before Iraqis Take over Security," *USA Today*, December 14, 2004, p. 1.

13. Quoted in Bassem Mroue, "Top Iraqi General Says Bush Misinformed about Soldiers," Associated Press, December 26, 2004.

14. Tom Squitieri and C. Mark Brinkley, "Long Way to Go before Iraqis Take over Security," *USA Today*, December 14, 2004, p. 1.

15. Quoted in Stephen Farrell, "Iraqi Forces Find Harsh Boundary between Rehearsal and Reality," *London Times*, December 6, 2004.

16. Ibid.

17. Quoted in Tony Capaccio and Jon Steinman, "U.S. Commander Says Iraqi Training behind Schedule," Bloomberg News Service, December 7, 2004.

18. Statement by the Minister of State for National Security Affairs, Dr. Qassim Dawood, on December 2, 2004, and conveyed by the Government Communications Directorate.

19. Quoted in Tony Capaccio and Jon Steinman, "U.S. Commander Says Iraqi Training behind Schedule," Bloomberg News Service, December 7, 2004.

20. Quoted in Bradley Graham, "Commander Sees Shift in Role of U.S. Troops; Force Would Focus on Training Iraqis," *Washington Post*, December 7, 2004, p. A-01.

Chapter 8

1. Interview, May 12, 2005.

2. Quoted in Ann Scott Tyson, "Iraqi Insurgency Is Weakening, Abizaid Says," *Washington Post*, March 2, 2005, p. 5.

3. Steven R. Weisman and Joel Brinkley, "Rice Sees Iraq Training Progress but Offers No Schedule for Exit," *New York Times*, January 19, 2005, p. 1.

4. U.S. State Department, *Iraq Weekly Status Report*, January 12, 2005, p. 5.

5. U.S. Embassy in Iraq, Iraq Year in Review, 2004 Fact Sheet, "Iraqi Security Forces–3," and U.S. State Department, *Iraq Weekly Status Report*, January 12, 2005, p. 5.

6. Josh White, "Iraqis' Readiness Disputed in Hearing," *Washington Post*, January 20, 2005, p. A04.

7. U.S. Embassy in Iraq, Iraq Year in Review, 2004 Fact Sheet, "Iraqi Security Forces–3," and U.S. State Department, *Iraq Weekly Status Report*, January 12, 2005, p. 5.

8. Data found in Multinational Security Transition Command–Iraq (MNSTC–I)/State Department Iraq Year in Review, 2004 Fact Sheet.

9. U.S. Embassy in Iraq, Iraq Year in Review, 2004 Fact Sheet, "Iraqi Security Forces–3," and U.S. State Department, *Iraq Weekly Status Report*, January 12, 2005, p. 26.

10. Josh White, "Deaths of U.S. Contractors Probed; Man Killed with Colleague Complained about Lack of Payment," *Washington Post*, January 21, 2005, p. A12.

11. Bassem Mroue, "Iraqi Commander: Troops Ready in Six Months," Associated Press, January 27, 2005.

12. Dexter Filkins, "Mystery in Iraq as $300 Million Is Taken Abroad," *New York Times*, January 22, 2005, p. A1.

13. Quoted in Dexter Filkins, "Mystery in Iraq as $300 Million Is Taken Abroad," *New York Times*, January 22, 2005, p. A1.

14. Ibid.

15. Dexter Filkins, "Mystery in Iraq as $300 Million is Taken Abroad," *New York Times*, January 22, 2005, p. A1.

16. John Diamond, "Pride, Pickups Help Forge New Model Army," *USA Today*, March 9, 2005, p. 8.

17. Interview, May 12, 2005.

18. Quoted in John Hendren, "U.S. to Overhaul Training of Iraqi Forces," *Los Angeles Times*, January 20, 2005.

19. Bassem Mroue, "Iraqi Commander: Troops Ready in Six Months," Associated Press, January 27, 2005.

20. AFP News Agency, Baghdad Bureau, January 24, 2005.

21. Quoted in John F. Burns, "Five Bomb Attacks Kill Twenty-six as Vote by Iraqis Nears," *New York Times*, January 20, 2005, p. A1.

22. John F. Burns, "Tape in Name of Leading Insurgent Declares 'All-Out War' on Iraq Elections and Democracy," *New York Times*, January 24, 2005, p. A10.

23. Report by the offices of inspector generals of the Department of Defense and State Department, July 25, 2005, http://oig.state.gov/documents/organization/50145.pdf, pp. 9–10.

Chapter 9

1. *Iraq Weekly Status Report*, May 11, 2005, p. 7.

2. See Jonathan Frank and Bradley Graham, "U.S. Urges Iraqi Leaders to Answer Violence," *Washington Post*, May 14, 2005, p. A12.

3. Ibid.

4. *Iraq Weekly Status Report*, February 9, 2005, released by the U.S. State Department and available at http://www.defendamerica.mil; additional data provided by MNSTC–I and the U.S. Embassy in Baghdad.

5. *Iraq Weekly Status Report*, July 27, 2005.

6. MNSTC–I planners understood that the December total might be lower due to the extension of the police basic course from eight to ten weeks, one of several initiatives to raise the quality of the police and military forces.

7. John Diamond, "Pride, Pickups Help Forge New Model Army," *USA Today*, March 9, 2005, p. 8.

8. Report by the offices of inspector generals of the Departments of State and Defense, July 25, 2005, http://oig.state.gov/documents/organization/50145.pdf, p. 36.

9. Interview, May 12, 2005.

10. Robert Burns, "U.S. General: Iraq Insurgency on Decline," Associated Press, March 17, 2005.

11. Hannah Allam, "Iraq Arms Scandal Unfolds," *Philadelphia Inquirer*, July 15, 2005, p. 1.

12. U.S. Department of Defense, *Report to Congress Measuring Stability and Security in Iraq*, report to Congress is submitted pursuant to the section titled "Measuring Stability and Security in Iraq" of House Conference Report 109-72 accompanying H.R. 1268, Emergency Supplemental Appropriations Act for Defense, the Global War on Terror, and Tsunami Relief, 2005, Public Law 109-13, July 20, 2005.

13. Ashraf Khalil, "Tough Times for Fifth Brigade of Iraq's Army," *Los Angeles Times*, July 12, 2005.

14. MNSTC–I response to inquiry.

15. U.S. Department of Defense, *Report to Congress, Measuring Stability and Security in Iraq*, submitted pursuant to the section titled "Measuring Stability and Security in Iraq" of House Conference Report 109-72 accompanying H.R. 1268, Emergency Supplemental Appropriations Act for Defense, the Global War on Terror, and Tsunami Relief, 2005, Public Law 109-13, July 2005.

16. Interview, May 12, 2005.

17. *Iraq Weekly Status Report* for February 25, 2005. Available at http://www.defendamerica. mil.

18. Report by the offices of the inspector generals of the Departments of State and Defense, July 25, 2005, http://oig.state.gov/documents/organization/50145.pdf. This series of excerpts takes key points from the entire ninety-six-page report and rearranges them to provide a clear picture of the key problems the report mentions.

19. Ibid., pp. 26–27.

20. *Iraq Weekly Status Report* for February 25, 2005. Available at http://www.defendamerica. mil.

21. For the comments of CPATT and other Coalition advisers and discussion of possible changes, see Appendixes G, H, and I to the report by the offices of inspector generals of Departments of State and Defense, July 25, 2005, http://oig.state.gov/documents/organization/ 50145.pdf. Thirty of the key recommendations of that report are still worth noting, both in judging Iraq's future progress and for any future options involving the creation of large-scale police and security operations in nations where insurgency and terrorism present serious problems:

Recommendation 1: Coalition authorities should plan and implement training focused on qualitative standards rather than on the numbers of trained IPs [Iraqi police]. This redefinition of objectives should be made explicit in a revised mission statement for CPATT [Civilian Police Assistance Training Team]. (Action: MNF–I in coordination with MNSTC–I and Embassy Baghdad.)

Recommendation 2: Coalition and Mission Iraq officials should support and encourage efforts by the Iraqi transitional government (ITG) to strengthen MOI [Ministry of Interior] control over the IPS [Iraqi Police Service] through recentralization of administrative processes and development of relevant SOPs. (Action: MNSTC–I and Embassy Baghdad.)

Recommendation 3: A working group of qualified instructors, specifically to include Iraqi representation, should design a range of courses suitable to the training needs of in-service IPS personnel. Mutually established parameters for candidate selection should be integral to this process. Changes in curricula for IP training must be negotiated in advance with the MOI and be implemented only after Iraqi agreement to such changes. (Action: MNSTC–I in consultation with the Iraqi Ministry of Interior.)

Recommendation 4: Coalition authorities should pursue agreement with the MOI to incorporate the existing emergency response unit, Bureau of Dignitary Protection, and provincial SWAT units into the public order battalions, special police commando units, and mechanized brigades. (Action: MNSTC–I in coordination with Embassy Baghdad.)

Recommendation 5: Appropriate parties need to explore the merits, feasibility and conceivable sources of any U.S. government funding to cover MOI salary shortfalls during the current fiscal year. This determination should take into account possible outyear implications for such support. (Action: MNF–I in consultation with MNSTC–I and Embassy Baghdad.)

Recommendation 6: A joint Coalition/MOI assessment should be conducted to determine operation and maintenance costs of Coalition-built and/or renovated training facilities and to determine how and whether those costs can be sustained. (Action: MNSTC–I in collaboration with Embassy Baghdad and in consultation with the MOI.)

Recommendation 7: Coalition and MOI leaders/trainers should identify a mutually agreeable target number or percentage of IPS trainees who demonstrate ambition and talent for subsequent leadership training. (Action: MNSTC–I in consultation with the MOI.)

Recommendation 8: A joint committee of Coalition and MOI officials should screen and select officers for advanced training based on mutually established qualification standards. (Action: MNSTC–I in conjunction with MOI.)

Recommendation 9: The Coalition recruiting program should be placed under the direction of the MOI, with MNC–I and CPATT providing assistance. (Action: MNF–I in consultation with MNC–I, MNSTC–I, and Embassy Baghdad.)

Recommendation 10: Coalition authorities should assess the extent and quality of Iraqi Ministry of Interior's records relevant to the vetting process, and then conclude a nonbinding memorandum of agreement with the Ministry on access to and utilization of such material. (Action: MNSTC–I in coordination with Embassy Baghdad and consultation with the MOI.)

Recommendation 11: Coalition and Iraqi authorities should establish a nonbinding agreement that states the MOI is responsible for vetting candidates for Coalition-sponsored police training. (Action: MNF–I in consultation with MNSTC–I and Embassy Baghdad and in collaboration with MOI.)

Recommendation 12: Coalition planners, in coordination with the MOI, should require that cadets first graduate from one of the police academies prior to entering public order brigade (POB) or emergency response unit (ERU) training. An in-service police training program should be developed for "currently serving" POB and ERU members who are not graduates of a police academy. (Action: MNSTC–I in coordination with the MOI.)

Recommendation 13: Contractual arrangements with expatriate instructors should specify that individually devised training courses will be submitted in advance for consideration and possible approval by MNSTC–I and CPATT. (Action: MNSTC–I.)

Recommendation 14: A nonbinding agreement should be negotiated by the U.S. government with the Iraqi Ministry of Interior that specifies that only applicants in possession of MOI-issued identification cards, explicitly stating that the bearer is a member of the IPS, will be accepted for training by the Coalition. (Action: MNSTC–I in coordination with Embassy Baghdad.)

Recommendation 15: Tables of organization and equipment should be developed for police stations and deployable police units throughout the country. (Action: MNSTC–I in coordination with MOI.)

Recommendation 16: Coalition authorities should establish internal controls to track transfer and accountability of equipment to the IPS. (Action: MNF–I in coordination with MNSTC–I and MNC–I and in consultation with MOI.)

Recommendation 17: Coalition resources, in close coordination with counterparts in the MOI and IPS, should develop an operational IPS readiness reporting system for the MOI. (Action: MNSTC–I in coordination with MOI.)

Recommendation 18: Coalition commanders should conduct a requirements analysis to determine the number of international police liaison officers (IPLOs) who can be gainfully engaged under prevailing circumstances and adjust the number of these mentors accordingly. (MNSTC–I in consultation with Embassy Baghdad and INL [State Department Bureau of International Narcotics and Law Enforcement].)

Recommendation 19: Standard operating procedures should be developed for the IPLOs to define the relationships and responsibilities among the police liaison officers and military police. (Action: MNSTC–I in consultation with Embassy Baghdad and INL.)

Recommendation 20: The Department of State must keep Coalition governments apprised of developments at JIPTC [Jordan International Police Training Center], specifically those that relate to provision of training staff at that facility. (Action: Department of State's Bureau of Near Eastern Affairs in consultation with INL.)

Recommendation 21: The Department of State should decide whether and where an ILEA should be established in the Middle East. If Jordan is selected as a venue, negotiations for such a transformation of JIPTC should proceed quickly. (Action: Department of State's Bureau for Near Eastern Affairs in consultation with INL.)

Recommendation 22: Coalition commanders should obtain from the Iraqi Ministry of Interior a written commitment to assume responsibility for direct payment of the salaries of Iraqis trained by the Coalition at JIPTC. (Action: MNF–I in coordination with MNSTC–I and Embassy Baghdad and in consultation with MOI.)

Recommendation 23: Embassy Baghdad should work with the Iraqi Ministry of Interior to define areas in which Coalition advisors can play useful roles. (Action: Embassy Baghdad in collaboration with IRMO and MOI and in consultation with MNSTC–I.)

Recommendation 24: Top priority should be given to recruiting "3161" personnel qualified to fill positions as defined jointly by Embassy Baghdad and the Iraqi Ministry of Interior, then to assigning a full complement of such advisers to the Ministry of Interior. (Action: Embassy Baghdad through IRMO.)

Recommendation 25: Embassy Baghdad should obtain from the MOI a written commitment to assure Coalition authorities can access data relevant to tracking and mentoring IPS personnel trained in U.S. government-funded programs. (Action: Embassy Baghdad in consultation with MNSTC–I.)

Recommendation 26: Coalition and MOI officials should develop standard operating procedures for personnel administration of the Iraqi Police Service. (Action: MNSTC–I in coordination with Embassy Baghdad.)

Recommendation 27: The Department of State should assign one or more INL officers to work directly within CPATT to ensure INL perspectives are considered in the development of the IPS. (Action: Department of State in coordination with Embassy Baghdad and MNSTC–I.)

Recommendation 28: MNSTC–I should perform an assessment of security and IPS infrastructure development by province to identify opportunities where additional responsibility for IPS training can be transferred to provincial police. (Action: MNSTC–I in consultation with the MOI.)

Recommendation 29: The Department of State should propose that the National Security Council establish an interagency working group with representatives from the Departments of State, Defense, and Justice. The working group should identify issues to be addressed for the transfer of police training responsibilities from DoD to DoS. (Action: Department of State, Bureau of Near Eastern Affairs, in consultation with Embassy Baghdad, MNF–I, MNSTC–I, and INL.)

Recommendation 30: The Departments of State and Defense, in consultation with the Office of Management and Budget (OMB), should prepare a memorandum of agreement (MOA) to define funding arrangements for future U.S. involvement in Iraqi Police Service-related programs. (Action: Department of State's Bureau of Resource Management (RM) and Department of Defense's office of the undersecretary for policy in consultation with OMB.)

22. U.S. Department of Defense, *Report to Congress, Measuring Stability and Security in Iraq*, submitted pursuant to the section entitled "Measuring Stability and Security in Iraq" of House Conference Report 109-72 accompanying H.R. 1268, Emergency Supplemental Appropriations Act for Defense, the Global War on Terror, and Tsunami Relief, 2005, Public Law 109-13, July 2005.

23. Gerry G. Gilmore, "General Will Assess Iraqi Training, Not War Strategy," Armed Forces Press Service, January 7, 2005.

24. Peter Spiegel, "U.S. Looking at Rethink of Strategy in Iraq," *Financial Times*, January 10, 2005.

25. Condoleezza Rice, testimony before the Senate Foreign Relations Committee, confirmation hearing for the position of Secretary of State, January 18, 2005, time code 3:25 to 3:37 p.m.

26. Ibid.

27. Eric Schmitt, "General Seeking Faster Training of Iraqi Soldiers," *New York Times*, January 23, 2005; also see Bradley Graham, "Army Plans to Keep Troop Level through 2006," *Washington Post*, January 25, 2005, p. A-1.

28. Interview, May 12, 2005.

29. Jim Garamone, "Multinational Security Command Trains, Equips Iraqi Forces," American Forces Press Service, January 21, 2005. The Ninety-eighth will be replaced by the Eightieth Division in the fall of 2005. The 100th Division is due to replace the Eightieth a year later, but the 100th is so undermanned that members of the Ninety-eighth were asked in the spring of 2005 if they would volunteer to return and serve in the 100th.

30. Greg Jaffe, "Change of Command; A Marine Captain Trains Iraqi Colonel to Take over Fight," *Wall Street Journal*, February 24, 2005, p. A1.

31. Eric Schmitt, "U.S. Commanders See Possible Cut in U.S. Troops in Iraq," *New York Times*, April 11, 2005, p. A11.

32. Quoted in Ann Scott Tyson, "Iraqi Insurgency is Weakening, Abizaid Says," *Washington Post*, March 2, 2005, p. 5. General Richard A. Cody made similar comments on March 18, 2005; see *Washington Post*, March 18, 2005, p. A20.

33. Even at the top of these ministries, a single Coalition adviser might have to deal with four offices, when the adviser effectively had a full-time job dealing with just one.

34. U.S. Department of Defense, *Report to Congress Measuring Stability and Security in Iraq*, report to Congress is submitted pursuant to the section entitled "Measuring Stability and Security in Iraq" of House Conference Report 109-72 accompanying H.R. 1268, Emergency Supplemental Appropriations Act for Defense, the Global War on Terror, and Tsunami Relief, 2005, Public Law 109-13, July 20, 2005.

35. John Hendren, "U.S. to Overhaul Training of Iraqi Forces," *Los Angeles Times*, January 20, 2005.

36. For an independent verification of the value of such efforts in operational practice, see Mike Dorning, "Trainer Leads from the Front," *Chicago Tribune*, April 8, 2005, p. C1.

37. Report by the offices of inspector generals of Departments of State and Defense, July 25, 2005, http://oig.state.gov/documents/organization/50145.pdf, p. 37.

38. Report by the Offices of Inspector General of Departments of State and Defense, July 25, 2005, http://oig.state.gov/documents/organization/50145.pdf, p. 37.

39. U.S. Department of Defense, *Report to Congress Measuring Stability and Security in Iraq*, report to Congress is submitted pursuant to the section entitled "Measuring Stability and Security in Iraq" of House Conference Report 109-72 accompanying H.R. 1268, Emergency Supplemental Appropriations Act for Defense, the Global War on Terror, and Tsunami Relief, 2005, Public Law 109-13, July 20, 2005.

40. Interview, May 12, 2005.

41. *Iraq Weekly Status Report*, July 20, 2005.

42. The text of the UN report was forwarded to the author by ABC News. The MNSTC–I data are taken from http://www.mnstci.iraq.centcom.mil/facts_troops.htm, as accessed on May 14, 2005.

43. U.S. Department of Defense, *Report to Congress Measuring Stability and Security in Iraq*, report to Congress is submitted pursuant to the section entitled "Measuring Stability and Security in Iraq" of House Conference Report 109-72 accompanying H.R. 1268, Emergency Supplemental Appropriations Act for Defense, the Global War on Terror, and Tsunami Relief, 2005, Public Law 109-13, July 20, 2005.

44. Ibid.

45. Statement of Joseph A. Christoff, "Rebuilding Iraq: Preliminary Observations on Challenges in Transferring Security Responsibilities to Iraqi Military and Police," submitted to the U.S. House of Representatives Subcommittee on National Security, Emerging Threats, and International Relations on March 14, 2005, p. 13. Christoff is the director of international affairs and trade at the Government Accountability Office.

46. Report by the offices of inspector generals of Departments of State and Defense, July 25, 2005, http://oig.state.gov/documents/organization/50145.pdf, p. 28.

47. Ibid., pp. 29–30.

48. This is from MNSTC-I's response to an inquiry.

49. This is adapted from a briefing on MNF-I priorities of the commanding general, May 15, 2005.

50. Report by the offices of inspector generals of Departments of State and Defense, July 25, 2005, http://oig.state.gov/documents/organization/50145.pdf, p. 13.

51. To review the press archives by date, see http://www.mnstci.iraq.centcom.mil/advisor.htm.

52. Eric Schmitt, "Many Iraqi Troops Not Fully Trained, U.S. Officials Say," *New York Times*, February 4, 2005, p. 8.

53. Interview, May 12, 2005.

54. "Commander Gives His Take," *Houston Chronicle*, January 29, 2005, p. 29. This is a print version of questions presented to Abizaid by the editorial board of the *Houston Chronicle*.

55. Greg Jaffe, "Change of Command; A Marine Captain Trains Iraqi Colonel to Take over Fight," *Wall Street Journal*, February 24, 2005, p. A1.

56. Ibid.

57. Statement of Joseph A. Christoff, "Rebuilding Iraq: Preliminary Observations on Challenges in Transferring Security Responsibilities to Iraqi Military and Police," submitted to the U.S. House of Representatives Subcommittee on National Security, Emerging Threats, and International Relations on March 14, 2005, p. 12.

58. Quoted in Ann Scott Tyson, "Iraqi Insurgency is Weakening, Abizaid Says," *Washington Post*, March 2, 2005, p. 5

59. Quoted in Rowan Scarborough, "Bomb Makers' Skills in Iraq Seen as Eroding," *Washington Times*, March 9, 2005, p. 6.

60. Jackie Spinner, "U.S. Prisons in Iraq Nearly Full with Rise in Insurgent Arrests; Detainee Releases Suspended until after January 30 Elections," *Washington Post*, January 21, 2005, p. A12; Bradley Graham, "U.S. to Expand Prison Facilities in Iraq," *Washington Post*, May 10, 2005, p. A15.

61. Quoted in Liz Sly, "Iraqi Army Takes First Step Toward Relieving GIs," *Chicago Tribune*, March 6, 2005.

62. Ibid.

63. Ann Scott Tyson, "Iraqi Unit Brings Calm to a Rebel Stronghold," *Washington Post*, April 28, 2005, p. A14.

64. Steve Fainaru, "Handoff to Iraqi Forces Being Tested in Mosul," *Washington Post*, April 7, 2005, p. A1; Peter Grier, "Iraqi Troop Training: Signs of Progress," *Christian Science Monitor*, March 29, 2005, p. 1.

65. Quoted in Edward Wong, "U.S. Uncovers Vast Hide-Out of Iraqi Rebels," *New York Times*, June 4, 2005.

66. Jonathan Finer, "Insurgents Reportedly Ready to Talk; Former Iraqi Official Says Two Groups Willing to Discuss Ending Violence," *Washington Post*, June 8, 2005, p. A16.

67. U.S. Department of Defense, *Report to Congress Measuring Stability and Security in Iraq*, report to Congress is submitted pursuant to the section entitled "Measuring Stability and Security in Iraq" of House Conference Report 109-72 accompanying H.R. 1268, Emergency Supplemental Appropriations Act for Defense, the Global War on Terror, and Tsunami Relief, 2005, Public Law 109-13, July 20, 2005.

68. Ibid.

69. Bradley Graham, "A Report Card on Iraqi Troops," *Washington Post*, May 18, 2005, p. A10.

70. Ibid.

71. Report by the offices of inspector generals of Departments of State and Defense, July 25, 2005, http://oig.state.gov/documents/organization/50145.pdf, p. 36.

72. U.S. Department of Defense, *Report to Congress, Measuring Stability and Security in Iraq*, submitted pursuant to the section entitled "Measuring Stability and Security in Iraq"

of House Conference Report 109-72 accompanying H.R. 1268, Emergency Supplemental Appropriations Act for Defense, the Global War on Terror, and Tsunami Relief, 2005, Public Law 109-13, July 2005.

73. General Peter Pace in response to a question posed by Senator Carl Levin before the Senate Armed Services Committee on June 29, 2005.

74. Peter Maass, "The Way of the Commando," *New York Times*, May 1, 2005.

75. John F. Burns, "Ten Sunnis Suffocate in Iraqi Police Custody," *New York Times*, July 13, 2005.

76. Ibid.

77. David Axe, "U.S. Forces Rebuild Ragged Local Police," *Washington Times*, April 13, 2005, p. 13.

78. John Hendren, "General Says U.S. Pullback Depends on Iraq's Police," *Los Angeles Times*, May 19, 2005; John F. Burns and Eric Schmitt, "Generals Offer Sober Outlook on War," *New York Times*, May 19, 2005, p. A1.

79. Ibid.

80. Anne Barnard, "Deaths Spur Calls to Overhaul Iraqi Police," *Boston Globe*, March 31, 2005, p. 1.

81. CPATT briefing on Police Partnership Program (P3), June 2003.

82. CPATT briefing, June 2005.

83. CPATT, June 2005.

84. Ibid., June 2005.

85. James Janega, "Too Much Border, Not Enough Patrol," *Chicago Tribune*, April 19, 2005.

86. U.S. Department of Defense, *Report to Congress Measuring Stability and Security in Iraq*, report to Congress is submitted pursuant to the section entitled "Measuring Stability and Security in Iraq" of House Conference Report 109-72 accompanying H.R. 1268, Emergency Supplemental Appropriations Act for Defense, the Global War on Terror, and Tsunami Relief, 2005, Public Law 109-13, July 20, 2005.

87. MNSTC–I briefing, current as of May 23, 2005.

88. Report by the offices of inspector generals of Departments of State and Defense, July 25, 2005, http://oig.state.gov/documents/organization/50145.pdf, p. 13.

Chapter 10

1. Quoted in Judy Aita, "Multinational Force Still Needed by Iraq, Foreign Minister Says," Washington File UN Correspondent, May 31, 2005.

2. For a detailed example of such a statement, see the text of the speech by Minister of Defense, Dr. Saadoun al-Dulaimi, Brussels, June 22, 2005.

3. Speech by Minister of Defense, Dr. Saadoun al-Dulaimi, Brussels, June 22, 2005.

4. For reporting on this issue, see Ellen Knickmeyer, "Iraqi Alliance Seeks to Oust Top Officials on Hussein Era," *Washington Post*, April 18, 2005, p. A1.

5. Robert Burns, "Rumsfeld Visits Iraq to Warn New Leaders to Avoid Delays," *Boston Globe*, April 12, 2005; Ellen Knickmeyer, "Rumsfeld Urges Iraqi Leaders Not to Purge Security Forces," *Washington Post*, April 13, 2005, p. A12; Jim Michaels and Rick Jervis, "Iraqi Factional Divide Broadens," *USA Today*, April 19, 2005, p. 10; Ellen Knickmeyer, "Iraqi Alliance Seeks to Oust Top Officials of Hussein Era," *Washington Post*, April 18, 2005, p. A1; Steve Negus, "U.S. Opposes Calls to Purge Former Ba'athists from Iraqi Security Forces," *London Financial Times*, April 12, 2005.

6. Slobodan Lekic, "Explosions in Iraq Kill 160, Injure 570," Associated Press, September 14, 2005, http://www.sfgate.com/cgi-bin/article.cgi?f=/news/archive/2005/09/14/international/i102842D85.DTL.

7. Excerpt from the text of the speech by Minister of Defense, Dr. Saadoun al-Dulaimi, Brussels, June 22, 2005.

8. See Hannah Allam, Warren P. Strobel and John Walcott, "Amidst Doubts, CIA Hangs on to Control of Iraqi Intelligence Service," *Knight Ridder*, May 8, 2005.

9. Comments are from various interviews. See also Eric Schmitt, "U.S. Commanders See Possible Cut in Troops in Iraq," *New York Times*, April 11, 2005, p. A1.

10. Excerpt from the text of the speech by Minister of Defense, Dr. Saadoun al-Dulaimi, Brussels, June 22, 2005.

11. Interview, May 12, 2005. The breakdown of Iraqi forces by sectarian and ethnic group within the army, security forces, and police is uncertain; the MNF–I and MNSTC–I did not collect such data.

12. Excerpt from the text of the speech by Minister of Defense, Dr. Saadoun al-Dulaimi, Brussels, June 22, 2005.

13. Ibid.

14. *USA Today*, March 29, 2005, p. 7.

Chapter 11

1. "Iraq Coalition Casualty Count," http://icasualties.org, September 19, 2005.

2. *Institute for Policy Studies*, Iraq Task Force, http://www.ips-dc.org, September 19, 2005. The figures are for August 31, 2005.

3. See Hamza Hendawi, "Insurgents Show Hostility to Extremists," *San Diego Union-Tribune*, April 10, 2005; Jan Michaels, "Insurgents Come Looking for Deals to Enter Politics," *USA Today*, April 14, 2005, p. 10.

4. Information is from interviews. For later signs of tension, see Hannah Allam and Mohammed al Dulaimy, "Iraqis Lament a Cry for Help," *Philadelphia Inquirer*, May 17, 2005, p. 1.

5. Ellen Knickmeyer and Jonathan Finer, "Iraqi Sunnis Battle to Defend Shiites," *Washington Post*, August 14, 2005, p. A01.

6. Karl Vick, "Mess Tent Blast Kills Nineteen GIs," *Washington Post*, December 22, 2004, p. 1.

7. John F. Burns, "Allawi Predicts More Strife, but Says Voting Will Go On," *New York Times*, December 21, 2004.

8. Lowell E. Jacoby, "Current and Projected National Security Threats to the United States," statement for the record, Senate Select Committee on Intelligence, February 16, 2005.

9. Quoted in Rowan Scarborough, "Bomb Makers' Skills in Iraq Seen as Eroding," *Washington Times*, March 9, 2005, p. 6.

10. Eric Schmitt, "Insurgency Loses Ground," *New York Times*, March 19, 2005, p. 7; CNN.com, "Myers: Insurgency Same as Year Ago," April 27, 2005, http://www.cnn.com/2005/World/meast/04/27/myers.insurgency/index.html.

11. Steve Negus, "Iraqi Insurgency Flagging after Defeats," *London Financial Times*, April 5, 2005; Jill Carroll, "Evolution in Iraq's Insurgency," *Christian Science Monitor*, April 7, 2005; Adrian Bloomfield, "UK Troops May Be First to Hand over in Iraq," *London Daily Telegraph*, April 5, 2005.

12. Robert Burns, "U.S. General: Iraq Insurgency on Decline," Associated Press, March 17, 2005.

13. Statement of Joseph A. Christoff, "Rebuilding Iraq: Preliminary Observations on Challenges in Transferring Security Responsibilities to Iraqi Military and Police," General Accountability Office, Washington, D.C., March 14, 2005, GAO-05-43IT, p. 1.

14. Greg Jaffe and Yaroslav Trofimov, "Iraqi Insurgents Change Their Focus," *Wall Street Journal*, April 21, 2005, p. 8.

15. Scott Johnson and John Barry, "A Deadly Guessing Game," *Newsweek*, May 16, 2005.

16. MNSTC–I response to inquiry.

17. Iraqi Coalition Casualty Count, http://www.icasualties.org/oif/IraqiDeaths.aspx, accessed May 9, 2005. To put these figures in perspective, the same source counted a total of 21,447 to 24,324 Iraqis killed during the war to date.

18. "Report to Congress, Measuring Stability and Security in Iraq," submitted pursuant to the section entitled "Measuring Stability and Security in Iraq" of House Conference Report 109-72 accompanying H.R. 1268, Emergency Supplemental Appropriations Act for Defense, the Global War on Terror, and Tsunami Relief, 2005, Public Law 109-13, July 2005.

19. "Three Children Die; Toll Grows," *Jordan Times*, June 2, 2005, p. 1.

20. Carl T. Williams, "Suicide Attacks Rising Rapidly," *Los Angeles Times*, June 2, 2005, p. 1.

21. "Iraq War Deaths," *Washington Post*, June 28, 2005, p. A12; Robin Hindry, "Iraq by the Numbers," Associated Press, June 27, 2005, 9:29:22.

22. Eric Schmitt, "Revels Said to Have a Pool of Bomb-Rigged Cars," *New York Times*, May 9, 2005.

23. Louise Roug and Patrick J. McDonnell, "Eight U.S. Troops Killed in Iraq," *Los Angeles Times*, May 9, 2005, p. 1. This count uses the Associated Press figures, which differ slightly from the U.S. Department of Defense count.

24. Some estimates were far higher. See Omar Fekeiki and Ellen Knickmeyer, "Two Suicide Bombings Kill at least Twenty-four in Iraq," *Washington Post*, May 7, 2005, p. A12. Web sources accessed as of May 6, 2005, included http://www.defenselink.mil/news, http://www.casualties.org, and http://www.iraqibodycount.net.

25. Eric Schmitt, "Revels Said to Have a Pool of Bomb-Rigged Cars," *New York Times*, May 9, 2005.

26. Omar Fekeiki and Ellen Knickmeyer, "Two Suicide Bombings Kill at least Twenty-four in Iraq," *Washington Post*, May 7, 2005, p. A12.

27. Some estimates were far higher. See Omar Fekeiki and Ellen Knickmeyer, "Two Suicide Bombings Kill at least Twenty-four in Iraq," *Washington Post*, May 7, 2005, p. A12. Web sources accessed as of May 6, 2005, included http://www.defenselink.mil/news, http://www.casualties.org, and http://www.iraqibodycount.net.

28. Jonathan Finer, "Marines Kill 100 Fighters in Sanctuary near Syria," *Washington Post*, May 10, 2005, p. A1; Ellen Knickmeyer, "They Came Here to Die," *Washington Post*, May 11, 2005, p. A1; Rick Jervis, "Iraq Insurgents' Strength Surprises U.S. Troops," *USA Today*, May 11, 2005, p. 7.

29. John Hendren, "General Says U.S. Pullback Depends on Iraq's Police," *Los Angeles Times*, May 19, 2005; John F. Burns and Eric Schmitt, "Generals Offer Sober Outlook on War," *New York Times*, May 19, 2005, p. A1; Bryan Bender, "Insurgency Seen Forcing Change in Iraq Strategy," *Boston Globe*, June 10, 2005, p. 1.

30. James Glanz, "Insurgents Wage Precise Attacks on Baghdad Fuel," *New York Times*, February 21, 2005.

31. Sabrina Tavernise, "Data Shows Faster-Rising Death Toll among Iraqi Civilians," *New York Times*, July 14, 2005, p. 1.

32. Ibid.

33. Ibid.

34. Analysis provided by Gary E. Langer of ABC News.

35. John Hendren, "General Says U.S. Pullback Depends on Iraq's Police," *Los Angeles Times*, May 19, 2005; John F. Burns and Eric Schmitt, "Generals Offer Sober Outlook on War," *New York Times*, May 19, 2005, p. A1.

36. Merle D. Kellerhals Jr., "General Myers Says Iraqi Political Success Tied to Security Success," Washington File, May 31, 2005.

37. Quoted in Tony Capaccio, "Syria Increasing Efforts to Seal Border with Iraq," Bloomberg.com, July 6, 2005.

38. General John Abizaid in remarks to the Washington press, January 26, 2005, http://www.state.gov.

39. For the text of such Sunni statements, see http://www.memri,.org/bin/opener_latest.cgi?ID=SD88805.

40. Scott Johnson and Melinda Liu, "The Enemy Spies," *Newsweek*, June 27, 2005.

41. See Bradley Graham, "U.S. Officers in Iraq Put Priority on Extremists," *Washington Post*, May 9, 2005, p. A1; Rowan Scarborough, "War in Iraq Looks Like Last Stand for Al Qa'ida," *Washington Times*, May 11, 2005.

42. For another discussion of this issues, see Jeffrey White, "Assessing the Iraqi Insurgency—Part I, Problems and Approaches," PolicyWatch, March 24, 2005, http://www.washingtoninstitute.org/templateC05.php?CID=2282; Michael Eisenstadt, "Assessing the Iraqi Insurgency—Part II, Devising Appropriate Analytic Measures," PolicyWatch, March 25, 2005, http://www.washingtoninstitute.org/templateC05.php?CID=2284.

43. Ijet Travel Risk Management, "Iraq—A Look Ahead," March 3, 2005, p. 2.

44. Karl Vick and Jackie Spinner, "Insurgent Attacks Spread in Iraq," *Washington Post*, November 16, 2004, p. 1; Rowan Scarborough, "Stifling Iraqi Revels a Long-Term Project," *Washington Times*, November 16, 2004, p. 1; Edward Wong and James Glanz, "Rebels Attack in Central Iraq and the North," *New York Times*, November 16, p. 1.

45. Anthony Shadid, "Troops Move to Quell Insurgency in Mosul," *Washington Post*, November 17, 2004, p. 1.

46. John Hendren, "General Says U.S. Pullback Depends on Iraq's Police," *Los Angeles Times*, May 19, 2005; John F. Burns and Eric Schmitt, "Generals Offer Sober Outlook on War," *New York Times*, May 19, 2005, p. A1.

47. For a good description of the problems in such areas, see Louise Roug, "Other Iraq Hot Spots May Flare," *Los Angeles Times*, June 7, 2005.

48. Statement of Joseph A. Christoff, "Rebuilding Iraq: Preliminary Observations on Challenges in Transferring Security Responsibilities to Iraqi Military and Police," submitted to the U.S. House of Representatives Subcommittee on National Security, Emerging Threats, and International Relations on March 14, 2005, p. 11.

49. Karl Vick, "Troops, Iraqi Police Attacked in Sunni Heartland," Edmund Sanders; "Flare of Violence Kills Four in Samarra," *New York Times*, December 9, 2004; *Washington Post*, December 9, 2004, p. 28; Josh White, "Town Reflects Rising Sabotage in Iraq," *Washington Post*, December 9, 2004, p. 1.

50. Gordon Corera, "Iraqi Charter and the Insurgency," BBC Online, August 26, 2005, http://news.bbc.co.uk/1/hi/world/middle_east/4186766.stm.

51. *United Press International*, "682 Iraqis Seized at Saudi Border," August 31, 2005, http://www.sciencedaily.com/upi/?feed=TopNews&article=UPI-1-20050831-11100000-bc-saudi-iraqinfiltrators.xml.

52. For interesting views of the Sunni groups in the insurgency, see Amatzia Baram, "Who Are the Insurgents? Sunni Arab Rebels in Iraq," Special Report 137, Washington, D.C., U.S. Institute of Peace, April 2005; and W. Andrew Terrill, Nationalism, Sectarianism, and the Future of the U.S. Presence in Post-Saddam Iraq," Carlisle, Strategic Studies Institute, U.S. Army War College, July 2003.

53. See Luke Baker, "Wild West a Constant Thorn for U.S. Troops," *Jordan Times*, June 2, 2005, p. 4. Also see http://www.icasulaties.org.

54. ABC News, e-mail update from Baghdad, September 12, 2005.

55. See John F. Burns, "On Way to Baghdad Airport, One Eye on the Road and One Eye on the Insurgents," *New York Times*, May 29, 2005, p. 14. Speaking from personal experience, riding the "Rhino" does not give one a feeling of security.

56. Toby Dodge, "Iraq's Future: The Aftermath of Regime Change," London, International Institute of Strategic Studies, Adelphi Paper 372, 2005, pp. 53–54.

57. Ibid., pp. 54–56.

58. Steven Negus, "Iraqi Insurgent Groups Appoint New Spokesman," *London Financial Times*, July 5, 2005.

59. Ibid.

60. Ibid.

61. Walter Pincus, "CIA Studies Provide Glimpse of Insurgents in Iraq," *Washington Post*, February 6, 2005, p. A19.

62. Anthony Shadid and Steve Fainaru, "Militias Wrestling Control across Iraq's North and South," *Washington Post*, August 20, 2005, http://www.washingtonpost.com/wp-dyn/content/article/2005/08/20/AR2005082000940.html.

63. Ibid.

64. Toby Dodge, "Iraq's Future: The Aftermath of Regime Change," London, International Institute of Strategic Studies, Adelphi Paper 372, 2005, pp. 16–17.

65. Statement by Thair Al-Nakib, spokesman for the office of prime minister, March 22, 2005.

66. See Anna Ciezadlo, "Fragmented Leadership of the Iraqi Insurgency," *Christian Science Monitor*, December 21, 2004, p. 1.

67. Richard Oppel Jr., "In Northern Iraq, the Insurgency Has Two Faces, Secular and Jihad, but a Common Goal," *New York Times*, December 19, 2004, p. 30.

68. Jeffrey White, "Assessing the Iraqi Insurgency—Part I, Problems and Approaches," PolicyWatch 978, March 24, 2005. Also see Jeffrey White, "The Elections and Insurgency," http://www.washjingtoninstitute.org/templateC05.php?CID=2247.

69. Interview with Pan-Arab Print Reporters, December 21, 2005, http://www.state.gov.

70. Jeffrey White, "Resistance Strategy in the Trans-Election Period," PolicyWatch 945, Washington Institute for Near East Policy, January 24, 2005.

71. Richard A. Oppel, "One Hundred Rebels Killed," *New York Times*, May 10, 2005, p. A1; Neil MacDonald, "Could Bigger Sunni Role Stop Attacks?" *Christian Science Monitor*, May 6, 2005, p. 1; Caryle Murphy, "Security Forces Are Targeted," *Washington Post*, May 6, 2005, p. A19.

72. Brinda Adhikari of ABC News summarizes Zarqawi's background as follows: He was born Ahmed al-Khalayleh on Oct. 20, 1966. His father was a traditional healer, and he and his nine siblings grew up poor. He took the name Zarqawi as homage to his hometown of Zarqa, Jordan. In 1983 he dropped out of high school. People there remember him as a petty criminal, simple, quick-tempered, and barely-literate gangster. In 1989 he went to Afghanistan to fight. He and Bin Laden rose to prominence as "Afghan Arabs"—leading foreign fighters in the "jihad" against Soviet forces. After the Soviets pulled out, he worked as a reporter for a jihadist magazine.

Abu Musab al-Zarqawi returned to Jordan around 1992 and was convicted of hiding weapons and of conspiring to overthrow the monarchy and establish an Islamic caliphate. Imprisoned until 1999, fellow inmates say he devoted hours of study to the Koran. He also is said to be a specialist in poisons. Not long after his release, he fled the country. His movements have been difficult to track. Western intelligence has indicated that Zarqawi had then sought refuge in Europe. German security forces later uncovered a militant cell which claimed Zarqawi as its leader. The cell members also told their German interrogators their group was "especially for Jordanians who did not want to join Al Qa'ida."

After Europe he is believed to have moved to Afghanistan and to have set up a training camp in the western city of Herat near the border with Iran. Students at his camp supposedly became experts in the manufacture and use of poison gases. It is during this period that Zarqawi is thought to have renewed his acquaintance with Al Qa'ida. He is believed to have fled to Iraq in 2001 after a U.S. missile strike on his Afghan base. U.S. officials argue that it was at Al Qa'ida's behest that he moved to Iraq and established links with Ansar al-Islam, a group of Kurdish Islamists from the north of the country.

He was first identified as a suspect at large in a plot to attack U.S. and Israeli targets in Jordan, culminating in the 2002 slaying of U.S. diplomat Laurence Foley. Jordan tried him in absentia and sentenced him to death for allegedly plotting attacks on American and Israeli tourists. He is believed to have traveled extensively since 9/11, reportedly spending time in Iran, Pakistan, Syria, Lebanon, and Turkey.

In the run up to the Iraq War in February 2003, U.S. Secretary of State Colin Powell told the United Nations that Zarqawi was an associate of Osama Bin Laden who had sought refuge in Iraq. On August 29, 2003, Ayatollah Sayed Mohamad Baqir Al-Hakim, the head of the Supreme Council for the Islamic Revolution in Iraq (SCIRI), was killed in a car bomb blast in the holy city of Al-Najaf in southern Iraq. It was one of the bloodiest attacks. U.S. authorities pinned the blame on Zarqawi. In February 2004, the U.S. military released a letter it claimed to have intercepted in which Zarqawi apparently asks Al Qa'ida to help ignite a sectarian conflict in Iraq. In October 2004 his group, Tawhid and Jihad, declared allegiance to Al Qa'ida.

He is suspected of direct involvement in the kidnapping and beheading of several foreigners in Iraq—even of wielding the knife himself. In May 2004 the American contractor Nick Berg, taken hostage in Baghdad, was among the first to be beheaded. The CIA believes with a "high degree of confidence" that it was Zarqawi who read out a statement and then carried out Berg's murder. Those killed in this fashion include another American, a South Korean, a Bulgarian, and a string of others. A Turkish hostage was shot three times in the head. In the days leading up to the January 30 Iraqi election, the terror leader declared a "fierce war" on democracy and was believed to be the voice in audiotapes urging people not to vote. In April 2005 U.S. forces said they had recently come close to capturing him in Iraq. See also Amnesty International's "Iraq in Cold Blood: Abuses by Armed Groups," July 2005, p. 13.

73. See Amnesty International's "Iraq in Cold Blood: Abuses by Armed Groups," July 2005, p. 14.

74. Carl T. Williams, "Suicide Attacks Rising Rapidly," *Los Angeles Times*, June 2, 2005, p. 1.

75. Al Pessin, "US General: Iraq Insurgency Fueled by Foreigners and Money," *Voice of America*, June 21, 2005, http://www.voanews.com/english/2005-06-21-voa42.cfm.

76. Patrick Quinn and Katherine Schrader, "Foreigners Blamed for Iraq Suicide Attacks," Associated Press, July 1, 2005.

77. Patrick Quinn and Katherine Schrader, "Foreigners Blamed for Iraq Suicide Attacks," Associated Press, July 1, 2005.

78. U.S. Department of State Office of the Coordinator for Counterterrorism, "Country Reports on Terrorism 2004," Department of State Publication 11248, April 2005, pp. 61–62.

79. US Department of State, Office of the Coordinator for Counterterrorism, "Country Reports on Terrorism 2004," Department of State Publication 11248, April 2005, pp. 94–95.

80. Fiona Symon, "Zarqawi: Mastermind or Myth," *Financial Times*, June 16, 2004, updated January 6, 2005.

81. See Ellen Knickmeyer, "They Came Here to Die," *Washington Post*, May 11, 2005, p. 1.

82. Interview on the *PBS Newshour with Jim Lehrer* with General Richard Myers, July 12, 2005, available at http://www.pbs.org/newshour/bb/military/july-dec05/myers_7-12.html.

83. Kirk Semple, "U.S. Discloses the Capture of a Top Terrorist in Iraq," *New York Times*, July 15, 2005.

84. Responsibility is difficult to pinpoint and is often claimed through postings on the Internet or various Islamic extremist Web sites.

85. See Susan Glasser, "Martyrs in Iraq Mostly Saudis," *Washington Post*, May 15, 2005, p. A1.

86. Susan Glasser, "Martyrs in Iraq Mostly Saudis," *Washington Post*, May 15, 2005, p. A1; Global Terror Alert Web sites at http://www.globalterroralert.com/ and http://www.globalterroralert.com/iraqconflict.html; PRISM (Project for the Research of Islamist Movements) Web site at http://www.e-prism.org/pages/1/index.htm.

87. "Iraqi TV Reports Confessions from Foreign Fighters," *USA Today*, November 8, 2004, p. 8; "Iraq to Exhibit Foreign Fighters," *Miami Herald*, October 29, 2004; John Hendren, "Few Foreigners among the Insurgents," *Los Angeles Times*, November 16, 2004, p. 1.

88. Detailed descriptions have been provided of such activities by captured Iraqi insurgents and Al Qa'ida activists in the Iraqi TV show, *Terrorism in the Hands of Justice*. See Caryle Murphy and Khalid Saffar, "Actors in the Insurgency are Reluctant TV Stars," *Washington Post*, April 5, 2005, p. A18.

89. Andy Mosher, "Rebels Threaten to Kill Abducted Diplomat," *Washington Post*, July 7, 2005, p. 15.

90. Bradley Graham, "Top Iraq Rebels Elude Intensified U.S. Raids," *Washington Post*, February 15, 2005, p. A1; and Dan Murphy, "After Temporary Gains, Marines Leave Iraqi Cities," *Christian Science Monitor*, March 3, 2005.

91. Robert Worth, "Jihadists Take Stand on Web, and Some Say It's Defensive," *New York Times*, March 13, 2005, p. 22.

92. Ibid.

93. For detailed quotes of the Iraqi Al Qa'ida ideology, see "The Iraqi Al Qa'ida Organization: A Self Portrait," http://www.meri.org/bin/opener_latests.cgi?ID=SD88405/.

94. Jeanne Meserve, "Officials: Bin Laden Message to al-Zarqawi Intercepted," CNN.com, March 1, 2005.

95. Walter Pincus, "Analysts See Bin Laden, Zarqawi as Independent Operators," *Washington Post*, March 5, 2005, p. A15.

96. Rowan Scarborough, "Letter Reveals Terror Group's Woes in Iraq," *Washington Times*, May 4, 2005, p. 3.

97. Robert Worth, "Jihadists Take Stand on Web, and Some Say It's Defensive," *New York Times*, March 13, 2005, p. 22.

98. See http://www.tajdeed.org.uk/forums/showthread.php?s=7838f482c3c844b637da2 53a006e17bf&threadid=33974.

99. This analysis was prepared by Hoda K. Osman of ABC News.

100. Ibid.

101. Salah Nasrawi, "Al-Zarqawi Blasts His Mentor for Urging Restraint in Attacks on Civilians, Shiites in Iraq," Associated Press, July 12, 2005.

102. Ibid.

103. Jeffrey Flieshman, "Zarqawi Reportedly Called for a Shift in Strategy," *Los Angeles Times*, May 19, 2005; Jonathan Finer, "Violence Blamed on Zarqawi Allies," *Washington Post*, May 19, 2005, p. A24.

104. BBC Online, "US Predicts Zarqawi Africa Flight," August 25, 2005, http://news.bbc. co.uk/1/hi/world/africa/4185596.stm.

105. "Iraq: The Threat of Ansar al-Sunnah," *Jane's Intelligence Digest*, January 7, 2005.

106. Dan Murphy, "In Iraq, a Clear-Cut bin Laden-Zarqawi Alliance," *Christian Science Monitor*, December 30, 2004.

107. John F. Burns, "Tape in the Name of Leading Insurgent Declares 'All-Out War' on Iraqi Elections and Democracy," *New York Times*, January 24, 2005.

108. The author is indebted to Ahmed Hashim for his pioneering analysis of the speeches, sermons, and literature on this topic.

109. Quoted in Ann Scott Tyson, "Iraqi Insurgency is Weakening, Abizaid Says," *Washington Post*, March 2, 2005, p. 5.

110. Edmund Sanders, "Loyalists of Rebel Cleric Flex Muscle," *Los Angeles Times*, March 31, 2005.

111. Edmund Sanders, "Power Struggles Stall Iraqi Provincial Councils," *Los Angeles Times*, April 6, 2005.

112. Solomon Moore, "Recent Violence Stirs Sectarian Tensions in Once Quiet Basra," *Los Angeles Times*, April 20, 2005.

113. Yaroslav Trofimov, "Sadr's Protesters Pose a Dilemma for Iraqi Rulers," *Wall Street Journal*, April 11, 2005, p. 20.

114. Anthony Shadid, "An Old U.S. Foe Rises Again," *Washington Post*, April 8, 2005, p. A1.

115. John F. Burns and Robert F. Worth, "Iraqi Campaign Raises Question of Iran's Sway," *New York Times*, December 15, 2004, p. 1.

116. Edward Wong, "Leaders of Iraq Back Militias, Widening Rift with Sunnis," *New York Times*, June 9, 2005; Tom Lasseter, "Militia Backed by Iraqi Leaders Accused in Attacks," *Philadelphia Inquirer*, June 10, 2005, p. 1.

117. Quoted in Edward Wong, "Leaders of Iraq Back Militias, Widening Rift with Sunnis," *New York Times*, June 9, 2005.

118. Quoted in Jonathan Finer and Naseer Nouri, "Sectarian Divide Widens on Iraq's Constitutional Panel," *Washington Post*, June 9, 2005.

119. "Might the Sunni Arabs Relent?" *The Economist*, May 28, 2005.

120. Tom Lasseter and Yasser Salihee, "Campaign of Executions Feared in Iraq," *Philadelphia Inquirer*, June 28, 2005, p. 1.

121. Ashraf Khalil and Patrick J. McDonnell, "Iraq Violence Taking a Sectarian Twist," *Los Angeles Times*, May 16, 2005, p. 1; Mona Mahmoud, "Sunni Clerics Found Dead; Shi'ite Religious Leader Killed," *USA Today*, May 18, 2005, p. 3.

122. Ali Rifat, "Al-Sadr Vows Revenge on Sunnis over Stampede Deaths," *The Sunday Times*, September 4, 2005.

123. Quoted in Tony Capaccio, "Syria Increasing Efforts to Seal Border with Iraq," Bloomberg.com, July 6, 2005.

124. Louise Roug, "Islamic Law Controls the Streets of Basra," *Los Angeles Times*, June 27, 2005.

125. Ellen Knickmeyer, "Sunni Faction Halts Work on Iraqi Charter," *Washington Post*, July 21, 2005, p. 1.

126. Toby Dodge, "Iraq's Future: The Aftermath of Regime Change," London, International Institute of Strategic Studies, Adelphi Paper 372, 2005, pp. 51–52.

127. Steve Fainaru and Anthony Shadid, "Kurdish Officials Sanction Abductions in Kirkuk," *Washington Post*, June 15, 2005, p. A01.

128. Ibid.

129. Ibid.

130. Quoted in Steve Fainaru and Anthony Shadid, "Kurdish Officials Sanction Abductions in Kirkuk," *Washington Post*, June 15, 2005, p. A01.

131. Karl Vick, "In Turkey, New Fears that Peace Has Passed," *Washington Post*, May 10, 2005, p. A12.

132. James Glanz, "Kurdish Suspects Reveal International Links, Officials Say," *Washington Post*, July 11, 2005.

133. Acting Assistant Treasury Secretary Daniel Glaser's testimony before the House Armed Services Subcommittee on Terrorism, Unconventional Threats and Capabilities and the House Financial Services Subcommittee on Oversight and Investigations, July 28, 2005.

134. Interviews and Monte Morin, "Crime as Lethal as Insurgency in Iraq," *Los Angeles Times*, March 20, 2005, p. A1; Sabrina Tavernise, "Iraq's Violence Sweeps away All Norms," *New York Times*, May 6, 2005, p. 1; Solomon More, "A Nation's Unnoticed Abductees," *Los Angeles Times*, May 6, 2005.

135. Caleb Temple's testimony before the House Armed Services Subcommittee on Terrorism, Unconventional Threats, and Capabilities and the House Financial Services Subcommittee on Oversight and Investigations, July 28, 2005.

136. Ibid.

137. Acting Assistant Treasury Secretary Daniel Glaser testimony before the House Armed Services Subcommittee on Terrorism, Unconventional Threats and Capabilities and the House Financial Services Subcommittee on Oversight and Investigations, July 28, 2005.

138. Thomas E. Ricks, "General: Iraqi Insurgents Directed from Syria," *Washington Post*, December 17, 2004, p. 29; Bill Gertz, "Commander Says Syria Must Curb Terrorist Support," *Washington Times*, December 17, 2004.

139. Quoted in Rowan Scarborough, "Bomb Makers' Skills in Iraq Seen as Eroding," *Washington Times*, March 9, 2005, p. 6.

140. Briefer Tom Casey, U.S. State Department daily briefing, May 9, 2005.

141. Richard Beeston and James Hider, "Following the Trail of Death: How Foreigners Flock to Join Holy War," *Financial Times*, June 25, 2005.

142. Jeffrey Flieshman, "Zarqawi Reportedly Called for a Shift in Strategy," *Los Angeles Times*, May 19, 2005; Jonathan Finer, "Violence Blamed on Zarqawi Allies," *Washington Post*, May 19, 2005, p. A24.

143. Hassan M. Fattah, "Syrians Clash with Fighters Linked to the Insurgency," *New York Times*, July 5, 2005.

144. Quoted in Tony Capaccio, "Syria Increasing Efforts to Seal Border with Iraq," Bloomberg.com, July 6, 2005.

145. Ibid.

146. Acting Assistant Treasury Secretary Daniel Glaser testimony before the House Armed Services Subcommittee on Terrorism, Unconventional Threats and Capabilities and the House Financial Services Subcommittee on Oversight and Investigations, July 28, 2005.

147. David Shelby, "U.S. Envoy Warns Syria to Change Pro-Terrorist Policies on Iraq," *The Washington File*, September 12, 2005, http://usinfo.state.gov/mena/Archive/2005/Sep/12-180993.html.

148. Quoted in Albert Aji and Zeina Karam, "Syria May Have Its Own Terrorists," *Washington Times*, July 7, 2005, p. 17.

149. Warren P. Strobel, "Iraq is No. 1 Extremist Training Spot, Studies Say," *Philadelphia Inquirer*, July 5, 2005.

150. Ibid.

151. Ibid.

152. Quoted in Dominic Evans, "Saudi Arabia Says Ready to Beat Militants from Iraq," Reuters, July 10, 2005.

153. Quoted in Judy Aita, "Multinational Force Still Needed by Iraq, Foreign Minister Says," Washington File UN correspondent, May 31, 2005.

154. Richard Beeston and James Hider, "Following the Trail of Death: How Foreigners Flock to Join Holy War," *Financial Times*, June 25, 2005.

155. Quoted in Robin Wright, "U.S. Doubts Zarqawi Went to Syria; Damascus Suspected in Role of Lebanese Journalist's Death," *Washington Post*, June 4, 2005, p. A12.

156. Ghaith Abdul-Ahad, "Outside Iraq but Deep in the Fight; A Smuggler of Insurgents Reveal's Syria's Influential, Changing Role," *Washington Post*, June 8, 2005, p. A01.

157. Ibid.

158. Quoted in Ghaith Abdul-Ahad, "Outside Iraq but Deep in the Fight; A Smuggler of Insurgents Reveal's Syria's Influential, Changing Role," *Washington Post*, June 8, 2005, p. A01.

159. Suzan Fraser, "Iraq's Neighbors Discuss Border Control," *Guardian Unlimited*, July 19, 2005.

160. Quoted in Suzan Fraser, "Iraq's Neighbors Discuss Border Control," *Guardian Unlimited*, July 19, 2005.

161. Douglas Jehl, "U.S. Ties Funds for Insurgents to Four Nephews of Hussein," *New York Times*, July 22, 2005.

162. Stuart Levey before the U.S. Treasury Department Washington press corps, July 22, 2005.

163. Acting Assistant Treasury Secretary Daniel Glaser testimony before the House Armed Services Subcommittee on Terrorism, Unconventional Threats, and Capabilities and the House Financial Services Subcommittee on Oversight and Investigations, July 28, 2005.

164. Rowan Scarborough, "Syria Seen as Stepping Up Aid to Iraq-Bound Insurgents," *Washington Times*, July 6, 2005, p. 5.

165. Quoted in Richard Beeston and James Hider, "Following the Trail of Death: How Foreigners Flock to Join Holy War," *Financial Times*, June 25, 2005.

166. Richard Beeston and James Hider, "Following the Trail of Death: How Foreigners Flock to Join Holy War," *Financial Times*, June 25, 2005.

167. U.S. State Department press release, "Iraq Needs Political, Economic, Military Approach," May 24, 2005, 07:28 See also http://www.state.gov/s/d/rm/46700.htm.

168. Richard Beeston and James Hider, "Following the Trail of Death: How Foreigners Flock to Join Holy War," *Financial Times*, June 25, 2005.

169. Nicholas Blanford, "Sealing Syria's Desolate Border," *Christian Science Monitor*, December 21, 2004.

170. Elliot Blair Smith, "Violence is off the Chart in Area on Iraqi Border," *USA Today*, April 19, 2005, p. 10; Oliver Poole, "Iraqi Forces Desert," *London Daily Telegraph*, April 25, 2005, p. 1.

171. Ellen Knickmeyer, "They Came Here to Die," *Washington Post*, May 11, 2005, p. A1; Richard A. Oppel, "One Hundred Rebels Killed," *New York Times*, May 10, 2005, p. A1; Neil MacDonald, "Could Bigger Sunni Role Stop Attacks?" *Christian Science Monitor*, May 6, 2005, p. 1; Caryle Murphy, "Security Forces Are Targeted," *Washington Post*, May 6, 2005, p. A19.

172. See International Crisis Group, "Iran in Iraq: How Much Influence?" Crisis Group Middle East Report No. 38, March 21, 2005, p. 6; Doug Struck, "Official Warns of Iranian Infiltration," *Washington Post*, July 26, 2004; Associated Press, December 15, 2004; and Annia Ciezadlo, *Christian Science Monitor*, December 16, 2004.

173. International Crisis Group, "Iran in Iraq: How Much Influence?" Crisis Group Middle East Report No. 38, March 21, 2005, http://www.crisisgroup.org/home/index.cfm?id=3328&l=1. Text drawn from Crisis Group interview, Mashhad, November 2, 2004.

174. Translation of the Al Fayhaa TV interview by the Middle East Media Research Institute, Special Dispatch Series, No. 849, January 19, 2005.

175. Thomas E. Ricks, "General: Iraqi Insurgents Directed from Syria," *Washington Post*, December 17, 2004, p. 29.

176. International Crisis Group, "Iran in Iraq: How Much Influence?" Crisis Group Middle East Report No. 38, March 21, 2005, http://www.crisisgroup.org/home/index.cfm?id=3328&l=1. Text drawn from Crisis Group interview, Mashhad, November 2, 2004.

177. John F. Burns, "Registering New Influence, Iran Sends a Top Aide to Iraq," *New York Times*, May 18, 2005.

178. Andy Mosher, "Iraqi Official Says Iran Will Not Train Troops," *Washington Post*, July 12, 2005, p. A16.

179. Quoted in Umit Enginsov and Burak Ege Bekdil, "U.S. Warns Ankara against Cross-Border Raids on Kurds," *DefenseNews*, July 25, 2005, p. 36.

180. Ibid.

181. Challiss McDonough, "Jordanian Police Arrest Suspect in Aqaba Attack," *Voice of America*, August 23, 2005, http://www.voanews.com/english/2005-08-23-voa23.cfm.

182. Dale Gavlak, "Jordan Seeks Arrest in Aqaba Rocket Attack," *Los Angeles Times*, August 27, 2005, http://www.latimes.com/news/nationworld/world/wire/sns-ap-jordan-aqaba-attack,1,282074.story?coll=sns-ap-world-headlines.

183. James Glanz, "In Jordanian Case, Hints of Iraq Jihad Networks," *New York Times*, July 29, 2005.

184. Richard A. Oppel Jr., "Iraq Accuses Jordan of Allowing Financing of Insurgency," *New York Times*, August 22, 2005.

185. James Glanz, "In Jordanian Case, Hints of Iraq Jihad Networks," *New York Times*, July 29, 2005.

186. Ibid.

187. John F. Burns, "Iraqi Government Calls for an End to Mosque Raids," *New York Times*, May 17, 2005, p. A1.

188. Ibid.; Paul Garwood, "Twenty Killed in U.S. Strike on Militants," *Washington Times*, May 18, 2005, p. 18.

189. BBC Online, "Calls for calm after Shia clashes," August 25, 2005, http://news.bbc.co.uk/2/hi/middle_east/4183334.stm.

190. GlobalSecurity.org, "Mogtada al-Sadr," http://www.globalsecurity.org/military/world/iraq/al-sadr.htm.

191. Ellen Knickmeyer, "Sunnis Step off Political Sidelines," *Washington Post*, May 22, 2005, p. A1.

192. Sinan Salaheddin, "Sunni Clerics Urge Iraqis to Join Security Forces," Associated Press, April 2, 2005, 04:29.

193. Robert F. Worth, "Sunni Clerics Urge Followers to Join Iraqi Army and Police," *New York Times*, April 2, 2005, p. A5.

194. Ibid.

195. See Amnesty International's "Iraq in Cold Blood: Abuses by Armed Groups," July 2005, p. 13.

196. Steven R. Weisman and John F. Burns, "Some Sunnis Hint at Peace Terms in Iraq, U.S. Says," *New York Times*, May 15, 2005.

197. John F. Burns, "Shi'ites Offer to Give Sunnis Larger Role on Broader Panel Writing a Constitution," *New York Times*, May 26, 2005.

198. Quoted in Jonathan Finer and Naseer Nouri, "Sectarian Divide Widens on Iraq's Constitutional Panel," *Washington Post*, June 9, 2005.

199. Ibid.

200. Reuters, "Iraq's Parliament Ends Talks on Constitution," September 6, 2005, http://today.reuters.com/news/newsArticle.aspx?type=worldNews&storyID=2005-09-06T123550Z_01_MCC645239_RTRIDST_0_INTERNATIONAL-IRAQ-CONSTITUTION-DC.XML.

201. Ellen Knickmeyer, "Talibani Offers Amnesty to Insurgents," *Washington Post*, April 8, 2005, p A22. For further details, see Sharon Behn, "Talibani Set Strategy to Divide and Conquer Terror," *Washington Times*, April 18, 2005, p. 12; BBC News interview with Talibani, April 18, 2005, 3:28 a.m.; Yaroslav Trofimov, "Iraqi Leaders Consider Amnesty for Insurgents," *Wall Street Journal*, April 15, 2005, p. 8.

202. For typical press reports, see James Glanz, "New Iraqi Forces Gain Ground but Face Pitfalls," *New York Times*, April 6, 2005.

203. For a detailed description of the kind of ongoing violence involved, see Salih Saif Aldin and John Ward Anderson, "Suspect's Death Invokes Saddam Era," *Washington Post*, April 9, 2005, p. A18.

204. "US State Department, Country Reports on Human Rights, 2004, "Iraq," http://www.state.gov/g/drl/rls/hrrpt/2004/41722.htm.

205. Report by the offices of inspector generals of the State Department and Department of Defense, July 25, 2005, http://oig.state.gov/documents/organization/50145.pdf, p. 33.

206. For descriptions of these efforts, consult the weekly archives of the weekly MNSTC–I publication, *The Advisor*. See also the press releases of U.S. units. For example, see Spc. Erin Robicheaux, "First Iraqi Army Brigade Receives Human Rights Training," HQ-MND Baghdad, Release 20050426-03, April 26, 2005.

207. Salih Saif Aldin and John Ward Anderson, "Suspect's Death Invokes Saddam Era," *Washington Post*, April 9, 2005, p. A18.

208. See Peter Maass, "The Way of Commandos," *New York Times*, April 31, 2005.

Chapter 12

1. Yochi J. Dreazen, "Security Remains Main Hurdle to Iraq Rebuilding," *Wall Street Journal*, May 9, 2005, p. 4.

2. MNSTC–I response to inquiry.

3. Saad Sarhan and Omar Fekeiki, "U.S. Forces Gives Iraqis Full Control of Najaf," *Washington Post*, September 7, 2005, p. A20.

4. Roula Khalaf, "Iraqi Forces to Take Over Shia Cities Soon," *Financial Times*, September 15, 2005.

5. *Newsweek*, "Sixty-one Percent of Americans Disapprove of the Way Pres. Bush Is Handling Iraq," August 6, 2005, http://biz.yahoo.com/prnews/050806/nysa006.html?.v=20.

6. Eric Schmitt, "Military Plans Gradual Cuts in Iraq Forces," *New York Times*, August 7, 2005, section 1, p. 1, column 5.

7. Kim Senupta, "US Sends More Combat Troops to Iraq Ahead of Referendum," *The Independent*, August 25, 2005.

8. Jim VandeHei, "Talabani Says Iraqis Could Replace Many U.S. Troops," *Washington Post*, September 12, 2005, p. A20.

9. Tony Carpaccio, "U.S. to Fly Missions in Iraq for up to Five Years, General Says," Bloomberg.com, September 14, 2005.

10. Quoted in Liz Sly, "Iraqi Army Takes First Step toward Relieving GIs," *Chicago Tribune*, March 6, 2005.

11. Quoted in Dexter Filkins, "Thirty-one Americans Die as Marine Copter Goes down in Iraq," *New York Times*, January 27, 2005, p. 1.

12. PIO, NATO Training Mission–Iraq (NTM–I), Baghdad, Iraqna: 07901939223, March 21, 2005.

13. Full transcript of speech available at http://www.defenselink.mil/transcripts/2005/tr20050210-1569.html.

14. MNSTC–I response to inquiry.

15. Ibid.

16. Eric Schmitt, "New U.S. Commander Sees Shift in Military Role in Iraq," *New York Times*, January 16, 2005, p. 10.

17. Ibid.

18. Quoted in Eric Schmitt, "General Seeking Faster Training of Iraq Soldiers," *New York Times*, January 23, 2005, p. 1.

19. CNN.com, "Rumsfeld: Insurgency Slows Progress," http://www.cnn.com/2005/world/meast/03/20/Iraq.anniversay/index\.html.

20. Eric Schmitt, "U.S. Commanders See Possible Cut in U.S. Troops in Iraq," *New York Times*, April 11, 2005, p. A11; Donna Miles, "Troop Strength Assessment in Iraq Expected This Summer," *The Advisor*, April 2, 2005, pp. 8–9; Rowan Scarborough, "Top U.S. Officer in Iraq to Study Reducing Troop Levels," *Washington Times*, April 1, 2005, p. 3.

21. Greg M. Grant, "New Strategy Details Security Handover in Iraq," *Jane's Defense Weekly*, April 27, 2005, p. 5.

22. Edward Wong and James Glanz, "Iraqi Leader Says Iraqis Can Secure Some Cities," *New York Times*, July 13, 2005.

23. "Troop Withdrawals Could Begin Next Year, Casey Says," Gerry J. Gilmore, American Forces Press Service, Iraq, July 27, 2005; CNN, "General: U.S. could start Iraq pullout in spring–Depends on political, security progress, commander says," July 27, 2005; "Pullout from Iraq could happen in spring," Matt Kelley, *USA Today*, July 27, 2005.

24. John Hendren, "General Says U.S. Pullback Depends on Iraq's Police," *Los Angeles Times*, May 19, 2005; John F. Burns and Eric Schmitt, "Generals Offer Sober Outlook on War," *New York Times*, May 19, 2005, p. A1.

25. John Hendren, "U.S. to Overhaul Training of Iraqi Forces," *Los Angeles Times*, January 20, 2005.

26. Robin Wright and Josh White, "U.S. Plans New Tack after Iraq Elections; Aim Is to Accelerate Deployment of Iraqi Forces on Front Lines Against Insurgents," *Washington Post*, January 23, 2005, p. A20.

27. E-mail to the author of May 5, 2005.

28. Quoted in Jim Garamone, "Rumsfeld Discusses State of Iraq," *The Advisor*, February 19, 2005, p. 2. Available at http://www.mnstci.iraq.centcom.mil.

29. Quoted in Eric Schmitt, "Many Iraqi Troops Not Fully Trained, U.S. Officials Say," *New York Times*, February 4, 2005, p. 8.

30. Interview, May 12, 2005.

31. John Hendren, "General Says U.S. Pullback Depends on Iraq's Police," *Los Angeles Times*, May 19, 2005; John F. Burns and Eric Schmitt, "Generals Offer Sober Outlook on War," *New York Times*, May 19, 2005, p. A1.

32. The fieldwork for the survey was carried out by a team from the Central Organization for Statistics and Information Technology in Baghdad (COSIT). The team was trained by researchers from the Norwegian NGO Fafo-AIS, which also carried out the solid analysis of the data compiled. The survey was funded by the government of Norway and the UN Development Program. The three volumes of the report, including the tabulation report, analytical report and socioeconomic atlas, are available in Arabic and English at http://www.iq.undp.org/ilcs.htm. For press comment, see Richard Beeston, "The Aftermath of the Invasion of Iraq," *The Times* (UK), May 13, 2005, http://www.timesonline.co.uk/article.

33. The results of the survey appear in three volumes: a tabulation report, which presents the main results of the survey in tabular form; an analytical report, and a socioeconomic atlas, which depicts the situation in Iraq using maps and diagrams. See http://www.iq.undp.org/ilcs.htm.

34. UN Development Program, "Iraq Living Conditions Survey—2004 Analytical Report," p. 118.

35. Christopher Foote, William Block, Keith Crane, and Simon Gray, "Economic Policy and Prospects in Iraq," *Journal of Economic Perspectives* 18 (3), Summer 2004, pp. 47–70.

36. Iraqi Planning Ministry/UN Development Program, May 2005; summary by Robin Weiner of ABC News.

37. See http://www.usaid.gov/iraq/accomplishments/watsan.html.

38. Iraqi Strategic Review Board, Ministry of Planning and Development Corporation, "Iraq's National Development Strategy, 2004–2007," June 30, 2005, p. 14.

39. See http://www.eia.doe.gov/emeu/cabs/iraq.html.

40. U.S. State Department, "Report on Iraq Relief and Reconstruction," Section 2207, July 2005, p. 57.

41. For a discussion of the futility of placing too much emphasis on NATO, see "NATO Fails to Agree on Iraq Training Mission," *Washington Post*, July 29, 2004, p. A18.

42. Bradley Graham, "Commanders Plan Eventual Consolidation of U.S. Bases in Iraq," *Washington Post*, May 22, 2005, p. A27.

43. Quoted in Eric Schmitt, "Many Iraqi Troops Not Fully Trained, U.S. Officials Say," *New York Times*, February 4, 2005, p. 8.

44. Rowan Scarborough, "Metrics Help Guide Pentagon," *Washington Times*, April 5, 2005.

45. Ibid.

46. Greg Jaffe and Yaroslav Trofimov, "Iraqi Insurgents Change Their Focus," *Wall Street Journal*, April 21, 2005, p. 8.

47. Scott Johnson and John Barry, "A Deadly Guessing Game," *Newsweek*, May 16, 2005.

About the Author

ANTHONY H. CORDESMAN holds the Arleigh A. Burke Chair in Strategy at CSIS. He is also a national security analyst for ABC News and a frequent commentator on National Public Radio and the BBC. The author of more than thirty books on U.S. security policy, energy policy, and the Middle East, his most recent publications include *The War after the War: Strategic Lessons of Iraq and Afghanistan* (CSIS, 2004); *The Military Balance in the Middle East* (Praeger, 2004); *Energy Developments in the Middle East* (Praeger, 2004); and *The Iraq War: Strategy, Tactics, and Military Lessons* (CSIS, 2003).

Recent Titles by Anthony H. Cordesman

2004

The Military Balance in the Middle East
Energy and Development in the Middle East

2003

The Iraq War: Strategy, Tactics, and Military Lessons
Saudi Arabia Enters the Twenty-First Century: The Political, Foreign Policy, Economic, and Energy Dimensions
Saudi Arabia Enters the Twenty-First Century: The Military and International Security Dimensions

2001

Peace and War: The Arab-Israeli Military Balance Enters the 21st Century
A Tragedy of Arms: Military and Security Developments in the Maghreb
The Lessons and Non-Lessons of the Air and Missile Campaign in Kosovo
Cyber-threats, Information Warfare, and Critical Infrastructure Protection: Defending the U.S. Homeland, with Justin G. Cordesman
Terrorism, Asymmetric Warfare, and Weapons of Mass Destruction: Defending the U.S. Homeland
Strategic Threats and National Missile Defenses: Defending the U.S. Homeland

2000

Iran's Military Forces in Transition: Conventional Threats and Weapons of Mass Destruction